Eyewitness Accounts of the American Revolution

Memoirs of the American Revolution
William Moultrie

The New York Times & Arno Press

MEMOIRS

OF THE

AMERICAN REVOLUTION

Engraved by G.Parker, from an Original by C.Fraser.

William Moultrie Esq.r

Late

Governor of S. Carolina, and Major Gen.l

in the american revolutionary war.

MEMOIRS

OF THE

AMERICAN REVOLUTION,

SO FAR AS IT RELATED TO

THE STATES OF NORTH AND SOUTH CAROLINA, AND GEORGIA.

COMPILED FROM THE MOST AUTHENTIC MATERIALS, THE AUTHOR'S PERSONAL KNOWLEDGE OF THE VARIOUS EVENTS, AND INCLUDING AN EPISTOLARY CORRESPONDENCE ON PUBLIC AFFAIRS, WITH CIVIL AND MILITARY OFFICERS, AT THAT PERIOD.

—————

BY WILLIAM MOULTRIE,

LATE GOVERNOR OF THE STATE OF SOUTH CARO-LINA, AND MAJOR GENERAL IN THE ARMY OF THE UNITED STATES DURING THE AMERICAN WAR.

—————

VOL. I.

NEW-YORK

PRINTED BY DAVID LONGWORTH,

FOR THE AUTHOR.

1802.

[*Copy-right Secured.*]

South Carolina District, to wit,

BE IT REMEMBERED, that on the sixth day of May, Anno Domini one thousand, eight hundred and two, and in the twenty-sixth year of the Sovereignty and Independence of the United States of America, Major General William Moultrie, of the said District, hath deposited in this Office the title of a book, the right whereof he claims as Author, in the following words :

" MEMOIRS

OF THE

AMERICAN REVOLUTION,

So far as it related to the States of

NORTH AND SOUTH CAROLINA AND GEORGIA,

By WILLIAM MOULTRIE,

Late Governor of the State of South Carolina, and Major General in the Army of the United States during the American War."

———

In Conformity to the Act of the United States, entitled ' An Act for the encouragement of Learning by securing the Copies of Maps, Charts and Books to the Proprietors and Authors of such Copies during the time therein mentioned."

THOMAS HALL,

Clerk of South Carolina District.

PREFACE.

TO THE PEOPLE OF SOUTH CAROLINA
AND GEORGIA.

MY FRIENDS AND FELLOW-CITIZENS,

HAVING had the honor of acting a very conspicuous part of the revolution of America, in the
states of South Carolina and Georgia, and having a
great many documents by me, the authenticity of
which cannot be doubted, and having read several
authors on the subject, and found them very defi-
cient, I have taken upon myself that arduous task,
thinking it incumbent on me to hand down to posterity the particulars of this great event: in doing of
which, I shall give a plain detail of facts as they
happened, by extracts, from orders and letters, and
my own knowledge. I shall likewise be constrained
to publish letters from some of my friends, which,
although private, yet they contain so much of the
subject I am writing upon, that I cannot dispense
with them, as they bring to light a number of anecdotes which happened in the war, that otherwise
would have been intirely lost. I therefore hope my
friends will pardon the liberty I have taken; and beg
the candid reader to make allowances for any inac-
curacy that may be in them, as they never were intended for publication, and were wrote in the hurry
and confusion of war.

I AM the more induced to this undertaking, as I
believe no one else is furnished with such materials,

and because whenever the chain shall be broken, for want of documents, my memory can link them together and carry on the subject. In the course of this reading, it will be found how ignorant we were in the art of war, at the commencement of our revolution.

I MUST acknowledge myself indebted to Doctor David Ramsay, author of the Revolution of South Carolina, for many particulars respecting public papers, which he, at a great deal of pains and trouble, had collected while I was a prisoner of war.

THE original private letters and papers are in the hands of the author.

[*As the author of the Memoirs has not arranged his work under any particular divisionary heads or chapters, but has pursued his work through one unbroken narrative, the publisher, to facilitate the turning to any particular passage of consequence the reader may occasionally wish to peruse, has annexed the following table of contents, referring to the pages, and pointing out where the relations of the most prominent events may be examined.*]

CONTENTS.

VOL. I.

sion of the public mail from England—
The Provincial Congress summoned to
meet—Their resolution to raise a regiment of cavalry rangers—Arrival of
Lord William Campbell—His conversation with Captain M'Donald—Character of the latter—His visit to St. Augustine—His narrow escape—Lord William Campbell goes on board the Tamar
sloop-of-war—Meeting of the Council
of Safety—William Moultrie, Esq. appointed Colonel of the 2d regiment
of provincial troops—Meeting of the
Georgia Congress—The provincials take
17000 lbs. powder from a vessel off St.
Augustine—Recruiting parties sent into
Virginia and North Carolina,
The Council of Safety send a talk to the
Catawba Indians—Dorchester made an
armed post—Fort Johnson taken possession of—Public stores, records, &c.
sent to Dorchester—Presents sent to
the Cherokees to prevent an Indian
war—Taken by the Tories—Hostilities
began by sinking two British schooners
near Hogg-Island—Charlestown blocked
up by British ships of war—All supplies
from the city denied them—The Ame-

———◦※◉———

CONTENTS.

VOL. II.

nel Hayne—Devastations in Ninety-six district—Colonel Ferguson marches towards the western parts of South Carolina—The back country inhabitants arm to oppose him—Battle at King's-mountain—Ferguson mortally wounded, and his troops surrender—Account of the enemy's loss, and cause of their disaster—Observations on militia-men in general, and what only should be expected from them—Maxim of the old king of Prussia—Influence and effect of this defeat on the plans of Cornwallis—The Americans roused by this fortunate event—Cornwallis retreats to Winnsborough—Colonel Washington takes a fort near Camden and one hundred and twelve prisoners—General Sumpter's activity with militia companies through South Carolina—His lenient conduct to Major Weyms—His advantage over Colonel Tarleton—Wounded—General Greene appointed to command in the southern department—Character of this officer—He arrives at Charlotte—Takes command of an ill provided and dispirited army—Divides it, and intrusts one half to General Morgan—Which are detach-

APPENDIX,

Containing letters and public papers, referred to in
the course of the Memoirs.

MEMOIRS

OF THE

AMERICAN REVOLUTION.

THE American Revolution took its rise in Boston: The people of that Province, being grievously oppressed by the British Parliament, who had passed several laws to restrain their trade, and shut up their ports; upon which they had several meetings of the inhabitants at Boston; and on the 13th of May, 1774, they came into the following Resolutions:...' That it ' is the opinion of this town, that if the other Colo- ' nies come into a joint Resolution, to stop all im- ' portation from, and exportation to Great Britain, ' and the West-Indies, till the Acts for blocking this ' harbor be repealed, the same will prove the salva- ' tion of North America and her liberties: and on ' the other hand if they continue their exports and ' imports, there is high reason to fear, that fraud, ' power, and the most odious oppression, will rise ' triumphant over our just rights, social happi- ' ness, and freedom; and, moreover, that this vote

' be transmitted by the moderator to all our sister
' Colonies, in the name, and in behalf of this town.'

On the vote being received in Charlestown, a
meeting of all the inhabitants then in town was requested to meet at the Corner,* when a great number was convened, a Chairman was chosen, and the
vote was laid before them. The business was of so
much consequence, that, after some conversation, the
present meeting thought it best to call as many of
the inhabitants together as they could get, by sending expresses to every part of the country to request
their attendance in Charlestown, on the 6th of July,
1774, on business of great importance : accordingly,
on that day, a great number met in Charlestown, under the Exchange ; when they were convened, the
proceedings of the British Parliament against Massa-
chusetts, and the vote of Boston were laid before them :
they then chose a Chairman, and went immediately
into the consideration of what measures should be
adopted : after passing seven or eight Resolves, respecting the oppressive Acts of the British Parliament, they then Resolved, that Henry. Middleton,
John Rutledge, Christopher Gadsden, Thomas Lynch,
and Edward Rutledge, Esqrs. be, and they are hereby appointed Deputies on the part and behalf of

....

* A large tavern, situated at the N. E. corner of Broad
and Church-streets, commonly called " The Corner."

this Colony, to meet the Deputies of the several Colonies, in North America, in general Congress, on the
first Monday in September next, in Philadelphia, or
at any other time and place that may be generally
agreed upon ; there to consider of the Acts lately
passed and the Bills pending in Parliament with regard to the port of Boston and the Province of Mas-
sachusetts, &c.

THEY also Resolved, that a Committee of ninety-
nine persons be now appointed, to act as a General
Committee, to correspond with the Committees of the
other Colonies, and to do all matters and things necessary to carry those Resolves into execution ; and
that any twenty-one of them met together, should
proceed upon business ; their power to continue till
the next general meeting :...A Committee of ninety-
nine were then chosen from the different Parishes
and Districts, in an adequate proportion.

THE Delegates appointed by this Convention shortly after sailed for Philadelphia, and were joined by
others from different Provinces, invested with the
same powers, and for the same purposes. Georgia
did not send Deputies to the first meeting of the Colonies.

THE Representatives of the several Provinces having met, were called a Congress, and they proceeded
to pass sundry Resolves which were binding upon all
the Colonies who had sent Deputies ; and in this

manner was the first Legislative body established i.
America, as a general Representation : on the 26th
of October, 1774, the Continental Congress having
finished their business, our Delegates returned home,
and gave an account of what had been done in Congress, to the General Committee ; who, after setting
some little time and considering of the Report made
by our Delegates, found matters had become more
serious.   They, therefore, determined to call a Provincial Congress, by sending out Writs of Election
to every Parish and District, to Elect Representatives (agreeably to the Election Law) to meet on the
11th day of January, 1775.   After the mode was
agreed upon, they were then at a loss how to appor-
tion the number of Representatives to each Parish
and District: Col. Geo. G. Powel in the Chair of the
Committee ; Col. Charles Pinckney proposed to give
thirty members to Charlestown, and then he said,
' Let the country take as many as they pleased ;' upon which, the country gentlemen, talking over the
matter, they agreed, that six members from each
Parish, would be quite sufficient, and as many as
they could get conveniently to attend : except for the
four large Districts, viz. Ninety-six ; between Broad
and Saluda rivers ; and Broad and Catawba rivers ;
and Eastward of Wateree river, should have ten
members each.   It was then Resolved, that Charlestown should send thirty members ; and that each

Parish and District should send the proportion agreed upon, to the Provincial Congress.

THIS is the manner in which the Representation of this Country was established at the Revolution, without respect to numbers or property: I am well acquainted with this circumstance, because I was present when it was agreed upon: it was thought political and right, to give these large Districts ten Representatives, the better to unite them with the lower country; and as they contained a large extent of territory, and but few inhabitants, that they should have a member from every part of their District, by which their Constitutents might be the better informed about the nature of the dispute with Great Britain and America, which they could not know, being settled so far from the Capital, and from each other; by this mode, our Representation was increased from 49 to 184: accordingly, the General Committee sent out Writs for electing members, agreeably to the Election Law, to some influential gentlemen in every Parish and District throughout the Province, for the Representatives elected to meet in Charlestown, on the 11th of January, 1775. On the Writs being returned to the General Committee: the following gentlemen* were elected for the different Parishes and districts.

* Most of the members of the House of Assembly, in the King's government, were Elected members of the Provincial Congress.

14

JOURNALS

OF THE

PROVINCIAL CONGRESS

OF SOUTH-CAROLINA.

A LIST

OF THE SEVERAL MEMBERS OF THE PROVINCIAL
CONGRESS, HELD AT CHARLESTOWN, IN
SOUTH-CAROLINA, ON THE ELEVENTH
DAY OF JANUARY, 1775.

For the Parish of St. Philip and St. Michael,
Charlestown....Col. Charles Pinckney, Mr. John
Neufville, Roger Smith, Esq. Mr. Peter Bacot, Mr.
Daniel Cannon, Col. Henry Laurens, Mr. Thomas
Corbett, Thomas Heyward, jun. Esq. Christ. Gads-
den, Esq. Isaac Huger, Esq. Thomas Savage, Esq.
John Edwards, Esq. Miles Brewton, Esq. Peter
Timothy, Mr. Joseph Verree, Arthur Middleton, Esq.
Mr. Edward Weyman, Mr. John Ernest Poyas, Mr.
Anthony Toomer, Mr. Cato Ash, Mr. James Brown,
Mr. Daniel Legaré, sen. Mr. Joshua Lockwood, Capt.
Owen Roberts, Mr. Theodore Trezevant, Mr. Mark
Morris, Rev. Mr. Wm. Tennent, Mr. John Ber-
wick, Mr. Felix Long, Mr. Michael Kalteisen.

For the Parish of Christ-Church....John Rutledge,
Esq. Arn. Vanderhorst, Esq. Clement Lemprierre,

Esq. John Sand. Dart, Esq. Gabriel Capers, Esq. Mr. Isaac Legaré.

FOR St. John's, Berkley-County....James Ravenell, Daniel Ravenell, Job Marion, John Frierson, Esqrs. Mr. Gabr. Gignilliat, Mr. Francis Marion.

FOR St. Andrew's....William Scott, Thomas Bee, William Cattell, Esqrs. Col. Thomas Fuller, Capt. Benjamin Stone, Isaac Rivers, Esq.

FOR St. George, Dorchester....David Oliphant, Benjamin Waring, William Sanders, John Matthewes, jun. Esqrs. Mr. Richard Waring, Mr. Richard Walter.

FOR St. James', Goose-Creek....Thomas Smith, sen. Esq. Col. Benjamin Singleton, John Parker, Benjamin Smith, John Izard, John Wright, Esqrs.

FOR St. Thomas, and St. Dennis....James Aiken, Isaac Harlestown, John Huger, John Moore, William Parker, John Syme, Esqrs.

FOR St. Paul's....Thomas Ferguson, Benjamin Elliot, George Haig, Charles Elliott, Robert Williams, Robert Ladson, Esqrs.

FOR St. Bartholomew's.... Hon. Rawlins Lowndes, Col. James Parsons, William Skirving, Esq. Philip Smith, Esq. James Skirving, jun. Esq. Mr. Edmund Hyrne.

FOR St. Helena....Mr. Thomas Rutledge; Mr. John Barnwell, jun. Mr. Dan. Heyward, jun. Capt.

John Joyner, Mr. Daniel De Saussure, Col. William Moultrie.

FOR St. James', Santee....Colonel Daniel Horry, Paul Douxsaint, Esq. Thomas Horry, Edward Jerman, Thomas Lynch, jun. Capers Boone, Esqrs.

FOR Prince George's, Winyah....Thomas Lynch, Elias Horry, jun. Benjamin Huger, Joseph Allston, Benjamin Young, Esqrs. Mr. Paul Trapier, jun.

FOR Prince Frederick's....Theo. Gaillard, Thos. Porte, Esqrs. Capt. Adam M'Donald, Mr. Anthony White, Mr. Samuel Richbourg, Mr. Benjamin Screven.

FOR St. John's, Colleton County....William Gibbes, Charles C. Pinckney, Thomas Evance, Esqrs. Mr. Thomas Legaré, jun. Capt. Thomas Tucker, Mr. Benjamin Jenkins.

FOR St. Peter's, Purrysburg....Col. Stephen Bull, William Williamson, Esq. Cornelius Dupont, Gideon Dupont, Thomas Middleton, Esqrs. Mr. Philotheos Chiffelle.

FOR Prince William's....Col. Benjamin Garden, Isaac Motte, Esq. John Ward, John Bull, William Bull, Isaac Macpherson, Esqrs.

FOR St. Stephen's....John Gaillard, Philip Porcher, Esq. Peter Sinckler, Charles Cantey, Gabriel Marion, Esqrs. Mr. James Sinckler.

FOR St. Marks's, viz. 1 Ninety-Six District....Col. John Savage, Col. James Mayson, Major And.

Williamson, Le Roy Hammond, Esq. Patrick Calhoun, John Lewis Gervais, Edward Rutledge, John Purves, Richard Rapely, Esqrs. Mr. Francis Salvador.

FOR the District between Broad and Saluda rivers....Major John Caldwell, John Colcock, Rowland Rugely, Esq. Jonathan Downes, Esq. Mr John Satterthwaite, Mr. James Williams, Mr. John Williams, Mr. John M'Nees, Mr. Charles King, Mr. George Ross.

FOR the District between Broad and Catawba rivers....Hon. Henry Middleton, John Chesnut, Esq. Robert Goodwin, John Winn, Henry Hunter, Esqrs. Mr. Thomas Woodward, Mr. Thomas Taylor, Mr. John Hopkins, Mr. William Howell.

FOR the District Eastward of Wateree river....Col. Richard Richardson, Jos. Kershaw, Esq. Mathew Singleton, Thomas Sumpter, Aaron Loocock, William Richardson, Robert Patton, Esqrs. Mr. Robert Carter, Mr. William Wilson, Mr. Ely Kershaw.

FOR Saxa Gotha District....Hon. William Henry Drayton, Hon. Barnard Elliott, Benjamin Farrar, Esq. William Arthar, Jonas Beard, William Tucker, Esqrs.

FOR the Parish of St. Mathew....Col. Tacitus Gaillard, Col. William Thomson, Rev. Mr. Paul Turquand, Mr. John Caldwell, Mr. George King, Mr. Simon Berwick.

For St. David's....Hon. G. G Powell, Claudius Pegues, Esq. H. W. Harrington, Alex. M'Intosh, Samuel Wise, Esqrs. Col. George Pawley.

------::: ❀ :❀: ❀ :::------

EXTRACTS.

On the 11th day of January, 1775, the gentlemen who, on the 19th ultimo, and 9th instant, had been elected Deputies, by such of the inhabitants of this Colony as were qualified to vote for members of the Commons House of Assembly, met in PROVINCIAL CONGRESS, at Charlestown, where

THEY unanimously chose Col. CHARLES PINCKNEY, to be their President.

AND Peter Timothy, a member, to be their Secretary.

THE Congress then proceeded to take under consideration the important affairs of the Colony, and the present critical situation of America: and having deliberated thereon for seven days, they, in that time, entered into several necessary resolutions, and formed many useful regulations; of which the following were ordered to be printed and made public.

ORDERED, That the AMERICAN BILL OF RIGHTS, as declared by the Continental Congress, be taken into immediate consideration.

THE BILL OF RIGHTS.

....

' WHEREAS, since the close of the last war, the British Parliament, claiming a power of right, to bind the people of America, by statute, in all cases whatsoever, hath in some acts expressly imposed taxes on them, and in others, under various pretences, but in fact for the purpose of raising a revenue, hath imposed rates and duties payable in these Colonies, established a board of commissioners with unconstitutional powers, and extended the jurisdiction of courts of admiralty, not only for collecting the said duties, but for the trial of causes merely arising within the body of a County.

' AND, whereas, in consequence of other statutes, judges, who before held only estates at will in their offices, have been made dependant on the crown alone for their salaries, and standing armies kept in times of peace. And, whereas, it has lately been resolved in Parliament, that by force of a statute, made in the thirty-fifth year of the reign of King Henry the Eighth, colonists may be transported to England and tried there upon accusations for treasons and misprisions, or concealments of treasons committed in the Colonies; and by a late statute, such trials have been directed in cases therein mentioned.

' AND, Whereas, in the last session of Parliament,

three statutes were made : one intitled, ' An Act to
' discontinue in such manner, and for such time as
' are therein mentioned, the landing and discharging,
' lading' or shipping of goods, wares and merchan-
' dize, at the town, and within the harbor of Boston,
' in the province of Massachusetts-Bay, in North
' America." Another intitled, " An Act for the bet-
' ter regulating the government of the Province of
' the Massachusetts-Bay, in New-England.' And another intitled, ' An Act for the impartial administra-
' tion of justice, in the cases of persons questioned
' for any act done by them in the execution of the
' law, or for the suppression of riots and tumults, in
' the Province of the Massachusetts-Bay, in New-
' England.' And another statute was then made,
' For making more effectual provision for the govern-
' ment of the Province of Quebec, &c.' All which
statutes are impolitic, unjust, and cruel, as well as
unconstitutional, and most dangerous and destructive
of American rights.

' AND, whereas, assemblies have been frequently
dissolved, contrary to the rights of the people, when
they attempted to deliberate on grievances; and
their dutiful, humble, loyal, and reasonable petitions
to the crown for redress, have been repeatedly treated with contempt by his majesty's ministers of state.

' THE good people of the several Colonies of New-
Hampshire, Massachusetts-Bay, Rhode-Island and

Providence Plantations, Connecticut, New-York, New-Jersey, Pennsylvania, Newcastle, Kent, and Sussex, upon Delaware, Maryland, Virginia, North-Carolina, and South-Carolina, justly alarmed at these arbitrary proceedings of Parliament and administration, have severally elected, constituted, and appointed Deputies to meet and sit in general Congress in the city of Philadelphia, in order to obtain such establishment, as that their religion, laws, and liberties may not be subverted: whereupon the deputies so appointed being now assembled, in a full and free Representation of these Colonies, taking into their most serious consideration the best means of attaining the ends aforesaid, do in the first place, as Englishmen, their ancestors, in the like cases have usually done, for asserting and vindicating their Rights and Liberties, DECLARE,

‘ THAT the inhabitants of the English Colonies in North America, by the immutable laws of nature, the principles of the English constitution, and the several charters or compacts, have the following RIGHTS........

‘ RESOLVED, N. C. D. I. That they are entitled to life, liberty, and property: and they have never ceded to any sovereign power whatever, a right to dispose of either without their consent.

‘ RESOLVED, N. C. D. II. That our ancestors, who first settled these Colonies, were at the time of their emigration from the mother country, entitled to all the rights, liberties, and immunities of free and natural born subjects, within the realm of England.

'RESOLVED, N.C.D. III. That by such emigration, they by no means forfeited, surrendered, or lost any of those rights, but that they were, and their descendants now are, entitled to the exercise and enjoyment of all such of them, as their local and other circumstances enable them to exercise and enjoy.

'RESOLVED, IV. That the foundation of English liberty and of all free government, is a right in the people to participate in their Legislative Council: and as the English Colonists are not represented, and from their local and other circumstances cannot properly be represented in the British Parliament, they are entitled to a free and exclusive power of legislation in their several Provincial Legislatures, where their right of representation can alone be preserved, in all cases of taxation and internal polity, subject, only to the negative of their sovereign, in such manner as has been heretofore used and accustomed: but from the necessity of the case, and a regard to the mutual interests of both countries, we cheerfully consent to the operation of such acts of the British Parliament, as are bona fide, restrained to the regulation of our external commerce, for the purpose of securing the commercial advantages of the whole empire to the mother country, and the commercial benefits of its respective members, excluding every idea of taxation internal or external, for raising a revenue on the subjects in America without their consent.

' RESOLVED, N. C. D. V. That the respective Colonies are entitled to the common law of England, and more especially to the great and inestimable priviledge of being tried by their peers of the vicinage, according to the course of that law.

' RESOLVED, VI. That they are entitled to the benefit of such of the English statutes, as existed at the time of their Colonization; and which they have, by experience, respectively found to be applicable to their several local and other circumstances.

' RESOLVED, N. C. D. VII. That these, his Majesty's Colonies are likewise entitled to all the immunities and privileges granted and confirmed to them by royal charters, or secured by their several codes of Provincial Laws.

' RESOLVED, N. C. D. VIII. That they have a right peaceably to assemble, consider of their grievances, and petition the King; and that all prosecutions, prohibitory proclamations, and commitments for the same, are illegal.

' RESOLVED, N. C. D. IX. That the keeping a standing army in these Colonies, in times of peace, without the consent of the Legislature of that Colony in which such army is kept, is against law.

' RESOLVED, N. C. D. X. It is indispensibly necessary to a good government, and rendered essential by the English Constitution, that the constituent branches of the Legislature be independent of each other; that, therefore, the exercise of legislative power in several Colonies, by a council appointed, during pleasure, by the crown, is unconstitutional, dangerous, and destructive to the freedom of American Legislation.

' ALL, and each of which, the aforesaid Deputies in behalf of themselves, and their constituents, do claim, demand, and insist on, as their indubitable rights and liberties; which cannot be legally taken from them, altered or abridged, by any power whatever, without their own consent, by their Representatives in their several Provincial Legislatures.

' IN the course of our inquiry, we find many infringements and violations of the foregoing rights; which, from an ardent desire that harmony and mutual intercourse of affection and interest may be restored, we pass over for the present, and proceed to state such acts and measures as have been adopted since the last war, which demonstrate a system formed to enslave America.

' RESOLVED, N. C. D. That the following acts of Parliament are infringements and violations of the rights of the Colonists; and that the repeal of them is essentially necessary, in order to restore harmony between Great-Britain and the American Colonies, viz.

THE several acts of 4 Geo. III. ch. 15. and ch. 34....
5 Geo. III. ch. 25....6 Geo. III. ch. 52....7 Geo. III.
ch. 41. and ch. 46....8 Geo. III. ch. 22. which impose
duties for the purpose of raising a revenue in America,
extend the powers of the admiralty courts beyond
their ancient limits, deprive the American subject of
trial by jury, authorise the judge's certificate to indemnify the prosecutor from damages, that he might
otherwise be liable to, requiring oppressive security
from a claimant of ships and goods seized, before he
shall be allowed to defend his property, and are subversive of American Rights.

' ALSO, 12 Geo. III. ch. 24. intitled, ' An act for
' the better securing his Majesty's dock-yards, maga-
' zines, ships, ammunition, and stores.' Which declares a new offence in America, and deprives the
American subject of a constitutional trial by jury of
the vicinage, by authorising the trial of any person
charged with the committing any offence described
in the said act out of the realm, to be indicted and
tried for the same in any shire or county within the
realm.

' ALSO, the three acts passed in the last session of
Parliament, for stopping the port and blocking up the
harbor of Boston, for altering the charter and government of Massachusetts-Bay, and that which is
intitled, ' An act for the better administration of
' justice,' &c.

' Also, the act passed in the same session, for establishing the Roman Catholic religion in the Province of Quebec, abolishing the equitable system of English Laws, and erecting a tyranny there, to the great danger, from so total a dissimularity of religion, law, and government, to the neighboring British Colonies, by the assistance of whose blood and treasure, the said country was conquered from France.

' Also, the act passed in the same session for the better providing suitable quarters for officers and soldiers in his Majesty's service in North-America.

' Also, that the keeping a standing army in several of these Colonies, in time of peace, without the consent of the Legislature of that Colony in which such army is kept, is against law.'

Resolved, That this Congress do approve the above declaration of American Rights.

Ordered, That the Association formed by the late Continental Congress, be taken into immediate consideration.

THE ASSOCIATION.

••••••••••••••••••••

' WE his Majesty's most loyal subjects, the delegates of the several Colonies of New-Hampshire,
Massachusetts-Bay, Rhode-Island, Connecticut, New-
York, New-Jersey, Pennsylvania, the three Lower
Counties of Newcastle, Kent, and Sussex on Delaware, Maryland, Virginia, North-Carolina, and South-
Carolina, deputed to represent them, in a Continental Congress, held in the city of Philadelphia, on the
fifth day of September, 1774, avowing our allegiance
to his Majesty, our affection and regard for our fellow-subjects in Great Britain and elsewhere, affected with the deepest anxiety, and most alarming apprehensions at those grievances and distresses, with
which his Majesty's American subjects are oppressed, and having taken under our most serious deliberation, the state of the whole continent, find that the
present unhappy situation of our affairs, is occasioned by a ruinous system of Colony-administration,
adopted by the British ministry about the year 1763,
evidently calculated for enslaving these Colonies, and,
with them, the British Empire. In prosecution of
which system, various Acts of Parliament have been
passed for raising a Revenue in America, for depri-
ving the American subjects, in many instances, of

the constitutional trial by jury, exposing their lives to danger, by directing a new and illegal trial beyond the seas, for crimes alleged to have been committed in America: And in prosecution of the same system, several late, cruel, and oppressive Acts have been passed respecting the town of Boston and the Massachusetts-Bay, and also an Act for extending the Province of Quebec, so as to border on the western frontiers of these Colonies, establishing an arbitrary government therein, and discouraging the settlement of British subjects in that wide extended country; thus, by the influence of civil principles and ancient prejudices to dispose the inhabitants to act with hostility against the free Protestant Colonies, whenever a wicked Ministry shall chuse so to direct them.

' To obtain redress of these grievances, which threaten destruction to the lives, liberty, and property of his Majesty's subjects in North-America, we are of opinion, that a non-importation, non-consumption, and non-exportation agreement, faithfully adhered to, will prove the most speedy, effectual, and peaceable measure :....And therefore we do, for ourselves, and the inhabitants of the several Colonies, whom we represent, firmly agree and associate under the sacred ties of virtue, honor, and love of our country, as follows:

' I. THAT from and after the first day of December next, we will not import into British-America from Great Britain or Ireland, any goods, wares, or merchandize whatsoever, or from any other place any such goods, wares, or merchandize, as shall have been exported from Great Britain or Ireland; nor will we, after that day, import any East-India tea from any part of the world; nor any molasses, syrups, paneles, coffee, or pimento, from the British plantations, or from Dominica; nor wines from Madeira, or the Western Islands; nor foreign Indigo.

' II. WE will neither import, nor purchase any slave imported after the first day of December next, after which time, we will wholly discontinue the slave-trade, and will neither be concerned in it ourselves, nor will we hire our vessels, nor sell our commodities or manufactures to those who are concerned in it.

' III. As a non-consumption agreement, strictly adhered. to, will be an effectual security for the observation of the non-importation, we, as above, solemnly agree and associate, that from this day, we will not purchase or use any tea imported on account of the East-India Company, or any on which a duty hath been or shall be paid; and from and after the first day of March next, we will not purchase or use any East-India tea whatever, nor will we, nor shall any person for or under us, purchase or use any of those goods, wares, or merchandize, we have agreed not to import, which we shall know, or have cause to suspect, were imported after the first day of December, except such as come under the rules and directions of the tenth article hereafter mentioned.

‘ IV. THE earnest desire we have, not to injure our fellow-subjects in Great-Britain, Ireland, or the West-Indies, induces us to suspend a non-exportation until the tenth day of September, 1775; at which time, if the said acts and parts of acts of the British Parliament, herein after mentioned, are not repealed, we will not, directly, or indirectly, export any merchandize or commodity whatsoever, to Great-Britain, Ireland, or the West-Indies, except Rice to Europe.

‘ V. SUCH as are merchants, and use the British and Irish trade, will give orders, as soon as possible, to their factors, agents, and correspondents, in Great-Britain and Ireland, not to ship any goods to them on any pretence whatsoever, as they cannot be received in America; and if any merchant residing in Great Britain or Ireland, shall directly or indirectly ship any goods, wares, or merchandize, for America, in order to break the said non-importation agreement, or in any manner contravene the same, on such unworthy conduct being well attested, it ought to be made public: and, on the same being so done, we will not from thenceforth have any commercial connexion with such merchant.

‘ VI. THAT such as are owners of vessels will give positive orders to their captains, or masters, not to receive on board' their vessels any goods prohibited by the said non-importation agreement, on pain of immediate dismission from their service.

'VII. WE will use our utmost endeavors to improve the breed of sheep, and encrease their number to the greatest extent, and to that end, we will kill them as sparingly as may be, especially those of the most profitable kind; nor will we export any to the West-Indies, or elsewhere ; and those of us who are, or may become overstocked with, or can conveniently spare any sheep, will dispose of them to our neighbors, especially to the poorer sort, on moderate terms.

'VIII. WE will in our several stations, encourage frugality, economy, and industry ; and promote agriculture, arts, and the manufactures of this country, especially that of wool ; and will discountenance, and discourage, every species of extravagance and dissipation, especially all horse-racing, and all kinds of gaming, cock-fighting, exhibitions of shews, plays, and other expensive diversions and entertainments. And on the death of any relation or friend, none of us, or any of our families will go into any further mourning dress, than a black crape or ribbon on the arm or hat for gentlemen, and a black ribbon and necklace for ladies, and we will discontinue the giving of gloves and scarfs at funerals.

' IX. SUCH as are venders of goods or merchandize, will not take advantage of the scarcity of goods that may be occasioned by this association, but will sell at the same rates we have been respectively accustomed to do, for twelve months last past....And if any vender of goods or merchandize, shall sell any such goods on higher terms, or shall in any manner, or by any device whatsoever, violate or depart from this agreement, no person ought, nor will any of us deal with any such person, or his, or her factor or agent, at any time thereafter, for any commodity whatever.

' X. In case any merchant, trader, or other persons shall import any goods or merchandize after the first day of December, and before the first day of February next, the same ought forthwith, at the election of the owner, to be either reshipped or delivered up to the Committee of the County, or town wherein they shall be imported, to be stored at the risk of the importer, until the non-importation agreement shall cease, or be sold under the direction of the Committee aforesaid; and in the last mentioned case, the owner or owners of such goods, shall be reimbursed (out of the sales) the first cost and charges, the profit if any, to be applied towards relieving and employing such poor inhabitants of the town of Boston, as are immediate sufferers by the Boston Port-Bill; and a particular account of all goods so returned, stored, or sold, to be inserted in the public papers; and if any goods, or merchandizes shall be imported after the said first day of February, the same ought forthwith to be sent back again, without breaking any of the packages thereof.

' XI. THAT a Committee be chosen in every county, city, and town, by those who are qualified to vote for Representatives in the Legislature, whose business it shall be attentively to observe the conduct of all persons touching this association; and when it shall be made to appear to the satisfaction of a majority of any such Committee, that any person within the limits of their appointment has violated this association, that such majority do forthwith cause the truth of the case to be published in the Gazette, to the end, that all such foes to the rights of British America may be publicly known, and universally contemned as the enemies of American liberty; and thenceforth we respectively will break off all dealings with him or her.

' XII. THAT the Committee of correspondence in the respective Colonies do frequently inspect the entries of their custom-houses, and inform each other from time to time of the true state thereof, and of every other material circumstance that may occur relative to this association.

' XIII. THAT all manufactures of this country be sold at reasonable prices, so that no undue advantage be taken of a future scarcity of goods.

' XIV. AND we do further agree and resolve, that we will have no trade, commerce, dealings, or intercourse whatsoever, with any Colony or Province in North-America, which shall not accede to, or which shall hereafter violate this Association, but will hold them as unworthy of the rights of freemen, and as inimical to the liberties of their country.

' AND we do solemnly bind ourselves and our constituents, under the ties aforesaid, to adhere to this Association until such parts of the several acts of Parliament passed since the close of the last war, as impose or continue duties on tea, wine, molasses, syrups, paneles, coffee, sugar, pimento, indigo, foreign paper, glass, and painter's colors, imported into America, and extend the powers of the admiralty courts beyond their ancient limits, deprive the American subject of trial by jury, authorise the judge's certificate to indemnify the prosecuter from damages, that he might otherwise be liable to, from a trial by his peers, requires oppressive security from a claimant of ships or goods seized, before he shall be allowed to defend his property, are repealed....And until that part of the act of the 12 G. 3. ch. 24. entitled ' An Act for the better securing his Majesty's dockyards, magazines, ships, ammunition, and stores ;' by which, any persons charged with committing any of the offences therein described, in America, may be tried in any shire or county within the realm, is repealed....And until the four acts passed in the last Session of Parliament, viz. that for stopping the port and blocking up the harbor of Boston...That for altering the charter and government of the Massachusetts-Bay...And that which is intitled, ' An Act for the better administration of justice, &c.'...And that ' For extending the limits of Quebec, &c.' are repealed. And we recommend it to the Provincial Conventions, and to the Committees in the respective Colonies, to establish such farther regulations as they may think proper, for carrying into execution this Association.

' THE foregoing Association being determined upon by the Congress, was ordered to be subscribed by the several members thereof; and thereupon we have hereunto set our respective names accordingly.

IN CONGRESS, PHILADELPHIA, OCT. 20, 1774.

Signed,

PEYTON RANDOLPH, *President.*

NEW-HAMPSHIRE. John Sullivan, Nathaniel Folsom.

MASSACHUSETTS-BAY. Thomas Cushing, Sam. Adams, John Adams, Robert Treat Paine.

RHODE-ISLAND. Stephen Hopkins, Samuel Ward.

CONNECTICUT. Eliphalet Dyer, Roger Sherman, Silas Deane.

NEW-YORK. Isaac Low, John Alsop, John Jay, James Duane, William Floyd, Henry Weisner, S. Boerum.

NEW-JERSEY. James Kinsey, William Livingston, Stephen Crane, Richard Smith.

PENNSYLVANIA. Joseph Galloway, John Dickinson, Charles Humphreys, Thomas Mifflin, Edward Biddle, John Morton, George Ross.

NEW-CASTLE, &c. Cæsar Rodney, Thomas M'Kean, George Read.

MARYLAND. Mathew Tilghman, Thomas Johnson, William Paca, Samuel Chase.

VIRGINIA. Richard Henry Lee, George Washington, P. Henry, jun. Richard Bland, Benjamin Harrison, Edmund Pendleton.

NORTH-CAROLINA. William Hooper, Joseph Hews, R. Caswell.

SOUTH-CAROLINA. Henry Middleton, Thomas Lynch, Christopher Gadsden, John Rutledge, Edward Rutledge.

RESOLVED, That this Congress do approve the American Association.

ORDERED, That the Resolutions of the late Continental Congress, on the 10th of September last, and the 1st 2d, 4th, and 6th Resolutions of the said Congress on the 14th of October last, be taken into immediate consideration.

The Resolutions above referred to.

'RESOLVED UNANIMOUSLY, That this Assembly deeply feels the suffering of their countrymen in the Massachusetts-Bay, under the operation of the late unjust cruel and oppressive acts of the British Parliament...that they most thoroughly approve the wisdom and fortitude, with which opposition to these wicked ministerial measures has hitherto been conducted, and they earnestly recommend to their brethren, a perseverance in the same firm and temperate conduct, as expressed in the resolutions determined upon at a meeting of the Delegates for the county of Suffolk, on Tuesday the 6th instant, trusting that the effect of the united efforts of North-America, in their behalf, will carry such conviction to the British nation of the unwise, unjust and ruinous policy of the present administration, as quickly to introduce better men and wiser measures.

‘ RESOLVED UNANIMOUSLY, That contributions from all the Colonies for supplying the necessities, and alleviating the distresses of our brethren at Boston, ought to be continued, in such manner, and so long as their occasions may require.

‘ RESOLVED, That this Congress do approve of the opposition made by the inhabitants of Massachusetts-Bay, to the execution of the late Act of Parliament ; and if the same shall be attempted to be carried into execution by force, in such case all America ought to support them in their opposition.

‘ RESOLVED, That it is the opinion of this body, that the removal of the people of Boston into the country, would be, not only extremely difficult in the execution, but so important in its consequences, as to require the utmost deliberation before it is adopted. But in case the provincial meeting of that Colony shall judge it ABSOLUTELY necessary, it is the opinion of this Congress, that all America ought to contribute towards recompensing them for the injury they may thereby sustain ; and it will be recommended accordingly.

'RESOLVED UNANIMOUSLY, That every person, or persons whomsoever, who shall take, accept, or act under any commission or authority, in anywise derived from the act passed in the last Session of Parliament, changing the form of government and violating the charter of the Provinces of the Massachusetts-Bay, ought to be held in detestation and abhorrence by all good men, and considered as the wicked tools of that despotism, which is preparing to destroy those rights, which God, nature, and compact have given to America.

'RESOLVED, That the seizing, or attempting to seize, any person in America, in order to transport such person beyond the sea, for trial of offences committed within the body of a county in America, being against law, will justify, and ought to meet with resistance and reprisal.'

RESOLVED, That this Congress do approve the above resolutions of the late Continental Congress.

ORDERED, That the President do return the most

cordial and grateful thanks of this Congress, to each of the late Delegates from this Colony to the late Continental Congress, for their able and faithful discharge in the said Congress, of the high trust reposed in them by their Country. And the same was done accordingly.

RESOLVED, That the unfeigned thanks of every American, are justly due to the worthy and patriotic members of the late Continental Congress, held at Philadelphia, for their wise and spirited exertions in behalf of American Liberty : And the representatives of this Colony now met in Provincial Congress, do hereby, in behalf of themselves, and in the names of their constituents, unanimously express their sense of the great services rendered them by those important proceedings.

ORDERED, That the Rev. Mr. Turquand, a member, be desired to celebrate divine service in Provincial Congress.

RESOLVED, That the President do return the thanks of the Congress, to the Rev. Mr. Turquand, rector of St. Mathew's Parish, for his devout and pious performance of divine service before the Congress. And the same was done accordingly.

RESOLVED, That it be recommended, by this Congress, to the inhabitants of this Colony, that they give a preference to their own flour and other manufactures : and that such articles be sold at reasonable rates.

RESOLVED, That it is the unanimous opinion of this Congress, that no action for any debt shall be commenced in the court of Common Pleas of this Colony, nor any such action pending there, which was commenced since last September Return, be proceeded in without the consent of the Committee of the Parish or District, in which the defendant resides, until it shall be otherwise determined in Provincial Congress. That the said Committees respectively, or a majority of such of them as shall meet (provided they are not less than three in the country Parishes and districts) do upon application give permission, for the bringing or proceeding on such suits, in the following cases, that is to say, where the debtors refuse to renew their obligations, or to give reasonable security, or are justly suspected of intentions to leave the Province, or to defraud their creditors, or where there shall appear to the majority of such Committees as aforesaid, any other reasonable cause for the granting such permission ; which Committees shall meet and sit on the first and third Saturdays in every month, at 12 o'clock at noon, or oftener, if it shall be found necessary, for the purpose of hearing and determining on such applications. That seizures and sales upon mortgages shall be considered on the same footing as actions for debts. That it be recommended to the Committees for each Parish and District, that they use their best endeavors to prevent any debtors from removing their effects out of the Colony, without the knowledge and consent of their creditors. That the Congress will indemnify the Committees for so doing. And that no summons shall be issued by any magistrate, in small and mean causes, without the like consent.

RESOLVED, That any eleven members of the Charlestown Committee, shall be a sufficient number to receive and determine upon applications relative to the issuing of writs and process, and proceeding on suits and mortgages, in the Parishes of St. Philip and St. Michael.

RESOLVED, That the following gentlemen be the Committees for the several Districts and Parishes herein after mentioned, for effectually carrying into execution the Continental Association, and for receiving and determining upon applications relative to law processes as aforesaid.

FOR the Parish of Christ-Church. Messrs. Gabriel Capers, Clement Lempriere, Sims White, Joseph Maybank, Robert Dorrel, Nathan Legaré, Isaac Legaré, Levi Duraud, and Joshua Toomer.

FOR the Parish of St. George, Dorchester. Messrs. John Joor, John Glaze, Daniel Stewart, Thomas Waring, William Dewitt, David Rumph, and William Morgan.

For the Parish of St. Andrew. Messrs. William Scott, Thomas Bee, William Cattell, Thomas Fuller, Benjamin Stone, Isaac Rivers, Henry Samways, Benjamin Fuller, and Richard Hutson.

For the Parish of St. James, Goose-Creek. Messrs. Benjamin Coachman, Henry Smith, John Davies, James Streater, Alexander Mazyck, Benjamin Mazyck, and Thomas Walter.

For the Parish of St. John, Berkley-County, Messrs. James Cordes, John Cordes, Elias Ball, jun. Richard Gough, Peter Witten, Peter Marion, and Stephen Mazyck, jun.

For the Parish of St. Paul. Messrs. Roger Sanders, Robert Miles, Allen Miles, Melchior Garner, Morton Wilkinson, Joseph Bee, and Edward Perry.

For the Parish of St. Bartholomew. Messrs. James Skirving, jun. Philip Smith, William Skirving, Edmund Hyrne, Thomas Hutchinson, Joseph Glover, Charles Shepheard, James Donnom, and William Mills.

For the Parish of St. John, Colleton-County. viz.

For John's-Island and Wadmelah-Island. Messrs. Abraham Waite, sen. James Laroach, William Boone, Thomas Ladson, Thomas Hunscomb, John Wilson, and John Holmes.   And,

For Edisto, in the said Parish. Messrs. Joseph Seabrook, Patrick Simpson, Joseph Fickling, Daniel Jenkins, James Murray, James Fickling, and Samuel Eaton.

For the Parish of St. James, Santee. Messrs.
John Barnett, Joseph Legaré, jun. Jonah Collins,
John Egan, Richard Withers, John Drake, and Col.
Elias Horry.

For the Parish of Prince-George. That is to say,

For George-town. Messrs. Paul Trapier, Samuel
Wragg, Paul Trapier, jun. Benjamin Young, Joseph
Allston, Thomas Godfrey, Anthony Bonneau, John
Withers, Hugh Horry, Daniel Tucker, and Robert
Heriot.   And,

For Little-River, in the said Parish. Messrs. Josias
Allston, Samuel Dwight, Dennis Hankins, Francis
Allston, and John Allston, jun.

For the Parish of St. Mathew. Colonel Tacitus
Gaillard, Col. William Thomson, Col. John Savage,
Rev. Paul Turquand, Messrs. George King, John
Caldwell, Simon Berwick, Henry Felder, Colonel
Michael Christopher Rowe, Messrs. Lewis Golson,
Adam Snell, and Christopher Zahn.

For the Parish of St. Helena. Messrs. Thomas
Rutledge, John Joyner, John Barnwell, jun. Daniel
Heyward, jun. Daniel De Saussure, William Rey-
nolds, James Dougharty, William Waite, Joseph
Jenkins, Francis Martingale, and Tunis Tebout.

For the Parish of Prince-Frederick. Messrs. John
James, Hugh Giles, Anthony White, jun. William
Gamble, Robert M'Cottery, John Witherspoon, Tho-

mas Potts, Francis Britton, William Michau, William Thompson, and William Snow.

For the Parish of St. Stephen. Messrs. Hezekiah Mayham, David Gaillard, John Pamor, jun. René Richbourg, John Dubois, John Peyre, and John Coutourier.

For the Parish of St. Peter. Messrs. Cornelius Dupont, John Louis Bourquin, James Thompson, John Chisolme, Adrian Mayer, John Buche, senior. and Charles Dupont.

For the Parish of St. Thomas and St. Dennis. Messrs. Daniel Lesesne, Edward Thomas, jun. Rev. Alexander Garden, Thomas Screven, Thomas Ashby, Thomas Dearington, and Benjamin Simons.

For the Parish of Prince-William. Col. Stephen Bull, Messrs. Benjamin Garden, Thomas Hudson, Joseph Brailsford, Ulysses Macpherson, John Ward, William Harden, William Bull, and John Wheatley.

For the Parish of St. David. Messrs. Henry William Harrington, George Pawley, Alexander M'Intosh, Claudius Pegues, Samuel Wise, Burwell Boyakin, George Hicks, Philip Pledger, and John Donaldson.

For Ninety-Six District. Col. James Mayson, Messrs. Andrew Williamson, Le Roy Hammond, Richard Rapley, Patrick Calhoun, Francis Salvador, John Purves, Benjamin Tutt, William Moore, John

Bowie, William Anderson, Hugh Middleton, David
Zubly, Moses Kirkland, William Calhoun, and
Arthur Symkins.

For the District in the Forks, between Broad and
Saluda Rivers. Col. Thomas Fletchall, Major John
Caldwell, Messrs. Charles King, John Williams,
John Satterthwaite, Jonathan Downes, James Wil-
liams, James Creswell, John M'Nees, Robert Cun-
ningham, George Ross, Samuel Savage, John Tho-
mas, John Ford, John Caldwell, John Gordon, and
John Prince.

For the District between Broad and Catawba
Rivers. Messrs. Thomas Taylor, Thomas Woodward, John Hopkins, John Chesnut, Robert Goodwin, William Howell, John Winn, Henry Hunter,
David Hopkins, Joseph Kirkland, and Robert Hancock.

For the District of Saxe-Gotha. Messrs. Benjamin
Farrar, Jonas Beard, William Tucker, Samuel Boyakin, Godfrey Drier, and Ralph Humphries.

For the District Eastward of the Wateree-River.
Col. Richard Richardson, Messrs. Robert Carter,
William Richardson, William Wilson, Mathew
Singleton, Thomas Sumpter, Joseph Kershaw,
Robert Patton, Richard Richardson, jun. John James,
sen. Samuel Little, John Marshal, and Isaac Ross.

Resolved, That a strict conformity to the requisition of this Congress, be recommended to the gen-

tlemen of the law, and all other persons, in regard to the issuing of writs and process, and proceeding on suits and mortgages.

RESOLVED, That it is the opinion of this Congress, that after the 10th day of September next, compensation shall be made by those who raise articles which may be then exported to those who cannot raise such articles, for the losses which they may sustain, by not exporting the commodities which they raise.

RESOLVED, That if the exportation of Rice should be continued after the 10th of September next, one third of the Rice made in this Colony, shall as it is brought to Charlestown, Beaufort, and Georgetown, be deposited in the hands of the Committees herein after appointed, at each of those places respectively, and sold by such Committees.*

RESOLVED, That the said Committees receive such of the following commodities, as shall be brought to them, the same being the produce of this Colony, merchantable, and not more in quantity or value than one third of the commodities of each kind, raised for sale in one season, by the owner of them (butter excepted) viz.

INDIGO, Copper of the best sort, at thirty shillings

* The exportation of Rice was prohibited by Congress, which put an end to the business of the Committees for exchange of property.

per pound...and other kinds in proportion to that value.

HEMP, at eight pounds per hundred weight, exclusive of the bounty.

CORN, at twelve shillings and six-pence per bushel.

FLOUR, of the best sort, at four pounds ten shillings ; and of the second sort, at four pounds per hundred weight.

LUMBER, inch pine boards, per 1000 feet, at twenty pounds, in Charlestown ; and fifteen pounds in Beaufort and Georgetown ; and other plank and scantling in proportion.

PORK, at thirteen pounds per barrel.

BUTTER, at three shillings per pound.*

AND, that in case the price of Rice should be higher or lower than fifty-five shillings per hundred weight, when the said commodities are deposited with such Committees, the price of such commodities shall be raised or lowered, from the above rate, in proportion to such rise or fall of the price of Rice.

RESOLVED, That the said Committees shall pay for the said commodities in the order they are brought to them, according to the foregoing rates ; either in money arising from the sale of Rice as it shall be delivered to them, if such Rice shall be sold and the money received, or in Rice if the owner of such commodities chooses to take it, or in certificates set-

---

* This was the paper currency of the State, and was depreciated to 7 for 1 of specie.

ting forth the quantity and value of the commodities which the Committee have received, and to whom they belonged ; and that such person, or the person holding such certificate, may receive the said sum in his turn, as money shall be received for Rice brought to the Committee, which certificates shall pass and be received as money.

RESOLVED, That the persons making Indigo, shall produce to the Committee of the Parish or District, in which it shall have been made, on oath, samples of it, according to its different qualities.

RESOLVED, That the person bringing any of the said commodities to the said Committees in Charlestown, Beaufort, and Georgetown, shall at the same time produce a certificate, from the Committee of the Parish or District where such commodities shall have been made or raised (which certificate, such Committee, being satisfied of the truth thereof, on oath of the party, shall give) specifying, that the commodities so brought, are only one third according to the quantity and quality of the commodity of that kind, raised in this Colony, in one season, for sale, by the owner, requiring such certificate.

RESOLVED, That the commodities brought to the said Committees, shall be at the risk of the persons bringing them down, until they shall be sold or exchanged as aforesaid. And that the Rice-planter, on delivering a third of his Rice, as it shall be brought to market to the Committee, shall have his proportion of such commodities as aforesaid, in the order they shall have been brought down, delivered to him or disposed of as he shall think proper.

RESOLVED, That the Committees settle their accounts of this business in November, 1776, and pay to the Rice-planters the balance of money (if any) belonging to them, which shall be in the hands of the said Committees. And in case the Rice so delivered shall not be sufficient to sink the said certificates, the same shall be made good out of the next crop of Rice.

RESOLVED, That persons making any other commodities than those above enumerated, which cannot be exported, shall be put upon a footing, in point of compensation for their losses by a non-exportation, with the makers of the commodities above specified.

RESOLVED, That the following gentlemen be Committees, to exchange Rice for other commodities after the 10th day of September next, if the non-exportation of Rice should be continued after that day, viz.

FOR Charlestown. Christopher Gadsden, Isaac Huger, William Gibbes, William Parker, Aaron Loocock, Roger Smith, Maurice Simons, John Poaug, Esqrs. Messrs. Thomas Legaré, sen. Edward Simons, Edward Blake, Samuel Prioleau, jun. Hugh Swinton, John Champneys, William Hort,

John Brewton, Alexander Chisolme, Alexander Chovin, William Livingston, and John Baddeley.

For George town, Winyah. Paul Trapier, Samuel Wragg, Benjamin Young, Joseph Allston, Thomas Godfrey, Robert Heriot, Esqrs. Messrs. Paul Trapier, jun. Anthony Bonneau, John Withers, Hugh Horry, Daniel Tucker, Samuel Smith, George Croft, James Gordon, George Heriot, and Thomas Mitchell.

For Beaufort, Port-Royal. Col. Stephen Bull, Messrs. Thomas Hughes, William Kelsall, Andrew Deveaux, William Elliott, Nathaniel Barnwell, jun. John Fripp, William Waite, George Barksdale, James Cuthbert, John Edwards, jun. James Frazer, Charles Givens, and John Joyner, jun.

RESOLVED, That in case of a general exportation or non-importation, these resolutions respecting compensation shall cease.

RESOLVED, That it be recommended to the inhabitants of this Colony, to raise cotton, hemp, flour, wool, barley, and hops.

RESOLVED, That after the first day of March next, no lambs or sheep be killed for sale.

RESOLVED, That stores in Charlestown, Beaufort, and George-town, be taken, and storekeepers employed to buy all the wool that may be brought to them, at three shillings per pound for unwashed, and five shillings for clean wool; that it be sold out at the same rates, to any person who shall undertake to manufacture it : And that such store-keepers receive, and expose to sale, for the benefit of the persons, bringing them down, all linen, woollen, and cotton manufactures of this Colony.

RESOLVED, That the present Representation of this Colony, shall continue until the next general meeting of the inhabitants, under the title of the PROVINCIAL CONGRESS. That it shall be adjourned from time to time by the President. That it be summoned to convene for the dispatch of business, upon any emergency, by a vote of the Charlestown General Committee. At which Committee, every member of this Congress, who may happen to be in town, shall attend, and shall be considered as a member.

RESOLVED, That any forty-nine members of the Provincial Congress, be a sufficient number to proceed on business.

RESOLVED, That any twenty-one members of the Charlestown Committee, assembled, be a sufficient number to proceed upon business.

RESOLVED, That when vacancies shall happen in any parish or district, by the death, removal, or refusal to act as a member of the present Congress, or the above mentioned Committees, the same shall be filled up by the inhabitants of such Parishes or Districts respectively.

RESOLVED, That it be strongly recommended to the parochial and District Committees, to use their utmost endeavors, to obtain liberal donations for the relief of the suffering people in the town of Boston and Colony of Massachusetts-Bay. And that all such donations as may be collected from time to time, be transmitted to the General Committee in Charlestown.

RESOLVED, That the Hon. Henry Middleton, Esq. Thomas Lynch, Christopher Gadsden, John Rutledge, and Edward Rutledge, Esqrs. or any three of them, be, and they are hereby, appointed and authorized to represent this Colony on the 10th day of May next, or sooner, if necessary, at the American Congress, to be held at Philadelphia or elsewhere; with full power to concert, agree upon, direct and order such further measures as in the opinion of the said Deputies, and the Delegates of the other American Colonies to be assembled, shall appear to be necessary, for the recovery and establishment of American rights and liberties, and for restoring harmony between Great-Britain and her Colonies.

RESOLVED, That this Congress will pay the expenses of the said Deputies, in going to, attending at, and returning from the said American Congress.

RESOLVED, That a Committee be appointed to prepare a proper address to his Honor the Lieutenant-Governor, touching the sitting of the General Assembly.

THE Committee reported the address to the Lieut. Governor, which having been amended, is as follows: To the Honourable WILLIAM BULL, Esq. Lieutenant-Governor and Commander in Chief, in and
over His Majesty's Colony of South-Carolina.

MAY IT PLEASE YOUR HONOR,

WE his Majesty's faithful and loyal subjects, the Representatives of all the good people in this Colo-
ny, now met in Provincial Congress think ourselves indispensably obliged to address your Honor, for redress of a grievance, which threatens destruction to the Constitution, and ruin to the inhabitants of this Country: we mean, the long, and still continued, disuse of General Assemblies; contrary, not only to every principle of free Government, but di-
rectly against a law of this Province.

To enumerate all the unhappy consequences which must follow a denial of the right of the peo-
ple, to appear, frequently, by their Representatives in General Assembly, must be unnecessary. Your Honor, who has, as a private person, enjoyed the blessing of freedom and good government amongst us, can want no information on that head.

TAXES continuing to be raised and paid, and laws to be executed, against the sense of the people, are but a part of our grievances.

MORTIFYING as these considerations are, the causes are more so; being, according to our best information, no other than a refusal of the House of Assembly to obey Ministerial Mandates, contrary to their consciences, and subversive of the rights of their constituents; and his Majesty's Council, composed chiefly of place-men, paying an implicit and servile obedience to unconstitutional instructions. Such acts tend, immediately, to a total abolition of Assemblies; for, if freedom of debate, and a constitutional independence be denied to them, they cannot possibly be useful; probably they will become dangerous.

WE forbear to trouble your Honor with reasons, in support of the request which we now, as of right, make, in behalf of all the good subjects of his Majesty in this Colony, that the holding and sitting of the General Assembly be no longer delayed, but that it be permitted to sit, for the dispatch of public business, as formerly.

WE pray your Honor to be assured, that by this our humble address, we do not intend to question his Majesty's prerogative, of calling, proroguing and dissolving the General Assembly, but only to request, that this power be exercised FOR THE GOOD OF THE PEOPLE.

    By Order of the Provincial Congress.

      CHARLES PINCKNEY, *President.*

IN PROVINCIAL CONGRESS,

CHARLESTOWN, *Jan.* 17, 1775.

THE address having been presented by the Congress, his Honor the Lieut. Governor was pleased to return the following answer:

GENTLEMEN,

I KNOW no legal Representative of the good people of this Province, but the Commons House of Assembly, chosen according to the Election Act, and met in General Assembly....As gentlemen of respectable characters and property in this Province, I acquaint you, that the General Assembly stands prorogued to the 24th instant. I have always endeavored to make the law of the land my rule of government in the administration of public affairs, and I shall not omit observing it in meeting the General Assembly according to the prorogation; with whom I shall, under the guidance of my duty to the King, and zeal for the service of the Province, do every thing in my power, that can contribute to the public welfare.

WILLIAM BULL.

CHARLESTOWN, *Jan.* 17th, 1775.

RESOLVED, That it be recommended by this Congress, to all the inhabitants of this Colony, that they be diligently attentive in learning the use of arms; and that their officers be requested to train and exercise them, at least, once a fortnight.

RESOLVED, That it be recommended to the inhabitants of this Colony, to set apart Friday the 17th February next, as a day of fasting, humiliation and prayer, before Almighty God, devoutly to petition him to inspire the King with true wisdom, to defend the people of North-America in their just title to freedom, and to avert from them the impending calamities of civil war.

RESOLVED, That the several ministers of the gospel throughout the Colony, be requested to prepare and deliver suitable discourses upon this solemn occasion.

RESOLVED, That every member of the present Congress, who may be in town, do meet at the Commons House of Assembly, and proceed from thence in a body, to attend divine service in St. Philip's Church: and that the President do request of the Rev. Mr. Robert Smith, that he will prepare and preach on that day, a sermon, suitable to the importance of the occasion.

RSEOLVED, That the President do accept of the most hearty thanks of this Congress, for the unwearied attendance he has given on the service of it, and for the very satisfactory conduct which he has pursued during the course of its important transactions.

RESOLVED, That the thanks of this Congress be returned to the member, who performed the duty of Secretary, for his faithful and diligent attention to that service.

THE Congress then adjourned until it shall be summoned to convene by the Charles-town General Committee.

THE Provincial Congress met at the State-house,
on the 17th of February, being the day appointed by
Congress, as a day of fasting, humiliation, and prayer, every place of worship in Charlestown was crowded with the inhabitants; and Congress went to St.
Philip's in a body, from the State-house, agreeably
to their resolve, and most of them in their military
array; on their entering the church, the organ
begun a solemn piece of music, and continued playing till they were seated; it was an affecting scene,
as every one knew the occasion, and all joined in
fervent prayer to the Lord, to support, and defend
us, in this our great struggle in the cause of LIBERTY
and our Country; and the Rev. Dr. Smith* (at the
request of the Provincial Congress) delivered an excellent and suitable discourse upon the occasion;
which very much animated the men; whilst the fe-
male part of the congregation were affected quite in
a different manner; floods of tears rolled down their
cheeks, from the sad reflection of their nearest and
dearest friends and relations entering into a dreadful civil war; the worst of wars! and, what was
most to be lamented, it could not be avoided.

AGREEABLE to a recommendation of the Provincial Congress, the militia were forming themselves
into volunteer uniform companies; drums beating,
fifes playing; squads of men exercising on the out

* Bishop Smith.

skirts of the town; a military spirit pervaded the whole country; and Charlestown had the appearance of a garrison town; every thing wore the face of war; though not one of us had the least idea of its approach; and more especially of its being so near to us, for we were anxiously looking forward to a reconciliation; when, on the 19th day of April, war was declared against America, by the British troops firing upon the inhabitants at Lexington; an account of which flew over the whole continent; and now the hopes of a reconciliation were at an end; and recourse to arms was the only and last resort.

In this situation were we when the battle of Lexington was fought, without arms or ammunition: some there were in the King's stores, but we could not get them without committing some violent act. A few gentlemen went to Capt. Cochran (the King's store-keeper) and demanded the keys of him: he said ' He could not give them up, neither could he hinder them from breaking open the doors;' this hint was enough; there was no time for hesitation; and that night a number of gentlemen went and broke open the doors, and carried away to their own keeping, 1200 good stand of arms: Lieut. Governor Bull offered a reward of one hundred pounds sterling to any person who would discover the persons concerned in the business; but to no purpose.

We had now got the arms, but no ammunition;

the next thing to be done, was the breaking open
the magazines ; as we were fairly entered into the
business we could not step back, and the next day
we broke open the magazines, and found in that at
Hobea, 1700 lb. at the Ship-yard, 600 lb. some little
at Fort Charlotte, in the back country, and in private
stores, the whole making about 3000 lbs. of powder,
which was all we had to begin our great Revolution.
On the same day the battle of Lexington was fought,
a Packet arrived at Charlestown from England : the
public letters were taken out by the secret committee, the particulars I have from Mr. Corbet, as follows :

'I was a member of the secret committee of the
'State ; and some time in 1775, a Packet arrived
'from England (it was about the time that disputes
'ran high with Lord William Campbell, the then
'Governor, and it was resolved by that committee
'to get possession of the Mail, that was expected in
'that Packet; and for that purpose the member who
'should first know of the Packets coming in, should
'give notice to the others, and be ready at the Post-
'Office, to get possession of the Mail ; as I lived at
'the south end of the Bay, I was the first mem-
'ber who knew of her coming, and immediately
'gave notice thereof to such as I could first find
'in time to intercept the Mail. On its arrival, Wm.
'Henry Drayton, and John Neufville, they two and

'myself, immediately went to the Office, kept then
'by Stevens, and demanded the Mail, he perempto-
'rily refused it, and we as peremptorily demanded it,
'declaring that we would take it by force if not deli-
'vered quickly, having authority for that purpose;
'he said we might do as we pleased, but that he
'should not deliver it : we then took possession of it,
'(for which he entered a regular protest against us,)
'we carried it to the State-house, and summoned
'the rest of the Committee ; when the Mail was open-
'ed, it contained (besides private letters) dispatches
'to Gov. Dunmore, of Virginia, Gov. Martin, of
'N. Carolina, Gov. Campbell, of S. Carolina, Gov.
'Wright, of Georgia, and Gov. Tonyne, of Augustine,
'(the private letters were all returned to the Post-
'Office unopened) the others were opened, and read,
'and found to contain the determination of England
'to coerce America; and directing the respective
'Governors to prepare such Provincial forces as they
'could, to co-operate when they should come : these
'dispatches were thought of so much consequence,
'as to be sent by express to Congress; and I have
'understood that it was the first certain accounts of
'the determination of the Councils of England, to
'subjugate the Colonies by force ; and the effect
'was that Congress resolved to raise an army, and
'prepare seriously for defence.

Yours, &c.   THOMAS CORBET,'

ABOUT this time a letter from Governor Wright to Gen. Gage, going to the northward, was intercepted by the secret committee, and opened; in it was found a request to Gen. Gage to send a detachment of his Majesty's forces to awe the people of Georgia; the secret committee took out his letter, and put another in the cover, (with his name counterfeited) in which they mention to Gen. Gage, ' that he had wrote for ' troops to awe the people, but that now there was ' no occasion for his sending them, that the people ' were again come to some order:' thus were the Americans obliged to take great strides to defeat the purposes of the British Government.

IN consequence of the battle of Lexington, the general committee immediately summoned the provincial Congress to meet on the first day of June, which was twenty-three days after the day appointed for their meeting. This long interval between the summons and the meeting gave the members time, cooly and deliberately to reflect, to consider, and prepare their minds for the events of war; there was no alternative. The reasons given for their call were:

'I. THE British troops in the province of Massachu-
' setts did, on the 19th day of April last, commence
' civil war in America, with force of arms, seizing and
' destroying the property of the people of that Colony,
' making hostile assaults upon their persons, whereby
' many of them fell in battle, in defence of their pro-

' perty, and the liberty of America ; a conduct in the
' British troops amounting, in effect, to a direct and
' hostile attack upon the whole people of this Conti-
' nent, threatening them with all the calamities of
' slavery.

' II. BECAUSE this Colony cannot discharge her
' duty in defence of American freedom, unless we
' put it into a state of security against any attack by
' the British arms ; this Colony being in a manner so
' immediately defenceless, that if only a small mili-
' tary British force should arrive, while things are in
' so deplorable a situation, they might easily take post
' in Charlestown where the continuance of the pro-
' vincial Congress and general committee would
' thereby become not only endangered, but impracti-
' cable, and there not being any body of men to en-
' force the execution of the American Association,
' there is every probability that in such a situation of
' affairs, it would be immediately violated ; a circum-
' stance that might be of the most fatal consequence
' to America.'

' III. BECAUSE there are just grounds to apprehend
' an insurrection of the slaves, and hostilities from
' the Indians instigated by the tools of a wicked ad-
' ministration.'

' IV. BECAUSE the formal military and naval forces
' lately sent from Great-Britain to reinforce the army
' in Boston, manifest the accursed design of the

' British Ministry to endeavor to quell the American
' troubles by arms, and not to quiet them by the
' laws of reason and justice. Thence, despairing of
' a redress of grievances by dutiful and peaceable ap-
' plication, long, unavailing, presented to his Bri-
' tanic Majesty, we see no alternative but that we sub-
' mit to abject slavery or appeal to the Lord of hosts,
' in defence of the common and unalienable rights,
' peculiar to Englishmen.'

AT this summons the people were greatly alarmed,
and their minds so much agitated, they were anxiously waiting for the day of the meeting that they
might consult with their countrymen, on what was
best to be done at this critical juncture; they saw
that a war was inevitable; and that it was to be with
that country which first planted them in America,
and raised them to maturity; a country with which
they were connected by consanguinity; by custom,
and by manners; by religion; by laws, and by language; a country that they had always been taught
to respect and to consider as amongst the first in the
world. A rich and powerful nation, with numerous
fleets, and experienced admirals sailing triumphant
over the ocean; with large armies and able generals
in many parts of the globe: This great nation we
dared to oppose, without money; without arms;
without ammunition; no generals; no armies; no
admirals; and no fleets; this was our situation when

the contest began: On our first meeting they determined upon a defensive war; and the fourth day it was resolved to raise two regiments of five hundred men each; and some confidential gentlemen were immediately sent to the West-India Islands, in small fast sailing vessels, to procure powder. They were so successful as to bring home ten thousand pounds, which was a very seasonable supply. The military ardor was so great, that many more candidates presented themselves, from the first families in the Province, as officers for the two regiments then were wanted; every one was zealous in the cause; those who through infirmities and particular domestic situations could not take the field, went into the cabinet and other civil employment; and in this way did we divide ourselves in different departments.

THE day after the officers of the first and second regiments of foot were ballotted for, it was resolved to raise a regiment of cavalry rangers of five hundred men. The pay and rations of the officers in the British service had at that time ; the soldiers had one shilling sterling per day ; the rangers had much more, as they were to find their own horses: In regard to the regiment of rangers, it was thought not only useful, but political to raise them, because the most influential gentlemen in the back country were appointed officers, which interested them in the cause: The officers of the first and second regiments were taken from the low country...their names are as follows...

FIELD OFFICERS OF THE FIRST REGIMENT.

Christopher Gadsden, Col. Isaac Huger, Lieut. Col. Owen Roberts, Major.

FIELD OFFICERS OF THE SECOND REGIMENT.

William Moultrie, Col. Isaac Motte, Lieut. Col. Alexander M'Intosh, Major.

CAPTAINS OF THE FIRST AND SECOND REGIMENTS.

Charles Cotesworth Pinckney, Bernard Elliott, Francis Marion, William Cattell, Peter Horry, Daniel Horry, Adam M'Donald, Thomas Lynch, William Scot, John Barnwell, Nicholas Weleigh, James M'Donald, Isaac Harleston, Thomas Pinckney, Francis Huger, William Mason, Edmund Hyrne, Roger Parker Sanders, Charles Motte, Benjamin Cattell.

FIELD OFFICERS OF THE REGIMENT OF RANGERS.

William Thomson, Lieut Col. James Mayson, Major.

CAPTAINS OF RANGERS.

Samuel Wise, Eli Kershaw, Edward Richardson, Ezekiel Polk, Robert Goodwin, Thomas Woodward, John Caldwell, Moses Kirkland, John Purvis.

FIRST LIEUTENANTS IN THE FIRST AND SECOND REGIMENTS.

Anthony Ashby, James Ladson, Richard Singleton, Thomas Elliott, William Oliphant, John Vanderhorst, Robert Armstrong, John Blake, Glen

Drayton, Richard Shubrick, Richard Fuller, Thomas Lesene, Benjamin Dickenson, William Charnock, John Moat, Joseph Joor, James Peronneau, John A. Walter, Thomas Moultrie, Alex. M'Queen.

THE commissions for second lieutenants were given to the captains of each company.

FIRST LIEUTENANTS OF THE REGIMENT OF RANGERS.

John Lewis, P. Imhoff, Charles Heatley, Alexander Cameron, Richard Winn, John Donaldson, Hugh Middleton, Lewis Dutarque, Francis Boyakin, Samuel Watson.

THE provincial Congress having now raised troops it was necessary to have some civil executive body to carry on the business of the Colony, during the recess of Congress; accordingly, the following thirteen gentlemen were elected as a council of safety, viz. Col. Henry Laurens, Col. Charles Pinckney, the Honorable* Rawlins Lowndes, Thomas Ferguson, Miles Brewton, Arthur Middleton, Thomas Heyward, jun. Thomas Bee and John Huger, Esq. Col. James Parsons, Honorable William Henry Drayton, Benjamin Elliott and William Williamson, Esqrs.

THE council of safety had great power and authority vested in them; the entire command of the army, to contract debts, to stamp and issue money,

....
* Those called Honorable were Judges.

to liquidate and pay all accounts, and to sign commissions for the army and navy.

DURING the sitting of Congress, Lord William Campbell arrived, as governor of the province: Congress waited upon him in a body, with a congratulatory addre٬ ٬, and stating the case of their grievances: He returned for answer; ' I know of no repre-
' sentatives of the people of this province; except con-
' stitutionally appointed, convened in general as-
' sembly; and am incompetent to judge of the dis-
' pute, which at present, unhappily subsists between
' Great Britain, and the American Colonies.

' IT is impossible during the short interval since
' my arrival, that I should have acquired such a know-
' ledge of the state of the province, as to be at pres-
' ent able to make representations thereupon to his
' Majesty; but you may be assured, no representa-
' tion shall ever be made by me, but what shall be
' strictly consistent with truth, and with an earnest
' endeavor to promote the real happiness and pros-
' perity of the province.'

HIS lordship being in the habits of intimacy with several of the members and officers of the provincial troops, he told them we were doing wrong, that he was in hopes all matters would be adjusted; he had so little mistrust, and so willing to oblige, that he even gave commissions to the volunteer companies; these assurances were repeated for some days, when sus-

picions arising with regard to his Lordship's sincerity
a stratagem was devised for the trial of it. Captain
Adam M'Donald of the first regiment, and an associate, introduced themselves to his Lordship, as Mr.
Cheney and Dick Williams, from the back country,
who pretended to be sent to him by the people that
were friends to the King, to know how to conduct
themselves.

THE conversation between Lord William Campbell,
Mr. Cheney, and Dick Williams (properly Captain
Adam M'Donald) was as follows :...

AFTER the common civilities were over, Mr.
Cheney asked the governor (who made an apology
for his absence when they first called) if Mr. Kirkland was well, and if he had sent him any word what
to do ?

Lord William. WHERE you not before the committee to day ?

Cheney. YES.

Lord William. WHAT did they say to you ? what
did they take you up for ?

Cheney. BECAUSE I came down for a life-guard to
Mr. Kirkland.

Lord William. THEY could not hurt you for coming
in company with Mr. Kirkland.

Cheney. I denied it, at first, that I came in company with him.

Lord William. I am sorry for that, you should

always tell the truth: You need not to fear the committee; they can do you no harm; is that one of your acquaintance, *(pointing to Capt. M'Donald)*

M'Donald and Cheney. Yes.

Cheney. This is Dick Williams.

M'Donald. I am serjeant to Kirkland; I am as much concerned as any of them; I want to get out of town early to-morrow, and I am afraid I shall be taken up by the committee; I will carry any message or letter safe to Fletchall, Brown, or Cunningham.*

Lord William. I have nothing to send them, but tell them to keep all the men in good order, to make a circuit and ride constantly round to one another.

M'Donald. I suppose you correspond with one another.

Lord William. Yes, yes.

M'Donald. I suppose they must not take up arms now.

Lord William. No, not without they have ammunition plenty, and think they are strong enough.

M'Donald. They are not strong enough, and have not ammunition enough; for Drayton is there, and getting them over fast.

Lord. William. If they are not strong enough, tell them by no means to take up arms yet; and that they will be released in a little time.

* Attached to government.

M'Donald. How?

Lord William. I could not have told you some time ago, but I can tell you now : I received a letter this day from the King, and he is resolved to carry his scheme into execution from one end of the continent to the other.

M'Donald. Will he send any soldiers here, between this and the fall.

Lord William. Yes, he will, and this will be a place settled for soldiers, and a seat of war, shortly.

M'Donald. I am much afraid, lest the committee should take me up and punish me, or put me to death.

Lord William. There is not the least fear of that, they dare not do any such thing.

M'Donald. But where shall I be safest, can you put me on board the man of war ? but if I go there, what can I do with my wife and family.

Lord William. (*Addressing himself to Cheney.*) I will put you on board the man of war, to-morrow.

M'Donald. But where shall I be safest ?

Lord William. No where safer than in town, for the militia are all in an uproar, and ready to turn the soldiers out of the barracks ; they are all now at variance, and will be more so shortly.

M'Donald. Are you certain it is so ?

Lord William. You may depend upon it as a fact.

M'Donald. Where is Kirkland going now ?

Lord William. HE has not determined any thing yet ; supplies are expected shortly.

Cheney. SUPPOSE they take me up again to night ?

Lord William. WHAT if they do !

M'Donald. THEY will tar and feather him.

Lord William. THAT is a bug-bear, why do not they tar and feather me.

M'Donald. YOU are a great man, and the King will send soldiers to protect you, if he gives up every where else, to punish them for you, but he will not mind such poor fellows as we are, and if we were to be put to death, no more notice will be taken of it.

Lord William. YOU will not be hurt ; they dare not do any such thing ; and they begin to repent of what they have done.

M'Donald. THE committee want Capt. Kirkland very much.

Lord William. WHAT will they do with him, if they get him ?

M'Donald. I heard that they said they would put him to death.

Lord William. WHAT had he done ?

M'Donald. I heard that he accepted a commission, and quitted it in an improper manner, and had deserted the cause, and deserved death ; that he was a great villian.

Lord William. PHO ! pho ! pho ! they are a parcel of profligates, and worse than nothing, if I may name it (*holding up his hands, and lifting his eyes*) and what have they done, but got the people to sign a paper, and it is of no more consequence, than that (*snapping his fingers*) if they don't like it, and they will be all punished for it shortly.*

CHENEY was a dissaffected person, and known to be so by Lord William; he was apprehended and confined by the committee, but was promised to be released, provided he would introduce Captain M'Donald, as Dick Williams, a friend to Kirkland.

CAPT. Adam M'Donald was a very bold adventurous man; and would undertake any thing for the good of the service. Soon after his interview with Lord William Campbell, the council of safety got him to go to St. Augustine, in East-Florida, to see the situation of the place, and to find out what number of troops were there in garrison. He set out immediately for Georgia, and from thence, went on foot to St. Augustine, in the garb of an overseer, and offered himself as a manager for an Indigo plantation; my brother John Moultrie, who was then Lieut. Governor, and Commander in Chief, heard of him, and sent for him; he had the confidence to

....

* Moses Kirkland had taken a commission in the American service, but was disgusted at some one being put over his head; he quitted, and went over to the British: he got privately to Charlestown, from the back country, and discovered himself to Lord William Campbell, who put him on board of a man of war.

go, although he had been intimately acquainted with
him on the Cherokee expedition, and was first Lieut.
to the Major's company ; nay, staid in the tent with
him at times ; they had some conversation on the
culture of Indigo, and the Governor, who suspected
him, talked to him about old times, to try to find
him out ; but to all the talk, M'Donald pleaded ignorance.   He told me, ' that the Governor eyed him
' so very closely, that he began to be alarmed, and
' was very glad when he got out of the house ;' he
immediately left St. Augustine, and pushed for Georgia ; and well he did so ; had he stayed a few hours
longer, he would have been taken, and in all probability, hanged as a spy.

WHEN the provincial Congress were informed of
the conversation, it excited general indignation ; and
Capt. M'Donald, with several members of Congress
were immediately sent to demand a perusal of his
lordship's last dispatches from England, and his correspondence with the back country.   This he positively refused : A motion was then made in the
Congress, for taking the Governor into custody,
which was for some time debated, and at last rejected by a considerable majority.   His lordship suspecting, and fearful of his personal safety in Charlestown, took the provincial seal with him and went on
board the Tamer sloop of war, then lying in Rebellion Road, and from thence, on the 15th of Sept. af-

terwards dissolved by proclamation the assembly he had called; who were in fact already dissolved in the eyes of the people; for, on the 16th of June, 1775, the council of safety, nominated, and appointed by the provincial Congress, met.

PRESENT.

HENRY Laurens, Charles Pinckney, Rawlins Lowndes, Thomas Ferguson, Miles Brewton, Arthur Middleton, Thomas Heyward, Thomas Bee, John Huger, James Parsons, William Henry Drayton. Benjamin Elliott, William Williamson, Esqrs.

HENRY Laurens was elected president, and Peter Timothy, Esq. secretary, with a salary of one thousand pounds currency a year.

THE council of safety met and proceeded upon business, before the provincial Congress had adjourned. Some of the council looked upon their post as the forlorn hope: the giving commissions, the stamping and issuing money, the giving orders to the military, &c. all were considered as acts of treason; some of them often said they were transacting business with halters about their necks; they would not give commissions in the usual form, but gave certificates, that run in the following manner.*

....

* The journals of the council of safety were long thought to be lost with their secretary, Mr. Timothy, who was cast away at sea; but Mr. Laurens, the president, kept them always with him, and they are now in the possession of his son,

*	*	SOUTH-CAROLINA.
*	*	'IN pursuance of the resolution of the provincial Congress, we do certify, that William Moultrie, Esq. is colonel of the second regiment in the provincial service"
*	*	
*	*	
*	*	
*	*	
*	*	Dated, 17th day of June, 1775. William Williamson, James Parson, Henry Laurens, Thomas Bee, Thomas Heyward, jr. Raw. Lowndes, William H. Drayton, Benjamin Elliott, Chas. Pinckney, Arthur Middleton, Miles Brewton, Thomas Ferguson.
*	*	
*	*	
*	*	

ON the 21st of June, the council of safety gave out the recruiting orders; but we did not wait for them, being urged by the members of the provincial Congress to begin to inlist men immediately after we were appointed officers, which we did; and by the returns* I made to the council of safety, on the 17th of July, which was exactly one month after the dates

....

who wishes the legislature would direct him to lodge them in some public office; they may be useful to some future historian: Mr. Laurens was kind enough to give me free access to them at his house in the country.

* Col. Gadsden was attending Congress at Philadelphia. I therefore had the honor of commanding the troops till the month of February, when he arrived and took the command.

of our commissions, we had recruited in, and near Charlestown, 470 men, which shews with what alacrity and spirit, they embarked in, and how zealous the people were in the cause.

On the 22d of June, the provincial Congress adjourned, and left the business of the colony to be carried on by the council of safety, as an executive body, and the general committee were to assist and support them in all their measures.

On the 23d of July, the council of safety sent proposals to Mr. Cameron (assistant to Mr. Stewart, who was agent for Indian affairs in the southern provinces) through Major Andrew Williamson, his particular friend, offering him a salary adequate to that which he got from John Stewart, Esq. besides making up any losses which he might sustain by joining in the American cause; Mr. Cameron refused to resign his commission, or accept of any employment in the colony service; and on receiving information of a report that prevailed, of an intention to seize his person, went off immediately from Ninety-six into the Cherokee country; his going off alarmed the back inhabitants very much, lest he should bring the Indians down upon them: but their minds were soon quieted, when they were informed by a letter to Williamson, which he had lately received from Mr. Cameron, telling him that Capt. Stewart had never given him orders to induce the Indians to fall upon

Carolina, but to keep them firmly attached to his majesty.

GEORGIA did not join the other colonies till July, 1777, when their Congress met.

' GEORGIA.

' THE alarming and critical situation of affairs ' upon the continent of America, having at length ' roused the attention of this province, and the several ' inhabitants thereof being desirous of uniting with ' their sister colonies in the great and important ' cause ; a general election was held throughout the ' province for delegates to sit in Congress, and the ' said delegates having so met in Savannah, on the ' fourth day of July, proceeding upon the considera- ' tion of such business as appears to be necessary ; and ' and among other things they have made choice of ' five delegates to represent this province in the grand ' continental Congress, now sitting in Philadelphia, ' viz. Archibald Buttock, John Houston, the Rev. ' Doct. Zubly, Noble Wimberly Jones, Lyman Hall, ' Esqrs. Signed in provincial Congress, this fifteenth day of July, 1775, by fifty-three members.'

JULY. About this time Wm. Henry Drayton, Esq. and the Rev. Mr. Tenant were called upon by the council of safety to make an excursion into the back country, to explain to the people, the causes of the present disputes between Great Britain and the American Colonies, and to endeavor to persuade them to sign the association. Many signed, others would not; however a treaty between them was agreed to, by which it was stipulated that the royalists should remain neuter; and both parties returned home. The council of safety entered into a resolve, that no person should leave the province without their permission,

THE want of powder was a very serious consideration with us; many schemes were advised and talked of, to procure that article; we knew there was none to be had upon the continent of America, as our delegates at Philadelphia had sent to this province for a supply.

THE council of safety formed a plan for making an attempt on the Island of Providence, and taking from thence the powder and other military stores; and had fitted out a small fast sailing sloop, of which Capt. Lamperer was appointed to take the command, and was joined by a number of volunteers, viz. Capt. Cochran Hatter, Tuff Joyner, Messrs. Tebout, Williamson and Jenkins; during this time and when the vessel was just ready to sail, information was received, that Capt. Loftus, in a brig, had sailed from London for St. Augustine and was hourly expected off that bar, loaded with military stores and Indians' goods; upon this the council of safety immediately sent off an express to Capt. Lamperer, who was then on board his vessel with his volunteers near Beaufort, to change his destination and proceed without delay

towards St. Augustine; they soon got sight of the brig*
lying off from the bar; the sloop bore down upon
her, keeping most of her hands below deck, till they
they came along-side (the brig not suspecting any
thing, and not knowing of the American revolution)
when they all jumped on board with their arms, and
ordered every man to be quiet, or they would be put
to death; there were sixteen soldiers on board asleep,
and away from their arms; when they awoke, the
were ordered to remain quiet, (for there was no intention to hurt them;) which they did.

OUR people, after taking out 17000 pounds of gun-
powder and seeing a vessel in St. Augustine harbor,
preparing to come out, they quitted the brig, and
made the best of their way home, leaving behind a great
deal more than one half of her cargo of military stores:
this consisted of strouds, blankets and plains, with
some field-pieces and 6000 pounds more of gunpowder. Had they brought off this brig, which they
could easily have done, she would have been a most
invaluable prize to us. However, the 17000 pounds
of powder which they brought home, gave us great
spirits; it increased our store of that necessary article to about † 31000 pounds.

* The brig could not get over the bar when loaded,

† From the West-Indies, in two seizures, S. Carolina and
Georgia got 39700 pounds of gunpowder.

FORT Charlotte, in Ninety-six district, remained in the hands of the royal government, garrisoned by a few men. A troop of rangers was sent there to take charge of the guns, powder, and military stores, and to send down the two brass field pieces that were there, and to endeavor to enlist the men in the service of the province.

COL. Thompson's regiment of rangers was soon compleated, as it was a service the country people preferred.

THE manual exercise laid before the council of safety by the field officers, in the service of the colony, was approved of, and recommended by the council of safety to the field officers of the militia, to adopt the same.

AUG. The officers of the first and second regiments, went out on the recruiting service into Virginia, North-Carolina, and the back parts of South-Carolina, and some remained in town to receive the recruits as they came down ; and to train and exercise them at the barracks in Charlestown. The council of safety now stamped and issued paper bills of credit of the colony.

THE Germans about the Dutch fork were very averse to the measures adopted by a majority of the people, on which Mr. Long and Mr. Waggoner, (both Germans) were requested to go into the back country among them, and explain to them the nature of the dispute, and the situation of America. They said they were unwilling to join, lest they should lose their little property of lands which they had got from the king, as a bounty for new settlers. They would not enter heartily into our measures till they were forced into it, by taking their property for the use of the public.

ABOUT this time, the Catawba Indians were alarmed, and could not tell what to make of it, on seeing such military preparations throughout the country; they sent down two runners to Charlestown, to be informed of the reasons. They had been told different stories and they came down to know the truth. The council of safety sent up by them a talk to their nation, acquainting them that our brothers on the other side of the water, wanted to take our property from us without our consent, and that we would not let them; and that we expected their warriors would join ours: The council of safety inform ed them that the people of Boston had had a great fight* with the red-coats, and had killed a great many of them. The Catawbas were requested to send the talk on to the Cherokees. The council of safety having received information that the inhabitants of Georgia had seized and taken from on board of Captain Mailand's ship, lying in their harbor, 12700lb of gun powder, they requested Wm. Henry

....

* Battle of Lexington.

Drayton and Miles Brewton, Esqrs. two of their council, to proceed immediately to Georgia to procure a part of that powder, and to purchase what other military stores they could get in that province. In a few days they returned, and brought with them 5000lb of powder, which the Georgians spared to us; besides a quantity of salt-petre, sulphur, blankets and plains, all of which they purchased and brought within land with them: The powder was landed at Tucker's Island, and immediately from thence 4000lb of this powder was put on board of a schooner commanded by Capt. Gambal, and sent to the delegates in Congress, at Philadelphia, for the use of the grand army. The other articles were brought within land to Charlestown; a party of soldiers were sent to escort them down.

As some of the people in the country were still unsettled in their minds with respect to the revolution, and some opposed directly to it; it was thought adviseable in order to fix the wavering, and intimidate the disaffected, to march a body of troops through the country by different routes; accordingly, the council of safety, on the 13th day of July, issued the following orders to Col. Thompson.

'On the 10th of August next, eight companies
' of the rangers shall rendezvous at some proper
' place by order of the colonel in the following routes:
' Three companies to the southward by Orangeburgh
' and the Three-Runs; thence down Savannah river

' to Purisburgh ; thence to Pon-Pon, and downwards
' by the high road: Three companies to the north-
' ward by Kingstree, Waccamaw and Pedee, to
' Georgetown, thence to Wambaw; and two companies
' through to Monk's Corner ; thence to Edisto Saw-
' Mills ; thence through Horseshoe and round Oto Pa-
' kers ferry, &c. Col Thompson with the first divi-
' sion to the southward : Major Mayson with the se-
' cond division to the northward ; the different divi-
' sions to meet at some convenient place within ten
' miles of Charlestown: Col. Thompson to order his
' officers to confine any person in the district Goals
' who is thought dangerous to the colony.'

HAVING now upwards of 30000 pounds of gun-powder in an about Charlestown, and always apprehensive of the British men of war,* lying in the Rebellion-
road, coming up to attack the town, it was thought
prudent to have some of the powder moved into the
country.

IN July the council of safety appointed a committee to survey the village of Dorchester, for making it
an armed post.

THE council of safety appointed a secret committee; William H. Drayton was chosen chairman: and
now they begin their military operations and issued
their first order :

* Two sloops, Tamer and Cherokee.

'In the Council of Safety, June, 17th 1775.

' Ordered,

' That Col. Moultrie, do make a return to this
' council, of the public arms already received, and
' now wanted for the two regiments of foot.

' By order of the council of safety.

' Peter Timothy, Sec'ry.'

' To William Moultrie, Esq.

' Col. of the 2d regiment of foot.

The reason for a return of arms being called for,
was, that the council had just entered upon the duties of their office, and wished to know the number
of arms that were already given out, and what remained in store ; as we had drawn arms from the
store-keeper as fast as we enlisted the men (before
the council of safety was appointed) because we expected every day to be attacked by the men of war :
if they only loosed their sails the alarm run through
the town immediately,   That ' the men of war were
coming to attack the town ;' these two sloops gave us
a great deal of trouble and uneasiness.

A letter from the chairman of the secret committee,

' Sir,   ' Charlestown, June 21, 1775.

' By directions of the secret committee, I inclose
' you two orders, by which you will be supplied with
' a quantity of ammunition for the use of the two re-
' giments of infantry in the service of the colony, not

' doubting of your prudence; they however think it
' their duty to recommend that the greatest care be
' taken of it; and as in a great degree the new levies
' are strangers, and their principles not certainly
' known, they cannot but intimate, that they think
' it advisable, that no soldiers should be placed sen-
' try over, or have any thing to do relative to the
' ammunition, but such as are known friends to the
' liberties of America.

' I am, &c.

' WILLIAM H. DRAYTON,

' Chairman of the secret committee,

' To Col. Moultrie.'

This letter shews in what an unpleasant situation
some men were, at the beginning of the revolution,
even doubtful of the fidelity of the soldiers that were
to fight our battles.

The officers who were constantly with them, had
no such fears or suspicions.

A Report prevailed at this time in Charlestown
that the British from St. Augustine intended a descent
upon Port-Royal Island, to take off the cannon and
military stores that were lodged there, before the
revolution; upon which the council of safety directed me to send off a reinforcement to that place;
which I did, of fifty men, under the command of
Capt. Cattel.

86

'To Capt. Wm. Cattel.

'August 14, 1775.

' You are to proceed with all expedition,
' with the men under your command, to Beaufort,
' Port-Royal, there to assist in defending that place
' and to take charge of the public powder, &c.

'William Moultrie.'

The report being unfounded, the detachment returned in a few days.

Fort Johnson, was still garrisoned by the British, under Col. Howarth's command, I was ordered to send and take possession of it: a day or two before the fort was taken, Col. Howarth, whom the inhabitants respected very much, was invited to go with a party into the country, to be out of the way, that no injury should happen to his person or character, he went, accordingly, not suspecting our intentions.

By the order I received from the council of safety, for taking Fort Johnson* they must have conceived it a hazardous and dangerous attempt by the number of men they required for that service.

' In Council of Safety.

' Sir,   'Charlestown, Sep. 13, 1775.

' You are to detach one-hundred and fifty men
' under such command as you shall judge most pro-

....

* The garrison we were certain had but six men and a gunner.

' per for the service; to embark this night at a proper
' time of the tide, to proceed with the utmost secre-
' cy and land at a convenient place on James' Island.
' Mr. Verree and Mr. Wm. Gibbs will be at Capt.
' Stone's, or in the neighborhood, attending the land-
' ing, in order to conduct the commanding officer to
' Fort Johnson, which he is to enter and take pos-
' session of, with as much secrecy and silence as possi-
' ble; taking especial care that none belonging to the
' fort escape, and that no intelligence be given but
' by his orders; when the officer, who shall be sent
' upon this service is in possession of the fort, he is
' immediately to give notice to this board and wait
' for orders; except only in case the man of war*
' now lying in the Rebellion-road, should make an
' attempt to attack the fort or proceed towards this
' town, when he is to do every thing in his power to
' prevent her progress: Capt. Stone, of James' Island,
' will order his company of militia to join the troops
' which you send, and the whole are to be detained
' till relieved by our order.

' By order of the council of safety.

' HENRY LAURENS, President.

' WILLIAM MOULTRIE, Esq.

' Col. of the second Regiment.'

IN consequence of receiving this order, I immediately issued the subsequent orders to the troops:

....

* Always in dread of this man of war.

' GENERAL ORDERS,

' 14th September, 1775, 4 'clock, P. M.

' ORDERRD, that captains Charles Cotesworth
' Pinckney's, Bernard Elliott's and Francis Marion's
' companies be immediately completed to fifty men
' each, from their respective corps, and hold them-
' selves in readiness to march in three hours. Col.
' Motte is appointed for this command, and will re-
' ceive his orders from the commanding officer.'

THE orders given to Col. Motte were similar to
those I received from the council of safety.

THIS detachment went on board their boats at 12
o'clock at night, at Gadsden's-wharf, and, dropping
down with the ebb tide, landed on James' Island, a
little above the fort, and marched in immediately unmolested; the garrison escaped to the men of war,
then in the road, but not before they had thrown
down all the guns and their carriages from off the
plat-form, which plainly shows that they had information of our intentions to take the fort.

So little were we acquainted with naval affairs, and
so highly impressed with the mighty power of a British man of war, that although we had got possession
of a strong fort and one hundred and fifty good regular troops, and the James' Island company of militia of about fifty men, yet the council of safety was
so fearful of the Tamer sloop of war mounting 14 or
16 6 pounders, attacking the fort, that they gave me

orders to send down two hundred and fifty men, as a reinforcement to Col. Motte, which I did by the following order.

'GENERAL ORDERS, Sep. 15, 1775.

'ORDERED, that Captains Benj. Cattel, Adam
'M'Donald, and John Barnwell's companies of the
'first regiment, and that Captains Peter Horry, and
'Francis Huger's companies be completed to fifty
'men each and to hold themselves in readiness to
'march: Major Owen Roberts to command this de-
'tachment.'

'To Major OWEN ROBERTS, of the first regiment,
'SIR,

'YOU are to proceed with your detachment to
'Gadsden's-wharf, where you will find two schooners
'ready to take on board your party; with them you
'will proceed to Fort Johnson on James' Island; on
'your arrival there you are to send an officer to Col.
'Motte to acquaint him: Then march to the fort
'and put yourself under his command; you are not
'to suffer any boats* to obstruct your passage.'

'To LIEUT. COL. MOTTE.

'SIR,

'I HAVE sent Major Roberts with two hundred

....

* Fear of the man-of-war boats.

' and fifty men to reinforce you. You are to defend
' the fort from all parties that may attempt to land,
' but if the man-of-war* should attack the fort, and
' you find you cannot make a stand against her, you
' are to withdraw your men to some place of safety,
' out of the reach of her guns; but you are to take
' care not to suffer any parties to land with an intent
' to damage the fort.'

At the same time Capt. Thomas Heyward, with a detachment of Charlestown artillery, went down with gin and tackles and had three cannon mounted immediately.

About this time the Cherokee sloop of war arrived. A little time after we were in possession of Fort Johnson, it was thought necessary to have a flag for the purpose of signals : (as there was no national or state flag at that time) I was desired by the council of safety to have one made, upon which, as the state troops were clothed in blue, and the fort was garrisoned by the first and second regiments, who wore a silver cresent on the front of their caps; I had a large blue flag made with a cresent in the dexter corner, to be in uniform with the troops : This was the first American flag which was displayed in South-

---

* Every order and every movement of our's shows how fearful we were of the man-of-war; all these orders were issued agreeably to the council of safety's directions.

Carolina: On its being first hoisted, it gave some uneasiness to our timid friends, who were looking forward to a reconciliation: They said it had the appearance of a declaration of war; and Capt. Thornborough, in the Tamer sloop of war, lying in Rebellion-road would look upon it as an insult, and a flag of defiance, and he would certainly attack the fort; but he knew his own force, and knew the weight of our metal; he therefore kept his station and contented himself with spying us.

LORD William Campbell, the Governor of the province, when he discovered from on board the Tamer sloop of war, that we were in possession of fort Johnson, he sent his secretary, Mr. Innis, in the man-of-war's boat to the fort, to demand 'by what authority we had taken possession of his majesty's fort;' he was answered ' by the authority of the council of safety,' he then made his bow and went off. After we had taken the fort we were in apprehensions, least these two small men of war should attack the fort or the town ; on the 16th Sept. orders were issued that all officers belonging to the two South-Carolina regiments should hold themselves in readiness, upon any alarm, to be immediately at the barracks. The long marches the recruits had taken from Virginia, North-Carolina, and the back parts of South-Carolina to Charlestown (in the month of September) was very unfavorable to their health at this season of the year; they were taken with fevers and other complaints, which soon filled our hospitals; we were obliged, on the 17th September, to move our sick over to Mount Pleasent, where they could breathe a purer air, and be kept under better regulations than it was possible in Charlestown, where liquor could not be kept from them; at this time we had recruited about 700 men. The magazine at Dorchester being now completed; on the 7th of October, I ordered a subaltern guard to attend Capt. Cochran, on board a schooner, to escort 10,000 pounds of powder to Dorchester and to see it safely lodged in the magazine under a militia guard.

It was thought prudent to send a part of our ammunition, ordinance, stores, and public records to be lodged at Dorchester, and to build fortifications round that town; commissioners were appointed to see the work executed, which was completed in November. On the 27th October, I ordered a detachment of colony troops to take post there as a guard to the powder, &c. that were lodged there, and to remain till they were relieved by two companies of rangers. About this time, at the request of Col. Powel, and others, a detachment of fifty men was sent to Charaws, to garrison a fort that was to be built there for the protection of the families of the well affected, against the tories, who were very numerous in that part of the country; this was an expensive work and of very little consequence. It was now thought necessary to have some armed schooners for the defence of our harbor and rivers, but it was very difficult to man them without taking the seamen from the first and second regiments, as they had already inlisted all the sailors in port ;* however it was absolutely necessary as the enemy had a schooner cruising on our bar, and we had information that the men-of-war's boats used to come up to town every night and get intelligence of our proceedings : Therefore, on 27th October, the council of safety ordered that thirty seamen from the first and second regiments be put on board the Defence schooner, commanded by Capt. Tuffs ; the schooner was stationed between Fort Johnson, and the town, to intercept the men-of-war's boats.

Soon after this, on 17th November, the colony raised a Regiment of Artillery and the command was given to Maj. Owen Roberts, with the rank of Lieut. Colonel, and Capt. Barnard Elliott, of the second regiment, was appointed Major : This regiment recruited very fast as their pay was greater than the infantry. We had now a camp on James' Island, near Fort Johnson, of at least five hundred men, well armed, well accoutered, and well clothed

---

* The sailors had no alternative, they must either inlist or starve, as the men-of-war had completely blocked up the port; the sailors were discharged from the vessels.

with a sufficient number of regular good tents: the
field officers and captains, each a tent and marquee,
and a tent and marquee for the subalterns of each
company. The officers tents were at their own expense: We now began to look, and act like soldiers, and keep up a strict discipline. The men
were taught the manual manœuvreing, and the exercise of the great guns, which made them matrosses
as well as infantry; they were as well clothed as
troops could be, and made a handsome appearance:
we thought it best to form our camp on James' Island,
for the benefit of the soldiers healths, and the better
situated to keep them from liquor, which it was impossible to do in Charlestown, notwithstanding our
strict discipline; and by being there, they were
ready to support Fort Johnson, should it be necessary.

Nov. We were busily employed in repairing and
enlarging our old batteries, viz. Brougton's, Lyttel-
ton's, Grenville's, and Cravan's; and building new
ones at Gadsden's, the Exchange, Beal's and Gibb's
wharfs, and we were very fortunate in the begining
of the revolution, in having a great number of large
cannon, and a great number of balls suitable in the
king's arsenal: we had some mounted on field carriages to move with facility to any part of the town
where they might be wanted; we had a great many
new carriages made for the battering cannon, the

old ones being quite rotten; we soon had the new carriages made, as the mechanics (almost to a man) were hearty in the cause and went cheerfully to work whenever they were called upon. Ten shillings currency per day was given for negro laborers, and several hundred were brought down from the country. When we wanted any work to be done we never sat down to calculate the expense; it was ordered to be done, and it was set about immediately; we had plenty of paper and money at command.*

WE were now building a battery about a quarter of a mile to the westward of Fort Johnson on a very commanding piece of ground, the command of this battery was given to Lieut. Col. Roberts.

IN the provincial Congress many new schemes were suggested for the defence of the colony, among them some very curious ideas were thrown out, such as sinking ships upon the bar, to prevent the enemy's vessels from coming in; some for one thing and some for an other ;† but the most extraordinary plan that ever was thought of, was the abandoning the town and to draw a line across Charlestown neck, somewhere between the quarter house and town to prevent the enemy from going into the country;

....

* We stamped and issued paper money.

† This was thrown out by some disaffected persons, as a tub to the whale; to amuse us, and prevent our going into any offensive military operations.

Congress went so far into this ridiculous business, as
to appoint commissioners for that purpose. Mr. Lowndes, Col. Powel, Mr. Cannon, and myself; Mr.
Rout was appointed clerk to the board by the commissioners. We had several meetings, and recommended a plan a little above Bell-Mount. When the
report come to be debated in Congress, a gentleman
very shrewdly observed, that we may as well build a
wall round a Cuckoo* to keep him in, as to suppose
these lines would prevent the enemy from going into the country ; this ridiculous idea of the line was
reprobated, and scouted out of the house ; then it
was determined to defend the town to the last extremity.

THE Cherokee Indians being deprived of their trade
through the southern provinces, were in very bad
humor, and we were apprehensive of an Indian war,
it was therefore proper they should be supplied with
powder and ball for their hunting season, to enable
them to procure our skins for their support; the
council of safety, therefore, to keep them in good
temper, sent one thousand weight of powder, and
lead in proportion, to be forwarded to them under an escort of rangers; but Patrick Cunningham
and John Bowman, of Ninety-six, at the head of a
party of tories, intercepted and took away the ammu-

----

* Owl.

nition &c. as appears by Moses Cotter's affidavit, taken before James Mayson, Esq.

' South-Carolina, }
' Ninety-six District. }

' Personally appeared before
' me, James Mayson, one of his majesty's justices
' of the peace, for the district aforesaid ; Moses Cot-
' ter, of the Congarees, waggoner, who being duly
' sworn on the holy evangelist, of Almighty God,
' makes oath, and says, that on Tuesday morning
' last, at about 9 o'clock he left the Congarees, with
' his waggon, containing the ammunition that was
' delivered him in Charlestown, by the honorable the
' council of safety, to carry to Keowee under an es-
' cort of Col. Thompson's rangers consisting of Lieut.
' Col. Charleton and Mr. Uriah Goodwin, a cadet,
' 2 sergeants and 18 privates, and continued on their
' journey there, without the least molestation or in-
' terruption, until about noon this day, when the de-
' ponent perceiving some men on horseback, ahead
' of the waggon, come towards him; a few minutes
' after, two of Patrick Cunningham's men, coming up
' to the deponent and asking him what he had in his
' waggon, the deponent answered, rum : Then up
' came a large body of armed men, in number, I
' suppose, at least one hundred and fifty, headed by
' Patrick Cunningham and Jacob Bowman. Cunning-

' ham ordered his men to halt, and then came up to
' the deponent and said, I order you to stop your
' waggon in his majesty's name, as I understand you
' have ammunition for the Indians to kill us, and I
' am come on purpose to take it in his majesty's
' name. He then ordered the deponent to take off
' his waggon cloth, which he refused; upon which
' Cunningham mounted the waggon himself, loosed
' the strings of the cloth, and took up a keg of the
' powder; ' there,' said he, ' is what we are in search of.'
' I immediately took the keg from him and laid it in
' the waggon. Cunningham said, ' it is in vain for
' you to attempt to hinder us from taking this ammu-
' nition, as you have no arms;' then he handed out
' every keg to his men who were along side the wag-
' gon and prepared with bags to receive it; after
' they finished with the powder, he, with Messrs.
' Griffin and Owen, and several others, took out the
' lead which they unfolded, cut into small pieces
' with their tomahawk's, and distributed it among
' the men. When the rangers were at some little
' distance behind the waggon, and were riding up
' pretty fast, Cunningham's party said, ' there comes
' the liberty caps; damn their liberty caps, we will
' soon blow them to hell;' and such like scurrilous
' language. Cunningham's men, as soon as Lieut.
' Charleton came up with his guard, retreated behind
' trees on the road side, and called out to him to

' stop and not to advance one step further, otherwise
' they would blow out his brains; at the same time,
' a gun was fired by one of their men, but did no
' damage. Lieut. Charleton, with his men, were soon
' surrounded by the opposite party, with their rifles
' presented, who said, 'don't move a step; deliver up
' your arms, otherwise we will immediately fire upon
' you.' Lieut. Charleton continued moving on, when
' Cunningham's men marched up to him, with their
' rifles presented at him, and repeated, ' deliver up
' your arms without moving one step further, or you
' are a dead man :' they then took his arms, together
' with his men's ; afterwards they tied Lieut. Charle-
' ton, Mr. Goodwin, and William Witherford, a pri-
' vate, by their arms.

' Lieut. Charleton seemed very much displeased
' at their behavior, and said ' he would rather have
' been shot, than used in such a manner, had he ex-
' pected it ; that he did not value his own life ; thought
' he had acted prudent by not ordering his men to
' fire on them, as it would be throwing away their
' lives, without answering any good purpose ; es-
' pecially as their party were so numerous, that he
' was sorry to see them behave in such a base man-
' ner, and that he would very willingly turn out his
' party against twice the number of theirs, and give
them battle :' Cunningham and Bowman, some little
' time after asked Lieut. Charleton, ' whether if they

'were to unloose him he would be upon his honor,
'not to go off:' to which he replied, 'I scorn to run,
'and all your force cannot make me;' they then
'marched off with the ammunition, and the 'prison-
'ers,' (as they called them,) and left the deponent,
'desiring him to return to the Congarees: but as
'soon as they were out of sight he took a horse from
'out the waggon and came to Ninety-six, to inform
'me of what had happened, and where he arrived
'this night about 8 o'clock. This unfortunate acci-
'dent of taking the ammunition, happened 18 miles
'below Ninety-six. Moses Cotter.

'Sworn, before me, this
'3d of Nov. 1775.' } Jason Mayson, J. P.'

A little after this powder was taken, Robert Cunningham (a brother to Patrick Cunningham) a very
popular man in the back country, declared he would
not be bound by the treaty made by Drayton and
Tenant; it was feared he would disturb the peace of
the country, he was therefore apprehended, brought
to town, and put in goal. During his confinement,
he was treated kindly, and visited by several gentlemen, who endeavored to persuade him from opposing his opinion against so large a majority of his
countrymen; he listened to their arguments and
at last agreed that if he was liberated he would return and be neuter. Accordingly, he was suffered to
return home. Patrick Cunningham had collected

that body of men who took the powder, to rescue his brother, but was too late.

UPON a report that the Tamer and Cherokee men-of-war, intended to pass the fort, and attack the town, I received the following order to fire upon the British, which was the first order given to fire upon them.

'BY ORDER OF CONGRESS.
'To Col. WILLIAM MOULTRIE, or to the commanding officer, at Fort Johnson.
'SIR,
    'You are hereby commanded, with the troops
' under your orders, by every military operation to
' endeavor to oppose the passage of any British na-
' val armament that may attempt to pass Fort John-
' son, until further orders by Congress, or the coun-
' cil of safety.
        ' I have the honor to be
            ' Yours, &c.
    ' WILLIAM H. DRAYTON, President.'
'Charlestown, Nov. 9th, 1775.'

MAJOR Andrew Williamson, who had the command of the militia at Ninety-six, went in pursuit of the party that seized the powder, but was obliged to retreat before superior numbers. In a letter from him to the council of safety, he informed them that he had had an action with the insurgents, under Major Robertson, for three days and three nights,

without refreshments, in his fortified camp at Ninety-
six, and was reduced at last to the necessity of making a treaty with them ; and at their own request
they agreed to a suspension of hostilities for twenty
days, with liberty for each party to send dispatches
unsealed to their superiors, informing them of their
situation. At this time, Colonels Richardson, and
Thompson were marching to form a junction to re-
leave Williamson. Of this the insurgents were informed, which induced them to agree to a suspension of hostilities : they had by some means or other,
kept up an intercourse with Lord William Campbell, who encouraged them to oppose us, by promises of great rewards ; they were also instigated by
Pearis, who had much influence in Ninety-six district : Congress was determined to send an army
among them, but first sent out by authority a declaration, viz.

' SOUTH-CAROLINA.

' (By authority of Congress.)

' IT has ever been the policy of America in gene-
' ral, and of this colony in particular, to endeavor to
' cultivate a good correspondence with the neighbor-
' ing Indians, and especially since the commence-
' ment of these present disputes with the British ad-
' ministration. This policy originated from a view of
' preserving at the cheapest rate, our borders from
' savage incursions ; of late this policy has been per-

' severed in, and our endeavors have been redoubled
' in order to oppose and to frustrate the designs of
' the British administration, by the hands of Indians
' to deluge our frontiers with the blood of our fellow
' citizens. Experience has taught us, that occasional
' presents to the Indians, have been the great means of
' acquiring their friendship : In this necessary service,
' government every year expended large sums of mo-
' ney. The late council of safety spared no pains to
' confirm them in their pacific inclinations, but from re-
' peated, constant, and uniform accounts, it clearly
' appeared that a general Indian war was inevitable,
' unless the Indians were furnished with some small
' supplies of ammunition, to enable them to procure
' deer skins for their support and maintenance, rath-
' er than draw on an Indian war, by an ill timed fru-
' gality in withholding ammunition; the late coun-
' cil of safety, in October, issued a supply of am-
' munition consisting of one thousand weight of pow-
' der and two thousand weight of lead, for the use
' of the Cherokee's, as the only probable means of
' preserving the frontiers from the inroads of the
' Indians.

' THE council more readily agreed to this measure,
' because, as they almost daily expected the Bri-
' tish arms would attack the colony in front, on the
' sea coast; they would be inexcusable if they
' did not, as much as in them lay, remove every

' cause to apprehend an attack at the same time from
' the Indians upon the back settlements.

' But this measure entered into by the council's
' principles of the soundest policy of christianity,
' breathing equal benevolence to the associators
' and non-associators, and arising only from necessi-
' ty, unfortunately has been made by some non-asso-
' ciators, an instrument for the most diabolical pur-
' poses. These weak men, to the astonishment of com-
' mon sense, have made many of their deluded follow-
' ers believe that this ammunition as sent to the In-
' dians with orders for them to fall upon the non-as-
' sociators, and taking advantage from the scarcity
' of ammunition among the individuals arising from
' the necessity of filling the public magazines, they
' invidiously represented that this ammunition ought
' not to have been sent to the Indians, while the in-
' habitants of the colony individually are in a great
' measure destitute of that article.

' Wherefore, in compassion to those who are de-
' luded by such representations, the Congress have
' taken these things into their consideration; and
' they desire our deceived fellow colonists, to reflect
' that the story of the ammunition being sent to the
' Indians with orders for them to massacre the non-
' associators, is absurd in its very nature; first, because
' the whole tenor of the council of safety, demon-
' strates that they were incapable of such inhu-

' manity as a body, and the character of each in-
' dividual, shields him against a charge of so cruel a
' nature.

' II. BECAUSE also, if men will but call reason to
' their aid, they must plainly see, that if the Indians
' were let loose upon the frontiers, they must indis-
' criminately, massacre associators and non-associa-
' tors, since there is no mark to distinguish either
' to the Indians. However, in order to' clear up all
' difficulties on this head, and ease the minds of our
' deceived friends; the Congress in a body, and al-
' so individually, declare, in the most solemn manner
' before Almighty God, that they do not believe that
' any order was ever issued, or any idea entertained
' by the late council of safety, or any member of it,
' or by any person under authority of Congress, to
' cause the Indians to commence hostilities upon the
' frontiers, or any part thereof: On the contrary,
' they do believe, that they, and each of them, have
' used every endeavor to inculcate in the Indians,
' sentiments friendly to the inhabitants without dis-
' tinction. It is greatly to be regretted, that fellow
' colonists, individually are not so well supplied with
' ammunition as would be adequate to their private
' inconvenience: But does not the unhappy situation
' of public affairs, justify the filling the public maga-
' zines, thereby securing the welfare, and forming
' the defence of the state, at the risk of inconvenience

' or safety of individuals, and out of the public stock
' is given to the Indians, which may be sufficient to
' keep them quiet, by, in some degree, supplying
' their urgent occasions, yet not sufficient to enable
' them to make war; ought our people, nay, they
' cannot have any reasonable ground, to arraign the
' policy by which they are, and may be preserved from
' savage hostility; or to complain that, because the
' whole colony, or the public individually, cannot be
' supplied with ammunition, that a small quantity
' ought not to be sent to the Indians. Men ought
' also to reflect that this small quantity is given, in
' order to render it unnecessary to supply the public
' individually on the score of defence against Indians.
' Men ought also to reflect, that when the public ma-
' gazines are well stored, supplies can be instantly,
' plentifully, and regularly poured upon those parts
' where the public service may require them.

' COMMON sense and common honesty, dictate that
' there is a probability that by a present of a small
' quantity of ammunition to the Indians they can be
' kept in peace: This present ought not to be held
' back at the hazard of inducing an Indian war,
' involving the colony in immense expense, breaking
' settlements, and unnecessarily sacrificing a number
' of lives.

'CHARLESTOWN, Nov. 19, 1775.'

Nov. 11. Capt. Blake under the cover of the Defence schooner, commanded by Capt. Tuffs, sunk two schooners at the mouth of Hog-Island creek, in order to block up that approach to the town. Capt. Thornborough, in the Tamer sloop of war, warped up to prevent them, but could not get near enough. Capt. Tuffs and he, exchanged a few long shot, but no damage was done; this was the commencement of hostilities in South-Carolina : it alarmed the town, and every one run to the Bay, to see 'the fight,' as they called it.

MATHEW Floyd, a messenger from Major Robertson, with dispatches to Lord William Campbell, the governor, then on board the Tamer sloop of war; which dispatches he pretended to have lost, and applied for permission to wait on his lordship, to relate to him the substance of an agreement to a cessation of arms, concluded on the 22d ultimo, at Ninety-six. He was permitted to wait on his lordship, attended by a person in behalf of the council of safety, who was to be present at the interview : Mr. Merchant, who attended Floyd, brought answer back, that Mr. Innis, the governor's secretary, said ' My lord desires you will return, and inform the persons who sent you, that as the other person is a friend to government, he must be detained until he has determined upon a proper answer.' In a day or two, Floyd returned, and was made a prisoner; among other things, Floyd said, that Lord William had desired him to ' tell the people in the back country to do every thing that they could for the best advantage; that he did not desire any effusion of blood; but whatever they should do would meet with his countenance.'

Nov. The men-of-war, lying in the road, entirely blocked up our port, and took all vessels that came in; the council of safety fitted out two pilot boats to go out through Stono inlet, and ply on our bar to warn all vessels from coming in; that the men-of-war would certainly take them; and they were directed to bring all letters up to town to be examined, to gain what intelligence we could. Capts. Vessey and Smith offered their service to take command of these boats gratis, and 1 serjeant and 9 privates from 1st regiment, and 1 serjeant and 9 privates from 2d regiment were put on board the two boats with their arms; these boats were very useful in getting intelligence and keeping the men-of-war's boats from cruizing about our inlets. Capt. Thornborough, of the Tamer sloop-of-war, took a schooner, belonging to Capt. Stone, fitted her out with a number of swivel guns and men, to take our two pilot boats, they got notice of it, however, and kept out of her way.

About this time, Capt. Tallemache arrived in the Scorpion sloop-of-war, and applied for 500 pounds of beef, but was refused, and informed that he could have provisions, only from day to day, according to the number of men they had on board. She had a large transport ship with her, that had been at Bermuda and Cape-Fear; from each of these places she brought off all the cannon and stores that could be taken; he had orders to seize all the cannon, where ever he could, in all the colonies.

WE had no doubt but that Beaufort would be the next place visited, and we were confirmed in our opinion, when a seizure was made of two Bermuda sloops, one of which hoisted a pendant immediately, from whence we concluded she was put in commission.

THE council of safety sent orders to Beaufort, to remove all the cannon and stores belonging to the fort to some secure place in land, without the reach of the men-of-war. Information was received in town, that the Scoffol* lights were coming down from the back country in great force, to carry off the ammunition, and public records, that were lodged at Dorchester; upon which, I received orders to send a reinforcement immediately to that place.

'Nov. 19th 1775.

'To Captain FRANCIS MARION.

'You are to proceed with all expedition, with

* Scoffol was a Col. of Militia, a man of some influence in the back country, but a stupid, ignorant, blockhead.

'yours, and Capt. Huger's companies to Dorchester,
' to reinforce the troops there, and to take special
' care in guarding and defending the cannon, gun-
' powder, and public records, at that place; you are
' to take the command of the whole of the troops at
' that place, till further orders. You are to apply to
' the committee at Dorchester, for a sufficient num-
' ber of negroes in the public service, to remove the
' cannon* lying near the water-side, to a spot more
' safe, and convenient, near the fort or barracks, &c.

' WM. MOULTRIE.'

ABOUT the 20th of November, the colony took into their service the ship Prosper, as appears by an
order I issued on the 21st.

'ORDERED, That six or eight seamen, go on
' board the Prosper ship to-morrow, to assist in rig-
' ging the said ship.'

ON the 27th, the Prosper was rigged, and had
20 nine pounders put on board, and manned by the
provincial troops, as appears by the following order:

' Nov. 27, 1775.

' (By authority of Congress.)

' SIR,

' You are hereby ordered to detach from
' the regiments under your command, forty such

---

* The cannon lay at too great a distance from the fort, they
could not be protected should a superior force come down.

' privates as are best acquainted with maritime affairs,
' and cause them to be embarked on board the colo-
' ny's ship Prosper; there to remain during one month
' (unless sooner discharged by proper authority) to
' do duty under the orders of the officers command-
' ing on board that ship, &c.'

   ' WILLIAM H. DRAYTON, President.
 ' To COL. MOULTRIE.

THE Prosper was fitted out as a guard-ship for the
harbor of Charlestown, to prevent the boats going
in and out of the port, to give intelligence; and to
be an additional force to Fort Johnson and our harbor. The command of her, was given to William
H. Drayton, Esq. a gentleman of great abilities, and
warm in the cause of America; but was no sailor,
and did not know any one rope in the ship from another.

AN order was issued by the council of safety, forbidding any person to supply the men-of-war with
provisions, and water; but from day to day, Capt.
Thornborough, of the Tamer, gave notice, ' That if
' his Majesty's agent* in Charlestown, was not per-
' mitted regularly, and without molestation, to sup-
' ply the king's ships, Tamer, and Cherokee, with
' such provisions as he thought necessary to demand,
' he would not from that day, so far as it was in his

---

    * Fenwick Bull.

' power, suffer any vessels to enter the harbor of
' Charlestown, or to depart from it.'

BY order of Lord William Campbell, a sloop belonging to Messrs. Samuel and Benjamin Legare
was seized.

DEC. 10. Mr. Fenwick Bull went down as a nota-
ry to protest against the proceedings relative to the
seizure of Messrs. Legaré's vessel, and on his return,
gave to the council of safety, a particular account of
the conversation which had passed between Lord
William Campbell, and the Captains of the three
sloops-of-war in Rebellion-road, and himself....Capt.
Tallemache was charged with having some of our
negroes on board; he declared ' he did not deny his
' having some of our negroes on board, but said they
' came as free men, and demanded protection ; that
' he could have had five-hundred who had offered ;
' that we were all in actual rebellion; and that he
' had orders to distress America by every means in
' his power; that had his advice been taken, Fort
' Johnson should have been attacked on the day of his
' arrival, if the attack had cost fifty men, and that
' this town should soon be laid in ashes ; but that it
' would soon be destroyed; that upon his honor he
' expected soon, two frigates and a bomb to arrive
' here.'

CAPT. Tallemache, with his transport, soon left the
port : The Tamer and Cherokee sloops-of-war, lying

in the road, were very troublesome to us, in blocking up our harbor, and enticing our negroes to run away and form a camp on Sullivan's Island; we were in. formed that nearly five-hundred had already encamped there : This was very alarming, and looked on as dangerous to the province at large ; and that it was absolutely necessary at all events to dislodge them from this place.

THE council of safety had received intelligence that there was a fording place from Haddrell's point to Sullivan's Island, they therefore desired I would send a strong detachment over; in consequence of which I issued the following order.

'Dec. 9, 1775.

'To MAJOR CHARLES COTESWORTH PINCKNEY.

'You are to proceed with all secret expedition
'with the men under your command, 4 capts. 8
'lieuts. 12 sergeants, and 150 rank and file to Sulli-
'van's Island, to ford over from Haddrell's point to
'the Island, there to surprize, seize, and apprehend
'a number of negroes who are said to have gone
'over to the enemy; together with every person
'who may be found on the Island; and to repel any
'opposition which may be against you in the exe-
'cution of this service, which service being perform-
'ed, the detachment with their prisoners, are to re-
'turn to town with all possible dispatch : If you can-

‘ not cross your party at Haddrell's point with safety,
‘ you are to proceed to the most convenient place to
‘ accomplish that end. You are to destroy the pest
‘ house, and every kind of live stock to be driven off
‘ or destroyed.

                                    ‘ WILLIAM MOULTRIE.’

MAJOR Pinckney went over to Haddrell's point,
with a detachment, agreeably to orders, and inquired
of all the inhabitants thereabout, and of some who
had lived there many years, and they all agreed that
they knew of no fording place there,* nor had ever
heard of one, and there being no boats to cross the
detachment; Major Pinckney informing me of these
circumstances, I sent him the following order.

                                    ‘ Dec. 9, 1775.
‘ SIR,
    ‘ You are to return immediately with the detach-
‘ ment to Charlestown, the intention of the expedition
‘ being entirely frustrated

                        ‘ WILLIAM MOULTRIE.’
‘ TO MAJOR PINCKNEY.’

THE Tamer and Cherokee still continued to block
up our port; we at last fell upon an expedient to

---

* There was a fording place for one or two men; but a body of men would soon render it impassible.

drive them quite off; which was to erect a battery at
Haddrell's point, that would give us the command of
the cove at the back of Sullivan's Island, and open to
us a safe passage from Haddrell's to the Island ; and
on the 19th of Decem. ' Ordered, that Major Charles
' Cotesworth Pinckney, 4 capts. 8 subalterns, and
' 200 rank and file from the first regiment, do hold
' themselves in readiness to march this afternoon.'

' CAPT. Beekman, of Col. Roberts' artillery, is also
' for this service, and to provide stores and ammuni-
' tion for four 18 pounders : The quarter master to
' furnish six days provisions.'

I went over with this detachment, and a great
many gentlemen volunteers ; we embarked from
Charlestown on a dark and very cold night, with
every thing necessary for erecting a battery (one
Gaboriel was our chief engineer but understood very
little of the business) we were all in high spirits expecting to surprize the men-of-war next morning ;
every one fell to work, and by day-light we were ourselves well covered, and in a few hours more, laid
our plat-forms, and some guns mounted; and shortly
after, opened our embrasures: The men-of-war immediately moved their stations a little further off;
however, we threw them a few long shot. The
erecting this battery, gave us the entire command
of the cove, and we could go on and off from Sullivan's Island as we pleased.

On the 30th of Decem. Major Cotesworth Pinckney*
and Capt. Beekman† took the distances: from the
battery at Haddrell's point, to the S. W. point of Sullivan's Island, is 1 mile, 240 yards: To the Tamer, 1
mile, 770 yards: To the Cherokee, 1 mile all but 88
yards: To Fort Johnson, 1½ mile, and 88 yards:
From the point of Sullivan's Island, to the Tamer,
570 yards: To the Cherokee, 726 yards: From the
Cherokee to Fort Johnson, is 1 mile, 44 yards.

1776. EARLY in January we were preparing to
build a fascine battery on Sullivan's Island, and on
the 10th, I issued the following order.

'ORDERS,

Jan. 10th, 1776.

'ONE capt. 2 subalterns, 2 sergeants, and 50 rank and
' file, from the 1st regiment, and 1 capt. 2 subalterns'
' 2 sergeants, and 50 rank and file, from the 2d reg-
' iment, hold themselves in readiness to take post on
' Sullivan's Island, there to remain as a covering
' party to the men, who were to be employed on the
' Island in building a fascine battery.'

As soon as the captains of the men-of-war discovered that we had got possession of the Island and
building a battery; they made the best of their way
out, and left the port to ourselves.

* Major General Pinckney.   † Late Col. Beekman.

VERY soon after, the two sloops-of-war left us, we were seriously alarmed at the appearance of two frigates anchoring near our bar; the alarm guns were fired; the sight of them confirmed what capt. Tallemache had informed Fenwick Bull of, on the 10th of December. At this time, we were pretty well prepared for the frigates, all our batteries about the town, and Fort Johnson were finished and ready for action, and we expected every hour to be attacked: our greatest fear was from the enemies which we had among us, setting fire to the town, at the same time that we were engaged with the frigates. The following order which I issued, after consulting with the council of safety, shows the apprehension we had from the danger of fire in town, while we were engaged with the frigates.

'GENERAL ORDERS,

'January 15th, 1776.

'WHEN the town shall be attacked or alarmed,
'1 subaltern, 1 sergeant, and 25 rank and file from
'Col. Pinckney's regiment,* are to take post at the
'State-house, with one of the fire engines, and a suf-
'ficient number of negroes with fire-hooks, axes,
'ropes, &c. to observe if any fire should break out
'in town, and in that case, immediately to repair to

* The Charlestown Militia.

' to the place with the party and engine, and endea-
' vour to extinguish the fire.'

' One subaltern, 1 sergeant, and 20 rank and file, from
' Col. Pinckney's regiment, with a fire-engine, ne-
' groes &c. to take post at Branford's corner,* to ex-
' tinguish any fire that may break out in town.

' One subaltern, 1 sergeant, and 20 rank and file,
' from Col. Pinckney's regiment, with one engine,
' negroes &c. at Grimke's corner,† to put out any
' fire that may break out in town.

' One subaltern, 1 sergeant, and 20 rank and file,
' from Col. Pinckney's regiment, with engine, ne-
' groes &c. at Rantowle's corner,‡ to put out any fire
' that may break out in town.

' One subaltern, 1 sergeant, and 20 rank and file,
' from Col. Pinckney's regiment, with engine, negroes,
' &c. at Ramage's corner,§ to put out any fire that
' may break out in town.

' One subaltern, 1 sergeant, and 20 rank and file
' from Col. Pinckney's regiment, with one engine, ne-
' groes, &c. at Brewton's corner,‖ to put out any fire
' that may break out in town.

' If any fire should break out at night in town,
' some persons from the guard house are to go up

* Meeting, and Trad street, S. W.   † Meeting, and
Queen-street, S. W.   ‡ Church, and Queen-street, N. E.
§ Broad, and Church-street, N. E.   ‖ Church, and Trad-
street, S. W.

'in the upper gallery of St. Michael's Church steeple,
'and there hold out a lanthern on a pole pointing to-
'wards the fire. Messrs. Manigault, and Thomas
'Smith,* one to be at the State-house, and the other
'at Ramage's corner, as directors to the engines, and
'give orders as they shall think necessary for extin-
'guishing fires.

'COL. Pinckney's regiment to be drawn up in
'Church-street, facing eastward their centre near
'the pump at Ramage's corner.

THE fusiliers of Col. Pinckney's regiment, take
'post at the battery, on Beal's wharf.

'CAPT. Cannon's company of Col. Pinckney's re-
'giment, to take post at the battery on Prioleau's
'wharf.

'THE artillery company to take post at Brough-
'ton's battery.†

'CAPT. Darrel's company to take post at Lyttleton's bastion.‡

'THE magazine guard to be completed to 1 capt.
'2 subalterns, 3 sergeants, and 50 rank and file.

'THAT 1 captain, 2 subalterns, 3 sergeants, and
'50 rank and file to remain at the barracks, as a.

* Two very respectable old citizens, who offered their services to do what they could. They had been fire-masters under the royal government.

† The point between east and south Bay.

‡ Mechanic battery.

' guard to the women and children,* that may retire
' to the barracks.

' THAT the grenadier company of the 2 regiment,
' do march to Grenville's bastion, south end of the
' Bay.

' MAJOR Bernard Elliott to take command of the
battery North end of the Bay.†

' LIEUT. D&Treville, to take post in the battery,
' on Beal's wharf.

' COL. Motte, with the remainder of the second
' regiment (4 or 500 men) to march and take post
' near Gadsden's house, to prevent the enemy from
, landing.

' THE detachment from Dorchester, under Capt.
' Hayne's to draw up at the State-house, fronting
' east, there to wait for orders.

' COL. Roberts to take command of Grenville's
' bastion.

' LIEUTS. Olyphant and Blake of the second regi-
' ment, are appointed to carry orders; all orders de-
' livered by them are to be obeyed.'

THESE two frigate's kept us to our alarm posts for
several days; at length they disappeared and we
went to our works again.

CONGRESS in November 1775 after sending out

----

* It was strongly recommended, to the women and children
to go to the Barracks, to be out of the way of the shot from the
men-of-war.

† Cravens bastion.

their declaration, determined to raise an army to quell the insurgents; they sent a large body of militia and regulars, under the command of Colonels Richardson and Thompson; they were joined by 6 or 700 North-Carolina militia, under the command of Colonels Polk and Rutherford, and 200 regulars, under Col. Martin : this strong body of men had instructions to 'apprehend the leaders of the party ' which seized the powder, and to do all other things ' necessary to suppress the present, and to prevent ' any future insurrections;' they seized the leaders of the insurgents and dispersed their body; a number retired over the mountains, and some to St. Augustine.

JAN. We were still going on with our military operations, and as fast as we finished our batteries, the guns were mounted, and powder drawn from Dorchester to supply them ; Charlestown was quite a garrison town, and our advanced posts were filled with troops, and a number of the militia were brought from the country to garrison Charlestown.

ABOUT this time a battery was built at Georgetown, and six heavy pieces of cannon mounted.

WE received orders from the council of safety to fire upon any British ships.

'IN COUNCIL OF SAFETY, 12th Jan. 1776.
' SIR,

' WE desire you to order the commanding officer

'of the detachment on Sullivan's Island,* as soon as
'the intended temporary battery is in readiness, to
'fire upon any ships of war, boats, or other vessels
'belonging to the enemy attempting to approach,
'pass, or land troops upon the Island ; and in the mean
'time to use all the force in your power to prevent
'the enemy's landing or passing by.

   'By order of the council of safety.

    'HENRY LAURENS, President.'
'Col. MOULTRIE.'

JOHN Stewart, Esq. agent for Indian affairs in this
southern department, being in West-Florida, it was
feared that he would stir up the Indians against us,
therefore. Mrs. Stewart his wife, and Mrs. Fenwick
his daughter, were detained as hostages for his good
behavior, and that they should give intelligence. I
received the following order :

 'IN CONGRESS, Charlestown, Feb. 3d, 1776.

 'ON MOTION.

 'RESOLVED, that it be expedient, and necessary
'that the lady, and daughter of John Stewart, Esq.
'be restrained from absenting themselves from his
'house in Charlestown.

    ....

* It was then quite a wilderness, and a thick deep swamp,
where the fort stands, covered with live oak, myrtle, and palmetto trees.

'ORDERED, That a proper guard be placed and
'continued about the house of the said John Stewart,
'Esq. to prevent such absenting ; and that Col.
'Moultrie do place guards accordingly.

'RESOLVED. 5th Feb. 1776. That Mr. Fenwick
'have leave to take his wife into the country, he be-
'ing answerable that she shall not depart the Col.
'ony, and for her appearance at any time agreeably
'to the order of Congress, or the council of safety.

'ORDERED, That no person whatever, be suffered
'to visit Mrs. Stewart, without leave from Col. Moul-
'trie, or the commanding officer, for the time being,
'signified by introduction in writing, or by an officer
'appointed by him for that purpose ; and that if at any
'time Mrs. Stewart shall have occasion to go abroad
'with the permission of Col. Moultrie, or the com-
'manding officer, for that time being, she shall do so,
'attended by an officer for that purpose.

'PETER TIMOTHY, Sec'y.'

MRS. Stewart in a little time made her escape, and
Mr. Fenwick was sent to Gaol on suspicion of aiding
and assisting her to make her escape.

COL. Gadsden arrived from Philadelphia and took
upon himself the command of the troops, and on the
13th February, issued his first order.

' ALL orders issued by Col. Moultrie, antecedent
to this date, are expected to be strictly attended to.'

On the second of March, I was ordered down to Sullivan's Island, to take command; where we were building a large fort sufficient to contain 1000 men. As this was looked upon as the key of the harbor; a great number of mechanics and negroe laborers were employed in finishing this fort as fast as possible, we having got certain intelligence that the British were preparing, at New-York, for an expedition against Charlestown.

MARCH. Congress resolved to raise two regiments of riflemen, Lieut. Col. Isaac Huger is appointed Col. of the first regiment. Major M'Intosh, Lieut. Col. Benjamin Huger, Esq. Major.

CAPTAINS OF THE FIRST RIFLE REGIMENT.

Hezekiah Maham, Benjamin Tutt, Geo. Cogdell, William Richardson, John Brown, Francis Prince, David Anderson, Thomas Potts.

OFFICERS OF THE SECOND REGIMENT OF RIFLEMEN.

Thomas Sumpter, Esq. Lieut. Col. William Henderson, Esq. Major.

CAPTAINS OF THE SECOND REGIMENT OF RIFLEMEN.

James Duff, Richard Richardson, jun. Samuel Taylor, George Wage, and William Brown.

PAUL Trapier, jun. is appointed Captain of the Georgetown artillery company, and William Harden, Captain of the Beaufort artillery company.

THE affairs of the province became too unweildly
for the management of Congress, and the council of
safety or general committee: Every thing was running into confusion, and although our criminal laws
were still of force, yet they were virtually repealed
for want of proper officers to execute them, all those
under the royal authority being suspended from office, it was therefore thought absolutely necessary to
frame a constitution for the purpose of forming a
regular system of government, and for appointing
public officers for the different departments to put the
laws into execution. When the business was brought
before Congress, many members were opposed to
its being taken up by the present Congress, alleging
for the reason, the impropriety of the measure ; that
the present members were not vested with that power by their constituents; however, the provincial
Congress, determined upon a temporary one, setting
forth the grievances; they entered into the following
resolves, viz.

'I. THAT this Congress, being a full and free re-
'presentation of the people of this colony, shall hence-
'forth be deemed and called the General Assembly
'of South-Carolina, and as such shall continue until
'the 21st of October next, and no longer.

'II. THAT the general assembly shall, out of
'their own body, elect, by ballot, a legislative-coun-

‘ cil, to consist of thirteen members, (seven of whom
‘ shall be a quorum) and to continue for the same
‘ time as the general assembly.

‘III. That the general assembly, and legislative-
‘ council, shall jointly choose, by ballot, from among
‘ themselves, or from the people at large, a presi-
‘ dent and commander in chief, and a vice-president
‘ of the colony.

‘ V. That there be a privy-council, whereof the
‘ vice-president of the colony shall of course be a
‘ member and president of the privy-council, and
‘ that six other members be chosen by ballot, three
‘ by the general assembly, and three by the legisla-
‘ tive-council ; provided always, that no officer of the
‘ army or navy, in the service of the continent, or
‘ of this colony, shall be eligible.

‘ VII. That the legislative authority be vested
‘ in the president and commander in chief, the gen-
‘ eral assembly, and legislative-council.

‘ XI. That on the last Monday in October next,
‘ and the day following, and on the same days of
‘ every second year thereafter, members of the gen-
‘ eral assembly shall be chosen, to meet on the first
‘ monday in December then next, and continue for
‘ two years from the said last Monday in October.
‘ The general assembly to consist of the same num-
‘ ber of members as this congress does, each parish
‘ and district having the same representation as at

' present. And the election of the said members
' shall be conducted, as near as may be, agreeably
' to the directions of the election act. The qualifica-
' tion of electors shall be the same as required by
' law.

' XVI. That the vice-president of the colony,
' and the privy-council, for the time being, shall ex-
' ercise the powers of a court of chancery. And there
' shall be an ordinary, who shall exercise the powers
' heretofore exercised by that officer in this colony.

' XIX. That justices of the peace shall be nomi-
' nated by the general assembly, and commissioned
' by the president during pleasure.

' XX. That all other judicial officers shall be
' chosen, by ballot, jointly by the general assembly
' and legislative-council.

' XXI. That the sheriffs, qualified, as by law di-
' rected, shall be chosen in like manner by the gen-
' eral assembly and legislative-council, and commis-
' sioned by the president for two years only.

' XXII. The commissioners of the treasury, the
' secretary of the colony, the register of mesne con-
' veyances, attorney-general, and powder-receiver,
' shall be chosen by the general assembly and legis-
' lative-council jointly, by ballot, and commissioned
' by the president during good behaviour ; but shall

'be removed on the address of the general assembly
'and legislative-council.

'XXIII. THAT all field-officers in the army, and
'all captains in the navy, shall be, by the general
'assembly and legislative-council, chosen jointly,
'by ballot, and commisioned by the president; and
'that all other officers in the army and navy shall
'be commissioned by the president and commander
'in chief.

'XXVI. THAT the president shall have no pow-
'er to make war or peace, or enter into any final
'treaty, without the consent of the general assem-
'bly and the legislative-council.

'XXVIII. THAT the resolutions of the continent-
'al Congress, now in force in this colony, shall so
'continue until altered or revoked by them.

'XXIX. THAT the resolutions of this or any for-
'mer congress of this colony, and all laws now of
'force here, and not hereby altered, shall so contin-
'ue until altered or repealed by the legislature of
'this colony, unless where they are temporary, in
'which case they shall expire at the times respec-
'tively limited for their duration.

'XXX. THAT the executive authority be vested
'in the president, limited and restrained as afore-
'said.'

IN consequence of this temporary constitution, the
following appointments took place.

The Honorable {
Charles Pinckney, *Charles* *Cotesworth Pinckney*
Henry Middleton,
Richard Richardson, *James Brown*
Rawlins Lowndes,
Le Roy Hammond,
David Oliphant,
Thomas Ferguson, } Members of the legisla-tive-council.
Stephen Bull,
George Gabriel Powel,
Thomas Bee,
Joseph Kershaw,
Thomas Shubrick,
William Moultrie,
}

His excellency John Rutledge, Esq. president.

His honor Henry Laurens, Esq. vice president.

Hon. William H. Drayton, Esq. chief justice.

Hon. Thomas Bee, J. Mathews, and Henry Pendleton, Esqrs. assistant judges.

Alexander Moultrie, Esq. attorney-general.

John Huger, Esq. secretary.

William Burrows, Esq. ordinary.

Hugh Rutledge, Esq. judge of the admiralty.

George Sheed, Esq. register of mesne conveyances.

The Honorable James Parsons, William H. Drayton, John Edwards, Charles Pinckney, Thomas Ferguson, Rawlins Lowndes, members of the privy-council.

Mr. Rutledge being in Congress when he was elected, addressed them in the following manner :

'Gentlemen,

'The very great, unsolicited and unexpected hon-
'or, which you have been pleased to confer on me,
'has overwhelmed me with gratitude and concern.
'...Permit me to return you my most sincere thanks,
'for so distinguishing and unmerited a mark of your
'confidence and esteem. I have the deepest sense
'of this honor....The being called, by the free suf-
'frages of a brave and generous people, to preside
'over their welfare, is, in my opinion, the highest
'any man can receive : But, dreading the weighty
'and arduous duties of this station, I really wish
'that your choice had fallen upon one, better qual-
'ified to discharge them ; for though in zeal and in-
'tegrity I will yield to no man, in abilities to serve
'you I know my inferiority to many : Since how-
'ever, this, gentlemen, is your pleasure, although I
'foresee that by submitting to it I shall be ranked by
'our enemies amongst ambitious and designing men
'by whom, they say, the people have been deceived
'and misled; yet, as I have always thought every
'man's best services due to his country, no fear of
'slander, or of difficulty or danger, shall deter me
'from yielding mine...In so perilous a season as the
'present, I will not withhold them; but, in her

'cause, every moment of my time shall be employ-
'ed: Happy, indeed, shall I be, if those services
'answer your expectations, or my own wishes...On
'the candor of my worthy countrymen I rely to
'put the most favorable construction, as they hither-
'to have done, upon my actions...I assure myself of
'receiving, in the faithful discharge of my duty, the
'support and assistance of every good man in the
'colony; and my most fervent prayer, to the om-
'nipotent ruler of the universe, is, that, under his
'gracious providence, the liberties of America may
'be forever preserved,'

In a few days after, the legislative-council and
general assembly addressed their president in the
following words:

'We, the legislative-council and general assem-
'bly of South-Carolina, convened under the author-
'ity of the equitable constitution of government,
'established by a free people, in Congress, on the
'26th ult. beg leave, most respectfully, to address
'your excellency.

'Nothing is better known to your excellency,
'than the unavoidable necessity which induced us as
'members of Congress on the part of the people to
'resume the powers of government, and to estab-
'lish some mode for regulating the internal polity of
'this colony; and, as members of the legislative-

' council and general assembly, to vest you, for a
' time limited, with the executive authority. Such
' constitutional proceedings on our part, we make
' no doubt, will be misconstrued into acts of the
' greatest criminality by that despotism, which, lost
' to all sense of justice and humanity, has already
' pretended that we are in actual rebellion. But,
' sir, when we reflect upon the unprovoked, cruel,
' and accumulated oppressions under which Amer-
' ica in general, and this country in particular, has
' long continued; oppression which, gradually in-
' creasing in injustice and violence, are now by the
' inexorable tyranny prepetrated against the United
' Colonies, under the various forms of robbery,
' conflagration, massacre, breach of public faith, and
' open war...Conscious of our natural and unalienable
' rights, and determined to make every effort in our
' power to retain them, we see your excellency's ele-
' vation, from the midst of us, to govern this coun-
' try, as the natural consequence of such outrages.

' By the suffrages of a free people, you, sir, have
' been chosen to hold the reins of government...an
' event as honorable to yourself, as beneficial to the
' public. We firmly trust you will make the consti-
' tution the great rule of your conduct; and, in the
' most solemn manner, we do assure your excellen-
' cy, that, in the discharge of your duties under that
' constitution which looks forward to an accommoda-

' tion with Great-Britain (an event which, though
' traduced and treated as rebels, we still earnestly
' desire) we will support you with our lives and for-
' tunes.'

' AFTER passing a few necessary laws, the representatives of the people closed their sessions, on the
11th of April, 1776. On this occasion his excellency president Rutledge addressed both houses in the
following words :'

    ' Honorable gentlemen of the legislative-council,
      ' Mr. Speaker, and gentlemen of the general as-
      ' sembly,

    ' IT has afforded me much satisfaction to observe,
' that, though the season of the year rendered your
' sitting very inconvenient, your private concerns,
' which must have suffered greatly by your long and
' close application in the late Congress to the affairs
' of this colony, requiring your presence in the coun-
' try ; yet, continuing to prefer the public weal to
' ease and retirement, you have been busily engaged
' in framing such laws as our peculiar circumstances
' rendered absolutely necessary to be passed, before
' your adjournment....Having given my assent to
' them, I presume you are now desirous of a recess.
    ' ON my part, a most solemn oath has been taken,

' for the faithful discharge of my duty...On yours, a
' solemn assurance has been given, to support me
' therein....Thus, a public compact between us stands
' recorded....You may rest assured, that I shall keep
' this oath ever in mind...the constitution shall be
' the invariable rule of my conduct...my ears shall be
' always open to the complaints of the injured...Jus-
' tice, in mercy, shall neither be denied or delayed...
' Our laws and religion, and the liberties of Ameri-
' ca, shall be maintained and defended to the utmost
' of my power....I repose the most perfect confidence
' in your engagement.

'AND now, gentlemen, let me intreat that you
' will, in your several parishes and districts, use
' your influence and authority to keep peace and
' good order, and procure strict observance of, and
' ready obedience to the law....If any persons there-
' in are still strangers to the nature and merits of
' the dispute between Great-Britain and the colonies,
' you will explain it to them fully, and teach them,
' if they are so unfortunate as not to know, their in-
' herent rights....Prove to them, that the privileges
' of being tried by a jury of the vicinage, acquaint-
' ed with the parties and witnesses; of being taxed
' only with their own consent, given by their repre-
' sentatives, freely chosen by, and sharing the burden
' equally with themselves, not for the aggrandizing
' a rapacious minister, and his dependent favorites,

‘ and for corrupting the people, und subverting their
‘ liberties, but for such wise and salutary purposes,
‘ as they themselves approve; and of having their
‘ internal polity regulated, only by laws consented
‘ to by competent judges of what is best adapted to
‘ their situation and circumstances, equally bound
‘ too by those laws...are inestimable, and derived
‘ from that constitution, which is the birth-right of
‘ the poorest man, and the best inheritance of the
‘ most wealthy....Relate to them the various unjust
‘ and cruel statutes which the British parliament,
‘ claiming a right to make laws for binding the colo-
‘ nies in all cases whatsoever, have enacted, and the
‘ many sanguinary measures which have been, and
‘ are daily pursued and threatened, to wrest from
‘ them those invaluable benefits, and to enforce such
‘ an unlimited and destructive claim. To the most
‘ illiterate it must appear, that no power on earth
‘ can, of right, deprive them of the hardly-earned
‘ fruits of their honest industry, toil and labor...even
‘ to them the impious attempt to prevent many thou-
‘ sands from using the means of subsistence, provid-
‘ ed for man by the bounty of his Creator, and to
‘ compel them, by famine, to surrender their rights,
‘ will seem to call for divine vengeance....The en-
‘ deavors, by deceit and bribery, to engage barba-
‘ rous nations to imbrue their hands in the innocent
‘ blood of helpless women and children, and the at-

'tempts, by fair but false promises, to make igno-
' rant domestics subservient to the most wicked pur-
' poses, are acts at which humanity must revolt.

'SHEW your constituents, then, the indispensa-
' ble necessity which there was for establishing some
' mode of government in this colony; the benefits
' of that, which a full and free representation has
' established ; and that the consent of the people is
' the origin, and their happiness the end of gov-
' ernment....Remove the apprehensions with which
' honest and well-meaning, but weak and credulous
' minds, may be alarmed ; and prevent ill impres-
' sions by artful and designing enemies....Let it be
' known, that this constitution is but temporary....
' till an accommodation of the unhappy differences
' between Great-Britain and America can be obtain-
' ed ; and that such an event is still desired, by men
' who yet remember former friendships and intimate
' connections, though for defending their persons
' and properties, they are stigmatized and treated as
' rebels.

' TRUTH, being known, will prevail over artifice
' and misrepresentation....Conviction must follow its
' discovery....In such a case, no man who is worthy
' of life, liberty or property, will or can refuse to
' join you in defending them to the last extremity...
' disdaining every sordid view, and the mean paltry
' considerations of private interest, and present

'emolument, when placed in competition with the
'liberties of millions; and seeing that there is no
'alternative, but absolute unconditional submission,
'and the most abject slavery, or a defence becom-
'ing men born to freedom, he will not hesitate
'about the choice....Although superior force may,
'by the permission of Heaven, lay waste our towns,
'and ravage our country, it can never eradicate,
'from the breasts of free men, those principles
'which are ingrafted in their very nature...such men
'will do their duty, neither knowing or regarding
'consequences; but submitting them with humble
'confidence to the Omniscient and Omnipotent ar-
'biter and director of the fate of empires, and trust-
'ing that his Almighty arm, which has been so
'signally stretched out for our defence, will deliver
'them in a righteous cause.

'THE eyes of Europe, nay of the whole world, are
'on America....The eyes of every other colony are
'on this...a colony, whose reputation for generosity
'and magnanimity, is universally acknowledged. I
'trust, therefore, it will not be diminished by our
'future conduct; that there will be no civil discord
'here; and that the only strife amongst brethren
'will be, who shall do most to serve and to save an
'oppressed and injured country.'

IMMEDIATELY after the address, the council of

safety and general committee were abolished, and the different departments of government filled up with officers regularly appointed, all of whom took the oath prescribed by the constitution, and immediately entered on the duties of their offices: The chief justice, William Henry Drayton, Esq. begun his, with a long and learned charge to the grand jury.

THIS new system opened such a scene of regularity, as confounded and astonished the disaffected, and gave great pleasure to the friends of the revolution.

THE president and privy-council were left as an executive body, with great power ; they continued to carry on the fortifications ; issue money ; to examine accounts ; and to pay all liquidated demands.

WE had information that an expedition was preparing at New-York, and that we should soon be visited by a British army and navy. All the mechanics and laborers about the town were employed, and a great number of negroes brought down from the country, and put upon the works ; every one seemed to be busy, and every thing went on with great spirit.

FRIGATES always hovering on our coast.

LETTER FROM THE PRESIDENT.

'April the 26th, 1776.

'SIR,

'HAVING received information that two men-of-
'war are at anchor off the racoon-keys, I desire that
'you will send a proper officer, and a sufficient num-
'ber of men through Santee-creek, to reconnoitre
'them; and as soon as possible, report what obser-
'vations they make of this matter. It is not impossi-
'ble that an attempt may be made to get some sheep
'or cattle from Bull's-Island; and if so, measures
'should be taken to prevent such a step.

'I am, &c.

'COL. MOULTRIE.'   'JOHN RUTLEDGE.'

———

TO THE PRESIDENT.

'SIR,

'I have just now received your orders to send
'a party to Bull's-Island; which I shall do imme-
'diately, though we are in want of boats; I have or-
'dered Capt. Peter Horry with a detachment for
'that service.   'I have the honor to be, &c.

'WILLIAM MOULTRIE.'

'HIS EXCELLENCY THE PRESIDENT.'

AT this time it was the general opinion, especially
among the sailors, that two frigates would be a sufficient force to knock the town about our ears:
notwithstanding our number of batteries with hea-

vy cannon; but in a few weeks (28 June) experience taught us, that frigates could make no impression upon our palmetto batteries.

APRIL. General Armstrong arrived from the northward, and took command of the troops in South-Carolina; he was a brave man, and a good officer, but not much acquainted with our manner of defence which was principally forts and batteries, with heavy pieces of cannon : we had at that time at least, 100 pieces of cannon mounted in different parts of our harbor.

MAY 31. Expresses were sent to the president from Christ-church parish, informing him that a large fleet of British vessels were seen off Dewee's Island, about twenty miles to the northward of the bar; and on the first of June they displayed about fifty sail before the town, on the out side of our bar. The sight of these vessels alarmed us very much, all was hurry and confusion, the president with his council busy in sending expresses to every part of the country, to hasten down the militia : men running about the town looking for horses, carriages, and boats to send their families into the country; and as they were going out through the town gates to go into the country, they met the militia from the country marching into town ; traverses were made in the principal streets ; fleches thrown up at every place where troops could land ; military

works going on every where, the lead taking from
the windows of the churches and dwelling houses,
to cast into musket balls, and every preparation
to receive an attack, which was expected in a few
days.

JUNE 4. General Lee arrived from the northward,
and took the command of the troops ; his presence
gave us great spirits, as he was known to be an able,
brave, and experienced officer, though hasty and
rough in his manners, which the officers could not
reconcile themselves to at first : it was thought by
many that his coming among us was equal to a reinforcement of 1000 men, and I believe it was, because he taught us to think lightly of the enemy, and
gave a spur to all our actions.   After Gen. Lee had
waited upon the president, and talked with him upon
his plan of defence, he hurried about to view the
different works, and give orders for such things to
be done as he thought necessary ; he was every day
and every hour of the day on horse back, or in boats
viewing our situation and directing small works to
be thrown up at different places ; when he came
to Sullivan's Island, he did not like that post at all,
he said there was no way to retreat, that the garrison would be sacrificed ; nay, he called it a ' slaughter pen,' and wished to withdraw the garrison and
give up the post, but president Rutledge insisted
that it should not be given up.   Then Gen. Lee

said it was 'absolutely necessary to have a bridge of 'boats for a retreat;' but boats enough could not be had, the distance over being at least a mile. Then a bridge was constructed of empty hogsheads buoyed at certain distances, and two planks from hogshead to hogshead; but this would not answer, because when Col. Clark was coming over from Haddrell's, with a detachment of 200 men; before they were half on, it sunk so low, that they were obliged to return : Gen. Lee's whole thoughts were taken up with the post on Sullivan's Island; all his letters to me shew how anxious he was at not having a bridge for a retreat; for my part, I never was uneasy on not having a retreat because I never imagined that the enemy could force me to that necessity; I always considered myself as able to defend that post against the enemy. I had upwards of 300 riflemen, under Col. Thompson, of his regiment, Col. Clark, with 200 North-Carolina regulars, Col. Horry, with 200 South-Carolina, and the Racoon company of riflemen, 50 militia at the point of the island behind the sand hills and myrtle bushes; I had also a small battery with one 18 pounder, and one brass field-piece, 6 pounder, at the same place, which entirely commanded the landing and could begin to fire upon them at 7 or 800 yards before they could attempt to land, this would have disconcerted them very much, besides had they made their landing good, the riflemen would have hung upon their flanks for three miles as they marched along the beach, and not above fifty yards from them.

Col. Thompson had orders that if they could not stand the enemy they were to throw themselves into the fort, by which I should have had upwaids of 1000 men in a large strong fort, and Gen. Armstrong in my rear with 1500 men, not more that one mile and an half off, with a small arm of the sea between us, that he could have crossed a body of men in boats to my assistance, this was exactly my situation ; I therefore felt myself perfectly easy because I never calculated upon Sir. Henry Clinton's numbers to be more then 3000 men ; as to the men-of-war, we should have taken every little notice of them if the army had attacked us.

Gen. Lee one day on a visit to the fort, took me aside and said, ' Col. Moultrie, do you think you can ' maintain this post.' I answered him 'Yes I think I ' can,' that was all that passed on the subject between us : another time Capt. Lamperer, a brave and experienced seaman, who had been master of a man-of-war, and captain of a very respectable privateer many years ago visited me at the fort after the British ships came over our bar ; while we were walking on the platform looking at the fleet, he said to me : ' well Colonel what do you think of it now ;' I replied that ' we should beat them,' ' Sir said he ' when

'those ships (pointing to the men-of-war) come to
'lay along side of your fort, they will knock it down
'in half an hour,' (and that was the opinion of all
the sailors,) then I said, 'we will lay behind the ru-
'ins and prevent their men from landing.'

GEN. Lee, I was informed, did not like my having
the command of that important post, he did not
doubt my courage, but said 'I was too easy in com-
'mand,' as his letters shew; but after the 28th June
he made me his bosom friend : our fort at this time
was not nearly finished ; the mechanics and negro
laborers were taken from all the works about the
town, and sent down to the Island to complete our
fort, we worked very hard, but could not get it nearly finished before the action.

'IN THE COUNCIL OF SAFETY, June 21st, 1775.
'TO WILLIAM MOULTRIE, ESQ.
'Or the commanding officer of the second regiment
'of foot.
'SIR,
'You are hereby directed forthwith to issue orders
'for levying in this and the adjacent colonies, proper
'men, not exceeding fifty in each company, to serve
'for six months certain, and not longer than three
'years, in the regiment of foot under your command;
'observing the articles agreed upon by the provincial
'Congress for ordering and governing the forces of

' this colony. And it is recommended to all the good
' people of this, and the neighboring colonies, to give
' you, and the officers under your command, all neces-
' sary aid and assistance therein....Given under our
' hands at Charlestown, in South-Carolina, the day a-
' bove mentioned :

' Charles Pinckney, William Williamson, Henry
' Laurens, Rawlins Lowndes, William H. Drayton,
' James Parsons, Arthur Middleton, Thomas Fer-
' guson, Miles Brewton, Benjamin Elliott, Thomas
' Heyward, jun.'

' By order of Congress.

' November 20th, 1765.

' Sir,

' Lieut. Colonel Roberts is ordered with a part of
' the corps of artillery, to take post at the battery, at
' Fort Johnson, and the new battery to the westward
' of it ; you are therefore ordered to afford the lieut.
' colonel all necessary assistance to make the best de-
' fence possible, at those places.

I am, Sir,

' Your most humble servant,

' Wm. H. Drayton,

' President.'

' To Col. Moultrie,

' Or the commanding officer at Fort Johnson..'

'December the 17th, 1775.
'IN THE COUNCIL OF SAFETY.
'SIR,

'You are directed to confer with the honorable
'William Henry Drayton, and Doctor Oliphant, upon
'taking post, and erecting a fascine battery for four
'cannon, 18 pounders, at Haddrell's Point, with all
'convenient dispatch: And for this service you will
'order a detachment from the provincials, consisting
'of 200 privates, commanded by a major; one ser-
'geant is necessary...You are likewise to order Capt.
'Beekman of the artillery regiment upon this service,
'and that he provide all necessary stores for the can-
'non, with all dispatch possible.

'By order of the council of safety.

'HENRY LAURENS, President.'

'COLONEL MOULTRIE.'

'SULLIVAN'S ISLAND, June 3, 1776.
'TO HIS EXCELLENCY THE PRESIDENT.
'SIR,

'WE have seen this day, two large ships, a large
'top-sail schooner, and a tender. The tender has
'been very busy in sounding from the inlet at our
'advance-guard, all along to Long-Island: It seems
'as though they intended their descent somewhere
'hereabout. Our fort is now enclosed: It is the o-
'pinion of every one, that we should have more men

' at this post; but, as I know they cannot be spared
' from the capital, I must make the best defence
' I can with what I have got; and doubt not, but that
' I shall give 4 or 500 men a great deal of trouble be-
' fore they can dislodge me from this post.

' I shall be glad you would order those boats over,
' which I had fitted up for this post : Capt. Coppithorn
' has them.

' I am your Excellency's most obedient servant.

'WILLIAM MOULTRIE,

'Col. of the second Regiment.

'June 4th, 1776.

' SIR,

'CAPT. Beekman is sent down to take the com-
' mand of the battery at Haddrell's point; if he should
' want a reinforcement from Sullivan's Island, you
' will send it, if it can be spared.

' Yours, &c.

' TO COL. MOULTRIE,   'J. RUTLEDGE.'

' SULLIVAN'S ISLAND, 7th June, 1776.

' SIR,

'A FLAG was just now sent from the men-of-
' war, but before they came to the shore, by some
' unlucky accident they were fired upon by some of
' our sentries, contrary to orders : I am sorry it should
' have happened, but now, no help for it. I sup-

'pose it only a piece of ceremony they intended....I
'expect they will begin very shortly; several of the
'fleet have gone northward, perhaps to land some
'troops: I doubt not your excellency will provide ac-
'cordingly. Your most obedient

'WILLIAM MOULTRIE
'Col. of the second Regiment.'
'To the President.'

'June 7, 1776. half past 6 o'clock, P. M.
'SIR,

'I AM very sorry, that a flag has been fired upon,
'by one of your sentries;...pray send off a flag im-
'mediately, by a discreet officer, with a proper letter
'to the commanding officer of the British fleet, ac-
'quainting him, that this act was committed by mis-
'take, and contrary to orders, and that a messenger
'shall be properly received, and that I have given this
'direction, the moment I was apprized of the fact:
'But, take care, to prevent a repetition of such con-
'duct in the sentries; at the same time, do not suffer
'any, under the appearance of a flag, to make dis-
'coveries of what the enemy ought not to know.

'Yours in haste,

J. RUTLEDGE.'
'HONORABLE COL. MOULTRIE.'

‘ SULLIVAN'S ISLAND, June 8, 1776.

‘ To the commanding officer of his Britannic
‘ majesty's fleet, now lying in five-fathom hole,
‘ South-Carolina.

‘ SIR,

‘ I SEND this flag by Capt. Huger, to assure you
‘ that the firing on a flag coming from your ship yes-
‘ terday, was the effect of error in the sentinel. A
‘ guard placed on the shore in order to receive your
‘ messenger, attempted to convince him of the mis-
‘ take, by displaying a white cloth at the end of a
‘ musket. I acquainted the president and commander
‘ in chief of this accident, whose orders I received
‘ immediately to inform you that a messenger, if you
‘ think proper to send one, shall be properly received.

‘ I have the honor to be your most obedient

‘ WILLIAM MOULTRIE,

‘ Col. of the second regiment.’

A second flag was sent, with a proclamation of
pardon to all that would return to their allegiance.

———

‘ THURSDAY MORNING, 6 o'clock.

‘ SIR,

‘ I AM extremely obliged to you for your ac-
‘ tivity and alertness : I beg you will order Long-Is-
‘ land to be reconnoitred well, and perhaps you will
‘ see a probability of attacking them with advantage

' from the main:...but this must be left to your own
' prudence. I have ordered the two rascally carpen-
' ters who deserted, to be searched for; if they can
' be found, I shall send them bound to you: I do not
' myself, much like the scheme of retreating by boats,
' it cannot, I think be done without confusion; but I
' think you ought to have two means of retreat; for
' which reason, I must beg that you will be expedi-
' tious in finishing the bridge: And all the boats I can
' procure shall be likewise sent to you...if possible I
' will visit you to day.

' I am, dear sir, yours,

' To Col. Moultrie.   'Charles Lee.'

———

'Charlestown, 8 o'clock, June 8th.

'Sir,

' As we have received information that a body of
' the enemy have landed, and are lodging themselves
' on Long-Island, and as the nature of the country is
' represented to me as favorable to riflemen, I must
' request that you immediately detach Thomson's and
' Sumpter's regiments; Capts. Alston's, Mayham's,
' and Coutirier's companies to that Island, with or-
' ders to attack, and if possible, dislodge this corps of
' the enemy;...but you must above all, take care, that
' their retreat across the breach from Long-Island to
' Sullivan's Island, is secured to them in case of ne-
' cessity. For which purpose, you are desired to move

' down to the point, commanding the breach, two
' field-pieces;...the sooner it is done the better:...you
' are therefore to exert yourself in such a manner that
' the attack may be made at break of day.

' I am, sir, yours,

' To Col. Moultrie.   ' Charles Lee.

' Major General.'

———

Charlestown, June the 8th, 1776.

' Sir,

' I have ordered a considerable reinforcement of
' riflemen to join Colonel Thomson, which, with the
' advantages of ground, ought to make you totally
' secure....I shall be with you as soon as possible in
' the morning. Mr. Bellamy will, I hope, be able to
' fin ish you a bridge to morrow.

' I am sir, your most obedient servant,

' To Col. Moultrie,   ' Charles Lee.'

' Sullivan's Island.'

———

June 9th, 5 o'clock.

' The command of all the regular forces and mi-
' litia of this colony, acting in conjunction, with them
' being invested in Major General Lee ; orders issued
' by him are to be obeyed.   J. Rutledge.'

' To Col. Moultrie.'

'June the 10th, 1776.

'Sir,

'You will receive a number of flats, ropes, and 'planks for the construction of bridges for your re-'treat...You are to give a receipt and be answerable 'for them.   'I am, sir, yours,

'Charles Lee, Major General.

'Col. Moultrie.'

'P. S. I find my last night's letter was not ,sent; I beg you would send a few expert scouts to 'discover what the enemy have done, or are doing; 'If it can be done with the least probable advantage, 'put my last nights orders in execution to night.

————

Sullivan's Island, 7 o'clock, June 10th, 1776.

'Sir.

'I just now received your orders for detaching 'Thompson and Sumpter's regiments, Allston, May-'ham and Coutirier's companies. By the date of 'your letter it seems as if you intended this busi-'ness to have been done this morning, but your let-'ter came too late to hand for that purpose. I shall 'send the detachment to our advance guard, there 'to remain with their boats for crossing them, hid 'till night, then shall embark them for Long-Island, 'where they may be reconnoitreing till day-light.

' I shall be obliged to your excellency to send us
' some person to finish our gate.

' I am, sir, your most obedient,
' WILLIAM MOULTRIE,
' Col. 2d. regiment.'

' To General LEE.'

———

' June the 10th, 6 o'clock, P. M.

' SIR,

' I AM just returned from an excursion into the
' country....As the large ships are now over the bar,
' and as your bridge must be finished ; I would wish
' you would lay asside all thoughts of an expedition
' against Long-Island, unless your scouts bring
' such intelligence as almost to insure a successful
' stroke.   ' I am, sir, yours,

'CHARLES LEE.'

' To Col. MOULTRIE,
' Sullivan's Island.'

———

' June the 10th, 1776, 8 o'clock.

' SIR,

' As the Commodore's ship has passed the bar,
' and as it is absolutely necessary for your, and the
' common safety, that the bridge of retreat should
' be finished this night ; I would have you by all
' means to lay aside all thoughts of the expedition
' against Long-Island ; unless you receive assurances

' from your scouts, that you may strike an important
' stroke.　　　　　　　Yours, CHARLES LEE,
　' To Col. MOULTRIE.　　　　　Major General.'

———

' June the 11th, 1776.
' SIR,

　' As the main body of Horry's regiment are at
' Point Haddrell, Mayham and Coutirier's compa-
' nies should be included in the detachment to be
' sent to the main.　　　　　' CHARLES LEE.'

　' To Col. MOULTRIE.'

———

' June the 11th, 1776.
' SIR,

　' I WAS much surprised that this morning the
' engineer should make a report to me, that a bridge
' of retreat was impracticable, as I understand that
' a few days ago, yourself and the other field officers
' gave it as your opinions that it might be effected.
' If I had boats, I should send them according to your
' request, but they are not to be had. The flats,
' ropes, and anchors were sent in consequence of
' your former opinion. As I think your security
' will be much greater by posting a considerable bo-
' dy of riflemen on the continent than on the Island;
' I must desire that you will immediately detach
' 400 of them to the continent: They are to post
' themselves, or rather extend themselves from the

'left of Point Haddrell, towards Long-Island; by
'which means they will be able to prevent the enemy
'from erecting works, to cut off your retreat. I
'would order the whole body off the Island, but ap-
'prehend it might make your garrison uneasy....You
'must order this body to be alert in patroling, and
'if there is not natural cover in this range, they
'must throw up artificial ones. I request that this
'order may be instantly obeyed.   I am, sir, yours,
                               'CHARLES LEE.

'I HAD rather you would make up this detach-
'ment, 500....I hope the point of your Island, op-
'posite to Long-Island is secured against the enemy
'lodging there. I have ordered boats to be found if
'possible.   C. L.'

'To Col. MOULTRIE.'

———

                    CHARLESTOWN, June the 13th, 1776.
'SIR,
    'As I am extremely solicitous for the honor and
'safety of you and the troops under your command, and
'as I am myself persuaded that your danger or safety
'depends entirely on the strength or weakness of the
'corps stationed on the other side the creek; I must
'request that when the necessary works proposed
'are finished, you will detach, at least, another hun-
'dred of men to strengthen this corps. I wish you
'would send me an exact state of your ammunition,
'that you may be supplied accordingly. His excel-

' lency the president, complains that several boats
have been lost at your station: as so much depends
' on these boats, I must desire that you will put
' them under a sufficient guard: Oblige the officer
' commanding the guard, to give a receipt for their
' number, and be accountable for them.

> ' I am sir your most obedient servant.
> 'CHARLES LEE.'

' To Col. MOULTRIE.'

———

'HADDRELL'S POINT, June the 15th, 1776.
' SIR,

' I have stationed Brigadier General Armstrong
' at this place; you are to make all your reports to
' him, and in all respects to consider him as your
' commanding officer.

> ' I am sir, you most obedient servant,

' To Col. MOULTRIE.   CHARLES LEE,

———

'SULLIVAN'S ISLAND, 16th June, 1776.
' SIR,

' COL. Thompson is now with me, and informs
' me that he has taken particular notice of the move-
' ment of the enemy, he observed about 10 o'clock,
' 200 grenadiers, and a small battalion, (which he im-
' agines came from Dewee to cover the landing of the
' rest) where they posted themselves, about one mile
' from our advanced guard, and waited until about

'seventeen hundred men were landed. They then
'marched off to Dewees' Island, he observed every
'six men carried something like a tent; they are
'still landing as fast as the boats can bring them.
'Col. Thompson begs that he may have at least his
'own men which are over with you (one hundred)
'without whom he cannot undertake to prevent their
'landing on this island, should they attempt it. We
'are all in high spirits, and will keep a good look out
'to prevent a surprise. Col. Thompson requests as
'a favor, if you have time, that you would come over
'and take a ride on the island to observe what a
'length of ground we have to defend.

'I am yours, &c.

'WILLIAM MOULTRIE.

'Col. 2d regiment.'

'To Gen. ARMSTRONG.'

'HADDRELL'S POINT, 16th June, 1776.

'DEAR COLONEL,

'I SHALL do my utmost to comply with yours
'and Col. Thompson's request, respecting the resi-
'due of his regiment, no passage over, unless you
'can send some boats in the morning. I wish the
'situation of the bridge may not be fatal to us, as
'we must assist each other. Let Mr. De Brahm be
'early at work there, as it must be defensible. Does
'not the movement of the enemy towards Dewees'

'look like an intention to use one of the creeks to-
'wards Haddrell's, probably Bolton's landing? I
'expect Gen. Lee early here to-morrow. Dear Col.
'be vigilant, keep your troops alert; I see no rea-
'son why you may not also reinforce Col. Thom-
'son; nay, if they appear indeed to land on Sulli-
'van's it must be done, and the point at the island
'where they may best land, prudently and vigorous-
'ly defended at all events. Let the Col. know this.

    'May Heaven attend you all

        'JOHN ARMSTRONG.'

'Col. MOULTRIE.'

           'June 21st, 1776.

'SIR,

  I AM extremely concerned to hear that the tra-
'verse which I had ordered to be thrown up, and
'which is really of the greatest importance, should
'be so illy executed as to threaten a speedy fall...
'surely Mr. De Brahm the engineer must be ac-
'quainted with the degree of talus necessary in all
'works...for God sake enjoin him to correct the evil
'before it is too late...at any rate devise the means
'of preventing its ruin...I must likewise express my
'concern when I am told that your gunners are suf-
'fered to fire at the enemy when it is almost impos-
'sible that their fire should have any effect...I must
'desire you, sir, that you must establish it as an

' eternal rule, that no piece of ordnance, great or
' small, should be fired at a greater distance than
' four hundred yards...but all orders will be in vain
' unless you make an example of the first who dis-
' regards your orders. Is Bellamy with you? Has
' he begun the second bridge? I hope you will keep
' him on the island until he has finished the work.

 ' I am, sir, your most obedient servant.

' CHARLES LEE.'

 ' P. S. Those two field pieces at the very end of
' the point, are so exposed that I desire you will
' draw them off to a more secure distance from the
' enemy...in their present situation it appears to me,
' they may be carried off when ever the enemy think
' proper.'

 ' To Col. MOULTRIE.'

———

' CHARLESTOWN, June the 21st, 1776.

' SIR,

 ' I hope you will excuse the style of my last let-
' ter, I must once more repeat that, it did not arise
' from any diffidence in your judgement, zeal, or
' spirit ; but merely from an apprehension that your
' good nature, and easy temper, might, in some mea-
' sure counteract those good qualities which you are
' universally known to possess. As you seem sensi-
' ble that it is necessary to exert your powers, I do

' not, I cannot wish this important post in better
' hands than yours : once more therefore excuse my
' manner of writing...I wish Mr. Bellamy had (when
' he was desired to give in a list of all he wanted)
' left nothing to ask for at this time. Mr. Cochran
' is now employed in finding out the planks he re-
' quests ; you shall have it as soon as possible. Capt.
' Tuffts was ordered to put himself under the com-
' mand of Gen. Armstrong...I shall write to the gen-
' eral to night, to order him to station him in such
' a manner as to be of the greatest use to you, as
' likewise to spare you all the necessary assistance :
' To-morrow I expect Mulenburgh's regiment, and
' I flatter myself that we shall be able to devise some
' means of baffling the enemy, should your post be
' really their object.

 ' I am, sir, with the greatest respect, your most
' obedient humble servant,

' Charles Lee.'

P. S. ' We have hoes and spades, but no helves
' to them ; so Gen. Armstrong must return those he
' borrowed : We shall endeavor to replace them.'

 ' To Col. Moultrie,

  ' Fort Sullivan.'

———

' Charlestown, June the 22nd, 1776.
' Sir,

 ' Inclosed is a letter for Col. Thompson ; I send

' it open that you may read it : for allowing for the
' difference of his circumstances as a rifle officer, the
' spirit of the order is to extend to the whole ; no
' vague uncertain firing either of rifles, muskets, or
' cannon is to be permitted. Soldiers running at
' random wherever their folly directs, is an absolute
' abomination not to be tolerated ; for heaven's sake,
' sir, as you are in a most important post ; a post where
' you have an opportunity of acquiring great honor...
' exert yourself ; by exerting yourself, I mean, when
' you issue any orders, suffer them not to be trifled
' with: every body is well persuaded of your spirit
' and zeal, but they accuse you of being too easy in
' command ; that is, I suppose, too relaxed in disci-
' pline, than which, in your situation, give me leave
' to say, there is not a greater vice. Let your orders
' be as few as possible but let them be punctually
' obeyed. I would not recommend teasing your men
' and officers with superfluous duties or labor ; but I
' expect that you enforce the execution of whatever
' is necessary for the honor and safety of your garri-
' son : should any misfortune happen which can be
' attributed to negligence or inertness on this head,
' the weight of censure will scarcely fall less heavily
' upon you, than should it arise from a deficiency of
' courage : but, as you are known to possess suffi-
' ciently of this last attribute, your friends are only
' apprehensive on the other score. You will excuse

' the prolixity and didactic style of this letter, as it
' arises not only from my anxiety for the public, but
' in some measure for my concern for the reputation
' of a gentlemen of so respectable a character as
' Col. Moultrie ; but enough of this at present :...be-
' fore you employ your engineer in any work, satisfy
' yourself well that he understands the principle of
' the work he undertakes, and the mode of executing
' it : for instance, does he understand what is the
' necessary degree of talus for the traverse in the
' fort? If I recommend the construction of an ad-
' vanced fleche on the right flank of your fort to im-
' pede the enemy's approaches, will he comprehend
' it? if he does not, I will send Mr. Byrd. I shall
' order some timber for this purpose to be carried to
' you : I desire you will post a commissioned officer
' (and a good officer) at the beach, to prevent the
' monstrous disorders I complain of.

  ' I am, sir, your most obedient servant,
' To Col MOULTRIE,   CHARLES LEE.'
 ' Sullivan's Island.'

  HADDRELL'S POINT,* June 25th, 1776.
' DEAR COL.
 ' THIS moment I was about to write you to
' learn the occasion and utility of the firing from the

---

 * About one mile from the fort, is an almost navigable
river between us.

' point ;...I hope some of your officers have been up
' to see and give the necessary directions....The bar-
' ron's conjectures may be right but their breast-
' works may as naturally be designed as a defence
' against any effort made upon our part. I am of
' opinion they will not attempt to land on Sullivan's,
' until the armed vessels are first before your fort.

' THE state of the bridge and marsh is like to give
' me great trouble ; part of the last detachment I or-
' dered to your island, has this morning absolutely
' refused until the passage between the two places is
' safely passable...I am a little surprized that your
' sergeant, agreeable to orders of yesterday, did not
' meet the men I sent to stake out the best path
' through the marsh on your side the bridge ; nor
' could the men I sent find any boards laid down,
' as you remember was ordered on Saturday night....
' this is the third day that for want of boats I could
' not get this detachment over, now part have refu-
' sed. I sent an express to Gen. Lee, and in the
' mean time desiring to know whether any new
' amendments for the bridge are going on, on your
' side the water ; and farther notice as the move-
' ments of the enemy may require. I am obliged to
' throw up works in a kind of chain, near four miles
' from this camp. The enemy constantly striving
' to find new landing places on the main.

'I am, dear sir, yours,
'JOHN ARMSTRONG,'

' CHARLESTOWN, June the 23d, 5 o'clock.
' SIR,

' I HAVE sent Capt. Cochran (a very active man)
' to your Island, to devise the means of establishing
' a second communication with the continent : Prit-
' chard's flat, he says is already at the Island : Mul-
' enburg's regiment will be here to night, we shall
' be then very strong : I will be down with you to-
' morrow with a body of workmen, and put you, I
' hope, in a state of great security. Upon the whole,
' I think you will be safe, if your people do their du-
' ty : There can be nothing to fear to night : I hope
' your garrison will remain in spirits : on my part, I
' promise every attention...and am, with the greatest
' truth, yours   CHARLES LEE.'

' To Col. MOULTRIE.'

' CHARLESTOWN, June the 25th, 1776.
' SIR,

' THE gentleman that delivers you this letter, is
' Baron Massenbourg, one of the continental engi-
' neers. I desire you will furnish him with the num-
' ber of workmen, and with every material he may
' require to carry on his works.

' I am, sir, your most obedient humble servant.
               'CHARLES LEE.'

' To Col. MOULTRIE,
' Sullivan's Island.'

' SIR,

'I HAVE sent you the carpenter; it is your
' fault if he escapes again : keep a guard over him :
' send the express boat back immediately.

'Yours,   CHARLES LEE.'

'P. S.   Finish the bridge.'

'To Col. MOULTRIE.'

———

'CHARLESTOWN, June the 27th, 1776.

'DEAR sir,

'COULD you not contrive this night to
' take up the enemy's buoys? I have ordered Gen.
' Armstrong to send an hundred volunteers to ease
' Col. Thompson's regiment of their heavy duty, for
' I find, that a part of Col. Horry's regiment had
' most magnanimously refused to take this duty on
' them : We shall live I hope to thank them....I am
' in hopes your bridge will be finished this night;
' you can then be reinforced at pleasure.

'I am, dear sir, yours,

'CHARLES LEE.'

'To Col. MOULTRIE.'

———

'CHARLESTOWN, June the 27th, 1776.

'DEAR Sir,

'SOME boats will possibly pass by you
' to night from town on a scouting expedition, before
' 12 o'clock at night, their orders are to intercept

' some of the enemy's boats, and gain some impor-
' tant intelligence: I must desire, therefore, that you
' enjoin the whole sentinels on your Island not to
' challenge any boats passing from town, or to fire
' upon them, which would defeat the whole scheme ;
' on their return, if they meet with any success, they
' shall have orders to greet you with two cheers ; and
' if the wind or tide is against their return to town,
' they will put into your post, and remain with you
' this night : I hope your bridge is finished, as I in-
' tend to reinforce you considerably.   Yours,

' CHARLES LEE.'

' To Col. MOULTRIE.'

———

' POINT HADDRELL, June the 28th, 1776.
' DEAR COLONEL,
      ' IF you should unfortunately expend your
' ammunition without beating off the enemy or driv-
' ing them on ground, spike your guns and retreat
' with all the order possible : but I know you will be
' careful not to throw away your ammunition.*

'CHARLES LEE,
' To Col. MOULTRIE.'   Major General.'

———

'June 28th, 6 o'clock, A. M.
' DEAR COL.
      ' I SHALL send you immediately a reinforcement.

....

* This letter was written to me during the action.

'If the bridge cannot be finished without taking down
'the old...take it down without ceremony, but it
'would be better to have both.

'Yours,   CHARLES LEE.'

'To Col. MOULTRIE.'

'ARMSTRONG'S, June 28th, 3 o'clock P. M.
'DEAR COL.

'MR. Byrd makes reports of your conduct which
'does you infinite honor; they are indeed such as I
'expected. I have sent for more ammunition for
'you, and ordered a large corps of riflemen to rein-
'force Col. Thompson.

'Your's,   CHARLES LEE.'

'To Col. MOULTRIE.'

'THE following letter from president Rutledge,
'wrote with a pencil on a small slip of paper, was
'sent in the height of the engagement.

June 28th.

'DEAR SIR,

'I SEND you 500 pounds of powder. I should
'think you may be supplied well from Haddrell's...
'You know our collection is not very great. HONOR
'and VICTORY, my good sir, to you, and our worthy
'countrymen with you.

'Yours,   J. RUTLEDGE.

'P. S. Do not make too free with your cannon.
'Cool and do mischief.'

'CHARLESTOWN, June 29th, 9 o'clock.

'DEAR COL.

'I SHOULD have thanked you and your brave gar-
'rison this morning, vis-a-vis at the fort...but am
'prevented by a great deal of business. I do most
'heartily thank you all and shall do you justice in
'my letters to congress. I have applied for some
'rum for your men. They deserve every comfort
'that can be afforded them. We have sent for more
'powder, inform me of all your wants.

'I am, dear Col. yours,

'CHARLES LEE.

'P. S. The General desires that Col. Thompson
'will send as soon as he can, a return of all occur-
'rences in his part of the Island.   J. N. Sec'ry.'

'To Col. MOULTRIE.'

————

'June 29th, 1776.

'DEAR SIR,

'MY very particular thanks are due to
'you, and the brave officers and men in your garri-
'son, for their heroic behaviour of yesterday. I beg
'that you will receive them yourself, and make them
'acceptable to the gentlemen, officers, and soldiers.
'Seeing the necessity of supporting you properly, I
'will strain every nerve to supply you with ammu-
'nition : no man would go a greater length than my-
'self in this matter; but, my good sir, you know the

'scantiness of our stock: I send you 1500 pounds,
' and think more cannot be spared: Indeed to do
' this, I have been obliged to get 2000 pounds from
' Dorchester: We must not wholly exhaust ourselves
' for the forts; small arms must decide the matter at
' last.

' I DAILY expect powder from Eustatia, then I
' hope to supply you plentifully; if those gentry think
' proper to re-visit you, after saying what I have done,
' you will not need any caution, to spare your pow-
' der: I beg and entreat of you only to fire your hea-
' viest guns very slowly, only now and then, and
' take good aim, if a brisk fire is kept up on your
' side, to attempt, by any means, to equal theirs,
' your ammunition will soon be expended, and what
' shall we do then...I, therefore, once more request
' most earnestly, that you will observe this advice: I
' send this powder upon Roberts' pressing it much,
' in consequence of a letter from Capt. Beekman;
' but yet I think it can not be wanted, I mean, what
' you have had, cannot have been near expended; I
' think you had 21 rounds to each gun, besides the
' 500 pounds sent yesterday, and surely nothing
' like that quantity could have been fired yesterday :
' I presume there must be a good deal made up for
' the guns, that were not fired, which Beekman has
'not thought of when he was writing to Roberts: pray,
' sir, have this matter investigated, and let me have

' a correct state of it by the bearer, Capt. Legaré,
' or any other good hand, coming up soon, let me
' have it; acquaint me if any thing, and whatever
' you may think material, or proper for me to know.
' I should mention, and you will please to communi-
' cate to the garrison, Gen. Lee's sentiment, which
' he thus expresses to me, ' Their conduct is such
' as does them the greatest honor, no men ever did,
' and it is impossible ever can behave better.' I hope
' you will caution the men with their field-pieces, at
' the advanced guard, and the riflemen also there,
' not to expend their ammunition in random shot, or
' unnecessarily.   Dear sir, yours,

                                      ' J. Rutledge.'

' To Col. Moultrie.'

—

                        ' Fort Johnson, 1st July, 1776.
' Dear Sir,

    ' I most heartily congratulate the colony on the
' drubbing you gave those fellows the other day, and
' only wish you had had powder enough, that it
' might have been complete.   Inclosed I send you a
' copy of a letter I sent Gen. Lee this morning, con-
' taining the information I received from five honest
' fellows, Americans, that got away last night.

    ' If they come up again they are determined to come
' as close to the forts as possible, in order I sup-
' pose to command us more easily from their tops, two

' of these men were on board the Commodore in the
' action, they say, your first fire killed a man in the
' tops, upon which the Commodore ordered them all
' out of the tops, from whence, they assured us there
' was not a gun fired. The Sphinx lost her bow-
' sprit by running foul of the Acteon, and they were
' obliged either to cut away their bowsprit or the
' Acteon's main-mast. These men all belonged to
' the Acteon, and two of them were drafted on board
' the Commodore just before the action. I fired three
' cannon at the Syren, merely to please several of my
' officers which fell far short as I expected. We ad-
' mired your behavior, but could do no more. My
' compliments to all your corps. We drink their
' healths every day...If you will send this account to
' Gen. Armstrong I shall be obliged to you.

Yours, sincerely,

'CHRISTOPHER GADSDEN.

' P. S. As soon as the action began, the Commo-
' dore ordered to be put into a place of safety, ne-
' gro Sampson, a black pilot.   C. G.'

'CHARLESTOWN, July the 1st, 1776.

' DEAR COLONEL,

' HUGER'S regiment have offered themselves to
' work at your fort. I believe a corps of blacks
' would have answered better, but the president and
' vise-president think otherwise. You must desire

‘ the baron, to throw up the redoubt I ordered near
‘ on the beach, to prevent their landing. The car-
‘ penter's I hope will soon finish the gate. I have
‘ applied for six horses, and hope I shall procure them
‘ for you. Five deserters are just arrived here from
‘ the ships-of-war. Inclosed I send you a list of the
‘ murders your garrison have now to answer for, but
‘ I hope it will sit light on their consciences.

‘ I am,

‘ Dear Colonel, yours,

‘ CHARLES LEE’

‘ P. S. I must request that your garrison may be
‘ kept more vigilant than ever, and that Col. Thomp-
‘ son and his corps do not relax; for it is almost pro-
‘ verbial in war, that we are never in so great dan-
‘ ger as when success makes us confident....Let the
‘ bridge be finished as soon as possible.’

‘ To Col. MOULTRIE’

‘ CHARLESTOWN, July 6th, 1776.

‘ DEAR COLONEL,

‘ I AM extremely concerned that the materials are
‘ not provided, which are necessary for carrying on,
‘ and finishing the works proposed in your fort and
‘ island; but at the same time I think the negroes
‘ you have with you, may be usefully employed...
‘ they may fill up the merlons which are not yet full
‘ ...they may palisade (for I believe you have palisades

' sufficient) the low and most assailable parts of your
' embrasures and angles :...Is your gate finished?
' ...How is your bridge?...I beg you will inform me.

' I am,

' Dear Colonel, yours,

'CHARLES LEE.'

' To Col. MOULTRIE,

' Sullivan's Island'

'CHARLESTOWN, July the 7th, 1776.

'GENERAL Lee's compliments to Colonel Moul-
' trie, and desires he may come to town as soon
' as he thinks proper; he hopes the air will cure his
' gout.'*

'July the 30th, 1776.

' DEAR COL.

'MR. Ferguson informs me, that he has fur-
' nished you with two hundred pair of negroe shoes:
' As a party is ordered on immediate service, I flat-
' ter myself you will have the kindness to spare them
' for the poor devils, who have so long a march be-
' fore them,† and are quite unshod: You will have
' time enough to replace them; I therefore request

....

* I had the gout before and at the time of the action, on the
28th of June.

† It was intended to march them to Augustine.

' that you will shew your charity on this occasion....
' and am, dear colonel, yours.

'Charles Lee.'

' To Col. Moultrie.'

June, 1776. On the morning of the 28th of
June, I paid a visit to our advance-guard (on horseback three miles to the eastward of our fort) while
I was there, I saw a number of the enemy's boats
in motion, at the back of Long-Island, as if they
intended a descent upon our advanced post; at the
same time, I saw the men-of-war loose their top-
sails; I hurried back to the fort as fast as possible ;
when I got there the ships were already under
sail; I immediately ordered the long roll to beat,
and officers and men to their posts: We had scarcely manned our guns, when the following ships of
war came sailing up, as if in confidence of victory ;
as soon as they came within the reach of our guns,
we began to fire; they were soon a-breast of the
fort...let go their anchors, with springs upon their
cables, and begun their attack most furiously about
10 o'clock, A. M. and continued a brisk fire, till
about 8 o'clock, P. M.

The ships were, the Bristol, of 50 guns, Commodore Sir Peter Parker : The captain had his arm
shot off, 44 men killed and 30 wounded.

THE Experiment, 50 guns: the captain lost his arm, 57 men killed and 30 wounded.

THE Active, 28 guns: 1 lieutenant killed, 1 man wounded.

THE Sole-Bay, 28 guns: 2 killed, 3 or 4 wounded.

THE Syren, 28 guns.

THE Acteon, 28 guns: burnt; 1 lieutenant killed.

THE Sphinx, 28 guns: lost her bowsprit.

THE Friendship, 26 guns; an armed vessel taken into service.*

THE Thunder-Bomb had the beds of her mortar soon disabled; she threw her shells in a very good direction; most of them fell within the fort, but we had a morass in the middle, that swallowed them up instantly, and those that fell in the sand in and about the fort, were immediately buried, so that very few of them bursted amongst us: At one time, the Commodore's ship swung round with her stern to the fort, which drew the fire of all the guns that could bear upon her: we supposed he had had the springs of her cables cut away : The words that passed along the plat-form by officers and men, were, ' mind the Commodore, mind the two fifty gun ships:' most all the attention was paid to the two fifty gun ships, especially the Commodore, who, I dare say, was not at all obliged to us for our particular atten-

* The killed and wounded on board of the men-of-war, was from their own account.

tion to him; the killed and wounded on board those two fifty gun ships confirms what I say. During the action, Gen. Lee paid us a visit through a heavy line of fire, and pointed two or three guns himself; then said to me, ' Colonel, I see you are doing very well ' here, you have no occasion for me, I will go up to ' town again,' and then left us.

WHEN I received information of Gen. Lee's approach to the fort, I sent Lieut. Marion, from off the plat-form, with 8 or 10 men, to unbar the gate-way, (our gate not being finished) the gate-way was barricaded with pieces of timber 8 or 10 inches square, which required 3 or 4 men to remove each piece; the men in the ships tops, seeing those men run from the plat-form concluded ' we were quitting the fort,' as some author mentions: Another says, ' we hung up a man in the fort, at the the time of ' the action;' that idea was taken from this circum-stance; when the action begun, (it being a warm day) some of the men took off their coats and threw them upon the top of the merlons, I saw a shot take one of them and throw it into a small tree behind the plat-form, it was noticed by our men and they cried out ' look at the coat.' Never did men fight more bravely, and never were men more cool;* their only

....

* Several of the officers, as well as myself, were smoking our pipes and giving orders at the time of the action; but we laid them down when Gen. Lee came into the fort.

distress was the want of powder; we had not more than 28 rounds, for 26 guns, 18 and 26 pounders, when we begun the action; and a little after, 500 pounds from town, and 200 pounds from Captain Tufft's schooner lying at the back of the fort.

THERE cannot be a doubt, but that if we had had as much powder as we could have expended in the time, that the men-of-war must have struck their colors, or they would certainly have been sunk, because they could not retreat, as the wind and tide were against them; and if they had proceeded up to town, they would have been in a much worse situation: They could not make any impression on our fort, built of palmetto logs and filled in with earth, our merlons were 16 feet thick, and high enough to cover the men from the fire of the tops : The men that we had killed and wounded received their shots mostly through the embrasures.*

AN author, who published in 1779, says 'the guns ' were at one time so long silenced, that it was ' thought the fort was abandoned; it seems extraor-' dinary that a detachment of land forces were not

....

* Twelve men were killed and 24 wounded. When Sergeant M'Donald received his mortal wound, he, addressing his brother soldiers who were carrying him to the doctor, desired them not to give up, that they were fighting for liberty and their country.

' in readiness on board of the transports, or boats,
' to profit of such an occasion.'

THE guns being so long silent, was owing to the
scarcity of powder which we had in the fort, and to
a report that was brought me, 'that the British
' troops were landed between the advance-guard and
' the fort;'* it was upon this information, that I ordered the guns to cease firing, or to fire very slow
upon the shipping; that we should reserve our powder for the musketry to defend ourselves against the
land forces, there being a great scarcity of powder
at this time.

AT one time, 3 or 4 of the men-of-war's broad-
sides struck the fort at the same instant, which gave
the merlons such a tremor, that I was apprehensive
that a few more such would tumble them down.
During the action, three of the men-of-war, in going
round to our west curtain, got entangled together,
by which the Acteon frigate went on shore on the
middle ground; the Sphinx lost her bow-sprit; and
the Syren cleared herself without any damage; had
these three ships effected their purpose, they would
have enfiladed us in such a manner, as to have driv-
en us from our guns: It being a very hot day, we
were served along the plat-form with grog in fire-
buckets, which we partook of very heartily : I never

* The advance, is about 3 miles from the fort at the east
end of Sullivan's Island.

had a more agreeable draught than that which I took out of one of those buckets at the time ; it may be very easily conceived what heat and thirst a man must feel in this climate, to be upon a plat-form on the 28th June, amidst 20 or 30 heavy pieces of cannon,* in one continual blaze and roar ; and clouds of smoke curling over his head for hours together ; it was a very honorable situation, but a very unpleasant one.

During the action, thousands of our fellow-citizens were looking on with anxious hopes and fears,† some of whom had their fathers, brothers, and husbands in the battle ; whose hearts must have been pierced at every broad-side. After some time our flag was shot away ; their hopes were then gone, and they gave up all for lost! supposing that we had struck our flag, and had given up the fort: Sergeant Jasper perceiving that the flag was shot away, and had fallen without the fort, jumped from one of the embrasures, and brought it up through a heavy fire, fixed it upon a spunge-staff, and planted it upon the ramparts again : Our flag once more waving in the air, revived the drooping spirits of our friends ; and they continued looking on, till night had closed the scene, and hid us from their view ; only the appearance of a heavy storm, with continual flashes and peals like thunder ; at night when we came to our slow firing (the am-

* 18 and 26 French pounders † At about 6 miles distance,

munition being nearly quite gone) we could hear the
shot very distinctly strike the ships: At length the
British gave up the conflict: The ships slipt their cables, and dropped down with the tide, and out of
the reach of our guns. When the firing had ceased,
our friends for a time, were again in an unhappy
suspense, not knowing our fate; till they received
an account by a dispatch boat, which I sent up to
town, to acquaint them, that the British ships had
retired, and that we were victorious.

EARLY the next morning was presented to our
view, the Acteon frigate, hard, and fast aground; at
about 400 yards distance; we gave her a few shot,
which she returned, but they soon set fire to her,
and quitted her: Capt. Jacob Milligan and others,
went in some of our boats, boarded her while she
was on fire, and pointed 2 or 3 guns at the Commodore, and fired them; then brought off the ships
bell, and other articles, and had scarcely left her,
when she blew up, and from the explosion issued a
grand pillar of smoke, which soon expanded itself at
the top, and to appearance, formed the figure of a
palmetto tree; the ship immediately burst into a great
blaze that continued till she burnt down to the water's edge.

THE other ships lay at the north point of Mor-

ris's Island* we could plainly see they had been pretty roughly handled, especially the Commodore.

THE same day, a number of our friends and fellow citizens, came to congratulate us on our victory
and Governor Rutledge presented Sergeant Jasper
with a sword, for his gallant behavior; and Mr.
William Logan, a hogshead of rum to the garrison,
with the following card. ' Mr. William Logan, pre-
' sents his compliments to Col. Moultrie, and the
' officers and soldiers on Sullivan's Island, and beg
' their acceptance of a hogshead of old Antigua rum,
' which being scarce in town at this time, will be ac-
' ceptable.' Mr. Logan's present was thankfully received. A few days after the action, we picked up,
in and about the fort, 1200 shot of different calibers
that was fired at us, and a great number of 13 inch
shells.

———

' June 30th, 1776.

' HIS excellency the president desires his very parti-
' cular thanks to the brave officers and men of this gar-
' rison, for their gallant behavior in the engagement
' of the 28th of June last.' ' Gen. Lee says no men
' ever did, and it is impossible that any can behave
' better: and that he will do us justice in his letters
' to the continental Congress. His excellency has
' sent a hogshead of rum to the garrison.'

....

* About 2 miles.

July 1. Yesterday, the lady of major Bernard Elliott, presented an elegant pair of colors to the 2d regiment, with these words :

' The gallant behavior in defence of liberty and
' your country, entitles you to the highest honors;
' accept of these two standards as a reward justly
' due to your regiment; and I make not the least
' doubt, under heavens protection, you will stand by
' them as long as they can wave in the air of Li-
' berty.'

The colors were presented by her own hands to the Colonel and Lieut. Colonel; she was thanked and promised ' that they should be honorably sup-
' ported, and never should be tarnished by the 2d
' regiment.'

There were never colors more honorably supported and never were colors better disposed of: they were planted on the British lines at Savannah : one by Lieut. Bush, who was immediately shot down: Lieut. Hume going to plant his, who was also shot down ; and Lieut. Gray in supporting them, received his mortal wound; and the gallant Jasper who was with them, on seeing Lieut. Hume shot down, took up the color and planted it ; he also received his death wound, however he brought off his colors with him, which was taken at the fall of Charlestown ; they were very elegant, one of a fine blue silk, the other a fine red silk richly embroidered : I am told they are now in the tower of London.

AFTER this, the legislature did me the honour to call the fort, FORT MOULTRIE.

OFFICERS who were in the fort on 28th June.

WILLIAM Moultrie, Col. Isaac Motte, Lieut. Col. Francis Marion, Maj. Andrew Dellient, Adj.

CAPTAINS, Peter Horry, Nicholas Eveleigh, James M'Donald, Isaac Harleston, Charles Mott, Francis Huger, Richard Ashby, Richard Shubrick, William Oliphant, John Blake.

LIEUTENANTS, William Charnock, Thomas Lessesne, Thomas Moultrie, Daniel Maryck, Jacob Shubrick, Thomas Dunbar, William Moultrie, jun. Thomas Hall, Henry Gray, Isaac Dubose, Richard B. Baker, Adrian Proveaux, Richard Mayson, Peter Gray, Basil Jackson, Gad Marion.

———

'PHILADELPHIA, July 20th, 1776.
'IN CONGRESS.

'RESOLVED, That the thanks of the United States
'of America, be given to Maj. Gen. Lee, Col. Wil-
'liam Moultrie, Col. William Thompson, and the
'officers and soldiers under their commands ; who,
'on the 28th of June last, repulsed, with so much val-
'or, the attack which was made on the State of
'South-Carolina, by the fleet and army of his Bri-
'tannic majesty.

'THAT Mr. President transmit the foregoing re-
'solution to Maj. Gen. Lee, Col. Moultrie, and Col.
'Thompson.

'By order of the Congress.

'JOHN HANCOCK, President.'

————

THE latter end of July the Declaration of Independence arrived in Charlestown, and was read at
the head of the troops, in the field by Maj. Bernard
Elliott; after which an oration was delivered by the
Rev. Mr. Pearcy.

JULY. About this time, Mr. Jonathan Bryan arrived
in Charlestown from Georgia, and informed Gen. Lee
that if he would send a detachment of troops to East-
Florida, he could easily take the town of St. Augustine; as there were but very few men in that garrison: upon which Gen. Lee hastily marches off the
Virginia and North-Carolina troops, at this inclement season of the year, (leaving Gen. James Moore
to command in Charlestown) without one necessary
article, nor a field piece, nor even a medicine chest;
he was followed by Gen. Howe and myself.

As soon as the British had retreated after the battle of Sullivan's Island, the state was left tranquil,
and free from any apprehension of another attack
soon; an expedition was planned against the Cherokee
Indians (who began to be troublesome) and carried
on by Col. Andrew Williamson; and a strong body

from North-Carolina, under General Rutherford, who came upon them through the mountains; and a body of men from Virginia, under Col. Christie; and another body from Georgia, under Col. Jacks: The detachment under Col. Williamson, had several skirmishes with them, before the other detachments came up. The Indians being attacked on all sides, sued for peace; which was granted them, upon their giving up all the lands to the eastward of the Oconee Mountains. If the British had set their Indian allies upon us a few months before Sir Henry Clinton and Sir Peter Parker made their descent on South-Carolina, they would have disconcerted us very much, by keeping thousands of our back country people from coming down; because they must have staid at home to protect their familes from the savages.

August 11th, a detachment of South Carolina troops was sent off for Georgia, with two field-pieces : when we got to Savannah, in Georgia, Gen. Lee proposed to me to take the command of the expedition against St. Augustine, and asked me whether my brother being there as governor, would not be an obstacle in my way : I told him my brother being there would be no objection with me ; but with respect to other matters, I did not see one thing in the place that we could get to aid such an expedition ; that if I undertook the expedition, I must have 800 men, and many things else ; and, at his request, I gave a list of such articles as I thought would be wanted: I told him I knew what it was to march an army through the wilderness : that I had been warring against Indians ; that I had seen an army of 3000 men reduced to only one days provision, and that, in an Indian enemy's country : Gen. Lee immediately sent to Augusta to have the articles got agreeably to the list I gave in ; and we were preparing for the march, when an express, in September, arrived from Congress, calling Gen. Lee immediately to the northward ; in two days after, he left Savannah, and ordered the Virginia and North-Carolina troops to follow him. This put an end to the East-Florida expedition.

The troops that went to Georgia, suffered exceedingly by sickness; at Sunberry, 14 or 15 were buried every day, till they were sent to the sea Islands, where they recruited a little.

On the 8th of September, Gen. Lee arrived in Charlestown, and the governor and council prevailed upon him to leave the North-Carolinians in this province, as a great part of the South-Carolina troops were in Georgia, and we should be left, with very few men, quite defenceless. He consented to leave the North-Carolina troops ; and before his departure, he issued the following orders.

' Orders, September 9th.

' Gen. Lee thinks it his duty before his departure,

‘ to express the high sense he entertains of the con-
‘ duct and behavior of the colonels and officers of the
‘ several battalions of South-Carolina, both as gen-
‘ tlemen and soldiers; and begs leave to assure them,
‘ that he thinks himself obliged to report their merit
‘ to the continental Congress.’

HITHERTO the South-Carolina battalions were upon the establishment of the colony; but it was found
very inconvenient to the service, that troops doing
duty together, should be governed by different laws :
it was recommended by Congress, to have the colony troops put upon continental establishment, which
was agreed to.

‘ IN GENERAL ASSEMBLY, Sept. 20th, 1776.
‘ RESOLVED, that this house do acquiesce in the
‘ resolution of the continental Congress of the 18th of
‘ June, and the 24th of July last, relative to the put-
‘ ting the two regiments of infantry, the regiment
‘ of rangers, the regiment of artillery, and the two
‘ regiments of riflemen, in the service of this state,
‘ upon the continental establishment.’

BY this resolve, the South-Carolina officers came
into the continental line as youngest officers of their
different ranks.

GEN. Lee left the southern States, and went to
the northward; upon which the command of the
southern troops devolved upon Gen. James Moore.

'ORDERS BY GEN. MOORE, Jan. 9th, 1777.

' THE detached situation of Fort Moultrie, Had-
' drell's point, this town, and Fort Johnson, from each
' other making it necessary that the command of the
' troops be divided ; Gen. Howe will command in
' town and Fort Johnson; Gen. Gadsden at Fort
' Moultrie and Sullivan's Island; and Gen. Moultrie
' to command the North-Carolinians, at Haddrell's
' point.'

GEN. Moore returned to North-Carolina, and left
the command of the troops of that State, to Gen.
Nash.

AN express arrived with orders for the North-Carolina troops to march to the northward.

' LETTER FROM GEN. NASH, March 9th, 1777.

' THE express returned last night and brought a
' letter for Gen. Howe, which I opened, not knowing
' you were in town : you will receive it by the bearer
' and will find that there is a necessity for the North-
' Carolina troops marching immediately. With your
' permission, I will give the necessary orders for pre-

'paring for a march as soon as possible : you will
'therefore much oblige me by signifying your orders,
'in writing, on the subject.'

' I am, &c.

'To Gen. MOULTRIE.'   ' F. NASH.'

FEB. Gen. Howe, commanding the troops in S.
Carolina and Georgia, he received advice from Georgia, that a body of regular troops under the command of Col. Fuser, were marching to invade Georgia...that a part of them were to come within land,
by water. Upon this serious alarm, Gen. Howe immediately went off for Savannah, and requested I
would order a strong detachment in vessels, within
land, to follow him : in consequence of which, I ordered one under the command of Lieut. Col. Marion, of about 600 men, in several vessels, with four
field-pieces, a large quantity of ammunition, stores,
intrenching tools, and provisions : they left Charlestown on the 28th of February, but before they arrived at Savannah, the enemy had retreated ; they had
penetrated as far as Ogechee-ferry, but Col. Elbert,
with about 200 men, prevented their crossing: a body of them demanded the fort at Sunberry ; but Lieut.
Col. M'Intosh, who commanded in the fort, desired
them ' to come and take it,' which they declined.

GEN. Scriven was killed in an ambuscade, marching up to oppose this body.

On the North-Carolina troops being ordered to the northward, Gen. Gadsden called a council to advise whether our troops should not be recalled from Georgia; accordingly, an express was sent to Gen. Howe.* Gen. Gadsden requested me to write to him, and send my letter with his, that our joint request would have the more weight.

'CHARLESTOWN, March 11th, 1777.
'DEAR SIR,
'I SEND an express to inform you, that Gen.
'Moore has received orders from the continental
'Congress to march the North-Carolina troops, to
'join Gen. Washington; upon which, Gen. Gadsden
'called a council, to advise whether our troops should
'not be recalled from Georgia, when it was deter-
'mined that they should be recalled; unless Georgia
'was actually invaded by a strong regular force,
'which I think cannot be the case at present: I
'therefore make no doubt of your ordering our men
'back, especially as you know the weakness of this
'place.†

....

* Gen. Howe and Gadsden were not upon the best footing.

† At this time by our orders and letters, it appears that at least 700 of our continental troops were then in Georgia, and not more than 4 or 500 left for the defence of Charlestown, Georgetown, and Beaufort.

'ONE of our continental frigates is now in our
'harbor, she is called the Randolph, carrying 36
'guns; twenty-six 12 pounders upon one deck, &c.

'GEN. Gadsden writes you by this express: I sup-
'pose he will mention to you our weak state, and
'press the return of our troops.

'I am, &c.

'WILLIAM MOULTRIE.'

THE North-Carolina troops, being ordered away,
and most of our regular troops in Georgia; gave
great uneasiness to the inhabitants for the safety of
Charlestown; but upon the arrrival of the Randolph
frigate, their fears were a little subsided; looking
upon her to be a great additional strength to our batteries, and protection to the harbor.

BY return of the express sent to Gen. Howe, I received the following answer.

'SAVANNAH, March 16th, 1777.

'DEAR SIR,

'I WROTE you a few days since that I had
'thoughts of returning all the troops of your state,
'except 200 of Sumpter's, which the weakness of this
'state, made it necessary to have here, till the arri-
'val of Col. Elbert, and Col. Scriven, who are ex-
'pected very shortly: The time of the enlistment of
'many of the men belonging to the battalion of this

' state, being expired, it is reduced to about 200,
' with which small number, in its present state, it
' would have been highly improper to leave it.

' THE troops who came by water, arrived only
' last night; they require a few days to refresh, for
' their long and inconvenient passage has made it ne-
' cessary.

' THOMPSON's are at Purisburgh, and will be or-
' dered to march to-morrow.

' I am, &c.

' ROBERT HOWE.'

' To Brig. Gen. MOULTRIE.'

———

SOME time in June, Gen. Howe returned from
Savannah to Charlestown ; every thing in the two
southern states being now quite quiet : at this time
the legislature was sitting.

AUGUST 21st, Gen. Gadsden resigned his com-
mision. Nothing material: only carrying on our
works by land and sea.

PRESIDENT'S LETTER TO GEN. HOWE,

' December 12th, 1777.

' SIR,

' THE trade of this port being likely to suffer
' great injury from the vessels of war,* which have

....

* The Carrisford, 32 guns, the Perseus, 20, and the Hinchenbrook, 16 guns.

' for some days past, been in sight of the town. In
' order to clear the coast and protect the trade, Capt.
' Biddle has agreed to go on a cruize with the Ran-
' dolph and several other vessels, engaged by the
' state, to be put under his command,* but it being
' thought expedient that a number of marines should
' be embarked in the vessels: the council have ad-
' vised, that you should be desired to order as many
' of the continental troops under your command as
' Capt. Biddle may apprehend to be necessary for
' this service, to be detached upon it. As I do agree
' in opinion with the council, I do, therefore, and in
' pursuance of their advice, request that you will be
' pleased to give the necessary orders for this pur-
' pose, and am,

' Yours, &c.

' To Gen. Howe.   ' J. Rutledge.'

———

Dec. The state of Georgia being now very
much disturbed by the inroads of the Florida scouts,
the Scopholites from Carolina, and their own disaffected tories: Gen. Howe thought it necessary to re-
visit that state; and about the thirteenth of December, set out for Georgia, but first issued the following order.

....

* Randolph, 36 guns, Capt. Biddle; Polly, 16 guns,
Capt. Anthony; Gen. Moultrie, 18 guns, Capt. Sullivan;
Fair American, 14 guns, Capt. Morgan; Notre Dame, 16
guns, Capt. Hall.

' December 13th, 1777.

' A council of war to be held as immediately as
' possible, at some convenient place in Charlestown,
' to take into consideration the matters which will be
' laid before them ; of this council, Brigadier Gen.
' Moultrie is to be president: the field-officers of the
' 1st, 2d, 4th and 5th regiments, members.'

' December, 13th, 1777.

' Gen. Moultrie's Orders.

' In consequence of Gen. Howe's orders, issued
, this forenoon; it is ordered that all the field-officers,
' in or near town, from all the continental regiments
' of this state, do meet at my quarters, precisely at
' four o'clock.'

' Gen. Howe's letter to Gen. Moultrie.
' Head-quarters, Charlestown, Dec. 13th, 1777.
' Sir,

' You will in consequence of orders issued this
' day, as immediately as possible hold a council of
' war, and lay his excellency the president's letter
' before them : the court are to give their opinion
' whether detachments from the continental troops
' can with propriety be sent upon the expedition pro-
' posed; if they can, what number can be spared ;
' how many officers, and what rank ; and how long
' it may be prudent to permit them to be absent; if
' the council determine, the reasons which guided

'their opinions are to be given at large, and signed
'by them: you will inform his excellency the presi-
'dent of their determination; and immediately trans-
'mit me a transcript of their proceedings by express.

'I am, &c.

'To Gen. MOULTRIE.   'ROB. HOWE.'

———

'December, 15th, 1777.

'In council of war, held the 13th instant,

'PRESIDENT, BRIGADIER GEN. MOULTRIE.

'COL. Isaac Huger, Col. Motte, Col. Roberts,
'Col. Pinckney, Col. Sumpter, Lieut. Col. Elliott,
'Lieut. Col. Marion, Maj. Peter Horry.

'THE council were of opinion that there would be
'no impropriety in sending the detachment required
'provided the remaining troops were thought suffi-
'cient for the defence of the state; but considering
'the present situation of the state, and of the seve-
'ral regiments, the council were also of opinion,
'that we have not men enough to defend the state
'should it be properly attcked.

'It is also my opinion that there is no impropriety
'in sending troops on that expedition provided there
'be enough to defend the state.

'Signed,

'WILLIAM MOULTRIE, President.'

———

GEN. Howe having received the opinion of the

court as above ; requested I would again call the
court ; which I did on the 19th December, of those
that could be got together : President Gen. Moultrie, Col. Huger, Col. Pinckney, Col. Roberts, Lieut.
Col. Marion, Maj. Peter Horry ; and laid before
the council, a letter from Gen. Howe, recommend-
ing them to reconsider the last opinion, because he
was 'certain the military would be highly censur-
' ed for not complying with the requisition of the
' Governor and Council.'

THE council of war, having deliberated upon the
matter, declare, 'they cannot alter their former
' opinion, and they would be unworthy of the com-
' mission they hold if they could be induced by
' the dread of censure, or any other motives to give
' an opinion contrary to their honor and conscience;
' at the same time the council beg leave to declare,
' in the strongest terms, that they are ready and
' willing to obey orders.'

'WILLIAM MOULTRIE, President.'

LETTER TO GEN. HOWE.
'CHARLESTOWN, Dec. 23d, 1777.
'DEAR SIR,
' THE council, (those of them that I could get
' together) are still of opinion that we cannot spare
' any troops: I sent a copy immediately to the presi-
' dent of the proceedings and opinions of the court.

' I WAITED on the president, and had some con-
' versation with him on the matter; he asks 150 men
' for the expedition : I have altered my opinion, and
' wish you would allow me to grant the request, and
' order the men ; it may be attended with good con-
' sequences, if otherwise, the state must take it upon
' themselves, as they have so earnestly requested the
' detachment. I send this by express, at the request
' of the president: I hope you will soon dispatch
' him, as they are impatient to know wether you will
' assist them or not.

' I am, &c.

' WILLIAM MOULTRIE.'

' MAJOR GEN. HOWE.'

LETTER FROM GEN. HOWE.

' SAVANNAH, Dec. 24th, 1777.

' DEAR SIR,

' MY sentiment respecting the determination of
' the council of war, coincide, in a great measure,
' with their opinion, but the importance of protecting
' the trade of your state, from which almost all
' America, at present, derive their supplies; joined
' to the earnest request of the executive authority of
' the state, which I, as a citizen, ought ever to res-
' pect, and when possible, attend to ; induces me to

' consent to furnish the 150 men desired by his ex-
' cellency the president.

'I am, &c.

'ROBERT HOWE.'

'GEN. MOULTRIE.'

IN conversation with the president, respecting the
naval armament ; he assured me, that there were a
number of vessels expected in, every day, with military stores, and other articles which we were very
much in want of ; that unless the men-of-war were
driven from our coast, they could not possibly get
in ; and also, by our vessel taking a short cruize,
they might pick up a prize or two of some English
ships out-ward bound to the West-Indies, loaded
with such stores as we wanted.

THESE reasons induced me to alter my opinion
from the council of war.

OUR little fleet consisted of the Randolph frigate,
of 36 guns, Capt. Biddle ; the ship General Moultrie,
18 guns, Capt. Sullivan ; the Notre-Dame brig, Capt.
Hall, 16 guns ; the Polly brig, Capt. Anthony, 16
guns ; and the Fair American, Capt. Morgan, of 14
guns : The troops were put on board, on 27th of
January, and in a few days the fleet sailed : They
were gone about 10 weeks, when they fell in with
the Yarmouth, a British 64 gun ship, which the
Randolph immediately engaged, and in a short time

after the action began, she blew up, and every soul on board perished, except 2 or 3 who were picked up on some of the wreck, by the Yarmouth's crew.

THE first regiment lost a fine company of fifty men, that were put on board as marines: The remainder of our fleet made the best of their way home;* and thus ended the expedition from which the president and privy council expected so much.

WHEN the captains of the British men-of-war Carrisford, &c. were informed of our preparations to attack them they quitted our coast, while they continued on it, some apprehensions were entertained of their going to Beaufort to take off our cannon and stores ; upon which a company of Col. Robert's artillery, were ordered to take post in the battery at that place.

JAN. 1778. AT this time the men-of-war's boat's crews [Carrisford and Perseus] were frequently in town, getting provisions and intelligence; we had so many tories then in town, that they could get good information from them, and so as to avoid our guards. Early this morning, 15th January, about 4 o'clock, A. M. a dreadful calamity happened in Charlestown : a fire broke out in a back house or kitchen in Union-street, near Queen-street, the wind blowing fresh at N. and N. N. E. and raged with such fury as to

* Some of them on their return home, picked up a few prizes.

baffle all efforts, and in a little time, it was communicated to the neighboring houses, and by the falling sparks of fire, houses in Broad, Elliott, and
Trad-streets, likewise took fire, and spread to the
houses in Church-street, Bedon's-alley, and East-
Bay, insomuch that on the Bay from Queen-street
to Grenville's-Bastion at the south-end thereof, only
5 or 6 houses escaped : About 6 o'clock that evening, the fire was in a great measure got under, after
having consumed 252 dwelling houses, besides kit-
chens and back stores: A list of which, with their
value as taken in the year 1776, viz :

Dwelling houses.		Currency.*
East-Bay,	56 - - - - - -	£ 177,425.
Broad-street,	29 - - - - - -	72,700.
Elliott-street,	51 - - - - - -	89,900.
Bedon's-alley,	15 - - - - - -	28,750.
Church-street,	17 - - - - - -	24,100.
Trad-street,	34 - - - - - -	73,200.
Union-street,	32 - - - - - -	20,760.
Chamber's-alley,	9 - - - - - -	9,500.
Unity-alley,	8 - - - - - -	3,500.
Queen-street,	1 - - - - - -	8,000.
	252.	£. 507,835.

* This is the currency of South-Carolina, five shillings to
the dollar.

IT was a very affecting scene to see the inhabitants running through the streets, looking for some place of shelter to put themselves and children in. We had strong suspicions, at the same time, that it was done by design: we had guards posted at every corner, and patroles going constantly through the streets the whole night. The next day was a sad spectacle, indeed! to behold the goods and property of different kinds, piled up in the streets in a promiscuous manner, and the proprietors harrassed out, and worn down with fatigue, standing to watch over their property, covered with blankets, and shivering with cold : and, to add more to their distress, it was so very cold, that the water which was thrown by the engines upon the tops of the houses to extinguish the fire, run down and hung in isicles along the eaves.

THE soldiers, headed by officers, exerted themselves in an extraordinary manner, to assist in extinguishing the fire; and had the thanks of the inhabitants given them, through me, in general orders. Notwithstanding this great calamity, still we were alarmed every night with the cry of fire ; it seemed as if they were determined that the town should be totally destroyed.

WE had information that the men-of-wars boats were in town every night ; and we had every reason to believe that they were the instigators of all the mischief that attended us.

THE following letters from the president, will show that the above suspicions were well grounded. [For the letter alluded to, and the answer to it, see the appendix.]

FEB. The legislature was now at this time very busily employed in framing a new constitution, and electing public officers. No military operations going on except keeping out guard-boats to endeavor to catch the men-of-war's boats, and some works going on about the lines and fortifications.

THE great numbers of the leading men from the back country, who were militia officers and men of influence, well attached to the American cause, were called down to Charlestown to attend the general assembly, and being detained there so long, that it gave time for the tories to collect, and disturb the peace of the country, which they effectually did, and began to embody in great numbers, so as to occasion a serious alarm.

A SIMILAR case happened in Georgia at the same time their general assembly were sitting; so that the tories in both states were playing the same game.

APRIL. Matters now in Georgia began to be very alarming, and it was absolutely necessary to call for some great exertions to save her from total ruin; Gen. Howe, who was there since the latter end of December, and early in April, began to call for the aid of South-Carolina, as his orders to me of different dates will shew : they saw the cloud blackening very fast, and ready to break down upon them with great violence, and the people of this state were also much alarmed; as the Scopholites began to make head.

A LETTER FROM MAJOR GEN. HOWE.

'HEAD-QUARTERS, SAVANNAH, April 7th, 1778.

' DEAR SIR,

' THE embodying of a number of insurgents from
' among the Scopholites of your state,* who have
' been joined by many of the disaffected in this, is a
' a circumstance so well authenticated both to the
' governor and myself, that it is not to be doubted.

' THEY crossed Savannah last Saturday, below
' Augusta, when luckily for themselves, they met
' with some trading boats coming down the river,
' which they pressed to facilitate their passage. Their
' numbers by the account, last night, could not be
' less than five or six hundred. They make prize of
' all as they march along. Their avowed intention
' is the forming a junction with the East-Floridians,
' who they say are determined shortly to attack this
' country. This plan, by a variety of different ways,
' we heard of before, and the raising of these people
' was a part of the story. It did not, however, ob-
' tain much credit; yet as their insurgency has actu-

....

* The Scopholites were some of the tories who were led by one Col. Scophol, Col. of militia, an illiterate, stupid, noisy blockhead.

'ally happened as was foretold, there would be rea-
'son to believe the rest, though no other matter con-
'tributed to render it probable, but the movements
'of the enemy at St. Augustine...their operations
'upon St. John's river, as well as some circum-
'stances relative to the troops at Pensacola, all seem
'to corroborate that some attack is intended. I there-
'fore think it incumbent on us, to prepare for the
'worst; and as the deplorably weak situation of this
'country renders it unequal to the least formidable
'attempt against it, I would wish you immediately
'to prepare, and have in readiness to march at a
'moment's warning, 200 men, and no time should
'be lost in having them in readiness. The situation
'of this country is a circumstance of exceeding anx-
'iety to me...assaillable on every side...and no where
'prepared for defence...many of the people disaf-
'fected to the cause; and those who wish it well, not
'united among themselves; exceedingly weak in
'numbers, as to militia, and these ill armed; and it
'is a melancholy truth that our regulars do not ex-
'ceed 550 effectives.

'I am, &c.

'ROBERT HOWE.'

'P. S. By some intelligence just now received, I
'am induced to desire you, to expedite the marching
'of the troops, as I immediately expect to have oc-
'casion for them.

'To Brig. Gen. MOULTRIE.'

A LETTER TO GEN. HOWE,

'CHARLESTOWN, April 10th, 1778.

' DEAR SIR,

' THIS state has been in commotion some days
' past, owing to the Scopholites : we have had our
' militia in pursuit of them, have killed and taken a
' few :...by your letter, their intention seems to be a-
' gainst Georgia, but I hope the Georgians will ex-
' ert themselves to prevent their further progress, and
' stop their junction with the Floridians, it will save
' us the trouble of marching to you. I can hardly think
' the people of Augustine are in a capacity to make
' any excursions ; their numbers being so few (from
' all the accounts we have been able to gather, they do
' not exceed 800 men) that unless they are greatly
' reinforced by Indians and tories, they had better
' stay at home and take care of their own castle. I
' have, agreeably, to your orders sent 150 men from
' Thompson's, and 50 from Sumpter's regiments in
' readiness to go off at a moment's warning : I hope,
' however, you will have no occasion for them. The
' people here seem to dread a foreign invasion ; not
' from any information, only from conjecture ; because
' when we were last attacked, it began in the interior
' parts of the country. Captain Senf, engineer, is
' lately arrived from the northward for this depart-
' ment ; if you should have any occasion for him, I will
' send him off with the detachment you have ordered.

'I am, &c.   'W. MOULTRIE.'

THE letter I wrote to the president on the 11th of April, requesting a loan of 20,000 pounds for the use of the quarter-master general's department, brought on a disagreeable altercation between the president and the deputy quarter-master general, (Lieut. Col. Francis Huger) so much that I was obliged to write to the president of Congress, requesting him to lay the matter before Congress.

[Letter to the president, see appendix]

LETTER FROM THE PRESIDENT.

' SIR,   April 14th, 1778.

' As it appears from the concurrent accounts of
' all the intelligence I have received, that the disaf-
' fected plan their hopes and expectations on being
' joined with a force from Florida ; and that their
' aim is to form the junction by crossing Savannah
' river, a considerable party having already taken
' that route, I submit to you, whether it would not
' be necessary and proper to post Thompson with
' his regiment at some convenient place on Savan-
' nah river to interrupt or prevent such a design,
' more especially as he would be enabled from thence,
' more expeditiously to remove to the immediate as-
' sistance of Georgia. The militia in all parts of the
' back country being in arms, and on their guard, I
' think no great danger is to be apprehended, unless
' a combined force should be effected, which must be
' by crossing Savannah river, the guarding of which

' might baffle their scheme. I did myself the plea-
' sure of calling at your house yesterday, to know
' your sentiments on this head, but you were from
' home. Some informations I have received, say it
' was talked of at St. Augustine, that a plan was
' concerted, while we were employed on these com-
' motions in the back parts to attack us from sea.
' This I think is the only ground to apprehend dan-
' ger.   ' I am, &c.

Brig. Gen. MOULTRIE.   ' RAWLINS LOWNDES'.

———

' CHALESTOWN, April 14th, 1778.

' SIR,

'   I AM very sorry I was not at home when you
' did me the honor to call upon me yesterday. I
' just now received yours, and have considered with
' attention what you mention with regard to posting
' Thompson's regiment on Savannah river, I cannot
' at present think it proper by any means, and I will
' therefore give you my reasons. That regiment
' consists of about one third the number of conti-
' nental troops in this state (150 of them in town
' which we cannot do without, unless the militia will
' take off some of our guards) and the sending them
' so far from the capital would be running too great
' a risk, besides the harrassing the troops : should
' any sudden attack be made upon our sea coast,
' we have only the continental troops to make head
' until the militia can be collected, which you know

' will take some little time ; should any attack be
' made on our frontier it cannot be half the conse-
' quence, and should the enemy attempt to move
' with an army through the back country, they must
' drag themselves so slowly along that before they
' could penetrate far we should be collected to op-
' pose them ; and should they move in small par-
' ties I think our militia quite sufficient to check
' their progress. I flatter myself that this bustle is
' not so serious as was first imagined, or I certainly
' should have heard from Gen. Howe ere this, to
' move on the troops, he had ordered to be in readi-
' ness. The Georgians are in motion and in pur-
' suit of the Scopholites, and I have not the least
' doubt but that they will prevent their junction with
' the Floridians, which will intirely defeat their
' plan. I am informed this state has three inde-
' pendent companies consisting of one hundred men
' each ; I think if your excellency will order half
' those men to take post at some proper place on
' Savannah river, they would be sufficient to guard
' that pass, and stop the communication between
' the insurgents of this state and Georgia : the other
' half of the men to garrison the different forts for
' which they were first raised.   I am, &c.

' WILLIAM MOULTRIE.'

' His Excellency RAWLINS LOWNDES.'

[Several letters are here omitted, for which the reader is referred to the appendix.]

Soon after the expedition under Capt. Biddle, the legislature resolved to purchase or build three frigates in France; and to have a commodore and three captains: accordingly, Alexander Gillon, Esq. was appointed commodore. and John Joyner, William Robertson, and John M'Queen, Esqrs. were elected captains; and in the year 1778, the commodore and his three captains, sailed to France, carrying with them a great deal of the country produce, to purchase, or build these vessels. Hitherto, the marine was carried on by the council of safety; but the legislature resolved to establish a navy-board, and to have gentlemen particularly for that department. who had more leisure and more professional knowledge: accordingly, Edward Blake, Roger Smith, Josiah Smith, George Smith, Edward Darrell, Thomas Corbet, John Edwards, George Abbot Hall, and Thomas Savage, Esqrs. were appointed commissioners of the navy, to transact the business in that department: they had power to fill up vacancies in the navy and marine, and to draw upon the treasury for any sums, to defray the expenses of building or fitting out vessels, &c. they were constantly employed in remitting produce to the commodore for the completion of his mission; but they were so frequently taken, that he could accomplish nothing more then to purchase, upon credit, a quantity of clothing and ammunition for the use of the state; and hire a large frigate from

the prince of Luxemburgh, for the term of 3 years,
on condition of allowing him one fourth of the prizes
captured while she was cruizing at the risk and expense of the state of South-Carolina: She was built
at Amsterdam, and was of a particular construction;
mounting 28 Swedish 36 pounders on her main-
deck; and 12 Swedish 12 pounders on her fore-cas-
tle and quarter-deck; her dimension equal to a 74
gun ship: 280 marines, and 69 seamen were engaged, on account of South-Carolina, to man this frigate : These men were kept at Dunkirk for several
months, until the ship could be got over the Texel;
as her great draught of water prevented her from
getting over the shoals, in any other position than
on her broad-side: The marines being on board,
would have been an encumberance. These men,
though in the service of South-Carolina, were sent
with other troops from Havre-de-Grace, without the
knowledge or consent of Commodore Gillon, on an
expedition against the island of Jersey: So many of
them were killed and taken in that enterprize, which
happened in January, 1781, that the frigate could
not go to sea till the August following: After many
difficulties, she went on a cruize in the European
seas; and took several valuable prizes; and on the
Amerisan coast, she took 10 prizes, and carried
them into the Havannah; where he was prevailed
upon by the Spaniards, to go with his vessel, and to

take the command of an expedition against the Baha-ma-Islands: The fleet consisted of 82 sail of Spanish and American vessels, and in May, 1782, the Baha-ma-Islands was reduced to the crown of Spain; for which service, Carolina got no recompense, nor for the prizes sent into the Havannah, or for the 4 other prizes that were first taken. Soon after this, she arrived in Philadelphia, where, after being completely repaired at an immense expense, she put to sea from that port, under the command of Capt. Joyner; on the second day of her sailing, she was captured by 3 frigates. There is no doubt, but that the British at New-York, got frequent intelligence about her; and knew the very day on which she was to sail and had 3 frigates in waiting for her: And shameful to say, she was taken without her making the least resistance, not even firing a gun: And for the hire of this ship, the state of South-Carolina, paid upwards of 100,000 pounds sterling, without ever receiving the least benefit from her.

WE now began to feel the want of salt; that necessary article, which we so unwisely threw into the river at the commencing of the revolution;* as an imported article from the dominions of Great-Britain; which was prohibited by our association.

....

* I saw a large ship lying near Hog-Island creek, loaded with salt; and a number of hands employed in throwing that cargo into the river.

In order to supply the state with salt, 8 gentlemen entered into partnership, and purchased 6 fast sailing Bermuda vessels, to be employed in importing salt: On their first voyage, they arrived safe, and brought in a supply of salt ; and they continued in that trade, for that particular purpose, till they were all taken.

LETTER FROM COL. PINCKNEY.

'CAMP AT FORT HOWE ON ALATAMAHA, May 24, '78.

'DEAR GEN.

'HERE we are still detained by the confounded 'delay of the South-Carolina galley, and provision 'schooner, who are not yet come round to this river ; 'and the reasonable and candid gentry of this state 'are throwing a thousand reflections on the general 'and the army, for not marching to attack the enemy, 'and storm Lines, without provisions and without 'ammunition. The whole army, except a very small 'garrison to take care of our sick, and secure our 'retreat, will however march from hence to Reid's 'bluff, three miles lower down, and on the other side 'of the river, to-morrow afternoon, or next day at 'farthest; and as by that time our ammunition 'and provision will have come round to this river, 'we shall proceed with all possible expedition for St. 'Mary's, where we shall have some amusement by 'the attack of Fort Tonyn ; notwithstanding any re-'flections which may be cast on the propriety of the

'present expedition at this season; it is now incon-
'trovertable, that the movements in Carolina, the
'capture of the Hinchenbrook and the other vessels,
'and the proposed expedition, have proved the sal-
'vation of the state of Georgia; however I cannot
'help lamenting to you, (and I owe it to candor and
'our friendship) that you have been much too par-
'simonious in your fitting us out for this expedition.
'What can be more cruel than crowding eight, ten,
'and twelve men into one tent, or oblige those who
'cannot get in, to sleep in the heavy dews? what
'is more inconvenient than to have only one camp-
'kettle to ten, twelve or fifteen men? and in this
'hot climate to have one small canteen to six or
'eight men? we think no expense too great to pro-
'cure men, but we do not think after we have got
'them, that we ought to go to the expense of pre-
'serving their health; having thus freely given you
'my sentiments concerning the articles we are in
'want of, I own I could wish, and the Gen. request-
'ed me to desire you to send round in a boat, or
'small schooner, 500 canteens, 100 camp-kettles,
'and 35 or 40 tents, I am sure they cannot be better
'employed, even if the state should lose them all;
'but I apprehend that cannot be the case, as they
'ought to be a continental charge. There has been
'a number of desertions from White's battalion of Bri-

‘ tish deserters :* I inclose you a plan of this curious
‘ fort and encampment, it is badly planned, and
‘ wretchedly constructed. By intelligence from Au-
‘ gustine, the enemy's force is as follows : 300 regu-
‘ lars at Fort Tonyn, on St Mary's ; 60 at St. Johns ;
‘ 320 at St. Augustine; 80 to the southward of Au-
‘ gustine, with some Florida rangers, a few Indians,
‘ and some Carolina tories. Nothing could be more
‘ fortunate than such a division of their force. I am
‘ this moment informed, that the governor of this
‘ state, has ordered from us, to the militia, two-
‘ hundred barrels of rice: he likewise ordered the
‘ gallies 30 miles higher up the river than this place ;
‘ when, on account of the shallowness of the water,
‘ they cannot come within 10 miles as high up as
‘ we are now : excellent generalship !...if you send
‘ a boat, the general would mean that the boat should
‘ come to Sunberry, where they will receive orders :
‘ we are very badly supplied with medicines : these
‘ articles not being sent, will not prevent our going
‘ on, but it will occasion the sickness of many, and
‘ render us less useful than we should otherwise be.’

‘ I am, &c.

‘ CHARLES C. PINCKNEY.’

‘ Brig. Gen. MOULTRIE.’

* Col. White's battalion, was composed chiefly, of British
deserters.

LETTER TO GEN. HOWE.

'CHARLESTOWN, May 31, 1778.

'DEAR SIR,

'I RECEIVED your letter a few days ago, dated
'Fort Howe, May 15: the contents are complied
'with; the orders for the waggons are paid, but
'with some reluctance; I shall be glad to hear from
'you whenever you are at leisure, and wish you
'could spare the time to give me a little account of
'your expedition with your numbers and the strength
'of your army, I wish this matter had been deter-
'mined upon two or three months ago, I fear the
'season is too far advanced; however, you must on-
'ly go the slower to work, and make it sure; should
'the men be too much fatigued, they will sicken ve-
'ry fast, so as to prevent you from carrying on your
'operations and succeeding in your attempt: if the
'season should be dry, I fear you will have a scar-
'city of water, when you draw near to Augustine,
'and what you get will be very bad and apt to throw
'the soldiers into disorders, which will probably car-
'ry them off fast; I wish you success, and doubt
'not but that you have taken every precaution to in-
'sure it: should a failure happen, it will be attended
'with bad consequences to these two southern states,
'of which you are well acquainted...many of the peo-
'ple in Charlestown wish you were all safe back, as
'they dread the inclemency of the season, and are

' fearful it will be fatal to a number of our men. Mr.
' Valentine the commissary has been with me to
' know how he is to get paid for the articles sent you
' to Georgia, by your order, amounting to upwards of
' 1500 pound, as the president has absolutely refused
' to allow it in his account...when he first shewed me
' your order, he was at a loss to know how to act,
' but I told him he must send the articles you wrote
' for, at all events. You will be pleased to inform
' me how this matter is to be settled.

' I am, &c.

' Maj. Gen. Howe.'   ' Wm. Moultrie.'

Letter from Gen. Gadsden,* which shows that
every article got for the continental troops, were
from the governor and council's order on the
state stores.

' Charlestown, June 4th, 1778.

' Sir,

' I received your favor, and immediately laid it
' before the council who desired me to give orders
' for fifty tents 250 canteens and two doz. kettles,
' which are all we can spare. The pork you say you
' have already ordered. Inclosed is the order for the
' above articles which will be charged to Congress.

' I am, &c.

' Christ. Gadsden.'

* Gen. Gadsden, after his resignation was one of the privy
council.

LETTER TO THE PRESIDENT OF CONGRESS.

CHARLESTOWN, June 5th, 1778.

' DEAR SIR,

' YESTERDAY I was honored with your favor of the
' 18th of May, with a copy of the resolves of Con-
' gress, dated the 15th of May : I return you thanks
' for your information respecting the president's pow-
' er of suspending any of the staff-officers within his
' state, should they give cause. We are much in
' the dark with regard to the resolution of Congress,
' relative to the army ; we may be guilty of errors
' and neglect of duty without the least intention of
' either ; which was the case with Col. Francis Hu-
' ger, who did not know that the president had any
' power over him, neither did any of the army know
' of such a resolution, till after the dispute : The pre-
' sident does not inform us of any resolutions which
' he receives, as I suppose he thinks we have them
' transmitted to us. I yesterday received a letter from
' Gen. Howe, dated Fort Howe, Alatamaha, May 23,
' he does not inform me what number of men he has
' with him : We have sent him 600 continentals from
' this state, and Col. Williamson is gone from Nine-
' ty-six, with 800 militia, and there are between 6
' and 700 continental troops belonging to Georgia, and
' some militia, with these he intends to proceed to
' St. Mary's, to dislodge the enemy from a strong
' post which they have established there ; he says

' it is absolutely necessary, or Georgia may as well
' be given up. In a letter I received from Col. C. C.
' Pinckney this day, he says ' notwithstanding any
' reflections which may be cast on the propriety of
' the present expedition at this season, it is now un-
' controvertible that the movements in Carolina, the
' capture of the Hinchenbrook and the other vessels,
' and the proposed expedition have proved the salva-
' tion of Georgia.' I fear Gen. Howe will not be able
' to push this matter as far as we could wish, for
' want of provisions, and other necessaries: I
' am now sending them a schooner load of salt pork,
' with tents, kettles, &c. I wish this movement had
' been made some months sooner; this is a most un-
' lucky season...I fear we shall expend a great many
' of our men (but not by fighting) and we can very
' illy spare them, as our inlistments run out very
' fast, and we cannot induce the men to enter again,
' &c.   I am, &c.

                              ' WILLIAM MOULTRIE,
                                        ' Brigd. Gen.
' The Hon. HENRY LAURENS.'

A LETTER TO GEN. HOWE.
' CHARESTOWN, June 5th, 1778.
' DEAR SIR,
       ' I RECEIVED yours, two days ago, and shall
' send off in a schooner to-morrow 150 barrels of

' pork; I cannot get as many canteens and kettles as
' you wrote for, there are not so many in the state
' store, but will send by this conveyance 250 canteens,
' and 24 kettles, which are all that can be spared:
' I shall order the row-boat to proceed with all expe-
' dition to Sunberry. You mention that Col. Pinck-
' ney had wrote me by the same opportunity, but
' have received no letter from him; I wish his had
' come to hand; as you say he was more particular
' than yourself. We have vessels frequently coming
' in with great quantities of goods, they are fallen in
' price, 2 or 300 per cent...we imagine the reason of
' so many getting in here is owing to the men-of-
' war and cruizers being called to the assistance of
' Augustine, on your movements towards that place•
' I heartily wish that you were provided with every
' thing necessary, that you might proceed on your
' intended expedition, before the season is too far ad-
' vanced: I fear for the troops in that climate in Ju-
' ly and August...I can pretty well guess the incon-
' veniences you must labor under, in procuring the
' necessaries proper for an army of 3,000 men; as I
' am informed you are to have, when Williamson
' joins you with his body of 800.

   ' I am, &c.

      ' WILLIAM MOULTRIE,

        ' Brig. Gen.'

' Major Gen. HOWE.'

LETTER TO COL. CHARLES C. PINCKNEY.

'CHARLESTOWN, June 5th, 1778.

'DEAR COL.

'SINCE I sealed up my letter to Gen. Howe I have
'received yours; and am very sorry to find that you
'are so illy provided with necesaries; I am also sorry
'to find the ammunition and provisions were so long
'a getting to hand, it must be owing to mismanage-
'ment...you charge me with parsimony in fitting you
'out for the expedition, and say I have only allowed
'a tent for eight, ten or twelve men, which I believe
'must be a mistake; I gave orders for 120 tents'
'which I thought sufficient for 600 men, especially,
'as quarter and regular guards and out posts, always
'build bowers in summer, for their shelter in these
'southern climates, which is done almost as soon as
'pitching a tent; I also sent a camp kettle for every
'five men: I am sorry to find you are badly supplied
'with medicines; that is a matter I am quite unac-
'quainted with; I ordered the surgeons to send from
'the hospital, a sufficient quantity for our troops;
'but I dare say, in putting them up they had no idea
'of supplying the Georgia troops also: I fear by a
'paragraph in your letter, that you and the Georgi-
'ans are not upon the best footing. The governor
'seems to be taking the bread out of your mouths:
'I cannot conceive why he should order the gallies
'so far up the river, was it to cover the crossing of

'the militia? or what could it mean; I am not much
'acquainted with the geography of that country,
'therefore, cannot form an exact idea of his inten-
'tion. From none of your letters can I collect what
'force you have with you, what number of continen-
'tals, and what number of militia, and who com-
'mands the Georgia militia. Williamson I suppose
'has joined you ere this, with eight-hundred men
'from this state. I am told, the troops with you,
'begin to be sickly; there is nothing like moving
'them about moderately; it will also keep the devil
'out of their heads, by changing the scene frequent-
'ly. I have sent my letter to Sunberry, with 250
'canteens, and 24 kettles, which is all I could pro-
'cure. I shall send off a schooner to-morrow, with
'150 barrels of pork, and 50 tents: the tents I sup-
'pose you will scarcely get till on your return. I am
'surprized you should talk of crowding so many men
'in tents, I would rather leave all tents and oblige
'them to build bowers; they are much healthier and
'very easily done: our whole army, in the Cherokee
'country, lived above a month that way; they would
'rather do it than be at the trouble of pitching and
'striking their tents every day, besides you have the
'less baggage to carry on: I shall be glad to hear
'from you when you are at leisure. I heartily wish

222

' you all success, and a great many laurels; though
' you have but a barren field to gather them from.
'I am, &c.

'WILLIAM MOULTRIE.'
'Col. CHARLES C. PINCKNEY.'

LETTER FROM GEN. HOWE.

'CAMP, AT REID'S BLUFF, June 7th, 1778.

'FORGIVE me, dear sir, if I cannot write to you as
'often as I wish :...Puzzled, perplexed, disappointed,
'and the devil and all...I have not one moment to
'spare, or spend as I wish...I have but advanced to this
'post, having been for several weeks waiting the ar-
'rival of the militia, who I have impatiently expected:
'I have marched off this day the Georgia brigades
'...I follow to-morrow, with Pinckney's. The ene-
'my, it seems, wait for us at St. Mary's. I shall
'endeavor not to keep them long ; had I been second-
'ed as I wished, something capital might have been
'effected ; I however, still am in hopes we shall (and
'indeed I doubt not) have a few knocks; as their
'post must be broken up for the safety of this state,
'and for theirs, must be defended, &c.

'I am, &c.

'ROBERT HOWE.'
'Brig. Gen. MOULTRIE.'

LETTER FROM GEN. HOWE.

' CAMP, AT REID'S BLUFF, June 12th, 1778.

' DEAR GENERAL,

' I HAVE just a moment to inform you I am set-
' ting off instantly upon my march to St. Mary's,
' where the enemy seem to expect us, and where I
' had long since been, had not ten thousand disap-
' pointments arisen, a few of them from accident,
' but more from the operations of this state, happen-
' ed to prevent and detain me: I have been wait-
' ing several weeks for the militia, which were to
' have proceeded rapidly, but are not yet arrived, ex-
' cept 400, that are encamped about 4 miles in my
' rear, waiting to be joined by the governor, who is
' behind, as we are informed, with a large body;
' but from him I have not directly heard for a long
' time, though I have written to him often, upon
' very important subjects; he has, I believe, exerted
' himself to spirit up the people; and I fancy has
' been greatly perplexed: I wished to see him before
' I moved, but I fear I shall not, unless he comes
' within half an hour; The brigade under Elbert I
' advanced to Sittilla, to take possession of the river,
' and by works thrown upon both sides to facilitate
' the advance, or cover the retreat of the army,
' which either may be requisite as soon as I join him,
' which will be (if nothing happens more then I ex-
' pect) the next day after to-morrow, I shall proceed

‘ to St. Mary's, where we shall meet Commodore
‘ Bowlan with the fleet, at an appointed place ; and
‘ if the enemy favor us so much as to make face, we
‘ shall endeavor to treat them with the attention they
‘ derserve, and we so ardently wish to bestow.

‘ I am, &c.

‘ ROBERT HOWE.’

‘ To Brig. Gen. MOULTRIE.’

———

LETTER TO GEN. HOWE.

‘ June 22d, 1778.

‘ DEAR GENERAL,

 ‘ As I think it my duty to give you every intel-
‘ ligence that comes to hand, more particularly that
‘ which relates to your present expedition : I thought
‘ it proper to send you an express, to inform you,
‘ that the day before yesterday, Capts. Bachop and
‘ Osborne (in two sloops, in 10 days from St. Au-
‘ gustine) were taken and brought in here, by a Con-
‘ necticut vessel, of 18 guns, with a small sloop, her
‘ tender.

 ‘ BY Bachop and Osborne we learn, that 1200
‘ men are marched out from Augustine, with a num-
‘ ber of Indians ; and 2 gallies, with 24 pounders,
‘ and other heavy cannon on board, are sent round
‘ to St. John's river : I have examined John Glass, a
‘ deserter from the first regiment, who seems to give
‘ a particular and good account of every thing there.

' He says they have 800 regular troops; 100 of
' Brown's; 150 militia; 95 Indians (some called them
' 200), 300 Scopholites, that are encamped up St.
' Mary's river, quite discontented and wish them-
' selves back again from whence they came.

' THIS force, with two field-pieces, is to dispute
' your passage over St. John's river, and perhaps
' meet you sooner. I would therefore humbly re-
' commend the keeping your little army together,
' and not to move them by brigades or divisions, as
' it may be of dangerous consequences in marching
' through such a country as you are now in ; the ene-
' my will always have their scouts about you and get
' fresh intelligence every day : and when they find
' you so detached, may be tempted to strike some
' blow, which, if they effect, will be of fatal conse-
' quences, by throwing your whole army into con-
' fusion: pray do not think yourself secure from such
' a surprize when you are within sixty miles of them,
' as I have known a body of men to march 48 miles
' in 24 hours, in this country :* I doubt not but that
' you will take every precaution : I hope you will ex-
' cuse my dropping these hints, you may be assured
' it is entirely owing to my anxiety for your safety.
' I was told yesterday that Williamson with his mili-

* Montgomery's highlanders in the Cherokee country, from
Twelve mile-river, to Sugar-town and back again.

' tia, was not above 9 miles from Savannah, and that
' the governor with his Georgians, were about Sun-
' berry : if this be the case, for God's sake ! when will
' you all join : if you still continue moving from each
' other, nothing but Augustine castle can bring you
' up ; would it not be best to halt the front, and let
' them secure themselves, and wait till they all come
' up, then you may go on slow and sure.'

' GLASS further informs me that the people at
' Augustine, are much alarmed, and are putting their
' effects on board of vessels : he says the outer line
' is not repaired at all ; and the inner one, near the
' town, is quite out of order ; that they have only a
' few pieces of cannon planted at the gate : but that
' they were pressing negroes to work for the king ;
' though he could not tell what work they were go-
' ing about : the fort at St. Mary's was evacuated.
' He says the best way to carry the town, is, by
' marching along the Musquito road (which is at the
' back of the town) from St. John's, about six miles
' beyond the town, where you may cross with ease ;
' then turn and march up, by which means you will
' keep the town between you and the castle ; there
' are no works at the back of the town. He was told
' the castle mounted 110 guns, and two mortars, one
' 24, and one 18 inches...he never was within it...the
' walls about 25 feet high ; the garrison tolerably well
' supplied with provisions, but the inhabitants very

' poorly. The best way from St. John's to town, is
' to take the beach, till you come near enough to take
' the Musquito road....No man-of-war at St. Augus-
' tine : the Galatea lost her rudder, and is gone to
' New-York. I was sorry to see, by a letter from
' Col. Pinckney, that our men begin to be sickly...
' that is all my uneasiness, except that the militia do
' not join you as heartily as they should ; I think if
' you were well united, and had every necessary, you
' might have an easy conquest of Augustine, but I
' fear the season is too far advanced; if your men
' should fall sick fast, as you approach the enemy, I
' think it would be much the best to retreat in time,
' before you get too near, as it will be very difficult
' then to come off; dragging a number of sick after
' you, you must expect the Indians and light troops
' to harrass your rear.

' I am, &c.

' WILLIAM MOULTRIE.'

' Major Gen. HOWE.'

LETTER FROM GEN. HOWE.

' FORT TONYN, 5th July, 1778.

' DEAR GENERAL,

' I HAVE been waiting for the galley first, and af-
' ter her arrival a tedious while for the militia of
' this state, and for the long expected coming of
' Col. Williamson and our countrymen with him. In

' short, if I am ever again to depend upon operations
' I have no right to guide, and men I have no right
' to command, I shall deem it then, as now I do,
' one of the most unfortunate accidents of my life.
' Had we been able to move on at once, and those I
' expected would have been foremost had only been
' as ready as we were, a blow might have been given
' our enemies, which would have put it out of their
' power to have disturbed us, at least not hastily;
' and perhaps have been attended with consequences
' more important than the most sanguine could have
' expected; but delayed beyond all possible supposi-
' tion, and embarrassed, disappointed, perplexed,
' and distressed beyond expression; the utmost we
' can now achieve, will be but a poor compensation
' for the trouble and fatigue we have undergone; ex-
' cepting we may be allowed to suppose (what I tru-
' ly think has been effected) that the movements we
' have made, have drove back the enemy, and pre-
' vented an impending invasion of the state of Geor-
' gia, which would otherwise inevitably have over-
' whelmed it, and also a dangerous defection of the
' people of both states. This good, I am persuaded,
' has resulted from it, and this is our consolation.
' The enemy were 2 or 3 days since at Alligator
' Creek, about 14 miles from this place: their for-
' ces, by all accounts, are at least equal either to the
' governor's troops or mine, and we are on contrary

' sides of the river, and not within 8 miles of each
' other. Ask me not how this happened, but rest
' assured that it has not been my fault: I believe,
' however, the governor will encamp near me to
' night, and if the enemy are still were they were,
' which I hope to know to night or to-morrow mor-
' ning, we shall probably beat up their quarters.

' I am, &c.

' Brig. Gen. MOULTRIE.'   ' ROBERT HOWE.'

———

LETTER FROM COL. CHARLES C. PINCKNEY.
' CAMP AT THE RUINS OF FORT TONYN,
' July 6th, 1778.

' DEAR GENERAL,

' OUR little army now too fully experience the
' sickliness of this confounded climate. The Caroli-
' nians have not been hitherto so sickly as the Geor-
' gians, but, taking the sick of both brigades into
' the account, our numbers are now one half less than
' what they were when first we joined at Fort Howe :
' our horses, too, having no grain to support them,
' die daily; we want 35 of the number we ought to
' have, to drag our artillery, ammunition, provisions,
' and little baggage ; so that if we do not retreat soon
' by water, we shall be in a situation of not being able
' either to retire or proceed by land ; a number of
' our officers and men are now ill. Governor Hous-
' ton talks of encamping near us to day ; he seems to

' be totally unmindful how we are to retreat ; nor
' do I think he is in the least anxious about the health
' of our troops. I think our operations, at farthest,
' should not extend beyond the River St. John's ; in-
' deed, from the report of the quarter master con-
' cerning the horses, I much doubt whether it will
' be possible for us to get as far...I do not think that
' Gov. Houston will cross St. Mary's with half the
' militia he mentioned to our state: We hear that
' Williamson has crossed the Alatamaha, I therefore
' suppose that he must be at Sitilla by this time ; I
' hope his troops will not feel the inclemency of this
' climate as mine have done.

  ' I am, &c.

   ' CHARLES COTESWORTH PINCKNEY.'

———

LETTER FROM COL. C. C. PINCKNEY.
' CAMP AT THE RUINS OF FORT TONYN, IN EAST-
  ' FLORIDA, July 10th, 1778·

' DEAR GENERAL,

  ' AFTER we have waited so long for the junction
' of the militia, we now find that we are to have as
' many independant commanders as corps. Gover-
' nor Houston declaring that he would not be com-
' manded; Col. Williamson hinting that his men
' would not be satisfied to be under continental com-
' mand ; or indeed any other commander but his
' own ; and Commodore Bowlan insisting that in the

' naval department, he is supreme; with this divided,
' this heterogeneous command, what can be done?
' even if the season, and every other military requi-
' site were favorable (but that is far from being the
' case) the continental troops have been so violently
' attacked by sickness, and the desolation made by
' it, is so rapidly encreasing, that if we do not retreat
' soon, we shall not be able to retreat at all, and may
' crown this expedition with another Saratoga affair,
' in reverse, but the many reasons which ought to
' induce us to return I cannot now enumerate; some
' of the principles I herewith enclose you: from
' thence you will learn that we have the strongest
' grounds to imagine that the enemy mean not to
' fight us seriously on this side of St. John's; skirmish
' with us, they may, perhaps hang upon our flanks,
' and harrass our rear; and, if we would give them
' an opportunity, attempt to surprize us: but to fight
' us on this side of St John's would be the most im-
' prudent thing they possibly could do, and all their
' movements shew they have no such intention.

' At another season with battering cannon, mor-
' tars, and the command of the rivers, much might
' be done; but I think our principal movements ought
' in such case to be by water; and we cannot begin
' too soon to build proper batteaus and vessels to car-
' ry on such an expedition. I hope we shall be able
' to retreat from this place, by water; if we do, the

' men who are ailing, and the convalescents, will in
' all probability, get better, before we reach Charles-
' town ; but if we are obliged to go back by land, I
' fear, much fear, that great part of the few that re-
' main well, will with the utmost difficulty, reach it,
' perhaps not at all : such an effect has the heat of
' the weather had upon our men, that as many fall
' sick on a march as when we halt...you would
' think we had all hospital waggons, and no baggage
' ones. Amidst all this sickness, I have the pleasure
' to inform you that Williamson's people have hith-
' erto continued very hearty ; but I cannot say the
' same of Gov. Houston's militia, who I am told, be-
' gin to grow sickly. I am informed that William-
' son's men are within a few miles of this river to
' night.   ' I am, &c.

' CHARLES C. PINCKNEY.'
' Brig. Gen. MOULTRIE.'

———

' At a council of war held in the camp, at Fort
' Tonyn, July 11th, 1778.

PRESENT,

'MAJOR Gen. Howe, Col. Elbert, Col. White, Col.
Tarling, Col. Rea, Lieut. Col. Roberts, Lieut. Col.
Scott, Maj. Wise, Maj. Habersham, Maj. Pinckney,
Maj. Grimkie, Col. Pinckney, Col. Eveleigh, Col.
Kirk, Lieut. Col. Henderson, Lieut. Col. M'Intosh,
Maj. Brown, Maj. Romand, Maj. Lane, Maj. Low.

'His excellency, Major Gen. Howe, opened the business; upon which the council was summoned, by laying before them the following informations: that the motions of the enemy from E. Florida, the post they occupied, and were endeavoring to occupy, the stations their men-of-war and armed vessels took posession of, the number of insurgents in South-Carolina and Georgia raising in arms, and forming a junction with the enemy, the information given by deserters and creditable persons escaped from Augustine, and also of spies sent there to make discoveries, upon oath; all uniting to prove that an immediate invasion against Georgia, in all appearance too formidable to be repelled by their force alone, induced the calling to the assistance of Georgia, a part of the continental troops of South-Carolina; and that that state with a conduct conformable to their usual spirit and generosity, had sent, with the utmost readiness, even more men than of right could be demanded of them, who, in concert with the continental troops of Georgia, had chased the enemy out of that country, obliged them to evacuate Fort Tonyn, from whence they had continually made inroads into Georgia, dangerous to the persons and property of its inhabitants: by which the troops had, in the general opinion, answered every purpose for which they had been called; but willing to have with him the opinion of the field-officers on every occasion, where they ought to be consulted, and ready to relinquish his own, should they offer any reasons which could authorize his doing so ; he wishes to propose to them several questions, but previously to this, he thinks it necessary to give them the following additional information, that drawing the enemy out of Georgia, and dislodging them from Fort Tonyn were the principal ends he aimed at, yet had the enemy in defence of that post or any other thought proper to oppose him with regulars, and he had been happy enough to defeat them in detail, he should have been ready to have availed himself of every advantage which might have resulted from it: that by information received from captains Moore, Heyrne, and Taylor, the roads were naturally bad; had been rendered much worse by the enemy's having broken them up, destroying the bridges, and by other methods, so that neither artillery or ammunition waggons can pass without great loss of time and labor; and that from appearances they conceive, and from other informations the general learns, that the enemy have abandoned all thoughts of opposition on this side of St. John's river. That the deputy quartermaster general has reported that the long march and hard service, had destroyed many horses, and rendered so many others unfit for use, that there is a deficiency of at least forty, for the absolute necessity of service. That the physician general, and all the surgeons of the army report, that at least one half the number of men we set out with are already sick, many of them dangerously so, and that by the increasing inclemency of the climate, the greater part of the army now well, will either by continuing here or advancing most probably be destroyed. That by information from the Commodore, the gallies cannot get into St. John's river without great time and labor spent to cut a passage through the Amelia narrows, and that if even such passage was effected, the accounts he had received all concur to make it probable that the enemy were ready to oppose his operations, when in the river, with a force superior to his. The General therefore thinks proper to propose the following questions :

1. As driving the enemy out of Georgia, and demolishing Fort Tonyn, were the objects principally aimed at, have not these purposes been effected?

RESOLVED unanimously in the affirmative.

2. As it appears from information above recited, that the enemy do not mean to oppose us in force on this side of St. John's river, is there any other objects important enough in our present situation to warrant our proceeding?

RESOLVED unanimously in the negative.

3. Is the army in a situation to cross St. John's river, attack the enemy, and secure a retreat in case of accident, though they should be aided by the

militia, now embodied under Gov. Houston, and Col.
Williamson ?

RESOLVED unanimously in the negative.

4. DOES not the sickness which so fatally prevails
in the army, render a retreat immediately requisite ?

RESOLVED unanimously in the affirmative.

THE Gen. then proceeded to inform the council
that the Governor had denied him the right to command the militia, even if a junction had been formed between them and the continental troops, notwithstanding the resolution of Congress declaring,
that ' as to the propriety of undertaking distant ex-
' peditions and enterprizes, or other military opera-
' tions, and the mode of conducting them, the Gen-
' eral, or commanding officer, must finally judge
' and determine at his peril.'

THE General therefore thinks proper to propose
the following questions :

1. CAN he with propriety, honor and safety to
himself, or consistant with service, relinquish the
command to the Governor ?

2. CAN the army, whilst the command is divided,
act with security, vigor, decision or benefit to the
common cause ?

RESOLVED unanimously in the negative.

Agreed to by all the officers.

LETTER FROM COL. PINCKNEY.

' SUNBERRY, July 23d, 1778.

' DEAR GENERAL,

' IT is with the greatest pleasure I embrace this
' opportunity of informing you that the sea air has
' already had a surprizing effect on the men with
' me; the weak and convalescents are getting strong
' daily, and the sick recovering fast. We have been
' hitherto, very much crowded in our vessels, but
' as the Georgia troops will be landed here, we shall
' soon have more room: I shall be able to procure
' the gallies of Georgia by Gen. Howe, and Commo-
' dore Bowlan's orders, to carry us to Port-Royal
' ferry, from thence, (without I receive orders to the
' contrary, as the Georgia gallies will go no further
' with us) I shall march the men to Charlestown; the
' sick and ailing I shall send round by water, together
' with our baggage, and that the men may be better
' accommodated on their short march, I shall send
' off in detachments of 40's and 50's, so that they will
' be able to sleep under cover in gentlemen's barns
' at night. I shall direct the commanding officers of
' these detachments, to draw upon you for money, to
' pay for what rations the men may want on their
' march: if you do not approve of any thing above
' proposed, an express will meet me (if you chuse
' to send one) time enough to bring me your orders
' at Port-Royal ferry, as our passage through the

' inland navigation is very tedious and slow, and I
' do not imagine we shall be able to get from this
' place these two days. I dare say it will be a fort-
' night before we arrive in Charlestown...I do not
' write to Gen. Howe, as I do not know whether he
' has left Georgia. One campaign to the southward
' is more fatiguing than five to the northward. The
' artillery I shall order to Fort Lyttleton at Port-
' Royal.

 ' I am, &c.

   ' CHARLES COTESWORTH PINCKNEY.'
' Gen. MOULTRIE.'

———

A LETTER TO COL. LAURENS,
President of Congress.

  ' CHARLESTOWN, July 26th, 1778.

' DEAR SIR,

 ' I DID myself the honor of writing to you on
the 20th instant, in which I informed you that
' our troops at the southward could not proceed any
' farther than St. John's river, if so far, since which
' by letters and a number of invalid officers that are
' returned to Charlestown, I am informed that the
' expedition is at an end; that it was impossible to
' proceed beyond St. Mary's river. The continental
' troops, which at first amounted to 1100, being re-
' duced to about 350 men fit for duty ; and that their
' horses were unable to draw their waggons, and

'Governor Houston refusing to put himself under
'the command of Gen. Howe; and Col Williamson
'with the Carolina militia, insisting on his command
'to be independent, that with such an army, with three
'separate commanders, nothing could be expected;
'therefore Gen. Howe called a council of officers, in
'which it was unanimously resolved to give over the
'expedition: I am told Governor Houston and Col.
'Williamson intend to proceed to St. John's, but for
'what purpose, I cannot conceive, as it can be of
'no advantage to march an army 40 miles through
'a dreary pine barren, and return again, at this sea-
'son of the year: I dare say Gen. Howe has given
'you a full account of the whole expedition. It seems
'to be absolutely necessary for the peace of these
'two southern states, to reduce Augustine; but it
'cannot be done at this season. I should humbly
'offer my opinion to you, who are well acquainted
'with the southern states, how I would prepare for
'this expedition: I would begin shortly to get ready
'a number of batteaus, pack-saddles, and bags to con-
'tain flour...with the batteaus I would convey most
'of the troops, the artillery and baggage under con-
'voy of the gallies within land, to St. John's river:
'the cattle to be drove on, under a strong guard of
'horse-men and light troops; where I would collect
'my whole force, within 30 miles of Augustine,
'there I would halt and prepare my army for this

‘ short march ; the men would be fresh and fit for
‘ immediate action : this should not be undertaken
‘ before the month of November, when the weather
‘ is moderate, and not very cold : this business can be
‘ done with three thousand men, and a small train of
‘ artillery, with some battering cannon to attack the
‘ castle. This plan I think cannot fail of success.

‘ GEN. Howe is hourly expected in town.

    ‘ I have the honor to be, &c.

               ‘ WILLIAM MOULTRIE.’

‘ The Hon. HENRY LAURENS.’

OCT. 6. COL. Francis Huger, quarter-master-
general, after Gen. Howe’s expedition was at an
end, made up his account, and resigned his commission....Col. Stephen Drayton appointed in his
place.

LETTER TO HIS EXCELLENCY, RAWLINS LOWNDES,
    ‘ CHARLESTOWN, November 14th, 1778.

‘ SIR,

    ‘ I AM sorry I was not at home the other day
‘ when your excellency did me the honor of calling
‘ upon me : I waited on you the next day, but was
‘ so unlucky as not to find you at home ; since which
‘ a general report prevails in town and seems to be
‘ credited by many, that this state is to be attacked
‘ soon, by a formidable force from New-York.

' The regard I have for my country, and my du-
' ty as a continental officer, obliges me to lay before
' your excellency, a few ideas that have occured to
' me, necessary for its defence, viz:

' The militia, already draughted, to be immediate-
' ly embodied, and marched with one month's pro-
' visions in three different divisions towards Charles-
' town, and posted in the following manner:

' The north division to be posted near Wither's, on
' Sewee Bay: The south division at Pon-Pon and
' Dorchester: the middle division about Monk's Cor-
' ner: by this disposition, the militia will be within
' two days march of the town; and two divisions can
' readily join, should we be attacked, northwardly
' or southwardly: and that a commissary be appointed
' for each division...that a number of small vessels
' and boats be taken into the public service, to trans-
' port cannon and stores into the country, and also
' for removing troops from one post to another.

' That all the bricks, lime, and timber, now in
' town, be taken for the public service...that 400 or
' 500 head of cattle, and a quantity of Indian corn be
' ordered to Haddrell's point, for the support of the
' troops that may be posted there, and also to supply
' Fort Moultrie.

' Five hundred negroes to be immediately im-
' pressed for the public works :...the cattle on the

' sea-islands to be drove off, and such of them as are
' fit, to be killed and salted for public use.

' ONE hundred waggons to be hired immediately,
' to be ready to come to town to assist in carrying
' off ammunition, &c. to Nelson's ferry, or any other
' place, if necessary.

' SOME of the large cannon to be mounted on field-
' carriages. All the armed vessels that are in port
' to be manned, and ready to go up Ashley and
' Cooper rivers, to prevent transports from running up
' those rivers to land their troops, and also to pre-
' vent the enemy from crossing those rivers to land
' on Charlestown neck.

' A NUMBER of hoes, axes, spades, saws, &c. to
' be sent to Forts Johnson and Moultrie.

' I DOUBT not but many of these things are already
' thought of, and perhaps all of them, and though
' it may not be thought necessary to put them into
' immediate execution; yet I think it will be highly
' proper to have them in view, should any invasion
' take place.

' I HOPE your excellency will excuse me for this
' trouble I have given you, and that my anxiety for
' the safety of the state, will be a sufficient apology :
' should any other matters occur to me for our de-
' fence, I must beg leave to take the liberty of com-
' municating them to you. I am, &c.

' WILLIAM MOULTRIE.'

‘ ZUBY-FERRY, November 27th, 1778.

‘ DEAR SIR,

‘ THE inclosed copy of a letter from Col. Elbert,
‘ received this moment, will inform you in what a
‘ a dreadful situation the state of Georgia is ; with-
‘ out assistance from this state it will absolutely be
‘ lost; exert yourselves to the utmost to hasten up
‘ the troops under the command of Col. Huger; let
‘ them march with all possible expedition ; baggage
‘ at this time is not to be considered, and provisions
‘ may be had at every house, let the men force on,
‘ and if some cannot march with the rest, let them
‘ proceed without the least delay; as this attempt
‘ upon Georgia is indeed a serious one : I think pro-
‘ per to direct that more troops should march south-
‘ wardly : you will therefore order either Hender-
‘ son’s regiment, or a number equal to them, taken
‘ by detachment, if this could be done with equal
‘ expedition : this will be left to you, still holding in
‘ mind, however, that much depends upon their
‘ speedy arrival. The situation of affairs makes it
‘ absolutely necessary, that the deputy quarter-mas-
‘ ter general should be furnished with powers to press
‘ waggons and horses : apply to the president for
‘ this, and if he grants it, the troops may force their

' way with expedition, which at this time is so essen-
' tial to service. Let 5000 pounds of gun-powder be
' immediately sent by land, and 500 by water, as
' consequential to our operations; you will therefore
' take measures accordingly. There is more than
' that quantity of continental powder in the hands of
' Mr. Livingston, agent; but, if not to be found, ap-
' ply to the state: the troops are not to wait for the
' powder:...with what powder comes by water, if 5000
' pounds of lead could be added, I should be glad, as it
' will probably be wanted. The dept. quarter master
' general, or his assistant, ought to attend the troops
' of this state, and a surgeon from the general hos-
' pital, with every thing requisite, should be instant-
' ly sent up. The commissary general ought to be
' ordered to lay up provisions of every kind at Mr.
' Dupont's, or some place contiguous thereto, I am
' too much hurried to determine where: you will
' therefore appoint the place.

' I am, &c.

' Brig. Gen. MOULTRIE. ' ROBERT HOWE.'

A LETTER TO GEN. HOWE, IN GEORGIA.

' CHARLESTOWN, Nov. 28th, 1778.

' DEAR SIR,

' I THIS day received yours by express, and am sor-

'ry to find the affairs are like to prove so serious with
'the Georgians; the inhabitants of this town could
'never be persuaded that matters would have come
'to such a length; now they seem frightened and
'think it may be their own case ere long, as the
'cloud from New-York, has not disappeared, but
'still hangs over our heads, and this attack upon
'Georgia confirms their ideas; by causing a diver-
'sion there, while we are to be invaded here.

'I HAVE sent an express to Col. Huger to expedite
'his march, leaving his baggage and weak men be-
'hind to come up more at leisure. I shall get Col.
'Henderson's battalion off I hope to-morrow; Thomp-
'son's regiment is not far from you, they are taking
'the shortest rout to Purisburgh. The President has
'given the deputy quarter-master general, a power
'to impress what waggons may be wanted for the
'expedition. I shall send 5000 pounds of gun-pow-
'der immediately by land; the rest you require
'shall be sent by water, it is rather unlucky that
'Col. Roberts sailed about an hour before the express
'came in, or I would have sent the powder by him.
'Capt. Spencer, deputy quarter-master's assistant,
'proceeds with our troops. The director-general,
'has ordered Dr. Fasseaux with a proper medicine
'chest to join our troops.

'I WILL consider and speak to the president re-

' specting the laying in stores at a proper place,
' some   where, as you mentioned.

'I am, &c.

'WILLIAM MOULTRIE.

' Major General HOWE.'

———

LETTER FROM RAWLINS LOWNDES, ESQ.
President.

' CHARLESTOWN, Nov. 29th, 1778.

' SIR,

 ' As the invasion of Georgia may presage a pre-
' meditated attack on this state, to which the present
' motions of the enemy may be a prelude, I shall be
' glad to have the aid and advice of the military, in
' consulting on the necessary steps to be taken, for
' the defence of this country ; and shall be much
' obliged to you, sir, if you, will, with your field-offi-
' cers who are in or near town, to whom it will be
' convenient, give me a meeting in council to-
' morrow, at 10 o'clock in the forenoon, to confer on
' this subject.

' I am, &c.

' RAWLINS LOWNDES.'

' Brig. Gen. MOULTRIE.

' GENERAL ORDERS, Nov. 29th, 1778.

' COLONELS Pinckney, Marion, and Elliott, are to
' attend the general to-morrow, at the state house,

' at 10 o'clock, to meet his excellency the president
' in council at that hour.'

A LETTER FROM GEN. HOWE.

' SUNBERRY, Dec. 8th, 1778.

' DEAR SIR,

' IT is impossible for me to give an account of
' the confused, perplexed way in which I found mat-
' ters in this state upon my arrival; nor has it been
' in my power to get them, as yet in a better train.
' I am sorry to inform you, that this town is not de-
' fensible for half an hour, should it be attacked the
' least formidably; and its present safety is entirely
' owing to the spirited conduct of the troops in the
' fort, and the want of enterprize in the enemy, who
' most certainly might have possessed it in a very
' short time, and with little loss, though the garrison
' had made (which I doubt not they would have done)
' the most spirited resistance: the enemy undoubtedly
' are at St. Simon's, where they are repairing the
' fort, and where the regulars remain; the Scopho-
' lites having been detached to convey their booty
' beyond St. John's, after which, as deserters say,
' they are to return: this story of their return, I
' I should not credit, had not a transport with troops
' put into Tybee, a deserter from which gives a par-
' ticular account of an intended descent upon this
' country, and makes it probable that the Floridians

' are waiting their arrival, and mean to second their
' efforts, when they arrive; the whole information
' given by this deserter, is contained in his deposi-
' tion, a copy of which, I herewith send you; the
' great firings we have heard at sea from different
' quarters, which appear like signals given, and an-
' swered, seem to confirm the accounts brought us
' by the man; and the number of men he mentions
' cannot well be on board so few transports, yet they
' may certainly bring enough to shake this state, in
' its weak unprepared situation, to its very founda-
' tion: in short, the troops these vessels can con-
' tain, must be too few for our state, and therefore,
' if they mean a descent at all, it must be intended
' for this country.

' I AM concerned to inform you, that notwithstand-
' ing these alarming appearances, and my very ear-
' ly applications for negroes to act as pioneers; I
' am as, yet, unfurnished with them; or indeed with
' any other assistance, however requisite, to carry
' on the works; without which, this state will pro-
' bably be lost. The gallies are likewise, in a con-
' dition, at this alarming crisis, truly deplorable.
' They are now given up to my direction, and I will
' exert myself to put them on a more respectable
' footing: all I can say is, that my strenuous endea-
' vors during my stay, shall not be wanting to make
' the best defence possible against the attempts of the

' enemy, and if I am but heartily supported by the
' state, which I hope I shall be, I flatter myself we
' shall make the purchase of this country dearer per-
' haps than our enemies expect.

' THOUGH I cannot think, without the most abso-
' lute necessity, of requesting of your state more con-
' tinental troops than have been ordered, yet should
' that necessity occur, being certain that my country
' will give to this, every generous support, I would
' have you hold Col. Henderson's regiment in con-
' stant readiness, to move upon the first notice ; and
' lest the exigence of affairs, should make still more
' assistance necessary, waggons and all other things
' requisite to the march of troops, should immediate-
' ly be got in readiness, that the men, when wanted,
' may move without delay.

' I am, &c.

' ROBERT HOWE.'

' Brig. Gen. MOULTRIE.'

' SAVANNAH, IN GEORGIA, SUNBERRY, Dec. 6th, '78.
' THE examination of William Haslam, a mariner,
' lately belonging to the transport ship, called the
' Neptune, of which one M'Dougal is commander, is
' as follows :

' THE examinant says, he arrived in the said ship
' last Friday at Tybee, having been out from Sandy-
' Hook that day, three weeks ; that the said ship was

' one of a fleet consisting of 20 sail, which were ly-
' ing at Sandy-hook, ready to sail; that a violent
' storm having come on, the ship Neptune, and
' another ship, parted with their anchors, and were
' obliged to put to sea; that after they came out
' Capt. M'Dougal opened his orders, which were to
' proceed to Tybee in Georgia, and there remain for
' forty eight hours, and if the rest of the fleet did not
' arrive in that time then to proceed to St. Mary's,
' and there wait until the fleet should arrive at
' Georgia; that he understood the army, on board the
' said transports, consisted of about 5,000 men, and
' thinks they would be ready to sail the next day af-
' ter he came away; that they were to come under
' convoy of the Phoenix, a 40 gun ship, the Vigilant
' (a large floating battery) a row galley, and one or
' two sloops of war; that the army was mostly com-
' posed of refugees from America, and that Gen.
' Skinner commands a part of them called the Jersey
' volunteers; but that there are among them, 3 bat-
' talions of British regulars, belonging to the 71st
' regiment; that the Neptune has on board of her,
' 100 men (besides mariners) who have, chiefly, their
' families with them, and say they came to winter
' in Georgia; that they are called the Jersey volun-
' teers, and are under the command of Col. Allen,
' who has large possessions either in Jersey or Penn-
' sylvania; that the Neptune is of no force but mus-

'ketry; that there was a large fleet, with about
' 10,000 men, left New-York about 3 weeks before
' them ; that he understood they were bound for Vir-
' ginia; that he had heard no talk lately of any thing
' coming against South-Carolina, but that it was the
' common talk that the 5,000 men before mentioned,
' were coming to winter in Savannah ; that last night
' and the night before, he heard a number of large
' guns fire out at sea, and takes it to be some of the
' fleet; that he had heard no other news, but that
' it was the common report, that the orders now were
' to burn and destroy all who would not submit.

'The above sworn to, before } WM. HASLAM.'
' me, the day above written. }

'J. HOUSTOUN.'

A LETTER FROM COL. HUGER.

'SAVANNAH, Dec. 28th, 1778.

'DEAR GENERAL.

'I AM just now turning out my regiment with
'Thompson's detachment, and few of the Georgia
'continentals, with orders to take the field immedi-
'ately. I am informed the shipping are coming
'nearer; if so we shall have an action, as I am convinc-
'ed they will attempt to land. It is a doubt with me,
'whether the militia will join us ; if so we shall
'not muster continentals and militia in town, more

'than six or seven hundred men. From the best
'intelligence received the last evening, the British
'fleet consists of 37 sail ; no expectation of any as-
'sistance from the country militia of this state; if
' any, but very little.

'I am, &c.

'ISAAC HUGER, Brig. Gen.

'Brig. Gen. MOULTRIE.'

———

GEN. HOWE'S ORDER OF BATTLE AT SAVANNAH.

'HEAD-QUARTERS, 29th Dec. 1778.

'GENERAL ORDERS, BY MAJOR GENERAL HOWE.

'PAROLE FIRMNESS.

'THE first brigade, is to be told off into 16 pla-
'toons of equal number of files ; the odd files to be
'formed in one platoon on the right wing of the
'brigade, to act as light infantry, according to exi-
'gences.

'Two field officers to be appointed to the com-
'mand of the right wing of both brigades.

'THE second brigade to be told off into 8 platoons,
'of an equal number of files ; the odd files to be form-
'ed on the left of the brigade, in order to act as
'light infantry, as will be directed, &c.

'COL. Huger will command the right wing of the
'army, composed of the first brigade, and light troops
'belonging to it.

'Col. Elbert is to command the left wing, com-
'posed likewise, of the second brigade, and light
'troops belonging to it.

'The artillery of both brigades, and the Park to
'be posted before, and during the action, as shall be
'directed, and defend their ground until further or-
'ders. The artillery when ordered, or forced to re-
'treat, is to fall into the road leading to the western
'defile, where Col. Roberts is to take as advanta-
'geous a post as possible, to protect the retreat of
'the line, &c.'

I insert so much of Gen. Howe's order of battle,
as to shew the strength of his army only consisted
of 24 platoons, and a few loose files, exclusive of
his artillery, which is agreeable to Gen. Huger's letter of 28th December.

When Gen. Howe perceived that the British, by
their movements, intended a descent upon Savannah,
he called a council of war of his field-officers, to advise with them, whether he should retreat from Savannah, or stay and defend the town with his troops:
the majority of the council were of opinion, that he
should remain in Savannah, and defend it to the
last. This was the most ill advised, rash opinion
that possibly could be given; It was absurd to suppose that 6 or 700 men, and some of them very raw
troops, could stand against 2 or 3,000 as good troops

as any the British had, and headed by Col. Campbell, an active, brave, experienced officer.

FROM every information which Gen. Howe received, he was well assured that the British troops
were at least that number: Gen. Howe should have
retreated with his 6 or 700 men, up the country, especially as he had certain information, that Gen.
Lincoln was marching with a body of men, to join
him, and did actually arrive at Purisburgh, on the
3d day of January, only 4 days after his defeat,
(which happened a few minutes after the action began.) It was a total rout, and the whole had nearly
been cut off from their retreat; the 2d brigade was
entirely so, those of them who made their escape,
were obliged to file off to the right, and cross the
Spring Hill causeway, and some were obliged to
swim Yamacraw creek, leaving their arms behind;
those who could not swim, were either killed or
taken. The loss of the arms to us, was a very
serious consideration. On this attack the British
landed about 2,000 men.

ON the 6th December, Gen. Lincoln arrives from
the northward, and issues the following order:

GENERAL ORDERS, BY GEN. LINCOLN.
' December 7th, 1778.
' THE honorable, the continental Congress, have
' been pleased to pass the following resolve:

' IN CONGRESS, September 26th, 1778.

' RESOLVED, that Major General Lincoln take the
' command in the southern department, and repair
' immediately to Charlestown, South-Carolina.'

GEN. Lincoln immediately after his arrival began
to prepare the troops to march to the southward, to
the relief of Georgia; knowing that the British had
arrived there in force, and informed of the very
weak state of Georgia. On the 24th instant, some
reinforcements came in from North-Carolina, and on
the 25th, Gen. Lincoln issued the following order:

'THE colonel or commanding officer of the regiment
' of new raised levies and militia, lately arrived from
' North-Carolina, will immediately call on the deputy
' quarter-master general, for such number of arms
' as are wanting in their respective regiments.'

THIS order shows the want of arms in the states,
even at this time, 4 years after the beginning of our
revolution: South-Carolina was better supplied with
arms and ammunition, than any state in the union;
their situation being at one end of the continent they
were more out of the way of the British cruizers,
and nearer to the islands from whence they drew
their supplies, and the Carolinians spared no pains
or cost, and run every risk to procure these necessaries. On the 26th instant, the following orders were
issued:

'GENERAL ORDERS.

'THE first and second regiments will hold them-
'selves in readiness to march at 6 o'clock to-mor-
'row morning.'

ON the 27th of Dec. we marched off the North and
South-Carolina troops, amounting to about 1200,
and arrived at Purisburgh on 3d January, 1779.

'GENERAL ORDERS BY GEN. LINCOLN, AT HEAD-
QUARTERS, AT PURISBURGH.

'January 3d, 1779.

'THE troops will immediately after dinner remove
'to the right, near the river at the lower end of the
'town, where they will take possession of the camp
'marked out by the deputy quarter-master general.

THIS evening, Gen. Howe joined us with his
suite, and gave us a particular account of his unfortunate affair in Savannah, he left the remains of his
troops on the other side of the river, at the two sisters, under the command of Col. Isaac Huger ; the
next day they were ordered to join us at this place.

HAD Gen. Howe retired from Savannah, and gone
up the country, we should soon have joined him, and
made a body of 2,000 men ; besides, such reinforcements were marching to us from Augusta, Ninety-
six, and many other parts of Georgia and Carolina,
that in a short time, we should have had an army of

4 or 5,000 men; with them we could have marched down to Savannah, before the British could have had time to fortify, and before they were reinforced by the troops under Gen. Provost, from Florida, and obliged them to leave the town and take to their shipping again. The loss of Savannah was not the only misfortune we met with in Gen. Howe's defeat, we lost the aid of almost all the citizens of that state, as the British immediately encamped the troops along Savannah river up to Augusta, and it also damped the ardor of the well effected in our state for a time, and I believe continued the war one year longer. Sometimes the most trifling circumstance of error in war, brings about great events; and the loss of Savannah was the occasion of the fall of Charlestown. On Gen. Lincoln's taking the command in the southern department, Gen. Howe was ordered to join the northern army. I thought it would be of great utility to our cause, if some gentlemen in the civil and the military departments, would have a private correspondence in which they could converse freely, and receive information from the cabinet and the field: I therefore called upon my particular friend, Col. Charles Pinckney, who was high in office, and a gentleman of very great influence, to correspond with me.

EXTRACT OF A LETTER TO COL. C. C. PINCKNEY, PRESIDENT OF THE SENATE, AND MEMBER OF THE COUNCIL OF SAFETY.

'PURISBURGH, Jan. 10th, 1779.

'DEAR SIR,

'I CHALLENGE you to open a correspondence be-
'tween Charlestown and our camp, if you accept I
'shall expect to hear from you, and shall continue to
'write you, and give you the earliest and best intelli-
'gence that comes in my way ; and shall hope you will
'answer me accordingly. We are (I mean the conti-
'nentals) encamped at Purisburgh, the N. Carolinians
'on the road leading to this place, about two miles
'from us. Our numbers are about 500 privates
'(continentals) and the North-Carolinians about
'1200 of all ranks; we are all in good spirits, and
'ready to receive the enemy, but are not strong
'enough to pay them the first visit; from all the
'intelligence we can get, their numbers on the op-
'posite side of the river to us, amount to about
'1500 and they occupy all the posts near us, over
'which we could possibly pass ; besides our men
'are undisciplined and many unarmed. I hope
'Richardson and others will soon join us : I think
'we should have 5,000 men before we cross the river,
'as we shall get immediately into action, I hope we
'shall drive those gentry on board their vessels ;
'we hear their drums beat every morning from our

' out posts; nay, hear their sentinels cough; I have
' no idea of the enemy coming over to us; their
' principal aim seems to be until they can strength-
' en themselves from the back parts of these two
' southern states; then perhaps they may endeavor
' to push us from hence : I hope our countrymen
' turn out cheerfully ; if they do not, I fear the war
' will be long and serious, and brought into our own
' state, which will be very unfortunate.

'A LATE instance I have had before my eyes;
' the poor women and children, and negroes of
' Georgia, many thousands of whom I saw on my
' journey to this place, (a spectacle that even moved
' the hearts of the soldiers) travelling to they knew
' not where.

' I FEAR we have lost Sunberry, and two gallies
' that took shelter under that battery, last Thursday,
' or Friday, as we heard a very heavy cannonade
' from that quarter. The officer commanding had
' about 120 continentals and some inhabitants with-
' in the fort,...refused to evacuate the post ; notwith-
' standing his receiving positive orders for that pur-
' pose, he Don Quixote-like, thought he was strong
' enough to withstand the whole force the British had
' in Georgia for which I think he deserved to be
' hanged.

' WE have the Congress and Lee, gallies, a ten
' gun sloop, and two schooners, now lying under this

' bluff (they pushed up here to get out of the way
' of the British) they may be of some service to cover
' our crossing, should it be expedient to land below
' this place, or to establish any post on the other
' side of the river. I believe they cannot go much
, higher than where they now aie.

' As it is absolutely necessary to keep open the
' communication between this place and Charlestown,
' I wish you would think of some way either legis-
' latively or otherwise, to keep the roads and bridges
' in good order; they are now wearing away very
' fast, notwithstanding we have had so much dry
' weather; how will they be when the rains set in,
' as they seem to begin to day? for God's sake let
' not your legislative or executive economy border
' too much upon parsimony: be generous to your
' militia, allow them every thing necessary to take
' the field; it is now time to open your purse strings;
' our country is in danger; be more bountiful than
' you have been hitherto in this present administra-
' tion; have the modesty to allow that very few of
' you have the least idea of what is necessary for an
' army, and grant what the officers shall ask for that
' purpose; they are certainly the best judges: ex-
' cuse me for this digression, but I cannot help be-
' ing warmed, when I think how ill the officers of
' this state have been treated, in being refused al-
' most every necessary they applied for; and had

' not Gen. Lincoln arrived here as he did, with the
' money, we should not have been able to take the
' field at this time, and our country might have been
' lost. I shall say no more on this head, as my
' warmth might carry me too far; and so to news
' again....Col. Campbell with the main body of the
' enemy, is posted at Abbercorne, 6 miles below this ;
' Gen. Lincoln had a letter from him, yesterday, in
' answer to one sent him in the morning, relative
'to the exchange of prisoners, or allowing the offi-
' cers their paroles until they can be exchanged from
'the northward,* but as to soldiers, he cannot give
'them up unless British soldiers be immediately
'given for them. Maj. Pinckney is to go on this
'business to-day or to-morrow. We have various
'accounts that a strong body of the enemy are gone
'to Augusta, say 1,000, but this not certainly to be
'depended upon; if true, I wish we were stronger
'here that we might spare a body to follow and cut
'them off from their retreat.   I am, &c.

       ' WILLIAM MOULTRIE·'

A LETTER TO COL. CHARLES PINCKNEY.

    ' PURISBURGH, January 14th, 1779.

DEAR SIR,

   ' THOUGH I fully intended to mention to you

....

* Gen. Lincoln wished to have the militia soldiers paroled.

' the necessity of filling our battalions, when I wrote
' you last, yet I find I have forgot it. I wish you
' would urge the necessity in the legislature, of giving
' a large bounty to inlist men for 12 or 18 months:
' had not you better give 3 or 400 dollars a man:
' the country will save money, and the militia be re-
' lieved from a very heavy burthen which they must
' certainly go through this winter. It appears to me,
' as if they must keep the field until spring; had they
' not better give large bounties, than be obliged to
' undergo so much fatigue, especially as by their
' taking the field, they do not save a penny; for, be
' assured, they are twice as expensive as regular
' troops, and your army is a very uncertain one;
' now were all our battalions full, the inhabitants
' might have rested quietly in their beds, and we
' would have been in Savannah, or perhaps have
' recovered it from the enemy; instead of which, they
' are advancing upon us; they have at this time a
' post on our side the river, called Yamassee bluff,
' not more then 4 miles below our camp; it is re-
' coned a secure place, surrounded by a deep swamp,
' and opposite Abbercorne bluff, one of their strong
' posts; they have a galley, a sloop, and a flatt,
' with boats lying between these two bluffs, to sup-
' port each other; however, I have detached from my
' brigade, a captain, and 40 men, to endeavor to get
' through the swamps, and surprize them; or to dis-

' cover what they are about ; I expect every moment
' to hear them begin to fire.

' A DESERTER came in yesterday, who informs us
' that the strength of the enemy are 3,000 from the
' northward, and 600 regulars from Augustine, be-
' sides their rangers : he also informs of Sunberry
' being taken at the time we heard the firing.

' WE hear nothing of the Georgians taking up arms
' against us ; most of them have delivered up their
' arms, and have submitted quietly to the British
' government, and I believe they will remain neuter,
' unless we go in with a considerable body, so as to
' insure success ; then perhaps they may join us.
' Richardson is encamped about 2 or 3 miles from
' this, with only 6 or 700 men ; he told Gen. Lin-
' coln he did not expect to keep them long, great
' numbers left him on their march to this place :
' this will show you what an uncertain body we
' have to depend upon, and how dangerous it will
' be to go into any enemy's country with such an
' army : we are told 1300 more North-Carolinians
' will be here in a day or two ; what an odd appear-
' ance this must make to these people, to find so
' very few of our men at this advanced camp : I
' wish it may not have a very bad effect : I am
' sorry to be informed that you have not made a
' house yet ; when you meet, you will have busi-

' ness of the utmost importance, and such as must
' be done speedily.

' I am, &c.

' WILLIAM MOULTRIE.'

LETTER TO COL. CHARLES PINCKNEY.

' PURISBURGH, January 16th, 1779.

' DEAR SIR,

' I WILL still continue to write you, until I hear
' whether you accept my challenge or not; therefore
' I will go on with giving you the intelligence as it
' comes to hand: in my last, I mentioned to you
' that I had sent a party to Yamassee bluff, where
' we thought the enemy had a post; but we were
' misinformed; our party went over the land; they
' discovered the enemy had been there, but had left
' it. By two deserters who came in last night, we
' are informed that the enemy are in force about
' 4,000 : 600 at Two-sisters; about 200 at Zuby-
' Ferry; their main body at Abbercorne : and 1,000
' Hessians at Savannah. These deserters inform
' that 1500 more are expected from Augustine, when
' they arrive, they intend to march for Charlestown.
' But for this last manœvre they must ask our leave :
' though we are not so strong as they are, yet we
' expect great reinforcements; Richardson's men,
' who arrived a few days ago, talk of going home

' soon; Richardson himself can scarce prevail up-
' on them to stay until their relief arrives. We
' had 4 or 500 North-Carolinians, who joined us
' two days ago, all these together, do not ex-
' ceed 2,500 men in our camp; it is serious to re-
' flect, that should the enemy cross the river on
' different places, we would have our hands full be-
' fore we can be reinforced. These deserters also
' tell us, that none but the light infantry were engag-
' ed at Savannah, that the battalions remained in
' order of battle, behind the barracks. The deser-
' ters tell us, that about 200 Georgians have already
' joined the enemy, and most of them horsemen;
' cannot our country raise a body of 4 or 500 men,
' to counteract them? they will be of infinite service;
' it behoves you all to exert yourselves now, and to
' find out resources to strengthen our army. I can
' think of no better than to fill up our regiments...
' at all events do not let our civil policy and economy
' ruin our country, as the Georgians have done.

' I wish the assembly would allow Capt. Senf, an
' additional pay, to enable him to live amongst us,
' he is a very useful man, and allowed on all hands,
' to be such a one as we want; he is an extraordi-
' nary field engineer; pray keep him if you can.

' I am, &c.

' William Moultrie.'

LETTER FROM COL. CHARLES C. PINCKNEY.

'CHARLESTOWN, Jan. 17th, 1779.

' DEAR SIR,

' I AM, in the first place, to thank you for your
' favors of the 10th and 14th instant; in the next, to
' ask you, how you could possibly pitch upon such a
' lazy fellow as you too well know me to be, to com-
' mence and carry on the friendly political corres-
' pondence, mentioned in your first letter? if you
' will not readily find a reason, I will...it must be, I
' think, that you are well assured from our long un-
' interrupted friendship and intimacy, I can refuse
' you nothing you can ask me; therefore, go on, my
' good sir, and be as particular as possible in all your
' letters to me ; to which, in return, I will endeavor
' (if public business and private laziness does not pre-
' vent me) to answer. As I have long known your mo-
' deration, I am well convinced you cannot expect
' my letters to be as full as yours, because I have
' not the same field for information, as you have ;
' but in the extent of things political, falling within
' my knowledge, and not inconsistent with my pub-
' lic duty to discover, you may always expect every
' satisfaction in my power to give you. By particu-
' lar request, I communicated the news, and seve-
' ral of your excellent observations on the present
' regulations wanted to advance the public service
' as set forth in your first letter, to some of our great

men; and gently touched on the string of parsimony, which you, and too many others have so often
' complained of; the former were acceptable, pleas-
' ing, and satisfactory; but the latter jarred a good
' deal, and was held inadmissible, nay, it was pret-
' ty generally held and agreed, that if it had not been
' for our money and our stores, and not altogether
' for the money you allude to, the army could not
' have marched in the good condition it did. It is
' true the late supply came very seasonably, and was
' very convenient to our domestic measures, in co-ope-
' rating with us for the public good; but for truth's
' sake, my friend, do not let this scanty remittance
' from the united treasury altogether eclipse our own
' well meant endeavors to promote the general wel-
' fare; let us participate in any merit that there may
' be, in having the army marched and maintained to
' their satisfaction, and it is all we ask:...enough of
' these discordant matters; let us return to some-
' thing else, and for the future resolve, each in his
' station, to use his utmost endeavors to advance any
' and every good plan that may be proposed and
' adopted for the defence and safety of our country;
' and leave the acrimony of reflection in oblivion.
' We have been using our best endeavors to make a
' senate and house of representatives, agreeably to
' our new constitution; the former by my joining
' them (much against my inclination, and declared

' sentiments, you well know ; having always prefer-
' ed a seat in the lower house; but which from en-
' treaty and remonstrance, I could not, consistent
' with my zeal and the public, at present withstand)
' has been made, and I have been honored with the
' chair ; but the latter I fear will be sometime in
' making a house.

' It seems to be the general opinion to enter in-
' to the most speedy and effectual measures for put-
' ting our militia on the best footing, and for com-
' pleting our state battalions : as far as I can judge
' from conversation, I believe money will not be want-
' ed to encourage the poor to act vigorously in the
' public defence, and the rich no doubt will so act
' from other motives. Gen. Lincoln has wrote the exe-
' cutive a long letter on the present state of affairs,
' and joins you in opinion fully on the proper mea-
' sures to be pursued ; he adds the necessity of send-
' ing more militia immediately to his camp: In con-
' sequence of which, 500 men are to march in a few
' days, and the drafts from Richardson's brigades
' are directed to hasten their march to camp: when
' these detachments join, and the additional North-
' Carolinians also, you will have a pretty strong
' camp. I agree with you in opinion, on the bad ef-
' fects that must ensue with our neighbors from the
' defection of our people, but I hope they will be in-
' duced from our future endeavors, to judge favora-

' bly. We are very anxious here about future events,
' and fear the enemy are, and will be soon, much
' stronger than is generally thought, from their oc-
' cupying so many strong posts, and other opera-
' tions: however we rely much on the prudence
' and spirit of our army in making an effectual de-
' fensive opposition, until we can be reinforced to act
' offensively. The roads and bridges the president
' has directed the several boards of commissioners
' to have put in immediate repair; which I hope will
' be accordingly done.

' I am, &c.

' CHARLES C. PINCKNEY.'

' To Brig. Gen. MOULTRIE.'

LETTER TO COL. CHARLES C. PINCKNEY.

' PURISBURGH, Jan. 26th. 1779.

' DEAR SIR,

' PERHAPS I may be too troublesome in writing
' you so often, I think this is the fourth letter since
' the 10th inst. and none from you; however, I will
' try once more before I give over, to establish our
' correspondence. I am informed that 300 of the
' militia from town, and Haddrell's point, with 50 of
' your artillery, and two field pieces, are ordered to
join us at Purisburgh, I could wish this order had
' been for those troops to have taken post at forts
' Johnson and Moultrie, and let us have the second

' regiment, and Roberts' artillery ; why I would wish
' this exchange, is, I think I see a large, severe, and
' serious piece of business before us, therefore, we
' should have as many disciplined troops as possible,
' the weight of the service will lay very much upon
' the Carolina troops ; those continentals from North-
' Carolina, are as undisciplined troops, as any militia ;
' then what are we to depend upon ? we should have
' twice the enemy's number to insure success.

' By letters and persons from Augusta, we are in-
' formed that some Georgians are embodied to the
' number of 3 or 400. Col. Hammond has about
' 300, Williamson has about 700, we have about 150
' Georgia continentals there, and we have detached
' 150 rifle men to join them ; with this body we may
' be able to force one of their posts near us, which
' will give us an opportunity of crossing the river ;
' when we do, our army will be much too small to
' attack the enemy, we can only fix upon some strong
' post so as to cover the country, and encourage our
' friends to come into us.

' In the first letter I wrote you, I pressed the ab-
' solute necessity of keeping up our roads and bridges.
' I hope you have thought of it; at this time they are
' so broken, that should we be obliged to retreat, we
' should lose all our stores and artillery; and we can-
' not be reinforced.   ' I am, &c.

' WILLIAM MOULTRIE.'

A LETTER TO COL. CHARLES C. PINCKNEY.

‘ January 26th, 1779.

‘ DEAR SIR,

‘ I AM happy at last on receiving a letter from
‘ you, yesterday, dated the 17th inst. I almost des-
‘ paired of success ; it has been a long time on the
‘ road ; I know your disinclination to trouble yourself,
‘ but had hopes from the regard I know you have for
‘ your country, to draw you into a correspondence,
‘ that may be of mutual advantage to us all, by in-
‘ formations received from each other in our different
‘ spheres* ; it was this, and our long friendship that
‘ induced me to desire you to step forth from your
‘ love of ease, and exert yourself in this critical mo-
‘ ment: I congratulate you upon your promotion to
‘ the senatorial chair ; it is a fine easy birth and will
‘ suit you well : I am in hopes that the two houses
‘ will keep up a constant union, and not differ about
‘ trifles at this juncture, when the force of every
‘ spring should play in unison. I am glad to hear
‘ that the legislative springs are set in motion.

‘ THE longer we keep the field, the more incon-
‘ veniency arises from having the militia part of our
‘ army ; an instance which happened two days ago, is
‘ a very striking one. One of Col. Kershaw’s men
‘ was upon the main guard, and had absented him-

* Col. Charles Pinckney was president of the senate, and
a member of the privy council.

'self for several hours, so long as that another was
'obliged to take his tour upon sentry, when he came
'to the guard, the captain very good naturedly chid-
'ed him; upon which the man gave him very rough
'language, the captain then ordered some of the
'guard to confine him, the man catched up his gun,
'cocked it, and presented it at the captain, swearing
'he would blow a bullet through him, upon which
'several of the guard standing bye, seized the gun
'and threw out the priming, the man struggling,
'at the same time endeavoring to fire her off, upon
'this he was confined; and now comes the grand
'affair: Col. Kershaw applies to Gen. Lincoln for
'a general court-martial, to try the offender; the
'court was accordingly ordered, and Col. Richard-
'son, one of the militia colonels, appointed president;
'the other members also from the militia corps: up-
'on convening the court, and tendering them the
'oath, as inserted in the continental articles of war,
'a demur was made to the oath; and that the pri-
'soner was not to be tried by those articles, but by
'the militia law: seven of the members refusing to
'take the oath, the matter was represented to Gen.
'Lincoln, who seemed to be a good deal surprised:
'I happened just then to call in upon him; he told
'me the story; I replied, that I did not think he
'could try the militia of this state, by the articles of
'war, as they were quite ignorant of it; neither did

' I believe they would take the field on that footing,
' unless their own legislature should pass a law for
' that purpose: he insisted that all the militia of other
' states, serving in junction with continental troops,
' and receiving pay from the continent, are subject
' to these articles: for the force of this argument, I
' refer you to the 17th section and 1st article of war.
' To end our dispute, he desired I would summons
' all the field officers of my brigade, to meet at my
' quarters, they met accordingly: the arguments
' that passed between him and myself, were again
' brought upon the carpet, when it was unanimously
' resolved by the field officers, that our militia was
' not liable to the continental articles, unless they
' received continental pay: Gen. Lincoln still think-
' ing himself right, and as a further argument he
' made use of, that they were in continental pay, was
' by a letter which he had received from the presi-
' dent, informing him, it was so; he seems a good
' deal staggered, and is at a loss how to act, at this
' critical time, when we are so near the enemy; he
' declares they are no more under his command, and
' therefore cannot furnish them with provisions; and
' that they were at liberty to go off when they pleas-
' ed: think of our situation, should the enemy be ac-
' quainted with it, it would be an invitation for them
' to cross the river; nay, before this, at two different
' posts, on which our security depended, the militia

' have gone off without acquainting us of their inten-
' tion : building upon their strength, we have weak-
' ened our little army much by detachments sent to
' Augusta, 350 men, to reinforce and spirit up that
' quarter. I think, however it is lucky the matter
' was started at this time, before we crossed the ri-
' ver, as some of us might have been sacrificed...as
' I mentioned to you before ; I see nothing so effect-
' ual for our security as the filling up of our conti-
' nental battalions; pray let me recommend that to
' be your first and most necessary care ; then after-
' wards any new matter that can give them assistance
' in the most speedy way, should be fallen upon.
' I hear from town that 500 horse-men are to be
' raised ; will not this hinder our recruiting for the
' regiments? if so, I wish it were deferred, for be
' assured all the solid business is to be done by the
' foot soldiers : but to return to the militia...I see no
' other use can be made of them but to take post on
' this side of the river, and defend their own country,
' when we shall be able to go on the other side and
' attack the enemy : they increase the strength of
' their different posts every day, and have extended
' themselves as far up as Hudson's bluff, about 16
' miles above the Two-sisters; their strong post is
' now at Two-sisters, the 71st regiment is there, 1400
' men, the others are at Ebenezer and Abbercorne ;
' this intelligence we got from a deserter yesterday ;

' he says they have left only 400 Hessians at Savannah,
' by their having such a number at the Two-sisters,
' it looks as if they had an inclination to pay us a
' visit, or to proceed up the country, to stop our pro-
' gress : we must keep our eyes about us here ; we
' are took weak to extend ourselves ; we depend up-
' on the militia to give us notice, should they attempt
' to cross, and this is but a very poor dependance,
' as they have lately quitted two very important posts,
' without giving us the least notice: I think the only
' speedy method you can fall upon to fill up our bat-
' talions, is by draught from the different districts,
' and allow them to send a substitute. We had a
' grand representation of an action; owing to 2 or
' 3 days rain, by general orders, ' all the arms that
' were loaded, must be discharged at retreat beating,
' and the cannon on board the gallies and armed ves-
' sels, should also be fired off.' The officers of the
' different corps, drew up their men on their respec-
' tive parades, and discharged their arms by platoons,
' which continued the firing for some time; before
' our firing was over, the enemy began theirs, at
' their lower post, Abbercorne, and it run along the
' river as far as you could hear them; the gallies be-
' gan as soon as the small arms were over, it kept
' the swamp in a continual roar for about half an
' hour; perhaps ere long we shall have this grand

' noise realized : I dare say the people within ten
' miles of this place, thought we were engaged.

 ' Poor old Mr. Bryan is gone a prisoner to New-
' York.   I am, &c.

      ' William Moultrie.'

 This letter shows what difficulties Gen. Lincoln
had to encounter, with having such an army,
mostly composed of militia, who were governed by
such a public law, that for the greatest military crime
they could be guilty of, they were only punishable
by a small pecuniary fine; with such an army, what
anxiety, perplexity, and difficulties must a general
be put too; how uneasy must he feel, when his military reputation was at stake, with such odds
against him, at a time when his camp were 3 miles
from an enemy, superior in force to him, and veteran troops : it was fortunate that a river and a
large swamp was between us : a militia army should
be brought into action immediately as they take the
field : they do not want for spirit ; but they soon tire
of a camp life...they then get home-sick, and off they
go, without giving the least notice, or obtaining
leave, because they know that the fine for their diso-
bedience is so trifling that they care not about it.
It was very fortunate for us, and impolitic in Lord
Cornwallis, to withdraw the paroles from the militia,

and to order them to take arms against their country, that being the case, they soon determined on which side to fight, they then joined their countrymen; whereas, had they been suffered to remain upon parole, I believe many of them would have been very well pleased to have staid at home quietly, but when once they had taken arms again in favor of their country, they were then obliged to keep the field as a place of security from being made, prisoners, and perhaps hanged. I believe one half of the militia of the state were upon parole at that time.

———

EXTRACT OF A LETTER TO COL. JOHN DART.

'January 20th, 1779.

'DEAR SIR,

'I HAVE nothing extraordinary to write you now;
'but that from Augusta we are informed the people
'are embodied there to nearly a thousand, including
'150 continentals; Col. Elbert is gone up that way
'to take the command; I hope their number will
'increase so as to assist us in crossing the river.
'God knows when we shall be strong enough; as to
'Richardson's militia they are worse than nothing,
'as they absolutely refuse Gen. Lincoln's orders:
'should we cross the river into Georgia with such an
'army, the few continentals might be sacrificed; we
'have nothing from the enemy these several days;
'they are lying still in their quarters and we in

' ours ; we frequently have flags going to and fro
' with necessaries to our unfortunate prisoners*....
' we are just going to send one with necessaries for
' poor old Mr. Bryan who is ordered to prepare him-
' self to go to New-York.

' I am, &c.

' WILLIAM MOULTRIE.'

LETTER FROM COL. CHARLES PINCKNEY.

' CHARLESTOWN, January 22d, 1779.

' DEAR SIR,

' I WROTE you a few days since, and yesterday
' was favored with yours of the 16th instant, the con-
' tents of which has been communicated to our
' friends agreeable to your commission ; I am glad
' the enemy have retired from Yamassee Bluff, and
' hope it will be the last Carolina territory they will
' tread. For God's sake my friend let us carry on the
' Fabian war as much as possible, until we can rein-
' force sufficiently to act otherwise. Our legislative
' powers are, at last, got to work, and I hope a few
' days will produce some acts that will answer public
' expectation, and give the people satisfaction. Bee
' is again, very deservedly, in the chair of the lower
' house, and I dare say will use his utmost endea-

....

* Prisoners taken in Savannah when Gen. Howe was defeated.

' vors to promote business with spirit and dispatch :
' the senate, you must know, from the nature and
' principle of their constitution ought, and I hope
' will act wisely ; though it is to be lamented, they
' are obliged to act now, without the assistance of
' yourself, Oliphant, and others of its members,
' whose aid would give a lustre to their proceedings.

' THE filling up the continental battalions seems
' to be the plan most relied on, to produce the best
' effects, in the way recommended by Gen. Lincoln ;
' the militia law will also undergo some material
' amendments, but I believe will not take such mili-
' tary strides, with respect to extraordinary powers,
' as some of our high flyers expect : God grant the
' means to be pursued may produce the best ends to
' promote the safety and happiness of our people.

' A FEW prizes have been brought in, within these
' few days, with some rum, sugar, &c. But these
' changes, instead of giving relief, from the present
' exorbitant prices of merchandize, generally add
' thereto ; Newton's rum and sugar, sold at public
' vendue, from 50 to 100 per cent. more than those
' articles could have been bought for, at vendue, three
' days before. It was such an unheard of proceed-
' ing one could almost be led to imagine our enemies
' have some secret commissaries to work, to raise the
' prices of these necessaries of life, and thereby add

' to the oppression and distresses of the people, to
' serve political causes.

' But as virtue shines brightest in enduring afflic-
' tions with manly fortitude. I hope these and eve-
' ry other endeavor of our enemies will fail, and ul-
' timately turn to our advantage.

' Strange, nothing yet from the Congress, whose
' last letter was the 3d December, nor have we
' heard from Virginia ; we hourly expect the last
' advices from those places. I intended to have said
' something more to you, but am summoned to bu-
' siness and so adieu. My best respects and com-
' pliments to my kinsman and friends, and believe
' me to be

' Your affectionate friend,

' Charles Pinckney.

' P. S. The governor has promised to lay Capt.
' Senf's case before the assembly, but I have heard it
' asserted he will not remain at any rate ; I wish he
' may be properly tried.'

' Brig. Gen. Moultrie.'

Letter from Col. Charles Pinckney.

' Charlestown, January 25th, 1779.

' Dear General,

' Yesterday I received your fourth letter, for
' which I thank you, and assure you I feel the cor-

' respondence so agreeable, that in a little time I
' shall be a-head of you; this is my third letter.

' WE are in a fair way, I hope, of filling the con-
' tinental regiments on our establishment, by grant-
' ing large bounties, and raising the pay of officers
' and of men already inlisted, and those to be listed:
' the law is not yet passed: a joint committee of
' both houses have agreed to these great outlines;
' vhich I hope will be very soon passed into a law;
' as soon as it does, I will endeavor .to transmit you
' a copy thereof; the bounty is 300 dollars.* I have
' hinted your hopes about the second regiment
' being sent to join Camp; I confess it did not
' meet my own judgement as right, with respect to
' the safety of our capital; nor did other gentlemen
' signify any approbation thereof: the last detach-
' ment of Charlestown, both the artillery and infan-
' try, I dare say, will answer every expectation of
' them. The information of your intended opera-
' tions I am anxious about, and wish soon to hear
' of its good success. Gen. Williamson we have
' not heard from for some time, but doubt not his
' well established zeal and activity in the public ser-
' vice; we expect some brilliant stroke from his
' quarter. The ordinance for raising the regiment

....

* Dollars much depreciated, 761 continental dollars for one
silver dollar.

‘ of horse, I wrote you about, is not carried into ef-
‘ fect; there is so much altercation about the parti-
‘ cularities of it, that it moves, I may say, with lead-
‘ en legs: I have much endeavored to give it the
‘ spur, as I have the greatest expectations of its util-
‘ ity. The militia, I am hopeful, will be more use-
‘ ful when they come to be more inured to camp ;
‘ at present, my friend, they require much indul-
‘ gence ; remember they are your peaceable neigh-
‘ bors and friends, and though willing to risque
‘ their lives and property in their country’s cause,
‘ yet it must be difficult and distressing to them to
‘ act the complete parts of veteran soldiers. The
‘ amendment of the law, by which they are, or ought
‘ to be governed is under consideration, but the ex-
‘ tension of penalties and powers, so much desired by
‘ some is not relished by the generality. May the
‘ result of this business promote the public weal.

‘ The 5th of February is pitched upon, by both
‘ houses, for the electing of state officers,* but though
‘ we are using our best endeavors to collect a suffi-
‘ cient number for that important purpose, agreeably
‘ to the constitution ; yet unless some of the mem-
‘ bers from camp, particularly two senators, do attend
‘ on that day, I fear the business will not be done.
‘ It is really necessary to the public service, and will

* Governor, &c.

' be a means of preserving a constitution which may
' be shaken, without a speedy choice of such officers.

' I am, &c.

' CHARLES PINCKNEY.
' Brig. Gen. MOULTRIE.'

EXTRACT OF A LETTER FROM COL. CHARLES
PINCKNEY.

' CHARLESTOWN, January 29th, 1779.

' DEAR SIR,

' YOUR two favors of the morning and evening of
' the 26th inst. I received last night, the latter
' contains important news indeed; the contents of
' which the town has been alarmed with, some little
' time before, by the imprudent exclamations of sev-
' eral people who ought to have known better. Port-
' Royal is looked on as conquered already, by the
' report of several people from the southward road
' yesterday, who say a heavy cannonade began about
' ten in the morning and was continued several hours.
' Gen. Bull (who was in town last night, but was re-
' quested to return to his duty, set off last night) is
' much alarmed and thinks Granville county is gone.
' He has authority to make use of the detachments
' from Charlestown, either to defend Port-Royal Isl-
' and, if not already taken, or in that way to stop the
' further progress of the enemy, but in all cases to
' consult with and follow such directions Gen. Lin-

'coln may please to give. It is thought the Charles-
'town detachment may be now so situated, as to be
'opportune for acting beneficially for the public ser-
'vice; if Gen. Ash is got no further than Pocotaligo,
'he may be assisting too, but we apprehend he had
'reached your camp; many people think, this move-
'ment of the enemy is to post themselves at Port-
'Royal, and there wait reinforcements from the
'northward; others, that it was done only to cause
'a division and to weaken your little army, that they
'might more easily pass the river; others, that it
'was to destroy the town and fort, plunder and re-
'turn to Tybee; but some with more penetrating
'looks and significant nods; that the vessels appear-
'ing in scull creek, as if intended, (Port-Royal was,
'or is, only a feint,) to cover a real design of land-
'ing suddenly on the Euhaws, march to a pass of
'consequence near Elliott's hill, on the southern
'road, and there throw up some field works, which
'with a few cannon will entirely cut off the com-
'munication from town to Gen. Lincoln's army,
'and put him between two fires; this last manœ-
'vre, is thought of so much consequence to the pub-
'lic safety, as to raise the public anxiety; but for
'my own part, I confess, from the opinion I have of
'more succours coming from the northward to the
'enemies assistance, that the enemy mean to make
'a strong lodgment there, which in its consequences

' may prove very prejudicial to the peace and safety of
' this country ; the ordinance for completing the con-
' tinentals passed both houses yesterday after some
' difficulty with respect to its operation. However it
' now rests in substance thus....that all persons who
' will enlist as soldiers in any of the continental re-
' giments for sixteen months, (a time thought suffi-
' cient by the lower house for two campaigns, but
' which was disputed by the senate for eighteen, as
' long as they thought the safety of the ordinance
' would suffer it) shall be entitled to the following
' bounty, viz. if enlisted in one month from the pass-
' ing of the law, 500 dollars,* if in two months, 400
' dollars, if in three months, 350 dollars, and if after
' that time, 100 dollars for sixteen months service.
' If these extra bounties do not procure the men,
' there is no other method at present pointed out,
' or ever I believe thought on to obtain them ; most
' being of opinion, this great encouragement will ef-
' fectually answer our expectation...God grant it may :
' but when I consider the struggle now making in
' the lower house, to allow each militia man 30 shill-
' ings per day, pay and rations &c. I fear this will be
' a great bar to the other. However it seems this
' regulation is much insisted upon by a strong party,

* This appears to be a very high bounty, but the paper
money was depreciated as low as 761 for one silver dollar.

' and I am doubtful whether when the bill reaches
' the senate, it will meet that opposition it merits ;
' add to this, the raising the corps of horse imme-
' diately, will as you justly observe, be an additional
' impediment ; therefore, so far as I have any influ-
' ence, you may depend I shall be active in prevent-
' ing the bad consequences, we seem to apprehend.
' The better regulation of the militia is also now be-
' fore the house of representatives ; and the matters
' I before informed you of will take place ; but with
' respect to the militia being subject to the articles of
' war ; I believe this will not be submitted to. How-
' ever as Gen. Lincoln in a letter to the governor
' (alluding to the case of colonel Kershaw's daring
' centinel, mentioned in your letter to me,) he in-
' sists upon this important point being brought to
' some legislative determination, one way or other ;
' I suppose you will soon know the turn it takes, I
' am sorry the general thinks the militia will be of
' no service without being subject to the articles of
' war, and therefore intends, to stop their provisions :
' You know, my friend, on former occasions they have
' rendered essential service to their country, under
' the present regulations ; and I cannot help thinking
' with a little proper management, such as treating
' them as you would win a coy maid, by gentle me-
' thods, you may at last expect a soldier-like perfor-
' mance of their duty ; have patience, and try to

' bear the misconduct of the refractory militia with
' that military philosophy every general ought to be
' possessed of, and I think the resulting consequen-
' ces will prove favorable ; do not think of bringing
' free men to the halter, or perhaps the receipt of a
' bullet by the sentence of a court martial, for prac-
' tices which they cannot be convinced are crimes :
' the punishment is more than adequate to the of-
' fence, and therefore highly improper in the case
' of freemen, who have never formally and volunta-
' rily resigned the rights of citizens to the benefits of
' the civil law, as is the case of the soldier in the
' regular service. I applaud your judgment, my
' friend, and also that of your brigade, who gave
' the opinion you mention ; see the operation of
' the continental articles over militia; a different
' judgment must have been of bad consequences,
' and therefore I hope you will have wisdom enough
' to maintain and pursue what your judgments have
' fixed as a principle. The pardon and amnesty
' so long expected by many, and dreaded by some
' few, is at last repealed in the lower house by a
' very great majority; the governor in his public
' speech recommended it to both houses; and the
' lower house in their address which I suppose you
' have seen, approve the recommendation : the sen-
' ate unanimously came into the measure to forward
' the good work ; originated and speeded the bill in

‘ their house ; but how amazing was the result, upon
‘ putting the common question, whether the bill
‘ should be read a second time ; some warm argu-
‘ ments and declamations were thrown out, and only
‘ eight arose to support the second reading : by
‘ which extraordinary conduct the bill was lost to
‘ the regret of many well wishers and supporters to
‘ the government.

‘ I am, &c.

‘ CHARLES PINCKNEY.’

‘ Brig. Gen. MOULTRIE.’

———

EXTRACT OF A LETTER FROM COL. C. PINCKNEY.

‘ CHARLESTOWN, Jan. 30th, 1779.

‘ DEAR SIR,

 ‘ I WROTE you yesterday, since which the gene-
‘ ral assembly has ratified the law, for filling the
‘ continental regiments. The general assembly have
‘ also ratified a law for reviving the laws for impress-
‘ ing boats, waggons, &c. for public service ; and
‘ for imprisoning suspected persons. The law for
‘ further regulation of the militia, is still under con-
‘ sideration ; as is the ordinance for raising the regi-
‘ ment of horse, but they (in my opinion happily at
‘ present, and until the recruiting service for the
‘ continental regiment goes on to completion) move
‘ slowly. There is likewise an ordinance, I am told
‘ before the lower house, for emitting one million of

'dollars immediately, and power to borrow five mil-
'lions more on loan, to answer the present extraordi-
'nary exigencies of government.

'THE public here, are much alarmed to day, by
'a report that Beaufort is in the possession of the
'enemy: If Beaufort should be taken, pray my
'good friend, give me your candid opinion what
'steps you think should be taken for the public safe-
'ty in the capital. The committee of both houses,
'in conference, on the state of public affairs, have
'resolved that it is necessary an army of 3,000 men
'should be immediately encamped near Charlestown,
'and ready to act on the shortest notice, for its de-
'fence. This report I believe will be agreed to, but
'from where the men are to be got, without prevent-
'ing the encrease of your army, I know not; but
'should the measure be adhered to, and measures
'pursued accordingly, pray what do you think of it?
'you well know the state and resources of our coun-
'try, and to which measure ought the preference to
'be given? your opinion I know will have weight;
'therefore pray be expeditious, explicit, and full in
'your answer to the questions.

'I am, &c.

'CHARLES PINCKNEY.

'Brig. Gen. MOULTRIE.'

To Col. Charles Pinckney.

'Port-Royal Ferry, Feb. 1st, 1779.

' Dear Sir,

' I arrived here last night, by desire of Gen.
' Lincoln, to endeavor to persuade our militia to go
' over to Beaufort, and to prevent the spiking up the
' cannon, but came too late, that business being
' done in too great a hurry, and the people moved
' off; it is lucky the militia from town are come
' up, as they have put spirits into those who hurried
' away so fast: I have nothing new to inform you
' from our camp, only that we have had a cessation
' for two or three days, on account of a conference
' between Col. Provost and Major Pinckney,* rela-
' tive to the exchange of prisoners : this matter was
' not concluded upon, when I left our camp.

' The enemy are gone up, it is said (in force 1500)
' within fifty miles of Augusta, (I need not mention
' to you, the news from that quarter, as I suppose
' you get it as often as we do) I hope ere this, we
' have got a body of 1500 men, now together, on the
' other side the river, and expect to hear of their
' skirmishing every day : Gen. Ash joined us last
' Sunday, with a body of 1157 men exclusive of of-

....

* Col. Provost and Major Pinckney could not agree....Col.
Provost expected we were to exchange British soldiers for citizens, who they had taken peaceably at their homes, and not
in arms.

'ficers; 234 of which are continentals. I hope be-
'fore long we shall be in motion; we have now a
'great freshet in Savannah river, which impedes
'our operations a little.

'I am, &c.

'WILLIAM MOULTRIE.

LETTER TO MAJ. GEN. LINCOLN.

'BEAUFORT, February 4th, 1779.

'DEAR SIR,

'I WROTE you a few days ago from Gen. Bull's,
'when I was there; the militia requested me to
'cross the river with them; which I readily con-
'sented to. The next morning, after leaving a
'proper guard to our camp, we began to cross the
'ferry, and got near three hundred over by sun set; we
'immediately marched off, and continued till we got
'within one mile of Beaufort; here I rested the
'troops a few hours, and then proceeded to the town
'which we entered at sun rise next morning : hav-
'ing ordered the troops into quarters, and reposed
'myself a little, I rode down to view the fort,* with
'Gen. Bull, and two or three other gentlemen ; we
'had scarce been a moment there when an express ar-
'rived informing that the enemy were in full march for

....

* The fort was blown up, and the guns spiked.

' Beaufort, and not more than five miles off; upon
' this I requested Gen. Bull to ride on to town, and
' have the men turned out; I followed immediately,
' and found them all paraded : and had another ac-
' count that the enemy were coming very fast. I
' then moved off the troops in order to meet them,
' and having marched two miles, was again inform-
' ed they were within four miles of us, I then pro-
' ceeded very slowly, looking for a proper piece of
' ground to form upon ; having soon found a very
' advantageous spot, I continued there, waiting an hour
' for the enemy, and was then informed, that they
' had, after halting awhile, altered their march, and
' were going towards our ferry, I followed them and
' had gone about three miles, when I learnt that they
' were upon their return from the ferry, in full
' march towards us, and not more than one mile
' distant; having sent my aid, Mr. Kinlock, to recon-
' noitre and bring me a particular account, he soon
' returned and informed me they were just at hand :
' I hastened our march to gain a swamp, which was
' near; but finding the enemy had already got pos-
' session of the ground I intended to occupy, I
' halted at about two hundred yards distance from
' the enemy, and drew up the troops to the right and
' left of the road, with two field-pieces, (6 pounders)
' in the centre, and one small piece, (2 pounder) on
' the right in the wood ; on the enemy's near ap-

'proach; I ordered Capt. Thomas Hayward to be-
'gin with the two field-pieces; and advanced my
'right and left wings nearer the swamp, and then
'the firing became pretty general: this action was
'reversed from the usual way of fighting, between
'the British and Americans; they taking to the
'bushes and we remaining upon the open ground:
'after some little time finding our men too much
'exposed to the enemy's fire, I ordered them to take
'trees; about three quarters of an hour after the
'action began, I heard a general cry through
'the line, of ' no more cartridges;' and was also in-
'formed by Captains Heyward and Rutledge, that
'the ammunition for the field-pieces was almost ex-
'pended, after firing about forty rounds from each
'piece: upon this I ordered the field-pieces to be
'drawn off very slowly; and their right and left
'wings to keep pace with the artillery to cover their
'flanks, which was done in tolerable order for un-
'disciplined troops: the enemy had beat their re-
'treat before we began to move, but we had little
'or no ammunition, and could not of consequence
'pursue: they retreated so hastily as to leave an
'officer, one sergeant, and three privates, wounded,
'in a house near the action, and their dead lying on
'the field. It is impossible as yet to be particular
'with respect to the latter. Two officers we have
'found and seven men they fought from behind

' the bushes. Capt. John Barnwell,* with a few light
' horse was of infinite service in giving us frequent
' intelligence of the enemy's motions, and attacking
' their rear; he had at one time Capt. Brewer, who
' is much wounded, two sergeants, and twelve pri-
' vates, prisoners; but a party of the enemy having
' rallied in their retreat; retook the captain, one ser-
' geant, and six men; the remainder, however, he
' brought off with twelve stand of arms. Barnwell
' had about fifteen men. It makes me happy to as-
' sure you, that our militia have that spirit which
' they have always been allowed to possess; noth-
' ing but discipline is wanting to make them good
' troops; the Charlestown artillery behaved gallantly;
' they stood to their pieces like veterans, and served
' them well, until I was constrained to order them
' to retire, in consequence of their ammunition be-
' ing nearly expended: I had in the action only nine
' continental troops; Capt. De Treville, two officers,
' and six privates, with one brass two pounder, and
' only fifteen rounds. I must, in justice to them, say,
' that they behaved well. It seems absolutely ne-
' cessary for me to remain here a few days longer,
' in order to have the wounded properly taken care
' of, and other matters put in a right channel.

' THIS moment died a valuable officer and good

....

* Now Gen. Barnwell.

' citizen, of the wound he received yesterday, Lieut.
' Benjamin Wilkins, of the Charlestown artillery :
' we have three other officers wounded ; Capt. Hay-
' ward in the arm, Lieut. Sawyer and Brown, both
' of the light infantry, with six or seven privates kill-
' ed in the field, and fifteen wounded. I cannot be
' very particular ; as yet have had no regular return
' made me. The enemy's brigade consisted of two
' companies of the 60th and one of the 16th regi-
' ment, all picked light infantry.

' WE had five deserters from them immediately
' after action, who informed us of several particulars
' already mentioned : also, that our second shot from
' the field piece-had disabled a Howitz, which they
' had fired but once.

' I am, &c.

' WILLIAM MOULTRIE.

' P. S. The Chehaw company was sent back be-
' fore the action, about 125 men, on a report that
' the enemy had landed there.'

BRIGADE ORDERS, BY GEN. BULL.

' Tuesday, February 2d, 1779.

' THAT Capt. Heyward do leave his tents standing
...take two days provisions with him...march with a
field-piece and half his detachment to cross the fer-

ry, and take post at the hither end of Cedar Causeway.*

' THAT Capt. Badley, of the light infantry, do leave his tents standing, with two or three privates to take care of them;...take the remainder of his detachment, with two days provisions,...cross the ferry, .to act as a covering party to Capt. Heyward.

' THAT the remainder of the army do·hold themselves in readiness to march at a moment's warning.

' THAT Col. Beekman, of the continental artillery, do cross the ferry, and take post at the Cedar Causeway, and take under his command the artillery now under Capt. Heyward. The artillery, with their field-pieces, to lead the line ; Col. Beekman will command this corps. The light infantry, commanded by Capt. Badley, to follow and support the artillery.'

ORDERS BY GEN. MOULTRIE.

' BEAUFORT, February 4th, 1779.

' GEN. Moultrie takes the early opportunity of returning his thanks to the troops, for their gallant and

* Instead of one field-piece and half the detachment, the general afterwards thought proper to make a verbal order, ' That two thirds of the detachment, with two field-pieces should cross the ferry.'

spirited behavior on the field, in the action of yesterday; and doubts not but they will always acquit themselves in the like spirited manner, especially when fighting in the glorious cause of liberty.

' A RETURN to be made immediately, of the killed and wounded, in the action of yesterday.'

Second Company,

S. Wilkins, John Fraser, mortally wounded.

John Anthony, John Calvert, Anthony Watts, John Green, John Laurence, wounded.

Third Company,

John Collins, John Righton, John D. Miller, wounded.

———

'CAMP, AT PORT-ROYAL FERRY.

' February 7th, 1779.

' RECEIVED the following, which was read to the men: Gen. Lincoln having learnt from Gen. Moultrie, the gallant and spirited behavior of the different corps engaged in the late skirmish with the enemy takes the first public opportunity of returning them his most sincere thanks.'

———

' ON the 15th January, 1779, President Lowndes issued orders to Maj. Grimball to detach 50 men from his battalion, with two field-pieces, to join

Gen. Lincoln. A meeting of officers was called, when it was resolved to turn the battalion out, and read the orders, to see if volunteers sufficient would turn out, if not, then to draw...16th January the battalion turned out, 80 volunteers offered, and were accepted by the president.

———

LETTER FROM COL. CHARLES PINCKNEY.

'CHARLESTOWN, Wednes. Ev. Feb. 3d, 1779.

'DEAR SIR,

'YOUR favor of yesterday, from Gen. Bull's camp
'is just come to hand. I am extremely sorry and
'much chagrined at the very unhappy situation of
'our affairs, at and about Port-Royal, and hope soon
'to hear, some little order and regulation to ad-
'vantage may be brought out of the present confu-
'sion. It is horrible to think of our late extraordi-
'nary proceedings in that quarter. The public have
'great hopes from your presence, and the assistance
'of the Charlestown militia now there, that the fort
'may still be saved, so as to protect Port-Royal I-
'sland.

'I HAVE lately wrote you several letters of the
'principal business now going on here, in the le-
'gislature ; but nothing material has happened
'therein since my last. The bill for the regiment
'of horse is not yet passed into a law, but it has so
'many advocates in both houses, who wish to expe-

' dite it, I think it will be ratified in a few days. A
' bill for amending the militia law, was this morning
' brought to the senate, and read the first time. Its
' principle objects are, to oblige the militia to march
' to the assistance of a neighboring state, under the
' penalty of 500 pounds, and three times the ax
' paid by the defaulter, and further obliging the de-
' faulter to serve 12 months in one of the continental
' regiments, or to find a substitute to perform that
' service. To oblige the militia, in times of alarm,
' to a more punctual obedience of orders, under the
' same heavy penalties, and nine months service as
' regulars. To have a summary trial for the con-
' viction of offenders and levying the fines ; and to
' establish the pay of each militia private at 25 shil-
' lings per day, for service in garrison or in the field.
' I am told the bill is to continue for 18 months, and
' that it met great opposition in the lower house.
' What fate it will meet with in the senate I cannot
' say, but hope every senator will have judgment
' enough to determine properly on the essential
' rights and privileges of their fellow-citizens as free
' men, and wisdom enough to maintain those rights
' with firmness. It is not the danger, or apprehen-
' sion of danger, at the present moment, that should
' oblige a patriot to part with essential rights ; and
' the present extraordinary proceeding puts me in
' mind of a spirited answer of the commons of Great-

' Britain, to the king, when they were told, ' That
' season was very improper to debate about rights
' and privileges, when news had been received that
' the enemy were to land an army in the kingdom,
' in a few days.' The answer was to this effect if I re-
' member right, from the parliamentary history, ' that
' if they were sure the enemy had an army in the
' heart of the kingdom, and were marching with has-
' ty strides to Westminster, they would not part with
' one of the least rights and privileges of the people.'
' This perhaps in the opinion of some may be going
' too far, but for my own part (who consider the
' present militia law as a very rigorous one, and one
' that would answer every purpose were it faithfully
' executed) I cannot, and will not, ever give my
' consent, to part with the constitutional freedom, and
' liberty of the people, in the mode pointed out by
' this before unheard of militia Bill. Recruiting
' goes on briskly I am told, for the regular regi-
' ments, and hope our expectations will be answered
' by the amazing bounties we have offered to get
' men.

  ' I HOPE we shall see you in town on Friday, if the
' public business will permit your absence from
' camp, as that is the day pitched upon for choosing
' a governor and other state officers. Your friends
' request to be remembered to you, Your son is

' now in town and well. I am, with compliments to
' all friends in camp,

     ' Your affectionate friend,

         ' CHARLES PINCKNEY.'

' To Brig. Gen. MOULTRIE.'

LETTER FROM GEN. LINCOLN.

    ' PURISBURGH, February 8th, 1779.

' DEAR SIR,

  ' From the latest accounts, I am informed, that
' the enemy have in the upper part of the country,
' near Augusta, about 1700 men; their views pro-
' bably are, to cut off our communication with the
' Indians, and engage them against us; to support
' the disaffected and stop our supplies; many of
' which we drew from that quarter. There are now,
' opposite Augusta, and the road there about, 2,000
' men; I am of opinion that we ought to leave here,
' and at the Two-sisters; the North-Carolina conti-
' nental troops and levies, and Col. Kershaw's militia;
' and march with all the others up to Augusta, attempt
' to cross, and secure as much of the state of Georgia
' as we can. I wish for your sentiments on the plan.

    ' I am, &c.

        ' BENJAMIN LINCOLN.

' Brig. Gen. MOULTRIE.'

LETTER TO GEN. LINCOLN.

'PURISBURGH, February 8th, 1779.

'DEAR SIR,

'I received yours of this day, by which I find the
'enemy have penetrated, with 1,700 men, as far up
'the country, as Augusta in Georgia. I agree with
'you in opinion, that should they be suffered to re-
'main there, they would increase by the disaffected,
'and possibly by the Indians ; by which means our
'supplies from that part of the country would be
'stopt. I therefore think it highly necessary we should
'leave 1,000 men, as a guard to this post, at the Two-
'sisters, and proceed up the river, with the remain-
'der of our army, (which you inform will be 3,000
'men) to cheek the progress of the enemy, and
'protect the friends of America.

'I am, &c.

'WILLIAM MOULTRIE.'

THE day after the action, I sent Lieut. Benjamin
Smith* with a flag, to the enemy's vessels, for Lieut.
Hazleton's baggage, who we had wounded and taken
prisoner, and also the other prisoners' baggage, and
received the following letter from him, viz.

....

* Now General Smith.

'PORT-ROYAL, Friday Evening, half past 7 o'clock.

'DEAR GENERAL,

'DOCTOR Fraser and myself arrived here at half
'after 3 o'clock, and proceeded (as soon as we could
'procure a boat and hands) towards the enemy; who
'lay in the same position they had done for several
'days past: we were met about a quarter of a mile
'from the Vigilant, (who lay nearest to us) by Capt.
'Mowbray, and another officer; the former received
'our dispaches, read them, and after getting into our
'boat, sent the other off with directions to bring us
'some refreshments. We were detained upwards of
'two hours, and in the course of the conversation,
'we discovered that the enemy believed us to be 500
'strong in the battle, that Capt. Murray (besides
'those we are acquainted with) was wounded. They
'highly applauded the bravery of those officers who
'were on horse-back. During the whole of the con-
'versation, he absolutely disavowed any action of
'plunder or intention to do so, giving a reason for
'the different houses being burnt; that they had ei-
'ther received very abusive language from the peo-
'ple on shore, (which he said was the case at Lau-
'rel-Bay) or had found some illiberal words written
'with chalk on the walls, against them: after the
'long conversation, an officer came from the vessel,
'and told us he would be very glad to meet us at

' old Talbert's, at 11 o'clock in the morning, when the
'things should be collected and delivered with a letter.

' WE saw a sloop and a large boat, sounding up
' the river, on a supposition that you intended leav-
' ing the Island. ' I am, &c.

' BENJAMIN SMITH.'
' Gen. MOULTRIE.'

WHEN I was preparing to leave Beaufort, and returning with the militia to their camp on the main,
I left Col. Beekman, with a detachment of the continental artillery, with the following order.

' BEAUFORT, Feb. 6th, 1779.

' SIR

' YOU will remain with the men under your
' command to transport all the stores and cannon
' in this place, and at Fort Lyttleton, to the main
' at Gen. Bull's camp; where you are to land them.
' Have the ammunition put in some proper house:
' having executed this with all proper expedition,
' you will withdraw with your party, to Gen. Bull's
' camp, and there wait until further orders. Such of
' the cannon, as may be, in your opinion, incapable
' of being rendered fit for service, are to be left be-
' hind.

' WILLIAM MOULTRIE.'
' Lieut. Col. BARNARD BEEKMAN.'

My reasons for this order was, that it was generally believed that the British would return to Savannah for a reinforcement; and that I was obliged to return immediately to Gen. Lincoln's camp, at Purisburgh; and that the militia would not remain on Port-Royal Island if I left them: I was therefore obliged to march them off to their old camp again, upon the main. Although the fort was blown up, yet it was not so totally demolished but that a great many of the stores were left unhurt, and the guns so lightly spiked, that you might draw out the spikes with a pair of pincers.

LETTER TO COL. CHARLES PINCKNEY.

'PURISBURGH, Feb. 9th. 1779.

' DEAR SIR,

' YESTERDAY I returned to this place, and I as-
' sure you not a little tired; I find my old bones
' yield much to fatigue; I hope, however, they will
' carry me through the war; then I will set me down
' in peace, and indulge myself the remainder of my
' days.

' I received your several favors of the 29th and
' 30th of January, and 3d of February. I hope the
' recruiting goes on fast: when 30 or 40 are got to-
' gether, they should be sent, with their arms and
' accoutrements, to camp, with all expedition. I
' wish we had 100 of the horsemen ready; they will

'be of infinite service; I saw the use of them at
'Port-Royal: do not be led away with the idea of
'having regular trained horsemen; we have not
'time for that; send them to us as they are listed;
'I wish and recommend strongly Capt. John Barn-
'well to have one company, if he cannot be appoint-
'ed one of the field-officers. You seem much dis-
'tressed about the loss of Beaufort, and think that
'if the enemy had that place they would take the
'whole country: I am quite of a different opinion;
'I allow it will be a convenient harbor for them, but
'they cannot land on the Main if the militia will
'but do their duty, and watch their motions: would
'you believe it? that the enemy had not more than
'300 men when our people took fright, spiked up
'the guns, blew up the fort, and ran away: I am
'happy I went down the country at the time; and
'wish it had been two days sooner, as I think I have
'put spirits in the militia, and convinced them that
'these red-coats are not so invincible as they ima-
'gined, and that the militia can beat them with a
'little superiority of numbers, and a confidence in
'their officers. I applied to go down, for a few days,
'to endeavor to arrange matters properly for your mi-
'litia; but was told I could not be spared, as we should
'move from hence to-morrow, to follow the enemy;
'we shall leave 1,000 men here, to guard this post and
'the Two-sisters; and proceed to Augusta, with a-

' bout 3,000 men, where we expect to be joined by
' Gen. Williamson and Col. Elbert, with 1500 more:
' I have heard privately that the enemy have made
' some proposals to our disaffected people about
' Ninety-six; but they are afraid to step forth while
' the enemy are on the other side of the river; by
' our movements we shall stop that communication;
' and I dare say increase our numbers before we get
' into Georgia, which will be ere long. You need
' not be under any uneasiness for the capital, as we
' know the enemy have full half their army up the
' river, and we shall always hang about them till we
' can catch an opportunity to give them a blow,
' which, I hope, will be a decisive one. I would
' have you keep a body of men near Charlestown, to
' be enabled to make head, should the enemy turn
' that way with a part of their army.

' I AM astonished to hear of such wild imagina-
' tions getting into people's heads, as you mention;
' they must all certainly be frightened out of their
' wits, to think that the enemy, by taking post on
' any hill on the road, can prevent our passing these
' little rivers at their heads, or many other places,
' when we have a superior army, and the whole
' country open to us: be not afraid of such manœu-
' vres; the enemy are not strong enough to play
' that game.   I am, &c.

' WILLIAM MOULTRIE.'

LETTER TO GEN. BULL.

'PURISBURGH, Feb. 9th, 1799.

' DEAR SIR,

' You will immediately upon the receipt of this,
' order Capt. Heyward,* to march to Purisburgh,
' with their field-pieces, and to wait there till further
' orders : you are also desired, to signify, to Col.
' Beekman, that he is to finish his present business
' with all possible dispatch ; and that, having finish-
' ed it; he is to expedite Capt. Treville, and his
' party, with the field-pieces, to join the army un-
' der Gen. Lincoln, wherever it may be : Captain
' Treville may hear of our movements, at the Two-
' sisters.

' I am, &c.

' WILLIAM MOULTRIE.'

LETTER FROM GEN. BULL.

' CAMP AT PORT-ROYAL FERRY, Feb. 10th, 1779.

' DEAR SIR,

' I HAVE this moment received your favor of yes-
' terday and have ordered Capt. Heyward to march
' with his corps and two field-pieces, to Purisburgh.
' He will begin his march to-morrow morning,

....

* Capt. Heyward commanded a detachment of the Charlestown artillery.

' though he says the men are not well pleased with
' the order; and they say they cannot stay from
' Charlestown longer than the first of March.....
' Capt. De Treville has also received his orders to
' march, with his detachment and field piece....
' Lieut. Col. Beekman is here, and brought from
' the fort all the shot and stores, but the flat sunk,
' by which means the powder is lost, the large boat
' also sunk, with one of the 26 pounders, near the
' fort. Last night the enemy's fleet had fallen fif-
' teen miles down the river; whether they are on
' their return to Savannah, or on their way to Beau-
' fort, I shall be able to judge as soon as they move
' two or three miles farther down, which they must
' do either to get back into scull creek, or to go up
' Beaufort river.

' I am, &c.

' STEPHEN BULL.

' Brig. Gen. MOULTRIE.'

LETTER TO COL. CHARLES PINCKNEY.

' PURISBURGH, 10th Feb. 1779.

' DEAR SIR,

' LAST night Col. Elbert came into camp, and I
' am sorry to inform you, that our affairs, from that
' quarter, do not wear so pleasing an aspect as we
' have been made to believe; would you think it?
' Williamson and Elbert, have but 800 men; and

'the back people waiting to see the event be-
'tween the two armies; though I flatter myself they
'will come in to us, when we get up. Another bad
'piece of intelligence I am to give you, is, that a
'whole regiment of 400 North-Carolinians, say their
'time is out, and they intend to march this day
'homeward; if this should take place amongst them,
'as it has done with our militia, it will be of very
'fatal consequences to this state, and the continen-
'tals that must keep the field, may be cut to pieces.
'I am going to leave this place immediately. Gen.
'Rutherford, and Col. Kershaw, are to be left with
'their militia to guard this post.

'I am, &c.

'WILLIAM MOULTRIE.'

LETTER TO COL. CHARLES PINCKNEY.

'CAMP, 5 miles from PURISBURGH, Feb. 11th, 1779.
'DEAR SIR,

'I WROTE you yesterday of the bad situation of
'our affairs in the back country; since which they
'seem to thicken: this afternoon we had an express
'from Gen. Ash, inclosing one from Gen. Wil-
'liamson, by which we are informed, that the ene-
'my are endeavoring to cross the river at Augusta,
'and to make a push for our back country, where
'they are well assured that the disaffected will join

' them in great force ; Williamson informs of their
' collecting in bodies to join the enemy, about Nine-
' ty-six and Saluda ; we advanced so far as this yes-
' terday, in our way up to Augusta ; but upon in-
' telligence received after we had marched seven
' miles, we thought it expedient to return to this
' place, we had great reason to believe the enemy
' intends to make a push at Purisburgh ; we are
' greatly embarrassed to know which way to move ;
' if the enemy should penetrate into this part when
' we are gone upwards, they will have three or four
' days march of us ; by which means, without your
' utmost exertions, they would get to Charlestown.
' I cannot learn by all the letters from town, what
' number of men you have got together ; was I as-
' sured of that, I perhaps might give you a plan of
' defence : should we remain here and suffer the in-
' surgents to join the enemy, that will also be of ve-
' ry dangerous consequences ; yet I think this last
' seems to be the most rational plan ; as we shall be
' in a body to proceed and check the enemy any
' where : we know that should the back country be
' suffered to make head against us ; they will amount
' to a very considerable army : I sent an order for
' the Charlestown artillery to march to Purisburgh,
' but Gen. Bull informs me, they will not stay lon-
' ger than the first of March : I fear our militia law
' will ruin our country : in contending too much for

' the liberties of the people, you will enslave them
' at last; remember, my friend, it has always been
' the maxim of all communities, to abridge the peo-
' ple of some of those liberties for a time, the better
' to secure the whole to them in future. I would
' recommend by all means to collect 3,000 men about
' Charlestown ; were we assured we could make
' head against the enemy a few days in Charles-
' town, we could go on cheerfully any where ; and
' should an invasion happen, we could come to you
' in some force.

' I am, &c.

' WILLIAM MOULTRIE.'

LETTER FROM GEN. BULL.

' CAMP AT PORT-ROYAL, Feb. 12th, 1779.

' DEAR SIR,

' AGREEABLE to your order, the continental ar-
' tillery, under the command of Capt. De Treville,
' marched off for the Two-sisters, yesterday after-
' noon, with one field-piece : I also ordered the
' Charlestown artillery to march to Purisburgh which
' occasioned such uneasiness and dissatisfaction, that
' Capt. Heyward thought it best to represent the
' matter to me, and to suspend the order for their
' march, as he found the men were determined to
' disobey the order, and to stay out of Charlestown

'only until the first day of March, during which
'time they choose to serve in my camp. Yester-
'day seven sailors, deserters from the Lord George
'Germain ship of war, were brought in by a party
'from one of our picquets; they say that the fleet is
'on their way to Savannah; that their land troops
'lost, in the action with us on Port-Royal, forty killed
'and wounded, and that the night after the action, an
'express was sent by a boat to Savannah, for a rein-
'forcement, but the answer was, none could be
'spared, and that the fleet must return; they further
'said, that they have carried off above 300 negroes
'belonging to different people.

'I am, &c.

'STEPHEN BULL.'

'Brig. Gen. MOULTRIE.'

THE preceding letters show what a disagreeable,
unpleasant and dangerous situation Gen. Lincoln
was in while at Purisburgh, with his army, being
so near the enemy, whose force of veteran troops,
was superior to him; and his mostly composed of
militia who were so discordant, that they disobey-
ed every order which was disagreeable to them;
and left their posts and guards whenever they
pleased, and that with impunity; he therefore determined not to have any thing more to say to

them, and left the command of the militia intirely
to me, being the senior continental officer of the state,
in hopes they would more readily obey my orders,
but they still continued in their contumacy. He
therefore requested I would take a ride to Charlestown, and represent matters to the governor, and
wrote me the following letter.

'PURISBURGH, Feb. 14th, 1779.

'DEAR SIR,

'You will please to proceed immediately to
'Charlestown, and lay before his excellency the gov-
'ernor, the very weak state of this army. You will
'represent to him that every plan which hath been
'digested for offensive operations have been render-
'ed abortive; many of the militia have refused to
'come out, others have joined the army for a few
'days, but have left it when they thought proper,
'and even this post with impunity.

'You will shew, as the militia, by a late resolve
'of the assembly, are not to be considered under the
'same control with the army, that it is necessary
'the state undertake to defend some particular part
'of the country.

'You will recommend the necessity of sending
'1,500 militia to maintain this post, and cover the
'neighborhood thereof. And, on this being done,

' it is probable the continental troops may attempt
' some offensive operations.

' IF this should not be agreeable, you will please
' to urge the propriety of this state taking the de-
' fence of the upper part of this country.

' You will inform him, that the time for which
' the North-Carolina militia engaged for service, ex-
' pires with the tenth of April next ; I have written
' to the governor of that state, urging the neces-
' sity of their relieving their militia here, and of
' marching their levies as soon as their furloughs
' expire. Other letters pointing to the same object,
' I think ought to be written.

' PROVISION must be made by the militia of this
' state to take the place of those from North-Caroli-
' na, in case their men do not come up.

' IN short, you will point out the necessity of the
' utmost exertions until Congress can afford relief.

' You will suggest the propriety of sending all
' the continental troops in Charlestown and in the
' forts, and of supplying their places with the mili-
' tia, and the Charlestown artillery.

' I am, &c.

' B. LINCOLN.'

' Brig. Gen. MOULTRIE.'

ON receiving the above letter, I immediately
prepared myself and set off for Charlestown, and on

my arrival waited upon the governor. In conversation, after representing our situation in camp to him, he promised that we should be reinforced, &c. and wrote a letter to Gen. Lincoln, the purport of which is in a letter to Col. Charles Pinckney.

LETTER FROM GOV. RUTLEDGE.

'CHARLESTOWN, February 22d, 1779.

' DEAR SIR,

' INCLOSED is a letter for Gen. Lincoln, express-
' ing thereby the result of the conference yesterday.

' PRAY let there be a court of inquiry on De Tre-
' ville's conduct at Fort Lyttleton, and send me the
' report of it, as soon as you can.

'DOGHARTY is come down, with some witnesses,
' to attend the trial of Tweed, Groundwater, and
' their confederates; but they cannot be tried, until
' the negroes and sailors, who were with them are
' here: I wish you would therefore have those peo-
' ple (I mean the negroes and sailors) sent down
' as soon as possible, as the keeping of the wit-
' nesses is expensive to the state, and inconvenient
' to them ;...they may be sent, under proper guard,
' to Gen. Bull's camp, with orders to him to send a
' guard of his men with them to town. I have not
' mentioned to the general any thing about forming
' a camp, because, though I think one must be

' formed, my opinion is not yet settled as to time,
' place, numbers, &c.

' I am, dear sir, your obedient servant,

' J. Rutledge.'

' Brig. Gen. Moultrie.'

LETTER TO COL. CHARLES PINCKNEY.

' Purisburgh, February 27th, 1779.

' Dear Sir,

' I arrived here yesterday, after pushing ve-
' ry hard for camp, as I received several accounts
' on the road, that great matters were doing on the
' river Savannah, which I suppose you have heard
' in town ; nay, they were so particular as to inform
' me, that we had taken 300 prisoners at Augusta,
' and that Campbell was hemmed up at Brier-creek,
' the bridge being cut away ; that Gen. Lincoln was
' gone in with 250 horse ; you must imagine all this
' gave me great spirits, and hastened my march to
' camp; after riding fifty miles, I was greatly cast
' down by being told that Gen. Lincoln was return-
' ed to camp, that the enemy had crossed Brier-
' creek, and that we had taken very few prisoners,
' this disappointment mortified me very much.

' Our news in camp, at present, is by a letter
' from Gen. Ash, received last night at 12 o'clock,
' dated 25th instant, he informs he would be at
' Brier-creek yesterday; that the enemy retreated

' so precipitately from Augusta, as to leave twelve
' beef killed and skinned upon the ground ; they
' were informed, that Gen. Ash, had 11,000 men
' with him, and that Gen. Lincoln, was crossing
' below Brier-creek to cut off their retreat ; they had
' a pretty strong body ; their army consisted of 1,000
' regular troops ; 300 Col. Reed's new levies, 300
' Carolina royalists (as they call them) 500 Brown's
' and Georgians, with six brass field-pieces, two
' howitzers and four grass-hoppers ; which were a
' strong body and a handsome train of artillery ;
' however, a panic seized them, and they pushed
' for Brier-creek, which they accomplished before
' our horsemen could destroy the bridge, and they
' passed it, they burnt it down to prevent our pur-
' suit, they lost one field-piece in crossing, by the
' boat sinking : Gen. Ash has sent to have it taken
' up and brought to his camp : Provost marched up
' 1,000 men to reinforce them ; they are all now got
' down to the Two-sisters and Ebenezer ; where we
' reckon the main body of the army are, it is agreed
' on all hands, that the enemy have a body of 5,000
' men now with them ; it seems to be the prevail-
' ing opinion in camp, that they are going away ; for
' my part I cannot see the reason for it ; it is said
' the commodore has ordered all the transports to
' wood and water for sea ; but is not this a prudent
' step to provide for the worst, they know that our

' reinforcements will enable us to attack ere long ;
' at present we are inferior to them : I wish they
' were gone ; something must be done soon ; as
' there is a buzzing in the North-Carolina camp'
' that their time will be out on the 10th of April, and it
' will take them a month to march home, they there-
' fore expect to move on the 10th of March ; should
' this be the case, we shall be as badly off as ever,
' if our militia do not get here by that time : I think
' you should mention to the governor, to order his
' guards at bloody point, and places adjacent, to give
' him and us the earliest notice, when they observe
' the enemy's fleet in motion.

' I am, &c.

' WILLIAM MOULTRIE.'

LETTER TO COL. CHARLES PINCKNEY.

'PURISBURGH, March 2d, 1779.

' DEAR SIR,

' I OBSERVE in a letter from the governor to gen-
' eral Lincoln, that he intends forming a camp at
' Orangeburgh, of 2,700 men, the 13th instant ; and
' that he also intends augmenting them to 5,000,
' from Thomas', Lisle's, Neal's, and Williams' regi-
' ments, from the Ninety-six regiment, without in-
' terfering with the measures necessary for defend-
' ing the back country ; I think all seems to be se-
' cure thereabouts. By Col. Mason who arrived in

‘ camp yesterday, via. Augusta, I am informed that
‘ 350 horse, from our back country have joined Gen•
‘ Ash, he saw a great many of them himself, count-
‘ ed 250, all well mounted, and said 50 more were
‘ only sixteen miles behind those, this will make a
‘ body of near 500 horse, from this state, which will
‘ be a considerable reinforcement for Ash, and make
‘ his numbers about 2,300 men, exclusive of Wil-
‘ liamson’s division at Augusta. I am surprised to
‘ find by the governor’s letter, that he has not order-
‘ ed the 1,200 men to this post, which I understood
‘ him when in town, should be immediately done ;
‘ besides forming the camp at Orangeburgh of 5,000.
‘ I imagine he means Gen. Lincoln is to draw
‘ horsemen from that camp when it is formed ; but
‘ there seems nothing particular or explicit, in his
‘ letter on that head ; I wish when he writes again
‘ he will explain that matter. Lieut. Fotheringham
‘ being exchanged, returned to us yesterday ; he says,
‘ the enemy are fortifying Savannah, so as to de-
‘ fend it with a few men ; they have marched all their
‘ force up this way leaving only 200 in Savannah,
‘ and about 50 at Sunberry ; they talk much of pass-
‘ ing the river the latter end of this month, or the
‘ beginning of the next ; but I fancy they will think
‘ better of it ; if they do not they may get a good
‘ drubbing : I hope we will save them the trouble
‘ of crossing ere that time comes ; and meet them

' on their own ground ; I assure you our men long
' much to be at them ; but this you may depend up-
' on, we shall do nothing rashly or inconsiderately ;
' we well know what we have at stake.

' THE enemy informed Fothringham, that they ex-
' pected great reinforcements from New-York; but
' I believe this to be a puff. I would advise that or-
' ders be given to our militia guards, that are sta-
' tioned at Bloody-point and other places, where
' they can see the enemy's fleet at Cockspur, when
' they are preparing to sail, to send immediate no-
' tice to Charlestown, and to Gen. Lincoln : these
' little hints may appear trifling; however, they may
' be very useful; I therefore think it my duty to
' transmit them. My division of continental troops
' amount now to about 2,000 men, exclusive of con-
' missioned officers. I shall be pretty strong when
' the second regiment arrives, which I hope will be
' in two days; I am informed they marched from
' town last saturday : the artillery arrived yesterday :
' we expect a great many recruits in a few days.

' I am, &c.

' WILLIAM MOULTRIE.'

THE different divisions of our army formed seve-
ral camps, one at Purisburgh, commanded by Maj.
Gen. Lincoln, of between 3 and 4,000 men : one at
Brier-Creek, on the west side of the river, com-

manded by Maj. Gen. Ash, of about 2,300 men;
and one at Williamson's house, on Black Swamp, under Gen. Rutherford, of 7 or 800 men ; besides Gen.
Williamson's division at Augusta of about 1200 men:
all these together made a pretty strong army, and we
began to prepare to cross the river, and give the
enemy battle ; and Gen. Lincoln sent a messenger
to Gen. Ash, to meet him and myself at Gen. Rutherford's camp, to hold a council of war, upon a plan
of operations, and of crossing the river, and attacking the enemy : accordingly, about the first of march,
Gens. Lincoln, Ash, Rutherford, and myself, had a
meeting, and we agreed to march the army from
Purisburgh (first leaving a strong guard there, to
watch the enemy's motion) to Gen. Rutherford's
camp, and cross the river, to join Gen. Ash ; this
being settled, Gen. Lincoln and myself returned to
Purisburgh. At the council of war, in conversation
with Gen. Ash, he assured us that he thought himself perfectly safe where he was ; that he had taken
a good possition on Brier-Creek, that his camp was
very secure ; and that the enemy seemed to be afraid
of him, believing his numbers to be much greater than
they were ; he only asked for a detachment of artillery, with a field-piece or two, which Gen. Lincoln
immediately ordered, under the command of Major
Grimkie. On the 3d of March, in the evening, to
our great surprize and astonishment, Col. Eaton
having swam the river with his horse, came full

gallop into our camp, and told us that Gen. Ash, and his whole army were cut off: this to be sure occasioned grave faces in camp: presently after this, Gen. Lincoln received the following letter from Gen. Ash.

MATHEW'S BLUFF, March 3d, 1779.

' SIR,

' I AM sorry to inform you that 3 o'clock, P. M.
' the enemy came down upon us in force ; what num-
' ber I know not : the troops in my division, did not
' stand fire, five minutes ; many fled without discharg-
' ing their pieces; I went with the fugitives half a
' mile, and finding it impossible to rally the troops,
' I made my escape into the river swamp, and made
' up in the evening to this place ; 2 officers and 2 sol-
' diers came off with me ; the rest of the troops, I
' am afraid, have fallen into the enemy's hands, as
' they had but little further where they could fly to:
' luckily Major Grimkie had not got the artillery out
' of the boat, so that I shall keep them here with
' Gen. Rutherford's brigade to defend this pass un-
' til I receive further orders from you. This instant
' Gen. Bryant and Col. Perkins arrived. Col. Eaton*

....

* Col. Eaton was not drowned, but was the first who gave us an account of the defeat.

' was drowned crossing the river. Since writing the
' above, a number of officers and soldiers have arri-
' ved : we have taken a man, who says he was taken
' by them, and would not take their oath, and was
' formerly under Lee to the Northward. He inform-
' ed there were 1700 red-coats, in the action, also a
' number of new levies from New-York, Georgia
' militia and Florida scouts : that 1500 men had
' marched up to Augusta, to fortify that place; that
' they are fortifying Hudson's very strongly : that
' the day before they marched off, 7,000 men had
' arrived from New-York. Gen. Bryant and Ruther-
' ford are of opinion that it is better to retreat to
' your quarters; therefore I am inclined to march
' to night, when we get all our fugitives over.

' I am, &c.

' JOHN ASH.'

' Major. Gen. LINCOLN.'

GEN. Ash's affair at Brier-Creek, was nothing
less than a total rout; never was an army more
compleatly surprized, and never were men more
panic struck; as Gen. Ash's letter, and the evidences at the court shows : the poor fellows! most of
them threw down their arms, and run through a
deep swamp, 2 or 3 miles, to gain the banks of a
wide and rapid river,* and plunged themselves in, to

* Savannah.

escape from the bayonet; many of them endeavoring to reach the opposite shore, sunk down, and were buried in a watery grave; while those who had more strength, and skill in swimming, gained the other side, but were still so terrified, that they straggled through the woods in every direction; a large body of them were stopped early the next morning at Bee's-creek bridge, about 20 miles, by a detachment of the second regiment, under Capt. Peter Horry, marching to camp; who told me he had just heard of the affair at Brier-Creek, and saw a large body (2 or 300) of the fugitives coming in a hasty and confused manner, most of them without their arms, and Gen. Ash and Bryant with them...drew up his men at the bridge: Gen. Ash rode up to him, and requested that he would stop those men; that they were running away: Gen. Bryant said they were not running away; Gen. Ash insisted they were; Capt. Horry then asked of the two generals who was the commanding officer; it was answered Gen. Ash: then, sir, I will obey your orders: and presented fixed bayonets, and threatened to fire upon the fugitives, if they attempted to come forward, which stopped them: afterwards Capt. Horry proceeded to camp, with his detachment, and Gen. Ash and Bryant brought back the fugitives.

WE never could ascertain the number of men that were lost in this unfortunate affair, as many of them made no stay any where until they got to their own homes in North-Carolina. The loss of arms was almost total, and it was a very serious consideration with us, at that time, as we could not replace them. Col. Elbert, with a few continentals, and a field-piece or two, fought some little time, but they were soon surrounded, and made prisoners of.

THIS unlucky affair at Brier-Creek, disconcerted all our plans, and through the misfortunes of Gen. Howe and Ash, the war was protracted at least one year longer, for it is not to be doubted that had we have crossed the river with our army, and joined Gen. Ash, which we were preparing to do, we should have had a body of 7,000 men ; besides strong reinforcements were marching to us from every quarter sufficient to drive the enemy out of Georgia ; and all the wavering, and all the disaffected would have immediately joined us ; and it is more than probable that Carolina would not have been invaded, had this event taken place

———

LETTER FROM COL. CHARLES PINCKNEY.

'CHARLESTOWN, March 9th, 1779.

' DEAR SIR,

' I AM no military man, capable of forming the
' certainty of events from particular situations, by
' scientifical knowledge; but in so far as common
' understanding might be allowed to judge and to

' give an opinion, I foretold for several days before
' it happened, the unfortunate turn of our affairs
' would take near Brier-creek, and therefore was not
' disappointed when the dismal news of the defeat of
' our North-Carolina friends in that quarter arrived :
' we are still hopeful when particulars come to be
' known, things will turn out even better than your
' last healing letter indicates : but remember this is
' hopes only ; for by some letters now in town, we
' are told things are in a much worse situation than
' you speak of : such as the loss of Col. Elbert and
' all his regulars, killed or taken, the death of Col.
' Harris, the loss of all Neal's horse, except 28, and
' some of Col. Picken's party, and too many of poor
' Gen. Ash's ; this stroke I am hopeful will ulti-
' mately turn out to our common advantage, by mak-
' ing the militia more careful to prevent surprizes.
' I well know your zeal and active spirit will spur you
' on, as you hint, to change posts ; but, my friend,
' steady ! remember the Fabian policy ; this critical
' hour, in my poor opinion, should be no otherwise
' employed ; for the stake at risk is too great to
' lose, and Generals should never act from heat or
' revenge to punish a momentary insult, as it may
' lay them too open to be foiled by a skilful enemy,
' already prepared to meet and make the best advan-
' tage of the occasion...have patience, for I think the
' time must shortly come, when we shall have full

‘ satisfaction, through the means we are now using
‘ to obtain this desirable end : when the detachment
‘ of the second regiment joins you, together with a
‘ number of recruits from the various recruiting offi-
‘ cers, and the jolly tars now on their way up, for
‘ the artillery, the gallies and boats, all under the
‘ articles of war, your body of regulars must be
‘ considerable ; then when Ash’s men recover them-
‘ selves, Rutherford, and 1200 men from Richard-
‘ son’s battalion (most of whom are now in motion
‘ towards Augusta) Horry’s light dragoons raising
‘ fast, and the arrival of the northern troops, a strong
‘ party of which were seen a few days ago at the
‘ ridge, and the intended encampment at Orange-
‘ burgh are all joined, the militia also must be in
‘ great force. These are the means I allude to as a
‘ happy presage of bringing about the ends before
‘ mentioned ; and now I really think we shall soon
‘ accomplish, or be able to accomplish, something
‘ clever : God grant it may be so ; therefore, my
‘ good sir, let me repeat to you my opinion that we
‘ had better not make more haste then good speed.

‘ The governor has signified his intention of tak-
‘ ing the field, and joining the camp at Orangeburgh ;
‘ which, I believe, will have a good effect to increase
‘ our numbers there : we propose to raise 2 or 3
‘ companies of artillery of some excellent seaman
‘ and mariners now in town, who have offered their

' services to attend the camp with half a dozen field-
' pieces. His excellency is so sanguine in this busi-
' ness, that he thinks they will be ready to march
' and act in a very few days, from the assurances he
' has received on this head : I wish it may be so :...
'my good sir, where I am not restrained by the du-
' ties of my office* from communicating measures
' to you, I always do it with the greatest pleasure,
' and heartily thank you for your kindness in the
' same way to me, and hope it will reciprocally
' be continued to our mutual satisfaction : I have
' mentioned to the governor, what you desired about
' explaining his orders for the march of the 1200 men
' from Richardson's battalion, which he says he has
' done. Also about the out-posts giving timely no-
' tice to Gen. Lincoln of the movements of the en-
' emy's fleet.

' By a very late return from Gen. Williamson, his
' brigade now on actual duty in various posts and
' services, including the state independant compa-
' nies, amounts to upwards of 1600 men : if this body
' could be brought together soon, and with safety to
' the common cause, surely it might make a pow-
' erful stroke, in conjunction with our forces on foot.
' The late great loss of arms, and the daily call for
' them, makes us somewhat uneasy ; but, by some

* One of the Privy Council.

' measures lately taken to recruit our public stock,
' we are hopeful the service will not suffer on this
' account. Gen. Bull has orders to march 300 of
' his regiment, further and scour the country in his
' district, from his lower camp to his upper, which
' he says is 70 miles about your camp, and thinks he
' shall be able to put this in execution soon. This
' we think will be of important service to prevent
' the inroads of the small parties of the enemy's
' horse plundering as they do on this side of the
' river, and also prevent the disaffected from joining
' the enemy ; Capt. Dogharty has undertaken the
' command and is appointed to garrison Fort Littleton
' with 50 men besides officers, and thinks he can per-
' form that service with effect : we have the highest
' expectation of good in this business, from the well
' known zeal, activity and bravery of this officer,
' we hope he will be soon at his post, where I learn
' that the artillery are now in good order.

' I am &c.

' CHARLES PINCKNEY.

' Brig. Gen. MOULTRIE.'

ABOUT this time several attempts were made to
set fire to the town ; almost every night we were
alarmed with the cry of fire ; and 6 or 7 houses were
burnt on Trott's-point.

TWEED, Groundwater, and Remington were taken, going over to the enemy, and a law was passed by the general assembly to appoint a special court for their trial; they were tried by the sedition act. Remington, one of the accomplices, turned states evidence ; Tweed and Groundwater were found guilty, and sentenced to be hanged ; some interest was made for Groundwater, he had been captain of a small vessel, and had been of service in the begining of the war, in bringing in to us stores and many necessary articles which we were in want of; he was, however, strongly suspected of being concerned with Tweed in setting fire to the town on Trott's-point:* the inhabitants were so incensed against him, that he suffered, to appease the people.

WE were now in daily expectation of strong reinforcements from Virginia and North-Carolina, and Paulaski's legion from Philadelphia.

LETTER TO COL. PINCKNEY.

‘ PURISBURGH, March 11th, 1779.

‘ DEAR SIR,

‘ BY five deserters, that came in this morning
‘ from the enemy, we are informed, that the British
‘ troops are moving down the country to Savannah ;

....

* North end of the Bay, above Mey's-wharf.

' from whence they are to go round to Port-Royal;
' I think this is a very necessary piece of intelli-
' gence for you to be acquainted with; that you may
' order your manœuvres accordingly; for my part
' I think we shall have a much easier game to play
' than at present, as our posts will not be so exten-
' sive ;...as to keeping possession of every island in
' that part of the country, it cannot be expected, but
' the securing of the main land is very easy; by this
' movement we shall be better able to draw matters
' to a point, and arrange them on a more contracted
' plan ; which will suit our army a little better; it
' will be quite out of the way of the Scopholites.

' GEN. Lincoln sent a flag, a few days ago, to re-
' quest the favor of Gen. Provost, to give him an ac-
' count of the number of prisoners, and what officers
' were taken at Brier-creek; which answer was re-
' turned yesterday: he mentions in his letter, that
' he had 162 prisoners (privates) and 24 officers, a
' list of which he sent.   I am, &c.

'WILLIAM MOULTRIE.'

———

THE following is the copy of a LETTER to GEN.
LINCOLN, from a FRIEND which we had in the
BRITISH CAMP, at Savannah, some time in Feb-
ruary, 1799.
' SIR,

' AFTER overcoming many difficulties, I have

' again arrived safe at home : when I first started I
' met Col. Marberry who informed of the move-
' ments of the enemy via. Paris'-mill, to attack
' Gen. Ash ; he immediately sent off a man unarm-
' ed, but has failed or was taken. It is surprising so
' necessary a post as Paris'-mill was left unsecured,
' the strength of the enemy now at Savannah, &c.
' is as follows ; first and second battalion of the 71st.
' regiment, the light infantry, Delancy's New-York
' corps, York and Jersey volunteers, Carolina-royal-
' ists, part of the 16th and 60th, two Hessian bat-
' talions, Brown's Rangers, and the militia, consist-
' ing in the whole upwards of 4,000 : I send you in-
' closed a sketch of their different posts, &c. their
' intention, you may depend, if Gen. Vaughan*
' arrives, is to visit Charlestown, and I believe by
' the upper road, as they made many inquiries
' in my hearing relative to the road. If Vaughan
' does not come, they intend holding fast the coun-
' try below Hudson's ; and have a mode of govern-
' ment established : Col. Campbell gave me his hon-
' or, that he refused the command without the
' country was to be kept, and the expedition sup-
' ported ; giving as a reason that he must falsify his
' honor to the people, and deceive them : and I as-

....

* Gen. Vaughan was expected from New-York, with
5,000 troops.

' sure you every appearance shows it; the mer-
' chants are trading away in perfect security ; the
' northward fleet was expected every hour when I
' left town ; and when I was at Tuchefewking :
' I heard a feu-de-joye fired, which was either
' for an arrival, or the admiral falling down to carry
' Col. Campbell to England, where he is going, if
' Vaughan does not arrive soon; if he arrives he
' waits to have the honor of subduing South-Caroli-
' na ; he is a dangerous officer. You may depend
' there are 500 Indians on the Alatamaha, waiting
' to assist in the movements ; they killed a Major
' Skinner, through mistake, thinking he was as they
' termed it ' a rebel,' they expect all the Indians
' that Stuart and Cameron have influence over, to
' assist them on the frontiers of South-Carolina : I
' mentioned to the general, I thought it would be
' cruel to let the Indians loose, who would massacre
' indiscriminately ; he told me they were to have
' white men to command them ; and more to divert
' the army than to do execution. They have re-
' cruiting officers now out. For Gods sake ! let
' South and North-Carolina know it : they mean to
' make two corps of royalists, viz. the South and
' North-Carolina regiments ; Col. Maitland, with the
' light infantry, a small part of the 71st. Brown's
' corps, and Forney's militia, are posted at Paris'-
' mill, and I believe mean coming no higher; at

' present they have strong posts from Hudson's for-
' ward : they hear every thing that passes in your
' camp ; and the commanding officer showed me a
' letter wrote by Maj. Ross to his wife, giving an
' account of the number and situation of the army ;
' the night before the engagement, they knew Gen.
' Ash's waggons and carts crossed Savannah river, at
' Barton's-ferry ; and that Gen. Lincoln, and Gen.
' Ash, met at the white house ; I doubt not when
' they intend crossing, they will divert you with a
' a fleet off Beaufort or Charlestown : I write to have
' the town fortified by land for that is their aim ; and
' have all passes to it secured ; look out for spies, for
' they have them amongst you ; destroy this and eve-
' ry other paper you receive from me ; they know
' my hand writing, I cheerfully risk my life for
' my country ; in the field I never valued it....but a
' ROPE ! there is the rub : I had my horse stolen
' when I was down, which I expect to be satisfied
' for, through you, at a future day ; if you have fur-
' ther occasion for my services ; send me a horse,
' and the one thing needful ; and I will serve you
' at all risks.

' A DESCRIPTION OF THEIR POSTS.

' 1st. AT Paris'-mill they are encamped on the
' south side, and keep a strong picquet on the north ;

' they have what cannon they took at Brier-creek,
' and two field-pieces of their own.

' 2d. At Hudson's they have a strong fort, finish-
' ed round the house, and two 6 pounders, two how-
' itz, and some artillery, all placed on the left of the
' road as you come from Savannah : on the brink of
' the hill they keep a strong picquet.

' 3d. At Paces I saw no artillery, but a strong
' picquet on the brink of the hill the Savannah side,
' and another picquet at about 200 yards from the
' house.

' 4th. At the two sisters, some artillery on the
' hill to command the river, and a strong picquet
' on the road where it comes up to the house.

' 5th. At a branch this side of Ebenezer, about
' three miles on the south side, a rail battery and a
' strong picquet.

' 6th. At Ebenezer, a redoubt on the water on the
' north side ; a strong picquet at the bridge, two
' strong redoubts, another round the little house near
' the tavern, another down at the ferry ; another on
' the hill, the south side of the south pass, and a ve-
' ry strong picquet ; this place has a good train of
' artillery, and is very strong, more so than Savan-
' nah.

' 7th. Savannah has a redoubt on the road at the
' spring-hill one at each end of the barracks ; another
' down the road that leads to the governor's farm,

' each of which mount two 18 pounders; from each
' redoubt to the other is an abbatis, or a kind of che-
' vaux-de-frise of boughs of trees, to prevent an en-
' emy mounting formed into the town : it is impos-
' sible to tell you the strength of each post, as they
' vary according to circumstances, I believe they
' mean to dispute each post : there were not 250
' regulars in town whilst I was there, and they are
' strung all up the river : there is a good train of ar-
' tillery ; and they have put the town in the posture
' it ought to have been in three years ago.'

' The proceedings of a Court of Inquiry,* held at
Purisburgh, the 13th of March, 1779, by order of
Maj. Gen. Lincoln, and continued by different ad-
journments to the 16th.

' The court being met, the order was produced
and read as follows.

' After Orders, 9th March, 1779.

' A court of inquiry to sit to-morrow morning, to
examine into the affair of the 3d instant, at Brier-
creek, and the conduct of Maj. Gen. J. Ash, relative
to his command there. All witnesses to attend.

....

* The evidences on this court of inquiry, fhow how
wretchedly the militia armies were provided with arms and
accoutrements.

‘ President Brig. Gen. Moultrie,

‘ Gen. Rutherford, Col. Armstrong, Col. Pinckney, Col. Locke, Edmond Hyrne, D. A. General.

‘ Gen. Ash being asked by the President, if he wished to say any thing before the witnesses were examined; answered in the affirmative; and having observed that the court now met had been held at his particular desire, in order to refute some reports highly injurious to his character, proceeded to describe the situation of his camp, between Brier-creek and Savannah river, and about a mile higher than the spot where the brigade had been: the creek was fordable both above and below his camp; and above so narrow in many places, that a tree might have been felled over so as to permit men to pass. The camp which had been fixed upon in the absence of Gen. Ash, by Generals Bryant and Elbert, fronted up the fork; the left nearly touched the creek, and the right reached within about half a mile of the swamp that borders upon Savannah river. In advance about a mile was a field-officers picquet of one hundred men; which had been divided into several smaller ones, with a chain of sentries between each, and advanced sentries to the whole, and in the rear was posted the light infantry, with one brass four pounder near where the bridge had stood; a detachment of the horse, under Major Ross, joined the camp on the 1st of March (Gen. Ash being absent) part of whom had been sent out on the morning of the 3d, the day of the action, in order to reconnoitre the enemy : they were directed to go as far as Hudson's, or near it, the Gen. intending, when he should be reinforced by Rutherford, to attack that post, if there should appear, from their report, any prospect of success : they might plainly have perceived from several proofs, that a considerable corps of the enemy had moved, but did not return to give notice of it ; another body of horse were, as Gen. Ash had been informed by Gen. Elbert, upon his return to camp, on the 2d day, preceding the action, a few miles up Brier-creek ; and it appears since the action, by a witness whom Gen. Ash could produce, that this party, which was under the command of Col. Marberry, not only saw the enemy cross the creek, but even exchanged fires with them, and yet did not send any information of their approach : the first intelligence that Gen. Ash received of the enemy's motions was from an express, that was on his way up to Gen. Williamson's, who had scarcely communicated it, when a message from Col. Smith confirmed it : Col. Smith commanded a party that guarded the baggage about eight miles up the river : Gen. Ash immediately ordered the drums to beat to arms, drew up his men ; who, by fatigue parties, the baggage guard, and absentees, were reduced to about 600 in two lines ; and saw cartridges distribut-

ed among them ; and advanced about a quarter of a
mile to meet the enemy. They came down about
three in the afternoon, in three columns, six abreast;
the centre column which came down the road, at
least (the two other the Gen. could not discern so
plainly) begun to fire at three hundred yards distance, and having displayed when about 150 yards
off, kept up from that time a regular and general
fire, as well with small arms, as with several grass-
hoppers : the first line stood about five minutes
and broke, the second, which was the first to break,
was not at all engaged, but for a moment on the
right. Col. Young who commanded there, having
been ordered to extend to the right, to prevent our
being flanked. Gen. Ash then added, with respect
to his own vindication, that he had no intrenching
tools; that he had been too short a time upon the
ground to become well acquainted with the environs
of it; that the people were totally unprovided with
pouches or cartouch boxes to hold their ammunition
in, nor could he have prevented them from wasting
it, had they been supplied before the action. He acknowledged that he galloped off the field whilst the
Georgians were still engaged ; but adds that it was
in order to get in the front of his own people, with
a view of rallying them, and that finding, after riding
after them near three quarters of a mile, that they
could not be stopped , and that either death or cap-

tivity must be his fate, if he persisted, he had entered the swamp in order to make his escape towards the ferry, over which he had passed the day
before: with regard to his men being so panic struck,
he attributed it to the long fatiguing march they had
undergone; to the scarcity of provisions that had prevailed for many days before; to the total want of all
necessary accoutrements, and to the superior number of the enemy, which he imagines to have been
3,000. Upon being asked whether he heard any
officer say, aloud, that the enemy was turning his
flank, he answered, he heard several, but mentioned
Gen. Bryant in particular.

' MAJOR Dogherty, Gen. Ash's aid-de-camp, was
now called upon, to declare what he knew of the
affair, and particularly of the conduct of Gen. Ash
on the 3d....He had been with Gen. Ash all the preceding part of the day, and was with him when the
news of the enemy's approach arrived, he was immediately dispatched to order Col. Lyttle, with his
infantry, to the field; and then with a message to
Col. Young, the purport of which has been already
adverted to; found every thing in confusion upon
his return; and the general who had appeared cool
and composed in giving his orders, now endeavoring
to rally his men...he adds that the Georgians, and a
small part of the first line were still engaged; but
that the second line was entirely broken, for the

greater part of the men fled, as he believes, without having discharged their pieces.

' MR. Chapman was with the general when the
news arrived, went out to reconnoitre, returned, saw
the men served with cartridges ; saw them break in
a few minutes, and the general attempting to rally
them.

' MAJOR Pointer....He saw Gen. Ash endeavoring
to rally the men, and came up with him as he entered the swamp.

' COL. Perkins....He did not see Gen. Ash ; his
regiment, which was for a few minutes engaged with
the enemy, was entirely broken, when Major Pointer
left the field ; he does not think they had more than
15 minutes notice of the enemy's approach.

' CAPT. Falls....He came up to the general, in
consequence of the order that had been sent to Col.
Lyttle, with whom he was accidentally upon a visit,
having crossed over from Gen. Rutherford's brigade
a few hours before, with 15 light-horse ; was immediately sent out to engage the enemy ; went full
speed, and met them about half a mile of the place
where he had left the army drawn up : The general
appeared cool and composed, though hurried in giving his orders.

[The court adjourned to the 14th, to Mr. Porchers.*]

* The court adjourned to Mr. Porchers, 12 miles higher
up the river, for the convenience of the witnesses who were at
Rutherford's camp.

[The court met according to adjournment the 14th of March.]

' MR. John More, a volunteer, with Capt. Fall's light-horse....He saw the general endeavoring to stop several of the men; after the whole broke, saw him also gallop off, as he (Mr. More) imagined to make his escape.

' THE above witnesses had been all examined at the desire of Gen. Ash, who saying that there was no one besides present he wished to call upon, but Gen. Bryant could probably give some information : Gen. Bryant was accordingly desired by the president to relate what he knew of the matter....Gen. Bryant, said that on Saturday, the 26th of Feb. he marched towards the lower part of Brier-creek; that he had pointed out, as his opinion, the impropriety of encamping close upon the bridge ; that he thought the general had coincided ; but that the army, never-theless moved down, and encamped in an old field; the second line being at the distance of about 200 yards from the bridge ; this he imagines to have been in consequence of the generals orders; as he saw the brigade quarter-master, who would have acted from his own authority, laying out the encampment and assigning to the officers their different stations ; a detachment of 400 were sent out that evening under Col. Caswell to surprise a picquet of the enemy's. They passed the creek in a flat near where the bridge had been ; that on the 28th, which was Sunday, Gen. Ash left camp about 10 o'clock in the morning to meet Gen. Lincoln at Williamson's, but without (having crossed near the Two-sisters-ferry) giving him (Gen. Bryant) any orders : that the command now devolving upon him, he called a council of his field officers, and determined for several reasons in conjunction with them, to move the camp a mile higher up the fork. He could have wished to have encamped across the road ; but consulted the convenience of getting water on the left, so that his right did not reach within 200 yards of it : he immediately fixed places about three quarters of a mile in front for the picquets, which consisted of a field-officer, and 100 men, whilst the camp was further secured by a chain of sentries from the creek swamp across the road, and down the road to the light infantry in the rear ; these precautions they thought sufficient for that evening. On Monday, the 1st of March, Col. Williams, who was field-officer of the day, acquainted him (Gen. Bryant) that the enemy, both horse and foot, had been on their lines all night ; Gen. Bryant upon this, doubled all the picquets, but had no horse to send out till about 12 o'clock, when Maj. Ross was prevailed upon, though his men had suffered very much for want of provisions, and their horses for want of forage. He sent out a party of sixty men, to patrole in the neighborhood of Paris'-Mill,

the remainder of the day, and all next night, upon
Gen. Bryant expressing to him these apprehensions
of the enemy crossing some where there-about. On
Tuesday, the 2d of March; about 12 o'clock in
the forenoon Gen. Ash returned, and was waited
upon in an hour or two after, who introduced Maj.
Ross to him, acquainting Gen. Ash of the party
that was sent out the day before, and of their having
made no discoveries : As Gen. Bryant left Maj. Ross
with the Gen. he knew not what orders the Gen. may
have given him, but is certain that no horse were
sent out that night; and well remembers upon his
urging to Gen. Ash the danger that might result
from it, this was his answer : 'that the horse then
'in camp were so worn down with fatigue, that many
' of the riders are unarmed ; but that, if the enemy
'did not surprise them that evening, he would take
' care to have the country well patroled for the fu-
' ture:' here Gen. Bryant added how excessively uneasy he had been, when he considered the long fatiguing march the men had undergone ; how wretchedly they were equipped, and that the enemy were
ever receiving the best intelligence. Wednesday,
the 3d, (this was the day of the action) Gen. Bryant
said he was sent for, about 3 o'clock, P. M. by Gen.
Ash, and he heard the intelligence received from
Col. Smith, and immediately concured with Gen.
Elbert and the Gen. that it was advisable to march

out and meet the enemy: the brigadier quarter-master being out the way, Gen. Ash desired him (Gen. Bryant) to order the drums to beat to arms, and to see the men supplied with cartridges: before the latter part of his orders could be well executed, the picquets were fired upon: as the right of the line was some distance from the road, Gen. Bryant was apprehensive of the enemy's marching down that way and turning their right flank, and ordered, upon his expressing his apprehension to Gen. Ash, a regiment that way, to prevent it; in consequence of which Col. Perkins' regiment was ordered to move towards the road, as no alarm posts had been assigned: Col. Perkins found the Georgians in his front, and was obliged to place his regiment on their right: Col. Perkins', and one or two other regiments, were advancing towards the road, after having gone a straight line, about 100 yards, and not more from the place of encampment; when the enemy appeared in sight, three regiments fired pretty smartly, for a few minutes; Gen. Bryant saw the left break very soon, and Gen. Ash riding across the bottom through the men, in order, as he believes, to rally them; at this time the right was not yet broke, but the whole very soon gave way, and in great confusion, towards the creek: Gen. Bryant seeing them incline to the right, instead of going to the left, which he knew to be the only way of escaping, and having in tain endeavored to rally them did not follow them any longer, but took to the left, in order to make his escape: Gen. Bryant added, that he had received no orders with respect to forming the line: That what he had said of the enemy turning their flanks, was not aloud: that he believes the men's knowledge of their situation, added to the causes the general had mentioned, made them retreat so suddenly; and that he agreed with the general, as to the impractability of fortifying themselves; the want of boats, and the impossibility of rallying the men; he added moreover, that there was nothing like surprize or flutter about the general, and that he believed every thing was done which the circumstances admitted of.

'LIEUT. Col. Young said he had been formed to the right of the second line, and was ordered by the general, to extend the line, in order to prevent the enemy flanking: that he never saw the general afterwards; and that his men were drawn up some time before the enemy came down, and appeared eager to engage: that they soon broke, however, except 25, with whom he joined Col. Lyttle, and marched to the edge of the swamp.

'LIEUT. Col. Williams said he was on the right of the first line; he saw Gen. Ash once, and once only, which was when the firing first begun: the second line was soon in a great confusion, and got very soon too near to the first: to the reasons already mentioned why the men were so panic struck; he added, that the cartridges given out, did not, many of them, suit the calibers of the guns: he does not think they had above 15 minutes notice, and remembers Gen Ash saying the enemy were only after their baggage; when their approach was mentioned every precaution was not, in his opinion, taken against a surprize, as 200 horse had been in camp that morning, many of whom might have been employed as videts.

' Col. Clinch, of Eaton's, was on the left of the second line; his attempt to rally them in vain, answered by several whom he spoke to, that their general had left them, and it was time to shift for themselves: imagined that there was about 15 minutes notice, before the action, and did not see the general.

' Major Blount, of Casewell's, was on the left of the first line, which broke immediately after the second line: did not see Gen. Ash at all: believes there was about 15 minutes notice; and that the men were not yet all served with ammunition when the picquets were fired upon: not above 20 or 30 of his regiment discharged their pieces: he added that he joined Col. Clinch in the swamp, whom he heard exclaim against Gen. Ash, in the strongest terms, and asserted that Gen. Ash was a coward, and had ordered a retreat. Here Col. Clinch begged leave

to observe, that what he had said, had been collected from the common men, and neither built upon his own knowledge, or any others officer's information.

' COL. Eaton had no notice of the enemy's approach till they fired upon the picquets ;...drew up
in his encampment, and ordered to form two deep ;
...saw Gen. Ash once, but does not remember particularly what time ;...remembers very well that there
were no videts a-head of the picquets, and no light-
horse up at Paris'-mill that day, although it was the
general opinion of the camp that if the enemy did
cross at all it would be there.

' LIEUT. Col. Brevard said he had crossed with
Capt. Fall, and corroborated that gentleman's testimony : he said, moreover, that he saw a column of
the enemy coming down the road, in very close order, six a-breast ; he heard Gen. Ash say to some
one near the brass field-piece, that it was too late to
rally any of the men ; and adds, that the greatest
part were far a-head of General Ash, flying to the
swamp.

' MAJ. M'Lewain saw Gen. Ash once, between
the lines, but did not see him again till near the
swamp ; and remembers not to have seen many
people before him in the retreat. Mr. Carter was a
mile from camp when drums beat to arms, found
all in confusion on his arrival, and saw the general

but once at first. Maj. Sherlock said, that the notice they had of the enemy's approach was about fifteen minutes; that they marched out of their encampment before the cartridges were well served
out to the men; that they advanced one hundred
yards, then inclined to the right ; that proper posts
had not been assigned to the officers, nor would
they have had time to take them ; that he saw Gen.
Ash once at the head of Perkins' regiment, but that
the privates complained as they were going off, that
the Gen. had left them.

'LIEUT. Patton, of Capt. Fall's light-horse, confirms what Capt. Fall had said, and added, that the
picquets were absolutely surprised, and never fired at
all; that some of the sentries were found asleep
by the enemy, and that the firing which was heard
in camp, and attributed by several officers to be the
picquets, was between the enemy and them. This
Col. Brevard also asserted.

'GEN. Ash having heard the gentlemen above-
mentioned, from Gen. Bryant, go through their evidences, and having also heard a paper read, which
had been drawn up by Gen. Moultrie, and signed
by both him and Gen. Rutherford, and contained
the substance of what those gentlemen remembered
of the conference at the white house,* begged leave

* Mr. Williamson's.

to make a few observations; and began with re-
marking upon Gen. Bryant's evidence; that it was
too late to change the place of encampment the evening he arrived near the creek; but he is positive,
notwithstanding what may be asserted to the contrary, that he did, upon his departure from camp, on
the 28th February, leave verbal orders with Gen.
Bryant, to move the camp higher up the fork; and
to see that all proper guards and sentries were placed for the security of the army: adding, that he
would be back as soon as possible: he returned to
camp on Tuesday the 2d March, about 12 in the
forenoon; but being much taken up with some necessary dispatches, did not see Gen. Bryant till an
hour or two after. Gen. Bryant then informed him
of the parties that had been seen upon the lines all
night; who were as he believes nothing but horse
thieves; and also of the light horse that had been
detached to Paris'-mill; them Gen. Ash says, he
understood from General Bryant, were not only to
patrole but to take post there; as to the party
that was sent out on the morning of the 3d;
General Ash expected them back so early as
to be able to send them on some other service that
day; though he is certain, that had there been a day,
nay, even a week's notice of the enemy's approach;
the confusion among his men would have been the
same: Gen. Ash observed, that he was the first that

proposed they should march and meet the enemy, and asserted, that not a moment's time was lost after receiving the intelligence : with regard to what he said of their coming after the baggage only, it was before Col. Smith's message arrived : that what Gen. Bryant said of the danger of their flanks being turned, it was aloud, and when the action was already begun : that a post had been assigned the Georgians, which was to repair to the centre, whilst the other regiments had been ordered to draw up in their encampments (though not in general orders) and that as to any further order of battle being given, it was first necessary to observe the enemy's motions ; which his people did not give him time to do ; he well remembers their having been a space of about 70 or 80 yards between the two lines when they were first formed : Gen. Ash then added, in answer to two or three questions made him by the court ; that his orders with respect to crossing the river, were indeed discretionary, and he believes he should not have crossed the river had he not been advised by Gen. Williamson, and importuned by his own officers ; that in what he had said to Gens. Lincoln, Moultrie, and Rutherford, of his security at Brier-creek, he looked forward to the large and speedy reinforcements he had been promised, and to a supply of entrenching tools ; that he was unacquainted with the nature of the ground, having been

but very little time upon it, and may naturally have
been mistaken in his account of it, at the time of
Mr. Williamson's conference above mentioned : and
lastly, that the generals must have misunderstood
him, with respect to the number of boats, as he only said, by all he can recollect, that he expected
several large boats from Augusta with corn, which
might be detained for the purpose of transporting the
army over the river, if necessary.

[The court adjourned.]

[Tuesday the 16th, the court met according to adjournment, at Mr. Porcher's house.]

'Opinion of the court.

'The court having maturely considered the matter before them, are of opinion that Gen. Ash did not
take all the necessary precautions which he ought to
have done to secure his camp, and obtain timely intelligence of the movements and approach of the enemy ; but they do entirely acquit him of every impu-
tation of a want of personal courage, in the affair at
Brier-creek, and think he remained in the field as
long as prudence and duty required.

Signed,

'WILLIAM MOULTRIE, president.'

[The court adjourned, sine die.]

'THE Court of Inquiry, of which Major Huger
'is president, have reported, that, on a thorough in-

‘ vestigation of the matter laid before them, The
‘ court are of opinion that Capt. De Treville, in spik-
‘ ing up the guns, and evacuating the fort, at Port-
‘ Royal Island, did no more than his duty, and rather
‘ deserves praise than censure for his conduct on this
‘ occasion.’

Capt. De Treville had the command of the fort,
with about 20 continentals, and a number of militia ;
when the enemy appeared, the militia all left him;
he, therefore, spiked up the guns and blew up the
fort.

———

LETTER FROM COL. CHARLES PINCKNEY.

‘ CHARLESTOWN, March 18th, 1779.

‘ DEAR SIR,

‘ THIS being my birth day, and having reached
‘ forty-seven years, and consequently going down
‘ hill, as the saying is; my ideas since I got up this
‘ morning have been very serious, and full of thought
‘ and meditation, on the transitory state of things
‘ here, both moral and political. With respect
‘ to the former, may my future days be follow-
‘ ing the example of good old Isaac, in his even
‘ of life ; and with respect to the latter, may our
‘ present struggles for our rights and liberties,
‘ be crowned with the most happy success ; and be
‘ attended with the loss of as few lives as possible,
‘ especially in cool blood. The lives that are lost

‘ amidst the conflict in the field for contending lau-
‘ rels, with a few bright strokes of military philoso-
‘ phy, are easily and triumphantly got over; but,
‘ alas! the unhappy who suffer publicly; perhaps
‘ from mistaken principles (as in my humble opin-
‘ ion two poor fellows* did yesterday) the sad morti-
‘ fications and miseries of death, amidst a gaping
‘ crowd, occasion so pungent a sorrow to some dis-
‘ positions, that it requires much time to get the
‘ better of it. Our old friend M——, in his day,
‘ you know, used to say, such milky dispositions al-
‘ ways gave themselves a great deal of unnecessa-
‘ ry grief and trouble; and that for his part he ne-
‘ ver cared much about human events, but always
‘ laughed at them; how true he spoke I leave you
‘ to determine, from some anecdotes of his life
‘ within our memory; which to me, and I suppose
‘ to you also, seemed then to breathe a different
‘ idea inwardly, and that he really had his tender
‘ feelings as well as those he censured: I own these
‘ tendernesses have their inconveniences, and are
‘ now unfashionable, but they are so fascinating to
‘ me, that they may be faulty; I cannot cure the
‘ distemper, and you must my friend excuse me....
‘ The sad spectacle of yesterday, and the necessary
‘ reflections thereon, with respect to the evil con-

....

* Tweed and Groundwater.

' sequences that may possibly arise from retaliation,
' and which, I think, might have been avoided with-
' out hurting the cause we are struggling for, makes
' many serious countenances ; but though I much
' fear it, God grant they may be the last examples
' of this kind ; for surely, between you and I, whilst
' the enemy forbear to make similar examples, com-
' mon policy, with defference to the opinions of our
' superiors, ought to direct us to be passive there-
' in : but enough of this disagreeable subject.

> ' Yours, &c.

> ' CHARLES PINCKNEY.

' Brig. Gen. MOULTRIE.'

> ' March 19th.

' SINCE writing the foregoing I have received
' your favor of the 15th, and am glad to hear of the
' enemy bending their force downwards to Savannah ;
' even though they should take a trip to our borders ;
' especially as you say, you are of opinion we should
' manage them better there than where they are,
' which opinion I think just ; this movement I think
' should alter the orders for our grand camp at O-
' rangeburgh, and place it nearer the capital for fear
' of a coup-de-main, I think you military men call
' it : and perhaps may be so soon : but at present
' it is the ruling opinion that the other place is near
' enough to receive succors from, in due time,

' should they be wanted. I wish it may be so....
' The drafts from Richardson's battalion were first or-
' dered to join your post ; but when the enemy were
' at Augusta, those orders were altered, and the
' drafts were ordered first to join Williamson, as
' there appeared the greatest danger, were subject,
' nevertheless to Gen. Lincolns orders, to move
' downwards if he thought proper, and as these or-
' ders, I believe, are now in force, and the danger
' about Augusta not so great as it has been, no
' doubt you will be joined by this body of men,
' whenever the Gen. thinks proper; and consequent-
' ly, there can be no intricacy in these orders as
' you seem to hint ; but they are perfectly consistent.
' You imagine, and intimate, that we cannot keep se-
' crets, but I assure you, you are much mistaken :
' however, events will establish the facts, depend on
' it, my good sir, our best and most zealous endea-
' vors, are used for the public service : but, alas, we
' daily meet with so many untoward circumstances,
' and distressing bars to our well meant designs,
' that though they do not and cannot stop our per-
' severance, yet they clog and hinder our operations
' much. I dare say you military gentlemen have
' also your difficulties, but let us not despair, things
' will be better with us by and by. The governor
' with his suite, is to set out for the grand camp
' on Sunday or Monday next. By some deserters,

' the governor examined yesterday, who lately came
' from the enemy, they assert that the enemy are
' actually 5,000 strong, and expect reinforcements ; if
' so, I believe there can be little reason to think they
' are going quite off, as you hint, and hope we
' shall take your other hint, and endeavor to have
' 2 or 3,000 men in and about town, to prepare to
' defend ourselves against the worst. Suppose you
' were to send Gen. Ash, or any of his brigade of
' influence, about prevailing on these people* to re-
' main in town one or two months, on our militia
' pay, for the sole defence of the town : do not you
' think some good may arise from it ? if you think
' so, pray do it, and let me know your thoughts
' thereon, in time, that I may be prepared here to
' do the needful, to give them the necessary en-
' couragement : I really think good quarters, good
' pay, and proper persuasion might influence at least
' some hundreds of these people to act in town for
' the above time. Paulaski is certainly not far off,
' and the North-Carolina relief, and our friends from
' Virginia are as certainly hastening to our succor.

' I am, &c.

' CHARLES PINCKNEY.

' Brig. Gen. MOULTRIE.'

....

* Their time for service was almost out, and they talked of
going home to North-Carolina.

LETTER FROM COL. PINCKNEY.

' CHARLESTOWN, March 22th, 1779.

' DEAR SIR,

' I WROTE you lately; since which I have re-
' ceived your favor of the 19th instant, and am glad to
' hear that the enemy do not very soon intend a des-
' cent on Port-Royal, as we had reason to believe
' they would have done, from news we have received
' in town for several preceeding days, which was
' generally believed, as it came from Gen. Bull's in-
' formation. We are in hopes you are now gathering
' in force; it will oblige the enemy to stay within
' their own new acquired lines, without daring to
' act offensively beyond them. I heard last night,
' that the continental chest has received a fresh sup-
' ply of a million of dollars, and that another is said
' to be getting ready to follow. His excellency has
' been obliged to postpone his setting off for his
' camp until to-morrow noon: I am told that there
' are not above one thousand men in that camp; but
' that their number, in a few days, will be increased
' to double; and in due time, if orders are complied
' with, the given number (5,000) fixed on, may be
' there: be they more or less, I wish the camp had
' been ordered near Charlestown; and I in vain ur-
' ged it should be so, but could not prevail: If you
' join me in opinion, I wish you would write the go-
' vernor on it; for surely the present encampment

' at Orangeburgh, is, considering our present circum-
' stances of expecting an attack here, much too far
' to give that necessary assistance that might be wan-
' ted. I thank you for the sentences of the courts
' of inquiry of Gen. Ash, and Capt. De Treville, and
' am glad the gentlemen are acquitted in the manner
' specified : the former gentleman (who must cer-
' tainly be a good man, by his quitting an easy sta-
' tion, as he did, to assist us who were in distress) by
' this animadversive sentence will thereby be more
' cautious in future, and consequently be the better
' general, and so add to his own character : and the
' latter by meeting, though slightly with praise, in-
' stead of censure, for his supposed fault, must by
' this balmy sentence, be so animated, to act here-
' after with a becoming dignity, that he will so there-
' by, add to his character : and thus these decisions
' from their great wisdom, and happy tendency, will
' promote and advance the public good; the great
' end of all courts of justice.
        ' I am, &c.
                        ' CHARLES PINCKNEY.
' Brig. Gen. MOULTRIE.'

LETTER FROM COL. CHARLES PINCKNEY.
        ' CHARLESTOWN, 28th March, 1779.
' DEAR SIR,
        ' IT is now some days since I wrote you; not for

' want of inclination to write, but for matter to write
' on, that would be new to you ; however in the in-
' terim I have two of your favors, for which I thank
' you. The first brought me the disagreeable ac-
' count of our gallies being taken by the enemy,
' which is only a common event of the pro and con
' in the fortune of war, and therefore not difficult to
' reconcile. But, my friend, I cannot so easily get
' over the principle on which the plan of attack (so
' full of dangerous consequences to our cause, and
' from which so little could have arisen, had we been
' successful) was formed as a wise step ; but sup-
' pose my doubts on the occasion must arise from
' my ignorance in, rather than my knowledge of, the
' military science: I doubt not when you can find
' time you will convince me of my error in judg-
' ment. The second has raised our anxiety for the
' event of things important, by your information of
' both armies being in motion ; and it is our happi-
' ness to think, that by a defensive plan, the interior
' country will be well protected, from the number
' and bravery of our citizens and friends now in the
' different camps, which joined together, would
' make a considerable army. You wish the post you
' just now left, may be reinforced with militia ; this,
' in my opinion, cannot be conveniently done, other-
' wise than by detachments from the grand camp at

'Orangeburgh, under the governor, with whom no
'doubt, you will exchange a letter on the subject:
'he and his suite are now, and have been for se-
'veral days past there, and it is said his camp is
'growing very strong, but I cannot inform you of
'particulars. Our town is full of strangers* from
'all parts, which must come in by land, as our
'communication by water, is, and has been, for
'some time past, in a manner shut up: many no
'doubt are friends, but we have reason to think
'some are enemies; many of them are full of conti-
'nental money, good, bad, and indifferent, or not now
'passable, and gave the most unheard of prices,† for
'slaves and all kinds of merchandize. Our poor
'are at the last stage of patriotic patience under
'their present sufferings, for the scarcity, and high
'prices of beef, rum, sugar and necessaries of life;
'and upon the whole, my dear sir, we are put to our
'shifts to remedy the evil: to-morrow is fixed up-
'on as a day extraordinary to discuss and determine
'on something leading that way; pray God our re-
'solutions may be attended with some success. Our
'works at the back of the town are going on brisk-

....

* These were post-riders, from the northward.

† The post-riders being acquainted with the depreciation of
the money, before we could possibly know of it, brought millions of dollars with them, which they gave for our property,
to the ruin of a number of our honest and industrious citizens.

' ly, and we shall soon be inclosed, when I fancy
' Charlestown will be declared to be a garrison
' town, and proper steps taken, as far as lays in
' our power, to reap the advantages of such an
' establishment, whilst our enemies are so near us,
' and so formidable. There are a number of British
' deserters still in town, loitering about in their red
' coats; and we really do not know what to do with
' them. I wish the general, together with yourself
' and friends, would give us a hint what would be
' best to be done with them. The circulation of the
' continental bills, of the 20th May, 1777, and the
' 11th April, 1778, agreeable to the order of Con-
' gress and our executive, is now intirely stopped at
' our state treasury: this convulsion will, I fear, sen-
' sibly affect the poor and indigent: to alleviate the
' inconveniency of the poor in this respect, a num-
' ber of gentlemen, very able and well disposed, are
' forming a society, to take off their small sums, for
' a full and valuable consideration. I have almost
' filled my usual quantity of paper; I therefore, af-
' ter once more hinting to you, it is the wish of your
' real friends, that you were sent down to Charles-
' town, to preside, assist, and manage the defence
' of the same.

' I am, &c.

' CHARLES PINCKNEY.

' Brig. Gen. MOULTRIE.'

LETTER TO COL. CHARLES PINCKNEY.

'BLACK-SWAMP, April 6th, 1779.

' DEAR SIR,

' I RECEIVED yours this day, dated the 28th of
' last month; and in answer to what you say, relative
' to the principle on which the plan of attack was
' made; I assure you it seemed to have the fairest
' prospect of success; and had it succeeded would
' have been of infinite advantage to us; I will give
' you my reasons : the enemy had stationed their gal-
' ley and sloop at Yamassee bluff, opposite Aber-
' corne, where they commanded the pass down the
' river ; and in that situation they received all our
' deserters before we could overtake them, whilst a
' great number of negroes in this part of the coun-
' try got over to them in spite of our care ; it seem-
' ed absolutely necessary, therefore, to run some
' risk to remove them from thence, which had we
' succeeded in, we would have immediately followed
' up the blow upon the post at Abercorne ; which
' could not have failed of success ; as we had plen-
' ty of boats to have dropped down the river, with
' 1,000 or 1,500 men ; this manœuvre would have
' changed the face of affairs, and brought the enemy
' down the country ; but ' it is not in mortals to
' command success.' I hope after these reasons you
' will not think our plan very absurd : besides, as

' we thought* it necessary to move our camp to this
' part of the country,† we should have been obliged
' to destroy the gallies. These several reasons make
' it warrantable, in military matters, to run some
' risk. The Fabian maxim does not agree alto-
' gether with American dispositions and undisciplin-
' ed troops ; they soon grow tired and desert ; too
' much of which we have sensibly felt ; upwards of
' 100 men having left us, since we took the field,
' and a great many of those gone over to the ene-
' my ; now, would it not be better to amuse them
' by skirmishes ? where we have an equal chance of
' lessening their numbers, than to have our men go
' off to them ; by which means they get reinforced
' and we weakened ; the choice I leave to your own
' judgment. I am glad to find you so sanguine in
' your expectations of our militia. I wish we could
' see something favorable from them to give us
' spirits ; I, that seldom am out of hopes, am yet
' dejected on seeing their movements so very slow :
' consider, Ash's, and Rutherford's people‡ go off
' on Saturday, and we shall be left here by our-
' selves (continentals) if the enemy are enterprizing,

....

* We lost the Congress galley with 70 men, and the Lee
galley with 34 men.

† Twenty-five miles higher up the river.

‡ About 2,000 men.

' I know what will be the consequence. I am glad
' to hear the executive authority have at last taken
' upon themselves to endeavor to correct the many
' abuses that have arisen in Charlestown lately; I
' hope it will have the desired effect. I have spoke
' to Gen. Lincoln relative to the British deserters;
' he, as well as myself, is surprised that they are
' suffered to remain in Charlestown, as they all had
' passes to go on to the northward, some as far as
' Philadelphia; nay, they were ordered to go to
' North-Carolina, and that may be seen by all their
' passes, which they should be made to produce....
' Gen. Lincoln, on my informing him what you said
' about them, desired me to write to you, and he
' would write to Mr. Bee* on the subject, to order
' them all out of the state to proceed northwardly.

' I AM pleased to hear you are fortifying Charles-
' town; it is best to be prepared for war; I dare say
' you will all sleep with more ease when you have
' an idea of being in greater security: I hope we
' never shall have occasion to try the goodness of
' the works: should you be attacked you may de-
' pend some of us will hasten to your assistance;
' we could soon mount a number of horsemen, so as
' to throw in strong reinforcements in a few days.
' This stoppage of the continental money will be a

* The lieut. governor (the governor being out of town.)

'great hinderance to our army, as the Georgia
'chest has between 2 and 3,000,000 dollars in it,
'of those that cannot pass.

    'I am, &c.

        'WILLIAM MOULTRIE.'

LETTER TO GOV. RUTLEDGE.

'BLACK-SWAMP, HEAD-QUARTERS, April 16th, 1779.
'DEAR SIR,

    'I HAVE the honor to inform you, that we ar-
'rived at our camp two days ago; nothing extraor-
'dinary have happened since we left it: they are
'much pleased to hear of the reinforcement (1,000)
'you have sent, and that they are on their march;
'we expect them here to-morrow. I hope ere long
'you will send us such another, so as to enable us
'to go on with the plan, which Col. Pinckney and
'myself informed you of when I was last in Charles-
'town; which was to leave 1200 men to guard this
'part of the country; whilst we marched up to join
'Gen. Williamson, and come down the other side
'of the river, and drive the enemy from Georgia:
'this I think can be easily done, especially when
'joined by the North-Carolinians and Paulaski, who,
'I am told, was seen 10 miles from Georgetown on
'the 9th instant: as I did not know, when I was at
'Orangeburgh, what had passed between your ex-

' cellency and Gen. Lincoln, relative to the sending
' each his orders to Gen. Williamson, without the
' other's knowledge, I beg leave to suggest the im-
' propriety of such a measure, and whether it may
' not be productive of ill consequences, as one or two
' at present occurs.

' In your orders to Gen. Williamson, of the 5th
' instant, you direct him to make incursions into
' Georgia, whenever favorable opportunities offer,
' for harassing or annoying the enemy, whom he is
' to distress, to the utmost of his power : the parties
' making such incursions, are to destroy all the cat-
' tle, horses, provisions, and carriages they meet with
' in Georgia. This is contradictory to the idea held
' up to those unhappy ones who could not possi-
' bly get off with their little property in this camp,
' which was, that they should remain quiet at home
' until we should be able to cross the river and give
' them protection : what must become of the poor
' widows, orphans, and helpless old men ? should the
' order be indiscriminately put into execution? an-
' other part of your order says, ' you will order the
' Georgia militia, and other troops under your com-
' mand, to join you whenever you thought it neces-
' sary.' This part of the order, in my opinion, must
' be void of itself; as no orders from any person in
' this state, but Gen. Lincoln, can have any effect,
' especially as those people have put themselves in-

‘ tirely under his command ; and he has paid them
‘ to this time. I must beg your excellency to excuse
‘ the liberty I have taken of communicating my sen-
‘ timents to you on these matters ; it is done with a
‘ view to prevent any clashing of orders, or misun-
‘ derstanding. I am sorry to inform you that our
‘ desertions still continue. We have lost thirty in
‘ a fortnight, and all from the post at Purisburgh ;
‘ and have only ten in return, from the enemy. The
‘ prisoners sent us from Georgia, in exchange for
‘ those sent from Charlestown, are quite emaciated,
‘ and some of them reduced so low as to be carried
‘ from the boats to their quarters ; they complain
‘ highly of their ill treatment ; they say they were
‘ fed upon condemned pork and oatmeal, which the
‘ hogs would not eat ; sometimes (officers and all)
‘ were served with seven days fresh pork at one time,
‘ which was quite spoiled after two days ; our men
‘ die fast on board the prison-ships, are carried
‘ a-shore on the marsh, and buried so slightly as to
‘ be a horrid sight for those left alive, who see the
‘ buzzards picking the bones of their fellow soldiers.
‘ Does not this demand retaliation and a prison-ship ?
‘ I cannot help being surprised at Provost’s modesty,
‘ in complaining to Mr. Williamson of the ill usage
‘ of his people. Gen. Lincoln intends having the af-

' fidavits of our people taken, and remonstrating to
' Gen. Provost on their ill usage.

' I am, &c.

' WILLIAM MOULTRIE.'

———

LETTER TO COL. CHARLES PINCKNEY.

'BLACK-SWAMP, April 16th, 1779.

'DEAR SIR,

'I HAVE the pleasure to inform you, that I re-
'turned from Orangeburgh* three days ago, after a
'ride of two hundred and twenty miles, a very fa-
'tiguing jaunt, both to ourselves and horses, we
'were (Mr. Kinlock and myself) gone six days; one
'day we staid with the Governor, the others in tra-
'veling. We expect Col. Simons here to-morrow,
'with one thousand men of all ranks: this will be a
'reinforcement to us that will be very acceptable.
'The Governor has promised more as soon as they
'can be collected. I was sorry to see so few† left
'at Orangeburgh after this detachment marched off;
'though Col. Neal lay about four miles off, with
'two hundred and eighty men of his regiment, and
'was to march in that morning. Whilst I was there
'I could see the governor had a great deal of trouble,

....

* ' I was requested to go there by Gen. Lincoln, to have some
' conference with the Governor, upon a plan of operation.

† Three or four hundred.

' and I wish his zeal may not cause him to commit
' some improprieties. I think I see matters brewing
' that may bring on misunderstandings between the
' Governor and Gen. Lincoln ; such as orders issued
' from two commanders ; which may perhaps run
' retrograde to each other ; this may be of dangerous
' consequences at this critical juncture ; I shall not
' enter into particulars ; should it go further you
' shall hear. I am, &c.

' WILLIAM MOULTRIE.'

COPY OF GOV. RUTLEDGE'S ORDER TO GENERAL
WILLIAMSON.

' ORANGEBURGH, April 5th, 1779.
' SIR,

' I DESIRE you will embody as many more men of
' the Ninety-six regiment, as that you may have 1000
' rank and file from those regiments on duty. You
' will keep your force collected as much as possible,
' but order incursions into Georgia ; whenever a
' favorable opportunity offers for harrassing or annoy-
' ing the enemy, whom you are to distress to the ut-
' most of your power by the parties making such
' incursions, and such parties are to destroy all the
' cattle, horses, provisions, and carriages they meet
' with in Georgia. You will order the Georgia mi-
' litia, and other troops in that state, under your
' command, to join you when you find it necessary.

‘ You will use your best endeavors to prevent inter-
‘ course between the enemy and the inhabitants of
‘ this state ; and guard particularly against spies in
‘ and about your camp ; whom, if any should be
‘ detected, you will cause immediately to be hanged.
‘ You will order the prisoners of war, those who are
‘ accused of sedition, now in Ninety-six goal, to be
‘ safely conducted under a sufficient guard to this
‘ place.*   All those who have been tried and con-
‘ demned with the prisoners of war immediately.
‘ And those who may be tried, immediately after
‘ conviction.

‘ JOHN RUTLEDGE.’

ABOUT this time Lieut. Col. Provost sent a proposal to Gen. Williamson, to suffer a particular part
of the inhabitants of Georgia to remain at home unmolested by either side ; which proposal Gen. Williamson sent to Gov. Rutledge for his approbation...
when he received the following letter :

‘ ORANGEBURGH, April 11th, 1779.

‘ SIR,
   ‘ LIEUT. Col. Provost’s proposition of a tempo-
‘ rary neutrality, for a part of Georgia, is really too

....

* The prisoners were ordered to Orangeburgh, as a place
of greater security.

'absurd, and ridiculous to require a moments con-
'sideration: Indeed it scarce merits an answer; how-
'ever, as you have promised, I presume you will
'give him one; which need be nothing more than
'that you are expressly enjoined not to agree to it,
'for I desire that you will not relax a tittle in the
'executions of my instructions of the 5th instant,
'which I delivered to you here, viz. to order incur-
'sions into Georgia, whenever favorable opportunities
'offer for harrassing and annoying the enemy, whom
'you are to distress to the utmost of your power, by
'the parties making such incursions; and such par-
'ties are to destroy all the cattle, horses, provisions
'and carriages they meet with in Georgia. Instead
'of relaxing, I would have you as soon as possible
'put it out of the enemy's power to collect or secure
'cattle, horses, provisions, boats, or carriages, which
'is to gain time, to reingage the Indians (who, I
'hope, are sent off) to join ours: this appears to
'me, to be Lieut. Col. Provost's object.

'I am, &c.   JOHN RUTLEDGE.
'Gen. WILLIAMSON.'

A LITTLE before this time Gen. Lincoln had sent
into Georgia privately to desire those who had remained there and could not get away, to be quiet
until we could relieve them, and they should not be
molested by our army.

LETTER TO COL. C. PINCKNEY.

'April 18th, 1779.

'DEAR SIR,

'I WROTE you on the 15th instant, in which I
'mentioned, 'I think I see matters brewing that
'may bring on misunderstandings between some :'
'since which, I am happy to inform you, that all
'will be well again; and that we have now a pros-
'pect of opening the campaign in a fortnight with
'success, according to our old plan, which I men-
'tioned to you when last in town: which was to
'cross the river with five or six thousand men; and
'leave 1200 to guard this part of the country: this
'last command I am told is to fall to my lot; I am
'to be left here, if the enemy should make any mo-
'tions towards Charlestown, to march immediately
'to its assistance: it may be an active part of the
'army, or it may not, just as the matter turns up.

'I am, &c.

'WILLIAM MOULTRIE.'

'A Council of general Officers, held at Head Quarters, Black-swamp, April 19th, 1779.

'Present....Maj. Gen. Lincoln, Brigadiers Moultrie, Huger, and Sumner.

'GEN. Lincoln informed the council, that the
number of men in camp, with those at Gen. Williamson's camp, and five hundred promised from

Orangeburgh, and seven hundred from North-Carolina now in this state, amounted to five thousand men; and desired their opinion, whether after leaving one thousand here and at Purisburgh, it would be adviseable to collect the remainder near to Augusta, cross Savannah river, take some strong ground in Georgia; prevent, if possible, the enemy receiving supplies from the back part of the country, circumscribe their limits, prevent their junction with the unfriendly, and savages in Georgia, and in the back part of the state.

' The council are of opinion the measure is rational, and do therefore advise it.

' Signed,

' B. LINCOLN,

' WM. MOULTRIE,

' IS. HUGER,

' JETHRO SUMNER.'

ABOUT this time Capt. Morgan arrived from St. Eustatia, with a fresh supply of arms and ammunition which were much wanted; we could not have moved any where without them, as we lost, at the affair at Brier-creek, upwards of one thousand stand of arms; and we were obliged almost always to arm all the reinforcements that came from North-Carolina.

LETTER FROM LIEUT. GOV. BEE.

' CHARLESTOWN, April 11th, 1779.

' DEAR GENERAL,

' I RECEIVED yours by Capt. Prevaux, and wish
' we were strong enough to spare the whole regi-
' ment ; to you who so well know the importance of
' Fort Moultrie, I need only mention the impropriety
' of garrisoning it with militia, or recruits intirely ;
' which would be the case if any more of the se-
' cond regiment are sent away ; as it is, I think the
' garrison too weak already. If the enemy should
' make any movements this way by water, I think
' your presence in Charlestown, would be full as use-
' ful as where you are : but of this you and the Gen.
' are the best judges.

' I am, &c.

' THOMAS BEE.

' Brig. Gen. MOULTRIE.'

———

LETTER TO LIEUT. GOV. BEE.

' BLACK-SWAMP, April 20th, 1779.

' DEAR SIR,

' I RECEIVED yours, and agree with you intirely,
' that Prevaux's company could not be spared from
' town : as it is probable we may make some mo-
' tions soon, it will also put the enemy in motion ;
' I have therefore thought proper to order Colonel
' Marion down to Fort Moultrie, as I well know the

' importance of that post, and that it should not be
' left without a field-officer: I shall be left at this
' place with about 1200 men, that I shall always
' hold in readiness to move to Charlestown, with the
' utmost dispatch, should occasion require. I am
' happy to hear that Morgan is arrived with a num-
' ber of arms, they are much wanted; we could not
' possibly move without them : I hope there are
' other military stores arrived, muskets, powder,
' cloth, &c.

' I am, &c.

' WILLIAM MOULTRIE.'

GEN. Lincoln marched off to day (20th April)
with about 2,000 men, light troops and cavalry, for
Augusta, leaving his baggage and artillery behind
to follow ; and on his arrival at Augusta, I received
the following letter from him.

' MR. GALPHIN'S, April 22d, 1779.

' DEAR SIR,

' I ARRIVED here to-day between twelve and one
' o'clock. You will please to order to this place all the
' continental troops, excepting the 2d and 5th regts.*
' of South-Carolina, with all the artillery except the

----

* Detachments making about 220 men.

' two pounder. You will please also to direct the quar-
' ter master to move with his department, reserving
' such articles as may be absolutely necessary for
' you : no time should be lost in marching the
' troops, they must commence as soon as possible
' and pursue it with the greatest dispatch : the com-
' missary must be directed to take on rice, for three
' days, including the one in which they leave camp.
' Meat he must provide daily on the road. I will
' send waggons to meet the troops with corn and flour.
' The quarter-master must send some person for-
' ward to supply forage ; corn I suppose can be had
' in plenty. You will please to remain in your pre-
' sent encampment with the two regiments and Col.
' Simon's brigade of militia. And keep, as long as
' you have it in your power, a post at Purisburgh....
' If the enemy should discover an inclination to at-
' tempt you in force, and to move towards Charles-
' town ; you will please as soon as possible to possess
' yourself of the several passes, and delay them as
' much as is in your power, and give time for us to
' come up. I wish the matter, that the troops are to
' join us here, might be kept secret as long as
' possible.

' I am, &c.

' B. LINCOLN.

' Brig. Gen. MOULTRIE.'

LETTER TO GOV. RUTLEDGE.

' BLACK-SWAMP, April 23d, 1779.

'DEAR SIR,

' YESTERDAY afternoon a party of Indians, and
' white men all painted, (about thirty) came over the
' River at Yamassee ; and had almost taken one of
' our small guards of six men, two of them are still
' missing; they proceeded and burnt Capt. Hart-
' stone's house. Col. Henderson, who commanded
' there, sent off a party of forty men, but could
' not come up with them : if your excellency could
' send us thirty or forty horsemen, and some Ca-
' tawba Indians, they would be of infinite service ; the
' few horsemen we have here (about 20) are quite
' insufficient for the duties absolutely necessary for
' this post* and Purisburgh : Gen. Lincoln who left
' this place three days ago for Augusta, took away all
' the continental horse with him ; which were about
' thirty-five : I will send off to Gen. Bull, to-morrow,
' to keep some of his men on the scout in that part
' of the country; or these Indians I fear will do a
' great deal of mischief : we are informed that the
' enemy have about fifty Indians at Abbercorne : I
' hope your excellency will be able to spare us a
....

* Black-swamp, about 25 miles from Purisburgh, where we
kept a guard of 100 men, and relieved them every week.

' reinforcement before any movement takes place
' from hence.

' I am, &c.

' WILLIAM MOULTRIE.

April the 24th, 1779.

'I RECEIVED a letter late last night from Gen.
' Lincoln, in which I have orders to move all the
' continental troops to Augusta, excepting the de-
' tachments of the 2d and 5th regiments, amounting
' to 220; I shall march them off this afternoon :* I
' wish your excellency would order Gen. Bull's mi-
' litia to take the post at Purisburgh.

' I am, &c.

' WILLIAM MOULTRIE.

' His excellency JOHN RUTLEDGE, Esq.'

LETTER TO MAJOR HORRY.

' BLACK-SWAMP, April, 25th, 1779.

' SIR,

' As we have information that the enemy are in
' motion, and it is uncertain which way they intend;
' you are therefore to keep a strict guard : keep your
' horsemen patroling at some distance from you : if
' you find the enemy land in force, you will file off
' your detachment to the right, down Purisburgh

* Under the command of Gen. Huger, 1000 men with baggage, and artillery,

' road, and take post at Coosohatchie bridge : you
' must give me the earliest notice of your retreat, by
' two or three different horsemen :Mr. Kinlock will
' give you further information. If you should hear
' of any reinforcements to the enemy, you must give
' me immediate intelligence.

    ' I am, &c.

           ' WILLIAM MOULTRIE.'

EXTRACT OF A LETTER TO GEN. LINCOLN.

      ' BLACK-SWAMP, April 24th, 1779.

' DEAR SIR,

' YOUR letter of the 22d, from Mr. Galphin's,
' reached me late last night ; the one to Gen. Huger
' was immediately sent to him, and every step has
' been taken this morning, which could forward the
' march of the troops ; they will move off the ground
' early in the afternoon : the director-general hav-
' ing represented to me the impossibility of getting
' the hospital stores in readiness to move before to-
' morrow morning, a party of one hundred men will
' be left to guard them. I have given the quarter-
master and commissary the necessary directions ;
' and have reserved from each department such arti-
' cles as were indispensably necessary for the use of
' this camp.

    ' A LETTER from Colonel Henderson, dated Puris-

' burgh, 22d April, 12 o'clock at night, informs me,
' that a party of Indians, or people painted like In-
' dians, about thirty or forty in number, had come
' through the swamp at Yamassee that evening,
' above where the guard is usually posted, and had
' burnt down Hartstone's house. It is unfortunate
' that neither the guard which was posted at the en-
' trance of the swamp, nor the party they had re-
' lieved which was at Hartstone's house, when the
' Indians appeared, never fired a gun; by which
' means the alarm was not communicated in time,
' to allow the party that was sent after them to im-
' pede their retreat. The circumstance of their hav-
' ing bayonets, makes Colonel Henderson conjecture,
' that they were only Indians to appearance. Sav-
' ages they certainly were. I have written to the
' governor and informed him of this affair; desiring
' at the same time, that he would send us a rein-
' forcement of horse and a few Catawba Indians....
' Col. Henderson has information of fifty Indians be-
' ing at Abbercorne with the enemy; and that an ex-
' pedition was talked of.

> ' I am, &c.

> ' WILLIAM MOULTRIE.'

A LETTER from Gen. LINCOLN, to Gen. HUGER, who commanded the detachment, marching up the country, to join Gen. LINCOLN.

' CAMP AT ADAMS' FERRY, April 24th, 1779.

' DEAR SIR,

' I THIS moment arrived here, and in the night ' came into my hands, a letter, from which the fol- ' lowing is an extract.

' I HAVE just now received advice that the enemy ' have been strongly reinforced, and that they intend ' to cross the Savannah, at some place above Ebene- ' zer ; whilst another strong body advances, to cross ' higher up. This advice is received from three se- ' veral persons, and induces me to believe that some ' fresh troops are arrived, and that they mean to ' make an attempt to cross into this state.

' You will take every precaution on your march, ' that you are not surprised by the enemy ; they may ' possibly mean to prevent your joining us here : ' you will keep out scouts continually, and light troops ' far on your left ; keep compact ; encamp on strong ' ground, if possible : if you should find it necessary, ' you will file off to the right : do not let the enemy ' get between this post and you. Major Clayborne ' will give you further information.

' I am, &c.

' BENJAMIN LINCOLN.

' Brig. Gen. HUGER.'

GEN. Huger was marching from Black-swamp, with a strong detachment, to join Gen. Lincoln, near Augusta...this letter was to caution him against a surprise.

LETTER TO COL. DRAYTON, D. Q. Master-Gen.
'BLACK-SWAMP, April 25th, 1779.

'DEAR SIR,

'As we have not 500 pounds of powder left, you 'will immediately apply to Lieut. Gov. Bee for 1000 'pounds of the musket powder that Morgan brought 'in with him : I shall order a waggon to town for 'that purpose, from Gen. Bull's camp ; but should 'it be detained by any accident, you must send up 'the post-rider by the best and earliest opportunity.

'I am, &c.

'WILLIAM MOULTRIE.'

EXTRACT OF A LETTER FROM LIEUT. GOV. BEE.
CHARLESTOWN, April 29th, 1779.

'DEAR SIR,

'I AM favored with yours of the 20th and 25th 'instant, and gave Col. Drayton immediate orders 'for the powder. Morgan brought only powder and 'arms ;* the arms were good and are sent on to

* The arms put us all in high spirits, as they were much wanted.

' Gen. Lincoln; the powder was all for musketry,
' a further supply of those two articles I expect in
' town to-morrow; they were sent over land from
' Baltimore by Congress: clothing and other arti-
' cles for the troops are expected soon. The Gov.
' is again returned to Orangeburgh, from whence I
' hope he will be able to send to Gen. Lincoln; he
' intends seeing the general and concerting mea-
' sures with him before he crosses the river: before
' the Gov. left town he wrote you concerning seve-
' ral people about new-river, who convey intelligence
' to Georgia. I hope the detachments from Gar-
' den's and Skirving's regiments are with you by
' this time, if not, you will please to write to Gen.
' Bull to hurry them on; if you order him to join
' you also, he can give you full information about
' all the suspicious persons, in that part of the
' country, who ought either to be secured or well
' watched; as several of the guards* about the neck
' have given intelligence to their friends; would it
' not be best to draw them to your camp, or to some
' other place at a distance, and to send others in
' their room. After much difficulty, I hope to get
' away one of the galley's to-morrow, she will pro-
' ceed to join the Rattle-snake† at Beaufort, and

* What difficulties we were under, when our very guards
would give intelligence to the enemy.

† A privateer.

' they are to be under Gen. Bull's orders : I think
' these two vessels with the assistance of the guards
' about Pinckney's or Dawfushy-island, may put a
' stop to the enemy's plundering parties in that
' quarter ; will you consult with Gen. Bull on this
' subject ? rice having got up to 25 pounds per cwt.
' you had better secure what you want for the army,
' in your neighborhood before it rises there also.

' I am, &c.

' THOMAS BEE.

' Brig. Gen. MOULTRIE.'

LETTER TO COL. M'INTOSH....sent by Express.

' BLACK-SWAMP, April 29th, 1779.

' DEAR SIR,

' You must endeavor to join us, if you can with-
' out any great risk : I wish you could have given
' me an account of the enemy's number, I could
' better judge how to act ; the light horseman in-
' forms me you imagine them upwards of 300 men.
' I think you were right to retreat in time, as your
' force* would not be equal to theirs by any means.
' I expect soon to have accounts from you, and
' more particulars ; as you have no baggage you
' may cross the country to this.

' I am, &c.

' WILLIAM MOULTRIE.'

....

* A guard of only 100 men.

EXTRACT OF A LETTER FROM GEN. LINCOLN.

'HEAD-QUARTERS, April 30th, 1779.

' DEAR SIR,

' YOUR favor of the 27th and 29th I have receiv-
' ed: Maj. Huger and Maj. Pinckney will settle the
' matters about the prisoners, and the former take
' the necessary papers. Your information relative
' to the enemy's principal force being at Ebenezer,
' agrees with accounts received here. I am happy
' in believing every thing in your power will be done,
' let their movement be what they may, for the good
' of the service and the safety of the troops.

' I am, &c.

' B. LINCOLN.

'Brig. Gen. MOULTRIE.'

LETTER TO GEN. BULL.

' BLACK-SWAMP, April 29th, 1779.

' DEAR SIR,

' I AM to acquaint you that the enemy landed up-
' wards of 300 men at Purisburgh, which obliged
' Col. M'Intosh to retreat from that post. I am to
' request you would order a strong detachment of as
' many men as can possibly be spared from your
' men, to take post at Coosohatchie, and there wait
' to support us, should we be obliged to retreat to
' that place ; I must also request you will send for
' what field-pieces you have got in your camp, and

' have them carried to Coosohatchie. I fear the
' enemy will soon have more men over; as by four
' deserters who came in to day, I am informed
' their strong post is at Ebenezer.

' I am, &c.

' WILLIAM MOULTRIE.'

LETTER TO GEN. LINCOLN.

' BLACK-SWAMP, April 30th, 10 o'clock, 1779.

' DEAR SIR,

' FROM all the intelligence I have been able to
' gain ; I am induced to think that the enemy are
' landed in force at Purisburgh, and that they mean
' to enter our country : this added to the difficulty
' of getting proper and speedy information, makes
' it adviseable to quit this post for Coosohatchie....
' Our little army will accordingly march in half an
' hour. The baggage and hospital stores were sent
' off this morning.

' I am, &c.

' WILLIAM MOULTRIE.'

LETTER TO GEN. LINCOLN.

' COOSOHATCHIE, April 30th, 1779.

' DEAR SIR,

' I THIS moment arrived at this place. The
' men under my command I expect in half an hour :
' we are informed the enemy have 1500 men at Pu-

' risburgh, and it is said they are to have as many
' as will make 2,000 ; we have very few men in arms
' in this part of the country, and I fear if we are
' not strongly reinforced they will get to Charles-
' town ; I hope you will consider the situation of this
' state, and repair to Charlestown with your army
' as soon as possible.　　　I am, &c.

'WILLIAM MOULTRIE.'

LETTER FROM COL. ALEX. M'INTOSH.
'COOSOHATCHIE, April 30th, 1779.

' DEAR GENERAL;

' LAST night two deserters from the enemy came
' to Bee's-creek ; they were of the light-infantry :
' they say Col. Maitland commanded yesterday ; that
' he had the light-infantry, and the second battalion
' of the 71st regt. amounting to 8 or 900 men ; that
' they were to send for three field-pieces, and three
' six-pounders, with a reinforcement to make them
' up 1500 men; that they did not know the Colonel's
' plan, but that they heard it said that he intended
' to proceed to Charlestown, and that he had 30 or
' 40 Indians with him.　I have given Gen. Bull and
' Col. Skirving information of those particulars; the
' men are so lame that I cannot be up before to-mor-
' row night.　We are all safe.　　I am, &c.

'ALEXANDER M'INTOSH,
' Brig. Gen. MOULTRIE.'

LETTER TO GOV. RUTLEDGE.

'COOSOHATCHIE, April 30th, 1779.

' DEAR SIR,

' I ARRIVED here about two hours ago; I was
' lucky enough to remove all our baggage and most
' of our stores this morning early; myself marched
' off about 2 o'clock, and proceeded for this place; I
' had left the ground three hours, when the enemy
' was at my camp. I cannot tell their numbers, but
' I believe vastly superior to mine; so I think I may
' say, I escaped a trimming; but I naturally con-
' cluded after Colonel M'Intosh retired, they would
' come to look for me, knowing my weakness: yet
' weak as I was, I thought I should be of more ser-
' vice this way; which determined me to make a
' sudden retreat; in which I happily succeeded: I
' think it is absolutely necessary, that you should
' send some reinforcements to meet me, and that
' immediately, as I am in hourly expectation of be-
' ing alarmed by the approach of the enemy; I shall
' use my best endeavors to retard their march; but
' be assured it requires your utmost exertions; as I
' am vastly inferior to them; they, by all accounts,
' 2,000, and I have not 1200. I think if you could
' march out 2 or 300 regular troops to meet me,
' they would be of infinite service. You have not a
' moment to lose to collect a body together; as you

' well know what my troops consist of,* which should
' be double their number to cope with them.

' P. S. I have sent off to Gen. Lincoln this af-
' ternoon, to request he will return to this state.

' I am, &c.

' WILLIAM MOULTRIE.'

LETTER TO GEN. LINCOLN.

' COOSOHATCHIE, May 1st, 1779.

' DEAR SIR,

' I WROTE you last night, informing you that the
' enemy had marched to Black-swamp ; since which
' I have further accounts, by which I am told they
' are still at Purisburgh ; their numbers I can-
' not be informed of ; but from different accounts
' they are allowed to be from seven to fifteen hun-
' dred ; by deserters who have come from them, we
' are told they intend making up their number to
' 2,000, and to proceed immediately for Charlestown ;
' I have with me now here about 1,200 men. Gen.
' Bull tells me he expects 200 more to-day. I have
' sent dispatches to the Gov. at Orangeburgh, and
' to Charlestown : I will impede the enemy's march
' as much as possible : if you could spare us 1,000
' men, I think they would be sufficient to prevent
' their going to Charlestown. I am, &c.

' WILLIAM MOULTRIE.'

* All militia, except 250 continentals.

LETTER TO GOV. RUTLEDGE AT ORANGEBURGH.

'COOSOHATCHIE, May 1st, 1779.

' DEAR SIR,

' I WROTE you last night via. Charlestown, since
' which I am informed the enemy still remain at
' Purisburgh; their number I cannot get any certain
' acounts of; some say 1,500, others say less; by
' two deserters who came in yesterday, we are in-
' formed their number consists of the light infan-
' try, and the second battalion of the 71st, with three
' field-pieces, six-pounders; they also say, they are
' to make up their number to about 2,000, then pro-
' ceed immediately to Charlestown : I have here
' with me about 1,200 men : I wish your excellency
' would reinforce me speedily; and with as many
' field-pieces as possible. I will do my utmost to
' prevent the enemy from going to Charlestown.

' I am, &c.

' WILLIAM MOULTRIE.'

_____

To GOV. RUTLEDGE.

TULLIFINY, May 1st, 5 o'clock, P. M.

' DEAR SIR,

' SINCE I sent off Mr. Kinlock this morning to
' Charlestown, I am informed by Col. Bourquin that
' he had got information, from very good authority,
' that the enemy's numbers are 2,000; and that
' Gen. Provost is certainly with them; this makes

' me imagine they must be in great force: I receiv-
' ed a letter from Gen. Lincoln, of the 29th ult. in
' which he says ' it is agreed by all their accounts,
' that the enemy's main body is at Ebenezer :' he
' had not yet heard of my retiring to this place: I
' wrote him two letters yesterday, informing him of
' the same : I have also requested of him, to send
' me 1,000 men, but if I can get speedily rein-
' forced from the country, I will countermand my
' request. Gen. Bull gives me great hopes of 5 or
' 600 men in two days, which I hope will be time
' enough, without breaking in upon Gen. Lincoln's
' plan.

   ' Gen. Bull has just now informed me, that ano-
' ther account confirms the first, of the enemy's fleet
' having left Savannah.*

        ' I am, &c.

                ' WILLIAM MOULTRIE.'

          —————

TO GOV. RUTLEDGE AT ORANGEBURGH.

        ' TULLIFINY, May 2d, 1779.

' DEAR SIR,

   ' THIS morning, two deserters from the British
' camp; by whom I am informed that the enemy's
' main body is at Middleton-plantation (Turkey-hill)
' on Black-swamp; they say their numbers are about

....

   * It was feared that the enemy intended a diversion with
their fleet, either at Charlestown or Beaufort.

VOL. I   D 3

' 3,000, with six 9 pounders; and that Gen. Provost
' is with them: that they are to proceed up the ri-
' ver, after Gen. Lincoln. I wish they may continue
' of that opinion, as I think he may be able to give
' a good account of them: I am greatly too weak to
' face them, should they move this way. This ac-
' count nearly agrees with that given me by Capts.
' Hampton and Newman ; whom I sent out to recon-
' noitre: they saw one battalion at the Two-sisters ;
' about 300 at Middleton's ; and their main body at
' Williamson's : I think I made a lucky escape from
' them ; as the very evening I moved off from my
' ground, they moved towards me, and halted about
' 5 miles off; intending to attack me next morning ;
' but they were informed that I was gone. I wish
' I could have some field-pieces.

   ' I am, &c.

     ' WILLIAM MOULTRIE.'

To LIEUT. GOV. BEE, IN CHARLESTOWN.

    ' TULLIFINY, May 3d, 1779.

 DEAR SIR,

  ' I SEND you 4 prisoners of war ; if you examine
' them, they can give you all the information they
' have given me : from other intelligence, the enemy
' are with their whole force about Black-swamp:
' it is uncertain which way they will turn ; I keep
' out scouting parties close to them, to give me the

'first intelligence of their movements; which you
'shall be informed of as soon as possible. The ene-
'my begin to destroy every thing before them : they
'have burnt the two Dupont's houses, on the great
'swamp : if I could collect 100 horse, I could pre-
'vent it, in a great measure. I am much surprised
'that I have not heard from the governor, or your-
'self, since I arrived here : I am very much at a
'loss, to know what measures the enemy mean to
'pursue ; I think they have not any preparations for
'a sea expedition.*   I am, &c.

'WILLIAM MOULTRIE.'

LETTER, WITH A FLAG, TO GEN. PROVOST.

'TULLIFINY, May 2d, 1779.

'SIR,

'THE like reasons and motives that possibly in-
'duced Col. Campbell lately to claim the offices of
'humanity, to be extended to your sick, from the
'hands of Gen. Williamson, at Augusta, in a less
'degree now operates with me, and obliges me to
'sue for the like protection, and care to be extended
'to our sick in your hands, at the hospital, at Black-
'swamp : to the humane, the distressed never plead
'in vain; his feelings, are not biased by party dis-
'tinction, and names without meaning ; but actua-

* It was apprehended that they would have had boats at
Beaufort, and come within land to Charlestown.

' ted by the laudable motives of humanity, as well
' as christianity, he generously supports and pro-
' tects the weak and infirm ; and feels in the discharge
' of them, such an inbred satisfaction that words have
' not energy enough to express. The bearer, sir, of
' this, is Doctor Fayseaux, sen. physician to our
' hospital ; he has my authority to assure you, that
' if the dismission of our sick, will be any accomoda-
' tion to you, we, on our parts, will estimate them pris-
' oners of war, and make a return of them as such, the
' first opportunity : if on the contrary, the detention
' of them might be deemed more elegible, I will rest
' satisfied, from the known tenderness and generous
' feelings of Gen. Provost, that they will find, if not
' a friend, a guardian and protector.

' I have the honor to be, &c.

' WILLIAM MOULTRIE.'

_____

' HEAD-QUARTERS. SILVER-BLUFF, May 2d, 1779.
' DEAR GEN.

' I HAVE the honor of your favor of the 30th ult.
' A detachment of picked continental troops are or-
' dered to your assistance. I have written to the
' Governor at Orangeburgh, and requested that he
' would reinforce you by the militia, intended for
' this army, and Major Grimball's artillery. The
' enemy, I think, cannot mean to attempt Charles-
' town with the few troops they have thrown over

' the Savannah. But if on further information, it
' should appear that they really do, you will give me
' the earliest intelligence of it ; every attention will
' be paid to counteract their designs and secure the
' state.   ' I am &c.

                                   ' B. Lincoln.
' Gen. Moultrie.'

_____

Letter to Gov. Rutledge, Orangeburgh.
' Tullifiny, May 3d. 6 o'clock P. M. 1779.
' Dear Sir.

' I this moment received yours ; I was in hopes
' you would have acquainted me of a strong rein-
' forcement marching to this place : the militia in
' the country came in very slow indeed ; not 300 of
' Gen. Bull's are at their camps ; he however gives
' me hopes of receiving two or three hundred very
' shortly (in two days from Garden's) Maj. Huger
' who came from Gen. Lincoln's camp yesterday,
' informs me, that Col. Garden was to march this
' day from Savannah river with 150 of his men : I
' shall be very glad to have the Catawba Indians ;
' they will be of service as scouts. I am sorry to
' inform you, the enemy with parties of horse and
' Indians, are ravaging the country in a barbarous
' manner, killing people and burning a number of
' houses as they go on. I fancy them to be M'
' Guth's ; they have set fire to the houses of the

' two Dupont's, to Gignilliacks, and several other
' houses in that part of the country. If I had 100
' horsemen I would stop their progress. The main
' body of the enemy is now at and about the Two-
' sisters ; by accounts from deserters and prisoners,
' they have 3,000 men, reports say they intend to at-
' tack Gen. Lincoln ; other reports say, they intend
' for Charlestown. You may depend upon my ut-
' most exertions, to prevent their march that way,
' though at present I have not more than 1,200 men
' at this camp, which is vastly too few to stop the
' progress of so superior an army. I sent Dr. Fay-
' seaux, with a flag to Gen. Provost, requesting he
' would allow me to bring off some sick, which I
' I was necessarily obliged to leave behind, for want
' of waggons, and I would account with him for
' them, as so many prisoners of war, (which he very
' politely agreed to) or that he would order his sur-
' geons to take particular care of them. I have sent
' the waggons to-day for them (about sixteen). Dr.
' Fayseaux says the enemy have taken up the
' ground for their encampment, from Williamson's
' house, as far as the Two-sisters, which is about 3
' miles. Maj. Barnwell, with about 20 horse, went
' out just now after a party of the enemy's horse.
' This moment word is brought they are engaged.
' I have sent to reinforce ours. I long for the event.
' The event of the above has turned nothing only 2

' guns fired at 2 soldiers, who made their escape.
' I leave you to judge whether we stand in need of
' reinforcements or not.

' At 7 o'clock, P. M.

' COL. Laurens who is now with me, and who I
' sent out to reconnoitre on the Purisburgh road,
' went as far as Mr. Allison's, where they saw a
' field-piece in the road, at the road across where the
' Two-sisters road comes in, with a High-lander sen-
' try standing, he endeavored to go round into the
' wood to make discoveries, but found the sentries
' of the light troops and High-landers so far extend-
' ed on each flank, that he could not get near
' enough ; but I think by all appearance it looks as if
' the enemy intend for Charlestown, I wish you
' could send us a reinforcement.

' I am, &c.

' WILLIAM MOULTRIE.'

LETTER FROM GEN. AUGUSTUS PROVOST.

' HEAD-QUARTERS, May 2d, 1779.

' I AM just now honored with yours of this date...
' you may be assured that I shall give every assist-
' ance in my power to your sick : and to the end
' that neither injury nor insult be offered to them,
' your physicians and surgeons may attend to their
' duty unmolested...I will send a safe guard there
' to-morrow morning, to remain until your sick are

' removed; which if equally agreeable to you, I
' should wish to be soon; and you will please send
' the necessary carriages, with your best conve-
' niency.

' I have the honor to be, &c.

' A. PROVOST.

' Brig. Gen. MOULTRIE.'

LETTER TO GEN. LINCOLN.

' COOSOHATCHIE, May 2d, 1779.

' DEAR SIR,

' THIS morning two deserters came from the Bri-
' tish camp, by whom I am informed the enemy's
' main body is now at Turkey-hill, on Black-swamp;
' they say their numbers are about 3000, with six
' nine-pounders; that Gen. Provost is with them
' and that they are to proceed up the river, to look
' for you: I wish they may continue of that opinion,
' as I am much too weak to face them; and I am
' in hopes your numbers will enable you to give a
' good account of them: this agrees with the infor-
' mation I received from Captains Hampton and
' Newman whom I sent out to reconnoitre. I have
' sent express to the governor at Orangeburgh, and
' to Charlestown, to hasten up the militia to this
' place, at present I have not many more than when
' you left me: I think I made a lucky escape; as
' the day that I left Black-swamp, a strong body of

' them marched off for my camp that evening ; the
' quarter-master did not leave me a single waggon
' more than the regimental ones ; by which means,
' I was obliged to leave some of the sick in the hos-
' pital behind ; and some trifling matters of the com-
' missary's stores. The provisions in store I had
' served out to the troops before I marched off. I
' will take care to give you every information which
' comes to my hand. Dr. Fayseaux will go off
' this morning, with a flag, to take care of the sick
' left behind.   I am, &c.

' WILLIAM MOULTRIE.

ON my retreat from Black-swamp, on the 30th
April, I removed the troops under my command,
and the hospital (such as could be removed) upon
certain information by our scouts that the enemy
had crossed the river at the Two-sisters in great
force ; I marched with all expedition to Coosohatchie,
giving notice, at the same time, to Col. M'Intosh, who was posted at Purisburgh, to march immediately with all possible dispatch, and join me at
Coosohatchie ; which he did the same night, where
we encamped.

1st of May, I moved my camp to Tullifiny-hill,
being a much more eligible place to make a stand :
here Mr. Thomas Heyward, sen. went with me to re-

connoitre the country in the neighborhood; and to shew me all the fording places above and below his house. It being a very dry season, the river was very low, which allowed of several fording places : To all of them I placed some small guards to give me notice if the enemy moved that way ; leaving my rear guard of 100 men at Coosohatchie ; in this situation I was making every preparation to receive the enemy at Tullifiny-hill ; and sending out horsemen to reconnoitre the enemy in different directions, to give me notice of their approach ; at this place I was determined to engage them : our accounts to day, was that they were encamped about ten miles in our rear.

3d of May. As the enemy was so near, I was desiring one of my aids to go and bring off our rear guard from Coosohatchie to join us immediately ; but Col. John Laurens (who joined me two days before) being present, he requested me to permit him to go on that service ; which I readily consented to, thinking him to be a brave and experienced officer ; I told him at the same time, that I would send 150 good riflemen to cover his flanks, lest the enemy should be too close upon him ; I accordingly sent Capt. James with one hundred and fifty picked men, and 100 men of the out picquet to join him ; these altogether made a body of 350 men, which was one fourth of my little army : but instead of Col. Laurens' bringing off the guard, as he was desired, he

very imprudently crossed the river to the east side ;
and drew them up on the opposite bank of the river,
taking those 150 who were sent to cover his flanks,
and the 100 men of the out picquet and joined them
to the guard ; while he left the houses on the hill for
the British to occupy : in this situation did he expose
his men to their fire, without the least chance of doing them any injury ; after remaining some time he
got a number of the men killed and wounded ; and
was wounded himself ; he desired Capt. Shubrick,*
who commanded after he left the field, to stay a little longer and then to bring off the men : had not
Capt. Shubrick moved off at the very instant that
he did, his party would have been cut off from their
retreat and every man of them would either have
been killed or taken prisoner : we heard the firing
very distinctly at Tullifiny, and supposed it was our
retreating guard coming in : but presently Col. Laurens came up to me, wounded in the arm : I said to
him ; ' well Colonel what do you think of it ?' ' why
sir, said he, your men won't stand,' upon which I said ;
' if that be the case I will retreat ;' and immediately
after our rear guard came in, I ordered the bridge
to be broken up ; and begun my retreat, about 12
o'clock. We marched off in good order and reached Salt-ketcher chapel that night, the British en-

* Now Col. Shubrick.

camped at Pocotaligo 5 miles in our rear : had not
Col. Laurens discouraged the men by exposing them
so much and unnecessarily, I would have engaged
Gen. Provost at Tullifiny, and perhaps have stopped
his march to Charlestown : we were all at our posts on
a very commanding ground and expected every moment to be engaged. Col. Laurens was a young
man of great merit, and a brave soldier, but an imprudent officer; he was too rash and impetuous.

From Salt-ketcher, I moved at 12 o'clock at night ;
by this early movement I got far before the British,
and burnt all the bridges in my way, which retarded them very much.

LETTER TO GOV. RUTLEDGE.

' TULLIFINY, May, 4th, A. M. 1779.

' DEAR SIR,

' THE enemy are now on this side Bee's-creek,
' about five miles from this ; I hope your excellency
' will hasten your light troops to reinforce me. I
' cannot give you any account of their numbers, but
' it is generally thought 3,000. I wish you would
' send to Gen. Lincoln to march this way, as soon
' as possible : I shall send also.

' I am, &c.

' WILLIAM MOULTRIE.'

LETTER TO GEN. LINCOLN.

'TULLIFINY, May 4th, 10 o'clock P. M.

'DEAR SIR,

'THE enemy are now at Bee's creek, about five
'miles from this post, they have now made a halt,
'(I suppose for the heat of the day) their numbers
'I cannot well assure you of; but I think they are
'at least 3,000 : I wish you would move this way,
'as I am very unable to stand against them : if you
'would hasten some light-horse on, they will be of
'great service. I expect the governor will join me
'to-morrow from Orangeburgh with the Charles-
'town artillery ; as to what militia he had I cannot
'inform you : it seems absolutely necessary for you
'to make a speedy march to save this country.

'I am, &c.

'WILLIAM MOULTRIE.'

LETTER TO COL. C. PINCKNEY.

'ASHEPOO, May 5th, 1779.

'DEAR SIR,

'I HAVE arrived at this place after a severe
'march : the enemy keeping close to us, we are
'greatly too few to make head against them ; I will
'endeavor to make some stand here, though my
'numbers are much reduced from what they were
'yesterday ; as Skirving's and Garden's are gone to
'take care of their families and property, which is a

' very natural consequence; it is a melancholy sight
' to see the movements in this part of the country :
' pray have a vast quantity of provisions laid up in
' town ; as you certainly will have a great number
' of people with you ; have an embargo immediately
' laid on ; get all the rice you can in store. For
' God's sake, let us not want provision ; have your
' works round the town finished as fast as possible ;
' as the enemy march very rapidly, have a number
' of large cannon mounted on your lines ; I will en-
' deavor to avoid an action as much as possible ; in
' order to throw my little army into town ; I think
' if you exert yourself in town we shall keep them
' out. Gen. Lincoln informs me he has marched
' off a picked body of continental troops to reinforce
' me, but I cannot tell where they are ; I have sent
' him two expresses two days ago to request he will
' march with his whole army ; I am in hopes he
' is now moving this way : the enemy are now at
' Salt-ketcher, and occupy the ground which I did
' the first of the last night, but moved off at twelve
' o'clock and marched to this place. I have sent
' Capt. B. Cattel to the governor to desire him to
' join me here ; and I have ordered the fish-pond
' bridge to be burnt.

' I am, &c.

' WILLIAM MOULTRIE,'

Letter to Gen. Lincoln.

'Godfrey's, Savannah, May 5th, 1779.

' Dear Sir,

' I have just now arrived at this place, about sev-
' en miles from Salt-ketcher ; I left Tullifiny yester-
' day about two o'clock, after having a little skirmish
' with the enemy across Coosohatchie river with our
' rear guard which I reinforced with 150 riflemen
' and the out picquet about 100 more ; they soon
' drove our body with their field-pieces and mus-
' ketry after killing and wounding some of our
' people. Col. Laurens who commanded the party,
' was wounded in the arm, and his horse shot : I
' soon found myself under the necessity of retreat-
' ing ; they appearing too numerous for me ; I have
' had good information, their number are 4,000, and
' that they intend for Charlestown ; I must beg you
' would hasten to our assistance, or I fear the town
' is in danger ; my little army decreases ; every one
' running to look after his family and property ; the
' enemy carry every thing before them, with fire
' and sword ; many good houses they have already
' destroyed, and many more will be consumed, before
' they can be checked ; I am retiring from them as fast
' as possible, pray follow them ; and let us Burgoyne*
' them. I shall endeavor to make a stand at Ashe-

....

* Gen. Lincoln was at the taking of Burgoyne.

' poo ; as I will expect the governor will join me
' there. Yesterday I was but six miles a-head of the
' enemy. I made a forced march last night.

' I am, &c.

' WILLIAM MOULTRIE.'

LETTER TO GEN. LINCOLN.

' ASHEPOO, May 6th, half past 12, A. M.

' DEAR SIR,

' I HAVE wrote you a number of letters request-
' ing your movement to Charlestown ; but have
' heard nothing from you on that head ; excepting
' your sending me a reinforcement of picked conti-
' nentals ; it must be very°strong to be of any ser-
' vice ; as the enemy are moving to town with all
' their force ; I must again press your marching this
' way, with all possible dispatch. I expect the enemy
' will lay before the town, before you come ; I hope
' we shall be able to keep them out till your arrival ;
' their numbers are said to be 4,000 : I have sent
' to the detachment you ordered to join me, to give
' them the route of the enemy, and to be careful
' they do not fall in with them : on your march
' downwards, you must not take the route I came ;
' as I have destroyed all the bridges ; I am just
' now cutting away that at Ashepoo ; as the enemy
' are advancing fast ; they are only four miles from
' me now : I shall move to town : I expected the

' Gov. would have joined me here ; but know not
' where he is : I have given him caution of the ene-
' my's route : I once more beg you would hasten to
' our assistance.

' I am, &c.

' WILLIAM MOULTRIE.'

———

' HEAD-QUARTERS. JANETT'S-FERRY.

' GEORGIA, May 6th, 1779.

' DEAR SIR,

' THE troops reached this place to-day, on their
' march down the country, to your assistance. If the
' enemy mean any thing serious against Charlestown,
' and our aid should be needed, we, sooner to give
' you succor, keep the boats with us, by which we can
' recross the Savannah, with great rapidity ; by mov-
' ing on this side the river, we probably shall divert
' the attention of the enemy from you ; if we do not,
' we lose no time by this pursuit ; therefore it should
' be continued.

' IF the enemy should give public evidence of their
' designs against Charlestown I think, with your
' force, as you are in possession of strong passes,
' you will be able to stop their progress, and give us
' time to come up.

' I am, &c.

' B. LINCOLN.

' Brig. Gen. MOULTRIE.'

LETTER TO GOV. RUTLEDGE.

'DEAR SIR,

'JACKSONBURGH, May 6th, 1779.

'I THIS moment arrived at this place, where I
'propose staying to-day; I hope your excellency
'will be here; the people are very much alarmed
'in town: your presence seems absolutely necessa-
'ry. The last account I got of the enemy, they
'were encamped at Godfrey's (Savannah): I doubt
'not you will hasten your march; as, should the
'enemy get notice of you, they will attempt to cut
'you off.

'I am, &c.

'WILLIAM MOULTRIE.'

LETTER TO GEN. LINCOLN.

'CHARLESTOWN, May 8th, 1779.

'DEAR SIR,

'I ARRIVED here last night, after being pursued
'by the enemy for several days: they now seem to
'have given over the chase, and have halted at Salt-
'ketcher bridge. I am in hopes they have now got
'some of your horse among them; which will per-
'plex them a little; I have now 150 horse which I
'shall keep close to their heels; I have heard noth-
'ing of the reinforcements you were to send me;
'when I get them I will face about, and keep as
'near as prudence will allow, and harrass them

‘ with my horse. There is a strange consternation in
‘ town : people frightened out of their wits ; they long
‘ that you should, and I hope you will soon be among
‘ the enemy ; I have halted the troops at Dorchester,
‘ where I intend to form my camp, ready to support
‘ you ; had the enemy continued their march, I
‘ really believe they would have carried the town ea-
‘ sily. I do not doubt but that you are marching
‘ to our assistance.   I am, &c.

‘ WILLIAM MOULTRIE.’

I LEFT the troops at Dorchester, under the command of Colonel Daniel Horry, and went to town
myself with my suite ; when I arrived in town, I was
received with great joy and open arms, found every
thing in the greatest confusion ; and was informed
that the enemy had taken the Ashley river road ;
I then sent the following order to Col. Horry.

‘ CHARLESTOWN, May 8th, 1779.

‘ DEAR SIR,
‘ As the enemy are near at hand (we have in-
‘ formation of their being at fish-pond bridge) you
‘ will please order all your baggage to be in read-
‘ iness to move at a moment's warning : I expect to
‘ be up with you to night ; you will please order the
‘ troops to be in readiness.

‘ I am, &c.

‘ WILLIAM MOULTRIE.’

‘ Col. DANIEL HORRY, Dorchester.’

The troops were marched into town on the 9th May, and the same day I issued the following order.

' CHARLESTOWN, May 9th, 1779.

' A RETURN to be made immediately to the com-
' manding officer, by the commanders of the different
' corps, of the number of officers, with their ranks
' and dates of their commissions ; and also the non-
' commissioned officers, and the number of rank and
' file.

THE militia are now marching into town from different parts of the country.

MAY 8. At this time there never was a coun-try in greater confusion and consternation ; and it may be easily accounted for, when 5 armies were marching through the southern parts of it, at the same time, and all for different purposes : myself retreating as fast as possible to get into town, at first with 1,200 men ; but reduced to 600 before I got near the town ; the British army of 3,000 men commanded by Gen. Provost in pursuit of me : and Gen. Lincoln with the American army of 4,000, marching with hasty strides to come up with the British : Gov. Rutledge from Orangeburgh, with about 600 militia ; hastening to get to town lest he should be shut out ; and Col. Harris, with a de-tachment of 250 continentals, pushing on with all possible dispatch to reinforce me ; and my sending two or three expresses every day to the governor and to Gen. Lincoln, to let them know where I was; and to Charlestown frequently, to hasten their works and to prepare for an attack; in short it was nothing but a general confusion and alarm. And the militia from the north part of the country, from every parish making what haste they could to reinforce Charlestown; that I may truly say the whole country was in motion.

MAY 16. I made disposition of the troops on the lines. 'The Charlestown militia are to occupy the right wing of the line, extending from the half moon battery to the centre.

' THE country militia are to occupy the left wing.

' THE cannon upon the right wing to be manned by the Charlestown artillery; those upon the left by Col. Robert's artillery.

' COL. M‘Intosh will take post with the 5th regiment in the redoubt on the right side of the line.

' THE redoubt on the left to be occupied by 100 men from the 2d regiment under the command of Col. Marion.

' THE advanced redoubt on the left to be occupied by Col. Harris's detachment (250.)

' The remainder of the 2d regiment, with General Paulaski's infantry, to occupy the half moon in the center as a corps de reserve; and to sally out upon the enemy from time to time, as the service may require, without breaking the line: Gen. Count Paulaski will be kind enough, to take upon himself the charge of posting the army according to the above plan; and also the daily inspection of the whole during the siege.

' The commanding officers of the different corps ' are to take care that their men are furnished with ' 100 rounds per man.

' The quarter-master general is to furnish a number of hogsheads, for the purpose of holding water* for the use of the troops along the line.

' A Capt. two subalterns, two sergeants, and forty rank and file, and ten from the artillery, as a fatigue party to march down to Gadsden's-wharf, to mount some cannon there.

One Captain, two subalterns, two sergeants, forty rank and file, to be posted near the old lines as an advance guard.'

By my being so particular in entering my orders; I might be thought by some of my readers to be too prolix: but while I am writing I have in remembrance my young countrymen, who may perhaps be called to the field some day or other; and by turning over a leaf or two of my book will find some form or precedent, which may be useful to them in their military career.

....

* As there was not water near, I ordered this, that the militia should not have any pretence to quit the lines.

EXTRACTS OF LETTERS.

The following letters which I received on my retreat from Black-swamp from the governor, and
lieutenant governor Bee, and mine to them and to
general Lincoln will shew the exact situation of
the country at that time.

LETTER FROM LIEUT. GOV. BEE.

'CHARLESTOWN, May 1st, 1779.

' DEAR SIR,

' YOURS of the 29th April, directed to the gover-
' nor came to me this morning ; I have sent it for-
' ward by express to Orangeburgh, from whence,
' if necessary, I make no doubt you will be reinforced.
' I gave Col. Drayton an order ten days ago
' for the musket powder you desired. I hope to be
' able to send you about twenty-five or thirty of Col.
' Horry's light-horse, in the morning, under Capt.
' Couturier's command ; each of whom may carry
' ten or twelve pound of musket powder to you, I
' hope this manœuvre of the enemy is only to draw
' Gen. Lincoln's attention to this quarter ; but when
' they find he is in earnest above, they will return
' of course ; if otherwise it will be best to drive off
' what stock may fall into their hands, in time : I
' think Coosohatchie bridge will stop them for some
' time at least, till the militia can be collected be-
' low, I should think most of Gen. Bull's out-post

' may be called in, but you will be the best judge.
' Of this I shall desire him to consult with you on
' this head; and as he is under your command,
' you will issue orders accordingly.

' I am, &c.

' T. Bee.

' Brig. Gen. Moultrie.'

Letter from Gov. Rutledge.

' Orangeburgh, May 2d, 1779.

' Dear Sir,

' I have sent to have a parcel of Catawba's em-
' bodied, and brought down, as soon as possible;
' and will order them to you, when they arrive here.
' I wrote to the lieut. governor, desiring. that he
' would immediately send as many of Horry's horse
' as are mounted, and accoutred; and the rest as
' soon as they can be to your camp. I am persuaded
' that you will make the best disposition of the troops
' under your command; and take the most effectual
' measures for opposing the enemy, and preventing
' their ravaging any part of the country: and doubt
' not, that Gen. Bull (to whom I now write) will exert
' himself, in furnishing as many men as he can, from
' Skirving's and Garden's regiments, and in co-ope-
' rating with you.   I am, &c.

' J. Rutledge.

' Brig. Gen. Moultrie.'

LETTER FROM LIEUT. GOV. BEE.

‘ CHARLESTOWN, May 2d, 1779。

‘ DEAR SIR,

‘ I RECEIVED your favors of 30th April, and 1st
‘ of May, by Mr. Kinlock, at 9 o'clock last night,
‘ and was happy to hear you had arrived safe at
‘ Coosohatchie, and make no doubt but the govern-
‘ or will reinforce you, as speedily as possible, from
‘ Orangeburgh; you know our weakness in men
‘ here, in case the enemy makes any attempt by
‘ sea, too well, to wish any drawn from town, unless
‘ in the last extremity. I hope Garden's and Skir-
‘ ving's militia will collect with spirit, when the dan-
‘ ger is at their own doors; but reinforcements must
‘ be from Orangeburgh; I have not heard from them
‘ since the governor left town. I have ordered the
‘ galley, and the boat under her convoy, with stores,
‘ for your men, to go to Combahee-ferry, as a safer
‘ navigation, than Broad-river; as will also Horry's
‘ light-dragoons, who have been detained a day, for
‘ their carbines and saddles. Drayton proposes now
‘ to send a few pack-horses, with musket-powder
‘ with them.

‘ I am, &c.

‘ THOMAS BEE.

‘ Brig. Gen. MOULTRIE.’

G 3

LETTER FROM GOV. RUTLEDGE.

'ORANGEBURGH, Sunday Evening.

' DEAR SIR,

' IN consequence of your advice, received this
' afternoon ; I will march with Grimball's artillery,
' and all the force we have here (except about 50,
' who must remain ; and 50 more, who go as an es-
' cort to the waggons with corn, &c. for Gen. Lin-
' coln's camp) as soon as possible, to reinforce you.
' I hope to get off to-morrow, and no time shall be
' lost on the march.   You will, without doubt, take
' every step in your power, to procure all the rein-
' forcements you can, and throw every obstruction in
' the way, to annoy the enemy, and prevent their pro-
' gress and ravages.

'   ' I am, &c.

'   ' J. RUTLEDGE.

' Brig. Gen. MOULTRIE.'

———

LETTER FROM GOV. RUTLEDGE.

' EDISTO SAW-MILLS, at Mr. Charles Elliot's,

'   ' 12 miles below Orangeburgh.

'   ' Wednesday morning.

' DEAR SIR,

' WE began our march, with what force we could
' bring from Orangeburgh, yesterday morning, for
' your camp ; and shall proceed as quickly as the wea-
' ther and the roads will admit.   I hope to bring up,

' and have very close after me, 500 men (exclusive of
' officers) horse, foot, and artillery. I received yours,
' dated 3d of May at 6 o'clock, about 11 last night ;
' I hope you will be able to withstand the enemy, or
' stop their progress. I shall send Allston's, and some
' other horse, as soon as they come up (which I expect
' to day) a-head, to join you. I have sent another
' express for the Catawbas. I hope to see you soon.
                                    ' I am, &c.

                                              ' J. RUTLEDGE.
' Brig. Gen. MOULTRIE.'

———

LETTER FROM GOV. RUTLEDGE.

                    ' EDISTO SAW-MILLS. Thursday.
' DEAR SIR,

     ' SOME hours ago, on the march hither, I re-
' ceived yours of last night ; and soon after, a let-
' ter from Major Butler ; in which he says, he heard
' the enemy were at Ashepoo : therefore, as I think
' we cannot possibly assist you at Jacksonburgh (it
' being 24 miles from hence) I have ordered the
' troops here, to cross the river, (they being now on
' this side) and proceed, by forced marches, to
' Charlestown, over four-hole and Dorchester brid-
' ges, I think you had better move...when you do,
' move, down by Dorchester. You will continue to
' throw obstruction in the enemy's way, and advise
' me of these, and your motions, by express to

'Charlestown; for which I am just setting off; you
'will give all necessary orders for destroying bridg-
'es, &c.

'I am, &c.

'Brig. Gen. MOULTRIE. 'J. RUTLEDGE.'

LETTER FROM LIEUT. GOV. BEE.

'DEAR SIR,

'I WROTE you this morning by express, in an-
'swer to your favor by Mr. Kinlock; and this even-
'ing I received yours dated yesterday evening five
'o'clock. I hope you will receive the reinforce-
'ments General Bull gives you reason to expect,
'speedily, as the council were unanimously of opin-
'ion none could be spared from Charlestown, or the
'forts at present, for reasons which will occur readi-
'ly to yourself, and Mr. Kinlock will further explain;
'by a letter I have just received, from the governor
'at Orangeburgh, dated yesterday morning, he had
'no intelligence from your quarter, but an express
'with the intelligence I sent from Charlestown,
'was met about thirty miles from thence, so that he
'must have arrived by day light this morning, and
'I make no doubt he has ordered every assistance
'possible; I sent another express to him this morn-
'ing;...press the measure; Horry's light horse un-
'der captain Dubois certainly march to-morrow....
'The enemy's fleet that came last week from Tybee,

‘ are certainly gone for Jamaica. We have receiv-
‘ ed several accounts different ways of Mr. Kinlock,
‘ which will so fully explain any other matter to you,
‘ that it is unnecessary for me to add any thing more
‘ at present.

‘ I am, &c.

‘ THOMAS BEE.

‘ Brig. Gen. MOULTRIE.’

LETTER FROM LIEUT. GOV. BEE.

‘ CHARLESTOWN, May, 3d 1779.

‘ DEAR SIR,

‘ I WROTE you last evening by Mr. Kinlock, since
‘ which I have got off the galley and boat with stores,
‘ for Combahee ferry. Twenty two of Horry’s light
‘ horse, marched this afternoon for your camp and
‘ will hurry on the party, that went to Orangeburgh
‘ with the Governor, who are just returned. By a
‘ letter from the Governor dated Saturday, he had
‘ then received no accounts of the enemies move-
‘ ments across the river, but an express I sent from
‘ town, would reach here in a few hours after, so
‘ that I hope he has sent off all the men he had to
‘ you immediately, with the field-pieces, of which he
‘ has 10 in all; to-morrow morning I will get all the
‘ guns I can mounted on field-carriages, and hope to
‘ get some fit to send you. I have received a letter
‘ from the Governor, from Orangeburgh, dated yes-

' terday, by which I find he is marching all his
' forces, with Grimball's artillery, immediately to
' join you, so that you will have a fine parcel of
' field-peices, with some well-trained men into
' the bargain. Col. Horry has just assured me he
' will send off 20 light-horse, completely equipped
' by Thursday morning.   I am, &c.

' THOMAS BEE.

' Brig. Gen. MOULTRIE.'

LETTER FROM GOV. RUTLEDGE.

' WILLIAM's FERRY, Wednesday.

' DEAR SIR,

' I HAVE just now received your letter of yester-
' day I will hurry on the troops with all possible dis-
' patch to your support, though their numbers (from
' 400 to 500) are very short of what I could wish.
' Major Butler sets off in four hours, with all the
' light-horse fit to be hurried on for service, their num-
' bers uncertain, as we have not yet selected them ;
' he will lose no time in getting to you. I am sure
' it is unnecessary to exhort you, to dispute every
' pass with the enemy, and to throw every obstruc-
' tion in their way so as to allow General Lincoln
' time to come in their rear, before they penetrate
' into the country.   I am, &c.

' J. RUTLEDGE.

' Brig. Gen. MOULTRIE.'

LETTER FROM LIEUT. GOV. BEE.

'CHARLESTOWN, May 5th, 1779.

'DEAR GENERAL,

'A person has alarmed us this afternoon with
'an account of your retreating to Salt-ketcher last
'night; no express from you yet. We will work
'as we are in town; if a party is ready to advance
'and cover your retreat with some field-pieces, you
'will undoubtedly have the governor with you as
'soon as this reaches you.

'I am, &c.   'T. BEE.'

'Brig. Gen. MOULTRIE.'

ORDERS ISSUED, MAY 11th.

'3 Captains, 6 subalterns, 6 sergeants, and 150
rank and file from the country militia, to hold themselves in readiness to March at a moment's warning, in order if necessary, to reinforce the advance
guard.

'This day Count Paulaski's infantry came into
town from Haddrel's point the cavalry of his legion
came in with himself, on the 8th. We this morning had advice that the enemy were near our lines.
Gen. Count Paulaski, paraded his legion about (one
hundred and twenty, and some militia) and attacked
the advance of the British troops a little beyond the
old race ground in sight of our advance guard; but
he was soon overpowered; in this skirmish, he lost

his Col. (Kowatch,) killed and most of his infantry, killed, and wounded, and prisoners; and it was with difficulty, the remainder got in, with our advance guard. Gen. Provost's army soon appeared before the town gates, at the distance of about a mile, the advance of his army being about Watson's house, in the afternoon; when I ordered the cannon at the gate to begin to fire, which stoped their progress : We continued at the lines, standing to our arms, all night, and serving out ammunition to the country militia ; who only came in the day before, with the governor : we were in expectation of their attacking us that night. About 10 o'clock, or sooner, (it being very dark) some of the people on the right, imagined they saw the enemy near the lines, upon which a few hopping shots were fired; and immediately after, the firing run almost through the lines ; with cannon, field-pieces, and musketry : by which unfortunate mistake, Major Benjamin Huger, and 12 others, were either killed or wounded. By the death of Major Huger, his country lost a brave and active officer, an able statesman, and a virtuous citizen. This party was sent without the lines by the governor, as I was told, to stop a gap that was left open for a passage through the abbettis. This time the command was unsettled ; the governor looking upon it as his right to command the militia ; and I knew it to be my right to command the continental troops.

The governor's orders were carried about by some of his aids, in this manner...' you are to obey the orders of the governor; of Gen. Moultrie; and of the privy council,' (8 of them): this order I heard, as I was riding in haste through the gate, to give some directions: I turned myself around, without stopping my horse; cried aloud, ' no orders from the privy council are to be obeyed:' however the orders were delivered to many, along the lines. Lieut. Col. M'Intosh, of the 5th continental regiment, told me, particularly, that the orders were delivered to him, in that way ; and to which he replied...' he would not obey any orders from the privy council; he would obey none, but such as came from the general.' In this awkward, confused situation, were we, when the enemy were before our lines, and the unlucky mistake of the firing happened : when I was informed of the number of men killed and wounded by the accident, I expressed myself with some warmth ; and asked ' who gave the orders for those men to go without the lines,' some one replied, ' the governor ;' he being near at hand, denied his giving any such orders; upon which I said ' gentlemen (addressing myself to the governor and council, they being all together) ' this will never do; we shall be ruined and undone, if we have so many commanders ; it is absolutely necessary to chuse one to command: if you leave the command to me, I will not interfere in any civil matters you may have to do with the enemy; such as parlies, capitulations, &c. I will attend only to the military department.' upon this the governor and council unanimously chose me to the command: after this was done, I employed myself riding along the lines, and giving the necessary directions, and desired the troops and sentries to keep a good look out, but not to throw away their fire. About 3 o'clock in the morning, it being still very dark, I heard some person inquiring for me; I rode up, and was then told the governor wanted to see me; upon which I rode up to him; he then took me aside, and asked me ' whether we had not best have a parly with the enemy; and whether we were able to resist their force;' and asked about our number; I assured him that they were upwards of 2,200 men:* he replied, ' he did not think we had more than 1800 men; and that the enemy's force, as he was informed, was 7 or 8,000 men, at least; and should they force the lines, a great number of the citizens would be put to death.' He represented to me the horrors of a storm: he told me, that the states' engineer, (Col.

....

* I guessed about 2,200 men; but had not yet had a full return: since which some busy persons in town, alarmed the governor and council very much, by telling them, that the enemy had 7 or 8,000 men.

Senf) had represented to him the lines to be in a very weak state :* after some conversation, he proposed to me, the sending out a flag, to know what
terms we could obtain : I told him, I thought we
could stand against the enemy ; that I did not think
they could force the lines; and that I did not chuse
to send a flag in my name, but if he chose it, and
would call the council together, I would send any
message : they requested me to send the following,
which was delivered by Mr. Kinlock.

' GEN. Moultrie perceiving from the motions of
' your army, that your intention is to besiege the
' town, would be glad to know on what terms you
' would be disposed to grant a capitulation, should he
' be inclined to capitulate.'

ABOUT 11 o'clock, A. M. the following letter was
sent in from the enemy.

' SIR,
' THE humane treatment which the inhabitants
' of Georgia and this province, have hitherto receiv-
' ed, will, I flatter myself, induce you to accept of
' the offers of peace and protection, which I now
' make, by the orders of Gen. Provost ; the evils

---

* On our left they were only 3 or 4 feet thick....The para-
pets were not completed.

' and horrors attending the event of a storm, (which
' cannot fail to be successful) are too evident, not to
' induce a man of humane feelings, to do all in his
' power to prevent it : you may depend, that every
' attention shall be paid, and every necessary mea-
' sure be adopted to prevent disorders; and that such
' of the inhabitants, who may not chuse to receive
' the generous offers of peace and protection, may
' be received as prisoners of war, and their fate de-
' cided by that of the rest of the colonies.

' Four hours shall be allowed for an answer; after
' which, your silence, or the detention of the bearer
' of this, will be deemed a positive refusal.

' I have the honor to be, &c.

' J. M. Provost.
' Col. commanding the advance,
' Camp, at Ashley-Ferry.
' May 11th, 1779.

' Brig. Gen. Moultrie,
' or the commanding officer in Charlestown.'

On my receiving this letter, I showed it to the
governor, who immediately summoned his council
to meet at his own house, and requested I would
go with them; and bring Count Paulaski with
me : Col. Laurens was also sent for: and I sent to
Col. Cambray, the engineer, to work upon the
left of our lines, as fast as possible; because that

part was very incomplete : and also ordered the bringing up the ammunition from town, to the lines; as a number of the men had not more than three rounds, the preceeding night : they had come in but the night before, from the country : we scarcely had time to furnish them with arms and ammunition, when the enemy were at our gates. On the meeting of the council, the letter was read to them ; they argued the matter of giving up the town amongst themselves : Gen. Count Paulaski, and my self, advised them not to give up the town; that we had men enough to beat the enemy; and so did Col. Laurens : they then asked me our number, which I gave the governor an account of, corps by corps; and which he took down, on the back of the letter sent to me, from Col. Provost. They amounted to 3,180, at the lowest computation. I had mentioned more, in some of the corps, but it would not be allowed me : the governor was sure there must be some mistake in the returns; that he did not think we had more than 2,500 men on the lines.

AMERICANS.

Charlestown militia	780.
Grimball's artillery	150.
French	50.
Bull's brigade	400.
Col. Neal's regiment	150.

Two Continental regiments . . .	300.	⎫
Col. Harris's detachment . . .	250·	Continentals.
Col. Beekman's artillery . . .	60·	
Col. M'Intosh's 5th regiment . .	190.	⎭
Paulaski's, and Racoon	200.	
Simmons's brigade	600.	
Sailors	50.	

3,180.

A GENTLEMAN who had been reconnoitreing with
a party of horse, about Ponpon bridge and Parker's-
ferry, was asked his opinion, respecting the number
of the enemy; he gave them to the governor, corps
by corps, according to the information he had received; which account was taken down by the governor on the back of the same letter from Col. Provost, and is as follows:

BRITISH.

Royal Scotch Highlanders ·	1300 or 1500.
Hessians	500 or 700.
Royal Americans	200.
Delancey's 1st and 16th . .	200.
Troops from Augustine . .	900.
York Volunteers	
Light-horse	400.
Indians	120.

3,620.

THE gentleman also said, that he was informed, that besides those already taken down, there were a great many tories from North and South-Carolina, and Georgia, that had joined them : I then replied to him, ' that I believed they could not have more than 1,000, at most ;' he said ' he could not tell.'

DURING this business at the governor's house ; Captain Dunbar, of the second regiment, came, in great haste, to acquaint me, that Gen. Provost had observed our working on the lines, during the passing of the flags;* and that if I did not immediately desist, he would march his troops in : I sent orders to stop the working ; and urged the governor and council to conclude upon something, as the time was growing very short, and that I wanted to be at the lines : at length they resolved I should send the following message.

' CHARLESTOWN, May 12th, 1779.

' SIR,

' I CANNOT possibly agree to so dishonorable a
' proposal as is contained in your favor of yesterday ;
' but if you will appoint an officer to confer on terms,

----

* This is contrary to military rules, to work on the lines while flags are passing.

' I will send one to meet him, at such time and place
' as you fix on.

' I have the honor to be, &c.

' WILLIAM MOULTRIE.'

' Brig. Gen. PROVOST.'

ON my retreat from Black-swamp, Colonel Senf,
from the governor's camp, Orangeburgh, joined me
at Ponpon bridge, with the racoon company, commanded by Captain John Allston, of about fifty men
on horseback ; I ordered the stores at the Borough
to be burnt, with a quantity of rice that was in
them, to prevent its falling into the enemy's hands,
and the bridge to be destroyed ; I also ordered
Colonel Senf, with his men, to keep in my rear,
and to burn all boats and bridges, and throw every
obstruction in the enemy's way to retard their
march ; they were the last corps that came into the
town before the gates were shut.

WHEN the question was carried for giving up the
town upon a neutrality, I will not say who was for
the question, but this I well remember, that Mr.
John Edwards, one of the privy council, a worthy
citizen, and a very respectable merchant of Charlestown, was so affected as to weep, and said, ' what,
are we to give up the town at last ?'

THE governor and council adjourned to Colonel
Beekman's tent on the lines, at the gate. I sent for

Colonel John Laurens from his house, to request the favor he would carry a message* from the governor and council to General Provost ; but when he knew the purport, he begged to be excused from carrying such a message, that it was much against his inclination ; that he would do any thing to serve his country ; but he could not think of carrying such a message as that. I then sent for Colonel M'Intosh, and requested he would go with Colonel Roger Smith, who was called on by the governor, with the message ; they both begged I would excuse them; hoped and requested I would get some other person. I however pressed them into a compliance : which message was as follows.

' To propose a neutrality, during the war between Great-Britain and America, and the question, whether the state shall belong to Great Britain, or remain one of the United States? be determined by the treaty of peace between those two powers.'

COLONEL Provost was appointed one of the commissioners to confer with Colonel M'Intosh and Colonel Smith, and they held their conference a quarter of a mile from our gate : we could see them from our lines. Upon the above proposal being made, Colonel Provost answered, ' that they did not come in

---

* All the messages that were carried out, were signed by the gentlemen, and are now in my possession.

a legislative capacity, but if Colonel Smith pleased, he would show the proposal to the general.' Upon meeting them a second time, at 12 o'clock, Colonel Provost said ' he had nothing to do with the governor, that his business was with General Moultrie, and as the garrison was in arms, they must surrender prisoners of war.'

(Signed.)   ' ALEXANDER M'INTOSH,'

Lieut. Col. Comdt. of the 5th Regt. Cont.

' ROGER SMITH,

Lieut. Col. of the 1st bat. militia.

UPON this the governor and council looked very grave and stedfastly on each other and on me, not knowing what I would say. After a little pause, I said to the governor and council, ' gentlemen, you see how the matter stands, the point is this, I am to deliver you up prisoners of war, or not ;' some replied ' yes :' I then said, 'I am determined not to deliver you up prisoners of war,...WE WILL FIGHT IT OUT.' upon my saying this, Colonel Laurens who was in the tent, jumped up, and said, ' thank God! we are upon our legs again;' and as I was coming out of the tent, General Gadsden and Mr. Ferguson, two of the council, who were against giving up the town, followed me and said, ' act according to your own judgment, and we will support you.' I immediately ordered the flag to be waved from the gate, which was a signal agreed upon, should the conference be at an end. They did not perceive our flag wave, they therefore continued with theirs flying, some time longer, upon which I sent out Mr. Kinlock to inform them 'that I was very sorry they should be detained so long, that our flag had been waved some time ago; and that all conference was at an end.' After which I hurried on in preparing every thing for our defence.

IN justice to the citizens, they knew nothing of what was going forward in the council: they all seemed firm, calm, and determined to stand to the lines and defend their country.

THE next morning at day-light, to the great joy of the citizens; it was cried out, along the line, 'the 'enemy is gone.' There is no doubt they must have begun their retreat, with their main body immediately after the conference was at an end; leaving some of their light troops, to make a show before our lines, to divert us from treading too close upon their rear; and to move themselves off, under the cover of the night. Early next morning, not seeing any of them, it was conjectured they were gone; and Count Paulaski went out on horseback, and made two or three circuits at full speed; and not discovering any of them, returned in, and made his reports, and then collected the cavalry, and followed; but they had crossed Ashley-river before he got there : I had given orders to him, to endeavor to find out where Gen. Lincoln was, with his army.

IMMEDIATELY after Gen. Paulaski went out, I issued the following order.

May 13th.

' ONE colonel, 2 lieut. colonels, 2 majors, 10 captains, 20 subalterns, 20 sergeants, and 1,000 rank and file are to hold themselves in readiness, to march at a moment's warning ; and also 1 captain, 2 subalterns, and a sufficient number of men from the artillery, with 2 field-pieces and 100 rounds for each piece.'

THIS detachment I ordered to be in readiness, to reinforce Gen. Lincoln ; as soon as I could hear of him....On the 14th I received the following letter from Gen. Lincoln.

' May 10th, 1779, 4 o'clock, P. M.

' DEAR SIR,

' I JUST now received your favor of the 8th....
' We are making, and shall continue to make every
' exertion, for the relief of Charlestown. The bag-
' gage will be left...the inability of the men only,
' will put a period to our daily marches...I am un-
' happy to inform you, that the 1,000 horse you
' mention, are decreased to less than 150 ; a num-

467

' ber scarcely sufficient for our front and flank guards,
' and the other necessary duties of camp...pray sti-
' mulate your people to every exertion, for the de-
' fence of the town, until the troops here, can ar-
' rive. Our men are full of spirits ; I think they will
' do honor to themselves, and render service to the
' public....Do NOT GIVE UP, OR SUFFER THE PEOPLE
' TO DESPAIR.

   ' I am, &c.

      ' B. LINCOLN.

' Brig. Gen. MOULTRIE.'

A COPY of this letter was taken by the British on the 11th, near our lines, which we suppose obliged them to retreat so precipitately ; as they
found Gen. Lincoln was on his march downwards,
with about 4,000 men ; and had they staid two or
three days longer on the town-neck, they would have
been in a very unpleasant situation, between two
fires : and if they had retreated the same way back,
they would have met Gen. Lincoln's army : they
therefore filed off to the left, and went on the
islands.

  LETTER FROM GENERAL LINCOLN.

   ' May 12th, 1779, 5 o'clock, P. M.

' DEAR SIR,

  ' I HAVE heard nothing from Charlestown, since
' your favor of the 8th ; nor have I any thing more

' to say, than that I observed to you, in mine of the
' 10th: I hope our affairs in your quarter, wear a
' better face, then they did at the time you last
' wrote : we are now encamped about 35 miles from
' Wort's ferry, on Edisto :...we will join you as soon
' as possible.   I am, &c.

'B. LINCOLN.

'Brig. Gen. MOULTRIE.'

LETTER FROM GEN. COUNT PAULASKI.

[Translation.]

'SIR,

'I SHALL remain here, about the environs of
' Dorchester bridge. The 40 horse remaining, are
' not in a state to furnish me with the least necessa-
' ries to form a party of observation : all the vo-
' lunteers* have left me : I do not know if those I
' left near the ferry, and other places, have made to
' you any report. I repeat to you, my general, that
' it is very necessary to fortify the town better...at
' present we have the time, of course let us make
' use of it....I have sent all along the river a patrole...
' the instant I receive any information of Gen. Lin-

....

* Militia.

' coln, I will advance with my party. I have noth-
' ing more to say, but that

                    ' I am, &c.

                            ' C. PAULASKI.

' Brig. Gen. MOULTRIE.'

———

A LETTER TO GEN. LINCOLN.

            'CHARLESTOWN, 13th May, 1779,

                    ' Half past 12 o'clock.

' DEAR SIR,

' I WROTE you this morning, informing you that
' the enemy have very precipitately left this place,
' (the lines) since which, I find the reason was, that
' they took an express coming from you to me, in
' which, I suppose, they have discovered your motions
' and intentions. I therefore think it absolutely neces-
' sary to send you this intelligence, that you may
' conduct yourself accordingly. I will give you very
' frequent notice ; I herewith enclose you their
' general orders for their line of march, which we
' got from an orderly book taken from one of their
' sergeants, which may give you some idea of their
' numbers.

            ' I am, &c.

                    ' WM. MOULTRIE.'

' Maj. Gen. LINCOLN.'

Letter to Gen. Lincoln.

'Charlestown, 13th May, 1779, in the Evening.
'Dear Sir,

'This morning before day the enemy left their
'camp, at Strickland,* near our lines, as they moved
'very precipitately, we imagine they have got some
'intelligence of your coming, and are marching, either
'to attack you, or to get away before you come up.
'I send you this, to give you the earliest notice in or-
'der to prepare yourself for their reception. Their
'number, from all the accounts I can gather, is be-
'tween 3 and 4 thousand men; you know what regu-
'lar troops they have, therefore can tell the number of
'the others, amongst whom are about 100 Indians: a
'1000 men are ordered to hold themselves in readi-
'ness to march at a moment's warning, and are in-
'tended to co-operate with your army, as soon as I
'shall have received more certain intelligence. The
'enemy appear to have taken the Ashley-ferry road.
'I am, &c.

'Wm. Moultrie.'

'Maj. Gen. Lincoln.'

....

* The old race ground.

LETTER FROM GEN. LINCOLN.

'EDISTO MILLS, 14th May, 1779, 9 o'clock.

'DEAR SIR,

'I WAS early this morning honored with your
'two favors of yesterday's date. I hear that the
'enemy were the last evening on this side Ashley-
'ferry, what movements they have made to day, I
'cannot yet hear, but expect soon to know their si-
'tuation, and more of their designs. I shall always
'be obliged by being favored with the information
'you may, from time to time, obtain of their move-
'ments, views, &c.

'I am, &c.

'Brig. Gen. MOULTRIE.   'B. LINCOLN.'

————

LETTER TO GEN. LINCOLN.

'CHARLESTOWN, May 14th, 1779.

'DEAR SIR,

'THE enemy are now at Ashley-river; some few
'have extended themselves on James'-Island. The
'people in town are apprehensive that they mean to
'cross over the river to attack us in rear; but this
'I think cannot be done, as we have a number
'of armed vessels stationed on that part, and some
'of them of considerable force; I doubt not but you
'will keep a good look out for the enemy; they im-
'agine you do not exceed 1500 men. One of Count
'Paulaski's officers, who is upon parole, assures me

'Provost told him so ; upon some conversation which
'he had with him, he asked Captain Celeron where
'you would get more men ? Captain Celeron told me
'he saw the whole British army, and does not think
'they exceed 3,500 including 3 or 400 Indians. I
'should be glad to know where you are, and what
'reinforcement I shall send. I have about 3,000 men
'in town.

'I am, &c.

'WM. MOULTRIE.'

LETTER TO GEN. LINCOLN.

'CHARLESTOWN, May, 15th, 1779.

'DEAR SIR,

'I RECEIVED your favor from the mills. I can-
'not give you any further account of the enemy's
'motions ; all my intelligence hitherto, has been
'from Count Paulaski, who I suppose is now with
'you. I have marched off this morning, to join you,
'400 continental troops, including artillery, with four
'field-peices, three 4, and one 3 pounder, and about
'350 militia ; the militia are mostly those living
'where the enemy have made such havock, I have
'informed them they would have a chance of gather-
'ing their property, as I doubted not, when you sent
'out any parties to collect and stop plundering, they
'would be of the number. I shall be glad to hear
'from you as soon as possible, and whether I should

' send any more men. I shall hold all the country
' militia in readiness, to march at a moment's warn-
' ing.

'I am, &c.

' Wm. Moultrie.'

Letter to Gen. Lincoln.

'May 15th, 1779.

' Dear Sir,

' I wrote you about two hours ago, informing you
' the enemy were making their way towards Port-
' royal, since which, I have intelligence, they are
' encamped about three miles above Ashley-ferry,
' and some of them near the parish church ; by the
' length of their different encampments, as discribed
' by a sensible, faithful negro, it appears the enemy's
' whole force are there. I am at a loss whether to
' move the reinforcement to you or not, as the enemy
' may carry the town before you can be up. I think,
' however, I shall order them to move to the ferry-
' road, and gain all the intelligence they can, and
' there wait your orders.

'I am, &c.

' Wm. Moultrie.'

Letter to Gen. Lincoln.

' May 15th, at half past 1 o'clock.

' The governor and council have requested that I

' would detain the detachment in town, till they
' can be better informed, as they are apprehensive
' the enemy will cross over behind the lines. I have
' accordingly stopped their march, until I hear fur-
' ther from you. I have about 2,500, or 3,000 men
' in town.

' I am, &c.

' WM. MOULTRIE.'

LETTER TO GEN. LINCOLN.

' CHARLESTOWN, May 16th, 1779. 5 o'clock, A. M.
' DEAR SIR,

 ' SINCE I wrote you yesterday, a deserter came
' in, who informs me the whole British army are
' now on James'-Island, with all their artillery, stores,
' &c. as if they intended a lodgement there : I am
' informed they have a number of boats, such as
' schooners and large row-boats, which they have
' collected about the country : it looks as if they
' meant to attack the town from that quarter : I have
' countermanded the march of the detachment I had
' ordered to join you, as we must guard the town all
' around.

' I am, &c.

' WILLIAM MOULTRIE.'

BY the movements of the enemy at Wappoo and
on James'-Island, (which we could discern very plainly
from the church steeple) the citizens were appre..

hensive the town would be attacked from that quarter, which obliged us to alter our disposition, and change our front: and also we were fearful they would take possession of Fort Johnson ; upon which, I received the following letter from the governor, and issued the necessary orders.

LETTER FROM THE GOVERNOR.

'May 16th, 1779.

' DEAR SIR,

' I REQUEST that you will be pleased to give 'the necessary orders for having the guns at Fort ' Johnson re-spiked with steel spikes,* and the shot ' brought away to town : if time will hereafter ad- ' mit of our bringing off the guns, or throwing them ' into the river ; it will be expedient to do so ; but ' I find this will be a work of great labor and delay : ' in the mean time, pray do not let us lose a mo- ' ment, in doing what I now propose : it will take a ' very short time ; and from the inclosed observa- ' tions from Mr. Timothy, on the church steeple ; ' I do not apprehend there is any great danger in

....

* When the garrison was withdrawn from Fort Johnson, they were slightly spiked with nails.

446

'the attempt...Treville says he will effect it with a
'small party of picked men.

'I am, &c.

'J. RUTLEDGE.

'Brig. Gen. MOULTRIE.'

ORDERS TO JOHN M'QUEEN, ESQ.

'SIR,

'You will please to proceed with your vessels,
'down to Fort Johnson; and draw as near as you
'can, to cover a party, going over to bring off some
'cannon.

'WILLIAM MOULTRIE.'

ORDERS TO CAPT. DE TREVILLE.

'SIR,

'You are to proceed over to Fort Johnson, with
'25 men, to bring off the shot, and spike the can-
'non left therein....The party to be taken from the
'continental troops, completely armed.

'WILLIAM MOULTRIE.'

THIS party was surprized, and some of them taken
prisoners.

DISPOSITION OF THE SHIPPING.

'CAPT. Newal's ship to lay in the river, near
James'-Island creek.'

'CAPT. M'Queen's ship to lay between Fort Johnson, and Broughton's battery.'

'CAPT. Newton's ships to be stationed near Wappoo-creek.'

'EACH of those vessels to keep out their boats at night, to discover the enemy, (should they attempt to cross the river) and give notice, by firing 3 guns; and immediately to keep up a brisk fire upon the enemy, to prevent their landing in town.'

'THE gallies are to be stationed between the ships and the shore of Charlestown.'

'THE French ship to haul up Town-creek, so as to flank the lines.'

'THE detachment commanded by Col. Harris, to join General Lincoln's: Georgia brigade (250); Cols. Garden and Skirving's regiments; Capts. Waring and Linning's companies; detachment from Robert's, with 2 field-pieces; detachment from Major Grimball's, with 2 field-pieces; 100 riflemen, from the corps of Majors Ellison, Irvine. and Lyde; such of Col. Horry's regiment who have horses; and Capt. Allston's company, are to join this detachment.'

'THIS detachment to hold themselves in readiness to march at a moment's warning.'

[THIS detachment was countermanded, and ordered to join the line again.]

'THAT Col. Marion, with the detachment of the second regiment, under marching orders, do immediately repair to Fort Moultrie.'

'THE commissary to lay in two months provision, for 500 men, at Fort Moultrie.'

[WE were apprehensive the British would make some serious attempt upon Fort Moultrie.]

'CAPT. Darrel's company to repair to their own fort.'

'THE volunteer company to take post at the Exchange.'

'THE grenadier company to take post at the battery near Roper's-wharf.'

'THE true-blue company to take post at the fort, near the Governor's-bridge.'

'COL. Harris, with his detachment, to occupy the two redoubts, on the left of the line ; and reinforce the horn-work at the gate-way, with the like number of men, as are taken from thence, belonging to the second regiment.'

'COL. Garden's detachment to take post at Gadsden's-wharf.'

'THE artillery, under marching orders, with their 4 field-pieces, and the remainder of the second regiment, are to be posted at, or near the Beef-market, as a corps de reserve ; to be always ready to support any part of the town that may be attacked.'

'GEN. Count Paulaski's corps to join the reserve.'

' Capts. Allston's, Sinclair's, and Legaré's troops
are to patrole the streets ; six horses in each
patrole ; going different ways ; and when any alarm
shall happen, they shall repair to the place, and inquire the cause, and immediately acquaint the commanding officer thereof.'

' Col. John Harleston will remain at Cumming's-
creek with Capts. Linning's and Waring's companies,
and detach a corporal's guard to the little battery, to
the southward of his post.'

' All the troops in garrison are to be under arms
at 3 o'clock, and to continue until it is clear day-
light, every day.'

The enemy being on James'-Island and Wappoo,
only about 2 miles from us, (in sight, from the church
steeple) and having a sufficient number of boats, to
transport their troops at one time over to Charlestown, kept us continually upon the watch, and obliged us to break up our little army into a number
of small guards, to be posted round the town, (as the
foregoing orders show) to prevent us from being
surprised : and the whole of these orders show that
we were apprehensive of an attack every night.

LETTER FROM GEN. PROVOST.

'HEAD-QUARTERS, ASHLEY-FERRY.

'May 13th, 1779.

'SIR,

'THE anxiety of Capt. Celeron, for his ex-
'change; and the total want of necessaries, which
'can be illy supplied by us, at present, has induced
'me, to allow him, and Mr. De la Close* to return
'on their parole, to Charlestown: I have to request
'that Capt. Constable be sent back in his place, as
'soon as possible, to the head-quarters of the Bri-
'tish army; or that he may, agreeable to his parole,
'surrender himself a prisoner at Savannah, in twen-
'ty days from this date; if you do not chuse to comply
'with my application, any British lieutenant, in the
'place of Mr. De la Close, will be received in ex-
'change.

'I have the honor to be, &c.

'A. PROVOST.

'Brig. Gen. MOULTRIE.'   B. G.

LETTER FROM GEN. LINCOLN.

'HEAD-QUARTERS, FORD'S-FERRY, 16th May, 1779.

'DEAR SIR,

'I HAVE received your two favors of yesterday's
'date; I cannot learn, with any degree of certainty'

....

* Capt. Celeron and Lieut. De la Close, were of Paulaski's
legion, and were taken before the town, on the 12th instant.

' where the enemy are. I expect every moment to
' be relieved from my present doubts on that head.
' I think while the enemy are hovering about Charles-
' town, you had better remain there with the troops
' you had detached; but as soon as it is evident that
' they mean to leave it, you will please to follow
' them and join us. Our time yesterday was taken
' up in preparing ammunition for the militia. Col.
' Hammond, whom I sent with a party of horse to
' Salt-ketcher, is on his way, with about 100 negroes,
' whom the enemy were sending to Georgia. I ex-
' pect to write again in an hour or two, for I think
' in that time I shall know better the enemy's situ-
' ation, and more of their intentions than I have at
' present been able to learn. The accounts I have
' are vague and contradictory.

I am, &c.

' B. LINCOLN.'

' Gen. MOULTRIE.'

FROM THE SAME.

'HEAD-QUARTERS, PARKER'S-FERRY, May 17, 1779.

' DEAR SIR,

' THE army arrived here last evening; a party of
' our light-horse is at Jacksonburgh; about 300
' negroes have been taken from the enemy; I have
' ordered an account to be taken of them, and to
' whom they belong, by the quarter-master; after

'that is done, I shall send a copy of it to town,
'and the negroes to Colonel Ford's or Dorchester.
'I hope their owners will send for them as soon as
'they be known. Part of the enemy (by good in-
'formation) were yesterday at Governor Rutledge's
'plantation, under Colonel Provost, viz. High-
'landers, a party of Brown's corps, and a party
'of the green coats. General Provost is said to have
'passed either at Stono or Wappoo; the former (by
'some information I had last night) is the most pro-
'bable: you will please, as I said before, as soon as
'you can leave the town with safety, to tread on the
'heels of the enemy; and remember, at the same
'time, that it is possible that you may be driven to
'the necessity of retreating, the means of which,
'you will keep in your power.

'THERE are a number of people in the neighbor-
'hood who have taken protections; I have forbidden
'them to come into camp, for we cannot admit them
'as friends, and they will incumber the army if we
'consider them as enemies. I wish to know what,
'under the present situation of affairs, the civil au-
'thority of the state, would wish me to do in this
'matter; those whom I find dangerous to the army,
'I shall confine.

'I am, &c.

'B. LINCOLN.

'Brig. Gen. MOULTRIE.'

483

FROM THE SAME.

'BEACH-HILL, COL. PINCKNEY'S PLANTATION.

'11 o'clock, P. M. 18th May, 1779.

'DEAR SIR,

'WE just arrived here on our way to Bacon's
'Bridge, in the neighborhood of which, the troops
'will probably encamp this night. I wish to see
'you, either this evening, or in the morning. We
'have a body of light troops marching by the road
'on our right, and a party of horse gone to recon-
'noitre the enemy; on their return, I expect some
'further account of their situation, &c.

'I am, &c.

'B. LINCOLN.

'Brig. Gen. MOULTRIE.'

———

FROM THE SAME.

'BACON'S-BRIDGE, May 18th, 1779. 3 o'clock.

'DEAR SIR,

'I JUST now arrived at this place, where the
'troops are to be encamped; and will remain for the
'night...the party below last night, have taken 172
'negroes; many of them, I hear, are the property
'of his excellency Gov. Rutledge; I wish you would
'mention the matter to him, and request he would
'send some person to receive them. I beg to repeat

' my request, that you would give me the pleasure
' of seeing you as soon as possible.

    ' I am, &c.

        ' B. LINCOLN.

' Brig. Gen. MOULTRIE.'

———

LETTER FROM GEN. PROVOST.

   ' HEAD-QUARTERS, May 19th, 1779.

' SIR,

 ' I EXPECTED to have had the honor of a letter
' from you, in answer to mine, by Capt. Celeron,
' from Ashley-ferry.

 ' I AM now to acquaint you, that I have got about
' 50 of the Beaufort and John's-Island militia, or
' state troops, including officers ; who I am willing
' to exchange, for an equal number of ours, who
' may be now in your hands ; taking first, such as
' may have been taken, during our march through
' Carolina. There are, besides, 15 wounded, who are
' permitted to go to their own friends' houses, with
' a surgeon to attend them, until their recovery.

 ' I have the honor to be, &c.

      ' A. PROVOST.

        B. G.

 ' P. S. I must not omit to acquaint you, that a
' Sergeant Cooke, of the 60th regiment, has been
' this day, carried off from a Mrs. Roans, where he

' had been placed as a safe-guard :* as this has not
' been the first instance of the kind ; and as it is di-
' rectly contrary to all rule ; I beg leave to acquaint
' you, that if this sergeant is not returned to his
' corps, I shall never again allow of any safe-guard
' to any place, be the consequence what it will.

 ' Brig. Gen. MOULTRIE,

  ' or officer commanding in Charlestown.'

LETTER TO GEN. LINCOLN.

   ' CHARLESTOWN, May 21st, 1779.

' DEAR SIR,

 ' THE governor and council have agreed I should
' reinforce you with 1200 men ;† I have accordingly
' ordered them to be in readiness to march off this
' afternoon, with 4 field-pieces ; I hope they will be
' with you to-morrow morning : I am informed of
' 90 Catawba Indians on their march to join you :
' I cannot hear any more of Kershaw's 500 men.

   ' I am &c.

    ' WILLIAM MOULTRIE.

' GEN. LINCOLN.'

      ....

 * A safe-guard left any where, is always looked upon, by
all parties, as a sacred person, and never should be molested :
he was taken by some of the militia...he was returned.

 † It was agreed between Gen. Lincoln and myself, that
when we wrote about our numbers, we should write double of
what they really were ; therefore the detachment was only
600. This was to perplex the enemy, should they take our
letters.

LETTER FROM GEN. PROVOST.

'HEAD-QUARTERS, May 21st, 1779.

' SIR,

' I AGREE to the exchange you propose....I am
' sorry Capt. Constable should be excepted against,
' as from the best information I have been able to
' procure, I am persuaded there is not any just rea-
' son can be given for his detention, or the hardships
' he has been made to experience : the crime alleg-
' ed against him, was never proved, or in any legal
' or satisfactory manner brought home to him ; and
' as it was supposing him to have been the author of it
' ...it was previous to his being admitted to parole, and
' whilst he was in confinement. I beg to recom-
' mend this man's affair to your candor. Sergeant
' Cooke has been returned. The pilot boat may be
' sent when you please to John's-Island, for the pur-
' pose you mentioned ; but I had rather it should be
' sent to Wappoo-creek, and notice given to the se-
' veral ladies and families, to meet it there ; but if
' you incline the former, you will please to let me
' know the landing you wish to send it to : I should
' ever be happy to gratify every request of yours ; and
' to soften, as much as is in my power, the rigors
' of war, to suffering individuals. Inclosed you will
' receive a list of the prisoners on this, and on John's-
' Island : there are about 20 more, whose names I
' cannot now send you, but they shall attend to-mor-

' row at Glen's-landing. Major Moore of the Geor-
' gia brigade, was sometime since, sent into Carolina
' for Major Fleming: on Fleming's arrival here,
' Major Moore will be free to act. For any number
' you send us, exceeding that which we have here to
' deliver you, you shall have an order on the com-
' missary general, of prisoners in Georgia, who at
' the same time will have direction to give passports
' to such prisoners, to the head-quarters of the
' American army in this province, sending lists and
' duplicates to this....I wish for the relief of both, to
' include in the exchange, those people who were
' some time ago taken on their way to join the royal
' army in Georgia, and are now in confinement in
' Carolina: humanity should incline to this measure;
' on that score I recommend it to you.

  ' I have the honor to be, &c.

         ' A. PROVOST.

' Brig. Gen. MOULTRIE.

    LETTER TO GEN. PROVOST.

     ' CHARLESTOWN, May 21st, 1779

' SIR,

  ' I BEG leave to propose in exchange for Captain,
' Celeron, Captain Whitley of Colonel Brown's corps
' and Lieutenant Dawkins for Lieutenant De la Close
' of Count Paulaski's legion. I am sorry to inform
' you, that Captain Constable is excepted against

'by the state, whose prisoner he is, as having been
'guilty of breaking his parole, and thereby rendered
'incapable of being exchanged. I herewith send you
'a list of prisoners of war now in our hands, and
'should be much obliged to you, if you would in
'return, favor me with a list of such of our people
'as may have been made prisoners by your army,
'during your march through a part of this state. I
'am intirely unacquainted with any circumstances
'relating to Sergeant Cooke; he is, in all probability,
'made prisoner by a party from the army under
'General Lincoln. I should esteem it as a favor,
'if you would permit a surgeon's being sent from
'hence, in order to attend our sick and wounded,
'on John's-Island; as there are several ladies upon
'the island who are desirous of returning to Charles-
'town, with their families, they may, if you think
'proper, embrace the opportunity of returning, by
'the pilot-boat that carries the surgeon. Captain
'Cattell and Mr. Hall, will wait your answer.

'I have the honor to be, yours, &c.

'WM. MOULTRIE.'

'Brig. Gen. PROVOST.'

LETTER TO GEN. PROVOST.

'CHARLESTOWN, May 22d, 1779.

'SIR,

'MR. Dawkins being amenable to the laws of this

' state, against which he has offended, cannot be con-
' sidered as a prisoner of war, and the exchange I
' yesterday proposed, with respect to him, cannot
' take place ; I am sorry that I was not sooner made
' acquainted with such circumstances as make it
' improper to exchange him. Lieutenant Ellis
' will, if you think proper, be given for Lieutenant
' De la Close ; Captain Constable having violated
' his parole, is, and will be considered as unexchange-
' able by the state ; circumstances respecting his
' guilt and treatment, I am as yet a stranger to.
' Major Fleming will be at liberty to act, whenever
' Major Moore shall have joined the American army,
' of which, immediate notice will be given. An or-
' der upon your commissary of prisoners in Savan-
' nah I cannot receive ; but a number of your men,
' prisoners with us, will be given for an equal num-
' ber of ours, prisoners with you, delivered at Wap-
' poo. The persons taken on their way to join the
' army of his Brittanic majesty, are not under my
' direction, having been delivered up to the civil
' authority of the state. Mr. Wright, who is now
' on parole, will, if agreeable to you, be exchanged
' immediately ; his name added to your list of pri-
' soners, will make the number 63.

 ' I have the honor to be, yours, &c.

    ' WM. MOULTRIE.'

LETTER FROM GOV. RUTLEDGE.

'May 22d, half past 5 o'clock, P. M.

' DEAR SIR,

'MR. Timothy will inform you of a discovery
' which he has just made, of some boats of the ene-
' my at Wappoo (according to Mr. Tucker's ac-
' count, to whom you gave a flag, and who went
' with it to Wappoo to-day) Gen. and Col. Provost
' were both at Wappoo, with Maitland and others ;
' may it not be very probable, if Mr. Timothy's eyes
' do not deceive him with respect to the number of
' boats, that a surprize may be attempted this after-
' noon, or rather in the evening, or to night...con-
' sequently proper to give the necessary orders to
' guard against such a measure...you will, if you
' think proper, give such orders.

'I am, &c.

' J. RUTLEDGE.

' Brig. Gen. MOULTRIE.'

———

LETTER FROM A. PROVOST.

' HEAD-QUARTERS, 23d May, 1779.

' SIR,

'BEING too much taken up, as to attend to the
' number of private flags constantly flocking in, that
' I am to desire, that none may be permitted or

'sent, unles it is upon public business, and those
'will only be received in Wappoo-creek.

'I have the honor to be, &c.

'A. PROVOST.'

'Brig Gen. MOULTRIE.'

ABOUT this time individuals were continually in-
treating and teazing Gen. Provost and myself, for
private flags from one army to the other, to see their
friends, or to look after some little property ; we
were constantly interrupted, so that we could
scarcely attend to other business. I cannot but say
that I was not displeased, when General Provost
put a stop to it, as on my part I could not refuse
my fellow citizens that favor.

LETTER TO GEN. LINCOLN.

'CHARLESTOWN, May 23d, 1779.

'DEAR SIR,

'By an exchanged officer* who came yesterday,
'I am informed that the enemy's main body are at
'James'-Island ; he saw about 400 men by them-
'selves, about 200 of which were Hessians ; some
'others are gone to James'-Island : by his account,
'they seem much dispersed : I think they may be
'attacked with great advantage about Ashley-river :

* Mr. Adams.

' he says they were in great bustle yesterday about
' Wappoo ; and it was thought by some, that you
' were moving towards them : they are collecting a
' number of boats about the Island, it is thought, to
' make their retreat : you see by the inclosed, that
' they have their vessels coming round to them : if
' we can destroy them, it will be a great stroke : I
' have sent Mr. ——, to conduct any party you think
' proper to send : you will see by the governor's let-
' ter the plan appears easy and reasonable.

' I am, &c.

' WILLIAM MOULTRIE.

' Gen. LINCOLN.'

———

LETTER FROM GEN. PROVOST.

' HEAD-QUARTERS, 24th May, 1779.

' SIR,

' I AM just now honored with yours ; with respect
' to the exchange of Mr. W——, I am sorry it is not
' in my power to comply with the request, as it is de-
' termined to exchange no more gentlemen, until we
' have satisfaction for the treatment some of our's
' have received among you, particularly, till it is
' agreed to exchange Captain Constable and Lieuten-
' ant Dawkins, for officers of their rank. On the
' contrary, I intend very soon to summon in, every

' gentleman that has been admitted to parole, during
' my march from Georgia.'

' I have the honor to be, &c.

' A. PROVOST.

' Brig. Gen. MOULTRIE.'

———

LETTER FROM GEN. LINCOLN.

' DEAR SIR,

' I WISH to see you this evening at the ferry house;
' I will cross the ferry and meet you between 9 and
' 10 o'clock. I have something to communicate,
' which I dare not commit to writing, and which
' ought not to be delayed.

' I am, &c.

' B. LINCOLN.

' Brig. Gen. MOULTRIE.'

———

LETTER FROM GEN. PROVOST.

' HEAD-QUARTERS, 27th May, 1779.

' SIR,

' HAVING received information that Capt. Knowles
' of his majesty's navy, had fallen into your hands,
' I am to propose his exchange for Major Habers-
' ham, who shall immediately be ordered at liberty,
' and permission for him to return to the American
' army. Or any other Major that may be in our
' hands. I have to request likewise, to be furnished

‘ with a list of those officers of the navy that may
‘ have been taken at that time, or since.

‘ I have the honor to be, &c.

‘ A. Provost.

‘ Brig. Gen. Moultrie.’

———

LETTER FROM GEN. LINCOLN.

‘ 13 MILE-HOUSE, MRS. ELLIS’, 30th May, 1779.

10 o’clock, A. M.

‘ DEAR SIR,

‘ THE enemy are throwing up some works at
‘ Stono-ferry, where they are collecting their schoon-
‘ ers and boats. I hope our armed vessels will keep
‘ them from getting to sea in their craft, while we
‘ watch their motions on the land.

‘ I am, &c.

‘ B. LINCOLN.

‘ Brig. Gen. Moultrie.’

———

LETTER FROM GOV. RUTLEDGE.

‘ May 31st, 1779.

‘ DEAR SIR,

‘ ON my return home just now, I was informed by
‘ one of the aids, of a message from you, that you
‘ intended sending a flag to General Provost, and
‘ wished to know, if Lieutenant Knowles might be
‘ exchanged for Major Habersham, or some other

' officer, in the enemy's hands; but I cannot consent
' to a proposition of this kind: I chuse to reserve
' Mr. Knowles, in order to exchange him, at a pro-
' per time, for any officer of the navy of this state,
' who may be taken.

' I am, &c.

' J. Rutledge.

' Brig. Gen. Moultrie.'

———

From Gen. Lincoln.

' 13 Mile-house,* June, 1st. 1779.

' Dear Sir,

' I received yours of yesterday's date last even-
' ing. I am glad to hear that your armed vessels are
' gone round; two of the enemy's gallies are in
' Wadmalaw, and it is said, more are expected.
' They attacked a pilot boat and a small schooner,
' sent up yesterday by Captain Anthony, (on a sup-
' position that they were not vessels of force) and
' soon obliged our people to leave their little craft.
' We marched yesterday morning towards the ene-
' my; but on their being reconnoitered by Count
' Paulaski; he thought them too strongly posted and
' of too great force for us to attack, and therefore or-
' dered the troops to retire. For particulars I refer

* Stono.

‘ you to Major Oliphant, who will wait on you with
‘ this and give you them.

‘ I am, &c.

‘ B. Lincoln.

‘ Gen. Moultrie.’

———

From Gen. Huger.

‘ Camp, Stono, 1st June 1779.

‘ Dear Gen.

‘ Yesterday morning I was detached with one
‘ thousand foot to attack a post of the enemy’s, at
‘ Stono-ferry (this side of the river) with Count Pau-
‘ laski and Horry’s horse; the light infantry and a
‘ party of Williamson’s foot, to begin the attack on
‘ their right flank; General Butler, with a party of
‘ his Brigade on their left; the 1st and 6th Carolina
‘ continentals, with four field-pieces with me; I was
‘ to charge them in front, and endeavor to force their
‘ lines, supported by General Lincoln, and the re-
‘ mainder of the army a mile in our rear. Count
‘ Paulaski on reconnoitering their works, found them
‘ entrenched with a line on their front, and flanked
‘ by batteries completely manned, with very large
‘ reinforcements from General Provost, too strong
‘ for us to attempt, therefore ordered me to retreat.
‘ A deserter shortly afterwards joined us, and said

' Colonel Provost was strongly posted at the ferry,
' with fifteen hundred ready to receive us.

' I am, &c.

' ISAAC HUGER.

' Gen. MOULTRIE.'

FROM COUNT PAULASKI.

[Translation.]

' FARR'S PLANTATION, June 2d, 1779.

' ON reconnoitering the enemy we have had a
' skirmish. Two of my officers are wounded, and
' the enemy retired near a thick wood. We had de-
' termined to re-attack them in their lines, which
' were formed near the ferry; but on their receiving
' reinforcements made us change our intention. To-
' day we are informed that there are some of the en-
' emy's gallies in the river. I cannot find a favorable
' opportunity to act.

' I remain, &c.

' C. PAULASKI.

' Gen. MOULTRIE.'

LETTER TO GEN. PROVOST,

' JAMES'-ISLAND, 4th June, 1779.

' SIR,

' I WAS honored with your two favors of the 27th
' inst. Captain Knowles being captured by a ship of
' war of this state, must consequently be a prisoner

' of war to this state. To exchange him for any
' other than a naval officer of South-Carolina, would
' be prejudicing our marine, as it would be an injury
' done our officers ; and though you may not know
' any difference betwixt continental and state prison-
' ers, you must allow the propriety of our making
' the distinction. I am sincerely sorry Captain
' Knowles' private affairs should suffer by his cap-
' tivity, and would with pleasure, be of service to him,
' where my being so, did not interfere with my duty
' to my country. I cannot think, because we are
' unwilling to ill treat the officers of our navy, to
' favor one of your's, you will put your threat in
' execution, of sending to New-York the prisoners
' with you and in Georgia : a little reflection must
' convince you of the injustice, as well as cruelty of
' such a proceeding. I must observe to you also,
' that there are numbers of British prisoners in the
' United States, and that unnecessary hardships and
' severity shewn our people, unfortunate enough to
' be in your power, will demand a like treatment to
' such of your's as the fortune of war may have
' placed in our hands. With this I send you a list of
' prisoners with us, who may be exchanged as soon
' as agreeable to you. I likewise send you a letter I
' received from Mr. P———, by which you will learn
' his opinion of his situation; Mr. M'———, if not
' with you already, is on his way to your camp. I

' will give notice to the gentlemen, a list of whose
' names you have sent me, and copies of whose
' paroles I have received, that you expect they will
' repair immediately to the head-quarters of his
' Britanic majesty's army on John's-Island. You
' have sent by mistake, two copies of Mr. M'Pherson's
' and Mr. Lyn's paroles ; so that I have received six
' copies of paroles, and not eight, as you mention.
' I know nothing of Captain Harrison, where he
' is, or who he is. Captain O——, though indulged
' on parole, is not at liberty to act. The money
' brought from the last flag, from you, I have sent
' to our commissary of prisoners of war, who will
' deliver it as directed : I shall esteem it as a favor,
' of your permitting Mrs. S——, Mrs. E——, and
' families, to leave John's-Island. I will send a boat
' for them...where and when you may appoint, if you
' grant them permission:

> ' I have the honor to be, yours, &c.

> > ' WILLIAM MOULTRIE.'

FROM GEN. PROVOST.

> HEAD-QUARTERS, 5th June, 1779.

' SIR,

' I HAVE the honor of your's of yesterday, and beg
' leave in the most sincere manner, to return my
' best thanks to you and the other gentleman, from
' whom Captain Knowles receives civilities. As

' Captain Knowles is always employed with the
' army, I judged it fell to our share to exchange him,
' as much as to the navy ; and therefore proposed to
' give Major Habersham, a gentleman of character
' also, for him, or any other of that rank, you might
' pitch upon. I still think, it might be managed in
' this way, notwithstanding the distinction made by
' your governor ; and wish, for the sake of both the
' gentlemen, it might be so done ; Captain Knowles
' to act on the arrival of the other gentlemen
' with your army. Inclosed, I send you a list of
' prisoners* of war upon parole, who I desire may
' have directions to repair forthwith, to my head-
' quarters, to have their paroles renewed in more
' ample form, than the hurry of a march would admit
' of.   I have the honor to be, &c.

' Brig. Gen. MOULTRIE.   A. PROVOST.'

LETTER FROM THE PRESIDENT OF CONGRESS,
WITH RESOLVES.

' PHILADELPHIA, May 15th, 1779.

' MAJOR Gen. Lincoln's ill state of health, has in-

---

* A list of which I shall keep to myself, of 16 prisoners,
most of whom followed the British army to get a protection,
instead of being paroled ; some of them we found in town after
the evacuation, and some of them went off with the British.
Their petitions to the legislature, praying for mercy after we
came into town, will point out many of them.

' duced Congress to permit him to retire from a cli-
' mate and service unfriendly to its recovery.

' I HAVE now the honor of transmitting to you, a
' copy of an act of the 13th instant, appointing you
' commander in his absence, during the continuence
' of the Southern army to the southward of North-
' Carolina ; and until the further order of Congress.

' ACCEPT my best wishes, that this appointment
' may be productive of fresh laurels, and that you
' may again be the instrument of encreasing the ho-
' nors and security of your country.

'I have the honor to be, &c.

' JOHN JAY, President.

' Brig. Gen. MOULTRIÉ.'

' IN CONGRESS, May 13th, 1779.

' RESOLVED that Brig. Gen. Moultrie, be com-
' mander, in the absence of Major Gen. Lincoln, of
' the Southern army, during its continuence to the
' southward of North-Carolina ; with the allowance
' of a Major General, on a separate command, until
' the further order of Congress.

' Extracts from the Minutes.

' CHARLES THOMSON, Sec'ry.'

ANSWER TO THE PRESIDENT OF CONGRESS.

' CHARLESTOWN, June 7th, 1779.

' SIR,

' I HAVE been honored with yours of 15th May,

' inclosing the copy of a resolution of Congress ; by
' which I am, in the absence of Gen. Lincoln, ap-
' pointed commander in chief of the Southern army,
' during its continuence to the southward of North-
' Carolina : the present posture of affairs will, I
' trust, prevent Gen. Lincoln from availing himself
' of the permission granted him by Congress ; but
' should the state of his health require , at any fu-
' ture time, his return to the Northward, and de-
' prive us of an officer to whom the country is so
' much indebted, be assured, sir, that my ambition
' will be to supply so great a loss, to the best of my
' abilities ; and that my utmost endeavors will be ex-
' erted for the welfare of this state, and in defence
' of our common cause : permit me, in the mean
' time, to make, through you, my most sincere ac-
' knowledgements to Congress, for this proof of the
' confidence they are pleased to honor me with.

' I have the honor to be, &c.

' WM. MOULTRIE.

' His excellency JOHN JAY, ESQ.
' President of Congress.'

LETTER TO GEN. PROVOST.

' CHARLESTOWN, June 8th, 1779.

' SIR,

' CAPT. Knowles having been frequently em-
' ployed with your army, does not, I conceive, ren-
' der him the less a sea-officer, and as it is not at all

' impossible, but that some officer of our navy may fall
' into your hands ; the reasons urged by the governor
' for not exchanging him on the terms you propose,
' must appear a very proper one : let me, however,
' assure you sir, that Capt. Knowles shall, in the mean
' time, meet with every degree of attention that is
' due to a gentleman ; and that the circumstances of
' the present juncture will admit of.   Mr. W——, is
' on his way to Georgia ; but with respect to the
' other gentlemen, whose names are included in your
' list, as several deny their having been made prison-
' ers of war : it is absolutely necessary that an au-
' thentic copy of each parole should be sent.

'I have the honor to be, &c.

'WM. MOULTRIE.'

FROM GEN. LINCOLN.
'NEAR 13 MILE-HOUSE, STONO-FERRY.
'June 8th, 1779.

'DEAR SIR,
'IF the boats which were a few days ago at
' Ashley-ferry, have been sent to town, I wish you
' would give orders for all of them immediately to
' return to the ferry : and that they be kept under a
' good guard, on the Charlestown side, with orders,
' if the enemy should approach, to go up or down the
' river, as the tide may favor, and rather than let them
' fall into their hands, destroy them.   The enemy

' seem to have in contemplation some movements;
' they will be attentively watched, and our troops
, ready to march on the shortest notice.

'I am, &c.

'B. LINCOLN.

'Gen. MOULTRIE.'

THE occasion of this letter, was, that we were apprehensive the enemy would endeavor, by surprise, to take our boats, to help themselves off.

FROM THE SAME.

'CAMP, June 8th, 1779.

'DEAR SIR,

' I HAVE not heard, since the return of Gen.
' Huger, any thing relative to the fleet, seen off Sto-
' no-inlet; if you discover that which looks like a
' movement, pray give me the earliest notice of it.
' Col. Richardson, who is stationed near Rantowle's-
' bridge, with a number of infantry and militia-horse,
' informs me, that a schooner or two, not far below
' it, were, the day before yesterday, loading, with
' what he could not ascertain, and that a detachment
' from Kershaw's regiment, had deserted their post :
' viz, 1 capt. 1 subaltern; and 27 privates.

'I am, &c.

'B. LINCOLN.

'Gen. MOULTRIE.'

FROM THE SAME.

'HEAD-QUARTERS, 13 MILE-HOUSE, STONO.

'June 9th, 1779.

'DEAR SIR,

'I DO myself the honor to inclose you a copy'
'of the two acts of Congress;* one passed March
'17th, the other May 13th; the former permitting
'me to return Northward: the other appointing you
'to the command here; a copy of which, I suppose
'has been sent you also: I congratulate you on the
'honor done you, and most cordially wish you full
'support; and that these states may be soon extri-
'cated from their present embarrassments.

'I am, &c.

'B. LINCOLN.

'Gen. MOULTRIE.'

———

TO GEN. LINCOLN.

'CHARLESTOWN, June 10th, 1779.

'DEAR SIR,

'THIS will be handed you by the Marquis De
'Bretigny; who will give you a piece of intelligence†
'of very great consequence to us; which should not
'be communicated to writing: you will, I doubt
'not, inform him of your plan of operations, for the

•••••••••••••••••••••••••••••••

* Two acts, same as sent me by the president of Congress.
† Relative to Count D'Estaing's coming to our assistance.

' reasons which he will mention to you. I send you
' Mr. Timothy's observations from the church stee-
' ple ; it seems as if the enemy had a mind to amuse
' us this way ; perhaps to play some other game : I
' shall watch their motions closely, and doubt not,
' but you will observe them narrowly : I have sent a
' reinforcement of 40 men to Fort Moultrie,* which
' will make the garrison 300 strong.

' I am, &c.

' WM. MOULTRIE.

' Gen. LINCOLN.'

ABOUT this time, Gen. Lincoln was very much
displeased, because some ill natured persons had
been casting reflections on him, for his having
marched up to Augusta with the main body of his
army ; and leaving the low country exposed to the
enemy ; and putting Charlestown in such imminent
danger : these reflections were thrown out by persons who were not acquainted with Gen. Lincoln's
motives for taking that step, in which he was perfectly justifiable ; as the council of general officers,
held at Black-swamp on 19th of April, advised the
measures as being rational and proper. Gen. Lincoln was a brave, active, and very vigilant officer ;

----

* We were apprehensive the enemy would attempt to surprise Fort Moultrie ; we therefore always kept a strong garrison there, with Gen. Marion.

and always so very cautious, that he would take no
step of any consequence, without first calling a council of officers, to advise with them on the measures.

LETTER FROM GEN. LINCOLN.

'NEAR 13 MILE-HOUSE, June 10th, 1779.

' DEAR SIR,

' IN your's of the 8th, you express a wish that I
' should still retain the command of the army in this
' state ; the same motives which led me here, would
' retain me, so long as my health should permit me
' to act : if there was the same prospect of rendering
' services to my country, as when I took command
' in this department ; but as it appears, from the un-
' kind declarations daily thrown out in your capital,
' that I have lost the confidence of the people ;
' whether justly or not, must be determined on some
' future day, without which, I can render little service
' to the public.   I ought to retire ; for whenever this
' happens to be the case, I think a man should sa-
' crifice his own feelings to the public good, and
' resign the command into the hands of those that
' will render them more essential services.   From
' the attachment of the people to you, and your know-
' ledge, judgement, and experience in military mat-
' ters, I have great confidence, that you will command
' with honor to yourself, and with the approbation of
' your country ; that you may, and that it may soon

' be relieved from its present distresses, is the sin-
' cere wish of

' Dear sir, &c.

' B. LINCOLN.

' Gen. MOULTRIE.'

LETTER FROM GOV. RUTLEDGE.

' June 11th, 1779.

' DEAR SIR,

' You will hear what the bearer, Mr. M——— says
' with respect to the James'-Island company,* and the
' want of guards on Jamess'-Island, and about Wap-
' poo. Don't you think it would be best to bring
' that whole company to town, and send some other
' to do duty at those places instead of them, as they
' behave in such a manner; according to this man's
' account, they are of no kind of service, and guards
' are absolutely necessary, at James'-Island and
' Wappoo, to prevent a surprise.

' Your's, &c.

' J. RUTLEDGE.

' Gen. MOULTRIE.'

* They would mount scarcely any guard, but contented
themselves in the day to ride patrole, opposite to John's-Island,
where the enemy where encamped....nay, some of them went
over to the British camp at night, in small canoes, and others
went to their homes; so that they could not be depended upon ;
it was therefore necessary to remove them to Charlestown, and
put others in their room.

About the 15th of June, General Lincoln came to town from his camp at Stono, to consult with the governor and council, upon a plan of operation to attack the British lines at Stono-ferry, with his troops and a strong detachment from Charlestown, to go over to James'-Island, to co-operate with occasionally. After the plan was agreed upon, he sent me the following order, and returned to his camp at Stono.

LETTER FROM GEN. LINCOLN.

'CHARLESTOWN, June 16th, 1779.

' SIR,

' You will please to hold the troops in this garrison,
' in readiness to march on the shortest notice, with
' 50 rounds of cartridges to each man, 18 or 20 in
' their cartridge-boxes, and the remainder in good
' boxes to be put in waggons, which are to be held
' in readiness to move also ; the remainder of the
' fixed ammunition, so as to complete 100 rounds to
' be kept ready to follow as soon as possible. You
' will please immediately to procure a return of all
' the ordnance in town, their different calibers, and
' the quantity of fixed ammunition to each, and send
' me a copy as soon as possible. You will also call
' for a return of the artillery men, and if the number
' is not sufficient for the ordnance, you will please, by
' inlistment, or by draught, to complete their num-

'bers, for it is necessary, that the men should be,
'as early as may be, trained to the use of the guns,
'I am, &c.

'B. LINCOLN.

'Gen. MOULTRIE.'

———

LETTER FROM GOV. RUTLEDGE.

'CHARLESTOWN, June 17th, 1779.

'DEAR SIR,

'MR. W—— set off some time ago for Savannah,
'according to engagement. It does not appear to
'me that any other persons, whose names are men-
'tioned on the list inclosed in General Provost's let-
'ter of the 5th instant, are prisoners of war on
'parole, for several of them, to whom I have spoken,
'deny themselves to be so ; it is therefore necessary,
'in order to satisfy me what the nature of their parole
'is, and what directions I should with propriety give
'respecting them, that an authentic copy of each
'man's parole be transmitted to me.

'I am, &c.

'J. RUTLEDGE.

'Gen. MOULTRIE.'

———

LETTER FROM THE GOVERNOR.

Thursday, half past 3, P. M.

'DEAR SIR,

'THE council have agreed that 1200 men shall go

' from this town, as proposed by Gen. Lincoln, of
' which you will please to acquaint him, that he may
' be preparing his disposition : you will, of course,
' take the necessary measures for your's ; and for
' informing yourself of every thing material to know
' with respect to landings, retreating, &c. if you
' want any thing done or ordered by me, or I can
' further any part of the service, only let me know
' how I may do it, and I will with the greatest rea-
' diness and pleasure.

' I am, &c.

' J. RUTLEDGE.

' P. S. Pray get Paulaski with all the horse to
' join Gen. Lincoln, as soon as you think they can ;
' I will send to Allston to do so.

' Gen. MOULTRIE.'

———

LETTER FROM GEN. PROVOST.

' HEAD-QUARTERS, June 17th, 1779.

' SIR,

' I AM again to propose the exchange of Capt.
' Knowles, for any Major you may pitch upon ; al-
' so Ensign M'Pherson of the 71st regiment, who was
' taken sick at Mrs. Heyward's, where it is believed
' he is still upon parole with his servant : These gen-
' tlemen may be sent to Purisburgh, from thence to
' Savannah, where the exchange may take place.
' What makes me so anxious for Capt. Knowles' ex-

' change, is, that I know his private affairs suffer by
' his captivity. We know no difference betwixt con-
' tinental and state prisoners ; to us they are all as
' one. I am therefore to inform you, that if this
' proposal is not now agreed to, I shall forthwith
' order the prisoners, both here and in Georgia, to
' be sent to New-York ; there to be e xchanged by th
' commander in chief : and as we have now at Flat-
' bush on Long-Island upwards of 400 officers, prison
' ers, I fancy it will be some time before your south-
' ern gentlemen return to you.

 ' I have the honor to be, &c.

' A. PROVOST.

' B. G

' P. S. You may have any field-officer for Capt.
' Knowles.*

' Gen. MOULTRIE.'

————

LETTER FROM GEN. PROVOST.

' HEAD-QUARTERS, 17th June, 1779.

' SIR,

 ' COLONEL Provost being absent at the time I re-
' ceived the honor of your last letter, relative to those
' gentlemen I had required to come to renew their

....

* The more anxious Gen. Provost was for exchanging Capt.
Knowles, the less inclined was the governor and council to exchange him, thinking he was of so much use to the British
army that they could not do without him.

' patroles, has prevented my sending an answer
' sooner. The inclosed, are all that the hurry of a
' rapid march would permit us to take ; I beg leave
' to refer you sir, to the paragraph of Colonel Pro-
' vost's letter, wherein, the reason he gives, I hope
' will appear such as to account to you for the
' seeming neglect of taking a verbal* word of honor,
' of people we then took to be gentlemen.

' EXTRACT OF COL. PROVOST'S LETTER.

' I AM sorry to find by your letter, that some per-
' sons (for they are not gentlemen) who were taken
' prisoners in our progress through Carolina, refuse
' to acknowledge themselves as such, and demand a
' copy of their paroles, in order to be convinced of
' their being prisoners ; it is a pity that General
' Moultrie did not see fit to mention their names,
' that he might have been furnished with authentic
' proofs of their villainy. On a march, it could not
' be expected that such persons would be dismissed
' with that formal regularity, which seems to be ex-

....

* A verbal parole ought to be held more sacred than a
written parole; because a generous conqueror had an unbounded
confidence in his prisoner. Officers are often paroled on the
field of battle, where there is not time for a written parole, in
that case, a gentleman will always consider himself as strictly
bound by his word, to the utmost extent of a written parole.
At the same time, it is to be understood, that your adversaries
conduct themselves with propriety, and agreeably to the customs
of war.

' pected. A gentleman's honor, to consider himself
' a prisoner in every respect, not to act against the
' king's troops, and to surrender himself when called
' upon, was deemed sufficient; his name was taken
' down and he was suffered to depart. I hope that
' neither Mr. P——nor Mr. M'—— are of the num-
' ber. Mr. W—— and D——, taken together by
' Major Barron, and a party sent to view the coun-
' try, Mr. H—— and many others, can hardly have
' forgot their engagements. I can put Mr. P——
' in mind of some circumstances relative to his own
' parole, that would put him to the blush, if he is
' guilty of denying it.'

' How far I am justifiable in my opinion, I leave
' you sir, to judge. I therefore again urge these
' people's returning to my camp, agreeable to my
' former summons ; otherwise they will be wholly
' blameable for any severity that may be inflicted in
' future, on those who may fall in our way. I am
' to mention a Captain H——, a mariner of your's,
' who was permitted to return on parole to Carolina ;
' the same indulgence was given to a Captain O——
' of our's, therefore, I wish to know if an exchange is
' admitted, and whether they are looked upon to be

' at liberty. I send with this, copies of paroles in my
' hands, eight in number.

' I have the honor to be, &c.

' A. Provost.

' Brig. Gen. Moultrie.'

———

From the Governor.

' June 18th, 1779.

' Sir,

' Inclosed are the minutes of the council, on the
' case of captain Knowles, also of Mr. M'——— and Mr.
' S———, who are the only prisoners mentioned on
' the list sent by General Provost, some time ago,
' and demanded as prisoners of war on Paroles, that
' appear to be so.

' I am, &c.

' J. Rutledge.

' Gen. Moultrie.'

The above letter shows that the governor and
council took upon themselves to judge of the validity
of a parole, and in their opinion a verbal parole was
of no consequence : in my opinion, a verbal parole
ought to be held more sacred than a written one, as
your adversary had an unbounded confidence in your
word.

From Col. Parsons, on his Parole.

'Dear Sir,   'June 18th, 1779.

' In answer to what Gen. Provost is pleased to
' say in his letter to you, to wit : that ' he could put
' me in mind of some circumstances relative to my
' parole (as he called it) that would put me to the
' blush, if I was guilty of denying it :' I think it be-
' hoves me to acquaint you, that after my arrival in
' town, in consequence of the governor's proclama-
' tion, I told him of every circumstance that then
' occurred to me to be material, that happened to
' me on the day, and at the time; that in a very po-
' lite manner I received unasked for, (but, as I ve-
' rily believe, upon a supposition that I came for it)
' a paper, purporting that I was at liberty to return
' to my family ; and that I was not to be molested
' in my person, family, or property ; and that I also
' shewed the governor that paper, and said, then
' and since, that if an express parole had been in-
' sisted upon, I would have given it, but that no
' such had been demanded from, or given by me ;
' and if I was to die this moment, I would declare
' with sincerity, and without blushing, that I do not
' recollect there was ; but I do now remember, which
' I take to be the circumstance Gen. Provost alludes
' to, that after the paper was delivered to me, which
' I shewed you also, signifying that I was at liberty
' to return to my family, and not to be molested, &c.

' I went back into the tent, and told Col. Provost
' that I thought it incumbent on me, to acquaint
' him, that I was not going to return, but intended
' to come on towards town, or to that effect; and
' that he politely answered, I might go where I
' pleased: under these circumstances, I confess I
' thought that whilst I reaped the benefit of the pro-
' tection, I ought not, nor would voluntarily take up
' arms; and now, though it has not secured me from
' being, since I got it, plundered of upwards of sixty
' negroes, many horses, geldings, mares, colts, cat-
' tle, sheep, household furniture, &c. I pretend not
' to judge for myself, but would rather suffer any
' hardships my broken spirits and constitution are
' able to bear, than even an enemy should have just
' reason to complain of my want of honor or candor,
' or that any man should suffer, in the least degree,
' from a justly conceived idea I had deviated from
' either; however, as the governor and council, it
' seems, have resolved that no inhabitant shall be
' considered as a prisoner of war, or exchangeable
' as such that was not taken in arms; as it is not in
' my power, of my own accord, to go and give a for-
' mal parole, and as an inquiry is ordered to be made
' and now on foot, whether I am not to be consider-
' ed, in consequence of my receiving the paper be-
' fore mentioned, as inimical to this country; I have
' it not in my power to dispose of myself, but ac-

' cording to the will of the ruling powers, and these,
' I will readily obey, if I shall be considered, even
' constructively, as upon parole, which may, for
' ought I can or will take upon me to judge, be the
' situation in which I ought to be considered.

'   I am, dear sir, your most obedient,

'   and very humble servant.

'   ' JAMES PARSONS.

' Gen. WILLIAM MOULTRIE.

FROM GOV. RUTLEDGE.

June 19th, half past 8, P. M.

' DEAR SIR,

'   GENERAL Lincoln, in a letter just received, has
' communicated to me the contents of his letter to
' you, brought, I presume, by the same opportunity,
' and added, " I beg your assistance in this matter."
' Inclosed are instructions to the captains of the gal-
' lies, and to the public boat-keepers, to follow your
' orders respecting the gallies and boats, as I think it
' probable, that the former may be useful, and the
' others necessary, on this occasion. You will
' therefore be pleased to give such orders, as you
' think proper, about them. If I can give any fur-
' ther, or other aid, I will readily, on knowing what
' may be desired.

'   I am sir, your most obedient servant.

' Gen. MOULTRIE.   J. RUTLEDGE.'

FROM GEN. LINCOLN.

'STONO-FERRY, June 19th, 1779.

' DEAR SIR,

' You will please, immediately on the receipt of
' this, (unless you should see some good reason) to
' throw over on James'-Island, all the troops which
' can be spared from town ; shew them to the enemy
' on John's-Island; carry your boats up Wappoo-
' cut, ready to throw your men on John's-Island, in
' case an opportunity should offer without risking
' too much. If you should hear any firing in the
' morning at Stono-ferry and find the enemy on
' John's-Island moving from you, you will endeavor
' to tread on their heels. I have written to Count Pau-
' laski, to aid you in your movements.

' I am, &c.

' Gen. MOULTRIE.   B. LINCOLN.'

TO GEN. LINCOLN.

' WAPPOO, June 20th, 1779.

' DEAR SIR,

' I THIS moment arrived at this place with about
' 700* rank and file, with one galley, not yet through
' the cut. I am very sorry I could not get to this
' place by the time you appointed: the want of boats,

* Besides a number of gentlemen volunteers, who went over
with me.

' vessels, &c. made it impossible ; especially as I
' hear you have had a skirmish with the enemy to
' day. I send to know your orders, and what plan
' we can co-operate in together. I shall not under-
' take any thing material, till I hear from you.

' I am, &c.

' WM. MOULTRIE.

' GEN. LINCOLN.'

————

BEFORE I had got half way over with the detachment from Charlestown to James'-Island, General
Lincoln had begun his attack on the British lines at
Stono-ferry, and the firing was intirely over before
we arrived at Wappoo-cut. General Lincoln, after
having some men killed and wounded, finding he
could make no impression on the British lines, drew
off his men, and retired to his camp, about two miles
back.

————

A LETTER from GENERAL LINCOLN, which accounts for his attacking the enemy before I
could get to Wappoo-cut. He was apprehensive
they would get off before he could have a stroke at
them.

' NEAR STONO, June 20th, 1779.

' DEAR SIR,

' FROM various accounts of deserters, and others,
' which we were informed of by a person of charac-
' ter, who left the enemy's lines the evening before

' the last, I was led to believe that they were retreat-
' ing, and by the same person who spent a day in
' their lines at Stono-ferry, that their whole force
' then did not exceed six hundred men : we thought
' it our duty to attack them this morning ; this
' resolution caused me to write to you yesterday,
' requesting you would attempt to divert them on
' John's-Island. The attack was made, which lasted
' about 56 minutes, during that time, we had some
' officers and men wounded, and some few men killed,
' among the former, was our brave and good friend
' Colonel Roberts, since dead of his wounds. The
' enemy did not choose to leave their lines, and being
' much better covered therein, than was expected,
' and having in the time of the action, received a very
' considerable reinforcement, I was induced to with-
' draw our troops, after securing our wounded, wag-
' gons and artillery, as I saw no prospect of continu-
' ing with any rational hope of success. In justice
' to the officers and men, I must say they behaved
' well in general. I wish the troops had been so
' broken to service as that they could have been
' brought to charge the enemy with fixed bayonets.
' The soldiers are in good spirits, and think that if
' they had had the enemy out of the lines, they
' could have flogged them easily.....I think they

' would : it is said by many of the officers* who saw
' the enemy's dead, that their loss is very consider-
' able. If your troops are on James'-Island, it will
' be well to keep them there, (if it can be done with
' safety to the town,) for probably you may aid there-
' by some future movements of ours. I yet think
' the enemy mean to leave their present post soon,
' and hope we shall have an opportunity of harrassing
' their rear. After a little rest, I shall be able to
' give you a more particular state of matters, than I
' can undertake at present, having been ten hours on
' horseback, without any sleep. I cannot get a list
' of the wounded officers, none were left dead on
' the field. Major Anerum is dangerously wounded,
' Colonel Lamoy and General Huger, had each a
' slight wound.

' There was a creek on the right of the enemy's
' works, which ran in front of the redoubts, and
' which was the real reason why our continental
' troops did not storm the works as was intended :
' we were wholly ignorant of there being such an
' obstruction in the advance of our troops, otherwise,
' our order of attack would have been reversed :
' however, it proved the bravery of our men, who

....

* Part of our army got into the enemy's lines, upon their
left, a party sallied out upon our left, where Colonel Henderson and Major Pinckney were with a detachment, they were
soon drove, leaving an officer and some men behind.

‘ marched to the very brink of the creek, and there
‘ remained exposed to the fire of the enemy, who
‘ were under cover, by their works. The order for
‘ retreat was not given, until the causeway, which is
‘ three-fourths of a mile long, and twenty-eight feet
‘ wide, leading from John's-Island, (and which you
‘ might clearly discern from our right) was completely
‘ covered from the woods down to the river, with
‘ the British reinforcements. The retreat was con-
‘ ducted in an orderly and regular manner, our
‘ platoons frequently facing about and firing by the
‘ word of command upon their pursuers, who, how-
‘ ever, very soon gave over the chase.

‘ I am, &c.

‘ B. LINCOLN.

‘ Gen. MOULTRIE.’

LETTER FROM GOV. RUTLEDGE.

‘ Sunday night, past 10 o'clock.

‘ DEAR SIR,

‘ I SEND Major Harleston, with a letter for you
‘ from General Lincoln, which I opened, understand-
‘ ing there had been an action ; I make no doubt you
‘ will not keep the troops on James'-Island, if you
‘ apprehend that the safety of the town would be in
‘ danger by your so doing. I wish to know by a
‘ line from you, by Major Harleston in the morning,

' what resolution you take, in consequence of what
' has happened or what may, before you write.

' Your's, &c.

' J. RUTLEDGE.

' Gen. MOULTRIE.'

LETTER FROM GEN. LINCOLN.

' HEAD-QUARTERS 13 MILE-HOUSE,

' DEAR SIR,   June, 21st, 1779.

' YOUR favor from Wappoo of yesterday's date, I
' received last night. I am of the same opinion, as
' when I wrote you yesterday: that it would be well
' to keep all the troops which can be spared from
' Charlestown, on James'-Island, ready to throw
' across to John's-Island, when a favorable oppor-
' tunity shall offer. I yet think that the enemy
' mean soon to remove, but expect to know more
' of the matter between this and the evening. As
' early as we can co-operate with a probability of
' success, I will give you the earliest notice of it.

' I am, &c.

' Gen. MOULTRIE.   B. LINCOLN.'

LETTER FROM GEN. PROVOST.

' HEAD-QUARTERS, JOHN'S-ISLAND,

' SIR,   June 21st, 1779.

' I EXPECTED before now to have had an answer
' to my two last, sent you on the 17th. The letters

' herewith now sent, were omitted. I shall be glad
' you would direct Captain Knowles to be delivered.
' There is also some money sent by this opportunity,
' which I suppose will be delivered as directed.

' I have the honor to be, &c.

' A. PROVOST.

' Gen. MOULTRIE.'

EXTRACT OF A LETTER FROM COL. GRIMKIE,
TO J. KEAN, ESQ.

' CAMP AT SOMMERS, June 21st, 1779.

' THE enemy having established themselves at
' Stono-ferry, on the Main ; maintained a garrison
' in their works, of about 5 or 600 men. It was of
' the utmost consequence that it should be in their
' possession, as it secured the navigation of the Sto-
' no-river, and facilitated their retreat to Georgia,
' towards which place all their movements pointed :
' they had already withdrawn their cavalry to John's-
' Island, where the main body of their army was en-
' camped : their transports had arrived from Savan-
' nah, and the baggage was embarking. The sea-
' son for action was almost exhausted ; and the heat
' of the weather, or the attendant disorders of our
' summer, would very shortly have put an end to
' the contention of the two armies, and compelled
' them to retire into Summer quarters. The cam-
' paign had as yet for us been unfortunate ; for af-

' ter the retreat of the army out of Georgia, a feeble
' and fruitless attempt was made on the enemy's gal-
' lies, in the river Savannah : a detachment of Geor-
' gia continental troops, and North-Carolina militia,
' amounting to 7 or 800 men, had been surprised,
' and totally routed at Brier-creek : and the march
' of Gen. Lincoln to Augusta, 120 miles from the
' town of Savannah, to cross the river there, into
' the state of Georgia ; had left the state of South-
' Carolina open to the irruptions of the enemy, who
' had appeared before, and summoned Charlestown to
' surrender ; spreading ruin and devastation from
' the Savannah, to the Ashley-river : a proper and
' well concerted attack upon the enemy at Wappoo,
' whilst they were divided in their force, was coun-
' termanded, almost at the very moment of the as-
' sault on their works : in consequence of which,
' Gen. Paulaski had withdrawn his legionary corps
' from the service, in disgust. Our army now en-
' camped at Sommers, mouldering away : the South-
' Carolina militia under Gen. Williamson, were re-
' tiring home privately, and individually ; and the
' time of the Virginia and North-Carolina militia,
' would expire in a few days. This was the situation
' of the two armies, when Gen. Lincoln called a
' council of war, on the evening of the 19th of June,
' wherein it was determined to attack the enemy's
' post at Stono-ferry, on the next morning : the ar-

' my was in motion at midnight; and having joined
' the battalion of light-infantry, under Lieut. Col.
' Henderson, which had been advanced towards the
' enemy's works; we arrived about an hour after
' day-break before the works, the front of the ene-
' my was covered by two square redoubts, and a bat-
' tery between them of three pieces of ordnance,
' which pointed down the road leading from the
' ferry, over Wallis-bridge, to Charlestown: their
' right was secured by a marsh, and a deep creek,
' over which led a very narrow causeway that was
' defended by a round redoubt, and one piece of ar-
' tillery, posted on the outside of this last work: a
' small breast-work on the bank of, and at right an-
' gles with the river, sufficient to cover about 80 or
' 100, with 2 field-pieces, protected the landing;
' and between this work, and their left square re-
' doubt, mentioned before, was almost equidistantly
' placed a small flank: the river covered their rear;
' and an abbattis surrounded the whole of their
' works. Our flanks were covered by the two batta-
' lions of light-infantry: the left of our line was com-
' posed of continental troops, under Gen. Huger,
' with 4 field-pieces; and the brigade of North and
' South-Carolina militia, with 2 field-pieces, under
' Gen. Sumner, formed our left: In the rear of this
' body was posted the Virginia militia, with 2 field-

' pieces in reserve; and the cavalry were posted up-
' on the right of the reserve, and rather more retired.

' The position of the enemy was nearly in the
' center of an old field. (extending about a mile along
' the river) and was advanced about 200 yards from
' its margin.

' Unfortunately for us, by the misinformation
' of our guides, we formed our line at the distance
' of three quarters of a mile from the enemy's works,
' which retarded the progress of the right of our ar-
' my, very much, as the ground over which they
' had to pass, was very fully wooded with a vast
' number of pine saplings ; the left advanced with
' more facility, as the ground over which they pass-
' ed, had never been cleared, and was wooded only
' with full grown, tall, and stately pines. Our light-
' troops soon drove in their picquets, who made lit-
' tle or no resistance : and the battalion commanded
' by Lieut. Col. Henderson on our left, in endeavor-
' ing to gain his position, fell in with two companies
' of the 71st regiment, which had been posted in the
' woods, with a design of checking those daily at-
' tacks, which our light troops had been accustom-
' ed to make upon them every morning. Lieut Col.
' Henderson, who was in column, when he first per-
' ceived the Highlanders, formed under their fire
' very deliberately, and returned it; then, ordering
' a charge with bayonets, drove the enemy with

' great precipitation into their works, leaving nearly
' half of their men killed or wounded on the field.'

To Gen. Paulaski.

' Hudson's, James'-Island, June 22d, 1779.

' Dear Sir,

' I was just now honored with your favor. I
' have ordered the batteau to the cut ready to bring
' over any horses. I shall have a bridge made over
' there, very soon; in the mean time, a dozen horse
' will be sufficient to assist us in patroling the island,
' these we can swim over the cut for the present ser-
' vice. Any information that may fall in your way,
' I make no doubt, but that you will acquaint me
' with.

' I am, &c.

' Wm. Moultrie.'

Orders to Capt. Pyne.

' Hudson's, June 22d, 1779.

' Sir,

' You will proceed with the three gallies under
' your command, to Stono-ferry, there you are to
' endeavor to destroy a bridge of boats* the ene-
' my have thrown over the river. In your pas-

....

* We were informed the enemy had a bridge of boats, at
Stono-ferry, from John's-Island to Stono, but it was not so :
they had boats at the ferry, but no bridge.

'sage up, and on your return, you are to sink,
'burn, and destroy any of the enemy's boats or
'vessels that you may meet with; if you should
'succeed in destroying the bridge of boats, you are
'to send me an account, either by land or water,
'as you shall judge best, and remain in some place
'of safety, until you receive your further orders.
'Should any troops be landed, the Marquis de
'Bretigney will take the command.

'I am, &c.

'WILLIAM MOULTRIE.'

To MARQUIS DE BRETIGNEY.

'SIR,

'June 22d, 1779.

'You will proceed with the gallies that may be
'ordered for the service intended, and will take
'the command of any troops on board, if a landing
'shall be thought practicable and necessary.

'I am, &c.

'WM. MOULTRIE,'

To GEN. LINCOLN.

'HUDSON s, June 22d, 1779.

'DEAR SIR,

'I AM to inform you that I have got three gallies
'through the cut. I mean to attack the enemy's

' bridge of boats to night ; this determination is so
' sudden, and so necessary to be executed immedi-
' ately, that I could not have any time to consult on
' any plan with you, as the enemy may make pre-
' parations for us. I think if we can cut off their
' communication, the remainder of the work will be
' easy. I have sent to General Paulaski, who is en-
' camped at Savage's, to be in readiness, should we
' have occasion for him. I imagine the gallies may
' get up about two or three o'clock in the morning.

'I am, &c.

'WM. MOULTRIE.'

_____

FROM CAPT. PYNE.

'RUTLEDGE-GALLEY, June 23d, 1779.

'SIR,

'LAST night the three gallies got under way from
' Wappoo, in order to proceed to Stono-ferry ; we
' passed by Gibbs' without any interruption ; on
' coming up to Stanyard's received a brisk fire from
' the enemy, with field-pieces and small-arms ; not-
' withstanding their perpetual fire, for three-quarters
' of an hour, we took a schooner from under their
' guns, and after silencing their guns, we went up
' the river, and met with another attack, at the next
' bluff, from a battery consisting of three field-pieces
' and a great deal of musketry : when we had si-

' lenced that battery, day-light coming on, and the
' tide being spent, were under the necessity of coming
' to anchor, off Mr. Thomas Eveleigh's plantation,
' where we now are: at sun rise we discovered about
' 1,200 men in camp, and on the causeway with
' cannon intrenched. The pilots informed me that
' we must pass within pistol shot of their intrench-
' ment, on which I thought prudent to acquaint
' your honor of their force: we now lay in safety,
' and shall remain until further orders. We like-
' wise discovered them sinking a large schooner
' under their cannon in the river, to obstruct our
' passage through. We amuse them sometimes with
' a round shot into their camp.

  ' From yours, &c.

     'JAMES PYNE. ⎫ Captains
     'ABEL FRISBIE. ⎬ of the gal-
     'Capt. BOUTARD. ⎭ lies.

 ' Gen. MOULTRIE.'

<hr>

To Capt. Pyne.

' SIR,   ' HUDSON's June 23d, 1779.

 ' As the enemy must be much alarmed from the
' firing last night, I would have you advise with your
' captains, to consider whether you can proceed any
' further with a probability of success, without risking
' too much. I leave to you, and their determination

' whether it is best to return: let me know what
' damage you have sustained.

'P. S. Since the above, I have received your joint
' letter, informing me of your success; on which,
' I congratulate you, and leave intirely to the deter-
' mination of yourself, and the other captains, whether
' to proceed or not.

' I am, &c.

' Wm. Moultrie.'

From Capt. Pyne.

' Sir,

' Rutledge-galley, June 23d, 1779.

' I received your's, and have consulted with the
' other captains of the gallies, and they all judge it
' best to return.

' I have the honor to be, &c.

' J. Pyne.

' Gen. Moultrie.'

To the Governor.

' Hudson's, June 23d, 1779.

' Dear Sir,

' The gallies returned last light, bringing with
' them their prize schooner: the enemy made great
' preparation for them on their way back; they had
' several batteries built, with two nine pounders

' mounted, and field-pieces ; had they not returned
' when they did, the banks of the river would have
' been so strongly fortified, as would have stopped
' them altogether. or at least done them great dam-
' age. When I found they were received so warmly
' the first night, I sent over land to Captain Pyne,
' desiring him to call the captains together, to know
' whether they should proceed or not, they agreed
' to return. I believe they killed some of the enemy
' and disconcerted their camp pretty much, &c. By
' the return of the boats made me, I have not more
' than will carry 320 men : I shall be obliged to
' your excellency, to order me as many more : Capt.
' Pyne informs they are in want of ammunition, &c.
                    I am, &c.

                               ' WM. MOULTRIE.'

                    ─────

            FROM THE GOVERNOR.

                              ' June 24th, 1779.

' DEAR SIR,

    ' I RECEIVED your's per Capt. Anthony, and
' am sorry to hear Boutard suffered so considerably :*
' I have desired Capt. Blake to take the necessary
' measures, for sending on immediately, the boats,

              ....

    * Boutard had six men killed, and a number wounded.

'cannon, ammunition, &c. you desire, which I
'doubt not, he will directly.

'I am, &c.

'J. RUTLEDGE.

'Gen. MOULTRIE.'

FROM GEN. LINCOLN.

'HEAD-QUARTERS NEAR STONO-FERRY.

'June 24th, 1779, 8 o'clock, P. M.

'DEAR SIR,

'I HAVE just received information that the ene-
'my have abandoned their post at Stono-ferry; when
'this movement took place, it is uncertain, as it
'was discovered this evening by a party who had
'been near their lines all day. If the enemy on
'John's-Island appear to be retreating, tread on their
'heels, if you can do it, without risking too much :*
'if they mean to keep their present station, watch
'them; and send to town for flats, suitable to trans-

....

* I had not boats, to take over the river, more than 320 at
one time, which would have been much too few to leave on the
Island, until I could make a trip or two more.

' port artillery ; and give me the earliest information
' in what state matters are : if they have moved, you
' will please to send a boat down the river, to watch
' their movements, in case they put to sea.

' I am, &c.

'B. LINCOLN.

' Gen. MOULTRIE.'

•••••••,••••••••••••••••••••••••••••••••••••
END OF THE FIRST VOLUME.
•••

MEMOIRS

OF THE

AMERICAN REVOLUTION

MEMOIRS

OF THE

AMERICAN REVOLUTION,

SO FAR AS IT RELATED TO THE

STATES OF NORTH AND SOUTH-CARO-LINA, AND GEORGIA.

COMPILED FROM THE MOST AUTHENTIC MATERIALS, THE
AUTHOR'S PERSONAL KNOWLEDGE OF THE VARIOUS
EVENTS, AND INCLUDING AN EPISTOLARY
CORRESPONDENCE ON PUBLIC AFFAIRS,
WITH CIVIL AND MILITARY OF-
FICERS, AT THAT PERIOD.

⚊⚊✦✧✦⚊⚊

BY WILLIAM MOULTRIE,

LATE GOVERNOR OF THE STATE OF SOUTH-CARO-
LINA, AND MAJOR-GENERAL IN THE ARMY
OF THE UNITED STATES DURING
THE AMERICAN WAR.

⚊⚊✦✧✦⚊⚊

VOL. II.

NEW-YORK:

PRINTED BY DAVID LONGWORTH,

FOR THE AUTHOR.

1802.

MEMOIRS

OF THE

AMERICAN REVOLUTION.

GENERAL Lincoln attacking the British lines at Stono-ferry, and I attacking them from James'-Island with the gallies, made their situation on John's-Island, rather unpleasant; and, no doubt, they expected we should make some other movements towards them; they therefore thought it best to quit that place, and get to a place were they could be supported by their shipping: accordingly they went from Island to Island, until they got to Port-royal, where they established a strong post at Beaufort; we never could get a sufficient number of boats to follow them, as they had possession of that part of the country where most of the boats belonged.

To Gov. RUTLEDGE.

'JAMES'-ISLAND, June 25th, 1779.

'DEAR SIR,

'By a letter I received this morning from Gen.
'Lincoln, I am informed that the enemy are moving,
'and have actually quitted Stono-ferry; this is con-
'firmed by private intelligence of my own; so that

' there is not left the least room for doubt : a party
' is sent down the river to perceive something of
' their motions, if possible ; and another party is
' this moment embarking, with a view of reconnoi-
' tering that part of the Island which is nearest us.
' Permit me, sir, to request an additional number of
' boats and flats ; they may be indispensibly ne-
' cessary.

' I am, &c.

' WM. MOULTRIE.'

FROM GOV. RUTLEDGE.
'CHARLESTOWN, June 26th, 1779.

' DEAR SIR,

' NOTWITHSTANDING repeated orders to the
' commissioners of the navy to have flats and other
' boats collected and sent to you, I apprehend there
' is, as usual, in all our operations, which com-
' monly renders them of less consequence than they
' otherwise would be, much delay ; and Major Har-
' leston having offered his service to go about and
' collect all that may be necessary, and proceed with
' them to your camp ; I have requested him to do
' so....I hope he will obtain a sufficient number of
' boats to transport Paulaski's horse, also Gen. Lin-
' coln's troops of infantry ; as well as yourself ; for
' if a blow of any importance is to be struck, (your
' men being too few) it seems requisite that you and

' they should co-operate with each other : you will
' of course, apprize them of the number of boats you
' have, and concert with them the most effectual
' plan for annoying the enemy. I understand they
' have not vessels enough to carry off all their own
' troops at once; (much less the negroes, and plun-
' der they have taken) so that some will probably
' wait for the return of the vessels.

' I am, &c.

' J. RUTLEDGE.

' Gen. MOULTRIE.'

———

TO GEN. LINCOLN.

' JAMES'-ISLAND, June 26th, 1779.

'DEAR SIR,

' FROM all the information I have been able to
' collect, and particularly from a deserter who came
' in this morning, and left the enemy about 5 o'clock
' yesterday afternoon it seems certain that they
' are all gone on board of their shipping : I had no
' opportunity of giving them a blow on their retreat,
' it was so sudden and so rapid : I had ordered a
' party, and a field-piece already in the boat, when
' I received a letter from Capt. Hall, informing me
' that the enemy were busily employed in throwing
' up some intrenchments at Mr. William Gibbs', and
' that a great body of them were there : this deter-
' mined me to countermand my order; the next

' account I had of them, was at night, when they
' were at Simons'-Island, and embarking; I then
' thought it needless to follow them, as it would be
' carrying my troops at too great a distance from
' town :* I have sent the gallies to endeavor to take
' some of their transports, or destroy them: Capt.
' Anthony and Milligan are going to observe the
' motions of the enemy, they will call on you for
' any orders you may have.

' I am, &c.

' WM. MOULTRIE.

' P. S. Since writing the above, two sergeants,
' deserters, are come in, they say the enemy have
' not vessels sufficient to carry them all off at once;
' the 71st and light-infantry are now halted at the
' meeting house; I have too few to attack them: I
' shall therefore send some flats and boats to the
' ferry, to facilitate your crossing : I will join you
' if you think necessary.'

On the 27th June, I ordered all my boats from
Wappoo-cut to Glen's-landing; and on the 28th embarked all my troops and landed them in Charlestown about noon. About the 30th instant, I was ordered out, to take the command of the army at Stono ; Gen. Lincoln wishing to come to Charlestown.

....

* We always kept in view ; that the enemy might come
round by water, and attack the town.

To Gov. Rutledge.

'Stono, July 3d, 1779.

'Dear Sir,

'From Gen. Williamson's information, I find
'it is impossible to keep his men in the field any
'longer; and the expectation of a relief for them, is
'intirely vanished; as I saw a letter from Col. Lyle,
'and others, in that part of the country, to William-
'son, informing him he could not get the men to
'march down this way; and as an excuse they have
'played the old stale game of Cameron's being in
'the Cherokees, with a number of white men and
'Indians, ready to fall on their part of the country;
'and also 1,000 tories coming from North-Carolina,
'&c. In short, I cannot tell what to advise, unless
'we could discharge all our back country militia,
'and begin a new plan with them, such as the le-
'gislature may adopt; I think it would be best : I
'have prevailed upon Williamson's men to stay un-
'til I hear from you; when I did not doubt but that
'they would be allowed to return home, especially
'as most of these men are the best of them, and have
'been in the field five months....I shall be glad to
'have your answer soon.

'I am, &c.

'Wm. Moultrie.'

To Gen. Lincoln.
' Stono, Sommer's, July 3d, 1779.

' Dear Sir,

'I have nothing extraordinary to write you
' from hence : by a letter from Colonel Horry, which
' is dated Port-royal-ferry, July 1st, I am informed
' that the enemy's army are not yet got to Beaufort,
' that only a party of marines, were on that island,
' and stationed opposite his post, but upon his ap-
' pearance they were called in, and went on board the
' Vigilant and two transports which lay there, that
' they had no more than 200 hundred men altogether
' at that place, including the Vigilant's crew. By
' three deserters from the enemy's gallies yesterday,
' I am informed that they are still on Edisto-Island,
' but they agree that their intention is to go for
' Beaufort. I think it not adviseable to move from
' hence, while they remain where they are. The
' North-Carolinians begin to move to day, their sick
' and weak, 202, the remainder will go next Sunday
' week. I fear I shall not be able to detain our mi-
' litia any longer. Williamson tells me his men
' seem determined to go in a few days ; no argument
' can prevail on them to stay. I herewith send you
' a letter from Governor Houston, with inclosed
' letters and papers from Colonel Dooley, I am un-
' acquainted with any plan you have directed, there-

' fore could say nothing to him. I shall be glad of
' your instructions.

'I am, &c.

'WM. MOULTRIE.'

FROM GEN. LINCOLN.

'HEAD-QUARTERS, CHARLESTOWN,
'July 4th, 1779.

'DEAR SIR,

'I RECEIVED your's of yesterday, this morning.
'I wish you would immediately send to Mr. Gol-
'phins 500 pounds of powder, lead, flints, and 100
'stand of arms, under the escort of the Georgia
'Brigade, which will remain in that part of the
'country, till further orders. After we came to the
'13 Mile-house, (Stono) I was informed that the
'enemy had left the state of Georgia; upon that I
'advised the inhabitants thereof, to collect and at-
'tempt to gain as much of it as possible. On this
'recommendation they have assembled 4 or 500 men,
'and wish to be aided in the attempt, but as our
'little army will soon be reduced; I have written
'to Colonel Dooley that he must at present content
'himself with covering the upper part of the country,
'for we cannot reinforce him, but with the few Geor-
'gia troops, whose times are near out and who it is
'said, can be engaged provided they can return. I
'think you judge right in keeping your ground until

' the enemy leave Edisto-Island, or at least till their
' main body do it.

' I am, &c.

' B. Lincoln.

' Gen. Moultrie.'

———

To Gen. Lincoln.

' Stono, July 5th, 1779.

' Dear Sir,

' I have just received information from different
' quarters, that the enemy are now upon Port-royal-
' Island. In consequence, I have ordered Colonel
' Pinckney's and the Georgia brigade, to be ready
' to march to-morrow morning early, and shall order
' General Sumner's to follow the next day; I shall
' march them in divisions, because it would be in-
' convenient to have them all together, when they
' came to cross the rivers. I propose forming my
' camp near Colonel Garden's, and keep my picquets
' on the river side; I shall order two field-pieces
' with each division, the remainder of the artillery
' I think may be as well sent to town ; but for this
' I shall wait your orders. I shall remain here a day
' or two longer, to know your pleasure relative to the
' Virginians and North-Carolinians whose times are
' near expiring. Mr. Houston was with me yester-
' day, and informed me that you promised some arms
' and ammunition to Colonel Dooley, for the state of

' Georgia. I shall be glad to know how many, and
' what quantity I shall send them. Williamson's
' men are anxious, and seem determined to get home.
' I wrote the governor concerning them. I shall be
' glad to have his answer.

' I am, &c.

' Wm. Moultrie.'

From Gen. Lincoln.

' Head-Quarters, July 5th, 1779.

' Dear Sir,

 ' Your favor of yesterday's date I received last
' evening: I am sorry that Colonel Pichin's men have
' left him, and that General Williamson's are like to
' follow their example. The governor informs me
' that the council cannot be persuaded, that the safety
' of the state will not admit of their being dis-
' charged. The governor and council have ordered
' a draught of one third of the militia, to march im-
' mediately to camp; on their arrival they will con-
' sent that those now therein shall be discharged.
' I suppose the consequences will be, that the militia
' will discharge themselves. You will endeavor to
' keep pace with the enemy; if they make a partial
' movement, and you cannot find means to attack
' them, I think you had better reinforce Col. Horry.
' I think, with you, that it would be hardly worth
' while to march the North-Carolina troops to Port-

' royal-ferry, for their time of service will be out
' soon after their arrival, and it would lengthen their
' march, which if possible, should be avoided this
' hot weather : I think, as your force decreases, you
' had better send some of your artillery to town.

' I am, &c.

' B. LINCOLN.

' Gen. MOULTRIE.'

———

FROM COL. DANIEL HORRY.

' PORT-ROYAL-FERRY, July 6th, 1779.

' DEAR SIR,

' CAPT. Dogharty (who has lately been with us
' for a day or two) went from hence to Beaufort, in
' cog. and was for a few hours at a friend's house ;
' who informed him that Gen. Provost was expected
' from Edisto every hour, with the remainder of his
' army : that about 2,000, including sick, wounded,
' convalescents, &c. were already at Beaufort, but
' kept on board ship : that Commodore Christie
' will not permit any boat on shore after retreat
' beating ; and that they had already wooded and
' watered ; this appears to us as if they meant a
' speedy embarkation.

' I am, &c.

' DANIEL HORRY.

'Gen. MOULTRIE.'

To Gen. Lincoln.

'Stono, July 5th, 1779.

'Dear Sir,

'I informed you some time ago, that I had
'directed Col. Drayton to have a number of bags
'(200) made for the purpose of carrying corn-meal
'from Augusta, to any place where it may be want-
'ed: As we are now bringing down meal, those
'bags would be of infinite service to us, and a great
'saving to the public, by more expeditiously loading
'the waggons, and by preventing great waste of the
'meal, which often happens from bad casks, and
'especially as each waggon may carry five bushels
'more, which is the difference between the casks
'and the bags: I shall be much obliged to you, to
'speak to Drayton about them: he informed me
'they were made some time ago, and sent up; but
'God knows where; he could not tell where they
'were sent to, nor by whom: if this is to be the
'case with other articles, our calls for money will
'be endless.   I am, &c.

'Wm. Moultrie.'

From Gen. Lincoln.

'Charlestown, July 6th, 1779.

'Dear Sir,

'I have been honored with your two favors of
'yesterday. I am fully with you in opinion, that

' part of the artillery ought to be sent on to town.
' I yesterday expressed my sentiments with regard
' to the North Carolina militia. I think you may
' want the Virginians with you, if you think you
' should not, you will also leave them behind. I have
' spoken to the governor often, perhaps too often,
' about the Williamson militia; I hope he will give
' you an answer. Colonel Drayton will explain to
' you the matter of the bags.

' I am, &c.

' B. LINCOLN.'

' Gen. MOULTRIE.'

FROM THE GOVERNOR.

' July 7th, 1779.

' DEAR SIR,

' I AM favored with your's of the 3d. inst. which,
' together with General Williamson's of the same
' date, I laid before the council. I have wrote fully
' on the matter to General Williamson, who will
' communicate the contents to you, &c.

' I am, &c.

' J. RUTLEDGE.

' Gen. MOULTRIE.'

To Gen. Lincoln.

'Stono, July 7th, 1779.

'Dear Sir,

'I recieved your favor, date the 5th inst.
'upon General Williamson's frequent representation
'to me, that he could not keep his men a day
'longer in camp, and upon telling me he thought it
'would be best for the service to discharge them,
'and suffer them to go home and send others down
'in their places, as the relief had absolutely refused
'to come; I accordingly issued an order for their re-
'turning home this day: I know they would go
'without my leave, had I not done it; (their num-
'bers 726.) I have sent four pieces of artillery to
'town, by Major Grimkie, we shall have two left,
'which will be quite sufficient for our little army.
'I shall also order the arms* down, about 300 stand.
'I wrote you that I would order Sumner's brigade
'to Port-royal-ferry, since which, I think they will
'be as useful here at present, as marching them to
'that place, especially as I am informed by two de-
'serters who came in last night, and who left the
'enemy two days ago, that they are on St. Helena-

....

* We were always obliged to keep a number of arms in
camp, as we were obliged frequently to arm the reliefs from the
militia.

' Island,* and their shipping laying in the sound.
' I will endeavor to keep pace with the enemy ; I
' have sent Colonel Pinckney, with about 250 men, to
' reinforce that post at Port-royal-ferry, and to take
' command there. General Sumner has applied to
' me for leave to go home, owing to his ill state of
' health ; he tells me he thinks he can be of more
' service, and that if he was in North-Carolina, he
' might recover, and be on the spot to forward on
' the troops to this place, as fast as possible, which
' he has promised me to do : I have accordingly
' given him leave to return home.

' ON Gen. Williamson's men being permitted to go
' home, to prevent the disagreeable necessity of their
' leaving camp without orders, I have requested the
' general (as I know his influence over these people)
' to return to that part of the country, and to send
' out the reliefs as soon as possible, which he has
' promised to do. I will be much obliged to you, to
' request of the governor to have some large flats
' stationed at Ponpon, Ashepoo, and Combahee rivers,
' to facilitate the marching of troops through those
' parts of the country ; it seems to be absolutely

....

* They could soon sail round to Charlestown, which was
my reason for remaining at Stono ; from whence I could readily
march down to town.

' necessary, as they are now obliged to go many
' miles round. I am, &c.

'Wm. Moultrie.'

To Gen. Lincoln.

'Dear Sir, Stono, July 7th, 1779.

' I wrote you this morning by Major Grimkie,
' since which I have received intelligence by letter,
' from Col. Mayson at Port-royal-ferry; that Capt.
' Dogharty was on the Island the 3d instant, and re-
' ports, from good authority, that Provost means to
' summer it there, and to take post on the Main,
' with 1,000 men, at all hazards : they have it amongst
' them, that your army is dispersed : I shall order
' Sumner's brigade off to morrow. I have ordered
' the several bodies of militia that are raised south-
' wardly, to join ours at Port-royal-ferry. I wish I
' could have about 20 light batteaus fixed upon wag-
' gon carriages always in camp; as we could some
' time surprise some of their posts on the Island.

' I am, &c.

'Wm. Moultrie.'

From Col. Horry.

'Port-royal-ferry, July 8th, 1779.

' Dear General,

' You will herewith receive John Livingston, a
' prisoner, which our party made yesterday, at the

'plantation of Dr. Fraser, on Port-royal-Island; he
'is a son to the widow Odengell, and has been with
'the enemy ever since they took possession of the
'town, and therefore may be a proper person for you
'to obtain intelligence from; he says he is only 15
'years of age, and stayed with his mother: the
'enemy from their talk, mean to remain on the Is-
'land and to take post with a party of 2,000 men on
'this side the river: that they intend next high wa-
'ter to come up here with one or two gallies, to at-
'tempt to prevent us from going on with erecting
'our little redoubt.

'I am, &c.

'D. HORRY.

'Gen. MOULTRIE.'

FROM GEN. LINCOLN.

'CHARLESTOWN, July 8th, 1779.

'DEAR SIR,

'I HAVE been honored with your two favors of
'yesterday's date.

'THE governor and council have ordered a draught
'of one third of the militia to serve three months af-
'ter they join camp: I hope this order will be put
'into execution, and that in future, your militia will
'be relieved regularly, for unless they are, it is not
'probable they will render us much service in camp;
'or remain there with any satisfaction to themselves.

' I do not think that the enemy mean to remain on
' Port-royal-Island, much less attempt to take post
' on the Main ; however, I think you perfectly right,
' in preparing for the worst. There is but little
' money in the military chest ; I wish you would
' take that, and let Mr. Rapely* return to town ; he
' will join you again, when the auditors return to
' camp : I will replenish the chest.

' I am, &c.

' B. LINCOLN.

' Gen. MOULTRIE.'

———

TO GEN. LINCOLN.

' STONO, July 8th, 1779.

' DEAR SIR,

' UPON my moving the troops to Port-royal-fer-
' ry, and my ordering the commissary and quarter-
' master's stores to follow: I find we have not a sin-
' gle waggon for that purpose ; I therefore request
' that you will order the quarter-master to send us
' ten waggons ; I shall also send to Port-royal-ferry
' for some regimental waggons ; I shall want some
' to remove the flying hospital immediately : our
' wounded officers and men cannot be removed at
' present, especially those with fractured limbs. I

* Mr. Rapely was pay-master.

' have wrote Doctor Oliphant* on the subject. I
' have 3 waggons load of arms (317 stands) they
' were given in by Gen. Butler,† who, I suppose,
' will deliver as many more to-morrow. Gen William-
' son has sent his spare arms up the country. Col.
' Thaxton's brigade‡ marched off this morning. I
' cannot leave this place, until I see the stores in a
' way of moving on.

' I am, &c.

' WM. MOULTRIE.'

To Gen. Lincoln.

' Stono, July 10th, 1779.

' Dear Sir,

' I received your favor, dated the 8th inst. in
' which you inform me that the governor and coun-
' cil had ordered a draught of one third of the militia ;
' I hope they will have something to bind them to
' their duty stronger than any thing we have had yet.
' At present I have no militia with me, but about 25
' of Colonel Hammond's ; all Goodwin's went off ex-
' cept the major, 3 lieutenants, and 5 privates, whom

....

* Director-general of the hospital.

† Of North-Carolina. This shows that when we had reinforcements from N. C. we were obliged to furnish them with
arms, and when their times were out, they delivered them up
again.

‡ North-Carolina.

' I discharged, and sent the officers home to collect
' more men. I should be glad to have some more
' bags for conveying corn-meal; as Col. Hammond
' informs there is a great deal ground up, and a large
' quantity of corn, which we may still have from
' Beach-Island. This is like to be our principal de-
' pendance this winter, as I am informed our wheat
' in the back country is totally lost. I received the
' military chest from Mr. Rapely, containing about
' 36,000 dollars; he is to return to day. I have
' just now received a letter from Col. Horry, inform-
' ing me that the enemy have landed at Beaufort,
' and mean to maintain the Island: they still talk of
' taking post on the Main: this last I give but little
' credit to: a party of our troops went on the Island,
' and brought off a young man, a prisoner, whom I
' have sent to town; he says they have landed their
' sick and wounded, and placed them in the court-
' house and goal, which they have converted into
' hospitals: this looks as if they intended staying
' there. Is it not scandalous to America, that a
' handful of men, with two small men-of-war, should
' ride triumphant, and distress these southern states?
' when perhaps our continental vessels are cruizing
' for the emolument of their commanders....Should
' not this be represented to Congress? At all events

VOL. II.   D

' I shall set off on Monday for camp at Port-royal.
' ferry. I fear we are beginning a new campaign.
          ' I am, &c.

                    ' WILLIAM MOULTRIE.'

                    ———

          FROM GEN. LINCOLN.
               ' CHARLESTOWN, July 10th, 1779.
' DEAR SIR,

    ' I HAVE been honored with your favor of yes-
' terday's date: Major Pinckney has returned from
' Port-royal-river, where he has been to negociate
' an exchange of prisoners: the enemy make a con-
' dition, previous to a general exchange taking place:
' that the officers who have absconded, and broken
' their paroles, and those taken, must be returned be-
' fore this business can be accomplished.

    ' I AM sorry that any officer who has the ho-
' nor to hold a commission, should conduct himself
' in a manner, so unjustifiable, and which in its con-
' sequences will do so much prejudice to their broth-
' er officers: those who were taken, I do not view
' in an unfavorable light, but I think from the tenor
' of their paroles they cannot act until exchanged.

    ' P. S. For particulars you must inquire of Major
' Pinckney.

          ' I am, &c.

                    ' B. LINCOLN.

' Gen. MOULTRIE.'

From Gen. Lincoln.

'Charlestown, July 11th, 1779.

' Dear Sir,

' Your favor of yesterday's date I received this
' morning. I hope that your conjectures, that we
' are now commencing a new campaign, are without
' foundation, for we are by no means prepared for
' such an event. We have at present neither men,
' stores or money; indeed the latter is so depreci-
' ated, that I apprehend that unless something is
' done to increase its value, it will not long answer
' the purpose of carrying on the war; if that fails us,
' our only resource is the VIRTUE of the people; how
' far that will avail us at this day, I leave you to
' judge.

' I am, &c.

' Gen. Moultrie.   B. Lincoln.

A great number of the preceding letters will
show what little dependance we could put upon the
virtue of the people.

—————

From Gen. Lincoln.

'Dear Sir,   Charlestown, 13th July, 1779.

' Sergeant Jasper with a party of men wait upon
' you, desirous of something being given them to do.
' Your being immediately on the spot, will better
' enable you to judge of the most advantageous man-

'ner in which they may be disposed of. It is theirs
'and my wish that they may be employed at your
'discretion*.

'I am, &c.

'B. LINCOLN.'

'Gen. MOULTRIE.'

TO GEN. LINCOLN.

'SHELDON, July 14th, 1779.

'DEAR SIR,

'I HAVE the honor to acquaint you that I arrived
'at this camp last night. I have ordered the Georgia

....

* At the commencement of the war, William Jasper entered
into my regiment, (the second) and was made a sergeant; he
was a brave, active, stout, strong, enterprising man, and a very
great partizan. I had such' confidence in him, that when I was
in the field, I gave him a roving commission, and liberty to pick
out his men from my brigade, he seldom would take more than
six: he went often out, and returned with prisoners before I knew
he was gone. I have known of his catching a party that was
looking for him. He has told me that he could have killed
single men several times, but he would not, he would rather
let them get off. He went into the British lines at Savannah,
and delivered himself up as a deserter, complaining at the same
time, of our ill usage to him, he was gladly received (they
having heard of his character) and caressed by them. He
stayed eight days, and after informing himself well of their
strength, situation and intentions, he returned to us again; but
that game he could not play a second time. With his little
party he was always hovering about the enemy's camp, and
was frequently bringing in prisoners. I have already spoken
of him on the 28th of June 1776, and shall say more of him
in another place hereafter.

' troops to move for Augusta. I have sent a flat
' from Ashepoo to Combahee, over land; and
' will have a large one finished in a few days.
' I do not write you any thing relative to our camp,
' or the enemy, as I have not had time to make the
' necessary inquiries. I therefore refer you to Col.
' D. Horry, who waits on you with this. We shall
' want him again.

' I am, &c.

' WM. MOULTRIE.'

To the Same.

' SHELDON, July 17th, 1779.

' DEAR SIR,

' I RECEIVED your favors of the 11th and 13th.
' The last information I received from the enemy,
' and from good authority, is, that they have sent
' some of their troops to Savannah, and have kept
' the 71st, the light-infantry, and some Hessians,
' posted in the following manner; the 71st at Beau-
' fort, and the Hessians at Mile-End, throwing up
' some works; this place is a narrow neck of land,
' about a mile from the town, not more than 300
' yards across, on each side is a navigable river,
' which makes it a very strong post indeed: the
' light-infantry, (between 3 and 400) are opposite
' Port-royal-ferry, in sight of one of our guards at

' the redoubt; the whole of their number does not
' exceed 1,000 men. It appears to me as if they
' would leave the place before long. I imagine they
' have not shipping enough to take them off at
' one trip, and are therefore obliged to wait the re-
' turn of the vessels which carri d the first division.

' As there are matters of the utmost consequence
' to come on the carpet, at the meeting of the
' general assembly, I propose to be in town, to at-
' tend the Senate, if you have no particular objec-
' tion : and will also give leave to as many officers,
' members of the assembly, to attend as can possi-
' bly be spared. The business here, in my opinion,
' will be only to wait on the motions of the enemy,
' which I think will be passive enough ; they only
' mean to keep possession of the Island in peace
' while they stay. I have sent off the Georgia troops,
' and have also detached Capt. Newman's company
' of horse, and Jasper's little party, to harrass and
' perplex the enemy in that state ; I have given them
' directions to join Col. Dooley, should he be under-
' taking any thing capital. I have been employed,
' these two days, in reconnoitering the country in
' this neighborhood: Col. Garden, with about 100
' men, has taken post at Gordon's plantation, on
' Scotch-neck, and detached about 20 men to Page's-
' point, where the battery is built: Col. Hammond
' is here with about 40 men ; these are all the mili-

' tia of this state, that are now in the field, near this
' place : I have changed my opinion, relative to
' commencing a new campaign, I rather think the
' enemy are lingering out the old one : Our camp
' will be very small in a fortnight, as the time of
' the North-Carolinians will expire, and I see no
' method taken by this state, to replace their num-
' bers : before I quit this, I will arrange matters in
' the best way I can : Col. Pinckney informs me
' that the 3rd regiment mutinied this morning ; their
' complaint is, the want of pay and cloathing ; it is up-
' wards of four months, and some of them five, since
' they have received any pay ; which must appear
' long to those who had always been paid regularly
' every month. I will be obliged to you to order the
' auditors to make a few copies of forms for pay-bills,
' such as Congress directs : several sets of pay-bills
' have been sent down, but are returned with this
' answer, " that they are not proper, and cannot be
' paid." I wish something would be done to bring
' their pay regularly about as usual.

> ' I am, &c.

> ' WM. MOULTRIE.

TO THE SAME.

' DEAR SIR,   ' SHELDON, July 18th, 1779.

' I WROTE you yesterday, since which, I have
' been informed that Gen. Scott is on his march from

' Salisbury to this place : as there is no immediate
' call for those troops this way, I would humbly
' submit my opinion to you, whether it would not be
' best to order them through the back country, to
' Augusta; where they can be supplied with every
' necessary, and keep the enemy in continual appre-
' hension ; besides encouraging and supporting our
' friends in that quarter : I fear if they march through
' this low country, at this extreme hot season, it
' will render many of them useless, for a considera-
' ble time. Col. Twig was with me yesterday, and
' says they are in want of ammunition at Augusta :
' I informed him that you had sent some to Col.
' Dooley : I wrote you yesterday that I proposed be-
' ing in town at the meeting of the general assem-
' bly : if you have no objection, I shall leave this
' next Friday.

' I am, &c.

' WM. MOULTRIE.'

FROM GEN. LINCOLN.

' HEAD-QUARTERS, July 19th, 1779.

' DEAR SIR,

' SENSIBLE of the necessity for your attendance
' in the Senate, it is my desire, yourself, and as ma-
' ny officers, members of the house, as can, consist-
' ent with the duties and welfare of the service, be
' spared, may, with all convenient speed, repair to

' town, after the meeting of the house. The audi-
' tors and pay-masters are to repair to camp this af-
' ternoon, in order to pay the army.

' I am, &c.

' B. LINCOLN.

' Gen. MOULTRIE.'

GEN. Lincoln wished all the officers of the army
that were members of the general assembly, to attend at the meeting, that they might be upon the
spot, to inform the Representatives with the difficulty there was in this state to keep an army together:
that it was a folly to depend upon the militia; that
it was impossible to keep them in the field: therefore some other method must be fallen upon to raise
an army, or else the country must be given up.

LETTER FROM COL. MAITLAND.

' BEAUFORT, July 19th, 1779.

' DEAR SIR,

' I SEND you by this flag of truce, a young man,*
' which Lieutenant Parham, one of your officers,

....

* This young man was left as a safeguard on the field, to
protect Captain Campbell from being killed by our soldiers, but
he had nearly been killed by their's: when we were obliged to
retreat, Captain Campbell could scarcely save him. 'Tis an
unpleasant situation to be placed as a safeguard on the field of
battle, over any one.

' was so good as to leave with Captain Collin Camp-
' bell of the 71st regiment, when wounded at Stono.
' The lad should have been returned long ere now,
' but our army's being in motion, and Captain Camp-
' bell at a distance from where I was, rendered it
' impossible. We are extremely obliged to Mr.
' Parham for his attention to Captain Campbell,
' who begs you will assure him, that he will ever
' retain a most grateful sense of his humanity and
' goodness. A Mrs. Odingsell of this island, has
' acquainted me that a small party of your people
' took her son, (a boy) from the plantation some
' time since, and that he still remains a prisoner.
' I cannot help thinking that this has been done
' without your consent, as the boy is only fourteen
' years old, and never carried arms ; however, if
' you hold him as a prisoner of war ; as his mother
' is extremely uneasy on his account, I shall take it
' as a favor, if you will release him, and send him
' here on his parole, until we can exchange him.

' By this opportunity, I also send you some letters ;
' amongst them is one for Miss C——, containing
' 160 pounds Carolina currency, and a 50 dollar bill ;
' a portmanteau containing cloaths, and a letter with
' 3 half joes, are also sent to Ensign M'Pherson, of
' the 71st, who was left sick at the widow Heyward's,
' these I beg you will order to be delivered him ; if
' there should occur to you any thing in which I

' can be of service to you here, I shall be happy in
' the opportunity of obliging you. There was a pro-
' posal made by Major M'Arthur, to Major Pinckney
' of yours, relative to the exchanging of Ensign
' M'Pherson for Doctor Halling. I should be happy
' to know whether you approve of this exchange
' taking place.

' I am sir, &c.

' JOHN MAITLAND,
Lieut. Col. 71st Regt.

' Gen. MOULTRIE.'

TO COL. MAITLAND.

' SHELDON, July 20th, 1779.

' SIR,

' I WAS honored with your favor of yesterday :
' the soldier who was left by Lieut. Col. Henderson
' of the 6th South-Carolina regiment, with Col. Camp-
' bell on the field at Stono, is returned, but without
' his arms. Lieut. Parham of the 1st regiment, was
' the gentleman who assisted another of your officers,
' when laying wounded on the field, and who, after
' repeated intreaties, received his watch of him :* if
' the officer still survives, and will send his name,
' Mr. Parham will immediately return his watch ;
' having, at same time, assured the owner that he

....

* A handsome gold watch.

' would receive it upon no other terms ; as it was
' for liberty, not for plunder that we fought. Mrs.
' Odingsell's son was brought off before I came to
' this place : I will endeavor, however, to get him
' restored to his mother ; upon his parole, at least,
' as soon as possible. I have received the several
' letters that accompanied your's ; that, containing
' 160 pounds, and a 50 dollar bill, and the other shall
' be delivered, as directed. Mr. M'Pherson's port-
' manteau, containing the articles specified in the
' letter, with the three half-joes shall be sent him, by
' the first opportunity : I am infinitely obliged to
' you, for your kind offer of service ; and shall be
' happy, in my turn, to have in my power to oblige
' you : I must beg you would excuse my being so
' frequently troublesome, in granting flags and pas-
' ses ; but, as there are a number of widow ladies,
' who flatter themselves with the hopes of recovering
' some part of their property on the Island, I cannot
' well refuse them. Not having seen Major Pinck-
' ney since his interview with Major M'Arthur, it
' is not in my power to say what passed between
' them, relative to the exchange.

' I am, &c.

' WM. MOULTRIE.'

JULY 20th. At this time, nothing material was
done ; the legislature was in session ; and our little

army remained at Sheldon, waiting upon the British, who had taken post at Beaufort, under the command of Col. Maitland. About the 4th of September, an officer came to town, from Count D Estaing's fleet, then off our bar, consisting of 20 sail of the line ; two 50 gun ships ; and 11 frigates, to acquaint Gen. Lincoln that the Count D'Estaing was ready to co-operate with him in the reduction of Savannah, and at the same time, to urge the necessity of dispatch ; as he could not remain long upon our coast, at this season of the year. This information put us all in high spirits : the legislature adjourned : the governor and council, and the military joined heartily, in expediting every thing that was necessary : boats were sent to Count D Estaing's fleet, to assist in taking the cannon and stores on shore : every one cheerful, as if we were sure of success ; and no one doubted but that we had nothing more to do, than to march up to Savannah; and demand a surrender : the militia were draughted ; and a great number of volunteers joined readily, to be present at the surrender ; and in hopes to have the pleasure of seeing the British march out, and deliver up their arms ; but, alas ! it turned out a bloody affair ; and we were repulsed from the lines, with the loss of 8 or 900 men killed and wounded : and I think I may say, that the militia volunteers were much disappointed ; as I suppose they did not go with the expectation of storming lines; I was pleased, when I was informed that in general they behaved well; and they could truly say, they had been in very severe fire. On the 5th of September, Gen. Lincoln ordered all officers and soldiers to join their respective regiments; and on the 8th the continentals were drawn from the forts, which were garrisoned by the militia: Gen. Lincoln goes off to take command of the army at Sheldon, about the 12th, and orders the troops, that were appointed to join the army, to follow as soon as possible; leaving myself the command of Charlestown, with a few continentals and the militia: Gen. Lincoln lay with his army at M'Millens', three miles from Savannah, from the 17th to the 23d September: on the 23d our army joined the French, and encamped before Savannah.

FROM GEN. LINCOLN.

' CAMP, BEFORE SAVANNAH, Sept. 24th, 1779.

' DEAR SIR,

' I AM very glad you detained the North-Caro-
' lina militia in town;* for they cannot, I think, arrive
' here in time. Ground was broken last night, very
' near the enemy's lines, towards their left, with very
' little interruption. The cannon† and mortars will

* A reinforcement just came in to us.
† The cannon and mortars were landed at Thunderbolt, about five miles from Savannah, and drawn to camp over land.

' soon be up, and ground opened in different places.
' I should invite you to camp, but think the matter
' will be determined one way or other, before you
' can possibly arrive. ' I am, &c.

' Gen. MOULTRIE.   ' B. LINCOLN.'

To GEN. LINCOLN.
' CHARLESTOWN, Sept. 26th, 1779.

' DEAR SIR,

' I HAVE just now been honored with your favor
' of the 24th inst. by which, I am glad to be informed
' that you have approached so near the enemy's lines,
' without any loss. I hope a few days more will de_
' termine them to surrender to the united forces of
' France and America. I should have been ex-
' tremely happy to have shared the glory, but the
' fates have forbid it. I hope soon to have the plea-
' sure of seeing some of your young gentlemen with
' the joyful news of the surrender of Savannah.
' Yesterday arrived another 500,000 dollars for the
' state of Georgia. I have ordered it to be lodged
' with Mr. Jervais in the same manner as the former,
' until I shall receive your orders thereupon.*   One

* At this time our money was very much depreciated, 1618
for one, and we talked of millions, and in fact, it was next to
nothing; there was one conveniency in it, which was, that a
couple of men on horse-back, with their bags, could convey a
million of dollars from one end of the continent to the other,
in a little time, with great facility.

' million and a half more, will be in to-morrow, for
' the purpose of exchanging the two emissions which
' were stopped in circulation.

' I am, &c.

' WM. MOULTRIE.'

THE army before Savannah was employed in making fascines, and building batteries; and the 4th of
October, at 5 o'clock, A. M. the batteries opened
upon the town with 37 pieces of cannon, on the land
side, and 16 from the water; and 9 mortars, to
throw shells at one and the same time. The French
army lay before Savannah, 7 days before Gen. Lincoln's army got up, and demanded a surrender on
the 16th September, and the garrison requested 24
hours, to consider on an answer: in the mean time,
Col. Maitland got into Savannah, with a strong reinforcement from Beaufort. The batteries continued
their fire, for 4 or 5 days, with very little intermis-
sion: Gen. Provost sent out to request leave to send
the women and children without the lines; but it
was denied, supposing he only wanted to gain time.
Count D'Estaing having been now a month with his
fleet on our coast, and close in shore; his officers
remonstrated to him, the dangerous situation the
fleet was in, and the hazards they run of being attacked by the British fleet, whilst theirs was in a
bad condition; and a great many of their officers

and men on shore : these representations determined the Count D'Estaing to call a council, in which
the opinion of the engineers was, that it would require 10 days more to work into the enemy's lines ;
upon which it was determined to try to carry them
by an assault ; and on the 8th, the following order
was issued.

Evening Orders, by Gen. Lincoln.

WATCH WORD...LEWIS.

' The soldiers will be immediately supplied with
40 rounds of cartridges ; a spare flint ; and have
their arms in good order.'

' The infantry destined for the attack of Savannah,
will be divided into two bodies : the first composed
of the light troops, under the command of Col. Laurens ; the second of the continental battalions, and
the first battalion of the Charlestown militia, except
the grenadiers, who are to join the light troops : the
whole will parade at 1 o'clock, near the left of the
line ; and march by the right, by platoons.'

' The guards of the camp, will be formed of the
invalids, and be charged to keep the fires as usual,
in camp.'

' The cavalry, under the command of Count Paulaski, will parade at the same time with the infantry, and follow the left column of the French troops,
and precede the column of the American light troops ;

they will endeavor to penetrate the enemy's lines, between the battery, on the left of the Spring-hill redoubt, and the next towards the river : having effected this, they will pass to the left, towards Yamacraw ; and secure such parties of the enemy, as may be lodged in that quarter.'

' THE artillery will parade at the same time; follow the French artillery, and remain with the corps de reserve, until they receive further orders.'

' THE whole will be ready by the time appointed, with the utmost silence and punctuality ; and be ready to march, the instant Count D'Estaing and Gen. Lincoln shall order.'

' THE light troops, who are to follow the cavalry, will attempt to enter the redoubt, on the left of the Spring-hill, by escalade, if possible, if not, by entrance into it ; they are to be supported, if necessary, by the first South-Carolina regiment : in the mean time, the column will proceed with the lines to the left of the Spring-hill battery.'

' THE light troops, having succeeded against the redoubt, will proceed to the left, and attempt the several works between that and the river.'

' THE column will move to the left of the French troops, taking care not to interfere with them.'

' THE light troops, having carried the works towards the river, will form on the left of the column.'

' IT is expressly forbid to fire a single gun before

the redoubts are carried, or for any soldier to quit his rank, to plunder, without an order for that purpose : any who shall presume to transgress, in either of these respects, shall be reputed a disobeyer of military orders, which is punishable with death.'

'THE militia of the first and second brigades ; Gen. Williamson's, and the second battalion of the Charlestown militia, will parade immediately, under the command of Gen. Huger, after draughting 500 of them ; the remainder of them will go into the trenches, and put themselves under the command of the commanding officer there : with the 500, he will march to the left of the enemy's lines, and remain as near them as he possibly can, without being discovered, until 4 o'clock in the morning, at which time, the troops in the trenches, will begin an attack upon the enemy : he will then advance, and make his attack as near the river as possible ; though this is only meant as a feint, yet should a favorable opportunity offer, he will improve it, and push into the town.'

'IN case of a repulse, after having taken the Spring-hill redoubt, the troops will retreat, and rally in the rear of the redoubt ; if it cannot be effected that way, it must be attempted by the same rout at which they entered.'

'THE second place of rallying (or the first, if the redoubt should not be carried) will be at the Jew's burying-ground, where the reserve will be placed : if these two halts should not be effectual, they will retire towards camp.'

' THE troops will carry on their hats, a piece of white paper, by which they will be distinguished.'

THE order for the attack, shows it was to have been made on the British lines at 4 o'clock in the morning, but by some means or other, it was delayed until it was clear day-light, which gave the enemy a very great advantage, because they could see our columns marching up, and knew where to direct their fire, consequently our troops suffered much, before they got up to the works ; and on their attack upon the Spring-hill battery, they were so crowded in the ditch, and upon the berm, that they could scarcely raise an arm ; and while they were in this situation, huddled up together, did the British load and fire upon them very deliberately, without any danger to themselves : a body of them came out, and formed a line to the left of their battery, within their abbettis, and kept up a warm fire upon our troops until they retreated : in all this confusion Lieuts. Hume and Bush planted the colors of the second South-Carolina regiment upon the ramparts, but they were soon killed. Lieut. Grey was on the ramparts, near the colors, and received his mortal wound; and the gallant Jasper was with them, and supported one of the colors, until he received his death wound, however he brought off one of the co-lors with him, and died in a little time after. The second regiment gained great honor in this affair: they lost Major Motte, marching up to the attack; and 3 lieuts. and Sergeant Jasper, killed in support-ing their colors on the ramparts; besides many others killed and wounded: of the Carolina troops, Major Wise and Capt. Shepherd was killed, and Capt. Warren wounded. Count D'Estaing received two wounds; and Count Paulaski, at the head of his cavalry, received his mortal wound, from one of the gallies.

Our troops remained before the lines, in this hot fire fifty-five minutes: the generals seeing no pros-pect of success, were constrained to order a retreat, after having 637 French, and 457 continentals killed and wounded: the Charlestown militia, although in a warm part of the fire, were fortunate enough to have only Captain Shepherd killed, and five or six wounded. General Huger made his attack at the same time, but had to wade through a rice field; he was received with music and a warm fire of cannon and mus-ketry, and after losing a few men, they retreated faster than they marched up. The assailants upon Savannah were about 2,500 French troops, headed by Count D'Estaing, and 4000 Americans, militia includ-ed, headed by Gen. Lincoln; the garrison was about

2,500, and of those, only 150 of them were militia. The British it was supposed, had information the day before, by a sergeant from the Charlestown Grenadiers, who went into them, and gave them a particular account of our plan of attack. They knew our force was to be led to the Spring-hill battery, and they were prepared accordingly by filling that post with as many men as it could possibly hold; and they knew that General Huger's attack was only to be a feint, they therefore drew almost all their troops from their left to their right. There cannot be a doubt, but that if the French and American armies had marched into Savannah when they arrived on the 17th, they would have carried the town very easily, because at that time, they had only the Spring-hill battery completed and no abbettis round the town; instead of which, they employed themselves in throwing up batteries for their cannon and mortars, which were of very little consequence till the 9th of October, before they made their attack, which gave the besieged three weeks to fortify themselves, and their success proves that they were not idle in that time. After this repulse, the idea of taking Savannah by regular approaches, was still kept up; but Count D'Estaing's marine officers being very uneasy at the situation of his fleet, pressed his departure, he then ordered all his cannon and stores on board, and embarked his troops from Thunderbolt, and left the coast of America.

WE were then in a much worse situation than before he arrived: the unfortunate militia of Georgia who had taken the British protection, could not go back to them again, after they had joined us, but were obliged to seek for shelter in a strange country, or live in the back woods of their own. This disappointment depressed our spirits very much, and we began to be apprehensive for the safety of these two southern states; it also depreciated our money so very low, that it was scarcely worth any thing.

GENERAL Lincoln retreated with the Americans as far as Ebenezer Heights, and, on the 19th of October, left the army to follow him to Charlestown. In November the small-pox broke out in Charlestown, after it had been kept out of the country near twenty years.

LETTER TO GEN. LINCOLN.

‘ CHARLESTOWN, Nov. 17th, 1779.

‘ DEAR SIR,

‘ I HAVE nothing new to write you; but new
‘ discoveries are made every day of the small-pox ;
‘ the persons are immediately removed to the pest-
‘ house. I expect it will continue to make its ap-
‘ pearance for some days to come ; but I hope we
‘ shall be able to put an entire stop to it soon.

‘ I am, &c.

‘ Gen. LINCOLN.   ‘ WM. MOULTRIE.’

THE small-pox breaking out in Charlestown, was a very good pretence for the militia not coming into town : in fact, they dreaded that disorder more than the enemy.

THE British finding they could make no impression upon the northern states, reversed the proverb of " taking the bull by the horns," and turned their thoughts on the southern states ; their late success in the repulse of the French and Americans from Savannah, and still keeping possession, encouraged them in the undertaking, and in December a large army embarked from New-York, under command of Sir Henry Clinton, convoyed by Admiral Arbuthnot, with several men of war : they had a long and boisterous passage, and arrived at Savannah on the 11th of February ; after staying there a few days, a strong detachment under General Patterson, was ordered to cross over to Purisburgh, and march through the southern parts of the state; whilst Sir Henry Clinton with the body of the army, came round with the fleet to Stono-inlet, and landed the troops on John and James'-Islands. We soon received accounts of the arrival of the British army at Savannah : at this time the legislature were sitting, they immediately adjourned, and all officers and soldiers were ordered to their posts.

LETTER FROM GEN. PROVOST.

'SAVANNAH, Feb. 19th, 1780.

' SIR,

' I HAVE received the honor of your letter of
' the 16th inst. and am much obliged to you for the
' favor : Captain Pemberton has been detained at one
' of our posts, from which he will be sent back, as
' soon as my letter arrives there. General Lincoln
' will also accept my thanks. I have been happy to
' find that our prisoners have been treated with
' civility, particularly Captain Constable, unjustly
' oppressed. I was to send back your's on parole,
' but a fleet and army being arrived, I have not had
' it in my power to effect it, they having demanded to
' defer their going : the other flag came in a canoe ;
' it has not been thought prudent to send her back
' as yet, from this place.

' I have the honor to be, &c.

' A. PROVOST.

' Col. DAN. HORRY.'

————

FROM GEN. LINCOLN.

' HEAD-QUARTERS, CHARLESTOWN,
Feb. 19th, 1780.

' DEAR SIR,

' You will please to proceed immediately to Ba-
' con's-Bridge, where you will form a camp of the
' militia of that part of the neighborhood, and of

' those who are ordered to this town ; if you should
' find it necessary, or for the safety of the troops
' under Colonel Marion, or for the defence of your
' post, you will call on him also : you will at all times
' keep hanging on the enemy's flanks, and oppose
' them at every advantageous pass. As the horse
' will be under your direction, you will give such
' orders as may be necessary for a co-operation of
' them and the infantry. You will cause to be re-
' moved, all the horses, beaves, sheep, swine, car-
' riages, boats, and indeed every thing which may
' comfort the enemy, or facilitate their march, saving
' such as may be necessary for the support of fami-
' lies left. You will throw up a work on the rising
' ground, on this side Bacon's-bridge, to command
' it. You will on approach of the enemy, previous
' to your leaving your post, effectually destroy the
' bridge. You will please to examine Stan's-bridge,
' and the swamp above it, and report your opinion of
' the practicability of passing it with heavy cannon.
' You will keep a small guard at Dorchester-bridge,
' and one on your right at Slan's-bridge. You will
' advise me daily of your situation and strength, and
' of the state of the enemy. You will keep the horse
' as near the enemy as possible.

' I am, &c.

' B. LINCOLN.

' Gen. MOULTRIE.'

To Gen. Lincoln.

'Bacon's-bridge, Feb. 22d, 1780.

'Dear Sir,

'I did not write you sooner, as I waited for
'the return of a party of horse that had gone out
'towards the enemy's lines at Stono, which returned
'last night. Major Jemison informs me he was
'within view of the centries of their picquets, posted
'at the Cross-roads, that he had not heard of any
'number coming out, except the first day or two,
'to drive in some stock. By the accounts he got,
'he believes there are not so many at Stono, as
'when they first took post there, that some of them
'are returned to John's-Island. I have not one mi-
'litia-man doing duty here. I am informed they
'are patroling in their different districts; they de-
'clare against going to town; from what I can un-
'derstand, they are afraid of the small-pox breaking
'out, when they are cooped up, which they say,
'will be worse to them than the enemy. When
'they collect here, I shall employ them in drawing
'off the stock, and destroying such provisions as
'cannot be brought away, from those plantations
'that are left to themselves. The rains have filled
'our rivers and swamps so much, that it is almost
'impossible for the enemy to drag their cannon and
'artillery stores along. I think they cannot pass
'this way; it therefore becomes us to look out, and

' expect them from some other quarter. I am told
' they have four gallies. I beg leave to suggest,
' whether it will not be more practicable for them to
' transport their army in flat-bottomed boats, under
' cover of these gallies, through Wappoo-cut, and
' land them on the west of the town ; then to march
' them round this way ; or whether they may not
' draw their flat-bottomed boats from Rantowle's to
' Ashley-river, drop down, and land near our lines ;
' or cross at Ashley-ferry and land on the causeway.
' I think the causeway should be cut across within
' grapeshot distance of the field-pieces, under Major
' Hog's command. I hope we will have some heavy
' pieces of cannon mounted on the west of the town,
' and that the creeks about Cumins' and the sugar-
' house be filled across. I am throwing up some
' works on a commanding hill at this place ; two
' field-pieces will make it very strong. We have a
' detachment of horse constantly waiting on the
' enemy, to observe their motions.

' I am, &c.

' Gen. LINCOLN.   WILLIAM MOULTRIE.'

———

To Gov. RUTLEDGE.

' BACON'S-BRIDGE, Feb, 22d, 1780.

' DEAR SIR,

  ' I RECEIVED your favor of the 20th inst. and
' forwarded the inclosed packets, agreeably to your

' request. Colonel Skirving was here at the time,
' in his way to town, but is gone back to execute
' your orders : not one militia-man at this place on
' duty : they are much averse to going to town :
' they are apprehensive of the small-pox breaking
' out, when the weather grows warmer, and they
' cooped up in town, would be worse to them than
' the enemy. I am informed they are doing patrole
' duty in their own districts ; if they were collected
' here, I would employ them in driving off the stock,
' and destroying the provisions which cannot be
' brought off. The continentals and state cavalry,
' I employ in waiting on the enemy. These heavy
' rains will retard the enemy's march this way, as
' all the rivers and swamps are full. I think we
' ought to have a watchful eye towards Wappoo-cut.
' I am informed they have four gallies and a number
' of flat-bottomed boats ; some heavy cannon should
' be mounted on the west of the town, and the
' creeks about Cumins' stopped. A detachment
' of our horse returned last night from the enemy's
' lines, but discovered no movements from that
' quarter.

' I am, &c.

' WM. MOULTRIE.

' His Ex. J. RUTLEDGE.'

To Gen. Lincoln.

'Bacon's-bridge, Feb. 23d, 1780.

' Dear Sir,

' I have the pleasure to inform you that Major
' Maham and Captain Sanders with a party of horse,
' took Captain M'Donald and eight privates yester-
' day, near their picquet; I shall send them down to
' day. We are much in want of ammunition: the
' people about the country have none.

    ' I am, &c.

       ' Wm. Moultrie.

' Gen. Lincoln.'

February 23d. The returns made me this day of
the troops under my command at Bacon's-bridge,
were, cavalry of all ranks 379, and the infantry under
Colonel Marion 227; total 606. My being so strong
in cavalry, kept the enemy pretty close to their
lines.

From Gen. Lincoln.

    ' Charlestown, Feb. 24th, 1780.

' Dear Sir,

' Your favor of yesterday, I have received, and
' the prisoners.

' Would it not be best to divide your horse, and
' keep two thirds, or more, over Stono-swamp, near
' where we encamped last year, and in the neighbor-

' hood; frequently shifting their ground; and al-
' ways have a party to watch the enemy's motions,
' to prevent surprise, and to give you the earliest no-
' tice; the other to watch them at Rantowle's, and
' look at them as far as Wappoo?

' I am, &c.

' B. LINCOLN.

' Gen. MOULTRIE.'

———

To GEN. LINCOLN.
' BACON'S-BRIDGE, Feb. 25th, 1780.

' DEAR SIR,

 ' I RECEIVED your favor, yesterday: I had ac-
' quainted Major Jemison that I would sent his corps,
' and Major Call's to some where near the places
' you mention; and where the most fodder is to be
' had: I should have removed them yesterday, but
' took the 2 majors, and a party with me, to recon-
' noitre the enemy on James' and John's-Islands: we
' proceeded to Wappoo-cut, from whence we had a
' very good view of their whole encampment; their
' left on Stono-river, extending their right, along the
' ditch, in Mr. Hudson's pasture, to the end of the
' ditch, near Wappoo-creek, which I take to be a
' quarter of a mile: by the stacks of arms and num-
' ber of men moving about, I judge them to be about
' 1,000 or 1,200, British and Hessians; in Stono-
' river, I saw 3 gallies and 3 schooners, and some

' small boats, sailing down the river ; 1 galley lay at
' the mouth of Wappoo-cut ; another lay at Hudson's-
' landing, and 1 at Fenwick's lower landing : they
' have thrown up a work near the Cut : I was in-
' formed by several persons, that 90 flat-bottom boats
' and canoes, went down Stono, towards the Cut a
' few days ago ; and yesterday, 6 proceeded down
' the river : for further particulars, I refer you to
' Major Jemison.

' I am, &c.

' WM. MOULTRIE.'

TO THE SAME.

' BACON'S-BRIDGE, Feb. 26th, 1780.

' DEAR SIR,

' I JUST now received two letters from Col. Skir-
' ving, both of which I send you enclosed : I also
' send down the prisoners mentioned in them : I al-
' so wrote to Col. Skirving, to send his militia, to
' endeavor to disperse the disaffected that are in
' arms : though should I want them in the mean
' time, I shall send for them. There are, as yet,
' no militia* at this post. I most earnestly request
' you will order me some ammunition ; as, not only
' the militia want it, but, that Major Venier report-

* The militia refusing to go to town, on account of the
small-pox.

' ed to me to day, that he had not more than
' four rounds per man, for his corps, &c.

'   ' I am, &c.

'   'Wm. Moultrie.'

From Gen. Lincoln.

'Head-Quarters, Charlestown, Feb. 28th, 1780.

'Dear Sir,

'   'I was last night favored with your letter of
' the 26th instant, inclosing two from Col. Skirving;
' a representation has this morning been made on
' the subject, to the governor: I shall order some
' ammunition to be sent you: the enemy are open-
' ing the ground near Fort Johnson: I expect our
' ship will disturb them before night.

'   'I am, &c.

'   'B. Lincoln.

'   'Gen. Moultrie.'

From Col. D. Horry.

'Camp, near Ashley-Ferry, Feb. 28th, 1780.

'Dear General,

'   'I am just returned from Lucas' old field, and
' Wappoo-cut; and with a small party, I went over
' to a point called Long-Island: the galley is at her
' old station, and about twenty-four or five at Mr.
' Hudson's-landing, with four armed schooners, and
' two other schooners, with a number of armed boats

' are now gone up to Stono ; probably with an intention
' to bring off the baggage from that post ; which we
' are told now consists of a command ; with 600
' men to guard their provisions and boats. The
' party we saw to-day, must consist of about 200 men
' including the galley's crew ; and from every intelli-
' gence we can obtain, the enemy will soon make a
' point of collecting at Fort Johnson ; where they
' are now busily employed erecting some works.

' I am, &c.

' D. HORRY.

' Gen. MOULTRIE.'

FROM MAJOR CALL.

' STONO, Feb. 29th, 1780.

' SIR,

'NONE of the enemy have been out since Sun-
' day ; when a pretty strong party advanced as far as
' Culp's-house, but returned, before the detachment
' of horse got down: I had all the country recon-
' noitered yesterday, between Ponpon-road and Mrs.
' Thomas' plantation, and not a man was to be seen,
' The officer who went down the Ponpon-road, re-
' ports that their drums beat, and horns sounded
' about 8 o'clock, where the picquet was usually
' kept ; after waiting some time, in expectation of
' their coming out, he moved up the Will-town
' road, found the guard drawn in, and the log-bridge

' torn up, which stopped his farther progress. The
' inhabitants seem to think they are gone, or about
' to leave Stono-ferry : several schooners were pass-
' ing to and fro yesterday from that place, to New-
' cut; which in some measure strengthens the ac-
' counts of the inhabitants : though those I saw had
' got too far to discover what number of men they
' contained. I have sent a party this morning, to
' get some certain intelligence, if possible, of their
' disposition, &c.

' I am, &c.

' RICHARD CALL.

' Gen. MOULTRIE.'

––––––

FROM GEN. LINCOLN.

' CHARLESTOWN, Feb. 29th, 1780.

' DEAR SIR,

' YOUR favor I have received, and am much
' surprised to find the militia so unreasonable as to
' wish to avoid this town : are not the North-Caroli-
' nians here, who have not had the small-pox ? have
' they views and interests to support that the inhabi-
' tants of this state have not ? surely no ! the safety
' of the town depends upon their coming to its assist-
' ance ; and I cannot give them the least encour-
' agement to hope that they will not be brought
' down : they must be brought down ; they ought
' to have been here before now, for they have noth-

' ing to apprehend from the small-pox : there has
' been this day, the strictest inquiry, by the com-
' missioners of the town ; the surgeons of the hos-
' pitals, and the officers of the army ; and they re-
' port to me that it is not in this place. Our garri-
' son is at present so weak, that I shall be obliged to
' send for the light troops the moment that you
' have a hundred or two of the militia join you.

' I am, &c.

' Gen. MOULTRIE.   B. LINCOLN.'

To GEN. LINCOLN.

' BACON'S-BRIDGE, March 1st, 1780.

' DEAR SIR,

   ' I THIS moment received intelligence from
' Major Vernier that all the enemy have crossed
' Wappoo ; and are approaching this way ; our horse
' are retreating towards us : should the intention of
' the enemy be for this post, I shall, on their com-
' ing near, have the bridge destroyed, and make a
' stand, as long as the force I have will permit :
' having been confined to my bed, ever since last
' Tuesday, I shall be obliged to leave the command
' to Col. D. Horry. In case of a retreat, I shall be
' glad to know whether you would have the light
' troops come to town, or remain in the country
' with the horse.   By order,

' PHILIP NEYLE, A. D. C.'

To the Same.

'BACON'S-BRIDGE, March 7th, 1780.

'DEAR SIR,

'By accounts received from Major Vernier and
'a prisoner taken this morning, the enemy crossed
'Wappoo last night at 8 o'clock, with 1,000 grena-
'diers and light-infantry : the last accounts we had
'of them, they were about 3 miles from Ashley-fer-
'ry ; we cannot learn what their intentions were,
'unless they designed to surprise Major Vernier's
'post.   By order,

'PHILIP NEYLE,   A. D. C.'

———

FROM THE SAME.

'CHARLESTOWN, March, 1780.

'DEAR SIR,

'I am happy to hear that you are better, and
'that probably you will soon be on your legs ; in or-
'der to hasten that, I have sent Gen. Huger to Ba-
'con's-bridge, to take all care from you; as soon as
'you are able, you had better come to town.

'I am, &c.

'Gen. MOULTRIE.   B. LINCOLN.'

On the 9th of March I left the command at Bacon's-bridge, to Gen. Huger, and came to Charlestown, where I was confined to the house for several
days, owing to my weakness from my late illness.

EXTRACTS OF LETTERS TO A PARTICULAR
FRIEND IN THE COUNTRY.

‘ CHARLESTOWN, March 19th, 1780.

‘ THE enemy are at Fenwick's place, at the
‘ mouth of Wappoo-creek, making batteries and
‘ other works directly opposite the town : their ship-
‘ ping lay off our bar ; and perhaps, may attempt to
‘ get in, to-morrow or next day : if they remain on
‘ our coast, much longer, they may be surprised by
‘ a Spanish fleet :* we are all in high spirits : the
‘ Virginia troops are expected in a few days.

‘ Yours, &c.

‘ WM. MOULTRIE.’

———

TO THE SAME.

‘ CHARLESTOWN, March 20th, 1780.

‘ THIS morning the enemy's ships (7 of them)
‘ got over our Bar ; and are now in Five-fathom-
‘ hole : perhaps they may begin their attack to-mor-
‘ row : I hope we shall give a good account of them :
‘ the enemy still remain at Wappoo ; we hear they
‘ are to march to day, this way.

‘ Yours, &c.

‘ WM. MOULTRIE.’

....

* Col. Ternant was sent to the Havannah, to endeavor to
get the assistance of a fleet and army, but could not succeed,
because they did not think he was authorized by the governor.

To the Same.

'March 21st, 1780.

'The enemy have got in ten of their men of war,* 'one of fifty guns, two of forty-four guns, and seven 'frigates and twenty gun ships. We expect in a 'day or two, to see some smart firing between them 'and our vessels and Fort Moultrie: we have seven† 'ships and three gallies to oppose them, if they will 'lay any time before the fort, I will engage we beat‡ 'them; but it is generally thought they will pass as 'fast as they can, and endeavor to take their stations 'above the town, in Cooper or Ashley rivers, where 'they will incommode us a little at our lines; but 'we are erecting batteries to keep them clear of us, 'which I hope will answer the purpose. I suppose 'we shall have their army soon on the neck, to 'blockade us; when that happens, you will hear but 'seldom from

'Your's

'Wm. Moultrie.'

....

* Three of them store ships.

† The Bricole of forty guns, the Providence and Boston frigates, each thirty-two guns, the Queen of France twenty-eight, L'Avanture and the Fruite, each twenty-six guns, brig General Lincoln twenty guns, and three gallies.

‡ General Pinckney was commanding officer of the fort at that time.

To the Same.

'March 22d, 1780.

'I wrote you yesterday; since which, we have
'altered our plan greatly; all our ships and gallies
'are ordered up to town, and their guns taken out
'and placed in the batteries, and manned by the
'sailors, by which means we have a reinforcement
'on shore, of 1,200 men, which adds greatly to our
'strength. We are to sink some ships, to stop the
'channel from the exchange over to the marsh, on
'the other side. The Virginia line, is expected in
'three or four days.

'The reasons for altering the plan fixed upon to
'dispose of our fleet, was, that Commodore Whipple
'did not choose to risk an engagement with the
'British fleet. I think he was right in the first in-
'stance, when stationed just within the bar to pre-
'vent the British fleet from coming over, as that
'was a dangerous place, but his second position,
'when he was to lay a little above Fort Moultrie,
'within point blank shot of the fort, with his ships
'across, to rake the channel: in that situation it
'would have been impossible for them to pass with-
'out losing some of their ships; I scarcely think
'they would have attempted it. The fleet was of little
'service to the besiegers in blocking up our port, as
'all the reinforcements that we got, or could expect to
'have, came in by land: it is true, Admiral Arbuthnot

' had the honor of having Fort Moultrie tamely given
' up to him, without firing a single gun, after Colonel
' Pinckney,* was withdrawn from that command.
' After the British fleet had passed Fort Moultrie, it
' was no longer of use to us, but rather a dead weight.
' We fired at them yesterday, which obliged them to
' move a little; two of their boats were sounding
' Ashley-river, but we soon made them retire.   The
' fleet still lays in Five-fathom-hole. We can manage
' them easy enough. We are sinking some vessels
' across the river, from the Exchange to the marsh
' opposite, which I think will stop the channel. We
' expect the Virginians every day. Yours, &c.

' WM. MOULTRIE.'

TO THE SAME.

' March, 26th, 1780.

' THE enemy are advancing slow; the head of
' their army is about John Cattel's, but I imagine
' they intend crossing over to Gibbs' place with
' their main body ; they are busily employed on the
' opposite shore, in making fascines and other things ;
' I suppose it will be a day or two yet, before they
' appear before our lines : they have three gallies at
' the mouth of Wappoo-creek, quite open to us.

' Yours, &c.

' WM. MOULTRIE.'

* Now General Pinckney.

To the Same.

'April 3d, 1780.

'The enemy are now before our lines,* and
'throwing up works very fast; they have four redoubts
'abreast finished; one at the broad road at Watson's,
'one at Hamstead, where St. Edmond Head's house
'stood, and one between those two, another they
'have on our left, near Cumin's-point; I suppose, to-
'night they will have one, where Tagart's house
'stood. We began to cannonade them yesterday,
'and shall continue every day; their batteries are
'not yet opened, but I suppose to-morrow or next
'day, they will begin; then you will hear a great
'deal of noise, but there is very little danger from
'this sort of fighting. I hope the obstructions laid
'across our river before the Exchange, will deter
'their shipping from coming up. We have estab-
'lished an hospital at Cainhoy meeting-house, for
'all those who are not able to do duty, to repair to.
'I forgot to mention to you, that the women walk
'out from town to the lines, with all the composure
'imaginable, to see us cannonade the enemy, but I
'fancy when the enemy begin, they will make
'themselves pretty scarce. We had a skirmish
'with the enemy, on their approach to our lines.

....

* They crossed Ashley-river, in force, above the ferry and
at Gibbs' within a mile or two of the town.

'Colonel Laurens commanded a corps of light
'troops, and fought them two or three hours, several
'were killed and wounded on both sides, and he was
'obliged to retire within the lines. Major Hyrne
'was wounded in this skirmish.

'Your's, &c.

'Wm. Moultrie.'

To the Same.

'April 7th, 2 o'clock, P. M.

'The Virginians are now landing at Gadsden's-
'wharf; we intend as soon as they land and march
'up, to fire thirteen guns, man the lines, and give
'three cheers.

'Your's, &c.

'Wm. Moultrie.

To the Same.

'April 8th, 1780.

'No doubt you have heard the firing yesterday'
'it was the British men-of-war passing Fort Moultrie'
'they are now lying by Fort Johnson; the fort has
'damaged them a little, and obliged them to burn
'one that got on shore; we cannot tell whether it
'is a man-of-war, or a store-ship,* but we see the
'people from the fort are very busy in picking up
'their plunder. We have not yet heard from the

* She was a store ship.

'fort, but I dare say they have little or no damage
'done them, and perhaps not a man killed. I sup-
'pose in a few days they will attempt to pass the
'town, then you must expect to hear a very great
'firing indeed, but we shall be pretty secure in our
'batteries. They have nine laying near us, but not
'more than seven men-of-war. Your's, &c.

'WM. MOULTRIE.'

To the Same.

'April 27th, 1780.

'WE are now closely blocked up, and only expect
'to be relieved by our friends. I have lost my
'brave and worthy aid, Philip Neyle,* killed by a
'cannon ball on the 18th inst. which took away a
'part of his head, since which, my poor brother
'Tom was killed on his return into our lines; they
'went out to sally into the enemy's entrenchments;
'they brought in twelve prisoners, and bayoneted
'fifteen or twenty more; my brother was the only
'man killed, and two wounded, in this sortie, of 300
'men. We two days ago had Colonel Parker killed,
'or else very little damage has yet happened; not
'above ten killed and forty wounded, notwithstanding
'the great number of cannon balls and shells that
'are thrown into the town.

'WM. MOULTRIE.'

* The only child of a crippled and aged father.

EVENING ORDERS BY GEN. LINCOLN.

March 26th.

' As General Moultrie is to direct the disposition
' of the artillery of the different batteries and works
' in and about the town, all orders relative thereto,
' issued by him, are to be obeyed.'

A JOURNAL OF THE SIEGE OF CHARLESTOWN.

Tuesday, March 28th, 1780.

THE enemy crossed Ashley-river, in force, above the ferry.

Wednesday, 29th.

THE enemy advanced on the neck. The light-infantry were this evening reinforced with two companies, and the command given to Colonel Laurens.

Thursday, 30th.

THE enemy came on, as far as Gibbs', where they continued skirmishing throughout the day, with our light-infantry: the enemy were reinforced in the evening, with two field-pieces, and ninety men, which obliged our party to retire into garrison about dark. Capt. Bowman of the North-Carolina brigade killed; Major Hyrne, and seven privates wounded. The enemy were all this day transporting troops from Old-town, on Wappoo-neck, to Gibbs'.

Friday, 31st.

THE garrison employed in mounting cannon; throwing traverses, &c.

Saturday, April 1st.

NOTHING material: the troops employed as yesterday.

Sunday, 2d.

LAST night the enemy broke ground, and this morning, appeared two redoubts; one nearly opposite the nine gun battery, on the right of the hornwork; and the other, a little to the left of the same, at about twelve hundred yards distance from our lines.

Monday, 3d.

THE enemy employed in completing their two redoubts, and erecting one on our left, at an equal distance from the rest.

Tuesday, 4th.

SEVERAL deserters within these three or four days, who say the enemy on Thursday last had upwards of twenty men killed and wounded; among the latter, a lieutenant colonel of the 60th regiment; Lord St. Clair badly; and that they are bringing their cannon on the neck: since the appearance of the enemy's works, they have been cannonaded: two ten inch and one seven inch mortars were removed from the Bay, and employed in retarding them. The

enemy all this day employed in finishing their redoubts, and throwing up a line of communication.

Wednesday, 5th.

LAST night the enemy continued their approaches
to Hamstead-hill, on which they erected a battery
for twelve cannon ; and a mortar battery a little in
the rear. The cannon and mortars employed as
usual, in annoying their works : the battery from
Wappoo, and the gallies, have thrown several shot
into town ; by which, one of the inhabitants in King-
street, was killed.

Thursday, 6th.

THE enemy approached from their centre redoubt
and erected a five gun battery on the angle, between
batteries No. 11 and 12. The Virginians,* under Brigadier General Woodford, got in by the way of Addi-
son's-ferry ; and some North-Carolina militia under
Colonel Harrington.

Friday, 7th.

THIS afternoon twelve sail of the enemy's vessels,
passed Fort Moultrie, under a very heavy fire ; one
of them, supposed to be a store ship...having met
with some accident, ran aground in the cove, where
she was blown up by her own people : the remainder were ten square rigged vessels ; viz. one fifty and

----

* About seven-hundred.

two forty-four gun ships; four frigates; two ships, supposed to be store ships; a schooner and sloop anchored under Fort Johnson.

Saturday, 8th.

THE enemy employed in finishing their batteries on the right.

Sunday, 9th.

THE enemy last night continued their approaches from their redoubt on the left, and threw up a battery for ten cannon, against the angle of our advanced redoubt, and the redan No. 7. Some shot were thrown at the shipping, by our batteries in town, but without effect.

Monday, 10th.

SIR Henry Clinton, and Admiral Arbuthnot summoned the town.

SUMMONS TO MAJ. GEN. LINCOLN.

'April 10th, 1780.

'SIR Henry Clinton, K. B. general and commander in chief of his majesty's forces, laying on the Atlantic, from Nova-Scotia, &c. &c. &c. and Vice-Admiral Arbuthnot, commander in chief of his majesty's ships in North-America, &c. &c. &c. regretting the effusion of blood, and consonant to humanity towards the town and garrison of Charlestown, of the havock and desolation with which they are threatened from the formidable force surrounding them by land and sea. An alternative is offered at this hour to the

inhabitants, of saving their lives and property contained in the town, or of abiding by the fatal consequences of a cannonade and storm.

' SHOULD the place in a fallacious security, or its
commander in a wanton indifference to the fate of its
inhabitants, delay the surrender, or should public
stores or shipping be destroyed, the resentment of an
exasperated soldiery may intervene ; but the same
mild and compassionate offer can never be renewed.
The respective commanders, who hereby summons
the town, do not apprehend so rash a part, as further
resistance will be taken, but rather that the gates
will be opened, and themselves received with a degree of confidence which will forebode further recon.
ciliation.

' HENRY CLINTON.
' M. ARBUTHNOT.'

————

FROM GEN. LINCOLN.
' HEAD-QUARTERS, CHARLESTOWN,
' April 10th, 1780.

' GENTLEMEN,
' I HAVE received your summons of this date ;
' sixty days have passed since it has been known that
' your intentions against this town were hostile ; in
' which, time has been offered to abandon it ; but

' duty and inclination point to the propriety of sup-
' porting it to the last extremity.

' I have the honor to be,

' Your Excellency's humble servant.

' B. LINCOLN.'

Tuesday and Wednesday, 11th and 12th.

THE enemy busied in completing their work and mounting their cannon.

Thursday, 13th.

BETWEEN 9 and 10 o'clock this morning, the enemy opened their cannon and mortar batteries. The cannonade and bombardment continued, with short intermissions, until midnight : the gallies and battery at Wappoo also fired. An embrazure at redan No. 7 destroyed ; a sergeant and private of the North-Carolina brigade killed ; a twenty-six pounder destroyed, and one eighteen pounder dismounted, in the flanking battery, on the right : some women and children killed in town. The enemy's cannon were chiefly twenty-four pounders ; and their mortars from five and an half, to ten inches : they threw several carcasses from eight and ten inch mortars, by which two houses were burnt.

Friday, 14th.

THE enemy began an approach on the right, and kept up a fire of small arms. Cannonade and bombard continued. One sergeant of the North-Carolinians killed by a cannon ball: one of the militia artillery killed, and one wounded : two matrosses of the South-Carolina artillery killed.

Saturday, 15th.

THE enemy continued approaching on the right : the mortars ordered to the right, and commence a firing immediately, to annoy them. A continual fire of small arms, cannon, and mortars. A battery of two guns, opened by the enemy at Stiles' place, on James-Island. Major Grimball's corps of militia, relieved from the advance redoubt, by a detachment of continental artillery, commanded by Major Mitchell.

Sunday, 16th.

IT is said the enemy attempted to land at Hobcaw-neck with two gun boats, but were prevented by Col. Malmadie. Two 18 pounders, a quantity of provisions, and other valuable articles got out of the wreck of the vessel near Fort Moultrie.

Monday, 17th.

A MAN, inhabitant of the town, killed by a cannon ball, and a woman wounded ; both from Wappoo battery.

Tuesday, 18th.

THE enemy continued a warm firing from their cannon, mortars, and small arms. Mr. Neyle, aid-de-camp to Gen. Moultrie, killed by a cannon ball. We advanced a breast-work to the left of the square redoubt, for riflemen, to annoy the enemy on their approach. Five men killed by small arms; and three wounded by a shell : a sentinel at the abbattis had his arm shot off by one of our own cannon : a twelve pounder* bursted in the horn-work, by which two men were much hurt. The enemy ceased throwing large shells. We hear that our cavalry under General Huger, have been defeated †; and that we lost between 20 or 30 killed and wounded; among the former was Major Vernier of Paulaski's legion. General Scott with the light-infantry crossed Cooper-river, into town : about 40 Virginians got in last night. The enemy continued their approaches to the right, within 250 yards of the front of the square redoubt : they threw during the night a great number of shells from sixteen royals and Cohorns, chiefly in the North-Carolina camp : one man killed, and two wounded.

Wednesday, 19th.

The enemy began an approach from the left battery, towards our advanced redoubt; and moved

* This was one of the guns belonging to the Acteon frigate, that got on shore while engaged with Fort Moultrie, in 1776, and was burnt. It is remarkable that eight or ten of those guns which we weighed, and mounted on our lines, were every one of them bursted, after two or three rounds : which makes me suppose that their being heated by the fire of the ship, and suddenly plunging into the water while red-hot, destroyed their metallic parts, and left only the dross behind.

† This was a shameful surprise, at Monk's-corner, in the open day.

some mortars into the former: they also advanced on Hobcaw-neck, and exchanged a few shot with our advance party. Two or three persons killed in town.

Thursday, 20th.

THE approaches continued on the left; their mortars removed from their left battery, into their approaches; an eighteen pounder dismounted at Captain Bottard's battery on the right; four of their gallies after dark, moved from Wappoo-creek to the shipping at Fort Johnson, under a very heavy fire from our batteries. The enemy retreated from Hobcaw across Wappataw-bridge, which it is said they have burnt. Two magazines in the batteries commanded by Capt. Sisk, blew up by shells, but no persons hurt.

Friday, 21st.

A flag sent to Sir Henry Clinton.

'CHARLESTOWN, April 21st, 1780.
'SIR,
'I AM willing to enter into the consideration of 'terms of capitulation, if such can be obtained as 'are honorable to the army, and safe for the inhabit-'ants. I have to propose a cessation of hostilities 'for six hours, for the purpose of digesting such 'articles.   'I have the honor to be,
'Your Excellency's, &c.
'B. LINCOLN.
'His Ex. SIR HENRY CLINTON.'

FROM SIR HENRY CLINTON.

'CAMP BEFORE CHARLESTOWN, April 21st, 1780.

'SIR,

'ADMIRAL Arbuthnot, who commands the fleet,
'should have been addressed jointly with me on
'this occasion. As I wish to communicate with him,
'and as I give my consent to a cessation of hostilities
'for six hours, I desire an aid-de-camp* may pass
'to the ships, with a letter, and my request, that the
'battery on James'-Island may desist firing.

'I have the honor to be, &c.

'H. CLINTON.'

'Maj. Gen. LINCOLN.'

ARTICLES OF CAPITULATION PROPOSED BY MAJOR GENERAL LINCOLN.

'CHARLESTOWN, April 21st, 1780.

ARTICLE 1. That all acts of hostilities and works
shall cease between the naval and land forces of
Great-Britain and America, in this state, until the
articles of capitulation shall be agreed on, signed, or
collectively rejected.

ART. 2. That the town, forts and fortifications
belonging to them, shall be surrendered to the commander in chief of the British forces, such as they
now stand.

....

* The aid was permitted to pass to the ships, from Gibb's,
round Ashley-river, to the vessels near Fort Johnson.

Art. 3. That the several troops garrisoning this town and forts, including the French and American sailors, the French invalids, the North-Carolina and South-Carolina militia, and such of the Charlestown militia as may choose to leave this place, shall have thirty-six hours to withdraw to Lamprier's, after the capitulation be accepted and signed on both sides; and that those troops shall retire with the usual honors of war, and carry off at that time their arms, field-artillery, ammunition and baggage, and such of their stores as they may be able to transport.

Art. 4. That after the expiration of the thirty-six hours mentioned in the preceding article, the British troops before the town shall take possession of it, and those now at Wappataw shall proceed to Fort Moultrie.

Art. 5. That the American army thus collected at Lamprier's, shall have ten days, from the expiration of the thirty-six hours before mentioned, to march wherever General Lincoln may think proper, to the eastward of Cooper's-river, without any movement being made by the British troops, or part of them, out of the town or Fort Moultrie.

Art. 6. That the sick and wounded of the American and French hospitals, with their medicines, stores, the surgeons and director-general, shall remain in the town, and be supplied with the necessaries requisite, until provisions shall be made for their removal, which will be as speedily as possible.

ART. 7. That no soldier shall be encouraged to desert, or permitted to inlist on either side.

ART. 8. That the French consul, his house, papers and other moveable property, shall be protected and remain untouched.

ART. 9. The continental ships of war, Providence, Boston, and Ranger, now in this harbor, with the French ship of war, the Adventure, shall have liberty to proceed to sea, with the necessary stores on board, and go unmolested, the three former to Philadelphia and the latter to Cape Francois, with the French invalids mentioned in article three.

ART. 10. That the citizens shall be protected in their persons and property.

ART. 11. That twelve months be allowed to those who do not choose to live under the British government, to dispose of their effects, real and personal, in the state, without any molestation whatever, and remove such parts thereof, as they choose, with themselves and families; and during that time, they, or any of them, may have in their option to reside occasionally in town or country.

ART. 12. That the same protection to their persons and property, and the same time for the removal of their effects be given to the subjects of France and Spain, residing amongst us, as are required for the citizens residing amongst us in the preceding article.

'B. Lincoln.'

SIR HENRY CLINTON AND VICE-ADMIRAL ARBUTH-
NOT TO MAJOR GENERAL LINCOLN.

'CAMP BEFORE CHARLESTOWN, April 21st, 1780.

'SIR,   8 o'clock at night.

'WE have in answer to your third article (for we
'cannot proceed further) to refer you to our former
'offer, as terms, which, although you cannot claim,
'yet we consent to grant. These however, must be
'accepted immediately, and responsible hostages, of
'the rank of field-officers, must be sent us as secu-
'rities, that the custom of war in these cases must
'be strictly adhered to, that no person of the garrison
'or inhabitant be permitted to go out, nothing be
'removed or destroyed, and no ships or vessels pass
'from the town. All dependant posts are to be in-
'cluded in the surrender, and the hostages to be as an-
'swerable for these as the town. Your answer is ex-
'pected at ten o'clock, at which hour, hostilities will
'commence again, unless our offers are closed with.

'H. Clinton.

'Maj. Gen. Lincoln.'   'M. Arbuthnot.'

ON the summons of Sir Henry Clinton, and Admiral Arbuthnot, General Lincoln called a council
of war, of field-officers, on the propriety of evacu-

ating the town. They were of opinion ' that it
' was unadviseable, because of the opposition made to
' it by the civil authority and the inhabitants, and be-
' cause, even if they could succeed in defeating a
' large body of the enemy posted in their way, they
' had not a sufficiency of boats to cross the Santee
' before they might be overtaken by the whole Bri-
' tish army.' The council therefore recommended a capitulation.

Saturday, 22d.

APPROACHES continued on our left in front of the
advance redoubt. The enemy kept up a heavy cannonade. Three men wounded.

Sunday, 23d.

APPROACHES continued on our right and left;
those on the right within twenty yards of the wet
ditch. About eight at night two deserters from the
enemy; they report them to have received a considerable reinforcement* from New-York, and that they
detached to day, ten companies of light-infantry
to get footing at Haddrell's-point, they say the enemy
have lost a number of men by our shells.

Monday, 24th.

A party composed of three hundred men, Virginians and South-Carolinians, under the command
of Lieutenant Colonel Henderson, made a sortie
upon the enemy's approaches, opposite the advance

* Lord Cornwallis with 2500 men.

redoubts at day light, they were completely surprised, and lost about fifteen or twenty men killed with the bayonet, besides twelve persons brought off, seven of whom were wounded. Captain Moultrie killed and two men wounded on our side. The enemy attempted to support their guards from the trenches ; but on receiving rounds of grape, made them retreat. The prisoners report their party to have been commanded by Major Hall of the 71st regiment, but no officers were to be found. Colonel Parker killed about eight o'clock, looking over the parapet; two privates killed and seven wounded. The greatest part of the 1st South-Carolina regiment came into garrison this morning, with Colonel C. Pinckney from Fort Moultrie.

Tuesday, 25th.

BETWEEN twelve and one this morning, a heavy fire of cannon and musketry, commenced from our advanced redoubt, and the right of the lines occasioned as it was said, by the enemy's advancing in column. It is certain they gave several huzzas, but whether they were out of their trenches, it is not clear; they kept up a very heavy and incessant fire with musketry, for thirty minutes. The enemy threw several light balls into town. Two o'clock P. M. Lord Cornwallis at Mount-Pleasant.

Wednesday, 26th.

THE Lord George Germaine, and a sloop, joined

the enemy's fleet. The enemy were very quiet all day, and last night; we suppose they are bringing cannon into their third parallel : they are strengthening their approaches : Lord Cornwallis took possession of Mount-Pleasant yesterday. Brigadier General Du Portail* arrived from Philadelphia. The garrison ordered to be served with the usual quantity of provision ; a plentiful supply having been received. One killed ; Captain Goodwin of the third South-Carolina battalion, and one private wounded.

On General Du Portail delaring that the works were not tenable, a council was again called upon for an evacuation, and to withdraw privately with the continental troops: when the citizens were informed upon what the council were deliberating, some of them came into council, and expressed themselves very warmly, and declared to General Lincoln, that if he attempted to withdraw the troops, and leave the citizens ; that they would cut up his boats, and open the gates to the enemy : this put a stop to all thoughts of an evacuation of the troops, and nothing was left for us, but to make the best terms we could.

* As soon as General Du Portail came into garrison, and looked at the enemy, and at our works, he declared they were not tenable ; and that the British might have taken the town, ten days ago : he wished to leave the garrison immediately, but General Lincoln would not allow him, because it would dispirit the troops.

Thursday, 27th.

ABOUT 1 o'clock in the afternoon, four of the enemy's gallies, an armed sloop, and a frigate, moved down the river, and anchored opposite the mouth of Hog's-Island creek. Five militia men, late of James'-Island, deserted last night from South-bay in a boat. Our post at Lamprier's-ferry, retreated across the river, in the night, to Charlestown, after spiking up four eighteen pounders, they were obliged to leave. One private killed, and five wounded.

Friday, 28th.

COLONEL Charles Pinckney is requested to assist General Moultrie in directing and disposing the artillery of the different batteries and works in and about town. Two deserters from the enemy at Hobcaw, brought over by our troops that retreated last night. Some supernumerary officers quitted the garrison. The enemy busy in throwing up their third parallel, within a few yards of the canal. Our fatigue employed in inclosing the horn-work : two privates killed ; Lieutenant Campaign of the North-Carolinians, and two privates wounded.

Saturday, 29th.

WE are throwing up a redoubt on the right of the horn-work. The enemy's batteries remarkably silent ; they seem to intend erecting two batteries in their third parallel ; one at the gate opposite the horn-work, and the other in front of Col. Parker's regiment. A heavy bombardment by the enemy during the night : a deserter from them ; who says that they are preparing a bridge to throw over the canal. Captain Templeton of the fourth Georgia battalion, wounded by a shell, of which he died.

Sunday, 30th.

THE deserter yesterday further tells us that the huzzas which occasioned the firing last Tuesday morning, were from the enemy's working parties, who thought we were sallying : their engineer, he says, had ordered them, in that event, to give three huzzas, and fall back upon the covering party's, who not having been apprised of it, received them as an enemy ; in consequence of which, a considerable number of them were killed and wounded : he affirms the account of the enemy's receiving a reinforcement from New-York, and says their detachment on Hobcaw, amounts to upwards of 2,000 ; that they look for their shipping up every night ; and are preparing a large number of fascines to fill up the canal. Lieutenant Hall of the North-Carolinians wounded ; his leg broke by a grape-shot, from our own batteries. Lieutenant Philips of the Virginians wounded in his thigh by a shell.

Monday, May 1st.

OUR fatigue employed in erecting another redoubt on the left of the horn-work, and completing the new works. The enemy appear to be about another

battery in their third parallel, opposite No. 12, on
our right. The garrison congratulated in the general orders of yesterday, on the certainty of large
reinforcements being at hand. Five men deserted
from the galley last night, Captain Montford of the
North-Carolinians wounded, and Mr. Lord,* a volun-

....

* Mr. Lord and Mr. Basquin, two volunteers, were sleeping
upon a matrass together, when Mr. Lord was killed by a shell
falling upon him, and Mr. Basquin at the same time, had the
hair of his head burnt, and did not wake till he was called upon.
The fatigue in that advance redoubt, was so great, for want
of sleep, that many faces were so swelled they could scarcely
see out of their eyes. I was obliged to relieve Major Mitchell
the commanding officer : they were constantly upon the look
out for the shells that were continually falling among them, it
was by far, the most dangerous post on the lines. On my
visit to this battery, not having been there for a day or two, I
took the usual way of going in, which was a bridge that crossed
our ditch, quite exposed to the enemy, in the mean time, they
had advanced their works within seventy or eighty yards of the
bridge, which I did not know of; as soon as I had stepped upon
the bridge, an uncommon number of bullets whistled about me,
on looking to my right, I could just see the heads of about
twelve or fifteen men firing upon me, from behind a breast-
work, I moved on and got in ; when Major Mitchell saw me,
he asked me which way I came in, I told him over the bridge,
he was astonished, and said, " sir it is a thousand to one that
you were not killed," and told me, " that we had a covered
way to go out and in," which he conducted me through on my
return. I stayed in this battery about a quarter of an hour, to
give the necessary orders, in which time we were constantly
skipping about to get out of the way of the shells thrown from
their howitzers, they were not more than one hundred yards
from our works, and throwing their shells in bushels on our
front and left flanks.

teer in the continental artillery, killed yesterday by a shell, in the advanced redoubt. A smart bombardment during the day.

Tuesday, 2d.

LAST night the enemy were making a ditch on the right, to drain our canal. A number of men killed and wounded within these last three or four days; their number not ascertained. A nine pounder bursted at battery No. 12, and a quantity of fixed ammunition blown up by accident at batteries No. 10 and 12. The enemy throw shells at us charged with rice and sugar.*

Wednesday, 3d.

OUR fatigue employed in fixing picquets, &c.

Thursday, 4th.

OUR rations of meat reduced to six ounces, coffee and sugar allowed to the soldiers. The fire from the enemy's cannon still slack, but they do not spare their shells.

Friday, 5th.

CAPTAIN William Mitchell of the continental artillery, badly wounded by a shell.

Saturday, 6th.

FROM all appearance, Fort Moultrie† is in the

....

* They were misinformed if they supposed us in want of those articles.

† Fort Moultrie was given up without firing a gun.

hands of the enemy ; a British flag was seen flying on the flag-staff.

Sunday, 7th.

THE above confirmed. Our principal magazine* near being destroyed, by a thirteen inch shell bursting within tenyards of it.

Monday, 8th.

A SECOND summons from Sir Henry Clinton in-informing us of the fall of Fort Moultrie, and that the remains of our cavalry were cut to pieces the day before yesterday. The embrazures of the enemies batteries in the third parallel† opened last night. Our meat quite out, rice sugar and coffee served out.

....

* The old magazine behind St. Philip's Church : in consequence of that shell falling so near, I had the powder (10,000 pounds) removed to the north east corner, under the exchange, and had the doors and windows bricked up. Notwithstanding the British had possession of Charlestown so long, they never discovered the powder, although their provost was the next apartment to it, and after the evacuation, when we came into town, we found the powder as we left it.

† When the enemy's third parallel was completed, we had sand-bags placed upon the top of our lines, for the riflemen to fire through. The sand-bags were about two feet long and one foot thick, we laid down first two of them, three or four inches one from the other, and a third laid upon the top of the two, which made a small loop hole for the riflemen to fire through, the British immediately followed our example : many men were killed and wounded through these holes.

FROM SIR HENRY CLINTON.

'CAMP BEFORE CHARLESTOWN, May 8th, 1780.
' SIR,

' CIRCUMSTANCED as I now am with respect to the
' place invested, humanity only can induce me to lay
' within your reach the terms I had determined should
' not again be proffered. The fall of Fort Sullivan,
' the destruction on the sixth instant, of what re-
' mained of your cavalry, the critical period to which
' our approaches against the town has brought us,
' mark this as the term of your hopes of succor,
' could you have framed any, and as an hour beyond
' which, resistance is temerity. By this last sum-
' mons therefore, I throw to your charge whatever
' vindictive severity exasperated soldiers may inflict
' on the unhappy people, whom you devote by per-
' severing in a fruitless defence.

' I SHALL expect your answer until eight o'clock,
' when hostilities will commence again, unless the
' town be surrendered, &c. &c.

' H. CLINTON.'

' Maj. Gen. LINCOLN.

FROM GEN. LINCOLN.

' CHARLESTOWN, May 8th, 1780.
' SIR,

' YOUR letter to me of this date, is now un-
' der consideration. There are so many different

' interests to be consulted, that I have to propose
' that hostilities do not again commence until twelve
' o'clock.

' B. LINCOLN.

' His Ex. Sir HENRY CLINTON.'

———

FROM SIR HENRY CLINTON.

, SIR,   May 8th, 1780.

' I CONSENT that hostilities shall not again com-
' mence before the hour of twelve, as you desire.

' I have the honor to be, &c.

' H. CLINTON.

' Maj. Gen. LINCOLN.'

———

FROM GEN. LINCOLN.

' SIR,   May 8th, 1780.

' As more time has been expended in consult-
' ing the different interests, then I supposed there
' would be, I have to request that the truce may
' be continued until 4 o'clock.

' B. LINCOLN.

' His Ex. Sir HENRY CLINTON.'

ARTICLES OF CAPITULATION PROPOSED BY MAJOR GENERAL LINCOLN.

CHARLESTOWN, May 8th, 1780.

ART. 1. That all acts of hostilities and works
shall cease between the besiegers and the besieged,

until the articles of capitulation shall be agreed on, signed, and executed ; or collectively rejected.

ART. 2. The town and fortifications shall be surrendered to the commander in chief of the British forces, such as they now stand.

ART. 3. That the continental troops and sailors, with their baggage, shall be conducted to a place to be agreed on ; where they shall remain prisoners of war, until exchanged : while prisoners, they shall be supplied with good and wholesome provisions, in such quantity as are served out to the troops of his Britannic Majesty.

ART. 4. The militia now in garrison shall be permitted to return to their respective homes, and be secured in their persons and properties.

ART. 5. The sick and wounded shall be continued under the care of their own surgeons, and be supplied with medicines, and such other necessaries as are allowed to British hospitals.

ART. 6. The officers of the army and navy shall keep their horses, swords, pistols, and baggage ; which shall not be searched ; and retain their servants.

ART. 7. The garrison, at an hour appointed, to march out with shouldered arms, drums beating, and colors flying, to a place to be agreed on, where they will pile their arms.

ART. 8. That the French consul, his house, papers, and other moveable property, shall be protected and untouched ; and a proper time granted to him for retiring to any place that may afterwards be agreed upon between him and the commander in chief of his British forces.

ART. 9. That the citizens shall be protected in their lives and properties.

ART. 10. That twelve months time be allowed all such as do not choose to continue under the British government, to dispose of their effects, real, and personal, in the state, without any molestation whatever ; or to remove such part thereof as they choose, as well as themselves and families : and that, during that time, they, or any of them, may have it in their option to reside occasionally in town or country.

ART. 11. That the same protection to their persons and properties, and the same time for the removal of their effects ; be given to the subjects of France and Spain, as are required for the citizens in the preceding article.

ART. 12. That a vessel be permitted to go to Philadelphia with the general's dispaches, which are not to be opened.

  (Signed)   B. LINCOLN.

FROM SIR HENRY CLINTON.

' SIR,   May 8th, 1780.

 ' As I wish to communicate with the Admiral ' upon the subject of your last letter, I have to de-

' sire that an aid-de-camp* may be permitted to
' pass to the fleet for that purpose.

' I have the honor to be, &c.

' H. Clinton.

' Major General Lincoln.'

——

FROM SIR HENRY CLINTON.

' May 8th, six o'clock, P. M.
' Sir,

' In order to give the articles of capitulation
' which you proposed, a due consideration ; I propose
' that the cessation of hostilities shall continue until to-
' morrow morning at eight o'clock ; and that in the
' mean time, every thing shall continue in its present
' situation : if you accede to this, you will please to
' give me immediate information of it.

' I have the honor to be, &c.

' H. Clinton.

' Major General Lincoln.'

——

FROM GEN. LINCOLN.

' May 8th, 1780.
,Sir,

' I ACCEDE to your proposal, that hostilities
' shall cease until to-morrow morning at eight o'clock,

....

* To pass from Gibb's, down Ashley-river, to the fleet
lying at Fort Johnson....it was granted.

' and that in the mean time all works shall continue
' in their present state.

(Signed)   ' B. LINCOLN.

' His Ex. Sir HENRY CLINTON.

FROM SIR HENRY CLINTON.

' SIR,   May 8th, 1780.

' YOUR answer to my letter proposing a contin-
' uation of the truce until to-morrow morning at
' eight o'clock, only accedes to the cessation of hos-
' tilities, and that in the mean time all works shall
' continue in their present state; but my proposition
' was, that, until that time, every thing should con-
' tinue in its present situation; and my meaning
' was, that there should not be an attempt made to
' remove any of the troops, or destroy any of the
' ships, stores, or other effects whatever, now in
' the town or harbor: If your idea is the same, I
' must request you will express yourself more ex-
' plicitly.

' I am, &c.
'H. CLINTON.

' Major General LINCOLN.'

FROM GEN. LINCOLN.

' SIR,   May, 8th, 1780.

' IN agreeing that the truce should be continued
' until eight o'clock to-morrow morning, and all

' works remain as they were, I meant to accede to
' your proposal, that every thing should continue in
' its present situation, which I again assent to.

' B. LINCOLN.'

' His, Ex. Sir HENRY CLINTON.'

WHILE these flags were passing, the militia looked
upon all the business as settled, and without orders,
took up their baggage and walked into town, leaving
the lines quite defenceless.

ALTERATIONS OF ARTICLES OF CAPITULATION
PROPOSED BY MAJOR GENERAL LINCOLN, AND
ANSWERED BY THEIR EXCELLENCIES, SIR HENRY
CLINTON, K. B. AND VICE ADMIRAL ARBUTHNOT.

ARTICLE 1. All acts of hostilities and work shall
cease until the articles of capitulation are finally
agreed to or rejected.

ART. 2. The town and fortifications, with the
shipping at the warves, artillery, and all public stores
whatever, shall be surrendered in their present state
to the commanders of the investing forces. Proper
officers shall attend from the respective departments
to receive them.

ART. 3. Granted.

ART. 4. The militia now in garrison shall be
permitted to return to their respective homes, as

prisoners upon parole, which, so long as they observe it, shall secure them from being molested in
their property by the British troops.

ART. 5. Granted.

ART. 6. Granted, except with respect to their
horses, which will not be allowed to go out of town,
but may be disposed of by a person left from each
corps for that purpose.

ART. 7. The whole garrison shall, at an hour to
be appointed, march out of town, to the ground between the works of the place and the canal, where
they will deposit their arms. The drums are not to
beat a British march, or colors be uncased.

ART. 8. Agreed, with this restriction, that they are
to consider themselves as prisoners of war on parole.

ART. 10. The discussion of this article, of course,
cannot possible be entered into at present.

ART. 11. The subjects of France and Spain shall
have the same terms as are granted to the French
consul.

ART. 12. Granted: and a proper vessel, with a
flag, will be provided for that purpose.

ALL public papers and records must be carefully
preserved, and faithfully delivered to such as shall
be appointed to receive them.

(Signed)   H. CLINTON.

M. ARBUTHNOT.

Camp before Charlestown, May 9th, 1780.

94

FROM GEN. LINCOLN.

' May 9th, 1780.

' Sir,

' In reply to your answer on the articles of capi-
' tulation, I must remark that in their present state
' they are inadmissable ; and have to propose those
' now sent, may be acceded to.

' If any further explanation should be necessary,
' I have to propose also, that two or three gentle-
' men be appointed to meet and confer on the sub-
' ject. I have the honor to be, &c.

' B. Lincoln.

' His Ex. Sir Henry Clinton.

ALTERATIONS OF ARTICLES OF CAPITULATION, PROPOSED BY MAJOR GENERAL LINCOLN.

Art. 2. The town and fortifications ; with the shipping at the wharves (excepting those which are private property) and all public stores shall be surrendered in their present state, to the commander in chief of the British forces

Art. 4. The militia now in garrison, shall be permitted to return to their respective homes, with their baggage unmolested ; and not to be considered as prisoners of war.

Art. 6. Such of the officers as may be unwilling to dispose of their horses, may keep them.

ART. 7. This article to stand as at first proposed : the drums beating a British march.

ART. 8. The French consul, never having borne
arms, and acting in a civil capacity, is not to be
considered as a prisoner of war.

ART. 9. The citizens, and all other persons, now
in town, who are inhabitants of this state, shall be
secured in their persons and properties, both in
town and country ; and not to be considered prisoners of war.

ART. 10. This article to stand as at first proposed : the persons who may claim the privileges
therein expressed, giving their paroles that they
will not act against the British government, until
they are exchanged.

ART. 11. This article to stand as at first proposed,
with the same restrictions as are mentioned in Art.
10. In order to prevent disputes, it is to be under-
.stood that all officers of the continental army, who
are citizens of this state, be entitled to all the benefits of citizens, with regard to the security of their
property. All public records now in town, will be
delivered to such persons as may be appointed to receive them. (Signed) B. LINCOLN.

Done at Charlestown, May 9th, 1780.

To Gen. Lincoln.

' May 9th, 1780.

' Sir,

' No other motives but those of forbearance and
' compassion induced us to renew offers of terms you
' certainly had no claim to. The alterations you
' propose, are all utterly inadmissable ; hostilities will
in consequence commence afresh, at eight o'clock.

' H. Clinton.'

' M. Arbuthnot.'

' Maj. Gen. Lincoln.

After receiving the above letter, we remained
near an hour silent, all calm and ready, each waiting
for the other to begin. At length, we fired the first
gun, and immediately followed a tremendous cannonade,* and the mortars from both sides threw out an
immense number of shells; it was a glorious sight,
to see them like meteors crossing each other, and
bursting in the air; it appeared as if the stars were
tumbling down. The fire was incessant almost the
whole night; cannon-balls whizzing and shells hissing
continually amongst us ; ammunition chests and
temporary magazines blowing up; great guns bursting, and wounded men groaning along the lines : it
was a dreadful night! it was our last great effort, but

* About 180 or 200 pieces of heavy cannon fired off at the
same moment.

it availed us nothing; after this, our military ardor was much abated ; we began to cool, and we cooled gradually, and on the eleventh of May we capitulated, and in the morning of the twelfth, we marched out and gave up the town.

To Sir Henry Clinton.

'Charlestown, May, 11th, 1780.

'Sir,

'The same motives of humanity, which inclined 'you to propose articles of capitulation to this garrison 'induced me to offer those I had the honor of send-'ing you on the 8th inst. They then appeared to 'me, such as I might proffer, and you receive, with 'honor to both parties. Your exceptions to them, 'as they principally concerned the militia and citi-'zens, I then conceived were such as could not be 'concurred with ; but a recent application from 'those people, wherein they express an unwillingness 'to comply with them, and a wish on my part to 'lessen as much as may be, the distresses of war to 'individuals, lead me now to offer you my acceptance 'of them.

'I have the honor to be, &c.

'B. Lincoln.'

To Gen. Lincoln.

' Camp before Charlestown, May 11th, 1780.

' Sir,

'WHEN you rejected the favorable terms which
' were dictated by an earnest desire to prevent effu-
' sion of blood, and interposed articles that were
' wholly inadmissable ; both the admiral and myself,
' were of opinion that the surrender of the town at
' discretion, was the only condition that should after-
' wards be attended to; but as the motives which then
' induced them, are still prevalent, I now inform
' you that the terms then offered, will still be grant-
' ed. A copy of the articles shall be sent for your
' ratification, as soon as they can be prepared, and
' immediately after they are exchanged, a detachment
' of grenadiers will be sent to take possession of the
' horn-work, opposite your main gate. Every ar-
' rangement which may conduce to good order in
' occupying the town, shall be settled before ten
' to-morrow, and at that time your garrison shall
' march out.

' I have the honor to be, &c.

' H. Clinton.'

ARTICLES OF CAPITULATION BETWEEN HIS EXCEL-
LENCY SIR HENRY CLINTON, &C. AND MARIOT
ARBUTHNOT, ESQ. VICE ADMIRAL, AND MAJOR
GENERAL LINCOLN.

ART. 1. That all acts of hostilities and work shall cease between the besiegers and the besieged, until the articles of capitulation shall be agreed on, signed and executed, or collectively rejected.

ART. 1. All acts of hostilities and works shall cease, until the articles of capitulation are finally agreed to, or rejected.

ART. 2. The town and fortifications shall be surrendered to the commander in chief of the British forces as they now stand.

ART. 2. The town and fortifications with the shipping at the wharves, artillery and all public stores whatsoever, shall be surrendered in their present state, to the commander of the investing forces. Proper officers shall attend from the respective departments to receive them.

ART. 3. The continental troops and sailors with their baggage, shall be conducted to a place to be agreed on, where they

ART. 3. Granted.

shall remain prisoners of war until exchanged; while prisoners, they shall be supplied with good and wholesome provisions in such quantity as is served out to the troops of his Britannic majesty.

ART. 4. The militia now in garrison shall be permitted to return to their respective homes, and be secured in their persons and property.

ART. 4. The militia now in garrison shall be permitted to return to their respective homes as prisoners of war on parole, which parole, as long as they observe, shall secure them from being molested in their property by the British troops.

ART. 5. The sick and wounded shall be continued under the care of their own surgeons, and be supplied with medicines and such necessaries as are allowed to the British hospitals.

ART. 5. Granted.

ART. 6. The officers of the army and navy shall

ART. 6. Granted, except with respect to the horses,

keep their horses, swords, pistols and baggage, which shall not be searched, and retain their servants.

which will not be allowed to go out of town, but may be disposed of by a person left for that purpose from each corps.

ART. 7. The garrison shall at an hour appointed, march out with shouldered arms, drums beating and colours flying, to a place agreed on, where they will pile the arms.

ART. 7. The whole garrison shall at an hour to be appointed, march out of the town, to the ground between the works of the place and the canal, where they will deposit their arms. The drums not to beat* a British march, or the colors to be uncased.

ART. 8. That the French consul, his house, papers and other moveable property, shall be protected and untouched, and a proper time granted to him for retiring to any place that may afterwards be agreed upon between him and the commander in chief of the British forces.

ART. 8. Agreed, with this restriction, that he consider himself as a prisoner on parole.

....

* We marched out with the Turk's march.

o

Art. 9. That the citizens be protected in their persons and property.

Art. 9. All civil officers and citizens who have borne arms during the siege, must be prisoners on parole, and with respect to their property in the city, shall have the same terms as are granted to the militia; and all other persons now in town, not described in this or other articles, are notwithstanding, understood to be prisoners on parole.

Art. 10. That twelve months time, be allowed all such as do not choose to continue under the British government to dispose of their effects, real, and personal, in the state, without any molestation whatever; or to remove such part thereof as they choose, as well as themselves and family; and during that time, they, or any of them, may have

Art. 10. The discussion of this article of course cannot possibly be entered into at present.

at their option to reside
occasionally in town or
country.

ART. 11. That the   ART. 11. The subjects
same protection to their of France and Spain shall
persons and property, and have the same terms as
the same time for the re- are granted to the French
moval of their effects, be consul.
given to the subjects of
France and Spain, as are
required for the citizens
in the preceding article.

ART. 12. That a ves-   ART. 12. Granted; and
sel be permitted to go to a proper vessel, with a
Philadelphia, with the gen- flag, will be provided for
eral's dispatches; which that purpose.
are not to be opened.

ALL public papers and records must be carefully
preserved, and faithfully delivered to such persons
as shall be appointed to receive them.

Done in the Camp before Charlestown,
        May 12th, 1780.
                    H. CLINTON.
                    M. ARBUTHNOT.

A LETTER FROM SIR HENRY CLINTON AND AD-
MIRAL ARBUTHNOT, TO GENERAL LINCOLN.

'HEAD-QUARTERS BEFORE CHARLESTOWN,

'SIR,   May 12th, 1780.

'WE have to request you will propose some
'proper contiguous building in the town, for the
'residence of the private prisoners of war, not to be
'on parole; those will be, of course, such as may,
'in discretion be asked.

'THE officers of the army and navy will go to the
'barracks at Haddrell's-point, and boats will be at
'the wharves to convey them at 3 o'clock.

'THE militia must depart as speedily as possible;
'and by a report of the numbers departing home-
'wards, on parole, by the several roads of the coun-
'try, boats shall convey their baggage to Stono-
'ferry; to Dorchester; to Strawberry-ferry; to
'Cain-hoy: themselves shall be escorted beyond
'our neighboring posts.

'WE beg from you, a general return of all per-
'sons bearing arms; and also all persons yet in
'town, in civil capacities.

'As soon as the detachment of grenadiers take
'possession of the horn-work, our deputies of depart-
'ments shall meet your's, who will deliver up to them,
'all public effects: and when your troops shall have
'quitted the town; the garrison destined to it, shall
'march in. Your officers shall be allowed to go to

' the extent of six miles from the barracks, but to
' pass no river, creek, or arm of the sea.

  ' We have the honor to be, &c.

      ' H. CLINTON.

      ' M. ARBUTHNOT.'

EARLY in the siege, General Lincoln requested,
and urged the necessity of the governor and council
leaving the town ; that their being in the country
would keep up the civil authority, and be more useful than they could possibly be, by staying in town :
the governor made many objections, and said the
citizens would say he left them in a time of danger ;
at last they fell upon an expedient that satisfied all
parties, which was, that the governor, and three of
his council, should leave the town ; and that lieutenant governor Gadsden, and the five others of the
council, should remain within the lines : this being
agreed to, on the twelfth day of April, Governor
Rutledge, the honorables Charles Pinckney, John
Lewis, Gervais and Daniel Huger left the town,
and went into the north part of the country. It was
very fortunate for the province, that the governor
was not made a prisoner in town : his presence in
the country, kept every thing alive, and gave great
spirits to the people, to have a man of such great
abilities, firmness, and decision amongst them : he
gave commissions ; raised new corps ; embodied the

militia, **and** went to Philadelphia, to solicit reinforcements : he returned, and joined the army ; he stayed by them ; enforced the laws of the province ;
called the legislature ; in short, he did every thing
that could be done for the good of the country.

A RETURN OF THE NUMBER OF CANNON, &c. IN
CHARLESTOWN, AT THE SURRENDER, ON THE
TWELFTH OF MAY, 1780, IN THE BATTERIES.

BATTERIES ON THE LINES.

		GUNS.
No. 1.	Beginning on the left.	10
2.		6
3.		6
4.		2
5.		6
6.		8
7.		4
8.		4
9.		2
10.		2
11.		2
12.		9
13.		7
14.		3
15.	Advance redoubt	6
16.	Cambray's battery	2
		79

BATTERIES ON THE WATER-SIDE.

		GUNS.
No. 1.	Liberty battery, where liberty-tree stood	6
2.	Lauren's wharf	10
3.	Cravan's Governor-bridge . . .	7
4.	Exchange	14
5.	Grenville's*	8
6.	Lyttleton's	12
7.	Broughton's	20
8.	Gibbs's-wharf	7
9.	Britigney, behind Gibb's house . .	4
10.	Sugar-house	7
		95
	Fort Moultrie	30
		125
	Four and six pounders	17
		142

GUNS.	POUNDS.	SHOT.
15 . . .	24 . . .	2817
31 . . .	18 . . .	7279
43 . . .	12 . . .	4990
68 . . .	9 . . .	4670
157		

About fifty thousand pounds of powder.

Mortars, (number not known.)

N. B. A number of the above guns were taken from the ships, two frigates and others.

. . . .

* South end of East-Bay.

ABOUT eleven o'clock, A. M. on the twelfth of May, we marched out between 1500 and 1600 continental troops, (leaving five or six hundred sick and wounded in the hospitals) without the horn-work, on the left, and piled our arms; the officers marched the men back to the barracks, where a British guard was placed over them; the British then asked where our second division was? they were told these were all the continentals we had, except the sick and wounded; they were astonished, and said we had made a gallant defence. Captain Rochfort had marched in with a detachment of the artillery to receive the returns of our artillery stores: while we were in the horn-work together in conversation, he said ' sir you have made a gallant defence, but you had a great many rascals among you,' (and mentioned names) ' who came out every night and gave us information of what was passing in your garrison.' The militia marched out the same day and delivered up their arms at the same place; the continental officers went into town to their quarters, where they remained a few days to collect their baggage, and signed their paroles, then were sent over to Haddrell's point. The militia remained in Charlestown. The next day the militia were ordered to parade near Lynch's pasture,* and to bring all their arms with

* Where the spring pump now stands.

them, guns, swords, pistols, &c. and those that did not strictly comply, were threatened with having the grenadiers turned in among them; this threat brought out the aged, the timid, the disaffected, and the infirm, many of them who had never appeared during the whole siege, which swelled the number of militia prisoners to, at least, three times the number of men we ever had upon duty: I saw the column march out, and was surprised to see it so large; but many of them we had excused, from age and infirmities; however, they would do to enrol on a conqueror's list. When the British received their arms, they put them in waggons, and carried them to a store-house, where we had deposited our fixed ammunition (about 4,000 pounds) and although they were informed by some of our officers that the arms were loaded, and several of them went off before the explosion took place, yet in taking them out of the waggons they threw them so carelessly into the store, that some at last set fire to the powder, which blew up the whole guard of fifty men, and many others that were standing by; their carcasses, legs, and arms were seen in the air, and scattered over several parts of the town. One man was dashed with violence against the steeple of the new independant church, which was at a great distance from the explosion, and left the marks of his body there for several days. The houses in the town received a great shock, and the window sashes rattled as if they would tumble out of the frames.

Most of our militia were still together; after delivering up their arms, they went in a body to assist in extinguishing the fire, that had communicated itself to the neighboring houses; and while they were working they were under the dreadful apprehensions lest the magazine should take fire, as the work-house and others that were next to it were in a blaze; at last some timid person called out, that ' the magazine was on fire,' this gave the alarm; every one took fright, both British and Americans, and instantly broke off from work, and run away as fast as possible through the streets, throwing down, and tumbling over each other, and others coming, after tumbling over them, in endeavoring to get as far from the expected explosion, as possible : I have heard some of them say, that although they were so confoundedly frightened at the time, they could not keep from laughing, to see the confusion and tumbling over each other : the alarm was soon brought into the town ; I was then in a house, joining St. Michael's church, with some company ; I advised the going out of the house, and walking to South-bay, because I was apprehensive, from the great shock which was felt in the houses, from the explosion of 4,000 pounds of powder, that, should the magazine blow up, which had 10,000 pounds of powder in it, many of the houses in town would be thrown down : on my way thither, I met a British officer, who asked me how much powder was in the magazine ; I told him 10,000 pounds: ' Sir,' said he, ' if it takes fire, it will blow your town to hell !' I replied, ' I expected it would give a hell of a blast !' The British were very much alarmed at the explosion ; all the troops were turned out under arms, and formed : they could not tell what was the matter : some of the British and Hessian officers supposed it was designed by us : I was abused, and taken up by a Hessian officer (whose guard was at Broughton's-battery) he was very angry, and said to me, ' you, General Moultrie, you rebel's have done this on purpose, as they did at New-York;' and ordered his guard to take me a prisoner, into a house near, and placed a sentry at the door, where a number of us were confined ; but I soon got a note over a back way, to General Leslie, acquainting him of my situation, upon which he immediately sent one of his aids to me, with an apology, that my confinement was contrary to orders, and ordered the sentry from the door : after a little time, the alarm subsided ; they went back, and stopped the progress of the fire : and if they had considered for a moment, they would have found that it was almost impossible for the magazine to take fire from the adjacent houses, because it was inclosed with a high brick wall; and the magazine itself was built of brick, and bomb proof.

To Gen. Patterson.

'Charlestown, June 15th, 1780.

'Sir,

'The surgeons, at Haddrell's-point, represent
'to me, a number of patients under inoculation;
'and many down with the yellow-fever; and no me-
'dicines, or the common necessaries of life, to as-
'sist them: they have sent a list of such medicines
'as are wanted, to the surgeons of our hospital, who
'say they cannot furnish them, being only supplied,
'from time to time, with what are immediately ne-
'cessary: and we are unable to purchase any, for
'the want of hard money: I am therefore to request
'the favor of you, to order the director-general of
'your hospital, to furnish the surgeons, with what
'medicines may be necessary, for the use of the
'officers and servants at Haddrell's-point.

'I have the honor to be, &c.

'W. Moultrie.'

To the Same.

'Sir, June 16th, 1780.

'I do myself the honor of informing you, that
the American commissary of prisoners, reports to
'me, that the British commissary refuses issuing

' provisions to the prisoners of war, as the returns
' from Haddrell's-point, exceed, by twenty-five, the
' real number: the reasons, I believe to be, is
, in the drawing rations for the general officers, each
' drawing six rations for himself and servants, when
' perhaps they have only one or two servants : I will
' inquire and have the matter cleared up. The
' officers at Haddrell's-point, are irregularly served
' with provisions, occasioned by the uncertainty of a
' boat at the precise time it should go off, which is
' sometimes attended with the loss of tide : the pre-
' sent boat is used with great risk, both to the men
' and provisions, as one hand is almost constantly
, employed to bale : I am therefore to request the fa-
' vor of you, to allow the officers at Haddrell's-point,
' to be supplied with provisions weekly ; and that
' you will be pleased to order the deputy quarter-
' master general to furnish the American commissa-
' ry of prisoners, a large canoe, for that purpose.

    ' I have the honor to be, &c.

                        ' WM. MOULTRIE.'

Copy of a Return of Prisoners made by the British.

RETURN OF THE REBEL FORCES, COMMANDED BY MAJOR GENERAL LINCOLN, AT THE SURRENDER OF CHARLESTOWN, THE TWELFTH OF MAY, 1780; NOW PRISONERS OF WAR.

REGIMENTS, OR CORPS.	Major Generals	Brigadier Generals	Majors of Brigade	Commissioned Officers									Regtl. Staff		Sergeants	Drummers	Rank and File
				Colonels	Lieut. Colonels	Majors	Captains	Lieutenants	Ensigns	Paymasters	Adjutants	Qr. Mas. ers.	Surgeons	Mates			
General Staff,	1	5															
Engineer do.	1																
South-Carolina Artillery.				1	1	1	8	7					1	1	10	1	62
North-Carolina do.							3	1							12	2	46
Charlestown Batt. of do.				1		1	3	5		1	1	1			10		146
Cannoniers,				1		1	3				1				2		159
1st Regt. of South-Carolinians,				1	1		7	6					1		25	14	176
2d do. do.				1			7	10					1	1	22	9	195
3d do. do.				.1			9	6					1	1	19	14	208
1st Regt. of North-Carolinians,				1	1	1	6	8	2				1	1	21	10	234
2d do. do.				1	1		7	7	4	1			1		19	15	245
3d do. do.				1			3	8					1		10	8	130
1st Regt. of Virginians,				1	1	1	5	7	5				1	1	20	26	268
2d do. do.				1	1	1	6	7	4				1	1	20	17	246
3d do. do.				2			7	7	3				1		24	10	198
1st Detachment of Virginians,															16	6	235
2d do. do.															9	5	218
4th Virginia Regiment,							2	2	2								
5th do. do.							3	3									
6th do. do.							2	4	4								
7th do. do.							3	2	1								
8th do. do.				1	1		2	2									
10th do. do.				1			2	3	2								
11th do. do.				1			2		3								
Light Dragoons,						1	3	1	1						5		31
Officers of Georgia,					1		3	1									
1st Batt. Charlestown Militia,				1	1	1	6	10			1		2		18		312
2d do. do.				1	1		6	10			1		2		20		446
S. and N. Carolina Militia,						4	7	36	43	10	3	3	2		44		1079
Citizens,																	40
French Company,							1	1					2		3		36
Spanish Company,																	
	2	5	3	16	9	21	145	162	41	1	7	6	18	6	329	137	4704

Civil List.	General Hospital Staff.	Quarter Master-General's Department.	Commissary General's Department.
1 Lieut. Governor,	2 Director-Generals	1 Qr. Master-Gen.	1 Commissary General,
3 Privy Council,	4 Physicians and Surgeons,	1 Assist. do.	1 Dep. Commissary General,
1 Commissary of Purchases,	9 Assist. Surgeons,	1 Dep. do. of forage	1 Conductor,
1 Clerk of the House of Representatives,	1 Apothecary-Gen.	2 Do of Hides,	1 Commissary of Stores,
1 Assistant Judge,	1 Apothecary,	1 Waggon Master-General,	1 Clerk of do.
1 Sheriff,	1 Apothecary's Mate,	3 Waggon-Masters,	1 Conductor of do.
1 Clerk of Sessions,	1 Chaplain,	1 Powd. Inspector,	
1 Clerk of Pleas,	2 Purveyors,	1 Arsenal Store-keeper,	
1 Ordinary,	1 Paymaster,	1 Purchaser of Wood,	
1 Aud. Gen. of accts.	2 Stewards,	2 Waggoners,	
1 Reg. of Conveyances	1 Waggoner.	1 Stable-keeper,	
1 Messeng. of Council,		1 Conductor.	
4 Clergymen.			

From Brig. Gen. Patterson.

CHARLESTOWN, June 17th, 1780.

' B. G. PATTERSON presents his compliments to
' General Moultrie, and begs he will do him the
' honor to call at his quarters, at any time most
' convenient to him this afternoon. He should wait
' upon the general himself, but is detained at home
' on very particular business, by appointment of
' several gentlemen of the town and country.

' Gen MOULTRIE.'

IN the afternoon, I waited upon General Patterson
who received me very politely; he wished to have
some conversation with me; he said he had had a
number of applications from our citizens, for different purposes, and wished to take my advice and
opinion upon them, he informed me he was entirely
a soldier, and very little acquainted with the civil
matters, and therefore begged to have some conversation with me respecting the prisoners on Haddrell's-point; after an hour's conversation, I left him,
and he very politely attended me down the stairs to
the outer door.

From Gen. Lincoln.

' CHARLESTOWN, May 18th, 1780.

' DEAR SIR,

' THE officers go this morning to Haddrell's-

' point, you being the senior, I have to request that
' you would make an arrangement of the barracks,
' and see that justice is done to all the officers, with
' respect to the rooms.

'   I am, dear sir, your's sincerely,
' Gen. MOULTRIE.   B. LINCOLN.'

WHEN we got to Haddrell's-point, it was very difficult to get quarters in barracks, for the
number of officers that were sent over ; they went
to the neighboring houses, within the limits of their
patroles* ; and many of them built huts about in the
woods, and in a very little time, were comfortably
settled with little gardens about them : the number
of officers (prisoners) at Haddrell's-point, and the adjacent houses, were two-hundred and seventy-four,
(Colonel Pinckney and myself were in excellent
quarters, at Mr. Pinckney's place, called Snee-farm)
it would be too tedious to insert their names, I will
only give a general return of all ranks, and the states
to which they belonged.

....

* I was, at this time, allowed to come to town when I
pleased.

Lines.	Brigadier Generals	Colonels.	Lieut. Colonels.	Majors.	Captains.	Lieutenants.	Ensigns.	Cornets	Surgeons.	Surgeon's Mates.	Paymasters.	Quarter Masters.	Muster Masters.	Total.
Virginia	2	4	5	6	27	35	26	2	4	2				115
N. Carolina	1	2	3	2	14	25	9		3	2				59
S. Carolina	1	2	1	1	23	24			2	2	1			55
Do. Artillery		1	1	1	2	12			1	1		1		19
Corps Eng.	1	1	1	1	2	1								7
Horry's horse						1								2
Polaski's leg.				3	1		1	1						6
Georgia line	1	1		1	4	1							1	9
Total	6	11	11	12	78	99	95	3	11	5	1	1	1	274

GENERAL Lincoln was furnished with a vessel, to carry him, and his suit, to Philadelphia; but before his departure, he appointed Captain George Turner, deputy commissary general of prisoners, for the southern department, who was allowed, for a time, to stay in Charlestown, to transact the business of his office.

To Capt. Turner.

' Sir,   ' Snee-farm, May 28th, 1780.

' I received your favor of the twenty-second
' instant, in which you recommend the appointing
' some proper person to act as issuing commissary ;
' that business is already done ; but I am sorry to
' say, that our provisions are very irregularly served
' out to us ; some times three days' bread, and two
' days' meat ; at other times, half day's rations of
' beef, and full rations of flour : in short, we have
' been almost starved : crabs and fish, have support-
' ed us hitherto : a very few of the officers have hard
' money ; and if they had they could not purchase any
' thing here ; the families have barely sufficient to
' support themselves : the officers here who have
' lately come from the Northward, inform it is cus-
' tomary for our prisoners with the British, to re-
' ceive their pay in hard money : as you are late-
' ly from there, you can inform us how that matter
' is ; I wish it could be brought about at this time.
' I observe you sign yourself commissary general of
' prisoners ; I shall be glad to know what instruc-
' tions you have, relative to the prisoners, that they
' may apply to you accordingly.

'I am, &c.

' Wm. Moultrie.

' Capt. George Turner,

' Dep. Com. Gen. of prisoners.'

THE officers, prisoners at Haddrell's-point, were very ungovernable indeed and it was not much to be wondered at, when two hundred and fifty of them from different states, were huddled up together in the barracks, many of them of different dispositions, and some of them very uncouth gentlemen; it is not surprising that their should be continual disputes among them, and frequent duels. General M'Intosh who was the senior officer that resided constantly with them, complained to me of their disorderly conduct and uncivil behaviour to each other, upon which, I wrote him the following letter.

'CHARLESTOWN, June 26th, 1780.

'SIR,

'I AM sorry to be informed that our officers
'behave so much amiss, as to make it necesary to
'hold court martials over them, and that they even
'dispute any authority we may have; I am there-
'fore to request, that you will let them know that I
'think myself fully authorized for that purpose, not-
'withstanding we are prisoners of war, and should
'any disorders happen, you will apply to me, and I
'will immediately order a court martial to be held,
'and approve or disapprove as I shall think right,
'and will transmit the sentence to Congress, for

' their approbation. The commandant* of the British
' troops agrees with me in opinion as to my right,
' and will allow me to send a flag to Congress for
' that purpose. I am sorry to inform you that the
' gentlemen must not apply for any more indulgen-
' ces for the present, as Mr. Pendleton's escape has
' put an end to all those matters.

' I am, &c.

' WM. MOULTRIE.

'Gen. M'INTOSH.'

HAVING received information that Doctor Houston, a prisoner of war to Sir Henry Clinton, who
had permission to go to Georgia upon his private
business, was arrested and sent to jail on a charge
of treason, I wrote the following letter to Lord Cornwallis :...

' CHARLESTOWN, June 29th, 1780.

' MY LORD,

' I HAVE the honor to inform your Lordship,
' that Doctor Houston, a continental officer, and
' prisoner of war upon parole to his Excellency Sir
' Henry Clinton, is now detained in Georgia on a
' charge of treason; three evidences appear against
' him, who, to support this charge, swear they saw

....

* Lord Cornwallis.

' him in the American camp, when that place was
' besieged, aiding and assisting the French and
' Americans ; my Lord, I look upon it my duty to
' require his discharge from his Excellency Sir James
' Wright, and that he may be permitted to return
' to the hospital in Charlestown, where he is much
' wanted ; I am therefore to request your Lordship
' will allow me to write to Georgia for that purpose.

  ' I have the honor to be, &c.

      ' WM. MOULTRIE.

' Lord CORNWALLIS.'

———

FROM LORD CORNWALLIS' AID.

    ' CHARLESTOWN, 29th, 1780.

' SIR,

  ' THE Earl Cornwallis has directed me to ac-
' quaint you, that he has not the least objection to
' your writing to Sir James Wright.*

    ' I have the honor to be, &c.

      ' HENRY HALDANE.

       ' Acting as aid-de-camp.

' Gen. MOULTRIE.'

....

* Gov. Wright and his chief justice, had just arrived at
Savannah, and began to exercise his civil functions with a high
hand, before the military had arranged their matters, which
gave great offence to Col. Clarke, who commanded there, as
Lord Cornwallis informed me.

To General Patterson.

'CHARLESTOWN, June 29th, 1780.

' SIR,

' COLONEL Pinckney, the officer appointed to
' superintend the South Carolina line, informs me
' that of the officers who were left with him for that
' purpose, one of them is dead, and two others very
' ill; he requests Captain Gadsden may be permit.
' ted to come to town to assist him; I therefore will
' take it as a favor if he may be allowed to come.

' I am, &c.

' WM. MOULTRIE.

' Gen. PATTERSON.'

WHEN the officers were first ordered over to Haddrell's-point, four from each line were allowed to remain in town, to take care that the sick and wounded were not neglected; but from information they
had received of some misconduct in our officers, or
Pendleton's escape, or some caprice, I cannot tell
which, I received the following order, after writing
the above to Gen. Patterson.

' CHARLESTOWN, June 30th, 1780

' BRIGADIER General Moultrie, Brigadier General
' Woodford and all the officers now prisoners of war,
' without exception, are to be in readiness to be

' conveyed from Drayton's-wharf,* to morrow morn-
' ing at six o'clock, where they are to remain
' until further orders. The servants that are now al-
' lowed at Haddrell's-point, are to remain there,
' provided General Moultrie makes himself absolutely
' responsible for their being accounted for in the
' exchange of prisoners: should any of them desert
' from Haddrell's-point they are on no account to be
' replaced. All indulgence of working is to be im-
' mediately stopped. Orders are issued for appre-
' hending all prisoners that may be seen in town
' without a pass from Mr. de Rossette commissary
' of prisoners. The rolls of the prisoners are to be
' called by the commissary or his deputy every morn-
' ing and evening, and the officer commanding the
' guard is to be accountable for any deficiencies. Any
' prisoner who shall attempt to make his escape will
' be confined on board of a prison-ship.

' By order of Brig. Gen. Patterson, Comdt.

'J. MONEY. Town Major.'

To Gov. WRIGHT.

' CHARLETOWN, June 30th, 1780.

' I HAVE just now received certain information from
' Doctor Houston, an officer in the continental service,

* Wrag's wharf, where Colonel Drayton deputy quarter-
master-general kept his boats and carts, while he lived in Mr.
Manigault's house,

' of his being a prisoner in your state, and arrested
' for treason by Anthony Stokes, Esq. chief justice
' of Georgia ; the evidences against him are three
' persons, who swear they saw him in the American
' camp, aiding and assisting the French and Ameri-
' cans at the time of the siege ; if this be his charge,
' I warn you of the consequences of proceeding on
' the trial, as should any injury be done his person,
' retaliation will certainly be made by Congress and
' their allies, on the subjects of his Britannic majesty.
' I inform you, he is a prisoner upon parole, to his
' Excellency Sir Henry Clinton, and had his
' leave to go to Georgia to settle some business,
' and to return agreeably to his parole ; I therefore,
' require his releasment from you.

> ' I have the honor to be, &c.
>
> ' WM. MOULTRIE.

' His Ex. Sir JAMES WRIGHT.'

THIS letter was sent open to Lord Cornwallis, who
ordered it on to Sir James Wright, to which I received no answer, but Doctor Houston was immediately released.

> FROM CAPT. TURNER.
>
> ' CHARLESTOWN, June 30th, 1780.

' SIR,

' I HAVE been honored with your letter of this

' morning, in which are these words : ' As you sent
' me word by Major Doctor Ellient that you did not
' think yourself accountable to me for your conduct
' as commissary of prisoners, I shall appoint some
' other person.' Give me leave to say, that the ap-
' pointing of another to the office, under present cir-
' cumstances, would create in me, no chagrin : un-
' provided as the department is, with every necessa-
' ry, I have found it a troublesome and unthankful
' office ; and nothing but the hopes of hearing from
' Congress, and a wish to serve my fellow prisoners,
' induced me to continue in it : as to the right of
' displacing me, I deny that it rests in any body
' here ; I hold myself accountable to none but Con-
' gress ; the commander of the southern department ;
' and the commissary general of prisoners ; and for
' your further satisfaction, I beg leave to inclose you
' a copy of my appointment. The message brought
' me this morning by your major of brigade, was
' to this effect : that you desired of me my account
' current, which you would transmit to Congress
' by the same opportunity that conveys your letter
' concerning Mr. Pendleton's breach of parole : I
' did not conceive this a proper demand, and there-
' fore desired Major Doctor Ellient to inform you,
' that I, myself, would transmit what accounts
' I had to Congress ; and beg to know if they could
' be sent with your dispatches. Before I conclude,

' permit me to observe, sir, that I believe I have acted
' up to my duty, and that you will not impute to my
' conduct, any personal pique, or the want of re-
' spect, which I have always had for your character.

' I am, &c.

' George Turner,

' Gen. Moultrie.'   D. C. P. S. D.

A few days ago, when Mr. Justice Pendleton
violated his parole, and left Charlestown, Lord
Cornwallis sent a message over to me at Haddrell's-
point, requesting to see me ; upon which, the next
day, I waited upon him, at General Patterson's quarters : (Mr. Motte's house) I was received by Lord
Cornwallis and General Patterson, very politely in
the drawing-room, up stairs ; after some little conversation respecting his rout through our back country, and telling me what a fine country we had, and
that he had taken all our stores, laid in different
places ; he then informed me that Mr. Pendleton
had broke his parole, and was gone off ; he therefore
hoped I would order him back, or the prisoners at
Haddrell's-point should suffer for it : upon which I
told him, I was not accountable for any man's parole but my own : he said he had a right to discriminate, and take some one in confinement, for Mr.
Pendleton : I told him he might do as he pleased,
but that his lordship was too much of a soldier, not

to know that every one was accountable but for his own parole, and for no other; besides, that Mr. Pendleton was a civil officer, I therefore could have nothing to do with him: I told his lordship that I would write to Congress, for them to decide upon the matter: upon which he was satisfied, and said he would forward the letter to Sir Henry Clinton; which letter I wrote, dated the thirtieth of June, and sent it to Lord Cornwallis, who forwarded it to Sir Henry Clinton; and by him, sent to the President, who laid my letter before Congress; and upon investigating the matter, they passed a resolve, justifying Mr. Pendleton's* conduct; and sent a copy of the resolve, to Sir Henry Clinton.

To the President of Congress.

'Charlestown, June 30th, 1780.

'Sir,

'I have the honor to inform you, that a few 'days ago, information was officially laid before me, 'by his Excellency Lord Cornwallis, and the Honora-

....

* Mr. Pendleton's case was this: that the day he made his escape, he was informed by a friend, who had it from a British officer, (Captain Constable) that if he did not get away that day, it was determined, by a party of tories (William Holliday, who kept the corner tavern, at their head) to take him from his quarters that night, and hang him at the town gate. Mr. Pendleton counterfeited Major Benson's hand, and made out his pass, by which he got off.

' ble Brigadier General Patterson, commandant of
' Charlestown, of the departure of Mr. Justice Pen-
' dleton, one of the judges of this state, from Charles-
' town, in violation of his parole, given by him, as a pri-
' soner of war, to his Excellency Sir Henry Clinton,
' shortly after the surrender of this place ; and I was
' desired, as I think it my duty to do, to lay the same
' before the honorable the Continental Congress.

' Such a violation of honor, as well as those rules
' and principles which all civilized nations have esta-
' blished and ever held sacred in the conduct of war,
' I am sure by the respectable body over which you
' preside will be deemed highly criminal, and as me-
' riting the severest punishment; as in its conse-
' quence the misery of thousands may be involved;
' and such an offence is an injury to mankind in
' general.

' I have also, Sir, to inform you, it is the earnest
' desire and expectation of his Excellency Lord Corn-
' wallis and the Hon. Brig. Gen. Patterson, that the
' Hon. the Continental Congress do interpose in this
' affair, and give the speedy remedy which is due in
' such cases by laws of nations and of war; and
' which they have formaly demanded through me ;
' intimating, at the same time, that unless Mr. Jus-
' tice Pendleton is by authority ordered immedi-
' ately to return to his parole, the prisoners now on
' parole will suffer for this offence.

' I THINK it my duty also, Sir, to intimate to you
' that the situation of the continental hospital, and
' the officers and privates, prisoners of war, is truly
' distressing, and such as calls for the immediate at-
' tention of Congress : as the bills left by Major
' General Lincoln, on his departure from this place,
' cannot be negociated, the hospital department, and
' the army, now prisoners, must want every ne-
' cessary and comfort, intended for them by the
' transfer of those bills ; and at a time, when, from
' the inclemency of the season and climate, and the
' hardships those men have already experienced,
' humanity, would make every exertion, to soften
' the hardships of war, and the rigor of captivity to
' the brave, and the good soldier : I would there-
' fore recommend, that the Congress do, as speedily
' as possible, obtain permission of a flag to Charles-
' town, by sea; in order to make the necessary pro-
' vision for the army here, and particularly the hos-
' pital; in such manner as may appear most expe-
' dient and proper, either by a transmission of money,
' or of bills, for the purchase of those necessaries,
' so much required.

' CAPTAIN George Turner, of the first South-Ca-
' rolina regiment of foot, is appointed commissary
' of prisoners, by Major General Lincoln, for the
' American army here : the bills of exchange* left

* Fifteen hundred pounds sterling.

' by General Lincoln, for the army, were given to
' him, to be negociated for that purpose; but holding
' himself in no wise accountable to me for his trans-
' actions in that department, I shall therefore ap-
' point another, until the pleasure of Congress is
' known.

'I have the honor to be, &c.

' Wm. Moultrie.

' His Ex. Samuel Huntington,

' President of Congress.'

From Capt. Roberts.

' Sir,

'I think it incumbent on me to acquaint you,
' for the information of the general, that the conduct
' of the rebels at the barracks at Haddrell's-point,
' during the course of this night, has been very irre-
' gular and improper. Not contented to celebrate
' this day, of their supposed Independence, with
' music, illuminations, &c. they have presumed to
' discharge a number of small arms; which, I ima-
' gine, it is thought they were not (nor indeed ought
' not to be, by the articles of capitulation) to be in
' possession of.

'I am, &c.

' J. B. Roberts,

' Captain of the sixty-fifth regiment;

' Commanding at Fort Arbuthnot.*

' Major Benson.

* Fort Moultrie.

FROM GEN. PATTERSON.

'CHARLESTOWN, July 6th, 1780.

'SIR,

'I AM extremely mortified to find myself
'under the necessity to transmit to you, the en-
'closed,* and in consequence of it, to beg, sir, that
'you will be pleased immediately to make the most
'particular inquiry; and report upon it, for the in-
'formation of the commander in chief, who is very
'much displeased, to see such an indecent abuse of
'lenity.

'I MUST also, sir, insist upon it, that the officers
'do immediately, and without exception, deliver up
'all their fire-arms to the commanding officer at Fort
'Arbuthnot.

'As soon as I am honored with your answer and
'report, a court-martial shall proceed to Haddrell's-
'point, to examine into the particular circumstances
'and persons, concerned in this gross outrage.

'I have the honor to be, &c.

'J. PATTERSON,

'Commandant.

'Gen. MOULTRIE.'

....

* Captain Roberts' letter.

To Gen. Patterson.

Christ-church Parish, July 6th, 1780.

'Half-past seven o'clock, P. M.

'Sir,

'As I am quartered five miles from the bar-
'racks, I did not receive your letter of this morn-
'ing (inclosing one from Captain Roberts, to Major
'Benson) until this moment: I will do myself the
'honor of answering it more particularly, to mor-
'row.   'I have the honor to be, &c.

'Wm. Moultrie.

'Brig. Gen. Patterson.'

———

To the Same.

'Christ-church, July 7th, 1780.

'Sir,

'In answer to your letter of yesterday with
'which you were pleased to honor me, I am to in-
'form you, that every continental officer in Christ-
'church parish who was well attended at the bar-
'racks at Haddrell's-point, in order to celebrate with
'decent festivity the anniversary of the Declaration
'of Independence, I had the satisfaction of being
'there, and can assure you I saw no "indecent abuse,
'or gross outrage" in any manner committed: with
'regard to music, except two or three fifes which
'played the Call for Dinner, there was none but what
'was brought by a person in your service, who with

' two others and some women danced for two or three
' hours in one of the rooms in the barracks, and went
' away about four o'clock in the afternoon. At five
' o'clock in the evening I departed, and am informed,
' that at eight some of the windows in the barracks
' were illuminated; I am sorry to find that some pis-
' tols were fired, which, at the same time, I disap-
' prove; I hope you will impute this to no intended
' affront, but to that exhilaration of spirit which in
' young men is too frequently the effect of convivial
' entertainments. This, sir, is a candid statement of
' the transaction of the 4th instant; and I am at a loss
' to conceive wherein we have so grossly erred in
' celebrating that day. It was by no means incon-
' sistent with our paroles to do so ; and the celebra-
' tion of particular festivals, even by prisoners, is not
' uncommon. I go no further back than the present
' war; the British troops have given us several pre-
' cedents of it ; the seventh regiment, now in Charles-
' ton, celebrated the anniversary of St. George's day
' when prisoners at Carlisle; and the convention
' troops kept the birth-day of his Britannic majesty
' both in the years 78 and 79, without the harsh ani-
' madversion of "indecent abuse of lenity "and " gross
' outrage." With regard to that part of your letter
' wherein you require me to order all the officers,
' without exception, to give up their fire-arms ; be-
' fore I do any thing in that matter, I must beg leave

' to observe, that by one of the articles of capitula-
' tion, the officers are to keep their pistols ; nor, in
' my humble apprehension, can they be deprived of
' them without a violation of that article. As to
' their fuzees, they were not fired on the fourth
' instant ; and I, some time ago, delivered you a let-
' ter, written by Sir Henry Clinton's order, and
' signed by Major Andre ; wherein his excellency
' permitted the officers to amuse themselves with
' their fuzees. Upon the whole of this matter, when
' my Lord Cornwallis, and General Patterson, come
' to review this affair, I trust they will not take it in
' the light, they seem to have done ; that they will
' not imagine any gross outrage was meant, where
' none was intended ; but impute it to the warmth of
' a cause which the continental officers at Haddrell's-
' point have embraced through principle ; in which
' some of them bled ; and for which all of them are
' now suffering.

 ' I have the honor to be, &c.

     ' WM. MOULTRIE.

' Gen. PATTERSON.'

———

FROM GEN. PATTERSON.

   ' CHARLESTOWN, July 9th, 1780.

' SIR,

 ' I SHALL, for the present, decline entering in-
' to the propriety of your letter to me of the seventh

' instant, on occasion of the festivity, in commemo-
' ration of the Declaration of Independence, cele-
' brated by the officers at Haddrell's-point: their
' situation as prisoners of war, I apprehend, gives
' us a right, by every law of nations, and of war, to
' expect from them, a decent behavior ; far short of
' illuminations, and other irregular demonstrations
' of joy ; and I think it my duty to shew my dis-
' approbation of their conduct, by immediately with-
' drawing the indulgence granted them, of being al-
' lowed their fowling-pieces : I am therefore, sir, to
' insist upon their being forthwith delivered up to
' the officer commanding at Fort Arbuthnot.

' I have the honor to be, &c.

' J. PATTERSON.
' Commandant.

' Gen. MOULTRIE.'

To GEN. M'INTOSH.

' SNEE-FARM, July 10th, 1780.

' DEAR SIR,

' As General Patterson declines entering into
' the propriety of my letter, on the seventh instant ;
' he thinks it his duty, immediately to withdraw the
' indulgence granted the officers, of being allowed
' their fowling-pieces. I am therefore to request you
' will order all the officers, immediately to deliver up
' to you their fowling-pieces (each officer marking

' his own piece) and send them over to the officer,
' commanding on Sullivan's-Island, that you may
' have them ready to deliver to his order.

'I am, &c.

' WM. MOULTRIE.

To CAPT. ROBERTS.

' SNEE-FARM, July 12th, 1780.

' SIR,

' IN consequence of a requisition from General
' Patterson, I have directed such of the officers at
' Haddrell's-point, as have fowling-pieces, to deliver
' them to General M'Intosh, who resides at the bar-
' racks ; and have desired him, as soon as they are
' brought in, to acquaint the commanding officer
' on Sullivan's-Island with it, that they may be deli-
' vered to his order.

'I am, &c.

' WM. MOULTRIE.'

ORDERS RECEIVED FROM THE COMMANDANT.

' August 6th, 1780.

' THE commandant, being determined, rigidly to
adhere to the terms of the capitulation on his part,
expect they will be as rigidly adhered to on the part
of the prisoners.

' No officer, under the rank of a general officer,
can be allowed to keep a horse, unless his state of

health is such as demands it ; in which case, a certificate from a physician, will be required, and an order from the commandant, be obtained for that purpose. Such horses as are the property of persons
not in the above direction, must be immediately disposed of : such as are not claimed as property, are
to be delivered up to the commanding officer of the
fort ; and such as have been taken from the inhabitants, are to be returned to them immediately.

' ALL complaints and applications, in order to
their being regurlarly attended to, are requested to
be made in writing, through the commissary of prisoners, to the commandant, by the general officer
commanding.

' A DEPUTY commissary of prisoners will be ordered on the Point, to facilitate the above.

' ORDERS will be given to the commissary of prisoners, to grant powder to the prisoners, restricting
them to the limits of six miles from the Point ; not
crossing any creek, river, or branch of the sea (general officers excepted) who have the range of the
parish, without the above restriction.

' No more than one servant, can be allowed to
each officer (general officers excepted, who will be
allowed three). Such servants as desert, cannot be
replaced ; but any officer detecting his servant
in the attempt, on his delivering him up to the commanding officer at Fort Arbuthnot, taking his receipt,

and sending it to the commissary of prisoners; will
have one ordered to him.

(Signed)   ‘ G. BENSON,
‘ Major of Brigade.’

—

To LT. COL. BALFOUR.

‘ September 1st, 1780.

‘ SIR,

‘ ON perusing the paper of the 29th August of
‘ Robertson, M'Donald, and Cammeron, published
‘ by authority, to my astonishment I find a para-
‘ graph to this effect: " The following is a correct
‘ list of prisoners sent on board the Sandwich yester-
‘ day morning," and underneath, the names of a
‘ number of the most respectable gentlemen, inha-
‘ bitants of this state; most of whose characters I
‘ am so well acquainted with that I cannot believe
‘ they would have been guilty of any breach of their
‘ paroles, or any article of the capitulation, or done
‘ any thing to justify so rigorous a proceeding against
‘ them: I therefore think it my duty, as the senior
‘ continental officer, prisoner under the capitulation,
‘ to demand a release of those gentlemen, particular-
‘ ly such as are entitled to the benefit of that act.
‘ This harsh proceeding demands my particular at-
‘ tention; and I do, therefore, in behalf of the Unit-
‘ ed States of America require that they be admitted
‘ immediately to return to their paroles; as their be-

'ing hurried on board a prison-ship, and, I fear,
'without being heard, is a violation of the 9th arti-
'cle of the capitulation. If this demand cannot be
'complied with, I am to request that I may have
'leave to send an officer to Congress to represent
'this grievance, that they may interpose in behalf of
'these gentlemen in the manner they shall think
'proper.

'I am, &c.

'WM. MOULTRIE.

ANSWER TO THE PRECEDING LETTER.

'CHARLESTOWN, September 4th, 1780.

'SIR,

'THE Commandant will not return any an-
'swer to a letter wrote in such exceptionable and
'unwarrantable terms as that to him from Gen. Moul-
'trie, dated the 1st instant; nor will he receive any
'further application from him upon the subject of it.

'By order of the Commandant.

'G. BENSON,

'Major of Brigade.

'Gen. MOULTRIE.'

TO LT. COL. BALFOUR.

'CHRIST-CHURCH PARISH, Oct. 16th, 1780.

'SIR,

'HOWEVER my letters may be thought by you

‘ to be wrote in “ exceptionable and unwarrantable
‘ terms,” yet I cannot be deterred from representing
‘ matters of such consequence, as I am now con-
‘ strained to do, in the strongest manner: though it
‘ is indifferent to me whether I write to you or the
‘ commissary of prisoners on trifling applications ; yet
‘ when my duty calls upon me loudly to remonstrate
‘ against a proceeding of so high a nature as a viola-
‘ tion of a solemn capitulation, I then think it ne-
‘ cessary to make application as near the fountain
‘ head as possible ; I therefore, sir, address myself
‘ to you to complain of a great breach of the capitu-
‘ lation in sending the continental soldiers on board
‘ of prison-ships (the truth of which I have not the
‘ least doubt of) as part of the agreement for which
‘ the town was delivered up to Sir Henry Clinton
‘ was, that the continental soldiers should be kept
‘ in some contiguous buildings in the town, as ap-
‘ pears by the following extract from their Excel-
‘ lencies’ Sir Henry Clinton and Admiral Arbuthnot’s
‘ letter of the 12th May, 1780, antecedent to the sur-
‘ render.

“ Sir,

“ We have to request you will propose some
‘ proper contiguous buildings in the town for the re-
‘ sidence of the private prisoners of war not to be
‘ upon parole ; these will be of course such as may
‘ in discretion be asked.” The barracks and some

‘ adjacent houses were then proposed and agreed
‘ upon; as a proof of which the soldiers have been
‘ confined in those buildings from the very instant of
‘ the surrender until this present removal, which I
‘ do most solemnly protest against, and complain to
‘ you, sir, of a direct violation of the third article of
‘ the capitulation, and demand that the continental
‘ soldiers be ordered back to the barracks and other
‘ houses in which they were first confined. In this
‘ demand I think I am clearly within the line of my
‘ duty, as well as in the demand I made for the citi-
‘ zens on the first of September last; and though they
‘ may not appear to you in the same military
‘ view, yet Lord Cornwallis and General Patterson
‘ would have held them clearly so, as they insisted
‘ I should write to Congress respecting Mr. Pendle-
‘ ton’s breach of parole, and considered me answera-
‘ ble for the whole militia in town, at the time of
‘ the capitulation, as being the senior officer after
‘ General Lincoln’s departure from hence. Should
‘ I be as unfortunate in this demand, as in that made
‘ for the citizens, I shall rest myself satisfied, that I
‘ have done my duty; and as these matters may be
‘ discussed at some future day, I flatter myself I
‘ shall stand acquitted to the world of any charge
‘ of neglect on my part.

‘ I am, &c.

‘ WM. MOULTRIE.’

This letter was delivered by Major Doctor Ellient, who received a verbal answer from the commandant, 'That he would do as he pleased with the prisoners 'for the good of his majesty's service; and not as 'General Moultrie pleases.'

———

From Doctor Oliphant.

'Charlestown, Nov. 14th, 1780.

'Dear General,

'I send by the bearer the few articles you re-'quire. Inclosed is the return of our sick for last 'month; the mortality is great; by much the greater 'number of deaths happen to those patients from on 'board the prison-ships: within these three days, 'there is an appearance of a jail fever from the ship 'Concord; she has been a prison ship throughout 'the summer. No less than nine of the sick, sent 'from that ship, died in the space of 24 hours; all 'of them bearing the appearance of a putrid malig-'nant fever. The unfortunate sufferers are the mi-'litia sent from Camden. I am much at a loss how 'to act in these our times of distress; my confine-'ment renders me incapable of giving such attend-'ance or service as I wish or ought to do. I have 'no person to look up to but you, sir; therefore I 'crave and entreat your assistance.

'I am, &c.

'D. Oliphant.

'Gen. Moultrie.'

To Lt. Col. Balfour.

'Christ-church Parish, 22d Nov. 1780.

' Sir,

'By a letter from Dr. Oliphant, and by returns
'from our general hospital, I am exceedingly shock-
'ed to know of so great a mortality among our un-
'fortunate prisoners; I cannot tell to what cause to
'attribute it ; but our Director General (on whom
'we principally depended for the good order and
'well governing of our hospital) being so long con-
'fined to his house by the board of police, conse-
'quently could not attend to his duty where he was
'so much wanted. I was led to believe, some time
'ago, by a letter from Dr. Fraser, that it never was
'your intention to prevent Dr. Oliphant attending
'the hospital : yet still he is restrained. I am so af-
'fected at the distresses of our poor soldiers, that I
'am at a loss how to address you on the subject ;
'but I must begin by calling on your humanity, and
'request you, for God's sake, to permit Dr. Oliphant
'to attend the hospital whenever he shall judge it
'necessary : and also beg you will order the pri-
'soners from on board the Concord ship (where
'they are infected with the jail fever) to some other
'vessels, if they cannot be permitted to be on shore.

' I am, &c.

' Wm. Moultrie.'

From Lt. Col. Balfour.

'Charlestown, Nov. 28th, 1780.

'Sir,

'I have received your letter of the 22d inst.
'in which you so pathetically call upon me to grant
'permission to Dr. Oliphant to attend your hospital
'whenever he shall judge it necessary, as you ap-
'prehend, his not attending to his duty, as the di-
'rector general of it, by reason of the restraint he
'is laid under by the board of police, has been one
'of the principal causes of the general mortality,
'which you say rages among the prisoners.

'I assure you, sir, that whenever, with proprie-
'ty, and consistent with my duty, I can remedy
'even an ideal grievance, my inclination sufficiently
'inclines me to it; therefore, although I do not
'think that Doctor Oliphant's absence, has been
'materially injurious to the hospital, no objection
'ever lay with me to his having visited it, at pro-
'per times, as often as he pleased.

'I am informed that an application to Colonel
'Hamilton, on behalf of the widow, and orphans of
'a friend of Doctor Oliphant's,* who became his se-
'curity, for the debt in question, was a prevalent
'motive with him, to take the steps he has done,
'to oblige the doctor to do justice; and although

....

* Major Huger.

' their husband and father fell, fighting in the cause
' of treason and rebellion, we do not wish to see them
' involved in ruin and distress.

' WITH respect to the last part of your letter, I
' was no sooner informed that there was a considera-
' ble sickness on board the Concord, than I ordered
' her to be inspected; and although it was reported
' to me that there was not any symptoms of the dis-
' ease you mention I removed the prisoners on shore.

   ' I am, sir,

      ' Your most obedient servant.

        ' N. BALFOUR.

' Gen. MOULTRIE.'

————

GENERAL OFFICERS BELONGING TO THE AMERICAN ARMY.

December 15th, 1780.

OFFICERS' NAMES.	RANKS.	DATES OF COM.
George Washington,	Com. in Chief,	June 15, 1775.
Israel Putnam, - -	Major Gen.	June 19, 1775.
Horatio Gates, - -	Ditto, -	May 16, 1776.
Nathaniel Greene, -	Ditto, -	Aug. 9, 1776.
William Heath, - -	Ditto, -	Aug. 9, 1776.
Wm. Earl Sterling, -	Ditto, -	Febr. 1777.
Arthur St. Clair, - -	Ditto, -	Febr. 1777.
Benjamin Lincoln, -	Ditto, -	Febr. 1777.
Marq. de la Fayette, -	Ditto, -	July 31, 1777.
Robert Howe, - -	Ditto, -	Oct. 20, 1777.

OFFICERS' NAMES.	RANKS.	DATES OF COM.
Alexander M'Dougal,	Major Gen.	Oct. 20, 1777.
Baron Stuben, - -	Inspect. Gen.	May 5, 1778.
William Smallwood,	Major Gen.	Sep. 15, 1780.
Sam. Holden Parsons,	Ditto, -	Oct. 23, 1780.
William Thompson, -	Brigadier Gen.	Mar. 1, 1776.
James Clinton, - -	Ditto, -	Aug. 9, 1776.
Wm. Moultrie, - -	Ditto, -	Sep. 16, 1776.
L. M'Intosh, - - -	Ditto, -	Sep. 16, 1776.
Henry Knox, - - -	Ditto, -	Dec. 27, 1776.
John Glover, - - -	Ditto,	These gentlemen, by resolve of Congress, of Feb. 21, are to rank according to the rank of their commissions in the army at that time.
John Patterson, - -	Ditto,	
George Weadan, - -	Ditto,	
Anthony Wayne, -	Ditto,	
Peter Mulhenbury, -	Ditto,	
George Clinton, - -	Ditto, -	Mar. 25, 1777.
Edward Hand, - -	Ditto, -	Apr. 1, 1777.
Charles Scott, - -	Ditto, -	Apr. 2, 1777.
Jedediah Huntington,	Ditto, -	May 12, 1777.
John Starkes, - - -	Ditto, -	Oct. 4, 1777.
Chev. du Portail, -	Do. chief Eng.	Nov. 17, 1777.
Jethro Sumner, - -	Brig. Gen. -	Jan. 9, 1777.
James Hogan, - -	Ditto, -	Jan. 9, 1777.
Isaac Huger, - -	Ditto, -	Jan. 9, 1777.
Mordecai Gest, - -	Ditto, -	Jan. 9, 1777.
William Irvine, - -	Ditto, -	May 12, 1779.
Daniel Morgan, - -	Ditto, -	Oct. 13, 1780.

To Col. Innis.

' December 25th, 1780.

' Sir,

' Mr. Gibbs, deputy commissary of prisoners,
' brought me an order yesterday from you, direct-
' ing " the officers, (general officers excepted) pri-
' soners of war, to be forthwith drawn within three
' miles of Haddrell's-point."

' In the third article of the capitulation, it is sti-
' pulated, " that the continental troops and sailors,
' with their baggage, shall be conducted to a place
' to be agreed on, where they will remain prisoners
' of war, until exchanged;" and the place agreed
' upon for the officers, by their Excellencies Sir
' Henry Clinton and Admiral Arbuthnot, and Major
' General Lincoln, before the gates were given up,
' was " Haddrell's-point, and six miles thereof;
' without passing any river, creek, or arm of the
' sea ;" a copy of which I transmit to you ; and, as
' a confirmation of this, all the officers' paroles (Gene-
' ral officers excepted*) were filled up to Haddrell's-
' point, or within six miles thereof, with the above
' restrictions ; and Colonel Balfour, in his first or-
' der as commandant, restrained the officers to six
' miles. As the officers are now situated agreeable to

....

* General officers restrained to twelve miles in their
paroles.

‘ the agreement, made under the capitulation, espe-
‘ cially as it is impossible to get proper quarters with-
‘ in the bounds you prescribe, and the barracks them-
‘ selves are so unfinished, as make them very cold
‘ and disagreeable in a winter season, I hope, sir,
‘ you will consider the great inconvenience the prison-
‘ ers must necessarily be put to by a removal ; and
‘ permit them to remain in their present quarters.

‘ I am, &c.

‘ WM. MOULTRIE.’

THE officers were allowed to remain in their quarters.

December, 1780.

GENERAL du Portail being now exchanged went
out from Haddrell’s-point; and, on his way to Philadelphia, visited General Greene’s camp.

To GEN. GREENE.

‘ CHRIST-CHURCH PARISH, Jan. 1st. 1781.

‘ SIR,

‘ THREE days ago I was honored with your fa-
‘ vor of the eighteenth of December last : I am sor-
‘ ry I cannot collect the returns which you require
‘ of me to transmit you by the favorable opportunity
‘ of General du Portail, who leaves this place so im-
‘ mediately as not to allow time ; I thought it,

' however, best to send you such as I had ready;
' which is a copy of one delivered to the British com-
' mandant, to send to New-York; and consists prin-
' cipally of the prisoners of war, under the capitula-
' tion of Charlestown; they stand upon the return
' as they are first to be exchanged, as settled by the
' general officers, prisoners here; which are to be
' those who have been longest in captivity; and the
' senior officer of the rank, proposed to be exchanged.

' I WILL have returns collected of all the prisoners
' of war in this state; and transmit them to you as
' soon as possible; those of the non-commissioned
' officers and privates can easily be procured, as
' they are all on board of prison-ships: my last re-
' turn of the continental soldiers amounted to about
' 1400.

' Your's, &c.

' WM. MOULTRIE.'

THE following proposal was made to my son, which
I found in his desk among his papers, after his
decease; in his own hand writing: viz.

'LIEUTENANT COLONEL BALFOUR'S PROPOSAL TO
GENERAL MOULTRIE.

' January 14th, 1781.

' MR. Moultrie, your father's character and your
' own have been represented to me in such a light
' that I wish to serve you both: what I have to say

' I will sum up in a few words. I wish you to pro-
' pose to your father, to relinguish the cause he is
' now engaged in, which he may do without the
' least dishonor to himself; he can only enclose his
' commission to the first general officer, (General
' Greene for instance) the command will devolve on
' the next officer ; which is often done in our service ;
' any officer may resign his commission in the field
' if he chooses : if your father will do this, he may
' rely on me, he shall have his estate restored to
' him, and all damages paid him : I believe you are
' the only heir to your father. And as for you, sir,
' if your father continues firm, I shall never ask you
' to bear arms against him. These favors, you may
' depend, I shall be able to obtain from my lord Corn-
' wallis ; and you may rely on my honor, this mat-
' ter shall never be divulged by me.'

THIS proposal from Colonel Balfour convinces
me, that the letter which I received from Lord
Charles Montague, some time after, did not origi-
nate with himself : when I shewed Lord Charles'
letter to my son, he then told me of Colonel Balfour's proposal to him. He told Colonel Balfour,
' He could not make such a proposal to his father,
for he was sure he would not listen to it.'

To Lt. Col. Balfour.

'January 24th, 1781.

' Sir,

'On my arrival in town, some days ago, I was
' informed that some of the British officers frequent-
' ed the American hospital, with an intention to in-
' list the men, to the great disturbance and disorder
' of the hospital; upon which I ordered captain Shu-
' brick to wait upon you, to acquaint you with their
' proceedings: you assured him it was contrary to
' your orders, and desired to have the officers' names,
' which I herewith inclose you: I could not procure
' them time enough to be sent before I left town.
' On my way to the boat, to return to this place, to
' my great surprise, I saw an officer, and a gentle-
' man dressed like a clergyman, leading a number
' of the continental soldiers down to the wharf;
' which I took to be two of the officers named on the
' inclosed list, as I was informed that morning they
' had inlisted many from the hospital; I hope, sir,
' as it was done in violation of your orders they will
' be directed to deliver those men back, and not be
' permitted to visit the American hospital on any
' pretence whatever.

'I am, &c.

'Wm. Moultrie.

FROM JAMES FRASER,

'CHARLESTOWN, Jan. 28th, 1781.

' SIR,

' I AM desired to inquire what letter General
' Greene received from you by General du Portail,
' as no letter of your's was sent here for inspection
' that was forwarded by that gentleman ; and, at the
' same time, beg to be acquainted why General du
' Portail visited General Greene on his way to Phila-
' delphia, the camp of the latter not being on his di-
' rect road to that place.

' By order of the Commandant.

' I am, sir,

' Your most obedient humble servant,

' JAMES FRASER,

' Com. Prisoners.

' Gen. MOULTRIE.'

———

TO GEN. GREENE.

' CHRIST-CHURCH PARISH, Jan. 30th, 1781.

' SIR,

' I DID myself the honor to write you on the
' 1st inst. in which I enclosed you a return of the
' officers prisoners of war at Haddrell's-point ; I now
' send you a return of all the prisoners in this state
' that I can get information of, as well militia as con-
' tinental, and those sent to Augustine. I shall be
' much obliged to you for some direction relative to

' the exchange of prisoners. I have made some
' partial exchanges, and shall be glad to know whe-
' ther I shall continue to exchange as I have done
' hitherto ; if so, be pleased to favor me with a list
' of such British prisoners as you have upon parole,
' that I may know how to guide myself in that busi-
' ness when it is proposed to me : about fifty privates
' have been proposed for exchange, but that I post-
' poned till I should hear from you, as you may give
' me some directions upon a more enlarged scale.
' By the resolutions of Congress of the 5th and 12th
' of August last, I am authorised to appoint a suit-
' able person to act as commissary of prisoners in
' Charlestown ; and am directed to return the name
' of the person, so appointed, to the commander in
' chief of the southern department. In pursuance
' of which resolution, I have nominated Mr. James
' Fisher for that office, and acquainted General
' Gates of the same for his approbation : I beg leave
' to recommend him to you as a gentleman who will
' exert himself to the utmost in the punctual and
' faithful performance of his duty.

' I AM happy to inform you, that by a letter from
' Mr. Matthews, a delegate for South Carolina, that
' a general exchange is agreed upon between their
' Excellencies Gen. Washington and Sir Henry
' Clinton ; and that it will soon take place. I am
' sorry that I cannot yet give you an account of the

' arrival of the flag from Philadelphia : we are in
' hourly expectation of seeing her.

' I am, &c.

' WM. MOULTRIE.

TO DOCTOR FRASER.

' CHRIST-CHURCH PARISH, Feb. 2d, 1781.

' SIR,

 ' I RECEIVED your's of the twenty-eighth of
' last month, the evening before last ; and, for the
' satisfaction of the commandant, enclose you a copy
' of the letter sent to General Greene, assuring him,
' at the same time, that I had not the least idea of
' sending a letter to the American camp, or any
' where else, in a clandestine manner, and contrary
' to my parole ; but doubted not it would be examined
' by the British officer who was to attend General
' du Portail without the lines ; and that if there had
' been the least impropriety it would not have been
' allowed to pass ; I left it open for perusal, and re-
' quested the favor of General du Portail, when it
' was examined, if he proceeded immediately on to
' Philadelphia, after he left the British lines, that he
' would seal up the packet, and forward it to General
' Greene : General du Portail informed me, he be-
' lieved (but was not certain) he would be under the
' necessity of going to General Greene's camp, to
' procure money and horses, to carry him on to

' Philadelphia; as to what rout he took when he
' left this, it was entirely at his own option; he best
' knew what his exchange allowed, and, I dare say,
' will anwer any objections that may be made on that
' head.

' I am, &c.

' WM. MOULTRIE.'

FROM DOCTOR OLIPHANT.

' CHARLESTOWN, Feb. 3rd. 1781.

' DEAR SIR,

' WITHOUT your support, it will be impossible
' for me to do my duty by our unfortunate sick. I
' am to acquaint you, that I received a message
' by Doctor Hayes from the commandant this morn-
' ing, desiring me to dismiss Mr. M'Clean,* our
' steward, from the service of the hospital; for he
' was determined he should not continue any longer
' in that place: no crime is laid to his charge: I
' conceive it contrary to my authority to dismiss him
' without a regular trial, as he has ever, to the best
' of my knowledge, acted as a faithful servant to the
' public. I look upon it I should commit the great-
' est act of injustice were I to pay any attention to
' the requisition.

....

* M'Clean was a faithful steward; his only crime to them
was his dissuading the men to inlist in the British service.

' THE physicians and surgeons were this day de-
' nied access to the sick in the hospital : no person,
' at 12 o'clock at noon, could pass or repass the
' gates, except the steward or his assistant, to fetch
' provisions for the sick : under such a choice of
' difficulties, I am much distressed how to conduct
' myself; permit me, therefore, if compatible with
' your situation, to entreat that you may come to
' town, and, if possible, put matters on a better foot-
' ing, for the relief of our unfortunate sick.

' I am your's, &c.
' DAVID OLIPHANT.

' Gen. MOULTRIE.'

FROM LT. COL. BALFOUR.

' CHARLESTOWN, February 8th, 1781.

' SIR,

' I HAVE before me your letter of the 4th inst.
' containing the complaint of Dr. Oliphant, respect-
' ing my directions for the dismission of the steward
' of your hospital, which is a point I must still insist
' on, as, by the report of the Deputy Commissary of
' Prisoners, he has been guilty of a conduct highly
' blameable from one under his situation.

' FOR the sole right, which you assert, Dr. Oli-
' phant has to give directions in the medicinal line
' of your hospital, I must conceive, as he is no lon-
' ger a prisoner of war, but detained here for the

'failure of private contract, in not liquidating his
'debts, that neither you nor he can have claims on
'his person to any advantages arising from the capi-
'tulation of Charlestown; and that therefore his be-
'ing at all allowed to officiate in his public capacity
'should rather be attributed to sufferance than claim-
'ed as a right.

'THE officers of your hospital being precluded,
'for a short time, admittance to it, as it was without
'my directions, was immediately rectified on com-
'ing to my knowledge; but, I must here remark,
'though against my inclination, that, in general, your
'people seem to be more solicitous for the causes
'of complaint, than anxious, on their own parts, to
'remove them. You have my full permission to
'write what you please, within the line of propriety,
'to General Greene, provided the same is submitted
'to proper inspection; and as this, sir, is an express
'condition of your parole, and I have some cause to
'think it has been violated in your letter by General
'du Portail to General Greene, I may hereafter,
'when I have completed my information, have occa-
'sion to write you more explicitly on this subject.
'General du Portail's making General Greene's
'camp, on his way to Philadelphia, was a direct
'breach of that passport, under which he had liberty

' to proceed there; of which I therefore think it my
' duty to inform the commander in chief.

' I am, &c.

' N. BALFOUR.

' Gen. MOULTRIE.'

———

LETTER FROM LORD CHARLES MONTAGUE.

' CHARLESTOWN, Feb. 9th, 1781.

' DEAR SIR,

' IT is a long time since I have had the pleasure
' of seeing you ; but the length of time has not ef-
' faced the civilities and marks of friendship I receiv-
' ed from you. I wish much to see you; you know
' I have again returned to this country for a short
' time.

' IF it is agreeable to you, I will either call upon
' you, or be glad to see you here, at No. 57, Old
' Church-street.

' I SEND this by my old servant Fisher.

' Your sincere friend.

' CHARLES MONTAGUE.

' Gen. MOULTRIE.'

———

TO LT. COL. BALFOUR.

' CHARLESTOWN, February 12th, 1781.

' SIR,

' I RECEIVED your's of the 8th inst. in which
' you inform me, you must insist upon the dismission

‘ of the steward of our hospital, as he has been guil-
‘ ty of a conduct highly blameable.*   I am sorry the
‘ steward has behaved himself in a manner unbecom-
‘ ing his station.   I wish I could have been inform-
‘ ed of it in time, to have prevented any ill conduct
‘ in future.   I claim the sole right of Dr. Oliphant’s
‘ giving directions in our hospital in the medicinal
‘ line, from a circumstance which, I imagine, you
‘ must be unacquainted with ; and, for your informa-
‘ tion, I inclose you a copy of Dr. Oliphant’s parole ;
‘ by which you will see, that, though exchanged, yet
‘ that exchange is not thoroughly completed, as he
‘ is there obliged to stay to do his duty in the hospi-
‘ tal ; therefore he is still a prisoner upon parole,
‘ and has still the direction of the hospital ;   and
‘ should he make satisfaction to those who have de-
‘ tained his person for a private contract, yet he
‘ could not leave the hospital without first obtaining
‘ permission from the American officer commanding
‘ in the southern department.   I was well assured
‘ that you were unacquainted with the physicians and
‘ surgeons being refused admittance† into our hospi-
‘ tal was the reason I wrote you on the subject, as I

....

* Dissuading the American soldiers from enlisting in the
British service.

† Because some British officers were then in the hospital endeavoring to enlist the men.

' have been informed that you wished more care was
' taken of the sick.

' I AM very sorry you should have cause to think
' I have violated my parole in the least; I stand ac-
' quitted in my own idea ; and I am sure a gentlemen
' of your candor will be of the same opinion, when
' you come to enquire more particularly into the cir-
' cumstances : the letter itself the most exact scru-
' tiny cannot take any exceptions to; and the send-
' ing a list of the prisoners I had your permission for
' so doing.

' GEN. du Portail is undoubtedly a gentleman of
' the strictest honor, and, I dare say, considered his
' going to Gen. Greene's camp as no impropriety, or
' he would not have taken that rout.

' I am, &c.

' WM. MOULTRIE.'

To MAJOR HARLESTON AND CAPT. PETER GRAY.

' HADDRELL'S-POINT, Feb. 27th, 1781.

' GENTLEMEN,

' You are at the receipt of this, to repair with
' your baggage, servants, &c. to the barracks near
' Haddrell's-point, there to take your quarters.

' I am your's, &c.

' JAMES PLACE.

' A. C. P.'

FROM MAJOR HARLESTON.

'DISTILLERY, Feb. 28th, 1781.

' SIR,

' As I conceive the enclosed mandate to be a
' flagrant breach of a most essential article of the
' capitulation, and as my refusal to obey it, may in-
' volve me in a contention I wish to avoid, I beg
' leave to address you on the subject, requesting an
' application may be made to the commandant for
' obtaining satisfaction in the premises ; and for si-
' lencing threats ; one of which was conveyed to me
' since the enclosed, in a verbal message, by a ser-
' geant, apparently calculated to irritate ; and which
' any attempt to execute, ought to be considered as
' discharging the party threatened from the obli-
' gations of a parole. I am led to observe, that the
' distance of this place from the barracks, in a di-
' rect line, does not exceed three quarters of a mile,
' nor does the circuitous rout imposed on me by the
' obstructions thrown in my way, protract the dis-
' tance to be more than two miles and an half.

' I am your's, &c.

' ISAAC HARLESTON.

' Gen. MOULTRIE.'

To Gen. Greene.

'Charlestown, February 28th, 1781.

' Sir,

' I have the honor to inform you, that I have
' made exchange for a number of continental officers,
' a list of whose names are herewith transmitted to
' you, and doubt not will meet with your approbation.
' I had proposed to exchange some militia, but Col.
' Balfour, commandant of Charlestown, did not
' choose to enter upon their exchanges, as that mat-
' ter would be settled in a general exchange ; which
' we are in hopes will soon take place.

' I shall esteem it as a particular favor if you
' would inform me, whether it is the custom, in our
' army, in making exchanges, to adhere to the old
' customs of war ; exchanging cavalry for cavalry,
' infantry for infantry, artillery for artillery ; or whe-
' ther we should go on as hitherto, by seniority and
' the longest in captivity.

'I am, &c.

' Wm. Moultrie.'

———

The Hon. Board of War, Philadelphia.

'Charlestown, March 1st, 1781.

' Gentlemen,

' I am honored with your favor of the
' 19th of December last, with invoice and bills of lad-
' ing of sundries for clothing the prisoners of war ;

' and also of three hundred and forty-four barrels of
' flour : all which are come safe to hand ; and a re-
' ceipt for three thousand six hundred and forty-
' seven dollars for the use of the officers ; the goods
' were a little damaged ; the flour I shall have sold,
' and the money appropriated, by employing the
' most necessitous people in making up the clothing ;
' and what balance may be left, shall be distributed,
' as directed to the continental troops and militia
' who were actually taken in arms : the money I
' have ordered to be paid to the officers, agreeable
' to rank ; which amount to nine days pay, including
' the hospital department. I am sorry I cannot send
' you an exact return of the prisoners of war, as
' many of them are inlisted in the British service ;
' I imagine, what remains, cannot exceed one thou-
' sand ; I heartily wish their supply had arrived a
' little sooner ; the officers are much in want ; their
' supplies were so trifling, as to be of very little ser-
' vice to them.

' I HEREWITH send you an account of disburse-
' ments for the vessel : we have done every thing in
' our power to have her dispatched.

' I have the honor to be, &c.

' WM. MOULTRIE.'

To Col. Balfour,

'Christ-church Parish, March 2d, 1781.

' Sir,

' I am again under the necessity of troubling
' you upon a subject on which I have too frequently
' wrote : I was in hopes matters had been so arrang-
' ed, as would require no farther application, but a
' letter I received last night from General M'Intosh,
' a copy of which I beg leave to enclose you, in-
' forms me that a British sergeant is ordered to be
' quartered in the barracks amongst the officers; and
' that they are to turn out of a particular room, to
' accommodate this sergeant ; the reason given is,
" that four of our officers, the other night, stole a
' boat, and went to town in her :" if this be true, I
' could wish they were pointed out, and punished ac-
' cording to the offence ; which, in my opinion, is of
' a very heinous nature, and deserves the severest
' treatment; but I cannot conceive the propriety of
' reducing the whole to a disagreeable situation for
' the ill conduct of a few. A parole is a sacred act
' between parties, which, if violated on either side, is
' void in itself; I cannot help observing, that this
' sergeant being placed among the officers upon parole,
' is unusual, and has the appearance of a guard : I
' hope, sir, you will consider it in that light, and
' have him removed. The officers are now exceed-
' ingly crowded, yet six of them must turn out to

' give a room to this sergeant: many of them are
' now under the necessity of building huts in the
' woods, for their better accommodation ; though
' we have had an exchange lately, yet their number
' was replaced by the gentlemen of the Maryland
' and Delaware lines.

' MAJOR Harleston and others have also informed
' me that they have received a positive order from
' Mr. Place, assistant commissary of prisoners, to re-
' pair with their baggage and servants near Had-
' drell's-point, there to take up their quarters. This
' order, I cannot but imagine, must arise from some
' mistake, as they are clearly within the line prescrib-
' ed by the capitulation; on a direct course not more
' than half a mile, and on a circuitous rout not more
' than two miles and a half.

' ANOTHER matter I must trouble you with ; Ge-
' neral M'Intosh, with a number of other gentlemen,
' are threatened by Mr. Scott to be turned out of his
' house, (which was allotted by the barrack master
' for the reception of the prisoners of war) and their
' baggage stopped for the payment of the rent. I
' hope, sir, when you come to consider of these se-
' veral matters, here related to you, that you will
' agree with me in opinion, that the placing a ser-
' geant * among gentlemen upon parole carries a

* The sergeant was withdrawn.

' suspicion of their honor ; that Major Harleston and
' others being ordered to the barracks is a violation
' of the capitulation; and that Gen. M'Intosh and
' other gentlemen being turned out of their quarters,
' and obliged to pay rent, would be an injustice done
' them. I find myself under some difficulty in not
' being permitted to send an officer to town to deliv-
' er any letter or message which I may have occa-
' sion to send you ; it leaves me in an uncertain si-
' tuation when my letters are to be sent to the assist-
' ant commissary of prisoners for his conveyance.

' I am, &c.

' WM. MOULTRIE.'

FROM LORD CHARLES MONTAGUE.

' March 11th, 1781.

' SIR,

' A SINCERE wish to promote what may be to
' your advantage, induces me now to write ; and the
' freedom with which we have often conversed makes
' me hope you will not take amiss what I say. My
' own principles, respecting the commencement of
' this unfortunate war, are well known to you, and,
' of course, you can conceive what I mention is out
' of friendship : you have now fought bravely in the
' cause of your country for many years, and, in my
' opinion, fulfilled the duty every individual owes to
' it. You have had your share of hardships and dif-

' ficulties, and if the contest is still to be continued,
' younger hands should now take the toil from you.
' You have now a fair opening of quitting that ser-
' vice, with honor and reputation to yourself, by go-
' ing to Jamaica with me. The world will readily
' attribute it to the known friendship that has sub-
' sisted between us : and by quitting this country for
' a short time, you would avoid any disagreeable
' conversations, and might return at leisure, to take
' possession of your estates for yourself and family.

' THE regiment I am going to command, the on-
' ly proof I can give you of my sincerity is, that I
' will quit that command to you with pleasure, and
' serve under you. I earnestly wish I could be the
' instrument to effect what I propose, as I think it
' would be a great means towards promoting that re-
' conciliation we all wish for: a thousand circum-
' stances concur to make this a proper period for
' you to embrace: our old acquaintance : my hav-
' ing been formerly governor in this province : the
' interest I have with the present commanders.

' I GIVE you my honor, what I write is entirely
' unknown to the commandant, or to any one else ;
' so shall your answer be, if you favor me with one.
' Think well of me.

' Your's sincerely.

' CHARLES MONTAGUE.

' Gen. MOULTRIE.'

To Lord Charles Montague.

'Haddrell's-point, March 12th, 1781.

'My Lord,

'I received your's, this morning, by Fisher;
'I thank you for your wish to promote my advantage,
'but am much surprised at your proposition; I flat-
'tered myself I stood in a more favorable light
'with you: I shall write with the same freedom
'with which we used to converse, and doubt not,
'you will receive it with the same candor: I have
'often heard you express your sentiments respecting
'this unfortunate war, when you thought the Ameri-
'cans injured; but am now astonished to find you
'taking an active part against them; though not
'fighting particularly on the continent, yet seducing
'their soldiers away, to inlist in the British service,
'is nearly similar.

'My lord, you are pleased to compliment me
'with having fought bravely in my country's cause
'for many years, and in your opinion, fulfilled the
'duty every individual owes to it; but I differ very
'widely with you, in thinking that I have discharged
'my duty to my country, while it is still deluged
'with blood and over-run with British troops, who
'exercise the most savage cruelties. When I en-
'tered into this contest, I did it with the most ma-
'ture deliberation, and with a determined resolution
'to risque my life and fortune in the cause. The

' hardships I have gone through I look back upon
' with the greatest pleasure and honor to myself : I
' shall continue to go on as I have begun, that my
' example may encourage the youths of America to
' stand forth in defence of their rights and liberties.
' You call upon me now, and tell me I have a fair
' opening of quitting that service with honor and re-
' putation to myself by going with you to Jamaica.
' Good God! is it possible that such an idea could
' arise in the breast of a man of honor. I am sorry
' you should imagine I have so little regard for my
' own reputation as to listen to such dishonorable
' proposals ; would you wish to have that man whom
' you have honored with your friendship play the
' traitor? surely not. You say, by quitting this
' country for a short time I might avoid disagreeable
' conversations, and might return at my own lei-
' sure and take possession of my estates for myself
' and family ; but you have forgot to tell me how I
' am to get rid of the feelings of an injured honest
' heart, and where to hide myself from myself ; could
' I be guilty of so much baseness I should hate my-
' self and shun mankind. This would be a fatal ex-
' change from my present situation, with an easy and
' approved conscience of having done my duty, and
' conducted myself as a man of honor.

' My lord, I am sorry to observe, that I feel your
' friendship much abated, or you would not endeav-

' or to prevail upon me to act so base a part. You
' earnestly wish you could bring it about, as you
' think it will be the means of bringing about that
' reconciliation we all wish for. I wish for a recon-
' ciliation as much as any man, but only upon ho-
' norable terms. The repossessing my estates, the
' offer of the command of your regiment, and the
' honor you propose of serving under me, are paltry
' considerations to the loss of my reputation : no,
' not the fee simple of that valuable island of Jamai-
' ca should induce me to part with my integrity.

' My lord, as you have made one proposal give me
' leave to make another, which will be more honor-
' able to us both ; as you have an interest with your
' commanders, I would have you propose the with-
' drawing the British troops from the continent of
' America, allow the independence, and propose a
' peace : this being done, I will use my interest with
' my commanders, to accept of the terms, and al-
' low Great Britain a free trade with America.

' My lord, I could make one proposal,* but my
' situation as a prisoner circumscribes me within cer-
' tain bounds; I must therefore conclude with allow-

....

* Which was to advise him to come over to the Americans:
this proposal I could not make when on parole.

' ing you the free liberty to make what use of this
' you may think proper. Think better of me.

' I am, my lord,

' Your lordship's most obedient

' Humble servant,

' WM. MOULTRIE.'

FROM LT. COL. BALFOUR.

' CHARLESTOWN, March, 1781.

' SIR,

' I TAKE this opportunity to transmit to your
' information the proceedings of a court of inquiry
' held here; in consequence of which, Lieut. Col.
' Grimkie and Major Habersham are committed close
' prisoners until Lord Cornwallis' pleasure shall be
' known. On perusing these proceedings, the lenity
' of British officers must forcibly strike you; as it
' must come within your own knowledge and feelings
' that breaches of parole have heretofore been over-
' looked; and their justice, if it were necessary, will
' be fully evinced in Mr. Place being dismissed from
' his office. You will be so good as to return the
' original letters,* which accompany these proceed-
' ings.

' I am now to address you on a subject, with
' which I am charged by Lord Cornwallis, who hav-

* Keane's Grimkie's and Habersham's.

' ing in vain applied to General Greene for an equit-
' able and general exchange of prisoners, finds it ne-
' cessary, in justice to the king's service, and those
' of his army, who are in this disagreeable predica-
' ment, to pursue such measures, as may eventually
' coerce it ; and his lordship has consequently or-
' dered me to send all the prisoners of war here,
' forthwith to some one of the West-India Islands ;
' which, I am particularly directed to inform you,
' cannot be delayed beyond the middle of next month ;
' and for this purpose, the transports are now al-
' lotted, of which an account will soon be transmitted
' you.

' I AM sorry to add, that the treatment our mili-
' tia received, when made prisoners by Brigadier
' General Marion, is such, as unless speedily redress-
' ed, will compel me, in justice to those unhappy
' persons, to a severe retaliation ; and, in that case,
' I shall be obliged to seperate the militia from the
' continental prisoners of war.

' I am your's, &c.

' J. N. BALFOUR.

' Gen. MOULTRIE.'

———

To COL. BALFOUR.

' CHRIST-CHURCH PARISH, March 31, 1781.

' SIR,

' I RECEIVED your's yesterday evening, dated

' *sine die*, 1781, with the proceedings of a court of in-
' quiry, ordered on Lt. Col. Grimkie and Major Ha-
' bersham and several letters relating thereto, and
' find every clause of so much consequence that I
' could expatiate very largely on each ; but my be-
' ing a prisoner prohibits me, I shall touch slightly
' upon them and leave the rest to those who are more
' at liberty. You inform me that Lt. Col. Grimkie
' and Major Habersham are close prisoners until Lord
' Cornwallis' pleasure shall be known. I observe, the
' court is of opinion they are guilty of a breach of their
' paroles, in corresponding by letters with a man not
' in the king's peace, and who is at Beaufort. I am
' informed, that the court were of opinion that the
' letters contained nothing criminal or of a bad ten-
' dency ; if merely writing a letter is to be construed
' a breach of parole, I believe there is scarcely an
' officer in the British or American service, who has
' been a prisoner any considerable time, but has vio-
' lated his parole. I am much at a loss to recollect
' any breaches of parole that have been overlooked ;
' my feelings cannot point them out to me. I here-
' with return the original letters which you require.

' THE subject of your next clause is of a very se-
' rious nature and weighty consequence indeed ; be-
' fore I enter particularly into that, I must request
' you will be so kind as to inform me, whether you
' deem the capitulation dissolved ? You tell me, Lord

' Cornwallis has frequently applied to General Greene
' for an equitable exchange of prisoners. I can also
' assure you, that General Greene, in a letter to Ge-
' neral M'Intosh, mentions that he proposed such a
' measure to Lord Cornwallis; and I can also assure
' you, that by a letter from a delegate in Congress
' we are warranted to say, that Congress has proposed
' a plan for a general exchange, which Sir Henry
' Clinton approved, and signified to Gen. Washing-
' ton his readiness to proceed on it; and, for ought
' we know, is at this moment taking place; how-
' ever, the sending of us to the West-India islands
' cannot expedite the exchange one moment; neither
' can the measure alleviate the distresses of those of
' your officers who are prisoners, as you must be well
' assured such treatment as we receive will be fully
' retaliated by Gen. Washington.

' I AM sorry to hear Gen. Marion should use any
' prisoners ill; it is contrary to his natural disposi-
' tion: I know him to be generous and humane.
' Before you proceed to extremities I must request
' you will permit me to send an officer to General
' Greene, with a copy of your letter, and the pro-
' ceedings of the court, with the letters relative to
' Lieut. Col. Grimkie and Major Habersham for his
' inspection.

' I am, &c.
' WM. MOULTRIE.'

PROCEEDINGS OF A COURT OF INQUIRY,

HELD BY ORDER OF LIEUTENANT COLONEL BALFOUR,
COMMANDANT OF CHARLESTOWN, &c.

CHARLESTOWN, March 23d, 1781.

MAJOR M'Arthur of the seventy-first regiment, President.

CAPTAIN Bean of the sixtieth regiment, Captain Blacke of the twenty-third regiment, members.

MAJOR Barry laid before the court the letters No. 1 and 2, addressed to Lieutenant J. F. Grimkie and Major John Habersham, Haddrell's-point.

MR. Charles Wroughton master of a galley stationed near Haddrell's-point, appeared before the court, and the following questions were put to him by Major Barry, viz:

Q. WHAT conversation had you with Captain Shubrick when he was a-long side the galley?

A. I ALWAYS speak all boats passing near the galley on their way to Haddrell's-point. Captain Shubrick, with two ladies, totally unknown to me, came in a boat a-long side the galley; as I had not the pleasure of knowing the ladies, I asked them for their passes, and Captain Shubrick made answer, 'That one was his lady, and he did not conceive that she had occasion for a pass,' or words to that purpose. I then asked Captain Shubrick if he had any letters, he answered 'No.' Lieutenant Johnston commanding the galley, then permitted the boat to go a-shore.

Q. (By the court.) WAS any person present at the time of your asking Captain Shubrick if he had letters ?

A. No, none to my knowledge, except those in the boat with Captain Shubrick.

ENSIGN Place, assistant commissary of prisoners, appeared before the court; and Major Barry put the following questions to him, viz :

Q. WHAT passed between you and Captain Shubrick, respecting the two letters ?

A. CAPTAIN Shubrick told me the officer of the galley had desired him to inform me that Mrs. Shubrick was in the boat, and he desired to know if I had any objections to her landing ; I said not, and proceeded, as usual, upon business, which was that of asking for letters; but I do not recollect I asked him for any, though he gave me several.

MR. Charles Wroughton further informed the court, that when he went a-shore, he was surprised to find Mr. Place had received letters from Captain Shubrick.

CAPTAIN Shubrick being called upon to answer to the evidence of Mr. Wroughton and Mr. Place, declared positively to the court, that he never was asked for letters, by the master of the galley or any one else on board ; that the orders he received from the galley respecting the ladies were strictly complied with. He further declared, that Mr. Place never asked him for letters but that he gave them to him. He further added, that he went to Mr. Place first to get permission for Mrs. Shubrick and the other lady to land; and when they were landed, he went a second time to Mr. Place and delivered the letters.

RESPECTING the letters No. 1 and 2, Lieut. Col. Grimkie and Major Habersham confessed to the court, that upon a strict and serious examination into the parole given to the officers at Haddrell's-point, they certainly have been guilty of a breach of that parole; but, at the same time, hoped the court would not consider it in a criminal light, nor as from a desire, by any means, to prejudice his Majesty's service, but merely to divert a few hours of tedious captivity.

LIEUT. Colonel Grimkie, in order to convince the court of the innocence of the correspondence, further informs the court, that the gazette alluded to in Mr. Kean's letter, was only a recapitulation or mention of those numerous and trifling reports, which commonly prevailed among the officers at Haddrell's-point.

LIEUTENANT Colonel Grimkie and Major Habersham further informed the court, that any news or information that was sent Mr. Kean, was prevailing at Haddrell's-point about six weeks before Mr. Kean received it, from which they conceived no design of hurt could be intended to his majesty's arms.

LIEUTENANT Colonel Grimkie and Major Habersham, respecting that part of the parole, viz : ' Or ' have intercourse, or hold correspondence with his ' enemies' they conceived it only extended to persons without the British lines, or such as were wavering in their principles.

AND further, in order to shew the real intention of the gazette, the motto prefixed to it, was
' *Dissipant nugæ curas edaces.*'

THE following letters from Mr. Kean were the cause of Colonel Grimkie's and Major Habersham's being confined ; they were delivered to the commissary of prisoners, and sent by him, to the commandant.

COPY OF MR. KEAN'S LETTER FROM BEAUFORT, TO LIEUT. COL. GRIMKIE AT HADDRELL'S-POINT.

' March 4th, 1781.

No. 1. 'SWEET are the gratulations of friendship, ' especially to a heart buried in sorrow ; your friend- ' ly letter has roused me, and from this moment I ' drive the fiend from me. SORROW, thou drawer ' of gloomy dejecting pictures, thou anticipater and ' prolonger of misery, thou desrtoyer of health, con- ' tent, and peace of mind, avaunt; nor ever more per-

' vade the sacred mansions of my friends. My heart
' has no room but for my mistress and my friends.
' I am not ordered to Charlestown ; no town, no
' charms shall keep me from you when I am ordered,
' if I can gain permission to come where you are.

' The amusements you prevailed on Habersham
' to send me have given me the greatest satisfaction ;
' was I to send you a gazette for this latitude how
' different would it be.

' I AM sorry to allay any joyous moments you may
' possess by repetition of losses ; however, for fear
' common fame might say more than there is occa-
' sion for, I will tell you myself. You know I am a
' provident lad, and not having occasion to make use
' of my crops of Indigo, for these last three years
' past, I had left them at Augusta, and they were
' coming down Savannah river in order to be turned
' into money for my travelling expenses, with all
' my present year's provision : the genius of the
' river, has taken a fancy to it, himself ; and has
' chosen to impurple his robe at my expense, say
' about 1,000 pounds sterling.

' I AM sorry for the reduction of your regiment,
' for I fear it was literally reduced ; your known
' abilities can never want employ ; we will strike out
' some plan for an exertion of your abilities, and our
' friendship shall be a stimulas to carry us to the
' pinnacle of fame ; I have a long race to run ere

' I gain the height you already have : Pliny says
' there are but two points of view worthy our atten-
' tion, the endless duration of fame, or the extent of
' life : those who are governed by the former, must
' pursue it with unremitting ardor ; those who are
' influenced by the latter should quietly resign them-
' selves to repose, nor wear out a short life in pe-
' rishable pursuits.

' WRITE me frequently, and tell Hab. not to fail
' to send me his monthly exercises.

' THAT you may enjoy a Mahometan paradise in
' this world, and such a heaven as is most pleasing
' in the next, is the wish of your sincere friend.

(Signed)　　　　　' JOHN KEAN.'

COPY OF A LETTER WROTE TO MAJOR HABERSHAM,
BY THE SAME.

' March 5th, 1781.

No. 2. ' I THANK you, my dear Jack, for your
' friendly congratulations ; and believe me, I have
' not received more true pleasure, since my capti-
' vity, than your letter afforded me : your gazette
' has roused my mind from a lethargy into which it
' was sunk by accounts so diametrically opposite, that
' I supposed there was nothing on this continent,
' save Mon. Rochambeau to make any opposition :
' indeed, to such a degree of apathy had I sunk, that,
' save yourself and two or three more, I cared not

‘ if the whole world had been perfectly annihilated :
‘ it is truly a rascally world.

‘ LECHMORE our present commandant, you know,
‘ is my particular acquaintance ; besides, you know,
‘ I am of a kind of placid disposition. Let me alone;
‘ do not come in my way, and I will let you do as
‘ you please; this is the reason I fancy why I have
‘ not been ordered to Charlestown.

‘ IT is certainly most convenient for me to be here,
‘ but it has exposed me to most severe trials ; figure
‘ to yourself an aged mother, a youthful sister, (all
‘ that remains of a once numerous family) looking
‘ up to me, the only male left of their line, and ad-
‘ ding their entreaties to those who stile themselves
‘ my friends, to become a subject : we should sin-
‘ cerely pray against temptation. I do heartily hope
‘ to be endowed with a sufficient degree of fortitude,
‘ to withstand every attempt : should I not, with
‘ those who know my situation, I shall receive some
‘ degree of credit, that I have so long withstood
‘ such powerful persuaders. Remember CORIOLANUS
‘ fell in the most virtuous time of the Romans : if I
‘ do, (which heaven forbid) it will be the most vir-
‘ tuous of my country.

‘ ADIEU to serious subjects! live all the little
‘ amusements that enable us to pass away our pro-
‘ bationary stay in this transitory world. I sincerely
‘ condole with you for your amazing loss, and, had

' I not bid farewell to serious subjects, I would tell
' you of one that I have met with.

' My poetical genius has left me a long time ; the
' mind ill at ease, cannot please, nor strike out any
' gay thought. I have sent you a copy from a good
' author, which, perhaps (as I imagine you have no
' library) may fill up a gap in your gazette. Re-
' peat the dose monthly of your amusement, it will
' awaken my genius perhaps.

' Adieu my friend, &c.

' JOHN KEAN.'

THE court having duly considered the evidence
for and against Lieutenant Colonel Grimkie and
Major Habersham, both of the American army,
is of opinion they are guilty of a breach of their paroles, in corresponding, by letters, with a man not in
the King's peace, and who is at Beaufort.

FROM LT. COL. GRIMKIE.

' SIR,

' IN obedience to your order of March the twen-
' ty-third, I repaired to Charlestown, and attended
' at Lieutenant Colonel Balfour's, for the purpose of
' explaining the nature of a correspondence, which
' I had held with Mr. Kean at Port-royal. Captain
' Barry's secretary informed me that a court of offi-
' cers had been ordered to investigate the matter,

' and that I must attend thereon : I was much sur-
' prised at the mode of inquiry pointed out, and ex-
' pressed my sentiments accordingly ; concluding
' with a desire that Colonel Balfour would suffer me
' to see him, as I was certain I could explain the
' whole occurrence to his satisfaction, without the
' mediation of a court : but this request was pe-
' remptorily objected to; and Captain Barry demand-
' ed, in a very importunate manner, a specific
' answer, whether I would appear before the court
' of officers, ordered to assemble on the occasion ?
' I reflected, as no other means of inquiry were left
' to me but this court, that I should gratify my ene-
' mies in a most essential point, and with the most
' singular advantage. Had I continued to refuse the
' explanation, in the way it was demanded of me,
' they might have represented, that, conscious of an
' intentional criminality in the correspondence allu-
' ded to, I had purposely avoided the inquiry, not
' daring to submit my conduct to the view of man-
' kind ; and that I preferred laying under the suspi-
' cion only of being guilty, rather than confirm it
' by my own examination : the natural consequences
' would have been, that I should have been conveyed
' to some place of confinement ; and, under the se-
' verest interdictions, have been precluded all mode
' of explanation and appeal : this conduct, I foresaw,
' would have contributed to the pregnant suspicions

'of mankind, and to my own condemnation. The
'subsequent part of their conduct towards me, evin-
'ces the propriety of my behavior upon this occa-
'sion, and the justice of this reflection : to remove,
'therefore, a calumny of the most illiberal kind, I
'was compelled to listen to their proposals of a court,
'sensible that nothing criminal could be alledged
'against me, SUPPORTED BY FACTS.

'CAPT. Barry laid before the court a letter written
'by Mr. Kean at Beaufort to me. There are few
'sentences, which, even in the cooler hours of rea-
'son, considered abstractedly, and unsupported by
'the general tenor of the subject, may not be per-
'verted, and which may not admit of several modes
'of construction. In the present precarious mo-
'ments which awaken suspicion and tend to create
'jealousies and distrusts : the fears of an enemy may
'be alarmed by the most trifling incidents. Several
'paragraphs of this letter were pointed out as ob-
'noxious, and which required an explanation. The
'most natural, as well as the most immediate and
'ready answers were given to every exceptionable
'part; but, nevertheless, words were deprived of
'their intrinsic meaning, and a sense imposed upon
'the different paragraphs foreign to the intention of
'the writer; for instance, the word amusement was
'said to mean information, and the Latin word *nugæ*,
'which literally and properly signifies trifles, was

'forced to assume the meaning of *folly.* This sus-
'picion I deemed excusable in people who had them-
'selves given such recent and notorious proofs, that
'they deemed themselves bound by no engagements
'in infringing the articles of a most sacred capitula-
'tion. They could not but be of opinion that their
'conduct not only merited, but would have justified
'any mode of retaliation. It is more than probable,
'that men devoid of the finer feelings of honor, would
'suspect a recrimination of injuries from a person
'whom they had also previously injured : such appre-
'hensions are natural to the weak, the base, and the
'guilty ; for they are incapable, from an irrecover-
'able badness of heart, to conceive a soul equal to
'the sufferings of injuries imposed on it ; and for a
'forbearance of its just resentment at the same mo-
'ment. To remove, therefore, these plausible jea-
'lousies, I candidly proposed to the court that they
'would permit me to write to Mr. Kean, whom I
'would request to send immediately the necessary
'papers to me ; and that they would defer the con-
'sideration of this matter until I could procure
'them ; they were absolutely necessary for an elu-
'cidation of the subject : they were absolutely ne-
'cessary for their information, and also for my de-
'fence and acquittal. So sudden and unexpected a
'proposal gave the alarm of the consciousness of my
'own innocence and the certainty of my acquittal ;

' but this reasonable demand was not listened to by
' the court. I am yet in doubt to resolve, whether
' this neglect proceeded from the native propensity
' of the court, or from the dictatorial mandate which
' was now delivered to them by captain Barry, and
' which they said proceeded from Lt. Col. Balfour.
' Capt. Barry told the court that the contents of the
' letters were by no means an object of their con-
' sideration; that it was wholly out of their province
' to judge of the criminality of the expressions; and
' that be the subject ever so innocent the fact alone
' of having corresponded constituted the guilt. He
' added, that Mr. Kean's letter sufficiently indicated
' that he was an enemy to the king, and that my pa-
' role provided that no correspondence or intercourse
' should be held with his enemies. I was astonished
' at this new doctrine and uncandid interpretation
' which was put upon the parole. I observed how
' inequitable it was to adopt a literal construction of
' the parole, and to assume a forced application for
' the terms of Mr. Kean's letter. That my concep-
' tion of the sense of the parole was very different;
' I was, indeed, bound not to communicate any in-
' telligence to an enemy of the king of Great Britain;
' but did not appear to preclude my writing to a
' friend, who was a prisoner upon parole, and within
' the enemy's lines as well as myself. Besides, the
' correspondence was perfectly innocent, and did no

'injury to the cause against which we were engaged.
'I had not endeavored to confirm Mr. Kean in the
'principles which he had adopted, as I was sensible,
'from the strength of his judgment and the upright-
'ness of his heart, that he would persevere in so just
'a cause. If I had mistaken the parole, and been
'too liberal in my construction of it, that the inten-
'tion ought to be weighed by the court. Supposing
'it possible that the interpretation given to the pa-
'role by Captain Barry should be thought the usual
'and received one, I must then confess that I had
'been guilty of a breach of it; but as it was without
'design, and without criminality, it could be deemed
'but an indiscretion, and, consequently, venial.

'In the course of this conference, you will be pleas-
'ed to observe that Mr. Barry changed his ground,
'who strenuously endeavored to establish the crimi-
'nality of the correspondence, by pointing out such
'passages as would bear a double meaning: but af-
'ter I had offered to produce the papers, he conclu-
'ded with assuring the court that it was not neces-
'sary to consider whether the expressions were cri-
'minal or not, but only whether a correspondence
'existed, for, in that alone the guilt lay. Upon
'the declaration of this positive command of Colo-
'nel Balfour, and the letters alone of Mr. Kean, was
'founded the sentence of the court; although I ob-
'serve that these proceedings positively declare an

‘ acknowledgement of a breach of my parole, and
‘ that they pronounced their sentence upon that con-
‘ fession, without making any mention whatever of
‘ the doubts which had arisen in my breast, concern-
‘ ing the propriety of their interpretation, or the con-
‘ ditionality of the acknowledgement.

‘ I MADE application to Captain Bluck for a copy
‘ of the proceedings of the court, which was refused
‘ me : I must confess my uneasiness at this refusal,
‘ apprehending some omissions, and that on so deli-
‘ cate a subject, the text might be attended with a
‘ variety of constructions ; it ought, therefore, to
‘ have been as full as possible, and the instances of
‘ misinterpretation, then before me, pointed out the
‘ necessity : since you did me the honor of the peru-
‘ sal of the proceedings of the court, I am sorry to
‘ say, I find my suspicions confirmed ; I have, there-
‘ fore, taken the liberty of representing to you the
‘ facts as they happened ; and supplied those disin-
‘ genuous omissions which I have discovered.

‘ IN consequence of their opinion, I was detained
‘ in the City-guard for ten days, without any allow-
‘ ance of provisions, fire, or candles, and it is proba-
‘ ble that if you had not interposed and represented
‘ the injustice of such proceedings, that the same
‘ injurious treatment would have existed to the mo-
‘ ment of my dismission. Major Habersham who
‘ was acquainted with Major M‘Arthur the president

' of the court, had two interviews with him after
' our confinement; wherein that gentleman very
' candidly disavowed the least suspicions of criminali-
' ty in our intentions, and advised us to write to
' Colonel Balfour. This advice I had reason to think
' was the result of a conference which he had held
' with that gentleman. He told us also, that were
' the papers produced which we had sent to Mr.
' Kean, it was more than probable we should imme-
' diately be dismissed. Such an inconsistancy of be-
' havior, filled me with more astonishment, than
' the injurious treatment I had received. At first
' the papers are refused to be seen, and a court forms
' a solemn sentence without them, though offered:
' Col. Balfour sends them word it is not necessary to
' consider the contents of the letters; and afterwards
' he thinks it requisite that they should be laid before
' himself. I treated this childish behavior with the
' contempt it deserved, and would not take any steps
' to produce the papers required. The confinement
' in a public prison, and the charge of the crime, of
' the deepest die, left open no door of reconciliation
' or further explanation on my part. One day's im-
' prisonment drew upon me the suspicions of the
' people, and the continuance of the punishment
' could avail no more. I presumed that as soon as
' Mr. Kean arrived in town, he would be able to ex-
' plain such matters as they were solicitous to make

‘ appear mysterious. The consequence of his letter
‘ was, that on the 17th April we were informed, that
‘ Col. Balfour was convinced that we had not inten-
‘ tionally been guilty of a breach of paroles, but that
‘ he could not release us until he had heard from
‘ Lord Cornwallis; to whom he had written upon the
‘ subject. This was a very extraordinary confession
‘ of our innocence, indeed, since no new matter was
‘ laid before Colonel Balfour which could have induc-
‘ ed him to have changed his opinion. I told Ma-
‘ jor Fraser that I imagined Colonel Balfour had been
‘ perfectly convinced of the purity of our intentions
‘ ever since he had received the proceedings of the
‘ court, which he candidly acknowledged ; whilst I
‘ had reason to believe that Colonel Balfour was con-
‘ vinced of the propriety of his own conduct, I re-
‘ mained satisfied, though I could not approve of it ;
‘ nay, sir, I even acknowledged the justice of the
‘ confinement I was suffering, whilst I was persuad-
‘ ed that Colonel Balfour's conduct proceeded from
‘ a mistaken principle, and not from the wanton ex-
‘ ertion of a temporary power. It is difficult to judge
‘ what were my feelings when I was informed that I
‘ was acknowledged not to be guilty intentionally or
‘ criminally, but that notwithstanding this declaration,
‘ I had not only been punished, but was to experience
‘ a continuance thereof : could language be more
‘ insulting or could actions be more malicious. Is

'it possible that any man can have so base, so ser-
'vile a spirit, as to exercise an office whose charac-
'teristic function is an indiscriminate infliction
'of punishment, without the additional property of
'dispensing justice or extending mercy? At length,
'after a confinement of five weeks, I was told by
'Major Fraser, that letters had been received from
'Lord Cornwallis, and that his lordship was of
'opinion, that we had not been guilty of a breach of
'parole; this part of their behavior deserves as
'little attention as credibility, though it was not the
'least extraordinary. It is well known that Major
'Benson, who attended General Scott, did not see
'General Greene, and that they did not know where
'to find Lord Cornwallis,* and therefore returned
'without having executed that part of their com-
'mission.

'I AM sorry, sir, that I was not acquainted with
'the opportunity you had of writing to General
'Greene, and of your intention of inclosing the

....

* The British in Charlestown, were very much at a loss
to know what was become of Lord Cornwallis : after the battle
of Guildford, they could get no account of him ; they therefore
fell upon this expedient, which was, to let General Scott go to
Virginia upon parole, but that Major Benson should atetnd
him until they came to Lord Cornwallis or General Greene ;
but in this they were disappointed, as a part of General Greene's
army met them and would not let them pass, but ordered them
back again, and General Scott returned to us at Haddrell's.
point.

' papers relative to me in your dispatches; had this
' explanation been included in your packet, it would
' have given a very different appearance to this affair
' than will be the result of the perusal of the British
' papers. I have therefore to request of you to
' communicate these facts to General Greene, before
' whom the British papers have been laid, and you
' will add to the obligations already conferred on me.
' I should have represented my situation to you at
' an earlier period, but reflecting that I had been
' refused a copy of the proceedings of the court, I
' did not imagine that permission would have been
' granted me to write to you; I therefore declined
' it until I should be released from my confinement;
' and I take this early period to offer you my warm-
' est acknowledgments for your interposition in my
' favor, to assure you how sensibly I am obliged to
you, and that

' I am, &c.

' J. F. GRIMKIE.'

' Gen. MOULTRIE.'

FROM COL. GRIMKIE.

' SIR,

' THE confinement I suffered, in the City-guard
' of Charlestown, having rendered the parole which
' I gave upon the surrender of that place null and
' void, and no other promise or parole having been

' given by me since, I thought myself at liberty to
' return to the duty of my country. I have inclosed
' you a copy of a letter written to me by Major
' Fraser the night before I left town, to which I re-
' turned no answer at all. The situation* in which
' you are, precluded me from asking your opinion
' upon a point of so much delicacy; I have therefore
' left my reasons for your perusal; hoping that I shall
' be vindicated in your opinion, which I highly
' esteem, and in that of the other officers, prisoners
' at Haddrell's-point.

' I am, &c.

' J. F. GRIMKIE.'

' Gen. MOULTRIE.'

COLONEL Grimkie went off and joined General
Greene's army.

———

TO LT. COL. BALFOUR.

'March 21st, 1781.

' SIR,

' YOU cannot possibly be more tired with read-
' ing my letters than I am of writing them ; yet I
' must intrude upon your multiplicity of business, and
' remonstrate against every violation of the capitula-
' tion, and represent every grievance which occurs to
' us, whether they are attended to or not. What I

* A prisoner.

'am now to remonstrate against, is a most violent
'and inhuman breach of the capitulation; which is
'the impressing the American soldiers from on board
'the prison-ships, taking them away by violence, and
'sending them on board the transports, to be carried
'from the continent of America;* many of them
'leaving wives and young children, who may possi-
'bly perish for want of the common necessaries of
'life; if I cannot prevail upon you to countermand
'this violation altogether, let me plead for those un-
'happy ones who have families to be exempted from
'this cruelty. I beg you will consider their situation
'and suffer your humanity to be partial in their favor.

' I am, &c.
' WILLIAM MOULTRIE.'

No answer to this letter.

To LT. COL. BALFOUR.
' April 3d, 1781.

' SIR,

' I AM to acknowledge the receipt of your's of
'yesterday's date, and as I cannot be permitted to
'send an officer to General Greene with my dis-
'patches, I have sent them down for your perusal,
'and request the favor you will forward them : I am

---

* Several hundreds of them were forced to inlist in Lord
Charles Montague's regiment, and were carried to Jamaica.

' also to request that I may be permitted to send to
' Congress your letter and my answer, relative to
' the sending the continental and militia prisoners of
' war to the West-Indies; which, if you agree to, I
' have sent down to be put immediately on board the
' flag going to Philadelphia, that she may not be de-
' tained one moment.

' I am, &c.

' WM. MOULTRIE.'

———

To GEN. GREENE.

' April 3d, 1781.

' SIR,

' I DO myself the honor to transmit to you the
' copies of two letters received from Lieutenant Colo-
' nel Balfour commandant in Charlestown and my
' answer thereto, relative to the sending the conti-
' nental and militia prisoners of war to the West-In-
' dies; and also the copies of the proceedings of a
' court of inquiry, ordered by Colonel Balfour, to ex-
' amine a charge against Lieutenant Colonel Grim-
' kie and Major Habersham, for a breach of parole :
' the letters and papers are numbered as follows,
' which if you find right, I request the favor you will
' signify to me by the return of the bearer.

' I am, &c.

' WM. MOULTRIE.'

FROM MAJ. FRASER.

'April 29th 1781, 8 at night.

'SIR,

'I BEG leave to acquaint you that a boat will be
'ready at Wragg's-wharf to-morrow morning, at
'half past eight o'clock, for the purpose of carrying
'you, Major Habersham, your servants and baggage
'to Haddrell's-point; where you will consider your-
'selves on parole, in the same situation with the rest
'of the officers there. I will thank you to commu-
'nicate this to Major Habersham.

'I have the honor, &c.

'C. FRASER. Town Major.

'Lieut. Col. GRIMKIE.'

———

TO MAJ. BENSON.

'April 30th, 1781.

'SIR,

'I RECEIVED your's at twelve o'clock, in which
'you inform me, that the commandant wishes to see
'me on business of consequence. I must request
'you will make my compliments, and I will wait on
'him to-morrow morning.

'I am, &c.

'WM. MOULTRIE.'

To Col. Balfour.

'Charlestown, May 2d, 1781.

' Sir,

' At your request, by letter from Major Benson,
' I came to town yesterday, on some business of con-
' sequence, on which I was informed you would
' wish to speak to me ; on my arrival I sent my aid-
' de-camp, Captain Shubrick, to acquaint you, and
' to know what hour you would wish to see me ;
' you appointed this morning at ten o'clock ; I ac-
' cordingly attended at your quarters, and after
' waiting some little time, was much surprised to
' find, instead of your speaking to me, a verbal
' message delivered by Major Barry ; by whom I
' was informed that you were then so busy that you
' could not see me ; but that he had it in charge to
' acquaint me, " That the continental and militia offi-
" cers were to be sent to Long-Island, (instead of
" the West-Indies, as had been threatened before)
" at the particular request of General Greene."
' However polite you may conceive this treatment,
' I look upon it quite otherwise ; and hope for the
' future, when a matter of so much consequence, as
' the total dissolution of a capitulation is to be trans-
' acted, that it will be done by letter, when no mis-
' understandings can be pleaded on either side ; and

' I therefore request that Major Barry's message
' may be transmitted to me in writing.

'I am, &c.

'WM. MOULTRIE.'

ARTICLES of a CARTEL for the exchange and relief
of prisoners of war, taken in the Southern department; agreed to at the house of Mr. Claudius Pegues on Peedee, the third of May, 1781; between
Captain Cornwallis, on the part of Lieutenant
General Earl Cornwallis'; and Lieutenant Colonel
Carrington, on the part of Major General Greene.

' I. THAT regular troops be exchanged for regulars, and militia for militia.

' II. THAT men inlisted for six months and upwards in continental or state service be looked upon
as regulars.

' III. THAT the mode of exchange be rank for
rank, as far as similar ranks shall apply.

' IV. THAT officers be exchanged by rotation,
according to date of captive ; but a reciprocal option
to be exercised as to subjects, in non-commissioned
and privates, by naming particular corps or particular persons.

' V. THAT no non-commissioned officer or private soldier admitted to parole, shall be considered
as a prisoner of war, but finally liberated, unless
paroled on the faith of a commissioned officer.

'VI. THAT officers who cannot be exchanged for want of similar ranks to apply, be immediately paroled to their respective homes until exchanged; subject to be recalled for a breach thereof, or for a violation of the cartel, by the party to whom they belong.

'VII. THAT passports be allowed for such supplies as may be sent from either side, to prisoners in captivity.

'VIII. THAT commissaries of prisoners be permitted to pass from each side into the opposite lines, and reside there, for the purpose of viewing and representing the situations of the prisoners; but removed by the respective commanding officers.

'IX. THAT prisoners shall not be sent from the continent whilst the articles of the cartel continue to be observed.

'X. THAT commissaries of prisoners shall immediately put in practice exchanges on the above principles, as far as the subjects on each side will go; and continue them in future as characters shall apply.

'XI. THAT the first delivery of American prisoners shall embark at Charlestown, on or before the fifteenth of June, and sail immediately for Jamestown, in James-river, where the first delivery of British prisoners shall embark, on or about the first week in July, and sail immediately to the nearest British port.

' XII. THAT the flag of truce shall be sacred going with the American prisoners, and returning with the British to the port where they are to be delivered.'

THIS cartel being agreed upon, Major Hyrne the American commissary of prisoners, came to Charlestown and proceeded upon the exchange of prisoners, and where similar ranks could not apply, the officers were paroled; some went to Philadelphia, others to Virginia with what soldiers were left, and the sick to the hospital.

I WAS allowed a small brig for myself and family, and such others as I chose to take on board; in consequence of which, by applications and intreaties of my friends, we had upwards of ninety souls on board that small brig; we sailed some time in June, and after a pleasant passage, arrived safe in Philadelphia; the other vessels all arrived in Virginia.

As soon as Colonel Grimkie joined General Greene's army, he solicited for a court of inquiry on his conduct at leaving Haddrell's-point; a court was accordingly appointed, of which Colonel Harrison of the Virginia line of artillery was president; and that they were unanimously of opinion, that Colonel

Grimkie had not broke his parole, and that he was justifiable in quitting Haddrell's-point; which was approved of by General Greene; and who was so strongly impressed with the justice and propriety of his conduct, that when he proposed to him to let him have a party of troops to bring off all his brother officers who were prisoners at Haddrell's-point, he immediately consented to it, and gave him a letter to General Marion on the subject, who was fully of opinion that the officers were absolved from their paroles; the general accordingly furnished him with a detachment, with which he proceeded to Haddrell's-point, and from which, he did not retreat, until he had made the British commissary prisoner within sight of the town, and until he had possession of the barracks and all the officers, and a number of the officers had proceeded on their way off, as far as the church, which was five miles from the barracks, and near the quarters where General Pinckney and myself staid; there they halted, and sent to know whether we would go off with them; we refused to go, though not one of us doubted the right or the propriety of the measure, because we were convinced that the British had violated the capitulation, against which we had often remonstrated, but we expected soon to be exchanged, and we thought it best to remain, rather than run any risk.

THE circumstance of General Greene's giving encouragement to those officers on parole to quit that parole, if they could do it with security to their persons, acknowledging thereby, as did every officer in our army, who were not prisoners, that every officer on Haddrell's-point, was freed from the parole which he had given, by the excessive outrages of the British, and their many and flagrant violations of our capitulation.

DURING the siege of Charlestown, on the 25th of April, Lord Cornwallis passed over to Mount-Pleasant with 2,000 men, by which movement we were completely invested; he soon afterward moved his main body to Brabants.*

WHILE the siege of Charlestown was pending, a French fleet under the command of Admiral Ternay, of seven ships of the line and five frigates and a number of transports, with five thousand as good troops as any in France, on board, hastening to our relief, but did not arrive in time; they were so near the coast as to take the vessel that was carrying Sir Henry Clinton's dispatches to New-York, with an account of the surrender of Charlestown. Their plan was to have gone into Ball's-bay, landed the troops at Sevee-bay, marched down to Haddrell's-point, and from thence, to cross over to Charlestown;

* Bishop Smith's seat.

which they could very easily have done, and would have effectually raised the siege and taken the British fleet in Charlestown harbor, and in Stono-inlet and in all probability their whole army.

COLONEL Buford was marching with a detachment of the Virginia line, between three and four hundred men, and a few of Washington's cavalry, to reinforce the garrison of Charlestown; but when he arrived at Nelson's-ferry, he received information of their surrender; upon which he began his retreat for N. Carolina. Lord Cornwallis who being incamped at Brabant's, in St. Thomas' parish some considerable time before the surrender, on the 18th May began his march for Huger's-bridge, with about 2500 men and 5 field pieces from thence to Leneau's-ferry, on Santee-river, where he found some difficulty in crossing; the Americans had destroyed most of the boats; some few were hid in the swamps, but the negroes discovered them and the army crossed; from whence Colonel Tarleton was sent off to George-town to drive off, or take any Americans that were to be found there. Lord Cornwallis proceeded on with the main body to Nelson's-ferry, where he was joined by Tarleton, whom he immediately detached with a body of about 700 infantry and cavalry in quest of Colonel Buford, who had begun his retreat from that place about ten days before. Colonel Tarleton (who had discretionary orders) left the army on the

27th, and the next day arrived at Camden, where he got intelligence of Buford; no time was to be lost to prevent his junction with a detachment of Americans that were incamped near the Catawba's. At two o'clock in the morning, the British being refreshed, continued their pursuit to Rugley's, and at daylight they were informed that the continentals had retreated about twenty miles towards the Catawba settlements to meet their reinforcements. In order to detain Colonel Buford on his march Captain Kinlock was sent off with a flag to summons him to surrender upon the same terms as the continentals had in Charlestown; informing him at the same time, that Colonel Tarleton had 700 infantry and cavalry: to which Colonel Buford sent back a message of defiance, at the same time continued his march while conversing with the flag; and at the near approach of the enemy he drew up his men in open order in the wood on the right of the road, his infantry in one line, with a small reserve and his colors in the centre; his artillery and waggons he ordered to continue on their march. Colonel Tarleton drew up his men in the following order at the distance of three hundred yards. Major Cochran commanded his right wing of sixty dragoons, and as many mounted infantry with orders to dismount to gall the flanks: Captains Corbet and Kinlock with the dragoons of the 17th and a part of the legion to charge the centre

while Tarleton with thirty chosen dragoons and some
infantry, were to attack their flanks and reserve:
the dragoons, the mounted infantry, and the three
pounder, were ordered to form in the rear as a reserve, as they came up with their tired horses: as
the British approached, the Americans were within
about fifty yards; the officers called out ‘ not to fire
until they were within ten yards,’ which Tarleton
said himself ‘ he was surprised to hear:’ in my
opinion this was a great error. Colonel Buford
committed two very capital mistakes in this affair:
the first was his sending away his waggons and artillery, which ought to have been his chief dependance. On the approach of the enemy he ought to
have formed them into a hollow square, with small
intervals between each ; in these intervals to have
placed platoons ; taking out the baggage and placed
it a little in the front of each platoon, which would
have served as a breast-work, and would have disconcerted the cavalry in their charge : his field-pieces
planted in the front angles of the square : an interval in the rear of the square for the cavalry, who
should face outward and be ready to sally when occasion should offer : six men in each waggon : with
this disposition the enemy could have made no impression upon him : nay, Tarleton would never have
attacked him. Another mistake was his ordering

his men not to fire upon the enemy (who were chiefly cavalry) till they came within ten yards of him.

A RETURN of rebels, killed, wounded, and taken, in the affair at Waxsaws, the 29th of May, 1781.

ONE lieutenant colonel, three captains, eight subalterns, one adjutant, one quartermaster, ninety-nine sergeants and rank and file, killed; three captains, five subalterns, one hundred and forty-two sergeants and rank and file wounded, unable to travel and left on parale; one hundred and thirteen killed, and one hundred and fifty-one so badly wounded as to be left on the ground; taken, three stand of colors, two brass six pounders, two royals, two waggons with ammunition, one artillery forge cart, fifty-five barrels of powder, twenty-six waggons loaded with new cloathing, arms, muskets, cartridges, new cartridge-boxes, flints and camp equipage.

(Signed,)   B. TARLETON.
Lieut. Col. Com. B. legion.

A RETURN of British killed and wounded in the affair at Waxsaws, the 29th of May, 1781.

CAVALRY, two privates killed; one subaltern and eight privates wounded. Infantry, two subalterns one private killed.

Lieutenant Pateschall of the seventeenth dragoons wounded; Lieut. M‘Donald and Lieut. Camp.

bell of the legion killed. Eleven horses killed and nineteen wounded.

(Signed,)   B. TARLETON
Lieut. Col. Com. B. legion.

MARSHALL Saxe says, page thirty, ' At the battle ' of Belgrade I saw two battalions cut to pieces in an ' instant; being surrounded by a thick fog, a strong ' blast of wind suddenly arose and dispersed it, when ' we immediately saw a battalion of Loraine and ' another of Neuperg upon a hill, separated from ' the rest of our army ; Prince Eugine at the same ' time, discovered a party of horse in motion up the ' side of the mountain, and asked me, if I could dis- ' tinguish what they were ? I answered, they were ' thirty or forty Turks ; then, repeated he, those ' two battalions are undone ; at which time I ' could perceive no appearance of their being at- ' tacked, not being able to see what was on the ' other side of the mountain, but galloping up at full ' speed, I no sooner arrived in the rear of Neuperg's ' colors, than I saw the two battalions present, and ' give a general fire upon a large body of Turks, at ' the distance of about thirty paces instantaneously ' after which the Turks rushed forward through the ' smoke without allowing them a moment's time to ' fly, and with their sabres cut the whole to pieces ' upon the spot. The only persons who escaped,

' were M. de Neuperg, who happened luckily to be on
' horseback, an ensign who hung to my horse's mane,
' and two or three privates ; the Turks of their own
' accord retired.   Upon the arrival afterwards of
' some cavalry and infantry, M. Neuberg desired a
' detachment to secure the clothing ; upon which
' sentries were posted at the four angles of the ground,
' occupied by the dead bodies of the two battalions,
' and their clothes, hats, shoes &c, collected in heaps
' together; during which time I had curiosity enough
' to count the number of Turks which might be de-
' stroyed by the general discharge of the two battal-
' ions, and found it amounted only to thirty-two."

THESE two instances show the superiority which
cavalry have over infantry.

THIS victory of Tarleton's gained him the highest esteem and confidence of Lord Cornwallis, who
recommended him in a very particular manner to
his majesty's favor. The total destruction of Buford's detachment left South Carolina and Georgia
without a single continental soldier but what were
prisoners of war : in this situation all military operations and all opposition to the British army were
suspended for a time : after this the principal object of
the British was to secure the submission of the inhabitants throughout the state, they accordingly sent
detachments, and took post at Camden, Georgetown,

Cheraws, Beaufort, and Congaree, and the citizens
sent in flags from all parts, (some excepted who were
in the back parts of the state still kept out) with
their submission to the British government, praying
that they may be admitted upon the same terms as
the citizens of Charlestown.

EARLY in June Sir Henry Clinton goes to New-
York with the main body of the British army, and
leaves about 4,000 of the troops under the command
of Lord Cornwallis, who came to Charlestown to arrange the civil matters, and in July or early in August returns to Camden, leaving Col. Nesbet Balfour
commandant in Charlestown.

ON the first of June Sir Henry Clinton and Admiral Arbuthnot as commissioners for restoring peace
to America, issued their proclamation, offering ' to
' the inhabitants, with a few exceptions, pardon for
' their past treasonable offences, and a reinstate-
' ment of the possession of all those rights and im-
' munities which they hitherto had enjoyed under a
' free British government, exempt from taxation,
' except by their own legislatures.'

THE people quite harrassed out and tired of war;
their capital fallen, and their army prisoners, no
place of safety for them to fly to with their families
and property; the British troops in possession of
their whole country, and no prospect of relief from
the neighboring states; in this situation they thought

all further resistance was useless, they therefore readily accepted of the pleasing offers, in hopes they would have been suffered to remain peaceably and quietly at home with their families, and to have gone on with their business undisturbed, as before; but how great was their astonishment three days afterwards, on the third of June, to see a proclamation from the British commander [See appendix, note 21.] setting aside all paroles given to prisoners not taken by capitulation, and who were not in confinement at the surrender of Charlestown, ' To be null and void ' after the twentieth of the same month; and the ' holders of them were called upon to resume the ' characters of British subjects, and to take an active ' part in forwarding military operations, or to be ' considered as rebels against his majesty's govern- ' ment.' This violation of all faith, this ill-grounded policy, enrolled into the American service, thousands of their citizens, who had indulged themselves with the pleasing hopes of remaining neuter until the end of the war; but they said, ' if we must fight let it be on the side of America, our friends and countrymen.' A great many exchanged their paroles for protections, and remained with the British: some few of them who were warm friends to the British government, prepared an address, [See appendix, note 22.] and carried it about town, to be signed by the inhabitants; many at first refused, some were persuaded, and others threatened that if they did not sign, they would be informed against : this to the timid was very alarming, lest they should be put in the provost, or otherwise ill treated, which obliged two-hundred and ten of the inhabitants to sign the address. In answer to their address they were promised the privileges and protection of British subjects, on subscribing a test oath to support the royal government.

THE capitulation of Charlestown was of very little benefit to the citizens who came under that compact, especially those who refused to sign the address ; the British found so many ways of evading or violating that contract, that it was rendered almost useless to the citizens ; but they were a little more cautious with the continental officers.

IF one or two citizens, in walking the streets of Charlestown, should happen to look at a British officer and smile, they were sure to be abused and perhaps sent to the provost.

GEN. Lincoln, during the siege of Charlestown, continued writing to Congress, to Virginia, and North Carolina, for reinforcements, representing the weak state of his army, and the dangerous situation that Carolina was then in, until we were completely invested ; at length Congress determined that a considerable reinforcement from their main army should be sent ; and Major Gen. Baron de Kalb with fourteen hundred continental troops of the Delaware and Maryland lines were ordered to the southward; they marched from head-quarters at Morristown in New-Jersey on the 16th April, 1780; embarked at the head of Elk in May, and landed soon at Petersburgh in Virginia, and from thence proceeded by land through the country towards South Carolina. Virginia made great exertions to expedite the movements of this little army. The South part of North Carolina being so much exhausted of provisions by the great bodies of militia armies of whigs and tories that had been moving about, that it was almost impossible, when Baron de Kalb got into that part of the country in July, to support his army; for many days they lived upon stewed peaches; there was scarcely food enough left to support the unhappy women and children that were obliged to stay at home.

In a letter from Baron de Kalb to Chevalier De la Luzerne, minister from France in Philadelphia; he says ' You may judge of the virtues of our small ar-
' my, from the following fact: we for several days
' lived on nothing but peaches; and I have not heard
' of a complaint: there has been no desertion.'

The State of North Carolina ordered a large detachment of their militia to take the field and to be relieved every three months: this army was intended to raise the siege of Charlestown, but too late for that purpose : they were, however, a very great check to the British and stopped their rapid progress over North and South Carolina. Upon Colonel Tarleton's near approach with his detachment to Mulinburgh county, Gen. Rutherford took the field, and in three days raised fifteen hundred men, which obliged Col. Tarleton immediately to retreat, and the militia returned to their homes : soon after, Lord Rawdon took post at Waxsaws : General Rutherford again raised a body of militia of eight-hundred men, and obliged his lordship to retreat.

THE North Carolinians were always active and ready to defend their country, but they were badly provided with suitable armor for defence ; they were obliged to turn their implements of husbandry, into those of war, by hammering up their scythes and sickles, and forming them into swords and spears : powder and lead was also scarce with them.

THE war was now carried from the lower, to the upper part of South Carolina, and into North Carolina, and the friends of independence were obliged to retreat before them into North Carolina : among the most conspicuous and useful of these, was Colonel Sumpter, who had formerly commanded the fifth South Carolina continental regiment ; a brave and active officer, and well acquainted with the interior parts of North and South Carolina ; the exiles from South Carolina joined their friends in North

Carolina, and made choice of Colonel Sumpter to command them : at the head of this small body of republicans, he returned into South Carolina, almost without arms or ammunition, and no stores to supply their wants, and when most of the inhabitants had given up the idea of supporting their independence : in this situation did he oppose himself to the victorious British army : they sometimes began an action with not more than three rounds per man, and were obliged to wait to be supplied with more, by the fall of their friends or enemies in battle ; when they proved victorious, they supplied themselves with arms and ammunition, from the killed and wounded.

At this sudden irruption of Americans into South Carolina, the British were greatly astonished, as all military operations on the part of America had ceased for upwards of six weeks, and they had represented, ' That the inhabitants from every quarter, ' had repaired to the detachments of the royal ar- ' my, and to the garrison of Charlestown, to declare ' their allegiance to the king, and to offer their ser- ' vices in arms, to support his government ; and in ' many instances they had brought in prisoners, their ' former oppressors and leaders : and that there ' were very few men in South Carolina that were ' not either their prisoners, or in arms with them.'

Lord Rawdon, who commanded at Camden, was

exceedingly irritated, vexed and disappointed, to
find the Americans were again embodying and making head against the British troops in South Carolina, and encouraging the British troops to desert, and
conceal themselves amongst the inhabitants: he
wrote the following letter.

'To H. RUGELY, MAJOR OF BRITISH MILITIA.

'NEAR THEIR HEAD-QUARTERS AT CAMDEN.

'SIR,

'So many deserters from this army have passed
'with impunity through the districts which are un-
'der your direction, that I must necessarily suspect
'the inhabitants to have connived at, if not facilita-
'ted their escape. If attachment to their sovereign
'will not move the country people to check a crime
'so detrimental to his service, it must be my care
'to urge them to their duty as good subjects, by
'useing invariable severity towards every one who
'shall show so criminal a neglect of the public in-
'terest. I am, therefore sir, to request of you that
'you signify to all within the limits of your com-
'mand my firm determination in this case: if any
'person shall meet a soldier straggling without a
'written pass, beyond the picquets, and shall not do
'his utmost to secure him, or shall not spread an alarm
'for that purpose, or if any person shall give shelter
'to soldiers straggling as above mentioned, or shall

' serve them as a guide, or shall furnish them with
' passes or any other assistance ; the person so of-
' fending, may assure themselves of rigorous pu-
' nishment, either by whipping, imprisonment or by
' being sent to serve his majesty in the West-Indies,
' according as I shall think the degree of criminality
' may require. I have ordered that every soldier
' who passes the picquets, shall submit himself to be
' examined by any of the militia who have a suspi-
' cion of him : if a soldier, therefore, attempts to es-
' cape, when ordered by a militiaman to stop, he is
' immediately to be fired upon as a deserter...single
' men of the light horse need not be examined, as
' they may be often sent alone upon expresses : nor
' is any party of infantry, with a non-commissioned
' officer at the head of it, to be stopped. I will give
' the inhabitants ten guineas for the head of any deser-
' ter belonging to the volunteers of Ireland ; and five
' guineas only, if they bring him in alive : they
' likewise will be rewarded, though not to that amount,
' for such deserters as they may procure, belonging
' to any other regiment. I am confident that you
' will encourage the country people to be more ac-
' tive in this respect.

' I am, sir,

' With much esteem, &c.

(Signed,)   ' RAWDON.'

LORD Rawdon on the report of the American army approaching, ordered all the inhabitants, in, and about Camden, to take up arms and join the British troops, and all those who refused were confined in a jail, upwards of one hundred and sixty persons were imprisoned; twenty or thirty of the most respectable citizens were put in irons, in close confinement.

COLONEL Sumpter's little party soon increased their number to one hundred and thirty-three, with these few he attacked a detachment of British troops and a large body of Tories, on the twelfth of July, 1780, at William's plantation, in Ninety-six district, commanded by Captain Huck; they were posted in a lane, both ends of which, was entered by the Americans at the same time. Colonel Ferguson of the British militia, Captain Huck, and several others were killed. Captain Huck did every thing he could to distress the inhabitants, by insult and injury; his profanity shocked them to a great degree, he had a particular hatred to the presbyterians, he burnt their meetings and dwelling houses, and destroyed their property, wherever he could find it; he was often heard to say, 'that God Almighty was 'turned rebel, but that if there were twenty Gods on 'their side, they should all be conquered.'

ON the twentieth of June, 1780, a large body of the Tories collected together at Rumsour's, in North

Carolina, under Colonel Moore, contrary to the advice of Lord Cornwallis, who had recommended to them to remain quiet till he had advanced into their settlements. General Rutherford marched against the insurgents, but was so short of lead, that he could arm only three hundred men ; he detached Colonel Lock with these, twenty-five miles, to discover the motions of the enemy, whilst he remained behind, in expectation of lead from the mines of Virginia. Colonel Lock, though greatly inferior to the enemy, was under the necessity of attacking them, which was done with great spirit and resolution. Captain Falls, with a party of horse, charged the enemy and threw them into great confusion, Colonel Lock had twenty-two of his men killed and wounded, Captain Falls and five other officers were killed; Colonel Moore proposed to Colonel Lock, to cease from hostilities for an hour, which was agreed to ; in the mean time Colonel Moore went off with his party. Soon after this party of Tories were dispersed, General Rutherford received information that Colonel Bryan of Rowan county, was at the head of another party, who were marching to join the British ; he went in pursuit of them, but they effected their purpose by marching down the east side of the Yadkin-river, and joined them at Camden. About this time, the extremities of North and South Carolina adjoining each other, were in great commotions ; large armed parties of

Whigs and Tories were continually moving about and frequently falling in with each other and fighting severe battles, so that the two countries were in one general confusion; and the animosities between the two parties were carried to great lengths; to enumerate the cruelties which were exercised upon each other would fill a volume of themselves. The British detachments that were marching through these two countries were not backward in their severities against the unhappy citizens, many of whom they hung up or otherwise cruelly treated or put to death in a wanton manner; in short the war was carried on with great barbarity: this treatment of the Americans by the British and their adherents, soon increased Gen. Sumpter's number to six-hundred: with these on the 30th of July, he made a spirited attack on a British post at Rocky-mount, but failed of success: however, in eight days after he made a successful attack on the post at Hanging-rock, which was defended by the Prince of Wales' regiment, and a large body of Tories under Col. Bryan: in this attack the Prince of Wales' regiment suffered exceedingly, and the Tories were intirely routed and dispersed: when Gen. Sumpter began this attack, he had not more than ten rounds of ball to a man; but before the action was over, he was amply supplied with arms and ammunition from the British and Tories that fell in the beginning.

It was now well known that an American army was marching from the northward for the relief of the southern states; this intelligence gave the Americans great spirits; they began to rear their heads and look forward to a recovery of their country: they first embodied in small parties, and chose their officers; with these they took the field, and often attacked the detachments of the British army that were moving about, and they were a very great check to the Tories, who were collecting to join the British. Col. Williams of Ninety-six district, a brave and active officer, and warm in the American cause, raised a large body of men, and frequently attacked the British parties. On the 18th of August, 1780, he attacked a large party of British and Tories at Musgrove's-mills on Enoree river, under the command of Col. Innis of the South Carolina royalists, whom he defeated; and wounded Col. Innis.

In the summer of 1780, a report prevailed which was much talked of among the officers, prisoners at Haddrell's-point, that Congress had given up the idea of contending any longer for the southern states, and that a peace was to be made with Great Britain, and that the two southern states were to be ceded to her: this gave some uneasiness for a time, until we got information of Congress having entered into the following resolve.

‘ In Congress, June 25th, 1780.

‘ Whereas it has been reported, in order to se-
‘ duce the states of North and South Carolina and
‘ Georgia, from their allegiance to these United
‘ States, that a treaty of peace, between America and
‘ Great Britain was about to take place, in which
‘ those two states would be ceded to Great Britain.
‘ Resolved unanimously, that the said report is in-
‘ sidious, and utterly void of foundation, that this
‘ confederacy is most sacredly pledged to support
‘ the liberty and independence of every one of its
‘ members, and in a firm reliance on the divine bles-
‘ sing, will unremittingly persevere in their exertions
‘ for the establishment of the same, and for the re-
‘ covery and preservation of any and every part of
‘ these United States that has been or may hereafter
‘ be invaded or possessed by the common enemy.’

‘ Extracts from the minutes.

‘ Charles Thomson, Sec’ry.’

On the twenty-seventh of July, 1780, General
Gates arrived from the northward, with orders from
Congress, to take the command of the continental
troops in North Carolina, hitherto commanded by
Major General Baron De Kalb. General Gates being a soldier of great reputation, and having had the
good fortune to capture General Burgoyne and his
army, much was expected from his military abilities;

it was not doubted that he would soon oblige the British to break up all their posts and retire into Charlestown, and that we should have possession of the whole country again. On the fourth of August, General Gates issued a proclamation which was very much approved of by the inhabitants. [See appendix, note 23.]

GENERAL Marion, who was lieutenant colonel commandant of the second South Carolina continental regiment, was in Charlestown at the beginning of the siege by Sir Henry Clinton, by some accident sprained his ancle, which rendered him unfit for service ; he therefore came under that general order issued by General Lincoln, ' That all supernumerary officers, ' and all officers who were unfit for duty, must quit ' the garrison and retire into the country.' Fortunately for Carolina he went out, and when he went, was so lame that he was obliged to sculk about from house to house among his friends, and sometimes hide in the bushes until he grew better ; he then crept out by degrees, and began to collect a few friends ; and when he got ten or twelve together he ventured out, and upon hearing of General Gates' army, he moved on and joined them: after the defeat of General Gates, he was obliged to quit the state, and go into North Carolina for a few days ; when he returned, he had about seventy volunteer militia with him, but most of them quite unarmed ;

he took the saws from the mills, and set the smiths to work, to turn them into horsemen's swords ; he frequently engaged when he had only three or four rounds to a man ; his little party would sometimes be reduced to five and twenty men...as is common with the militia, they grow tired, and have a pretence to go home, or sometimes without any pretence at all : he was very troublesome to Major Wemys, who had taken post on Peedee with a detachment of British troops, and had burned a number of the inhabitants houses on Peedee, Black-river and Lynch's-creek, supposing the owners had joined General Marion. The British by their impolitic conduct, recruited General Marion's little party very fast, who always lay in the woods, in the most unfrequented places, with nothing but their blanket to cover themselves ; he had his scouts out constantly, and when they brought him intelligence (which they frequently did) of any small party of the enemy, or any escorts with stores, he sallied out, and was sure to have them : Lord Cornwallis was heard to say, ' That he would give a good deal to have him taken.' And always praised him, as a good partisan officer.*

* General Marion and myself, entered the field of Mars together, in an expedition against the Cherokee Indians, under the command of Colonel James Grant, in 1761 ; when I had the honor to command a light infantry company, in a provincial regiment ; he was my first lieutenant...he was an active, brave and hardy soldier, and an excellent partisan officer.

EARLY in August, General Marion was detached
by General Gates with fifteen or twenty men, down
the country towards Georgetown, to inform the
well affected inhabitants of his arrival in South Carolina, with a respectable and well appointed army,
and to shew them his proclamation, calling upon
them to join the American army: he was ordered
to destroy all the boats, flats and crafts of every
kind which he could find, quite down to the sea, to
prevent the enemy's army at Camden, from escaping to Charlestown : on General Marion's arrival
near Georgetown, he was joined by Colonel Peter
Horry and Captain Logan of the continental line,
and some militia officers: the morning after General Gates' defeat, which General Marion knew
nothing of for several days, nor until he had surprised at Sumpter's old field, near Nelson's-ferry, a
captain and forty British soldiers, on their way to
Charlestown, escorting thirty American soldiers,
prisoners (part of General Gates' army) to Charlestown : at this time Marion had but thirty militia with
him, with these he released the prisoners, and retreated to Briton's-neck, on Peedee-river, to be farther
from the enemy, and in hopes of being joined by
more of the militia, and to get the released prisoners
armed, but they absolutely refused to stay any longer with him : so gloomy were American affairs
at this time that very few would join him ; and the

Tories were now gathering from all quarters; the nearest party of them were on little Peedee, under Captain Barfield; these were surprised in their camp, some killed, wounded and taken prisoners, with little or no loss to the Americans, and Marion again returned to Briton's-neck: the enemy beginning to perceive that he would be very troublesome to them, determined upon a plan to drive him off: two parties were sent after him from Santee and Georgetown, and Tarleton it was said, was on his way from Camden, on the same errand: on receiving information that the two first parties were very near, Marion with about fifty men, retreated to Whitemarsh, in North Carolina; the enemy did not pursue far, which gave Marion a few days to reflect and project further operations; he was informed that a number of Tories had assembled at Black-mingo, he returned into South Carolina, and attacked them at night, and both parties suffered considerably, Captain Logan and others were killed; the enemy were routed, and many escaped and got into Georgetown much terrified: soon after this, another party of Tories was heard of, under Colonel Tines; these were completely surprised in their camp; many were killed and wounded; their colonel and two other officers taken prisoners; when they were fired upon, they could not but think it was their own men in diversion; several were killed with cards in their hands.

THE enemy now began to see Marion's importance, and that now was the time to force him out of
the country : General Gates defeated and gone, and
Sumpter at so great a distance, either at Ninety-six
or Mecklenburgh, North Carolina, that he could
receive no assistance, a plan was concerted in Charlestown, which seemed to insure success ; it was made
no secret of, Col. Watson was sent from Charlestown with a detachment, and on his way to Marion
was joined by another, under Colonel Small : they
came up with the General a little below Wibo-swamp,
on Santee-river, where a skirmish ensued ; a second
took place at the lower bridge, on Black-river, and
a third at Sampit bridge. Colonel Watson got into
Georgetown very much harrassed and fatigued :
Colonel Small after the first skirmish, left Colonel
Watson near Wibo, and marched with his detachment to Camden. Colonel Peter Horry had a detachment of eighty picked men, all well mounted,
half riflemen, to hang on the enemy and harrass them
all in his power; he frequently ambuscaded them,
made many feints and false charges on the line,
fired on their advance guards, centinels and videts,
and at night gave them constant alarms. Colonel
Watson was so perplexed and vexed, that he com-

plained, and said it was unprecedented in war...* that the Americans dared not come to battle.

GENERAL Marion retired to Lynch's-creek, and was soon informed that Colonel Watson and a party of Tories were advancing fast upon him, the first in his rear, the second on his right, and that Colonel Doyle from Camden was in his front, three detachments from different directions, and all point ed towards Marion, with an intention to drive him out of the country. They knew he could get no support or assistance, and that he had but very few men with him: General Marion made known his situation to Colonel Peter Horry, and said if the enemy did drive him out of the country, he was determined to retire over the mountains, with as many as would follow him, and from time to time would gather a party and sally down the country, and do them as much injury as he could, until he was killed or they had left the country, he would not leave off warring against them: he said he was afraid that if he should be hard pushed, that many of his men would not leave their families and fly with him. General Marion desired Colonel Peter Horry to call the field-officers together privately, and lay the circumstances of their situation, fully before them ; to

* It was a little extraordinary, that Colonel Watson, who was said to be a good partisan officer, should complain of this mode of harrassing a party.

acquaint them of his determination, and to have their's, in order that he might know how far he could rely on them : he recommended that the officers should unite with him as a band of brother officers ; and that each should most solemnly pledge to the other, his sacred word and honor, to be faithful, and never submit to the enemy but with their lives.

THE field-officers then in camp, were Colonel Peter Horry, Hugh Horry, James Postell and Irvin: Majors, James Baxter and Swinton ; these met and resolved according to the wishes of the general, and without hesitation, said they were bound in honor to adhere to his fortune, whether good or bad ; and they all declared they would be faithful to each other, and would carry on the war as the general should direct: these determinations being made at a time when there was the greatest prospect of distress, was truly honorable to themselves and to their country. On General Marion's being acquainted with their resolutions, he said ' he was satisfied, and that one of the enemy's detachments should feel his force :' and in about an hour, he decamped, crossed Lynch's creek, and marched up Peedee to meet Col. Doyle's detachment; preferring to attack this party because if he should be defeated he had the country open for a retreat : the next morning arriving at a house on the road, he was informed that Colonel Doyle had encamped there that night, and that he had received an express from

Camden, informing him that General Greene was advancing fast towards that post, that he marched off before day in great haste for Camden, so fast that it was impossible for Marion to overtake him; he pursued for several hours, but in vain; he then wheeled about to look for Colonel Watson, said to be on little Peedee, but he had also received an express the same night as Colonel Doyle had, with the same information; and had immediately destroyed all his stores, waggons, carts, and every species of heavy baggage, and decamped early the next morning, and crossed little Peedee: Marion judging they would cross over to Georgetown and Santee, pushed on for Manigault's-ferry, to intercept them on their way to Camden: Watson crossed as Marion got to Manigault's-ferry, on the south side; he was informed that Watson had just crossed over to the north side, a few miles above, and pushing fast for Camden, he got safe in, without any further loss: the scene was now reversed; instead of Watson and Doyle pushing Marion out of the country, he faces about and pursues them towards Camden; their marches were too rapid for them to be overtaken.

GENERAL Marion in his pursuit of Watson, was joined by Captain Conyers, with a small party of dragoons, who informed him that he was sent by Colonel Lee, to let him know that he was on his way to join him, and that General Greene was actually advancing towards Camden: Marion retired to Snow's-Island, where he was joined by Colonel Lee with his legion, who proposed to the general, a plan to surprise the garrison at Georgetown, by night; Marion agreed to it, and allowed the colonel wholly to project and carry into execution.

JANUARY 25th, 1781, General Marion with his brigade of militia, retired to Snow's-Island, and was there joined by Colonel Lee with his legion. Colonel Lee formed a plan to surprise Georgetown, which was garrisoned with about three hundred regular troops, and some militia, under the command of Colonel Campbell: Captain Carnes and Captain Rudolph, with about ninety (mostly of Lee's infantry) were sent down from Snow's-Island, about forty miles from Georgetown, in a large boat, to drop down the river, towards the town, while General Marion and Colonel Lee were to have come down with the main body by land: just before day-break, on the second day, Captain Carnes with his party, landed at Mitchell's-point, about a quarter of a mile to the east of the town; they landed and marched on a bank through the rice field, and was in the town a little before day-light; the British knew nothing of them, until they were alarmed by a few popping shots, and then, very great confusion ensued; the officers running about for the men, and the men for the officers; in this hurry and confu-

sion, the guides got so alarmed and frightened, that
they lost their way to the fort, where the main body
of the British were quartered, or else the surprise
would have been complete. A party went to Colonel Campbell's quarters, took him out of bed, and
carried him of, without any other clothes than his
shirt, to about a quarter of a mile on the back of the
town, through bushes and briers ; he begged and
intreated so much that they would allow him to go
back and be paroled to Charlestown ; after a little
time, they had compassion upon him, and suffered
him to go back upon parole : by this time the enemy began to embody, and the firing was heard from
different parts of the town, and General Marion and
Colonel Lee not entering the town at the same time,
Captains Carnes and Rudolph thought it adviseable
to retreat : had our guides not missed their way to
the fort, it is more than probable this little detachment would have taken the whole garrison prisoners ;
some few men were killed on both sides. The cavalry under General Marion and Colonel Lee, did
not arrive, and as they met with a breast-work not
easily to be mounted, they proceeded no further, particularly, as the infantry had already retreated.

GENERAL Gates takes the command of the continental troops, and is joined by the North Carolina
militia, at the cross roads, forty-five miles from Camden, on the tenth of August, 1780, and was joined

by General Stevens on the fifteenth, with a brigade of Virginia militia: the American army now amounted to three thousand six hundred and sixty-three, and not more than nine hundred continental infantry and seventy cavalry; with this army General Gates moved towards Camden, being possessed with a belief that the British intended, and were preparing to retreat; he therefore was determined to be near at hand, to prevent them, or to be close in their rear, to harrass them as much as possible.

LORD Rawdon who commanded at Camden, sent an express to Lord Cornwallis in Charlestown, to inform him of the American army approaching: Lord Cornwallis immediately sets out, and arrives at Camden on the thirteenth of August, and takes the command of the army, and at the same time, four companies of light troops arrived form Ninety-six; they took three American soldiers, who informed that General Gates had given orders to move from Rugley's, to attack next morning: at ten o'clock, P. M. the British moved from their ground, and a little after two o'clock, the advance of the British charged the advance of the Americans, and a firing commenced; after some time they both retreated to their main bodies.

LORD Cornwallis' army consisted of seventeen hundred infantry and three hundred cavalry; on the night of the fifteenth he marched out to attack the

American army ; at the same time General Gates put his army in motion, to take a position on Sander's-creek.

THE American army was drawn up on the sixteenth of August, in the following order : the second Maryland brigade, commanded by Brigadier General Gist, on the right of the line, flanked by a morass ; the Virginia militia commanded by Brigadier General Stevens, on the left, flanked by the North Carolina militia, light infantry, and a morass ; and the North Carolina militia, commanded by Major General Caswell, in the centre : the artillery was posted in the intervals of the brigades ; Major General Baron de Kalb commanded on the right of the line ; Brigadier General Smallwood was posted as a corps-de-reserve, two or three hundred yards in the rear of the whole : General Sumpter was posted with a strong body (one hundred continentals, seven hundred militia and two field-pieces) on the opposite side of the Wateree-river, to prevent their retreat that way : in the morning a general engagement took place : the British appeared at about two hundred yards distant, all drawn up in front of the North Carolina troops ; the artillery was ordered to fire ; and General Stevens to attack the column which was displayed on the right ; he marched up with great bravery, and advanced with his brigade in good order, within fifty paces of the enemy, who were also advancing) and called out to his men, ' My brave fellows, you have bayonets as well as they ; we'll charge them.' At that moment the British infantry charged bayonet with a shout : the Virginians threw down their arms, and run off as fast as possible ; the North Carolina militia followed their example, except a few of General Gregory's brigade, who halted a little longer ; a part of Colonel Dixon's brigade fired a few rounds ; but the greatest part of the militia run off, without firing a single shot : this dastardly behavior of the militia, left the continentals to be attacked by the whole British infantry and cavalry : they fought bravely ; never did men behave better than the continentals ; and a great fire of musketry was kept up on both sides, with great obstinacy ; at length, Lord Cornwallis ordered his cavalry to charge, which soon put an end to the contest : General Gates endeavored to rally some of the militia, to cover the retreat of the continentals, but in vain. The cavalry pursued the fugitive militia, upwards of twenty-five miles, and made a dreadful slaughter among them ; the road on which they fled, was strewed with arms, baggage, the sick, wounded and dead ; the whole of the baggage which was ordered on the day before, fell into the enemy's hands, and eight field-pieces.

GENERAL Sumpter who was on the south side of the

Wateree until the sixteenth, and had been fortunate enough to take a small fort and a strong detachment going up with stores for the British troops at Camden when he heard of General Gates' defeat, he was retreating with his prisoners and captured stores up the river. Lord Cornwallis detached Colonel Tarleton with his legion and a body of infantry after him; he was overtaken on the eighteenth, on Fishing-creek; the British horse was in their camp before they knew, or had heard any thing of their being near them; it was a complete surprise, the greatest part of his troops fled to the river, some were killed and wounded, and others taken; the whole of his party were dispersed, and the British prisoners, about three hundred, were retaken, and all the stores conducted to Camden: Colonel Sumpter lost all his artillery.

THIS victory over General Gates, and the surprise of General Sumpter, occasioned great rejoicings and congratulations in Charlestown: [See appendix, note 24.] the troops were turned out and fired a fue de joye, whilst the poor prisoners were quite dispirited at the total defeat of their army; they lost all hopes of ever recovering their country again: most of the officers who were taken at Camden and Fishing-creek, were sent to Haddrell's-point, upon parole with the officers taken in Charlestown, which gave us an opportunity of knowing many particulars relative to these two unfortunate affairs.

THE situation of America in the southern department was truly deplorable, their army dispersed and taken. Lord Cornwalls, when he joined his army at Camden, found himself in a critical situation, and very difficult to retreat to Charlestown; he had been on the east side of Wateree-river, with but very few boats to cross his troops, and General Sumpter on the opposite side with six or seven hundred men to oppose his passage, and General Gates with three thousand six hundred men, only eight miles distant: Lord Cornwallis knowing the number of General Gates' army, and that they were mostly composed of militia, determined to risk a battle, and he, unfortunately for our cause, gained a complete victory.

GENERAL Marion always gave strict orders to his men, that there should be no waste of the inhabitants property, and no plundering: he was so conscious of his not having injured any one, that when a bill was brought before the legislature after the war, to indemnify the officers and to prevent vexatious suits against them, his name was inserted in the bill; upon which (being a member of the house) rose from his seat, and moved 'that his name should be struck out; 'that if he had injured any person he was willing to 'make them compensation.'

ABOUT this time General Sumpter's and Marion's

parties, and the inhabitants of the New Acquisition,* were almost the only American force to oppose the British troops in South Carolina : the inhabitants of the New Acquisition had never been made prisoners, neither did they take protection ; it was from them that General Sumpter recruited many of his men ; and after his defeat on the 10th of August, they went back to their settlements, and kept in small parties, for their own security: some of them joined Major Davie, who commanded fifty or sixty volunteers equiped as dragoons.

Soon after General Gates' defeat, the hot weather and the unhealthy season came on, which put an end to any further military operations by the British; nay, they had no force to oppose them ; the American army was quite broke up and dispersed ; they therefore had nothing to fear. Colonel Ferguson, an experienced, brave, active partisan officer, made an excursion near the mountains, with a few regular troops, in hopes to have recruited a large number of men for Lord Cornwallis' army, and to have

....

* The New Acquisition was a tract of country taken from North Carolina in 1772 ; the line between the two states had been long disputed, till by an order of the king and council, it was run, beginning at the corner tree, on the Salisbury road, and which took fourteen miles of the south part of North Carolina into South Carolina, and run parallel with the old line sixty-five miles.

trained and fitted them for the field; with these he was to have joined the main army, and at a proper season, to assist in reducing North Carolina. They continued some time near the western mountain, in hopes of intercepting Colonel Clark, on his return from Georgia.

COLONEL Clark, in September, 1780, raised a body of riflemen, and marched through the upper part of South Carolina, on his way to Georgia. The inhabitants of Ninety-six endeavored to dissuade him from his design of attacking the British post at Augusta; he persisted however, and made an attempt in which he failed, and was obliged to make a precipitate retreat, and leave the country altogether. This ill-timed attempt was of very great injury to the inhabitants about Augusta: Colonel Brown, who commanded there, treated the people with the greatest severity. Many of those who had joined Colonel Clark, and were supposed to have favored his design, were obliged to resume their arms for their own security, and join the Americans.

THE British now began to exercise their cruelties. In a few days after General Gates' defeat, Lord Cornwallis issued the following inhuman order, by which he let loose the dogs of war upon the poor inhabitants, and Tarleton, with his blood hounds, excelled in brutality. Unfortunate men, who were found peaceably and quietly at their homes, were cut to pieces: others taken out of the gaols and hung up without being questioned, or even having a hearing, and every species of cruelty was exercised throughout the country.

EXTRACT OF A LETTER FROM GOVERNOR RUTLEDGE, TO THE DELEGATES IN CONGRESS FROM SOUTH CAROLINA, DATED THE 8th OF DECEMBER, 1780.

' IT is really melancholy to see the desolate con-
' dition of Mr. Hill's plantation in the New Acquisi-
' tion; all his fine iron-works, mills, dwelling-houses,
' and buildings of every kind, even his negro-houses,
' reduced to ashes; and his wife and children in a
' little log hut. I was shocked to see the ragged,
' shabby condition of our brave and virtuous men,
' who would not remain in the power of the enemy,
' but have taken to arms. This, however, is but a
' faint description of the sufferings of our country;
' for it is beyond a doubt, the enemy have hanged
' many of our people, who from fear, and the im-
' practicability of removing, had given paroles, and
' from attachment to our side, joined it. Nay, Tarle-
' ton has since the action at Black-stocks, hung one
' Johnson, a magistrate of respectable character:
' they have also burnt a prodigious number of houses,
' and turned a vast many women, formerly of affluent
' and easy fortunes, with their children, almost naked
' into the woods. Tarleton, at the house of General
' Richardson, exceeded his usual barbarity; for, hav-

' ing dined in his house, he not only burnt it after-
' wards, but having driven into the barns a number of
' cattle, hogs, and poultry, he consumed them, toge-
' ther with the barn and the corn in it, in one gene-
' ral blaze. This was done because he pretended to
' believe, that the poor old general was with the rebel
' army; though had he opened his grave before the
' door, he might have seen the contrary. Colonel
' Charles Cotesworth Pinckney's family was turned
' out of his house: in short, the enemy seem deter-
' mined, if they can, to break every man's spirit, if
' they cannot ruin him; engagements of capitulations
' and proclamations, are no security against their op-
' pressions and cruelties.'

———

EXTRACT FROM LORD CORNWALLIS' ORDERS.

' I HAVE given orders that the inhabitants of
' the province who have subscribed, and have taken
' part in this revolt, should be punished with the
' greatest rigor, and also those who will not turn out,
' that they may be imprisoned, and their property
' taken from them, or destroyed. I have likewise
' ordered that compensation be made out of their
' estates, to the persons who have been injured or
' oppressed by them. I have ordered in the most
' positive manner, that every militia man, who has
' borne arms with us, and afterwards joined the ene-
' my, shall be immediately hanged. I desire you

' will take the most rigorous measures to punish the
' rebels in the district in which you command, and
' that you obey in the strictest manner the directions
' I have given in this letter, relative to the inhabitants
' of this country.'

' CORNWALLIS.'

THESE orders were sent to every post throughout
the country.

THE unfortunate Colonel Hayne was executed under this general order, as appears by Colonel Balfour's letter to General Greene.

EXTRACT OF COLONEL BALFOUR'S LETTER.

' I COME now to that part which respects Colonel
' Hayne; on which head, I inform you, it took place
' by the joint order of Lord Rawdon and myself, in
' consequence of the most express directions from
' Lord Cornwallis to us, in regard to all those who
' shall be found in arms, after being at their own re-
' quest, received as British subjects, &c.'

COLONEL Hayne subscribed a declaration of allegiance to the king of Great Britain, but with an
express condition, that he never should be called
upon to take up arms against his country : notwithstanding, he was soon called upon to take up arms
and join the British, and upon refusal, he was

threatened with close confinement; this induced him to consider himself as released of engagements with the British; and he took the command of a regiment of his countrymen; he was soon after taken by a party of British horse, carried into town, and in a little time, executed without a trial.

THESE were horrid times for poor Carolina! The loss of property was now of no consideration, whilst the blood of their citizens was streaming down from every pore.

IT was generally said, and believed, that in the district of Ninety-six alone, fourteen hundred unhappy widows and orphans, were left to bemoan the fate of their unfortunate fathers, brothers and husbands killed in the war.

THE mountaineers, a bold and hardy people, began to be alarmed at Colonel Ferguson's near approach to them with a large body of men, and being informed that they plundered all the Whig inhabitants and treated them ill, (they had never yet felt the effects of the war,) they spread the alarm throughout their country, and immediately every man took up his rifle, blanket and knapsack, saddled his horse, and went in pursuit of Colonel Ferguson, leaving some few in their rear to drive the cattle after them; and some hunters were kept out to supply them more plentifully with provisions. They soon fell in with Ferguson's encampment at the foot of King's mount,* the whole of their force making nine hundred and ten men. Though Colonel Campbell was said to command, yet Colonels Cleveland, Shelby, Sevier, Williams, Laccy, and Brenan, each commanded their own men, and an excellent disposition they made, so that their attack would have disconcerted the most experienced officer with the bravest troops. Colonel Cleveland, in going round the mountain, discovered one of the enemy's pickets, upon which he addressed his men: ' My brave fellows, we have beat ' the Tories, and we can beat them again; they are all ' cowards : if they had the spirit of men, they would ' join their fellow-citizens in supporting the indepen- ' dence of their country. When you are engaged, ' you are not to wait for the word of command from ' me : I will show you by my example, how to fight ; ' I can undertake no more : every man must consider ' himself as an officer, and act from his own judg- ' ment. Fire as quick as you can, and stand your ' ground as long as you can : when you can do no ' better, get behind trees, or retreat ; but I beg you ' not to run quite off : if we are repulsed, let us make ' a point of returning and renewing the fight : per-

....

* This took its name from one King, who lived at the foot of the mount with his family : it is near the corner where the North and South Carolina line intersects the Cherokee Indians boundary line.

' haps we may have better luck in the second attempt
' than the first. If any of you are afraid, such shall
' have leave to retire, and they are requested imme-
' diately to take themselves off.'

WHEN the firing began, the Americans were
scattered about the woods....They soon collected and
were all animated ; every one acted as he pleased :
the picket in a little time gave way and were pursued up the mountain to their main body: Colonel
Ferguson upon hearing the firing made ready his
men ; and upon the near approach of the Americans,
ordered his men to charge bayonets, which obliged
them to retire. Immediately after, Colonel Shelby
came up with his party unexpectedly, and threw in a
heavy fire, which obliged Colonel Ferguson to face
about, and engage Colonel Shelby, who he drove
back with fixed bayonets ; at the same time, Colonel
Campbell came up from another quarter and renewed
the attack : Colonel Ferguson again faced about and
obliged him to fall back. By this time the men who
first begun and retreated, returned and made another
attack. In short, Colonel Ferguson was so beset
from every point by a number of active, brave, determined men, that it was impossible for him to retreat ;
and extricate himself, he could not ; and surrender,
he would not. At length he received his mortal
wound, and soon after, his party asked for quarters,
which was granted, and they surrendered themselves

prisoners of war: ten of the most notorious, who deserved death by the laws of their country, were immediately hung up, in retaliation for a number of Americans whom the British hung at Ninety-six, Camden, and other places. In this action, the enemy lost, in killed, wounded, and taken, upwards of eleven hundred men, amongst them nearly one hundred regulars. The Americans lost very few, but amongst them the brave Colonel Williams, of Ninety-six district, and Major Cronicle; and it is easily accounted for: the British made use mostly of the bayonet instead of firing their pieces. It was impossible for those heavy armed troops to come up with the strong, active mountaineers, who were dispersed about the woods. Had Colonel Ferguson dispersed his men (who were equally acquainted with bush-fighting) and fought his adversaries in their own way, he would have had a better chance to make a retreat.

This battle, as well as many others under Generals Sumpter, Marion and others, proves that the militia are brave men, and will fight if you let them come to action in their own way. There are very few instances when they have drawn up in line of battle, that they could be brought to stand and reserve their fire until the enemy came near enough. The charge of the bayonet they never could stand, and it can never be expected that undisciplined troops could stand so formidable an attack: witness the affairs of General Gates, at Camden, and General Greene, at Guilford Court-house. It was a maxim with the old king of Prussia, that young troops should begin to fire at two hundred yards distance; by which he said 'they ' became animated, and enveloped with smoke, saw ' no danger, and rushed on like old soldiers.'

THIS affair at King's mount revived the drooping spirits of the Americans, and at the same time it was a very severe blow to Lord Cornwallis, to lose a brave, experienced and confidential officer, and eleven hundred men, was a serious consideration to him; after which he was obliged to contract his plans into very narrow limits, and he lost all hopes of recruiting his army from that part of the country.

SOON after General Gates' defeat, when the hot weather and unhealthy season was at an end, Lord Cornwallis left a small guard at Camden, and marched off with the main body of his army, and took post at Charlotte, in North Carolina. This proved to be a very uneasy position for him, as Generals Sumner and Davison encamped in the neighborhood with a large body of North Carolina militia; and any detachments that were sent out by him were sure to be attacked and driven in, or taken. Major Davies' party was considerably increased by volunteers from the low country: he was very fortunate in frequently falling in with their foraging parties and convoys, and taking them. The riflemen would often creep near to their camp, and shoot down stragglers : none dared to venture far from their guards. At last, Lord Cornwallis found his situation so very disagreeable, and being apprehensive for the safety of his army, marched off, and took post at Winnsborough.

THE defeat of Colonel Ferguson, and the retreat of Lord Cornwallis to Winnsborough, encouraged the American militia to collect and repair to the camps of their respective commanders : their turning out again obliged them to submit to strict discipline, and fight bravely ; for, if they should be taken a second time, they were sure to be hanged : their only place of safety was with the army. The state of North Carolina put their militia who were under General Smallwood under martial law.

EARLY in October, General Gates detached General Morgan from Hillsborough, with three hundred Maryland and Delaware troops, and eighty dragoons, to aid and support the militia of Mecklenburgh and Rowan counties ; from this detachment, Colonel Washington made an excursion with a small force, to Colonel Rugely's fort, about fourteen miles from Camden ; in which he had collected one hundred and twelve of the British militia : upon the appearance of Colonel Washington's force before the fort, he immediately surrendered the whole of his party, to a pine-log which they had been accustomed to see every day, elevated a few feet from the ground by its branches; but upon seeing a military force about it, their fears converted it into a field-piece, ready to fire upon them; this occasioned their surrender.

AFTER General Sumpter's defeat on the eighteenth of August, he again collected a number of volunteers, and took the field; and immediately after, thirty of his former party rejoined him, and one hundred of the militia, at his request, also joined him at Sugar-creek, and the militia from all parts came in to him, and put themselves under his command. General Sumpter's active, martial spirit would not allow him to lay still, whilst the British parties were roving about the country unmolested, robbing and murdering the inhabitants.

ALTHOUGH there was no continental army in South Carolina for several months, it can never be said she was a conquered country, whilst Generals Sumpter and Marion each kept a body of men in the field, in support of her independence. General Sumpter's party increased every day; he ranged about Enoree, Broad and Tyger rivers; often changing his ground which he could do with great facility and expedition, as his men were all on horseback; by thus moving about from place to place, he frequently fell in with the enemy, and skirmished with them when they least expected it, which gave him a great advantage. On the twelfth of November, 1780, he had a smart action with Major Weyms,

who commanded a body of infantry and dragoons:
he defeated them, wounded their commanding officer and took him prisoner ; and although this man
had ordered some of the citizens to be hanged, and
attended personally at their execution, burnt many
of their houses, and destroyed their property in a
wanton and cruel manner, yet he was treated politely, and suffered to go to Charleston upon his
parole ! Soon after this affair with Major Weyms,
on the seventeenth of November, 1780, Colonel
Tarleton attacked General Sumpter at Black-stocks,
near Tyger-river, with a considerable body of infantry and cavalry: this was a serious and severe conflict, in which the British lost three officers and a
great number of men ; the Americans lost but few ;
General Sumpter was among the wounded, by which
unlucky accident, we lost the service, for several
months, of a brave, active, and experienced officer, and one on whom the militia had the greatest
reliance ; his spirited and prudent conduct in the
several actions which he had had with the British,
procured him the entire confidence of his country,
and the thanks of Congress. [See appendix, note 25.]

CONGRESS authorized and requested General
Washington to appoint an officer to command in the
Southern department, in consequence of which he
nominated Major General Greene, a native of Rhode-
Island : this appointment gave great satisfaction to

every one ; his military abilities, his active spirit, his great resources when reduced to difficulties in the field, his having been quarter-master general to the army under the commander in chief ; all these qualities combined together, rendered him a proper officer to collect and to organize an army that was broken up and dispersed. General Gates' army that had been defeated near Camden, on the sixteenth of August, in the latter end of the year 1780, moved down to Charlotte.

GENERAL Greene immediately set off to take the command of the Southern army, and arrived in Charlotte, on the second day of December, 1780 ; on the eighth, the returns made to him of the army, amounted to nine hundred and seventy continentals, and one thousand and thirteen militia, and a respectable cavalry, which was the security of his army ; most of the continentals were the remainder of the Maryland and Delaware lines that had been defeated near Camden on the sixteenth of August ; they had been four years in service, and were as good troops as any the British had ; they were half starved, unpaid, and ill clad, and had been in this situation for several months, yet there was no murmuring and no desertion : with this army General Greene took the field, against a superior victorious British army, and many other difficulties he had to encounter ; the clothing, the pay and feeding the troops, were almost impossible to be effected : that country had already been so pillaged and robbed, that scarcely enough was left for the inhabitants ; the difficulty he had in procuring provisions for his army at Charlotte, induced him to divide his force ; he accordingly detached General Morgan with a strong body, to the western extremities of South Carolina, and marched on the twentieth of December, with the main body to Hicks'-creek, opposite Cheraw-hill ; by this disposition, he covered the two extremities of the country, and gave encouragement to the militia in those parts, to embody and join his troops. It was a very wise measure in General Greene to divide his army and separate them so far ; whereas, if he had kept them together, they would have been an object for the British to strike at, but in this detached, distant situation, Lord Cornwallis could have no apprehensions from them, of any successful operations against his superior force.

THE British established a post at Ninety-six, which they kept possession of thirteen months : moderate measures were first pursued with the inhabitants ; but some of the most notorious, infamous villians, who called themselves king's men, by shirking, creeping, and mean submission, insinuated themselves into the confidence of the British so much, that they were appointed officers of the militia : they then began to shew their resentment and take revenge upon their former friends and neighbors, for mere private disputes which had subsisted between them, long preceding this time : they robbed, they plundered, and even murdered the whig inhabitants : and, although frequent applications were made for redress, no attention was paid to them : this ill treatment, this violent usage, soon alienated the new subjects from their allegiance and obliged them to break their engagements to the British, and to resume their arms, and join the Americans.

LIEUTENANT Colonel Nisbet Balfour, a proud, haughty Scot, carried his authority with a very high hand; his tyrannical, insolent disposition, treated the people as the most abject slaves; he even issued an order ‘ That every man who was not in his house by a certain day, should be subject to military execution.

THE inhabitants, tired of their ill treatment and great oppression, and finding no security for their lives or property, sincerely wished for an American force to come among them. At this critical time, General Morgan, on the twenty-fifth of December, appeared amongst them with a body of troops; and on the twenty-ninth, detached Lieutenant Colonel Washington with his own regiment and two hundred militia horse, under Lieutenant Colonel M'Call, and dispersed a body of Tories who were plundering the Whig militia : Colonel Washington fell in with them near Hammonds' store; he immediately charged, and routed them; many were killed, and about forty taken prisoners. The next day Colonel Washington detached an officer with a small body of infantry and cavalry to pursue the fugitives, and to surprise a fort about seventeen miles from Ninety-six, in which General Cunningham commanded about one hundred and fifty militia, in which was a great deal of plunder taken from the whig inhabitants, besides forage grain, and other provisions for the British army. The Americans, after destroying the fort and all the provisions which they could not carry off, joined Colonel Washington again. Lord Cornwallis could not bear the idea of suffering General Morgan to remain in that part of the country, and draw the militia over to the Americans: he therefore detached Colonel Tarleton with one thousand infantry and two hundred and fifty cavalry, the flower of his army, with two field pieces, to dispossess General Morgan and drive him quite off. General Morgan got intelligence that Colonel Tarleton was in pursuit of him. The Americans endeavored to avoid an action, and were retreating as fast as possible, because they knew that Tarleton's force was greatly superior to theirs. The British having left a part of their baggage about twenty-five miles in their rear, under a guard of one hundred men to follow, pursued the Americans so closely that they could not get off without the loss of their baggage, which they were unwilling to part with. The last and best account which General Morgan got of Tarleton, was by a horseman who left them at about fifteen miles distance; and before he could have got to General Morgan, they must have been within ten miles of him: he immediately called some of his officers together to consult upon what was best to be done, when it was determined to try the event of a battle, and if they were not successful, they could but retreat, and give up their baggage. At their near approach, on the seventeenth of January, 1781, General Morgan drew up his men on an open pine barren in the following order: (the ground equal to both) the militia of about four hundred men formed the first line under General Pickens; the continentals of about five hundred (two hundred of whom were six months men, very raw troops) formed the second line, commanded by Colonel Howard, about two hundred yards in the rear of the first. Colonel Washington, with about seventy-five continental cavalry, and forty-five mounted militia, with swords, under Colonel M'Call, in the rear of the whole: in this disposition did they wait to receive the enemy. Colonel Tarleton, as he drew near, saw the Americans already formed: he halted and formed his men; they then advanced, and threw in a heavy fire upon the militia. General Pickens had ordered his men to reserve their fire, till the enemy came within fifty yards, which they did, with great firmness and success; but they were soon obliged to give way and retreat behind the second line. The British immediately advanced upon the second line, who received them very warmly, and a heavy fire commenced between them: at length, the second line began to give way. Colonel Washington perceiving this, immediately rode up close to the rear of the second line with his cavalry, and spoke to Colonel Howard, ' that ' if he would rally his men, and charge the enemy's ' line, he would charge the cavalry that were got ' among our militia in the rear.' Colonel Washington, riding up so close to the rear of our second line, stopped the British for a moment, which gave time to Colonel Howard to rally his men, and charge with fixed bayonets. This soon obliged the British to fall back upon their second line, and our militia at the same time recovered themselves and charged, which threw them into the utmost confusion; and Colonel Washington charged the enemy's cavalry, who were cutting down our militia, and soon drove them off. At the moment that the enemy were in this general confusion, Colonel Howard called out to them, to ' lay down their arms, and they should have good ' quarters. Upon this, upwards of five hundred laid down their arms, and surrendered themselves prisoners. The first battalion of the seventy-first, and two companies of light infantry, laid down their arms.

Upwards of two hundred were left dead upon the field, besides a great number wounded; eight hundred stands of arms, two field pieces, and thirty-five baggage waggons fell into the Americans hands. Colonel Washington pursued the British cavalry twenty-five miles; at fifteen miles, he came to where they had burnt their baggage waggons. So great was the consternation in which the British infantry were, at seeing their cavalry gallop off, that, either from pique or panic, numbers of them never fired a gun. In this action, six hundred were made prisoners; so that this large detachment of one thousand infantry, and two hundred and fifty cavalry from Lord Cornwallis' army, was almost entirely lost; very few got off, except the cavalry, and those who were left in the rear with the waggons.

This victory was so complete, that the Americans were astonished at it themselves. The Americans had only twelve men killed, and sixty wounded.

This defeat of Colonel Tarleton's at the battle of the Cowpens, chagrined and disappointed the British officers and Tories in Charlestown exceedingly. I happened to be in Charlestown at the time when the news arrived. I saw them standing in the streets in small circles, talking over the affair with very grave faces. I knew the particulars as soon as they did. Governor Rutledge sent in a person on some pretence with a flag; but in fact, it was to inform the Ameri-

can prisoners of our success : the person informed
me of the whole affair, which I communicated to the
officers at Haddrell's-point, on my return in the evening. The news gave great joy, and put us all in high
spirits. Some of the old British officers who were
made prisoners, and paroled to Charlestown, when they
came down, were exceedingly angry indeed, at their
defeat, and were heard to say, ' that was the conse-
' quence of trusting such a command to a boy like
' Tarleton.' There is no doubt but Colonel Tarleton
was a brave man, and a good soldier, but in this affair
he displayed neither generalship nor courage, but
galloped off with his two hundred and fifty horse,
when pursued by about seventy continental cavalry,
and forty-five militia horse, and left his infantry to
be made prisoners of. Colonel Tarleton should have
requested a court of inquiry to have cleared himself
of any charge of misconduct in this affair, notwithstanding his aquittal in a letter from Lord Cornwallis
to him.

EXTRACT OF A LETTER FROM LORD CORNWALLIS
TO COLONEL TARLETON.

' You have forfeited no part of my esteem as
' an officer, by the unfortunate event of the action
' of the seventeenth instant ; the means you used to
' bring the enemy to action, were able and masterly,
' and must ever do you honor ; your disposition was

' unexceptionable ; the total misbehavior of the troops,
' could alone have deprived you of the glory which
' was justly your due.'

THE thanks of Congress were given to General
Morgan and his officers and men. [See appendix,
note 26.]

THIS great victory at the Cowpens* changed the
face of American affairs, and raised the drooping
spirits of her desponding friends. In two actions
soon after each other, the British lost about two
thousand men : that at King's mount, on the seventh
of October, and that at the Cowpens of the seventeenth of January, 1781 : the latter was of more serious consequence to Lord Cornwallis, because it
deprived him of nine hundred of his best troops.

COLONEL Tarleton having been successful in surprising unguarded troops, and the more unguarded
militia, Lord Cornwallis had no doubt of his being
a brave and active officer ; and having a mean opinion of our militia, from their behavior at Camden,
he was, no doubt, flattering himself, that he would
receive accounts from Colonel Tarleton, of his having defeated General Morgan ; while he was pos-

* An account of the affair at the Cowpens, I had from an
American officer of great veracity and high rank, and one that
was very conspicuous on that day in the action.

sessed of this idea, to his utter astonishment, he got the unwelcome and unexpected intelligence of Tarleton's complete overthrow. What must his feelings have been, when he received this account of his favorite officer, and one in whom he had the greatest opinion, in regard to his military abilities, and who had with him upwards of twelve hundred of the pick of his army, that he should be defeated by about one thousand men, and half of them militia? His chagrin and his disappointment must have been great indeed, upon this occasion.

LORD Cornwallis, in hopes of retrieving the credit of his troops, and recovering the prisoners taken at the Cowpens, left all his baggage, and took only a few waggons, sufficient to carry the necessaries for his army, and went in pursuit of General Morgan; his long and rapid marches, soon brought him near to General Morgan; they came to the Catawba-ford on the evening of that day when the Americans crossed it; and before the next morning, a heavy rain made it impassable, by which fortunate event, General Morgan pushed on with his detachment and prisoners, and got off, and Major Hyrne proceeded with the prisoners. The hasty marches after General Morgan, induced General Greene to retreat from Hicks'-creek, lest the British should get between the two divisions of his army. This affair of Colonel Tarleton's, at the Cowpens, hurried Lord Cornwallis into his plan of subjugating North Carolina : before it was ripened into maturity, Major Hyrne, had been previously dispatched to receive the prisoners, and conduct them to Virginia.

GENERAL Greene left the main body of his army under the command of General Huger, with orders to proceed and rendezvous at Guildford Court-house. To facilitate his march, all the heavy baggage was ordered to Hillsborough, and he, himself, rode one hundred and fifty miles, to join General Morgan on the Catawba-river, who was at some considerable distance before Lord Cornwallis, where he could best command the two divisions of his army.

AT this time, General Greene joined General Morgan (who intended to have gone over the mountains, to avoid Lord Cornwallis) and directed the movements of both divisions of his army, so as to form a junction at Guildford Court-house.

As soon as the Catawba-river was fordable, Lord Cornwallis prepared for crossing ; and, in order to deceive the Americans, made several feints at different fording places, and early in the morning, on the first of February, he crossed over, near M'Gowans, which was defended by a party of militia, under General Davidson ; the British crossed the river, under fire of the militia, with shouldered arms, and formed on the opposite bank ; they then engaged the militia, but General Davidson being killed early in the action, his men were dispirited, and made a precipitate retreat: the militia about the neighborhood, although General Greene was amongst them, could not be persuaded to take up arms: all the fords were abandoned, and the British crossed without any opposition.

THE British having possession of the two southern states, began to extend their views to the conquering Virginia and North Carolina; and the more easily to accomplish their plan, Major General Leslie was detached from New-York to Chesapeak, with three thousand men. On his arrival there, Lord Cornwallis ordered him to march immediately to Charleston, with fifteen hundred men, and then to join his army: one frigate and two sloops of war, took possession of Wilmington; and Major Craig was detached with three hundred men, to take post there: this position was extremely convenient for Lord Cornwallis' army, from whence he could draw supplies for his troops, without any risk.

ABOUT this time, a large detachment was sent from New-York, under Major General Phillips and Brigadier General Arnold, the American traitor, who the British gave, for his treachery, the rank of brigadier in their army.

Now the British and American generals began to display their military skill; the one in pursuing, the other in retreating; marching and counter-marching, and various manœuvres were made; the one endeavoring to join the main body of his army under General Huger, whilst the other endeavored to bring on an action before the junction could be made. General Greene crossed the Yadkin, partly in flats, and partly by fording, on the second and third day of February, and secured all the boats on the north side of the river. Lord Cornwallis was close in his rear, but the want of boats, and the rapid rise of the river, from the excessive rains, rendered his crossing impossible. This was the second narrow escape General Morgan's detachment had from Lord Cornwallis.

THE British, disappointed at not crossing the trading ford on the Yadkin, were obliged to march to the upper fords, which are generally passable. This gave time for the junction of the two divisions of the American army. Whilst Lord Cornwallis and General Greene were opposed to each other in North Carolina, General Marion was not idle in the lower parts of South Carolina; he had a small party of mounted militia, and his principal range was between Santee and Cooper-rivers; his camp was in Santee-swamp, sometimes on the south side, at other times on the north of the river; always in a safe position, where he never could be surprised; from whence he sent out small parties, and frequently intercepted the convoys of provisions. He perplexed the British very much, by moving his camp so often that they could not tell where to find him ; and to hunt for him in the swamps, they were afraid, lest they should fall into an ambuscade. On the twenty-ninth of January, he sent out two small parties, under the command of Major and Captain Postell, to cross Santee, and take different routs ; the first destroyed a great quantity of stores at Manigault's-ferry ; the latter did the same at some other place. Soon after this, he got information of a number of waggons under a convoy, near Monk's corner ; he immediately marched off, surprised them, and destroyed fourteen waggons loaded with stores, took forty prisoners, most of them regular troops, without losing a man.

GENERAL Greene and General Huger formed a junction at Guilford Court-house, on the seventeenth of February, 1781, yet their numbers were so inferior to the British, that General Greene could not venture an action : he called a council of his officers, and the result of their opinion was, that he ought to retire over the Dan, and avoid an action as much as possible, until he should be reinforced.

LORD Cornwallis, well knowing the inferiority of the American army, endeavored to cut off General Greene's retreat into Virginia ; and with this view, he kept possession of the upper country, where the rivers were fordable, which obliged General Greene to keep below where the rivers were impassable ; and being informed that there were not sufficient numbers of boats to cross his army, was in hopes of forcing General Greene to an action, before he could cross the river.

GENERAL Greene, before he began his retreat from Guilford Court-house, very wisely made two divisions of his army. The light troops were composed of Lee's legion, and Colonel Howard's battalion (compleated); the cavalry commanded by Colonel Washington, and a corps of Virginia riflemen under Major Campbell, the whole together making about seven hundred men. These he put under the command of Lieutenant Colonel Williams, commandant of the Maryland line: he began his march from Guilford Court-house on the tenth of February. The main army and light troops took different routs to avoid a pursuit. The next day, the latter had a reincountre with the advanced of the British army, in which an officer and six or seven men of Tarleton's legion were made prisoners, and some few killed. The light troops manœuvred and skirmished with the British in order to deceive Lord Cornwallis with respect to the route of the main army, which gave General Greene time to send off his baggage. Lord Cornwallis by his close pursuit obliged the American light troops on the fourteenth to retreat forty miles; and General Greene on that day crossed the whole of his army, artillery and baggage into Virginia, over Boyd's and

Irvin's ferries, on the Dan, without any interruption and waited himself the arrival of the light troops, and saw them all safe over that night. The pursuit of the British was so close that the van of their army arrived at the river, as the rear of the Americans had crossed.

The British were extremely mortified and disappointed at General Greene's escape into Virginia before they could have a blow at him: they had thought it impossible. However, Lord Cornwallis consoled himself with driving General Greene off, and having entire possession of North Carolina. He dared not to follow the American army into Virginia, as he knew that state would be too powerful for him. He contented himself with staying in North Carolina, and calling upon the loyal inhabitants to make good their promise of rising in favor of the British government; and to make it more convenient for them to join him, he retired to Hillsborough, where he raised the royal standard, and by proclamation called upon all his friends to join him. General Greene, in order to frustrate Lord Cornwallis' plan of embodying the Tories, re-crossed the Dan on the twenty-third, and detached General Pickens with some light troops, and Lee's legion in pursuit of Colonel Tarleton, who, with a considerable force of infantry and cavalry had crossed the Haw-river to encourage and support the Tories. Colonel Pyles, who, with three hundred and fifty Tories, was marching to join the British, fell in with the American party : having no suspicions of their re-crossing the Dan, he took them for Tarleton's detachment. While they were under this mistake, the Americans attacked them to great advantage, and even when they were cutting them down, they were protesting their attachment to the king. About the same time, a party who were going to join the British, fell in with Tarleton's detachment, who took them for rebels, and cut them to pieces, so that the poor Tories were between two fires. Lord Cornwallis continued several days in that part of the country were Pyles was defeated, in hopes of picking up some of the stragglers belonging to the loyalists; but in that he was disappointed : he said himself, that he could find none but ' timid ' friends, or inveterate enemies.'

GENERAL Greene's re-crossing the Dan-river into North Carolina, obliged Lord Cornwallis to quit Hillsborough, a few days after he had issued his proclamation, inviting his friends to join him at that place, and was very much disappointed at not being reinforced by the loyalists, from whom he had great expectations. A large body of them, had marched to join him, but upon hearing that the American army had returned into North Carolina, and knowing the fate of their friends under Colonel Pyles, they were terrified, and returned home, to wait a more favorable time.

GENERAL Greene's retreat into Virginia, awakened the people of that state, and they began to be alarmed for their own safety: a great number of the militia turned out, but very few of them were armed, and many of them declined going into North Carolina. A small brigade of four or five hundred men, commanded by General Stevens, was all the reinforcements General Greene could get from Virginia; with these he re-crossed the Dan. Although General Greene's army was greatly inferior to Lord Cornwallis' yet he was obliged to go into North Carolina, to be a check upon the Tories, and to prevent, as much as possible, the British from getting supplies for their army. General Greene kept as close as he could, without coming to an action, as his cavalry could always secure him a safe retreat. For two or three weeks the two armies were manœuvreing, in marching and counter-marching: Lord Cornwallis endeavoring to bring on an action, whilst General Greene as studiously avoided it, until his reinforcements should arrive from Virginia and North Carolina. On the eleventh of March, General Lawson arrived from Virginia, with a brigade of militia, and four hundred regular troops, raised for eighteen months, besides two brigades of militia, commanded by Generals Butler and Eaton, from North Carolina: these gave the Americans a great superiority in numbers; and General Greene began now to prepare to give Lord Cornwallis battle, and broke up his corps of light troops, commanded by Colonel Williams, with thanks to them for their eminent services, while acting as a separate corps from the main army ; he ordered them to fall in the line, and join their respective corps ; and he then marched to Guilford Court-house, and issued the following order :

'THE great probability of coming to a general
'action in a short time, must be a consideration
'that will induce every officer and soldier to do his
'duty ; and if order and discipline are maintained,
'so great a confidence has the general in the brave-
'ry of the troops, that he flatters himself the efforts
'of his countrymen will be favored by heaven, and
'crowned with success.'

ON the fifteenth of March, 1781, the two armies were drawn out near Guilford Court-house for action : the Americans consisted of about four thousand, five hundred men, in three lines : the North Caro_ lina militia under Generals Butler and Eaton, of about one thousand men, formed the first line : the second line was commanded by Generals Stevens and Lawson, of about seventeen hundred Virginia militia : the third line was of the Maryland and Delaware continental troops, of about fifteen hundred men, commanded by General Huger, on the right, and Colonel Williams on the left : Colonel

Washington with his cavalry, and a body of the Delaware light infantry and some riflemen under Colonel Lynch, covered the right flank : Colonel Lee, with his legion, and some riflemen under Colonel Campbell, the left. After the cannonade begun the British advanced in three columns, and displayed the Hessians on the right, Colonel Webster's brigade on the left, and the guards in the centre. Webster's brigade attacked the front line, which gave way when their adversaries were at the distance of one hundred and fifty yards, many of them without firing a gun : the Virginians kept up a smart fire and did great execution, until they were ordered to retreat. General Stevens had posted some riflemen in the rear of his line, with orders to shoot every man down that quitted his post. General Stevens, when he saw the North Carolina militia give way, ordered his line to open intervals, to let them pass through, and gave out amongst his men, that they had orders to retreat, which prevented it having any bad effect upon them. The continental troops were next attacked, and the business between them and the British, became very serious. The cavalry under Colonel Washington, supported by the Maryland troops, commanded by Colonel Gunby and Colonel Howard, made such a charge, that they rode down the whole regiment of guards, in which a great many of their officers and men were

killed and wounded. This heavy charge, being
well supported by the infantry, obliged the British
to fall back; and when General Huger received orders to retreat, the Americans were pressing close
upon them. This action lasted one hour and an
half, when the Americans retreated. Lord Cornwallis kept the field, and General Greene retired
over the Reedy-fork, about three miles. This victory cost the British dear : their killed and wounded
were upwards of six hundred;* amongst the first
were two colonels, three captains, and a number of
subalterns: of the latter, two brigadiers, one colonel, and a number of other officers. The Americans had three hundred continentals, and one hundred of the Virginia militia killed and wounded, and
lost two field-pieces (six pounders) which had been
alternately in the possession of the two armies, during the action. At this victory, there were great
rejoicings in Charleston, the troops were turned
out, and a feu-de-joye was fired ; though some of

....

* It is remarkable that whenever the British and Americans
came to fair firing in battle, the first always lost double the
number of men ; and the reason is, perhaps, because the
Americans are bred to arms, and accustomed to fire at single
objects, and were they blind-folded, would naturally level
their pieces well ; whilst the British soldiers, who are taught
to fire by platoons, always fire too high or too low.

the British said that such another victory would ruin them. Lord Cornwallis' conduct after this affair proves that this victory gave him no advantage, and that it left him in a much worse situation than before it happened. Three days after the battle, he issued a proclamation, [See appendix, note 27.] setting forth his complete victory, and calling upon all the loyal subjects, to come forward, and take an active part in restoring good order and government, offering pardon to all who should surrender themselves by the twentieth day of April; and on that day, his lordship destroyed all his baggage, left his hospital and seventy-five wounded men, with a great number of loyalists in the neighborhood of Guilford, and marched off for the sea-coast, which shows that he thought himself in no condition to keep the field; and thirteen days before the expiration of his act of grace, he reached his shipping at Wilmington, and left the whole of the upper country in the power of General Greene's army. Lord Cornwallis was extremely mortified at not receiving some support from the Scotch Highlanders, settled at Cross-creek: although he marched through their settlements, and they were opposed to the American measures, yet they kept aloof from the British. On General Greene's being informed of Lord Cornwallis' movements, he immediately decamped, and followed him, and continued his pursuit as far as Ramsay's mill, on Deep-river, so rapidly that the British had just crossed, when the Americans arrived: they suffered much in this pursuit, for want of provisions. Lord Cornwallis remained three weeks at Wilmington, with the British army; then marched them to Hallifax, and from thence to Petersburgh in Virginia, on the lower route, where he met with no opposition; and on the twentieth of May he joined the British forces in Virginia, under Major General Phillips and Brigadier General Arnold.

GENERAL Greene, before he knew of Lord Cornwallis' determination to proceed to Virginia with his army, resolved to re-commence military operations in South Carolina, but first issued his general amnesty, inviting the loyalists to join him, and sent orders to General Pickens to collect the militia of his brigade, and to prevent supplies from going to the British at Ninety-six and Augusta: and Colonel Lee with his legion and part of the second Maryland brigade, was ordered to advance before the continental troops, to co-operate with General Marion. General Sumpter was now recovered of his wound, and as soon as he was informed that Lord Cornwallis had quitted the state in pursuit of General Greene, he collected a body of men, and penetrated into the heart of the country to encourage the friends of independence, and early in February he crossed the Congaree-river in force, and appeared before Fort Granbee, and destroyed all their stores. Lord Rawdon immediately marched from Camden for the relief of that post, upon which General Sumpter retired, and appeared before another British post near Colonel Thomson's; and the second day after, he attacked and defeated an escort convoying some waggons going from Charleston to Camden with stores: thirteen of the British were killed, and sixty-six were taken prisoners: the stores were sent down the river in boats, but were retaken on their passage. General Sumpter with three hundred horse, swam across Santee-river, and marched to Fort Watson at Wright's-bluff; but on being informed that Lord Rawdon was marching to its relief, he retired to Black-river, and on his return he was attacked near Camden by Major Fraser with a considerable force of regulars and militia, who he obliged to retreat after twenty of his men were killed.

GENERAL Sumpter hitherto performed all his eminent services with militia, but finding them so uncertain a body, and as the war was to be renewed in South Carolina, it was thought proper to have a more permanent body; therefore General Sumpter with the approbation of General Greene raised three small regiments of regular state troops for ten months, in March, 1781; with these and the continental troops, the war was renewed in South Carolina with great vigor and spirit, and more regularity. Colonel Harden with his friends and neighbors from about Beaufort, and the south parts of Carolina, and Colonel Baker from Georgia, with some of his friends and neighbors, about seventy-six in all, who had been with General Marion on the north side of Santee-river, resolved to visit their settlements, and in their way, fell in with about twenty-five of the royal militia at Four-holes, whom they took; the privates were paroled, the officers were carried off prisoners. Colonel Harden was very active in the southern parts of the state: he sent parties to the houses of the royal militia; some were taken, whilst others fled to Charleston; he had several skirmishes with the British, in which he was successful; he took Fort Balfour at Potataligo, he surrounded it, and persuaded them that his numbers were many more than they really were, which induced Colonel Fenwick, Lichmore and Rassal, to surrender the fort, with thirty-two regular dragoons and fifty-six militia-men, on the twelfth of April, 1781. Colonel Harden's friends and neighbors were extremely glad to see him with a body of Americans; (hitherto there had been none but British parties amongst them) they turned out cheerfully and joined; by which, his party soon became very formidable: he carried on the partisan war as Sumpter and Marion did, and was very troublesome to the enemy.

GENERAL Greene marched with the main body

of his army, on the seventh of April, from Deep-
river, in North Carolina, towards Camden : the
British were a good deal surprised, when they were
informed that Colonel Lee had gone through the
country and joined General Marion near Santee, and
that General Greene, with the Americans, had encamped on the nineteenth of April, near Camden.

THE British had established a line of forts on the
banks of the Santee and Congaree rivers, to secure
the provisions, and render their communication to
Camden more safe and easy. Fort Watson, at
Wright's-bluff, on Santee, was closely invested on
the fifteenth of April, 1781, by eighty militia, and
a body of continentals under Colonel Lee : the fort
was built on an Indian mount ; but Colonel Mayham contrived to raise another within shot, much
higher, with logs and rails, filled in with earth,
which he raised, so that they could look down into
the fort, and the besieged were intirely exposed to
the fire of our riflemen. On the twenty-third, the garrison consisting of one hundred and fourteen men,
commanded by Lieutenant M'Kay, surrendered by
capitulation. The American army of about seven
hundred continentals, took post at Hobkirk's hill, about
one mile from Camden, which lay in the fork of Wateree-river and Wateree-creek; was fortified with six
redoubts and a battery defended with nine hundred
men commanded by Lord Rawdon, who ordered

every man in garrison that could carry a musket to take arms; and on the twenty-fifth marched out to attack General Greene. So little did the Americans expect the British out of their lines, that the second in command, General Huger, told me that they had just come to their ground, and that a number of officers with himself were washing their feet, and a number of soldiers were washing their kettles in a small rivulet that run by their camp, when their picket was engaged with the enemy. They ran to camp as fast as they could, and the British was soon after them, when a general action took place, and it would probably have been a serious surprise upon General Greene, had it not been for Washington's cavalry, which were saddled, and only the bits of their bridles out of their mouths; they were soon got ready, and General Greene ordered them to charge the enemy's right flank, which they did, and soon got in their rear; this threw them into the greatest confusion, and gave General Greene time to make a good retreat to Gun-swamp, about five miles. Colonel Washington paroled a number of officers upon the field, and amongst them eleven surgeons who were dressing their wounded. General Greene immediately sent them in to Lord Rawdon, (knowing they would be wanted for the wounded) who was so pleased with General Greene's liberal conduct, that he immediately sent to the commandant in Charleston to allow General Moultrie to exchange the like number of his medical line, such as he pleased, and that they should be conducted to any American post that he required.

At one time Colonel Washington had made upwards of two hundred prisoners, but upon the American army retreating, he was obliged to relinquish them all to about fifty, which he brought into camp, and lost only three men. This gave me an opportunity of exchanging Doctor Fayssoux,* whom I had several times proposed for exchange, but was always refused : they did not like him, and threw every obstacle in the way of his exchange, even his private debts, although he told them he left a great deal more in their hands than would satisfy them all. Their principal dislike to Doctor Fayssoux was, that he was too faithful to his friends, and wrote and spoke too freely of his enemies, respecting their conduct in his department ; as a number of his letters to Doctor Oliphant, director-general of the hospital, shows, and one to Doctor Ramsay, which is an exact statement of their conduct in our hospital at that time. [See appendix, note 28.]

The Americans lost in this affair at Hobkirk's, about two hundred killed, wounded, and missing.

....

* Doctor Fayssoux was surgeon-general in the hospital.

THE next day Colonel Washington went down with fifty men, to reconnoitre the British lines; he showed but a few of his men, and kept his main body concealed in the bushes. His scheme answered very well; his intention was to draw out their cavalry. As soon as they saw this small party, Major Coffin sallied out in pursuit of them, with forty Irish volunteers: they immediately rode off and drew him into an ambuscade, and as they passed, the Americans rushed out from the bushes, and attacked them in the rear, and killed about twenty of them.

Soon after the action of the twenty-fifth, General Greene sent off a detachment to reinforce General Marion near Nelson's-ferry, to prevent supplies going to Camden, from Charleston or the country; and sent parties to the Wateree to take a position, to prevent supplies going in from that quarter.

On the seventh of May, 1781, Lord Rawdon received a considerable reinforcement, by the arrival of Colonel Watson with his detachment; and endeavored the next day to bring General Greene to another action, but that could not be effected. General Greene knew that Lord Rawdon was so surrounded, that he could not get supplies, and that he must soon quit Camden; he therefore declined an action; and Lord Rawdon knowing his situation was growing more critical every day, by the increase of the American forces, and that he would be the more closely invested, determined to evacuate Camden, and retreat to Charleston; and on the tenth, he burned the gaol, mills, and many private houses, and destroyed a great part of his baggage, and retired with his army to the south side of Santee-river, leaving his own sick and wounded, and as many Americans, who they had taken on the twenty-fifth of April : by which movement he gave up the whole of South Carolina, that was on the north side of Santee, Wateree and Congaree-rivers ; a large extent of country. Most of the militia within those limits, immediately joined General Greene.

LORD Rawdon invited the Tories to accompany him to Charleston, and promised them every assistance in his power ; but very few of them attended him : the greater part chose to stay, and trust to the mercy of their countrymen : those who went down with the British, were cruelly neglected. After their arrival in Charleston, they built themselves huts without the lines, which was called. Rawdontown : many of these unfortunate women and children, who lived comfortable at their own homes near Camden, died for want, in those miserable huts.

THIS evacuation, and the enemy's posts falling in such quick succession, and the British falling back to the low country, gave great spirits to all America. The day after Lord Rawdon left Camden, the post at Orangeburgh, consisting of seventy militia,

and twelve regular troops surrendered to General
Sumpter. After the surrender of Fort Watson,
General Marion and Colonel Lee crossed the Santee,
and moved up to Fort Motte, which lies about the
fork, on the south side of Congaree, where they
arrived on the eighth of May, and began their approaches, which were carried on very rapidly. They
informed Mrs. Motte, that they were afraid that they
should be obliged to set fire to her house, which
stood in the centre of the fort: she begged them
that they would not consider her house as of any
consequence in the general cause; and with great
patriotism and firmness, presented them with an
African bow, and quiver of arrows, and requested
they would burn the house as quick as they could.
With the arrows, and skewers with combustibles
tied to them fired from muskets, they soon put the
house in a blaze; and the garrison commanded by
Lieutenant M'Pherson immediately surrendered at
discretion. Mrs. Motte who had retired to a house
at a little distance from her own, was extremely
rejoiced at seeing the garrison surrender, although
at the expense of her own elegant house.

Two days after this surrender, the British quitted
their post at Nelson's-ferry, on the south side of
Santee-river, about sixty miles from Charleston,
blew up their works and destroyed a great part of
their stores. A few days after, Fort Granby, in

Granby, on Congaree-river, (which had been much harrassed by Colonel Taylor's regiment of militia) surrendered to Lieutenant Colonel Lee. The garrison commanded by Major Maxwell, consisted of about three hundred and fifty men, most of them militia : in all these different forts, the Americans took a large quantity of stores. Lord Rawdon being on the south side of Santee-river, marched immediately to the relief of Fort Granby, but after marching fourteen miles, he met officers of that garrison on their way to town as prisoners of war, and paroled to Charleston ; upon which, he returned.

GENERAL Marion with his brigade of militia, marched to Georgetown. As soon as he begun his approaches, the British left the place, and retreated to Charleston by water : General Marion soon after moved off, and left Georgetown under a small militia guard ; and one Manson, an inhabitant of the country, came with an armed vessel, and demanded leave for his men to land, which was refused : he then sent some on shore, under the cover of his guns, and set fire to the town, and burnt forty-four houses in that small place.

THE British had now lost all their posts in the three southern states, except that at Ninety-six, one at Fort Golphan, and one at Augusta, in Georgia. These were the only objects General Greene had to contend against.

MANY people from the upper part of Georgia, crossed Savannah-river and went to the northern states, and some over the mountains, and a great number of Carolinians and Georgians had submitted to the British, and were at first treated kindly, but they were called upon to take up arms against their countrymen, which they declined.

COLONEL Clark returned to Georgia at the head of a party, in September, 1780, and laid siege to Augusta, in which Colonel Brown commanded: Lieutenant Cruger marched with a detachment from the garrison of Ninety-six, to relieve Colonel Brown, which obliged Colonel Clark to retreat : after this, Colonel Brown treated all his adherents, and those supposed to be so, with the utmost severity : this ill treatment of the Americans was now become insufferable, and parties in different parts of the back country, were arming to oppose the British : Captain M'Koy marched with a large body, and posted them along the banks of Savannah-river, and frequently intercepted boats going up with supplies for the British : upon this, Colonel Brown detached an officer, twenty-five regulars and twenty militia : Captain M'Koy attacked them at Mathew's-bluff, killed the officer and fifteen of them ; the remainder retreated in haste.

AGREEABLY to General Greene's plan at Deep-river, of returning to South Carolina, General Pickens and Colonel Clark, with a body of militia, had for some time harrassed the British about Augusta.

The day after the surrender of Fort Granby, Colonel Lee marched with his legion to Augusta : the first place that surrendered to a detachment of his legion under Captain Rudolph, was Fort Golphan, with seventy men, a field-piece and valuable stores. The next post that was invested, was Fort Cornwallis at Augusta, commanded by Colonel Brown. Colonel Grierson who occupied an out-work that was dependent, relinquished his post, and endeavored to throw his force into Fort Cornwallis : thirty of his men were killed and many more taken prisoners, but himself and a few others got off into the fort. The approaches were carried on with great rapidity, and Colonel Brown, an active officer, defended it with great bravery : several batteries were erected, two of which were within thirty yards, that overlooked their parapet, and the riflemen shot into the fort, with great success, and every man that attempted to fire at the besiegers was immediately shot down. On the fifth of January, 1781, the garrison consisting of about three hundred men, capitulated after making a gallant defence.

The Americans lost Major Eaton, and about forty killed and wounded. Colonel Grierson, who was very obnoxious to the Americans, was shot down by an unknown hand, after he was a prisoner. One hundred guineas reward was offered to any person who would point out the offender, but in vain. No doubt Colonel Brown expected the same fate from his vindictive disposition towards the Americans, but he was furnished with a guard, although he had hanged thirteen American prisoners, and others he gave into the hands of the Indians to be tortured. On his way to Savannah he passed through the settlements where he had burnt a number of houses, and hung some of the relations of the inhabitants. At Silver-bluff, Mrs. M'Koy obtained leave of the American officer who commanded his safeguard to speak to him, when she thus addressed him: " Colonel Brown, in the late ' day of your prosperity, I visited your camp, and on ' my knees supplicated for the life of my son, but you ' were deaf to my intreaties, you hanged him, though ' a beardless youth, before my face. These eyes have ' seen him scalped by the savages under your imme- ' diate command, and for no better reason than that ' his name was M'Koy. As you are now a prisoner to ' the leaders of my country, for the present I lay aside ' all thoughts of revenge, but when you resume your ' sword, I will go five hundred miles to demand satis- ' faction at the point of it, for the murder of my son."

WHILE the detachments from General Greene's army were reducing the small posts, General Greene proceeded on with the main body to Ninety-six. This was a post of mnch consequence to the British, it

being situated in the middle of a fertile and populous
country : the fort was garrisoned by a large body of
regular troops commanded by Lieutenant Colonel
Cruger, a brave and gallant officer. The garrison
made a gallant defence. On the left of the fort was a
work in the form of a star ; on the right was a strong
stockade fort, and two block-houses : within the town,
flanked by those two works and picquetted all around,
and surrounded by a ditch and a high bank. There
were also several flushes in different parts of the
town : to all the works was a communication by covered ways.

On the twenty-third of May, 1781, the main body
of the American army encamped within half a mile
of the British post, and that night threw up two
flushes within one hundred and fifty yards of the star-
fort ; the next morning the enemy made a sally, and
being supported by the artillery and musketry from
the star-redoubt, obliged the besiegers to retreat. The
next night two strong block-batteries were erected at
the distance of about three hundred yards, which were
opened in the morning : soon after two batteries of
twenty feet high ; one within two hundred yards, and
the other within one hundred yards of the main fort.
Approaches were carried on at the same time on
the left, under the direction of Colonel Kozinsco, a
young gentleman of distinction from Poland. On
the fourteenth of May, a third parallel within fifty

yards of the ditch was completed, and a rifle-battery upwards of thirty feet high, erected at the same distance. On the seventeenth, the abbattis were turned, and two trenches and a mine were within six feet of the ditch. Great perseverance and bravery were exhibited on both sides; riflemen were employed, who immediately fired at any person that appeared, and seldom missed their aim. Many severe skirmishes took place between the covering parties and those from the garrison, who frequently sallied out.

On the third of June, a fleet arrived at Charleston from Ireland, having on board the third, nineteenth and thirtieth regiments of British troops; a detachment of guards, and a great number of recruits; the whole under the command of Colonel Gould. Lord Cornwallis had left orders to detain those troops in South Carolina if they should be wanted: accordingly, on the seventh of June, 1781, Lord Rawdon marched from Charleston with this reinforcement for the relief of Ninety-six. This was a dreadful prospect for these newly raised troops arrived from Europe, immediately from on board ship, who had not yet recovered the use of their legs, heavy armed and thick clad, to be forced to undertake a march of two hundred miles at this inclement season of the year: it is not to be doubted that numbers of them must have been left behind at the end of every day's march. They had been amused with the idea, that on their arrival in Carolina, they would have nothing to do but sit themselves down quietly, on some of the forfeited estates of the rebels.

GENERAL Greene had carried his works so near the British garrison, as almost to insure success; and the moment when he expected them to surren. der, intelligence was received that Lord Rawdon was near at hand with two thousand men. The wife of a British officer (an American) then in the garrison of Ninety-six, received a large bribe to convey a letter to Colonel Cruger, to inform him of their near approach, which she did: as she was well known to all the American officers, she rode about their camp, unsuspected of any ill design, and her servant with her, conversing with one and then with another, until she found an opportunity; gave a signal to the fort, it is said, by holding up a letter, upon which a man was sent out from the fort upon horseback, who got the letter, and galloped back into the fort with it: he had several shot fired at him, but without effect. General Greene attempted to retard Lord Rawdon's march, but his men were too few to carry on the siege, and stop the progress of the British troops: their near approach obliged General Greene to raise the siege, or attempt to carry the place by a coup-de-main; which last was agreed upon, and a disposition made on the eighteenth of June. Lieutenant Colonel Lee with the infantry of his legion, and Captain Kirkwood's light-infantry, made the attack upon the right: Lieutenant Colonel Campbell, with the first Maryland and first Virginia regiments, were to have stormed the star-redoubt, the ditch of which was eight or nine feet deep, the parapet eleven or twelve feet high, and raised with sand-bags near three feet more. The forlorn hopes were led on by Lieutenants Duval and Sheldon, and followed by a party with hooks and entrenching tools, to pull down the sand-bags. Had this been effected, the besieged could not have annoyed the assailants without exposing themselves to the American riflemen. The artillery soon made breaches in the redoubt on the right; it was therefore abandoned, and they took possession without loss. On the left, great exertions of resolution and bravery were displayed, but without success. The forlorn hopes entered the ditch through an incessant fire, and made every effort to get down the sand-bags. Both of the officers were wounded, and there was not more than one in six of the forlorn hopes but what were killed or wounded.

Lord Rawdon by his rapid marches was very near to Ninety-six at the time of the assault, which obliged General Greene to make a precipitate retreat over the Enoree. Lord Rawdon pursued General Greene, but finding it impossible to overtake the Americans, and supposing they had got to North Carolina or

Virginia, contented himself with the idea of having driven him quite out of the country. The arrival of the British reinforcement, and the retreat from Ninety-six, gave reason to suppose that the British would re-establish their posts which they lost to the southward of Santee. The destination of Lord Cornwallis' army having been known for some time, the British commanders in South Carolina were obliged to draw in all their posts within the limits of Santee, Congaree and Edisto rivers, and to confine their future operations within those bounds. The vicissitudes in war are many, and it is the part of a good general to know when to fight, and when to run away. See Lord Rawdon at one time pursuing General Greene with hasty strides, and he as hastily getting off; at another time when Lord Rawdon divides his force, General Greene faces about and offers him battle, whilst the other retreats as precipitately to Orangeburgh, and takes a strong position to secure himself from an attack.

WHILST General Greene lay near Orangeburgh endeavoring to bring Lord Rawdon to an action, he got intelligence that Colonel Cruger was marching the garrison of Ninety-six to join Lord Rawdon, which in his situation he could not prevent; he therefore retired with the American army to the high hills of Santee.

ON the post of Ninety-six being evacuated, the

whole of the upper country was in the possession of
the Americans, except a few of their small parties
moving about, that often fell in with ours, who generally routed them, and made many prisoners. Captain Eggleston with a part of Lee's legion, came up
with forty-nine British horse, and took forty-eight of
them. Colonel Lee with his legion, took all the waggons and horses belonging to the convoy of provisions.
Colonel Wade Hampton charged and routed a party
of British near Charleston; he also took fifty prisoners at Strawberry, and burnt four vessels loaded with
stores for the British army. Generals Sumpter and
Marion appeared before the camp at Biggen Church,
which consisted of five hundred infantry, and one hundred cavalry: their advance fell in with the enemy's
picquet, had a small skirmish, and were obliged to retire: in the evening they set fire to the church, with
all their stores, and retreated over Wadboo-bridge
towards Charleston. Generals Sumpter and Marion
with their brigades, Lee's legion and Hampton's state
cavalry pursued them closely. The cavalry came up
with them near Quinby-bridge, and took their rear-
guard with their military chest and all their baggage.
Some of the plank of the bridge being taken up, retarded the pursuit a little: however, the main body
came up with them at Quinby (Colonel Shubrick's
plantation) where they had possession of the negro-
houses and other out-houses. In this situation, they

were attacked with great spirit, till upwards of fifty Americans were killed and wounded; and finding they could not dislodge them from the houses, and hearing that a reinforcement was coming from town, via Hobcaw, they then ordered a retreat. Captain Armstrong with five of Lee's legion, rode into their camp, while the officers and men were dispersed, and charged several small parties, and came off with the loss of only two men.

About this time, every thing seemed to run retrograde with the British : they were very much perplexed and embarrassed, not knowing how to conduct their affairs. If they kept their forces together in the upper country, the Americans were sure to get between them and Charleston, and with small parties, surprise and take their supplies going up to them ; and if they divided their force, they were beat ; and the people that went over to them for protection, finding they could not be protected, joined the Americans again, so that the British interest declined daily. Disconcerted in all their schemes, driven from all their posts, in despair and vexation, to appease their wrath, the unfortunate Colonel Hayne was executed without a trial. At the time that Generals Sumpter and Marion were detached down the country, the main army was on the high hills of Santee, and the British returned to the fork of Congaree and Wateree. In this situation the two armies lay within fifteen miles of each other, with a rapid river between them : they knew that no sudden attack could be made on either side, as no boats were to be had. General Greene, whose martial active spirit would not allow him to remain idle, formed a plan to drive the enemy again from their post. As he could not procure boats where he was, he took a circuit of about seventy miles, where boats were to be had, and where the river was fordable in some places. Soon after he had crossed the river, he was joined by General Pickens with a body of the Ninety-six militia, and by the state troops under Colonel Henderson. General Marion with his brigade had been to Pon-pon, to support Colonel Harden in opposing the British, who had taken post near Combahee-ferry, and had issued orders to the inhabitants to bring their rice to the neighboring landings, that it might be carried to Charleston. Colonel Harden exerted himself to oppose their designs, and found it necessary to call in some other militia of the state: many skirmishes took place, in which the enemy lost a number of men. After this, General Marion joined General Greene.

THE American force being collected, marched the next morning to attack the British army commanded by Lieutenant Colonel Stewart. The British had retired from Congaree to Eutaw, about forty miles nearer to Charleston. The advance of the Americans fell in with two parties of the British who were rooting potatoes, about four miles from their main body ; they were charged by the legion of state troops, which obliged them soon to retire. It was unfortunate they fell in with these parties, otherwise their main body would have been completely surprised. They had not the least suspicion of General Greene's being any where near them: they immediately drew up their men, and General Greene drew up his little army consisting of about two thousand men, in two lines. The first consisted of the North and South Carolina militia, commanded by Generals Marion and Pickens, and Colonel Malmedy: the second consisted of the continental troops from North Carolina, Virginia and Maryland, commanded by General Sumner, Colonel Campbell and Colonel Williams. Colonel Lee with his legion covered the right flank, and Colonel Henderson with the state troops on the left. Colonel Washington with his cavalry, and Captain Kirkwood with the Delaware troops, were formed as a corps of reserve. The enemy was drawn up in a wood, their left among some scrub-oak trees. The front began to fire, and advance upon the British, till the action became general, and they in their turn obliged to give way. They were well supported by General Sumner's brigade, most of whom were raw troops, composed of militia-men, who were turned over to the continental service for their precipitate flight in former actions: Colonel Williams and Colonel Campbell were ordered to march up with trailed arms, and charge. Nothing could exceed the bravery of the officers and men on this occasion: they marched up through a heavy fire of musketry with such intrepidity as obliged the enemy to fall back. Colonel Henderson who commanded the state troops, was wounded early in the action; the command then devolved upon Colonel Wade Hampton, who made a very spirited charge, in which he took upwards of one hundred prisoners. In this confusion, Colonel Washington brought up the corps de reserve, and charged so briskly on the left as gave them no time to rally, and upwards of five hundred were made prisoners. Colonel Washington charged with his cavalry in a thick scrub-oak wood, which was very unfavorable for the horse: the British reserved their fire till the cavalry was almost upon them. When they gave fire, Colonel Washington's horse was shot under him, and he fell into their ranks. He received a wound with a bayonet, and would have been killed, but was saved by a British officer, and made prisoner. Most of his officers were either killed or wounded, and a great many of his men. After this, the enemy retreated to a strong brick-house and a piquetted garden at Eutaw, where they renewed the action. Four field-pieces (six-pounders) were brought up to fire upon the house, from whence the British were firing: they

sallied out and took the pieces. The Americans retired out of the reach of their fire, leaving a strong
picquet upon the field. The next evening, Colonel
Stewart destroyed a great quantity of stores, and retreated towards Charleston, leaving upwards of seventy of his wounded, and a thousand stand of arms.
They were pursued several miles, but could not be
come up with. About fourteen miles below Eutaw,
they were joined by a strong detachment under Major M'Arthur; however, they retreated down to Wan-
toot, (Mr. Ravenel's) twenty miles below Eutaw,
where they encamped some time. After this battle,
the British were so alarmed that they burnt their
stores at Dorchester, and the gates of the town were
shut. A number of negroes were employed in felling
trees across the road on Charleston-neck.

THE loss of the British at Eutaw, was upwards
of eleven hundred men : the Americans lost about
five hundred, including about sixty officers : Colonel Campbell of the Virginia line, was among the
slain, universally lamented.

AFTER the battle of Eutaw, the Americans retired
to their old camp on the high hills of Santee.

IN the latter part of the year 1782, General
Marion was encamped with his militia at Wadboo,
(a place belonging to Mr. Colleton) where he was attacked by Major Fraser, with two or three hundred
dragoons : Marion got notice of his approach, and

posted his men in the house and out-houses. They
came to the charge at full gallop, and were received
with such a warm fire from the houses, as obliged
them to retire very precipitately, leaving a captain
and several others on the ground, killed and wounded.

SHORTLY after, Colonel Maham appeared before
the post at Fairlawn (Sir John Colleton's place) with
a small party of cavalry, took upwards of eighty prisoners, and burnt the house, with all their stores:
and although the British were greatly superior in
force, yet they dared not to stir out of their works to
save their stores. Colonel Mayham was constrained
to burn the house, because his men were making too
free with the liquors.

CONGRESS honored General Greene for his conduct in the action at Eutaw, with a British standard
and a golden medal. [See appendix, note 29.]

THE latter part of the year 1781, about two months
after the battle of Eutaw, General Greene moved his
army into the lower country, to secure provisions for
his army: during the winter, the main body of his army was put in motion under the command of Colonel
Williams.

GENERAL Greene with two hundred horse, and two
hundred infantry, appeared near Dorchester. The
British, believing his whole army was near at hand,
immediately abandoned their post, and retired to the
Quarter-house, at Charleston-neck. General Greene's

army encamped on the west side of Ashley-river, about sixteen miles from Charleston, by which he secured for his army all the provisions in the southern parts of the state, except the sea-islands, on which the enemy had collected a great number of cattle. Very little of military operations were going on now, except some excursions with cavalry and infantry: one was made in February, 1782. While General Marion was attending the legislature of Jacksonborough, his brigade was surprised near Santee, by a party of British cavalry commanded by Colonel Thomson, in which Major Benson, Mr. Broughton and several others were killed.

On the nineteenth of March, 1782, Captain Rudolph and Lieutenant Smith, with twelve men, took and burned a British galley, in Ashley-river, which mounted twelve guns, and forty-three men. They disguised themselves, and passed for negroes going to market with poultry: they were allowed to come so near that they boarded her with ease, the enemy not suspecting them. Three or four were killed ; the rest were brought off prisoners.

While the American army lay on the south side of Ashley-river, the greater part of the men were so completely ragged, that their clothes would scarcely cover their nakedness: every little piece of cloth was taken up to tie about their waists; and that was not the worst of their grievances ; the want of provisions was severely felt by them. Sometimes they had meat without bread or rice, sometimes bread and rice without meat, and sometimes were without either. In this situation did they continue for several months, and only sixteen miles from Charleston, where the British army was in garrison, with a greatly superior force; fortunately, Ashley-river was between them. By their being encamped so long in one place at this season of the year, (July, August, September and October) they began to be sickly, discontented and mutinous. The long arrears of pay, and the want of provisions and clothing, was truly distressing, and very hard upon this brave little army, who had been marching and counter-marching, and fighting, almost the whole year round, that now they came to have a little respite, that they should be in want of every necessary; but it could not be otherwise: it was the unfortunate situation of the country at that time, which made it so. It is not surprising that these men were dissatisfied, and began to brood mischief: a few of them had formed a plan to deliver General Greene, their beloved commander, into the hands of the British; but the plot was discovered, and prevented from being carried into execution. Only twelve men were concerned in this wicked design, and only one (sergeant) executed.

WHILE General Greene lay encamped at Ashley-river, there were frequent communications between

Charleston and the army. Flags were passing almost every day upon public or private business. Governor Mathews, by assistance of Mr. Joshua Lockwood, got out a quantity of clothing and other necessaries for the army, which quieted them, and restored good order, and duty was cheerfully performed as before.

Soon after the British had taken possession of Charleston, Brigadier General Patterson was appointed commandant to superintend the civil affairs of the town : he conducted himself with politeness towards the prisoners : he shortly after went for New-York, and Lord Cornwallis nominated Lieutenant Colonel Nisbet Balfour to that office, with very extensive powers in all civil matters. While he was commandant, a board of police was established to determine all disputes in a summary way, (but under the control of the commandant, James Simpson, Esq. intendant of the board) a depreciation table was drawn up, ascertaining the value of the paper currency at different times. This had the appearance of justice and civil authority; but it created a great deal of mischief and discontent; many suits were commenced, and great numbers ruined.

The place allotted to confine their prisoners, was a part of the cellar under the Exchange, and called the Provost; a damp, unwholesome place, which occasioned amongst the prisoners much sickness, and some deaths. It was a horrid place to confine citi-

zens in. They had no respect to age or sex : they
were all huddled up together in one common room ;
American prisoners of war, and British felons. Two
young ladies of a respectable family, were confined
among the other prisoners, for several days, on a
groundless suspicion of giving intelligence to the
Americans. I had frequent applications from the unfortunate sufferers in the Provost, requesting I would
interest myself in their behalf, to get them released
from that loathsome place : in some of my applications I succeeded ; in others I could not. The unfortunate citizens of Charleston, who would not take
the British protection, on the slightest pretence
were hurried away to the Provost. The violent and
arbitrary administration of Colonel Balfour, lessened
the British party, and very much strengthened the
American interest.

THE first distinction of names in America at the
commencement of the revolution, was that of subscribers and non-subscribers ; the first were those
who signed the association agreed upon by Congress ;
the latter were those, who, from timidity, or attachment to the British government, refused to sign ;
they were but very few, and were looked upon in a
very odious light; their former friends would scarcely speak to them, or have any dealings with them :
these distinctions were made before we had any idea
of going to war.

THE next distinction was of a more serious nature, that of Whig and Tory. This was after the state had raised troops and established funds. The Whigs were in favor of America, the Tories for the British. Those in favor of Congress gave certificates for such articles as they were obliged to impress from their friends, which was paid for by the money then in circulation, and was esteemed at first as good as specie. What the Tories took, was looked upon as a robbery, because they had no funds to draw upon. Each party oppressed the other as much as they possibly could, which raised their inveteracy to so great a height, that they carried on the war with savage cruelty: although they had been friends, neighbors and brothers, they had no feelings for each other, and no principles of humanity left. When the British party prevailed, after the surrender of Charleston, they gave full scope to their interested and malicious passions. Some of the most abandoned characters came from their hiding places, called themselves king's men, and committed the most violent acts of cruelty and injustice, which was sanctioned by the British, provided they called themselves friends to the king, and the outrages were committed on such as were called rebels. Many houses were burnt, and many people murdered. The unfortunate Whigs were obliged with their families to quit their homes, and lie in the woods, as the only places of security. I will here give one or two instances of their cruelties, which will suffice for the whole.

WHEN General Greene returned to South Carolina in the spring of 1781, Major William Cunningham, of the British militia, came out of Charleston with a party, and kept bye-roads and private paths, till he got in the rear of the American army undiscovered into the district of Ninety-six. The many acts of cruelties which had been committed by the Tories, induced the Whigs to associate in small parties, and to arm in self-defence. Captain Turner and twenty men, had taken post in a house, and defended themselves till their ammunition was expended; they then surrendered, upon a promise of being treated as prisoners of war; notwithstanding, they were instantly put to death, by Cunningham and his party. Soon after, this same party attacked a number of the American militia commanded by Colonel Hayes, and set fire to the house in which they had taken shelter: they were reduced to the sad necessity of surrendering themselves prisoners, or be burnt. Colonel Hayes and Captain Daniel Williams were immediately hung upon a pole; this breaking, they both fell: upon which, Cunningham cut them to pieces with his own hands, and continued his savage barbarity on the others, till he was quite exhausted; then he called to his men to kill which of them they pleased. They instantly fell to, and put to death such of them as they disliked. Only two fell in the action; fourteen of them were deliberately put to death.

WHEN General Greene returned to South Carolina, in 1782, every thing was reversed. In a few weeks, the British were dispossessed of all their posts in the upper country, and the injured and exasperated Whigs had again the superiority. On their return to their homes, they found starving families, and desolate places. Sweet revenge comes now to reek her vengeance on those infamous, merciless, bloody villains that had gone before. The Whigs began to plunder and to murder.

THE conduct of those two parties was a disgrace to human nature, and it may with safety be said that they destroyed more property, and shed more American blood than the whole British army.

ABOUT this time, Governor Rutledge returned to South Carolina, and exerted himself in re-establishing good government: he issued his proclamation, strictly forbidding all violence. [See appendix, note 30.] Magistrates were appointed in every part of the state, not in the British possession: civil government was restored, and property secured. [See appendix, note 31.] A few weeks after, several hundreds came out of the British lines, and greatly reinforced the American militia. Many made their excuses for remaining with the British, on account of the situation of their families: others who took British militia commissions, said it was at the request of their neighbors, to keep them from having officers put over them, who would abuse and ill treat them. It is within my own knowledge, that several gentlemen took militia commissions, to protect their friends and neighbors from insult. Many of the citizens who had been lately exchanged and sent to Philadelphia and Virginia, and some who had been banished, returned to South Carolina; among them most of the civil officers of the state, and members of the former legislature: and the American army at Jacksonborough (a little village, about thirty-six miles from Charleston) induced Governor Rutledge to convene a new legislature; accordingly, he issued his writs for a new election, which was ordered to be held at the usual places, where it was practicable; and in other cases, as near as safety and other circumstances would permit. All those who had taken British protection, were excluded from voting, or having a seat in the legislature.

A GENERAL assembly was chosen, and met in January, 1782, and were addressed soon after their meeting, by Governor Rutledge.

THE SPEECH OF JOHN RUTLEDGE, ESQ. GOVERNOR
AND COMMANDER IN CHIEF OF THE STATE OF
SOUTH CAROLINA, TO THE GENERAL ASSEMBLY
MET AT JACKSONBOROUGH, ON FRIDAY, 18th JANU-
ARY, 1782.

' Honorable Gentlemen of the Senate,

' Mr. Speaker, and Gentlemen of the House
' of Representatives,

' SINCE the last meeting of a general assembly,
' the good people of this state have not only felt the
' common calamities of war, but, from the wanton
' and savage manner in which it has been prosecuted,
' they have experienced such severities as are un-
' practised and will scarcely be credited by civilized
' nations.

' THE enemy, unable to make any impression on
' the northern states, the number of whose inhabit-
' ants, and the strength of whose country, had baffled
' their repeated efforts, turned their views towards
' the southern, which, a difference of circumstances,
' afforded some expectation of conquering, or at least
' of greatly distressing. After a long resistance, the
' reduction of Charleston was effected, by the vast su-
' periority of force with which it had been besieged.
' The loss of that garrison, as it consisted of the con-
' tinental troops of Virginia and the Carolinas, and
' of a number of militia, facilitated the enemy's
' march into the country, and their establishment of

' strong posts in the upper and interior parts of it ;
' and the unfavorable issue of the action near Cam-
' den induced them vainly to imagine, that no other
' army could be collected which they might not ea-
' sily defeat. The militia, commanded by the bri-
' gadiers Sumpter and Marion, whose enterprising
' spirit and unremitted perseverance under many dif-
' ficulties are deserving of great applause, harrassed
' and often defeated large parties ; but the numbers
' of those militia were too few to contend effectually
' with the collected strength of the enemy. Regard-
' less therefore of the sacred ties of honor, destitute
' of the feelings of humanity, and determined to ex-
' tinguish, if possible, every spark of freedom in this
' country, they, with the insolent pride of conquerors,
' gave unbounded scope to the exercise of their ty-
' rannical disposition, infringed their public engage-
' ments, and violated the most solemn capitulations.
' Many of our worthiest citizens were, without cause,
' long and c osely confined...some on board of pri-
' son-ships, and others in the town and castle of St.
' Augustine...their properties disposed of at the will
' and caprice of the enemy, and their families sent
' to a different and distant part of the continent with-
' out the means of support. Many who had surren-
' dered as prisoners of war were killed in cool blood....
' several suffered death in the most ignominious
' manner, and others were delivered up to savages

' and put tt tortures under which they expired.
' Thus the lives, liberties and properties of the peo-
' ple were dependent solely on the pleasure of British
' officers, who deprived them of either or all on the
' most frivolous pretences. Indians, slaves, and a
' desperate banditti of the most profligate characters,
' were caressed and employed by the enemy to exe-
' cute their infamous purposes. Devastation and
' ruin marked their progress and that of their adhe-
' rents...nor were their violences restrained by the
' charms or influence of beauty and innocence...even
' the fair sex, whom it is the duty of all, and the
' pleasure and pride of the brave to protect...they,
' and their tender offspring, were victims to the in-
' veterate malice of an unrelenting foe. Neither the
' tears of mothers, nor the cries of infants, could ex-
' cite in their breasts pity or compassion. Not only
' the peaceful habitations of the widow, the aged and
' the infirm, but the holy temples of the Most High
' were consumed in flames, kindled by their sacrile-
' gious hands. They have tarnished the glory of the
' British arms, disgraced the profession of a British
' soldier, and fixed indelible stigmas of rapine, cru-
' elty, perfidy and profaneness on the British name.
' ...But I can now congratulate you, and I do so
' most cordially, on the pleasing change of affairs,
' which, under the blessing of God, the wisdom,
' prudence, address and bravery of the great and

' gallant General Greene, and the intrepidity of the
' officers and men under his command, has been hap-
' pily effected...a general who is justly entitled, from
' his many signal services, to honorable and singular
' marks of your approbation and gratitude. His suc-
' cesses have been more rapid and complete than the
' most sanguine could have expected. The enemy,
' compelled to surrender or evacuate every post which
' they held in the country, frequently defeated and
' driven from place to place, are obliged to seek re-
' fuge under the walls of Charleston, and on islands
' in its vicinity. We have now the full and absolute
' possession of every other part of the state ; and the
' legislative, executive and judicial powers, are in
' the free exercise of their respective authorities.

' I ALSO most heartily congratulate you on the glo-
' rious victory obtained by the combined forces of
' America and France over their common enemy.
' When the very general who was second in com-
' mand at the reduction of Charleston, and to whose
' boasted prowess and highly extolled abilities the
' conquest of no less than three states had been ar-
' rogantly committed, was speedily compelled to ac_
' cept of the same mortifying terms which had been
' imposed on that brave but unfortunate garrison. to
' surrender an army of many thousand regulars, and
' to abandon his wretched followers, whom he had
' artfully seduced from their allegiance by specious

'promises of protection, which he could never have
'hoped to fulfil, to the justice or mercy of their
'country :...on the naval superiority established by
'the illustrious ally of the United States...a superi-
'ority in itself so decided, and in its consequences so
'extensive, as must inevitably soon oblige the enemy
'to yield to us the only post which they occupy in
'this state:. .on the reiterated proofs of the sincerest
'friendship, and on the great support which America
'has received from that powerful monarch...a mo-
'narch whose magnanimity is universally acknow-
'ledged and admired, and on whose royal word we
'may confidently rely for every necessary assistance:
'...on the perfect harmony which subsists between
'France and America...on the stability which her in-
'dependence has acquired...and on the certainty that
'it is too deeply rooted ever to be shaken; for, ani-
'mated as they are by national honor, and united by
'one common interest, it must and will be main-
'tained.

'WHAT may be the immediate effects on the Bri-
'tish nation, of the events which I have mentioned;
'of their loss of territory in other parts of the world;
'and of their well-founded apprehensions from the
'powers of France, Spain and Holland, it is impos-
'sible to foretel. If experience can teach wisdom
'to a haughty and infatuated people, and if they will
'now be governed by reason, they will have learned

' that they can have no solid ground of hope to con-
' quer any state in the union ; for, though their ar-
' mies have obtained temporary advantages over our
' troops, yet the citizens of these states, firmly re
' solved as they are never to return to a domination,
' which, near six years ago, they unanimously and
' justly renounced, cannot be subdued...and they
' must now be convinced that it is the height of folly
' and madness to persist in so ruinous a war. If,
' however, we judge as we ought of their future by
' their past conduct, we may presume that they will
' not only endeavour to keep possession of our capi-
' tal, but make another attempt, howsoever improba-
' ble the success of it may appear, to subjugate this
' country :...it is therefore highly incumbent on us to
' use our most strenuous efforts to frustrate so fatal a
' design. And I earnestly conjure you by the duty
' which you owe, and the sacred love which you bear
' to your country ; by the constant remembrance of
' her bitter sufferings ; and by the just detestation of
' British government, which you and your posterity
' must forever possess, to exert your utmost faculties
' for that purpose, by raising and equipping, with all
' possible expedition, a respectable permanent force,
' and by making ample provision for their comforta-
' ble subsistence. I am sensible the expense will be
' great, but a measure so indispensable to the pre-
' servation of our freedom, is above every pecuniary
' consideration.

' THE organization of our militia is likewise a sub-
' ject of infinite importance. A clear and concise
' law, by which the burdens of service will be equally
' sustained, and a competent number of men brought
' forth, and kept in the field when their assistance
' may be required, is essential to our security, and
' therefore justly claims your immediate and serious
' attention. Certain it is, that some of our militia
' have, upon several occasions, exhibited instances
' of valor which would have reflected honor on vete-
' ran troops. The courage and conduct of the gene-
' rals whom I have mentioned, the cool and deter-
' mined bravery repeatedly displayed by Brigadier
' Pickens, and indeed the behavior of many officers
' and men in every brigade, are unquestionable testi-
' monies of the truth of this assertion ; but such be-
' havior cannot be expected from militia in general,
' without good order and strict discipline...nor can
' that order and discipline be established but by a
' salutary law steadily executed.

' ANOTHER important matter for your deliberation,
' is the conduct of such of our citizens as voluntarily
' avowing their allegiance, and even glorying in their
' professions of loyalty and attachment to his Britan-
' nic majesty, have offered their congratulations on
' the success of his arms, prayed to be embodied as
' royal militia, accepted commissions in his service,
' and endeavored to subvert our constitution and esta-

' blish his power in its stead...of those who have re-
' turned to this state in defiance of a law by which
' such return was declared to be a capital offence,
' and have abetted the British interest...and of such
' whose behaviour has been so reprehensible, that
' justice and policy forbid their free re-admission to
' the rights and privileges of citizens.

' The extraordinary lenity of this state has been
' remarkably conspicious : other states have thought
' it just and expedient to appropriate the property of
' British subjects to the public use, but we have for-
' borne to take even the profits of the estates of our
' most implacable enemies. It is with you to deter-
' mine whether the forfeiture and appropriation of
' their property should now take place. If such shall
' be your determination, though many of our firmest
' friends have been reduced for their inflexible attach-
' ment to the cause of their country, from opulence
' to inconceivable distress, and, if the enemy's will
' and power had prevailed, would have been doomed
' to indigence and beggary, yet it will redound to the
' reputation of this state to provide a becoming sup-
' port for the families of those whom you may deprive
' of their property.

' The value of paper currency became of late so
' much depreciated, that it was requisite, under the
' powers vested in the executive during the recess of
' the general assembly, to suspend the laws by which

' it was made a tender. You will now consider whe-
' ther it may not be proper to repeal those laws, and
' fix some equitable mode for the discharge of debts
' contracted whilst paper money was in circulation.

' In the present scarcity of specie it would be diffi-
' cult, if not impracticable, to levy a tax to any con-
' siderable amount towards sinking the public debt;
' nor will the creditors of the state expect that such a
' tax should, at this time, be imposed; but it is just
' and reasonable, that all unsettled demands should be
' liquidated, and satisfactory assurances of payment
' given to the public creditors.

' The interest and honor, the safety and happiness
' of our country, depend so much on the result of
' your deliberations, that I flatter myself you will
' proceed, in the weighty business before you, with
' firmness and temper, with vigor, unanimity and dis-
' patch.

' JOHN RUTLEDGE.'

To this speech the following addresses were returned by the two branches of legislature.

' THE ADDRESS OF THE HONORABLE THE SENATE IN
' ANSWER TO THE GOVERNOR'S SPEECH.

' May it please your excellency,

' We beg leave to return your excellency the
thanks of this house for your speech.

' Any words that we might adopt would convey
' but a very faint idea of the satisfaction we feel on
' the perfect re-establishment of the legislative, exe-
' cutive and judicial powers in this state.

' It is with particular pleasure, that we take the
' earliest opportunity to present to your excellency,
' our unfeigned thanks for your unwearied zeal and
' attention to the real interest of this country, and
' to testify our entire approbation of the good conduct
' of the executive since the last meeting of the gene-
' ral assembly.

' We see and revere the goodness of Divine Pro-
' vidence in frustrating and disappointing the attempts
' of our enemies to conquer the southern states; and,
' we trust, that, by the blessing of the same Provi-
' dence, on the valor and intrepidity of the free citi-
' zens of America, their attacks and enterprises will
' continue to be repelled and defeated.

' We reflect with pleasure on the steady resolution
' with which Charleston was defended by a small
' body of brave men against such a vast superiority of
' force, and we gratefully acknowledge the meritori-
' ous conduct and important services of the officers
' and privates of the militia, who stood forth in the
' hour of danger, and whose coolness perseverance
' and ardor, under a complication of difficulties, most
' justly entitle them to the applause of their country.

' We flatter ourselves that the blood which the

' enemy has inhumanly spilled, the wanton devasta-
' tion which has marked their progress, and the ty-
' rannical system that they have invariably pursued,
' and which your excellency hath so justly and pa-
' thetically described to us, will rouse the good peo-
' ple of this state, and will animate them with a spirit
' to protect their country, to save their rights and li-
' berties, and to maintain, at all hazards, their inde-
' pendency.

' IT is with inexpressible pleasure, that we receive
' your excellency's congratulations upon the great
' and glorious events of the campaign, on the happy
' change of affairs, and on the pleasing prospect be-
' fore us ; and we assure your excellency, that we
' concur most sincerely with you, in acknowledging
' and applauding the meritorious zeal, and the very
' important services which have been rendered to
' this state by the great and gallant General Greene,
, and the brave and intrepid officers and men under
' his command, and to whom we shall be happy to
' give the most honorable and singular testimonies
' of our approbation and applause.

' WE are truly sensible of the immense advantage
' which the United States derive from the magnani-
' mous prince their ally : we have the most perfect
' confidence on his royal word, and on the sincerity
' of his friendship ; and we think ourselves much in-
' debted to that illustrious monarch for the great and

' effectual assistance which he hath been pleased to
' give the confederated states, and by whose means
' they have been enabled to humble the pride of Bri-
' tain, and to establish their independency upon the
' most permanent basis.

' THE importance of the several matters which
' your excellency hath recommended to our consider-
' ation is so evident, that we shall proceed to delibe-
' rate upon them with all possible dispatch; and we
' flatter ourselves that our business will be carried on
' with temper, firmness and unanimity.

' J. L. GERVAIS, President.'

' THE ADDRESS OF THE HOUSE OF REPRESENTATIVES
' IN ANSWER TO THE GOVERNOR'S SPEECH.

' WE, the house of representatives of the state of
' South Carolina, in general assembly met, return
' your excellency our most cordial thanks for your
' very interesting speech to both houses at the open-
' ing of this session, the language of which, evident-
' ly bespeaks a heart glowing with ardent zeal for
' the interest and welfare of our common country.

' WE want words to express our heart-felt exulta-
' tion on the pleasing reverse in our affairs. On
' this spot, but a few months past, a military despo-
' tism prevailed, and tyranny, with lawless violence,
' was desolating our fair possessions; but we now,
' with ecstacy, behold a free government re-establish-

'ed, liberty, that greatest of temporal blessings, re-
'stored, and every citizen secured in the possession
'of his property by the firm barrier of the law of his
'country. This auspicious change is in a great de-
'gree owing to the prudence, firmness and good con-
'duct of your excellency.

'IF any thing can add to the sublime and refined
'enjoyment, which must arise from your excellen-
'cy's own reflections on your persevering, unabated
'and successful exertions towards rescuing your coun-
'try from the iron hand of oppression, be pleased,
'sir, to accept the most sincere and unfeigned thanks
'of your grateful fellow-citizens.

'THE black catalogue which your excellency has
'given of British barbarities, forms but a small part
'of the whole. Whenever the historic page shall be
'stained with their story, it will exhibit a nation de-
'void of faith; with whom oaths, treaties, and the
'most solemn compacts were considered as trifles:
'who, without scruple or remorse, had abandoned
'all regard to humanity, honor, justice and every
'ennobling sentiment of the human breast. It is
'hardly possible to conceive any circumstance that
'could aggravate the atrocious wickedness of their
'conduct. There is not left a step in the degrada-
'tion of national character to which they can now
'descend. The name of a Briton must hencefor-
'ward be a term of reproach among all nations.

' We should betray a great degree of insensibility,
' and be wanting in justice to his merit, should we
' omit this occasion of acknowledging, with the
' warmest gratitude, our obligations to the great and
' gallant General Greene. His atchievements in
' this state, while they rank him with the greatest
' commanders of ancient or modern date, will en-
' grave his name in indelible characters on the heart
' of every friend to this country. Our acknowledg-
' ments are also due to all the brave officers and
' men under his command. who have so often fought,
' bled and conquered for us. The Generals Sump-
' ter, Marion and Pickens, with the brave militia
' under their commands, those virtuous citizens who
' did not despair of the commonwealth in her greatest
' extremity, are deserving of the highest commend-
' ation. The friendly, seasonable and effectual aid
' recently afforded us by our great and illustrious
' ally, by means of which the General on whom the
' British nation seemed most to have placed their
' dependence. has been compelled to surrender the
' flower of the British army to our immortal com-
' mander in chief, must greatly increase the flame
' of gratitude which had been before kindled in the
' breast of every American, and which it will not be
' in the power of time or accident to extinguish.
' We perfectly concur in sentiment with your excel-
' lency, that, from our connection with this powerful

' and wise monarch, we may expect, with well-
' grounded confidence, that our independence will be
' shortly established upon an immoveable basis, nor
' need we harbor a single fear of its dissolution.

' AN union which originated from such liberal and
' generous motives, and which is founded on mutual
' interest, that best cement of nations, must and will
' continue. Whether the series of losses, disasters
' and defeats of the year past, will at length recover
' Britain from her delirium, time only can disclose;
' but as misfortune hitherto, instead of producing re-
' flection and prudence, has operated to increase her
' insanity, we agree in opinion with your excellency,
' that it is probable she will not only endeavor to keep
' possession of our capital, but make another attempt
' to subjugate the country...we shall therefore imme-
' diately enter upon the prosecution of the measures
' recommended by your excellency, as necessary for
' its safety; and being fully sensible how much de-
' pends upon the result of our deliberations, we will
' endeavor to proceed in the weighty business with
' firmness and temper, with vigor, unanimity and dis-
' patch.

   ' By order of the house,

        ' HUGH RUTLEDGE, Speaker.'

ON the execution of Colonel Hayne, the regular
officers of the continental army petitioned General

Greene that he would retaliate on the British officers.
[See appendix, note 32, 33.]

THE British emissaries had induced the Cherokee
Indians to commence hostilities against the Americans. They, with a number of white men disguised,
made an incursion into the district of Ninety-six,
murdered some families, and burnt some houses.
General Pickens collected three hundred and ninety-
four men, and marched into the Cherokee country,
burnt thirteen towns, killed upwards of forty Indians,
and took a great number of Indians prisoners, and
returned in fourteen days; not one of his party killed,
and only three wounded. This was the second time,
during the American war, that the Cherokees had
been chastised in their own settlements, and again
sued for peace, which they obtained upon a promise
not to listen to the British emissaries, and to deliver
up all who endeavored to instigate them to war
against the Americans.

IT now became necessary, agreeably to the constitution, to choose a new governor; when the honorable Christopher Gadsden was chosen governor, who
delivered a short speech, which he concluded as follows: ' The present times require the vigor and ac-
' tivity of the prime of life, but I feel the increasing
' infirmities of old age to such a degree, that I am
' conscious I cannot serve you to advantage: I there-
' fore beg, for your sakes, and for the sake of the pub-

'lic, that you will indulge me with the liberty of de-
' clining the arduous trust.' He was indulged in his
request. Then the general assembly elected the honorable John Mathews governor: he filled up all vacancies in the civil departments, and re-established civil
government in all its branches. They also delegated
to the governor the same extensive powers with similar limitations, which they had entrusted to his pre-
decessor, ' of doing all matters and things which were
' judged expedient and necessary, to secure the li-
' berty, safety and happiness of the state.'

THE legislature then proceeded to business. Laws
were passed for confiscating the estates and banishing
certain persons mentioned therein; and for amercing
the estates of others, as a substitution for the personal services of which their country had been deprived. The reasons that induced the assembly to
adopt the measures of confiscation, &c. were stated
by themselves in the preamble to the act, which is in
the words following: ' Whereas the thirteen British
' colonies, now the United States of America, were,
' by an act of the parliament of Great Britain, passed
' in or about the month of December, in the year of
' our Lord one thousand, seven hundred and seventy-
' five, declared to be in rebellion, and out of the pro-
' tection of the British crown; and by the said act
' not only the property of the colonists was declared
' subject to seizure and condemnation, but divers

' seizures and destruction of their property having
' been made after the nineteenth day of April, anno
' Domini one thousand seven hundred and seventy-
' five ; and before the passing of the said act, such
' seizures and destruction were by the said act de-
' clared to be lawful : and, whereas the good people
' of these states having not only suffered great losses
' and damages by captures of their property on the
' sea by the subjects of his Britannic majesty, but by
' their seizing and carrying off much property taken
' on the land : in consequence of such proceedings
' of the British crown, and those acting under its
' authority, the honorable Congress of the United
' States, after due and mature consideration, au-
' thorized the seizing and condemnation of all pro-
' perty found on the sea, and belonging to the sub-
' jects of Great Britain, and recommended to the se-
' veral states in which such subjects had property, to
' confiscate the same for the public use ; all political
' connection between Great Britain and the United
' States having been dissolved by the separation of
' these states from that kingdom, and their declar-
' ing themselves free and independent of her : in
' pursuance of which recommendation, most, if not
' all, have disposed of such property for the public
' use. And, whereas, notwithstanding this state has
' forborne even to sequester the profits arising from
' the estates of British subjects, the enemy, in viola

'tion of the most solemn capitulations and public
'engagements, by which the property of individuals
'was secured to them, seized upon, sequestered and
'applied to their own use, not only in several instances,
'the profits of the estates, but in other instances
'the estates themselves of the good citizens of this
'state, and have committed the most wanton and
'wilful waste of property both real and personal, to
'a very considerable amount.

'AND whereas. from a proclamation of Sir Henry
'Clinton, declaring, that if any person should ap-
'pear in arms in order to prevent the establishment
'of his Britannic majesty's government in this coun-
'try, such persons should be treated with the utmost
'severity, and their estates be immediately seized in
'order to be confiscated : and whereas, from a letter
'of Lord Rawdon to Lieutenant Colonel Rugely, de-
'claring, that every militia-man who did not use his
'utmost endeavors to apprehend deserters, should
'be punished in such manner as his lordship should
'think adequate to such offence, by whipping, im-
'prisonment, or being sent to serve his Britannic
'majesty in the West-Indies. From Earl Cornwal-
'lis' letter to Lieutenant Colonel Cruger, bearing
'date the eighteenth of August, 1780, declaring
'that he had given orders that all the inhabitants
'who had submitted, and who had taken part with
'their countrymen in the first action near Camden,

' although such submission was an act of force or
' necessity, should be punished with the greatest ri-
' gor...that they should be imprisoned, and their
' whole property taken from them or destroyed...and
' that he had ordered, in the most positive manner,
' that every militia-man who had borne arms on the
' part of his Britannic majesty, and who had after-
' wards joined his fellow-citizens, although he had
' been compelled to take up arms against them,
' should be immediately hanged ; and ordering the
' said Lieutenant Colonel Cruger to obey these di-
' rections in the district in which he commanded, in
' the strictest manner. And, from the general tenor
' of the enemy's conduct in their wilful and wanton
' waste and destruction of property as aforesaid, com-
' mitting to a cruel imprisonment, and even hang-
' ing, and otherwise putting to death in cold blood
' and an ignominious manner, many good citizens
' who had surrendered as prisoners of war, it is evi-
' dent that it was the fixed determination of the ene-
' my, notwithstanding their professions to the con-
' trary, to treat this state as a conquered country ;
' and that the inhabitants were to expect the utmost
' severities, and to hold their lives, liberties and pro-
' perties, solely at the will of his Britannic majesty's
' officers.

' And it is therefore inconsistent with public jus-
' tice and policy to afford protection any longer to

' the property of British subjects, and just and rea-
' sonable to apply the same towards alleviating and
' lessening the burdens and expenses of the war, which
' must otherwise fall very heavy on the distressed
' inhabitants of this state; Be it therefore enacted'...

THE Jacksonborough assembly was much censured by some, and thought to have been very severe
and cruel to their fellow-citizens, in passing the confiscation, banishment and the amercement laws : but
when it comes to be considered, the very men who
composed that legislature were yet in the field, and
many of them had been fighting during the whole
war; and some of them perhaps with their wounds
still bleeding ; and others just returned from captivity and banishment, it is not to be wondered at,
that they should be in an ill humor, and displeased
with their countrymen, who had entered into a solemn compact with them, to support the rights and
liberties of their country ; and that they should be at
that very time within the British lines, under their
protection, and some of them with British commissions in their pockets. The taking protection, and
remaining quiet was no great offence ; it was unavoidable with many. I advised several of my friends,
after the fall of Charleston (who were not in the continental army) to take that step, and to stay with
their families, till we could come in force to release

them : but to take protection, then a commission, and then to treat their countrymen worse and with more rigor than enemies themselves, was unpardonable; but for the honor of the Jacksonborough assembly, the most of those very men were members at the first meeting of the general assembly which met in Charleston after the evacuation. When they had got possession of their country again, and peace was restored, they were softened with pity, and had compassion for their fellow citizens, and listened with cheerfulness to the prayer of their petitions. I had the honor of being appointed chairman to a large committee from the senate, to meet a very large committee from the house of representatives, to hear the merits of their several petitions; and after sitting several weeks and giving every one a fair and impartial hearing, a report was made to the separate houses in favor of a great majority; and a great part of those names which were upon the confiscation, banishment and amercement lists, were struck off; and after a few years, on their presenting their petitions year after year, almost the whole of them had their estates restored to them, and themselves received as fellow-citizens.

ABOUT the middle of January, 1782, General Greene took post with the American army below Jacksonborough, and in April moved down to Beach-hill, near Bacon-bridge, where he remained till the seventh of July, when he came down and took pos t

at Ashley-river, about sixteen miles from Charleston:
on the fourth of April he received the following letter from General Leslie:

'HEAD-QUARTERS, April 4th, 1782.

'SIR,

'IT was with deep concern I viewed, in the pro-
'ceedings of your last assembly, acts for amercing
'the property of some persons, and confiscating that
'of others, whose principles had attached them to
'the cause of their sovereign. Yet, alarming as the
'public resolutions appeared, I was in hopes hu-
'manity, as well as policy, would have arrested
'their execution, and that I should not have been
'compelled to take measures for their counteraction,
'injurious to the country, and therefore painful to
'me. But when these hopes were disappointed, and
'I found the effects of the loyal and well-affected re-
'moved from their estates, and carried to parts far
'distant from them, I could no longer remain the
'quiet spectator of their distresses; but, in order to
'induce a juster line of conduct, I have employed a
'part of the force intrusted to my charge for their
'protection, in seizing the negroes of your friends,
'that restitution may be thereby made to such of
'ours as may suffer under these oppressive and ruin-
'ous resolutions. This, sir, was the object of the
'late excursion towards Santee, and these principles

' will greatly mark the future operations of this army,
' unless a relinquishment of this assumed right on
' your part should justify less destructive measures
' on mine.

' To point out to you, or the world, the distinction
' between temporary sequestration and actual confis-
' cation, would be impertinent; but it will by no
' means be so to observe on the opposite conduct
' pursued by each party in carrying into execution
' these very different measures; for whilst you have
' endeavored to involve, in perpetual ruin, the per-
' sons and estates of those who have differed from
' you in political sentiments, I can safely appeal even
' to those whose violent opposition to the king's go-
' vernment compelled the with-holding from them
' for a time their possessions in this province, for the
' great attention which has been invariably paid to
' their property...the connected state in which it has
' been preserved...and the liberal allowances that were
' made to their families, insomuch, that, while other
' estates were running to waste by the distractions of
' the country, these have greatly thriven at the ex-
' pense of government.

' Thus far I have deemed it necessary to urge the
' motives of humanity, policy and example, for your
' suspension of such rigorous procedures; and should
' you think a meeting of commissioners on each side
' might tend to lessen the devastations of war, and

' secure inviolate the property of individuals, I shall
' have a peculiar happiness in embracing proposals
' that may accomplish such benevolent purposes;
' but, if, notwithstanding this earnest representation,
' you should still persevere in executing these acts
' of your assembly, I trust this letter will hold me
' justifiable to the world for any measures which
' necessity may adopt in counteraction of steps unjust
' in their principles and personally distressful in their
' consequences; and that, whilst I only endeavor to
' secure to those, who with respectable steadiness
' have attached themselves to our cause, the full pos-
' session of their effects, or, in case of losses, to pro-
' vide an equitable restitution for them, I shall be
' clearly exculpated from all the horrors and calami-
' ties which the road you now point out unavoidably
' leads to.

  ' I have the honor to be,
   ' your most obedient
    ' and most humble servant,
  (Signed)   ' ALEX. LESLIE.
' To Major General GREENE.'

To this letter General Greene returned an immediate answer, ' that he had the honor to command
' the forces of the United States in the southern de-
' partment, but had nothing to do with the internal
' police of any state.' On which Lieutenant General

Leslie addressed himself to Governor Mathews, and
inclosed the letter which had been addressed to General Greene, to which Governor Mathews gave the
following answer:

‘ April 12th, 1782.

‘ SIR,

‘ I HAD the honor of receiving your letter of the
‘ eighth instant, inclosing one from you to Major Ge-
‘ neral Greene of the fourth, and his answer to you
‘ of the same date.

‘ THE manner in which you refer to your letter to
‘ General Greene, obliges me to view that letter as
‘ now addressed to me. I must therefore beg leave
‘ to observe upon it, previous to answering the one
‘ immediately addressed to me.

‘ YOUR remaining so short a time in this state, af-
‘ ter the surrender of Charleston, and not returning
‘ to it till most of the sequestered estates had been
‘ rescued from the hands of your sequestrator, has
‘ put it out of your power to speak of the manage-
‘ ment of them in this country from your own know-
‘ ledge, consequently what has been said by you on
‘ that subject must have been from information. The
‘ character of General Leslie has always been repre-
‘ sented to me in so favorable a light, that candor
‘ forbids me to entertain the most distant idea of his
‘ having intentionally represented matters so con-

' trary to fact, to answer even the greatest political
' purposes ; but it is evident that he has been most
' grossly imposed on by men in whom he had con-
' fided, and that they have betrayed him into an as-
' sertion which must injure his feelings whenever he
' is possessed of a true state of the management of
' those estates that were put under sequestration by
' order of Lord Cornwallis.

' I WOULD not, sir, give an hasty answer to your
' observations on this subject, and thought myself
' well justified in deviating from the rule of polite-
' ness in delaying an answer, that I might have an
' opportunity of investigating truth. I have taken
' much pains in my inquiries, the result of which has
' been the most indubitable proofs, that so far from
' these sequestered estates " having had the greatest
" attention paid to them...being preserved in a con-
" nected state...and greatly thriven," most of them,
' while under the management of your sequestrator,
' have been very greatly injured ; many have been
' nearly ruined, and others altogether so. What ex-
' pense the British government has incurred on their
' account I know not, but, I can with confidence as-
' sert, the sequestered estates have been very little be-
' nefited thereby.

' I WILL now appeal to a fact within your own know-
' ledge. You know that great numbers of the ne-
' groes, belonging to these esates, are now within

‘ your lines, and lost to their owners. And on few
‘ plantations is a four-footed animal to be found. How
‘ then do you prove that the estates have been pre-
‘ served in a connected state, when one half of some,
‘ two-thirds of others, and the whole of a few of the
‘ estates have been deprived of the negroes and stock
‘ that were upon them when put under sequestration?
‘ How do you prove that these estates have greatly
‘ thriven, and that the greatest attention has been
‘ paid to them?

‘ As to the liberal allowance made to the families
‘ of those persons whose estates were sequestered,
‘ this, sir, I must beg leave to say you have been as
‘ greatly deceived in, as the other parts of your in-
‘ formation. So far from the wives and children
‘ having been allowed the stipulated sums out of their
‘ husbands’ and fathers’ estates, the truth is, that
‘ after much intreaty, and in many instances very
‘ unbecoming treatment, some have obtained trifling
‘ sums compared with what they were entitled to,
‘ while others have been altogether denied.

‘ On this ground of investigation, I am ready to
‘ meet you, sir, whenever you think proper, when
‘ I will undertake to produce to you the proofs of
‘ every thing I have here advanced.

‘ Your observation on the opposite conduct of
‘ each party in carrying into execution the measures
‘ of sequestration and confiscation, so far from being

'founded in fact, evidently shew the uniform decep-
'tion into which you have been led. In the common
'acceptation of the word, it is true, sequestration
'means no more than a temporary privation of pro-
'perty; but your sequestrator general, and most of
'his officers, have construed this word into a very dif-
'ferent meaning; and, regardless of the articles of
'capitulation of Charleston, as well as of the most
'sacred contracts contained in marriage-settlements,
'every species of property, negroes, plate, household-
'furniture. horses, carriages, cattle, &c. have been
'indiscriminately torn from their owners by persons
'now under your immediate command, and have been
'either sent beyond seas, for the benefit of those who
'had taken...I had almost said plundered them, or
'now remain within your lines, and in either case
'lost to their owners.

'Now, sir, let us for a moment view the conduct
'of the legislature of this state in their late session.
'The most sacred regard has been paid by them to
'private contracts, neither marriage-settlements nor
'the faith of individuals have been violated, but left
'to their full operation. A provision also was made
'for the families of those whose estates have been
'confiscated. And although the property of British
'subjects within this state has been confiscated, yet
'the debts due to them from the citizens of this state
'have been left untouched. And be assured, sir,

' whilst I have the honor of holding the rank I now
' do, it shall be my particular business to see that
' this, as well as every other law of the state, is exe-
' cuted with lenity, fidelity and integrity.

' AFTER these observations, permit me, sir, to
' draw your serious attention to a candid and impar-
' tial view of the conduct of each party on the opera-
' tion of your sequestration and our confiscation acts,
' when I leave you at liberty and at leisure to judge,
' whether you find any difference between them, and
' if you do, whether confiscation on our part is likely
' to be productive of more ruinous consequences to
' those who are affected by it, than sequestration on
' your part has been to those unfortunate citizens of
' this state who have felt its effects.

' As to the assumption of a right on the part of
' the state, to treat its citizens according to their de-
' merits, I must beg leave to observe such language
' is only calculated to irritate, and by no means to
' accomplish the ends you aim at. And, sir, if you
' conceive ours to be no more than an assumed right,
' I have reason to suppose that no convention that
' can be entered into in the negociation that you pro-
' pose can be looked upon by you as binding, after it
' has been in the most solemn manner concluded.
' And, did I not suppose the expression had inadvert-
' ently escaped you, I should rest the matter here,
' and think no more about it. But the opinion I en-

‘ tertain of General Leslie forbids me to imagine him
‘ capable of deception.

‘ You entirely mistake my character when you
‘ suppose me to be intimidated by threats, and there-
‘ by deterred from executing the duties of the office
‘ with which the state has honored me. For, be as-
‘ sured, sir, the laws of this state trusted to me, must
‘ and shall be carried into execution...maugre the
‘ consequences.

‘ THE powers vested in me by the state are very
‘ extensive; but I shall ever be extremely cautious
‘ how I exercise them, and when I do I must be con-
‘ vinced that the exercise of my extraordinary powers
‘ is calculated to produce some proportionate benefit
‘ to the state.

‘ I WOULD recommend to you, sir, to consider well
‘ the consequences before you carry into execution
‘ the threats you hold out; for, remember, the estates
‘ reserved for marriage-settlements, and the debts
‘ due to those who have attached themselves to your
‘ cause, as well as the debts due to the subjects of
‘ Britain, are in my power, and that I can, in an
‘ hour's time, deprive them of every benefit to be
‘ derived to them from the benevolent intentions of
‘ the legislature of this state. My sensibility would
‘ be extremely wounded, should I be reduced to the
‘ painful necessity of exercising this power; but it
‘ rests with you, sir, whether I do or not. And I shall

' bo as ready as you are to appeal to the world for the
' rectitude of my conduct.

' Your proposition for suspending the operation
' of the confiscation act, without offering any equiva-
' lent, is inadmissable. If you have any thing seri-
' ous and solid to propose on this head, I am ready
' to appoint commissioners on my part to meet those
' of yours to confer on the business.

  ' I have the honor to be,
   ' sir, your most obedient
    ' and humble servant,
 (Signed)   ' John Mathews.
' Lieutenant General Leslie.'

After the capture of Lord Cornwallis' army in
Virginia, the Pennsylvania line marched to South
Carolina and joined General Greene, which enabled
him to send a detachment to Georgia, under the
command of General Wayne. That country had
been entirely laid waste by the desolations of war:
the rage between Whig and Tory ran so high, that
what was called a Georgia parole, and to be shot
down, were synonymous.

Armed parties were frequently making excursions
against the British detachments. Colonel Clark commanded a party of Georgia militia, and the twenty-
third of March, 1781, fell in with Major Dunlap,
near Ninety-six, with a detachment of British troops:

the major and forty-three men were killed, and forty-two taken prisoners.

In January, 1782, General Wayne was detached to Savannah-river with one hundred dragoons, under Colonel White ; he crossed at the Two-sisters' ferry ; having previously ordered the Americans at Augusta, to join him at Ebenezer : he was afterwards reinforced by three hundred continental infantry under Colonel Posey. The British commander hearing of the Americans, sent orders to all the different posts, to burn the provisions in the country, and retire within their works at Savannah. The provisions were so effectually destroyed, that the Americans were obliged to depend chiefly upon South Carolina for their support. The garrison at Savannah consisted of about one thousand regulars and some militia, under the command of Brigadier General Clarke. Notwithstanding, General Wayne appeared frequently before their lines, and attacked their picquets. Several attempts were made to surprise the advance of the Americans under Lieutenant Colonel Jackson, but without effect.

About this time, Governor Martin, of the state of Georgia, came with his council from Augusta to Ebenezer, and re-established the American government near the sea-coast. Soon after his arrival, he issued his proclamation, offering every British and Hessian soldier who would leave Savannah, two hundred acres of land and some stock; which had a very good effect.

On the twenty-first of May, 1782, Colonel Brown marched out of Savannah, with an intention of attacking the Americans but General Wayne got between him and Savannah, attacked him at twelve o'clock at night, and routed his whole party. Colonel Brown had forty men killed and twenty taken prisoners. The Americans had only five killed and two wounded.

On the twenty-fourth of June, 1782, a party of Creek Indians, with a British officer at their head, made an attack on General Wayne in the night. They conducted the affair with so much spirit, that they got possession of two field-pieces that were in the rear; the troops so rallied and recovered the two pieces. This was a smart action, in which they fought hand to hand with tomahawks, swords and bayonets: the Indians were routed; they lost one of their chiefs, and fourteen were killed. The Americans took a British standard and a number of horses. The American army interrupted the intercourse between the Indians and Savannah. A party of them were on their way to Savannah with a large quantity of skins and a number of horses, which were taken by General Wayne. Two of them were detained as hostages; the remainder were sent home with provisions and a friendly talk. This kind treatment, with the successes of General Greene and the surrender of Lord Cornwallis, detached the Indians from their friends the British.

EARLY in 1782, Great Britain was induced to abandon all offensive operations in America; and on the twentieth of May, 1782, General Leslie proposed to General Greene a cessation of hostilities, but this was declined for want of instructions from Congress: however, nothing of consequence was attempted on either side.

A SCHEME was now adopted of evacuating the smaller posts in the United States; Savannah being the first southern post which was evacuated. It was evacuated on the eleventh of July, 1782.

WHEN the merchants and others came to be informed of this determination, they obtained permission to apply to General Wayne for the security of their property. To their deputies he replied, ' that, ' should the British garrison eventually effect an evacu- ' ation, the persons and properties of such inhabitants ' and others, who choose to remain in Savannah, ' will be protected by the military, and resigned in- ' violate into the hands of the civil authority, which ' must ultimately decide.' The merchants and inhabitants of Savannah, having sent out a second flag, General Wayne, at the desire of the civil authority of the state, sent them for answer, ' that the ' merchants, not owing allegiance to the United ' States, will be permitted to remain a reasonable

' time to dispose of their goods and settle their af-
' fairs.' Major Habersham, who was charged with
this message, pledged himself that they might rely,
with the utmost confidence, on the terms proposed
to them.

On the eleventh of July, 1782, the British evacuated Savannah, and the Americans took possession.
Peace was restored to Georgia, after it had been
four years in the possession of the British. It was
supposed that state lost one thousand of its citizens,
and four thousand slaves.

Early in 1782, a report circulated that the British intended to evacuate Charleston very shortly.
The Americans were looking forward for that happy
event every week, which, however, did not take place
till the fourteenth of December. The moving such
a body of troops with their baggage and stores, the
property of the merchants and others, and the vast
property plundered from the Americans, was a work
of time, and required a great many vessels to take
them off which could not be easily procured. However, the Americans were in possession of the whole
country, except Charleston and about five miles without the gates. Major Ganey was at the head of a
small party of Tories about Little Peedee, who
hid themselves in the swamps, and would frequently
sally out, and distress the people in that neighborhood. On the twenty-eighth of April, a party of

them came out under the command of Captain Jones, and set fire to Colonel Kolb's house; he afterwards surrendered himself, upon a promise of his being treated as a prisoner. Notwithstanding, he had been so notorious a villain, that he was immediately put to death before his wife and children. Ganey was so troublesome, that General Marion made a treaty of neutrality with him in 1781. [See appendix, note 34.] Afterwards, the state gave them a full pardon for all treasons which they had committed, and a security for their property, on condition of their delivering up their plunder.

AFTER it was given out in general orders that Charleston would be evacuated, General Leslie wrote to General Greene, offering payment for rice and other provisions to be sent into Charleston; [See appendix, note 35.] at the same time threatening, that if it was not granted for money, that it should be taken by force.

ON the proposed evacuation, the merchants and others, who came with the British to Charleston, were in a disagreeable situation : they had contracted large debts with those without the lines, who were unable to pay; they therefore applied to General Leslie, for leave to negociate for themselves, which was granted. A deputation from them waited on Governor Mathews, who granted permission for them to reside in South Carolina eighteen months, to col-

lect their debts and settle their business. This indulgence was extended to a longer time by the legislature.

THE government refusing to send provisions to
Charleston, was the occasion of much specie being
carried away, besides losing the opportunity of sell-
ing a large portion of the produce at a very advanced
price. It was owing to their friendship for the
French nation, as it was believed, that the British
intended to supply themselves with a large quantity
of provisions, to carry on the war in the French
West-India Islands. General Leslie, finding that he
could not purchase, sent out large parties to seize
provisions near the different landings, and bring
them by water to Charleston. This was effected, in
some instances, before a body of men could be sent
to prevent it.

A LARGE party of the British were sent to Combahee-ferry to collect provisions; where they arrived
on the twenty-fifth of August, 1782. Brigadier General Gist was detached with about three hundred
infantry and cavalry to oppose them : he captured
one of their schooners, and prevented them, in a
great measure, from getting provisions. When the
two parties were near each other, Colonel John Laurens, being advanced with a small party, fell in with
a superior force which he engaged : he was too far
advanced to be supported by the main body. In this

affair he received his mortal wound, and died in the field. Several of his men were killed and wounded. The party were obliged to retreat. Soon after this, an attack was made on a party of British on James-Island, near Fort Johnson, by Captain Wilmot, who was killed with some of his party ; the rest retreated. This was the last blood which was shed in the American war.

When the evacuation of Charleston drew near, it was apprehended that the British army would carry off some thousands of negroes which were within their lines. To prevent this, Governor Mathews wrote a letter to General Leslie, dated August seventeenth, 1782, in which he informed him, ' that, if the ' property of the citizens of South Carolina was ' carried off from its owners by the British army, ' he should seize on the debts due to the British ' merchants...and the confiscated estates...and the ' claims on those estates by marriage-settlements... ' which three articles were not included in the confis- ' cation act.' This conditional resolution operated as a check on some, so as to restrain their avidity for plunder, and induced General Leslie to propose a negociation, for securing the property of both parties. The honorable Benjamin Gerard and Edward Rutledge Esqrs. were appointed commissioners in behalf of the state, and Alexander Wright and James Johnson, Esqrs. in behalf of the royalists. After sundry conversations, the commissioners on both sides, on the tenth of October, 1782, ratified a compact on this subject, of which the following are the principal articles:

'FIRST, That all the slaves of the citizens of South
'Carolina, now in the power of the honorable Lieu-
'tenant General Leslie, shall be restored to their
'former owners, as far as is practicable, except such
'slaves as may have rendered themselves particularly
'obnoxious on account of their attachment and ser-
'vices to the British troops, and such as had specific
'promises of freedom.

'THAT the faith of the state is hereby solemnly
'pledged, that none of the debts due to British mer-
'chants, or to persons who have been banished, or
'whose estates have been confiscated, or property
'secured by family settlements fairly made, or con-
'tracts relative thereto, shall now, or at any time
'hereafter, be arrested or with-held by the executive
'authority of the state...that no act of the legislature
'shall hereafter pass for confiscating or seizing the
'same in any manner whatever, if it is in the power
'of the executive to prevent it...and that its whole
'power and influence, both in its public and private
'capacity, shall at all times be exerted for that pur-
'pose.

'THAT the same power shall be allowed for the re-

' covery of the debts and property, hereby protected
' and secured by the parties or their representatives,
' in the courts of justice or otherwise, as the citizens
' of the state may at any time be entitled unto, not-
' withstanding any act of confiscation or banishment,
' or any other disability whatever...and that the same
' may be remitted to whatever part of the world they
' may think proper, under the same, and no other
' regulations than the citizens of the state may be sub-
' ject to.

' THAT no slaves restored to their former owners,
' by virtue of this agreement, shall be punished by
' authority of the state for having left their masters,
' and attached themselves to the British troops; and
' it will be particularly recommended to their respect-
' ive owners to forgive them for the same.

' THAT no violence or insult shall be offered to the
' persons or houses of the families of such persons as
' are obliged to leave the state for their adherence to
' the British government, when the American army
' shall take possession of the town, or at any time af-
' terwards, as far as it is in the power of those in au-
' thority to prevent it.

' THAT Edward Blake and Roger Parker Saunders,
' Esqrs. be permitted to reside in Charleston, on their
' parole of honor, to assist in the execution of the first
' article of this compact.'

In consequence of this agreement, Governor Mathews gave a commission and a flag to the honorable Thomas Ferguson and Thomas Waring, Esqrs. to reside near the British lines, with instructions to receive such negroes as should be delivered from the garrison. Edward Blake and Roger Parker Saunders, Esqrs. had also a commission and a flag given them to reside in Charleston, and forward the delivery of the negroes to the gentlemen who were waiting to receive them without the garrison. Governor Mathews requested the citizens of the state to attend for the purpose of receiving their negroes, and earnestly intreated that they would forgive them for having deserted their service and joined the British. Great were the expectations of the suffering inhabitants, that they would soon obtain re-possession of their property ; but these delusive hopes were of short duration. Notwithstanding the solemnity with which the compact had been ratified, it was so far evaded as to be in a great measure ineffectual for the end proposed.

EDWARD Blake and Roger Parker Saunders, Esqrs. having waited on General Leslie, were permitted to examine the fleet bound to St. Augustine ; but were not suffered to examine any vessel that wore the king's pendant. Instead of an examination' the word of the commanding officer, to restore all the slaves that were on board, in violation of the

compact, was offered as an equivalent. In their search
of the Augustine fleet, they found and claimed one
hundred and thirty six negroes. When they attended to receive them on shore, they were surprised to
find no more than seventy-three landed for delivery.
They then claimed this small residue of the original
number, to be forwarded to the other commissioners
without the lines, but they were informed by General Leslie, that no negroes would be delivered, till
three soldiers were restored that had been taken by
a party of General Greene's army. On that occasion, the following letter was written to Edward
Blake and Roger Parker Saunders, Esqrs:

'Head-Quarters, October 18th, 1782.

'Gentlemen,

'General Leslie was much surprised on finding
' that a large patrole from General Greene's army,
' two days ago, came down so near our advanced
' post on Charleston-neck, as to carry off three sol-
' diers who were a little way in the front. At the
' time this act of hostility was committed, Mr. Fer-
' guson and another person was at Accabee, where I
' believe they still remain, in expectation of receiving
' the negroes to be delivered up, without any sanction
' but that of the agreement entered into.

' I am directed to observe, that if a line of conduct
' on the part of General Greene so different from

' ours, is adopted, that it must of course put an end
' to the pacific intentions General Leslie means to
' follow in regard to this province, during the short
' time he is to remain in it.

' He wishes you will inform Governor Mathews,
' that he expects the soldiers taken away will be re-
' turned, and that the governor will take proper
' measures to have this requisition complied with.
' Until this is done, General Leslie must be under
' the necessity of putting a stop to the farther com-
' pletion of the agreement.

' I am, gentlemen,

' your most obedient,

' humble servant,

' J. Weyms, D. A. General.

' Roger P. Saunders and

' Edward Blake, Esqrs.'

This letter being forwarded to Governor Mathews,
he replied to it in a letter to General Leslie, in the
following words:

' October 19th, 1782.

' Sir,

' I was a few minutes ago favored with a let-
' ter from Messrs. Blake and Saunders, inclosing
' one to them from Major Weyms, written by your
' authority. As I do not like a second-hand corres-

' pondence, I therefore address myself immediately
' to you.

' I ADDRESSED a letter to you this morning, by
' which you will find, that I was not even then with-
' out some apprehensions of an intended evasion of
' the compact entered into on the tenth instant: but
' on the receipt of Major Weyms' letter, no room
' was left me for doubt; which obliges me, without
' giving farther trouble to those engaged in the busi-
' ness, and introducing farther altercation between
' us, to declare, that I look on that agreement as
' dissolved, and have accordingly ordered my com-
' missioners immediately to quit your lines. But, be-
' fore I take my final leave of you, permit me to make
' one or two observations on Major Weyms' letter,
' as probably the whole correspondence between us
' may one day be brought to public view.

' ON the twelfth instant I wrote to you, to know
' whether persons going to Accabee, to bring off
' their negroes when brought there, should be pro-
' tected from your armed parties; and farther, to
' permit me to send a party of militia to guard the
' negroes remaining unclaimed to some part of the
' country where they could be supplied with provi-
' sions. To this letter I have received no answer,
' which has obliged me to use the precaution of giv-
' ing flags to all persons who have applied to go to
' Accabee, as I could on no principle look on that

' ground as neutral until it had been mutually agreed
' on as such. Indeed, I was left to conclude the con-
' trary was intended on your part, both by your tedi-
' ous silence, and detachments from your army mak-
' ing excursions as far as Ashley-ferry, which was
' absolutely the case the morning of the day that the
' party from General Greene's army took the soldiers
' you so peremptorily demand of me. And, if I am
' rightly informed, hostilities were commenced by
' your party. But, be that as it may, I conceive it of
' little consequence, as either party had a right to
' commence hostilities on hostile ground, and be-
' tween enemies every spot must be considered as
' such until mutually agreed upon to be otherwise.
' Besides, it is a well-known fact, that there is not a
' day but some of your armed parties are on that very
' ground which you affect to hold neutral.

' WITH regard to Messrs. Ferguson and Waring
' remaining at Accabee unmolested; I hold myself
' under no manner of obligation to you for this for-
' bearance, as I informed you they were there under
' the sanction of a flag...that they were to remain
' there for the purpose of receiving the negroes sent
' out by the agents in Charlestown. They were there-
' fore authorised to continue there till you signified
' the contrary to them. Flags from you have re-
' mained within half a mile of our lines for several
' days, even on private business, without the least

' molestation whatever. Besides, sir, if your reason-
' ing, as far as it applies to those gentlemen, proves
' any thing, it proves too much, because, on the same
' principle, the other two commissioners, being in
' Charlestown, ought to make that neutral ground also,
' notwithstanding no stipulation for that purpose had
' been entered into. I never interfere with General
' Greene's military plans, therefore the paragraph
' which relates to his operations ought to have been
' addressed to him ; but I believe he pays as little
' regard to threats as I do.

> ' I have the honor to be,
> (Signed)   ' JOHN MATHEWS.
> ' Lieutenant General LESLIE.'

THIS was the unsuccessful termination of a benevolent scheme, originally calculated for mitigating
the calamities of war. Motives of humanity, together with the sacred obligation of the provisional articles of peace, prevented the state of South Carolina
from extending their confiscation laws. Instead of
adding to the list of the unhappy sufferers on that
score, the successive assemblies diminished their
number.

THE prospects of gain, from the sale of plundered
negroes, were too seducing to be resisted by the officers, privates and followers of the British army. On

their departure from Charlestown, upwards of eight hundred slaves, who had been employed in the engineer department, were shipped off for the West Indies. It was said and believed, that these were taken by the direction, and sold for the benefit of Lieutenant Colonel Moncrieff. The professional abilities of that distinguished officer cannot be too much applauded, nor his rapacity too much detested. The slaves carried off by the chief engineer were but a small part of the whole taken away at the evacuation, but their number is very inconsiderable when compared with the thousands that were lost from the first to the last of the war. It has been computed by good judges, that, between the years 1775 and 1783, the state of South Carolina was deprived of negroes to the amount of twenty-five thousand.

THE evacuation, though officially announced by General Leslie on the seventh of August, as soon to be adopted, did not take place till the fourteenth of December, 1782.

THE latter end of February, 1782, while I was at Philadelphia, I received my certificate of exchange, with my parole (cancelled) from Colonel Skinner : as they come from the first authorities, I here insert them that they may serve for precedents in future.

' THESE are to certify, that Brigadier General

' William Moultrie, in the service of the United
' States of America, and late prisoner of war to the
' British, was, on the ninth day of this month, re-
' gularly exchanged, with a number of other Ameri-
' cans, by composition for Lieutenant General Bur-
' goyne, of the British forces, and late a prisoner of
' war to the United States of America.

' GIVEN under my hand this nineteenth day of
' February, 1782.

' ABRAHAM SKINNER,
' Commissary General of Prisoners.
' To whom it may concern.'

' I DO hereby acknowledge myself to be a prisoner
' of war upon my parole, to his excellency Sir Hen-
' ry Clinton, &c. and that I am thereby engaged,
' until I shall be exchanged, neither to do, or cause
' any thing to be done, prejudicial to the success of
' the arms of his Britannic majesty : and I do further
' pledge my parole, that I will not intentionally go
' within twelve miles of any British garrison or post,
' and that I will surrender myself when required,
' agreeable to the terms of the cartel made on the
' third of May, 1782, for the exchange and relief of
' prisoners of war taken in the southern depart-
' ment*.

* For the Articles of a Cartel of Exchange, see page 198,
vol. ii.

' In witness whereof, I have hereunto subscribed
' my name this eighth day of July, in the year of
' our Lord, one thousand, seven hundred and eighty-
' one.

'Wm. Moultrie,
' Brigadier General,
' Charlestown, South Carolina.
' John Brown, A. Commissary of Prisoners.
' Geo. Gibbs, D. A. Commissary.'

General Burgoyne's exchange, released almost
a whole brigade of American officers, prisoners of
war. Only two of the South Carolina line were included in this exchange, which were Colonel C.
Pinckney* and myself.

Soon after my being exchanged, I prepared to set
off with my family for South Carolina, and early in
April left Philadelphia, and arrived at Waccamaw
in South Carolina in June, where I was informed
that General Greene's army lay at Ashley-river,
quite inactive, and no military operations going on.
I remained at Winyaw till late in September, at
which time I paid a visit to General Greene. It
was the most dull, melancholy, dreary ride that any
one could possibly take, of about one hundred miles
through the woods of that country, which I had

* General Pinckney.

been accustomed to see abound with live-stock and
wild fowl of every kind, was now destitute of all. It
had been so completely checquered by the different
parties, that not one part of it had been left unex-
plored; consequently, not the vestiges of horses, cattle, hogs, or deer, &c. was to be found. The squirrels
and birds of every kind were totally destroyed. The
dragoons told me, that on their scouts, no living crea-
ture was to be seen, except now and then a few
camp scavengers,* picking the bones of some unfortunate fellows, who had been shot or cut down, and
left in the woods above ground. In my visit to General Greene's camp, as there was some danger from
the enemy, I made a circuitous route to General Marion's camp, then on Santee-river, to get an escort
which he gave me, of twenty infantry and twenty cavalry: those, with the volunteers that attended me
from Georgetown, made us pretty strong. On my
way from General Marion's to General Greene's
camp, my plantation was in the direct road, where I
called and stayed a night. On my entering the
place, as soon as the negroes discovered that I was
of the party, there was immediately a general alarm,
and an outcry through the plantation, that 'Massa
was come! Massa was come!' and they were running
from every part with great joy to see me. I stood in

----

* Turkey buzzards.

the piazza to receive them: they gazed at me with astonishment, and every one came and took me by the hand, saying, ' God bless you, massa! we glad for see you, massa !' and every now and then some one or other would come out with a ' ky !' And the old Africans joined in a war-song in their own language, of ' welcome the war home.' It was an affecting meeting between the slaves and the master: the tears stole from my eyes and run down my cheeks. A number of gentlemen that were with me, could not help being affected at the scene. Many are still alive, and remember the circumstance. I then possessed about two hundred slaves, and not one of them left me during the war, although they had had great offers, nay, some were carried down to work on the British lines, yet they always contrived to make their escapes and return home. My plantation I found to be a desolate place; stock of every kind taken off; the furniture carried away, and my estate had been under sequestration. The next day we arrived at General Greene's camp ; on our near approach, the air was so infected with the stench of the camp, that we could scarcely bear the smell; which shows the necessity of moving camp often in the summer, in these hot climates. General Greene expecting the evacuation to take place every week, from the month of August, was the reason he remained so long on the same ground.

BEFORE I conclude my memoirs, I must make my last tribute of thanks to the patriotic fair of South Carolina and Georgia, for their heroism and virtue in those dreadful and dangerous times whilst we were struggling for our liberties. Their conduct deserves the highest applause; and a pillar ought to be raised to their memory: their fortitude was such as gave examples, even to the men to stand firm; and they despised those who were not enthusiasts in their country's cause: the hardships and difficulties they experienced were too much for their delicate frames to bear; yet they submitted to them with a heroism and virtue that never has been excelled by the ladies of any country; and I can with safety say, that their conduct during the war contributed much to the independence of America.

FROM J. BURNET, ESQ.

'ASHLEY-HILL, December 13th, 1782.

'SIR,

'THE general commands me to say, that 'his excellency the governor, intends passing the 'river at Cedar-grove, and to meet him on the 'other side of Ashley-ferry, at 12 o'clock to-mor-'row.

'GENERAL Greene wishes to leave this place be-

' fore 10 o'clock ; when he hopes to have the plea-
' sure of seeing you here.

    ' I have the honor to be, &c.

                    ' J. BURNET,

' The honorable   Aid-de-Camp.

' Major Gen. MOULTRIE,

    ' Middleton-place.'

EVACUATION.

ON Saturday, the fourteenth day of December, 1782, the British troops evacuated Charlestown, after having possession two years, seven months, and two days.

THE evacuation took place in the following manner: Brigadier General Wayne was ordered to cross Ashley-river,* with three hundred light-infantry, eighty of Lee's cavalry, and twenty artillery, with two six-pounders, to move down towards the British lines, which was near Colonel Shubrick's, and consisted of three redoubts. General Leslie who commanded in town, sent a message to General Wayne, informing him, that he would next day leave the town, and for the peace and security of the inhabitants, and of the town, would propose to leave their advanced works

....

* General Greene's army lay on the west side of Ashley-river, above the ferry.

next day at the firing of the morning gun ; at which time, General Wayne should move on slowly, and take possession ; and from thence to follow the British troops into town, keeping at a respectful distance (say about two hundred yards ;) and when the British troops after passing through the town gates, should file off to Gadsden's-wharf, General Wayne was to proceed into town, which was done with great order and regularity, except now and then the British called to General Wayne that he was too fast upon them, which occasioned him to halt a little. About 11 o'clock, A. M. the American troops marched into town and took post at the state-house.

At 3 o'clock, P. M. General Greene conducted Governor Mathews, and the council, with some other of the citizens into town: we marched in, in the following order: an advance of an officer and thirty of Lee's dragoons ; then followed the governor and General Greene ; the next two were General Gist and myself; after us followed the council, citizens and officers, making altogether about fifty : one hundred and eighty cavalry brought up the rear: we halted in Broad-street, opposite where the South Carolina bank now stands ; there we alighted, and the cavalry discharged to quarters: afterwards, every one went where they pleased ; some in viewing the town, others in visiting their friends. It was a grand and pleasing sight, to see the enemy's fleet (upwards of three hundred sail) laying at anchor from Fort Johnson to Five-fathom-hole, in a curve line, as the current runs ; and what made it more agreeable, they were ready to depart from the port. The great joy that was felt on this day, by the citizens and soldiers, was inexpressible : the widows, the orphans, the aged men and others, who, from their particular situations, were obliged to remain in Charlestown, many of whom had been cooped up in one room of their own elegant houses for upwards of two years, whilst the other parts were occupied by the British officers, many of whom where a rude uncivil set of gentlemen; their situations, and the many mortifying circumstances occurred to them in that time, must have been truly distressing. I cannot forget that happy day when we marched into Charlestown with the American troops; it was a proud day to me, and I felt myself much elated, at seeing the balconies, the doors, and windows crowded with the patriotic fair, the aged citizens and others, congratulating us on our return home, saying, ' God bless you, gentlemen ! you are welcome home, gentlemen !' Both citizens and soldiers shed mutual tears of joy.

IT was an ample reward for the triumphant soldier, after all the hazards and fatigues of war, which he had gone through, to be the instrument of releasing his friends and fellow citizens from captivity, and restoring to them their liberties and possession of their city and country again.

THIS fourteenth day of December, 1782, ought never to be forgotten by the Carolinians ; it ought to be a day of festivity with them, as it was the real day of their deliverance and independence.

[The following orders should have been inserted in the preceding part of this volume, but was omitted by mistake.]

RESOLUTIONS OF CONGRESS AND ORDERS FROM GENERAL WASHINGTON.

' HEAD-QUARTERS, SHUTT'S-HILL,

June 18th, 1780.

' As it is at all times of great importance, both for the sake of appearance and for regularity of service, that the different military ranks should be distinguished from each other, and more especially at the present, the commander in chief has thought proper to establish the following distinctions, and strongly recommends to all the officers to endeavor to conform with them as speedily as possible.

' THE major generals to wear a blue coat with buff facings and lining, yellow buttons, white or buff under clothes, two epaulets with two stars upon each, and a black and white feather in the hat.

' THE brigadier generals the same uniform as the major generals, with the difference of one star instead of two, and white feather. The colonels, lieutenant colonels and majors, the uniform of their regiments, and two epaulets; captains, the uniform of their regiments and an epaulet on the right shoulder; the subalterns, the uniform of their regiments and an epaulet on the left shoulder.

'THE aid-de-camps, the uniform of their rank and corps; or, if they belong to no corps, the uniform of their general officers: those of the major general and brigadier generals, to wear a green feather in their hats; those of the commander in chief, white and green.

'THE inspectors, as well sub, as brigade, the uniform of their ranks and corps, with a blue feather in the hat.

'THE corps of engineers, and that of sappers and miners, a blue coat with buff facings, buff under clothes, and the epaulets of their ranks: such of the staff, as have military rank, to wear the uniform of the rank, and the corps to which they belong in the line; such as have no military rank, to wear a plain blue coat, with a cockade and sword.

'ALL officers, as well warranted as commissioned, to wear side arms, either swords or genteel bayonets.

'By order of his Excel. General WASHINGTON.

'SCAMMEL, Adjutant General.'

APPENDIX.

NOTE I.

LETTER FROM THE PRESIDENT.

SIR,   April 6th, 1778.

I HAVE received letters and information from the
Congarees, which give good grounds to suspect that
some design is formed to disturb the tranquility of the
interior parts of this state. Several of the inhabitants
have suddenly and secretly withdrawn themselves
from their habitations, and have manifested, by other
parts of their behavior, that some enterprise is in
agitation, that may, if not timely attended to, surprise us at a disadvantage. I have ordered Colonel
Beard to keep a good look out, and to raise a proper
number of his militia, so as to be in readiness to oppose any sudden attempt that may be undertaken by
those people called Tories. I have taken the liberty
to direct him in case the matter should wear a serious
aspect and require a greater force than he can readily draw from his regiment, to apply for aid and succor to Colonel Thomson, who, I believe has a detachment of his regiment near those parts, as I intended
to apply to you to give the required assistance. I
wish the present appearances which have given this
alarm may blow over without producing any ill con-

sequences. Perhaps the late incursions of the Florida scouts in those parts, may have afforded an opportunity of tampering with the ill-affected, and of exciting ill humours amongst them. However this may be, it is prudent to be prepared against the worst.

I am, &c.

RAWLINS LOWNDES.

The honorable General MOULTRIE.

HITHERTO the state had paid and clothed the troops, and furnished every article that was necessary for military operations from their own stores, the continent having nothing here at the time, which blended the civil and military so much together, as brought on disagreeable altercations, and made it quite a heterogeneous command, because it constrained the commanding officer of the troops to apply to the president for the smallest article for the use of the army. In consequence of the above letter from the president, I wrote the following.

NOTE II.
LETTER TO THE PRESIDENT.

SIR,   April 11, 1778.

As there are disturbances in this and the neighboring states, and as the matter may grow more serious, I shall frequently have occasion for different articles from the public stores, for the use of the continental troops in this state. I have daily applications from the different commanding officers, sometimes for trifling articles, which I am sorry to trouble you with at every call; I shall therefore be obliged to you, to order the public store-keeper to deliver to my order, or to the deputy quarter-master general on his giving a receipt for the same, such articles as may be wanted for the troops or forts, in times of alarm or actual invasion. It is impossible I can have time to send to you by letter or otherwise for every article; should I be under that necessity, it would retard our business, and perhaps be the loss of the whole.

The deputy quarter-master general informs me, he is in want of twenty thousand pounds to pay the debts already incurred, and for future services: I shall be much obliged to your excellency for an order on the treasurer in favor of the deputy quarter-master general for that sum, for the use of the troops in this state.   I am, &c.

WILLIAM MOULTRIE.

To his Excellency RAWLINS LOWNDES.

NOTE III.

LETTER TO THE PRESIDENT OF CONGRESS.

SIR,   April 19th, 1778.

THE honorable Major General Howe being now in Georgia, the command of the continental troops in

this state devolves upon me : I therefore do myself
the honor of writing you to inform you of such
matters as fall within the line of my duty.

ANOTHER matter which occurred the other day,
was this : requesting the favor of the president to order the treasurer of this state, to advance to the deputy
quarter-master general, twenty thousand pounds for
the use of the continental troops in this state, he refused, until he could first see the quarter-master's accounts ; I desired the deputy quarter-master general
to send him his books for his perusal, which he accordingly did, by his clerk, but the president was not
well pleased on his not waiting upon him himself :
the deputy quarter-master general said, he had no
business with the president ; his business was with
the commanding officer: the president also desired
the accounts to be drawn out and placed in the hands
of the auditor of this state. I told him I thought the
auditor had no business with the accounts; that he
was not a competent judge whether they were right
or not; that the accounts were transmitted to the
board of war and to General Mifflin, who were the
proper judges, and who laid them before Congress.

THE president apprehended, by a resolution of Congress, passed February the ninth, 1778, that he had
the power of suspending Colonel Huger, but I differed entirely with him, and told him, that officer had
his commission immediately from Congress: he re-

plied, that ' he was only a deputy of General Miff-
' lin's.' I shall be much obliged to your honor to
represent these matters to Congress and have them
cleared up, as I should be extremely unhappy to
have any difference with the executive authority during my command. I yesterday received letters by
express from General Howe, acquainting me that he
is apprehensive of an invasion on the state of Georgia,
but does not mention any particulars; but, from flying
reports, the insurgents from our back country are
gone off, to the number of five or six hundred, to join
Kirkland, who has a body of men at Pensacola, and
Brown, at St. Mary's. They are to be supported by
troops from Augustine, with some Indians. General Howe has ordered me to send him two hundred
and fifty continental troops, and thirty matrosses with
two field-pieces. The president has ordered three
hundred men from Bull's, and four hundred from
Williamson's regiment, to rendezvous at Purisburgh,
ready to support them, which I think will be quite
sufficient, &c.

I have the honor to be, yours, &c.

WILLIAM MOULTRIE.

The Honorable HENRY LAURENS.

NOTE IV.

EXTRACTS OF A LETTER FROM GENERAL HOWE.

SAVANNAH, April 14th, 1778.

DEAR SIR,

THE situation of affairs here, makes it necessary to desire that the men under marching orders, repair, with all possible expedition to Purisburgh, where they will receive directions as to their further conduct. You will take care that they are provided with every military requisite, as this state cannot furnish them. You are, however, not to delay the march of the men, for any preparations of this sort, as I am exceedingly anxious for their arrival, and shall continue to be so, till they do arrive.

I HAVE written to the president, requesting the favor of him to supply you with such stores, or other requisites as the continental agent cannot furnish you with, and inclose you a memorandum of what just now occurs to me. When I wrote you before, though I thought it eligible to prepare for the worst, yet I had hopes that things would not have been so serious ; but the aspect they now wear, induces me to believe, that this state, deplorably weak in itself, will need every support yours can give it : I am therefore under the necessity of ordering fifty men from the first regiment, and also thirty men from the artillery, with two field-pieces, with every thing proper for action.

I am, &c.

ROBERT HOWE.

Brig. Gen. MOULTRIE.

NOTE V.

LETTER TO THE PRESIDENT.

CHARLESTOWN, April 18th, 1778.

SIR,

MAJOR General Howe has ordered me to send a detachment of two hundred and fifty men, and thirty matrosses with two field-pieces, from this state, to march immediately to Georgia : he has also sent me a list of military stores much wanted there, and has desired me to request the favor of you, to let us have such articles from the arsenal of this state as can be spared, and that we cannot be supplied with from the continental agent here. I herewith send you a list of the articles wanted, and also sixty tents for the detachment, and three hundred havre-sac. He desires me, by all means, to have the commissary, the pay-master and the deputy quarter-master general to be well provided with money ; all of which he must know cannot be done without the favor of this state lending the money, as we have no military chest here. I am sorry to be under the necessity of requiring a loan from the treasury, as I know the great demands upon it, and the little money in bank ; however, if we cannot be supplied, I fear it will be of very dangerous consequences to Georgia, as well as to this state, if not soon relieved by us. I have shown you General Howe's letter, in which you see how pressing he is to expedite the marching of the troops.

I have the honor to be, &c.

WILLIAM MOULTRIE,
Brigadier General.

To his Excellency RAWLINS LOWNDES.

NOTE VI.
LETTER FROM THE PRESIDENT.

SIR,   April 17th, 1778.

SEVERAL gentlemen being out of town, I am not able to make a council. Such part of the articles which you mention in your list that we can spare, consistent with a proper attention to our own safety, you shall have; but I cannot ascertain the quantity or species, until I make further inquiry. The tents, the iron and the lead, we shall be obliged to curtail, as also the cartridge-paper. The most difficult article is the cash, which we certainly are not in a condition to supply in any considerable amount.

I am Sir, &c.

RAWLINS LOWNDES.

Brig. Gen. MOULTRIE.

NOTE VII.

LETTER TO GENERAL HOWE.

CHARLESTOWN, April 18th, 1778.

DEAR SIR,

I RECEIVED yours by express, last night, and shall order the first detachment off to-morrow morning; the remainder of the first regiment and the artillery will march off on Monday, under the command of Colonel Charles C. Pinckney; he, I think you will be glad to see with the detachment. I applied to the president for the articles you wanted, as by your list sent me. He says, ' what we can spare, ' consistent with a proper attention to our own safety, ' you shall have, but I cannot ascertain the quantity ' or species, until I make further inquiry. The tents, ' (I applied for sixty,) the iron and the lead, we shall ' be obliged to curtail, and also the cartridge-paper. ' The most difficult article is the cash, which we ' certainly are not in a condition to supply, in any ' considerable amount.' The treasury, I know, is at a very low ebb just now, owing to the many large draughts for our navy. They are almost tired of advancing for the continent. I wish you had been more particular in your letter, relative to your apprehensions of Georgia. You have left us to guess at the number, situation and posture of the enemy. A part of our unfortunate fleet is returned...the General Moultrie and Morgan. They give us the particulars of the unhappy fate of the Randolph. She blew up in about fifteen minutes engagement, fighting at a most infernal rate. The ship she engaged was the Yarmouth of sixty-four guns. They were so near as to throw their hand granades from their tops upon each other's decks : in short, during the time of the action, it was one continual blaze of fire, &c.

I am, &c.

WILLIAM MOULTRIE.

NOTE VIII.

EXTRACT OF A LETTER FROM GENERAL HOWE'S AID-DE-CAMB.

SAVANNAH, April 18th, 1778.

SIR,

I am directed by General Howe to request of you, that you would have the remaining part of the continental troops, amounting to one half the number and allowed by the president and council of your state, in immediate readiness for marching, upon receiving the general's orders. The general is extremely anxious to have the stores he wrote for forwarded with all possible expedition, and which he trusts your diligence will exert itself not to permit to be delayed at a time of such critical danger.

I am, &c.

J. F. GRIMKIE, Aid-de-Camp.

To Brig. Gen. MOULTRIE.

NOTE IX.

Letter from Major Grimkie.

Savannah, April 21st, 1778.

Sir,

Inclosed you have the deposition of a person arrived in Savannah this evening, in three days from St. Augustine, which is of the utmost importance. I am sure, sir, that you will not only see the necessity of ordering up the remainder of the troops allowed by the governor and council, but that you will, without delay, execute the orders I inclosed you this morning. You will therefore be pleased to order them to rendezvous at Savannah as soon as possible. The person who makes this affidavit, is a gentleman of reputation, and has traded to Savannah ten or twelve years.

I am, &c.

T. F. Grimkie, Aid-de-Camp.

Brig. Gen. Moultrie.

NOTE X.

Georgia.

Captain James Mercer at Savannah, being duly sworn, maketh oath and saith, ' that the deponent ' about the seventeenth day of April, sailed from St. ' Augustine with a French lad, and set sail from ' thence with intent to come to this state, where he ' is now happily arrived; after mentioning to the peo-

' ple in Augustine that the deponent was bound to
' St. John's, the better to secure his safe passage and
' prevent suspicions of his coming to Georgia...That
' a number of troops under the command of, and with
' General Provost, had left Augustine, and were des-
' tined towards the Alatamaha, as the deponent was
' informed...That he believes about three hundred
' men, regular troops, were left to garrison at Augus-
', tine, as was said...That the deponent, on his arrival
' in Augustine, was informed there were about four-
' teen hundred men in Augustine; and the deponent
' saw some of the battalions reviewed...That about
' three hundred men from the back parts of South
' Carolina had arrived and encamped at St. Mary's;
' and that seven hundred more were expected, and on
' their march to join them; and that advice of the
' three hundred had been sent to Augustine...That an
' express had come from the Creek Indians, inform-
' ing, that they, the Indians, were coming down to join
' the people of St. Augustine, as was reported...That
' it was generally believed that an expedition was on
' foot against Georgia...That a number of French
' prisoners had been sent off, and that two cartels
' bound to Charlestown or to Georgia, were ready to
' sail, with a number of prisoners on board the vessels
' appointed for that purpose; and that no ships of war
' were off the bar of Augustine when he the deponent
' left the place, other than Bachop's sloop of twelve

' guns, in the harbor, bound on a cruize...That the
' deponent further said, that he saw and partook of
' plenty of salt provisions, but very little fresh, &c.

'JAMES MERCER.'

Sworn before me, 21st April, 1778.

WM. STEPHENS, Attorney General.

NOTE XI.

LETTER FROM COLONEL ELBERT TO GENERAL
HOWE, INCLOSED TO ME.

FREDERICA HARBOR, on board the Sloop Rebecca.

DEAR GENERAL,　　　　April 19th, 1778.

I HAVE the happiness to inform you, that about
ten o'clock this forenoon, the Brigantine Hinchenbrook, the Sloop Rebecca, and the prize brig, all
struck the British colors, and surrendered to the
American arms. Having received intelligence that
the above vessels were at that place, I put about
three hundred men, by detachments, from the troops
under my command at Fort Howe, on board the
three gallies...the Washington, Captain Hardy; the
Lee, Captain Braddock; and the Bullock, Captain
Hatcher; and a detachment of artillery with two
field-pieces, under Captain Young, I put on board a
boat. With this little army we embarked at Darien,
and last evening effected a landing at a bluff, a mile
below the town; having Colonel White on board the
Lee, Captain Melvin on board the Washington, and

Lieutenant Petty on board the Bullock; each with a sufficient party of troops. Immediately on landing, I dispatched Lieutenant Ray and Major Roberts with about one hundred men, who marched directly up to the town, and made prisoners three marines and two sailors belonging to the Hinchenbrook. It being late, the galley did not engage until this morning. You must imagine what my feelings were, to see our three little men-of-war going on to the attack of those three vessels who have spread terror on our coast, and who drew up in order of battle. But the weight of our metal soon damped the courage of those heroes, who took to their boats; and as many as could, abandoned their vessels, with every thing on board...of which we immediately took possession. What is extraordinary, we have not one man hurt. Captain Ellis is drowned, and Captain Mawberry made his escape. As soon as I can see Colonel White, who has not come up with his prize, I shall consult with him and the others on the expediency of attacking the Galatea, now laying at Jakyl.

I am, &c.

SAMUEL ELBERT.

NOTE XII.

LETTER TO GENERAL HOWE.

DEAR SIR, April 24th, 1778.

I RECEIVED yours by express, last night, and

heartily rejoice at your success under Colonel Elbert, and hope soon to hear of their taking the Galatea. I doubt not but this will rouse the drooping spirits of the Georgians, and I think it will stop General Provost's further progress. Our first detachment marched off a few days ago, and Colonel Charles C. Pinckney with the second, went off yesterday. I have the use of the state galley to send to Georgia ; I shall man her with some soldiers, and in her send you ten thousand pounds of powder, and the cannon-shot, with some cartridge-paper, &c. with some of your stores. I think they might get to Savannah sooner than if they went by land. I have ordered the remainder of Thomson's and Sumpter's regiments to be ready to march on my receiving your further orders. I cannot send you a general return of the troops by the express, but I will have them ready to send you by the next opportunity. Our number of continental troops belonging to this state, amount to about fifteen hundred. I doubt not but that you will have boats ready to convey the troops from Purisburgh to Savannah. I am much hurried in getting the stores on board the

galley. I therefore refer you to Colonel Charles C. Pinckney for particulars, &c.

I am, &c.

WILLIAM MOULTRIE.
Brigadier General.

NOTE XIII.

LETTER FROM MAJOR GRIMKIE.

HEAD-QUARTERS, SAVANNAH, April 26th, 1778.

SIR,

I HAVE to request your excuse if I did not deliver myself so explicitly as I was ordered to do in the last letter I wrote you by desire of Major General Howe. As I did not keep a copy, not having time to write it over again, I cannot refer to the order, nor do I at present recollect in what mode of expression I delivered myself. The order, sir, that it was my intention to transmit you, should have positively declared the necessity for the immediate march of the troops, forming the remaining part of the continental battalions in the state of South Carolina. You will please, therefore, to order the troops you refer to, whom you say you have directed to be ready to march at a moment's warning, and consists of the other parts of Colonel Thomson's and Sumpter's regiments. They are to proceed to Fort Howe, by the shortest road upon the Alatamaha, without touching at Savannah, &c.

By order of the General,

I am, &c.

J. F. GRIMKIE, Aid-de-Camp.

Brig. Gen. MOULTRIE.

NOTE XIV.

LETTER TO MAJOR GRIMKIE.

SIR,   CHARLESTOWN, May 1st, 1778.

THE excuse you request should rather be asked by me, as I neglected to inform you, that your orders were very explicit, and I accordingly put them in execution, excepting for Thomson's, in lieu of which I sent the first regiment, as they are better clothed and disciplined. I hope this last detachment will reach you by Sunday next. I can scarcely have time to order them to the Alatamaha: their orders were to proceed immediately to Purisburgh. I think it will still be the best way, as I have sent the galley round to Savannah, with a quantity of stores and officers' baggage. I am sending a schooner with about two hundred barrels of pork; if more should be wanted, we can spare it very well. I wish General Howe would order the galley back as soon as she has delivered her cargo, that she may be here ready, in case he should want any other assistance.

I am, &c.

WILLIAM MOULTRIE.
Brigadier General.

NOTE XV.

LETTER FROM GENERAL HOWE.

DEAR SIR,   SAVANNAH, May 3, 1778.

As the quantity of medicines, &c. sent up are by no means proportioned to the troops already here, and, consequently, must be very inadequate to the wants of the army, when the other detachments arrive, I must desire that a surgeon from the general hospital, with medicines and every necessary apparatus very liberally proportioned to the men sent, may, without the least delay, and by the shortest route, be ordered to join the army at Fort Howe.

I am, &c.

ROBERT HOWE.

Brig. Gen. MOULTRIE.

NOTE XVI.

LETTER FROM COLONEL CHARLES C. PINCKNEY.

SAVANNAH, May 4th, 1778.

DEAR GENERAL,

FROM every appearance here, it is probable we shall have something to do. The design of the Hinchenbrook, Rebecca, and the other vessels that were lately taken, was to attack Sunberry, while General Provost with some Augustine troops, penetrated into and ravaged the interior parts of this state ; but the capture of those vessels has, I believe, considerably damped their ardor : they, however, yet maintain their advanced post on St. Mary's, and, from a letter of Brown's, mean to maintain it. On board the Hinchenbrook was found three hundred suits of clothes belonging to my regiment, which were taken in Hatter : these, I presume, were intended for the insurgents. We have been in daily expectation of the arrival of the row-galley with the ammunition and stores, but it is not yet come. The General has countermanded your order relative to the waggons; has ordered me to take them on with me; indeed, we could no possibly do without, for they will be as necessary to us from Savannah to Alatamaha and St. Mary's, as they were from Charlestown to Savannah.

I am, &c.

CHARLES COTESWORTH PINCKNEY.

Brig. Gen. MOULTRIE.

NOTE XVII.

LETTER FROM GENERAL HOWE.

CAMP AT FORT HOWE, May 23d, 1778.

DEAR SIR,

THE strange delay of the Carolina galley with the military stores, has detained me much against my inclination, and to the great injury of the service. The enemy are determined to give us something to do at St. Mary's, where they are pretty well posted, and assisted with cannon. Had I not been detained, I should have prevented their being quite so well prepared; but, upon the whole, perhaps it is for the best, for should they exhaust their strength in out posts, the ultimate result may be much more important than at first we hoped. St. Johns, also, they are preparing to render formidable to us by posts on both sides of the river. We have sanguine hopes of

success upon these posts, that if we obtain, any further progress will depend intirely upon circumstances:
nothing too extensive, or risk, will be undertaken you
may depend upon it. It is, however, absolutely necessary to dislodge the enemy from those advanced
posts, or Georgia may as well be given up to the enemy. As I have been under the necessity of taking
on the schooner with the provisions, I would wish
you to procure another vessel, and forward to us at
least one hundred and fifty barrels of pork, or two
hundred if possible; and I recommend that expedition should be used upon this occasion. I have to
lament that you did not furnish the men with more
kettles. canteens and tents, when so many were in the
arsenal. I assure you the men suffer exceedingly, for
the canteens, particularly, in a country like this, when
a whole day's march may be made without one drop
of water. I would wish a row-boat with five hundred
canteens, two hundred kettles, and as many tents as
could be got, be dispatched with them, with orders to
proceed, both by night and by day, to Sunberry, where
they will receive orders, &c.

I am, &c.

ROBERT HOWE.

Brig. Gen. MOULTRIE.

383

NOTE XVIII.

Letter from the President of Congress.

YORK-TOWN, May 18th, 1778.

DEAR GENERAL,

On the thirteenth instant, I was honored with your favor of the twentieth of April; the next morning I presented it to Congress, and it was ordered with his excellency President Lowndes' dispatches, to a select committee. When a report is made, and I receive commands, you shall be immediately informed : in the mean time, I may safely assure you, the deputy quarter-master general is liable to suspension by the president, should he, which I hold to be impossible, give cause by improper conduct. I shall this day return thanks to Governor Livingston, for his attention to public interest, by suspending many staff-officers...among them, a person exactly upon a line with Colonel F. Huger, a deputy quarter-master, appointed by General Mifflin. I may as safely add, the president, refusing to grant money before preceding grants had been accounted for, is generally applauded, and, I presume, will be more especially noticed by the committee, &c.

I am, &c.

HENRY LAURENS.

Brig. Gen. MOULTRIE.

NOTE XIX.

LETTER FROM GENERAL HOWE.

CAMP AT FORT HOWE, STATE OF GEORGIA,

DEAR SIR,   May 15th, 1778.

I WAS obliged to draw upon the president for money to pay for waggons which the deputy quarter-master general of your state was by necessity of service obliged to purchase, and which, however, are a cheap bargain. I therefore wish you to wait upon the president, and exert yourself to have the orders paid, as the case of the men will be deplorable indeed, should they be disappointed; and the credit of continental officers so injured, that they will not be able to obtain any thing the service may require, however necessary it may be, &c.   I am, &c.

ROBERT HOWE.

Brig. Gen. MOULTRIE.

NOTE XXI. PAGE 210.
SOUTH CAROLINA.

PROCLAMATION by his Excellency Sir HENRY CLINTON, Knight of the most honorable order of the Bath, General and Commander in Chief of all his Majesty's forces within the colonies lying on the Atlantic ocean, from Nova Scotia to West Florida inclusive, &c. &c.

WHEREAS, after the arrival of his majesty's forces under my command in this province in February last, numbers of persons were made prisoners by the army, or voluntarily surrendered themselves as such, and such persons were afterwards dismissed on their respective paroles : and whereas, since the surrender of Charlestown, and the defeats and disperses of the rebel forces, it is become unnecessary that such paroles should be any longer observed ; and proper that all persons should take an active part in settling and securing his majesty's government, and delivering the country from that anarchy which for some time hath prevailed ; I do therefore issue this my proclamation to declare, that all the inhabitants of this province, who are now prisoners upon parole and were not in the military line (those who were in Fort Moultrie and Charlestown at the times of their capitulation and surrender, or were then in actual confinement, excepted) that, from and after the twentieth day of June instant, they are freed and exempted from all such paroles, and may hold themselves as restored to all the rights and duties belonging to citizens and inhabitants.

And all persons under the description before mentioned, who shall afterwards neglect to return to their allegiance, and to his majesty's government, will be considered as enemies and rebels to the same, and treated accordingly.

Given under my hand, at head-quarters in Charlestown, the third day of June, 1780; and in the twentieth year of his majesty's reign.

(Signed)   H. CLINTON.

By his Excellency's command,

(Signed)   PETER RUSSEL,

Assisting Secretary.

NOTE XXII. PAGE 210.

To their Excellencies Sir HENRY CLINTON, Knight of the Bath, General of his Majesty's Forces, and MARIOT ARBUTHNOT, Esq. Vice-Admiral of the Blue, his Majesty's Commissioners to restore Peace and good Government in the several Colonies in rebellion in North-America.

The humble ADDRESS of divers Inhabitants of Charlestown.

THE inhabitants of Charlestown, by the articles of capitulation, are declared prisoners on parole ; but we the under-written, having every inducement to return to our allegiance, and ardently hoping speedily to be re-admitted to the character and condition of British subjects, take this opportunity of tendering to your excellencies our warmest congratulations on the restoration of this capital and province to their political connexion with the crown and government of Great Britain; an event which will add lustre to your excellencies characters, and, we trust, entitle you to the most distinguishing mark of the royal favor. Although the right of taxing America in parliament, excited considerable ferments in the minds of the people of this province, yet it may, with a religious adherence to truth, be affirmed, that they did not entertain the most distant thought of dissolving the union that so happily subsisted between them and their parent country ; and when, in the progress of that fatal controversy, the doctrines of independency (which originated in the more northern colonies) made its appearance among us, our nature revolted at the idea, and we look back with the most painful regret on those convulsions that gave existence to a power of subverting a constitution, for which we always had, and ever shall retain the most profound veneration, and substituting in its stead a rank democracy, which, however carefully digested in theory, on being reduced into practice, has exhibited a system of tyrannic domination, only to be found among the uncivilized part of mankind, or in the history of the dark and barbarous ages of antiquity.

WE sincerely lament, that after the repeal of those statutes which gave rise to the troubles in America, the overtures made by his majesty's commissioners from time to time, were not regarded by our late rulers. To this fatal inattention are to be attributed those calamities which have involved our country in a state of misery and ruin, from which, however, we trust, it will soon emerge, by the wisdom and clemency of his majesty's auspicious government, and the influence of prudential laws, adapted to the nature of the evils we labor under; and that the people will be restored to those privileges, in the enjoyment whereof their former felicity consisted.

ANIMATED with these hopes, we entreat your excellencies interposition in assuring his majesty, that we shall glory in every occasion of manifesting that zeal and affection for his person and government, with which gratitude can inspire a free and joyful people.

CHARLESTOWN, June 5th, 1780.

[SIGNED by two hundred and ten of the principal inhabitants.]

NOTE XXIII. PAGE 222.

CHARLESTOWN, August 29.

Copy of a PROCLAMATION issued by General GATES at PEEDEE, the fourth instant.

By HORATIO GATES, Esq. Major General and Commander in Chief of the Army of the United States in the Southern Department of America, &c. &c.

A PROCLAMATION.

THE patriotic exertions of the virtuous citizens of America, having enabled me, under the protection of Divine Providence, to vindicate the rights of America in this state, and by the approach of a numerous, well-appointed, and formidable army, to compel our late triumphant and insulting foes to retreat from their most advantageous posts, with precipitation and dismay; I have judged it most expedient, at this period of my progress, to give assurances of forgiveness and perfect security to such of the unfortunate citizens of this state, as have been induced by the terror of sanguinary punishments, the menace of confiscation, and all the arbitrary measures of military domination, apparently to acquiesce under the British government, and to make a forced declaration of allegiance and support to a tyranny, which the indignant souls of citizens resolved on freedom, inwardly revolted at, with horror and detestation.

AND in order to afford an opportunity to the real friends of America to testify their affection and attachment to the cause of liberty, an invitation is hereby held out to them to assert that rank among the free and independent citizens of America, in which their former exertions and zeal had deservedly placed them, and to join heartily, when called upon, in rescuing themselves and their country from an opposition of a government imposed on them by the ruffian hand of conquest. Nevertheless, I cannot at present resolve to extend these offers of pardon and security to such, as in the hour of devastation, have exercised acts of barbarity and depredation on the persons and property of their fellow-citizens; nor to such, as being apprized of the security afforded to them by the army under my command, shall be so lost to a sense of honor and the duty they owe to their country, as hereafter to give countenance and support to that enemy, who, but for the disaffection of many of the apostate sons of America, had long ere this been driven from the continent.

The inhabitants of this state may rely on the assurance that an army composed of their brethren and fellow-citizens cannot be brought among them with the hostile vices of plunder and depredation. Such triumphs, under the color of protection and support, are left to grace the British arms alone: but they may rest satisfied, that the genuine motive which has given energy to the present exertions, is the hope of rescuing them from the iron rod of oppression, and restoring to them those blessings of freedom and independence which it is the duty and interest of the citizens of these United States, jointly and reciprocally, to support and confirm.

Given at head-quarters, on the river Peedee, this fourth day of August, in the year of our Lord one thousand seven hundred and eighty, and in the fifth year of our independence.

HORATIO GATES.

By the General's command,

CHRIST. RICHMOND, Secretary.

NOTE XXIV. PAGE 235.

To the right honorable CHARLES EARL CORNWAL-
LIS, Lieutenant General of his Majesty's Forces,
&c. &c.

The humble ADDRESS of divers loyal Inhabitants of
CHARLESTOWN.

WE, his majesty's dutiful and loyal subjects, inhabitants of Charlestown, finding ourselves disappointed in the expectation we entertained of your
lordship's returning shortly to this capital, whereby
we are precluded of personal access to your lordship,
take this opportunity, through the intervention of the
commandant, of tendering to your lordship our joyful congratulations on the total defeat and dispersion
of the rebel army, by his majesty's forces under
your command.

WHEN we reflect on the desolation and ruin with
which this province was threatened by the unrelenting cruelty of a formidable and menacing enemy,
we think ourselves fortunate that we had no idea of
our danger, until we were effectually relieved from
it by the glorious victory obtained by your lordship,
wherein the interposition of a protecting providence
is evident; which inspires us with gratitude to the
Supreme Ruler of the universe; and at the same time
excites in our minds a due sense of the manifold obligations we have to your lordship, for your dis-

tinguished conduct and courage, so eminently con_
spicuous in the accomplishment of that great event,
which has rescued this province from impending
destruction, and is no less advantageous to our most
gracious sovereign and the British empire, than honorable to your lordship; and which fame will trans_
mit to the latest posterity, with that tribute of praise
and admiration your lordship has so justly merited
on this important occasion.

ALTHOUGH a prevailing faction subverted our excellent constitution, and established a democratic
kind of government in its stead, yet, as that arbitrary system of rule was annihilated by the surrender of
this capital, and submission of the country, every
member of the community had an indubitable right
to consult his own happiness; and as the people
in general, induced by their predilection and veneration for the old constitution, have made an explicit declaration of their allegiance, and availed themselves of the protection of that government under
which they formerly enjoyed the highest degree of
civil and political liberty, as well as security in their
properties, we cannot but consider the late attempt
of Congress to subjugate the freemen of this province
to their tyrannical domination, an additional proof of
their restless ambition, and of the wicked machina-
tions of the contemptible remains of that expiring
faction, who have so recently exercised a despotic

and lawless sway over us; and we trust that every other hostile experiment, by the goodness of God, and your lordship's vigilance and animated endeavors, will be rendered equally futile.

THAT Heaven, propitious to your lordship's active zeal in the service of your king and country, may crown your future exertions with success, and incline our deluded sister colonies to partake of those blessings of which we have so fair a prospect, are the sincere and ardent wishes, not only of us, but we are persuaded of every other loyal inhabitant of Charlestown.

September 19th, 1780.

[SIGNED by one hundred and sixty-four persons.]

NOTE XXV. PAGE 249.

Saturday, January 13th, 1781.

THE committee, to whom was referred the letter of December seventh from Major General Greene, delivered in a report; whereupon,

CONGRESS taking into consideration the eminent services rendered to the United States by Brigadier General Sumpter, of South Carolina, at the head of a number of volunteer militia, from that and the neighboring states, particularly in the victory obtained over the enemy at the Hanging-Rock, on the sixth of August; in the defeat of Major Weyms and the corps of British infantry and dragoons under his

command, at Broad-river, on the ninth day of November, in which the said Major Weyms was made
prisoner; and in the repulse of Lieutenant Colonel
Tarleton, and the British cavalry and infantry under
his command, at Black-Stocks, on Tyger-river, on
the twentieth day of November last; in each of which
actions the gallantry and military conduct of General
Sumpter, and the courage and perseverance of his
troops, were highly conspicuous:

RESOLVED, therefore, that the thanks of Congress
be presented to Brigadier General Sumpter, and the
militia aforesaid, for such reiterated proofs of their
patriotism, bravery and military conduct, which entitle them to the highest esteem and confidence of
their country; and that the commanding officer of
the southern department do forthwith cause the same
to be issued in general orders, and transmitted to
General Sumpter.

NOTE XXVI. PAGE 258.
IN CONGRESS, MARCH, 1781.

Friday, March 9th, 1781.

ON the report of a committee, consisting of Mr.
Burke, Mr. Varnum and Mr. Bee to whom were
referred sundry letters from Major General Greene
and Brigadier General Morgan, the following resolutions were passed:

THE United States in Congress assembled, considering it as a tribute due to distinguished merit to give a public approbation of the conduct of Brigadier General Morgan, and of the officers and men under his command, on the seventeenth day of January last; when, with eighty cavalry and two hundred and thirty-seven infantry of the troops of the United States, and five hundred and fifty-three militia from the states of Virginia, North Carolina, South Carolina and Georgia, he obtained a complete and important victory over a select and well-appointed detachment of more than eleven hundred British troops, commanded by Lieutenant Colonel Tarleton; do therefore resolve:

THAT the thanks of the United States in Congress assembled, be given to Brigadier General Morgan and the men under his command, for their fortitude and good conduct displayed in the action at the Cowpens, in the state of South-Carolina, on the seventeenth day of January last:

THAT a medal of gold be presented to Brigadier General Morgan, and a medal of silver to Lieutenant Colonel Washington, of the cavalry, and one of silver to Lieutenant Colonel Howard, of the infantry, of the United States, severally, with emblems and mottoes descriptive of the conduct of those officers respectively on that memorable day:

THAT a sword be presented to Colonel Pickens, of the militia, in testimony of his spirited conduct in the action before mentioned:

That Major Edward Giles, aid-de-camp of Brigadier General Morgan, have the brevet commission of a major ; and that Baron de Glasbeck, who served with Brigadier General Morgan as a volunteer, have the brevet commission of captain in the army of the United States, in consideration of their merit and services.

Ordered, that the commanding officer in the southern department communicate these resolutions in general orders.

NOTE XXVII. Page 271.

By Charles Earl Cornwallis, Lieutenant General of his Majesty's Forces, &c.

A PROCLAMATION.

Whereas by the blessing of Almighty God, his majesty's arms have been crowned with signal success, by the complete victory obtained over the rebel forces on the fifth instant, I have thought proper to issue this proclamation, to call upon all loyal subjects to stand forth, and take an active part in restoring good order and government : and, whereas it has been represented to me, that many persons in this province, who have taken a share in this unnatural rebellion, but having experienced the oppression and injustice of the rebel government, and having seen the errors into which they have been deluded by falsehoods and misrepresentations, are sincerely desirous of returning to their duty and allegiance, I do

hereby notify and promise to all such persons (murderers excepted) that if they will surrender themselves, with their arms and ammunition, at head-
quarters, or to the officer commanding in the district
contiguous to their respective places of residence, on
or before the twentieth day of April next. they will
be permitted to return to their homes, upon giving a
military parole; and shall be protected in their persons and properties from all sorts of violence from
the British troops; and will be restored, as soon as
possible, to all the privileges of legal and constitutional government.

GIVEN under my hand at head-quarters, this
eighteenth day of March, A. D. 1781, and in the
twenty-first year of his majesty's reign.

(Signed)   CORNWALLIS.

NOTE XXVIII. PAGE 277.

LETTER FROM DR. FAYSSOUX TO DR. RAMSAY.

CHARLESTOWN, March 26th, 1785.

SIR,

IN compliance with your request, I now send you
some of the most remarkable facts relative to the
treatment the American prisoners the sick in particular, received, during their captivity in Charlestown,
from the British. The director general having been
confined by the British, the immediate charge of the
American hospital devolved on me, I can therefore

answer for the truth of this account, as every circumstance was within my own knowledge. From the surrender of Charlestown to the period of General Gates' defeat, I do not think we had any material cause of complaint.

THE regulations for the government of the hospital, the supplies of medicine and diet, were in general prescribed by ourselves and acceded to by the British.

AFTER the defeat of General Gates, our sufferings commenced. The British appeared to have adopted a different mode of conduct towards their prisoners, and proceeded from one step to another, until they fully displayed themselves, void of faith, honor or humanity, and capable of the most savage acts of barbarity.

THE unhappy men who belonged to the militia, and were taken prisoners on Gates' defeat, experienced the first effects of the cruelty of their new system.

THESE men were confined on board of prison-ships, in numbers by no means proportioned to the size of the vessels, immediately after a march of one hundred and twenty miles, in the most sickly season of this unhealthy climate.

THESE vessels were in general infected with the small-pox ; very few of the prisoners had gone through that disorder. A representation was made to the British commandant of their situation, and permis-

sion was obtained for one of our surgeons to inocu-
late them...this was the utmost extent of their humanity...the wretched objects were still confined on
board of the prison-ships, and fed on salt provisions,
without the least medical aid, or any proper kind of
nourishment. The effect that naturally followed, was
a small-pox with a fever of the putrid type ; and to
such as survived the small-pox, a putrid dysentery...
and, from these causes, the deaths of at least one
hundred and fifty of the unhappy victims. Such were
the appearances, and such was the termination of the
generality of the cases brought to the general hospital after the irruption of the small-pox...before the
irruption, not a single individual was suffered to be
brought on shore. If any thing can surpass the above
relation in barbarity, it is the following account :...

THE continental troops, by the articles of capitulation, were to be detained prisoners in some place
contiguous to Charlestown ; the barracks were pitched on as the proper place ; this was agreed to by
both parties....The British, in violation of their solemn compact, put these people on board of prison-
ships....Confined in large numbers on board of these
vessels, and fed on salt provisions in this climate in
the months of October and November, they naturally generated a putrid fever from the human miasma.
This soon became highly contagious. The sick
brought into the general hospital from the prison-

ships, generally died in the course of two or three days, with all the marks of a septic state. Application was made by Mr. de Rosettee, the British commissary of prisoners ; the vast increase of the numbers of deaths was pointed out, and he was requested to have proper steps taken to check the progress of a disorder that threatened to destroy the whole of the prisoners.

In consequence of this application, Mr. Fisher, our commissary of prisoners, and Mr. Fraser, who formerly practised physic in this country, but then acted as a British deputy commissary, were ordered to inspect the state of the prisoners in the vessels. This report confirmed the truth of what had been advanced...this can be proved by a very particular circumstance....My hopes were very sanguine that something would be done for the relief of those unhappy persons, but they were entirely frustrated by a person from whom I did not, and ought not to have expected it. Dr. John M'Namara Hays, physician to the British army, a person who had been taken by the Americans on the capture of Burgoyne, who had received the politest treatment from the Americans when a prisoner, and who had the generosity to acknowledge the usage he had met with...this person was ordered to report on the state of the prisoners... to my astonishment, I was informed his report was, that the prison-ships were not crouded, perfectly wholesome, and no appearance of infectious disorders amongst the prisoners.

I THEN determined to make one more effort for the relief of these unhappy persons...for this purpose I had two of the dead bodies kept in the area of the hospital, and, upon Doctor Hays' daily visit to our hospital, I marked to him the appearances of the subjects, whose bodies were highly tinged with a yellow suffusion, petechied over the breast and trunk, with considerable ecchymosis from extravasated or dissolved blood about the neck, breast and upper extremities. I inquired if it was possible a doubt could remain respecting the nature of their disorder, and expressed my surprise at the report he had made. The words of his reply were, ' that the confinement of the ' prisoners in prison-ships was the great eye-sore, ' and there was no help for that, it must be done.' The disorder in consequence continued until the cold weather; the number of deaths, joined with the number that were compelled by this treatment to inlist with the British, removed in a great measure the cause. Hitherto a number of our prisoners who were tradesmen had been permitted to remain in the barracks, or in the city, where they were employed by the British...about the month of January, 1781, they were all confined to the barracks, and there British emissaries were very busy amongst them, to persuade them to inlist in their new corps. About the same

time a supply of clothing, and some money to procure necessaries, arrived from the Congress for the
use of the prisoners.

Mr. Fisher, our commissary, was prevented from
distributing the clothing, and the prisoners were informed it was a deception, for no supplies had arrived
for their use. Their motive was, that by the com-
plicated distress of nakedness and imprisonment,
their patience would be exhausted, and inlistment
with them would ensue.

To prevent this, means were found to have several bales of the clothing brought to the picquets
which inclosed the barracks, and in sight of our soldiers ; this measure established the fact.

Disappointed from this quarter, the British
commandant or his ministers determined to observe
no measures but what would accomplish their own
purposes. All the soldiers in the barracks, including the convalescents, were paraded, and harangued
by Fraser, the British deputy commissary, and one
Low, a recruiting officer for one of the British corps.
The conclusion of the affair was, that such as chose
to inlist with the British should leave the ranks, and
the remainder go on board of the prison-ships. A
few who had been previously engaged withdrew from
the ranks ; the large majority that stood firm, after
three different solicitations without effect, had this
dreadful sentence pronounced by Fraser, ' that they

' should be put on board of the prison-ships, where
' they could not expect any thing more but to perish
' miserably; and that the rations hitherto allowed
' for the support of their wives and children, from
' that day should be withheld; the consequence of
' which would be, they must starve in the streets.'

HUMAN nature recoiled from so horrid a declaration...for a few seconds the unhappy victims seemed
stupified at the dreadful prospect; a gloomy and uni-
versal silence prevailed....This was followed by a loud
huzza for General Washington; death and the prison-ships was the unanimous determination.

THE hospital at this time was reduced to the greatest distress imaginable...the sick without clothing,
covering, or any necessary but one pound of beef and
bread...very little sugar, no wine, and rarely a small
allowance of rum.

WE had no resources, and the British would only
furnish the absolute necessaries of life. The officers
of the hospital, on the mildest representation, were
threatened and insulted, frequently prohibited from
visiting the sick, once I remember for three days.

IT was scarcely possible for men to support such an
accumulated load of misery; but when least expected, a relief was administered to us. A subscription
for the support of the sick was filled by people of
every denomination with amazing rapidity. Several
of the ladies of Charlestown, laying aside the distinc-

-tion of Whig and Tory, were instrumental and assi-
duous in procuring and preparing every necessary of
clothing and proper nourishment for our poor, worn-
out and desponding soldiers.

THUS, sir, I have furnished you with some of the
most material occurrences of that unhappy time.   I
have not exaggerated or written a single circumstance
from hatred or prejudice.   I could furnish you with
a long detail of cruelty and distress exercised on individuals....Major Bocquet's case, exposed in an open
boat for twelve hours in a violent fever, with a blister-
ing plaster on his back, extended at length in the bottom of the boat, then put into the dungeon of the provost with the vilest felons and murderers, left to lan-
guish under his complaint until his death seemed
morally certain, only released from his confinement
from the dread of a just retaliation...the moment his
recovery seemed probable, again hurried back to the
provost, there to remain until the general exchange
released him from their power.

THIS instance of severity exercised on an individual, whose only crime was a steady attachment to
the cause of his country, and a determined resolution to keep sacred the solemn oath he had taken in
its cause, would appear as nothing, were I to enumerate the scenes of woe and distress brought on
many citizens of this once happy country, by British
cruelty and unnecessary severity.   I am sure every

breast would be softened, even tears would fall from British eyes.

I am, sir, with esteem, yours, &c.

P. FAYSSOUX.

NOTE XXIX. PAGE 296.

BY THE UNITED STATES IN CONGRESS ASSEMBLED,
October 29th, 1781.

RESOLVED, that the thanks of the United States in Congress assembled, be presented to Major General Greene, for his wise, decisive and magnanimous conduct in the action of the eighth of September last, near the Eutaw Springs, in South Carolina; in which, with a force inferior in number to that of the enemy, he obtained a most signal victory.

THAT the thanks of the United States in Congress assembled, be presented to the officers and men of the Maryland and Virginia brigades, and Delaware battalion of continental troops, for the unparalleled bravery and heroism by them displayed, in advancing to the enemy through an incessant fire, and charging them with an impetuosity and ardor that could not be resisted.

THAT the thanks of the United States in Congress assembled, be presented to the officers and men of the legionary corps and artillery, for their intrepid and gallant exertions during the action.

THAT the thanks of the United States in Congress

assembled, be presented to the brigade of North Carolina, for their resolution and perseverance in attacking the enemy, and sustaining a superior fire.

THAT the thanks of the United States in Congress assembled, be presented to the officers and men of the state corps of South Carolina, for the zeal, activity and firmness by them exhibited throughout the engagement.

THAT the thanks of the United in Congress assembled, be presented to the officers and men of the militia, who formed the front line in the order of battle, and sustained their post with honor, propriety, and a resolution worthy of men determined to be free.

RESOLVED, that a British standard be presented to Major General Greene, as an honorable testimony of his merit, and a golden medal emblematical of the battle and victory aforesaid.

THAT Major General Greene be desired to present the thanks of Congress to Captains Pierce and Pendleton, Major Hyrne and Captain Shubrick, his aids-de-camp, in testimony of their particular activity and good conduct during the whole of the action.

THAT a sword be presented to Captain Pierce, who bore the general's dispatches, giving an account of the victory, and that the board of war take order herein.

RESOLVED, that the thanks of the United States in Congress assembled, be presented to Brigadier General Marion, of the South Carolina militia, for his wise, gallant and decided conduct, in defending the liberties of his country, and particularly for his prudent and intrepid attack on a body of the British troops, on the thirtieth day of August last, and for the distinguished part he took in the battle of the eighth of September.

Extract from the minutes,

CHARLES THOMSON, Secretary.

NOTE XXX. PAGE 303.
SOUTH CAROLINA.

By his Excellency JOHN RUTLEDGE, Esq. Governor and Commander in Chief of the said State.

A PROCLAMATION.

WHEREAS many persons taking advantage of the late disturbed and unsettled condition of the state, and hoping in the confusion and disorder occasioned by the calamities of war to escape punishment, have committed the most wanton and rapacious acts of plundering; some under color of indemnifying themselves for losses they have sustained; others, under pretence that the persons to whom such property belonged are Tories or enemies of the state; and others, from a wicked and inordinate desire of acquiring wealth by any means, however unjustifiable, and from any persons, whether friends or foes: and whereas the public safety requires that the most effectual measures should be taken for suppressing such an unwarrantable and pernicious practice, inasmuch as good and faithful subjects should be secured and protected in the full and free enjoyment of their property, and no man, although criminal, should be despoiled of his estate but by due course of law: I have therefore thought fit to issue this proclamation, strictly forbidding all persons from plundering, taking, or holding the property of others under any pretence, or for any cause whatever; warning persons possessed of such property, of the danger which they will incur by continuing to withhold it, and charging them immediately to restore such property to the owners of it, unless such owners are with the enemy; and in that case, to deliver it to the brigadier general of the district in which it is, as they will answer the contrary at their peril; for speedy and effectual punishment shall be inflicted on the offenders: and I do direct all justices of the peace diligently and faithfully to execute their office, and to use all lawful means that may be necessary for apprehending, securing, and bringing to justice such persons as are or may be accused of the above-mentioned, or any other criminal offence. I do moreover command all military officers of this state to give such aid and assistance to the civil magistrates, as they may require for that purpose: and I do exhort all those who know, or have reason to believe,

where any plundered property is concealed or se-
creted, or by whom it is possessed, to make discovery
and give information touching the same to the nearest magistrate, in order that proper steps may be
taken for the recovery thereof.

GIVEN under my hand and the Great Seal, at the
High Hills of Santee, this fifth day of August, 1781,
and in the sixth year of the independence of America.

JOHN RUTLEDGE.

By his Excellency's command,

JOHN SANDFORD DART, Pro. Secretary.

NOTE XXXI. PAGE 303.
SOUTH CAROLINA.

By his Excellency JOHN RUTLEDGE, Esq. Governor
and Commander in Chief of the said State.

A PROCLAMATION.

WHEREAS the forces of the United States having
compelled the troops of his Britannic majesty to
surrender or evacuate the several strong posts which
they held in the upper and interior settlements, and
retreat to the vicinity of Charlestown; and the enemy,
being therefore unable to give that protection and
support which they promised to their adherents, left
many inhabitants of this state, who had taken up
arms with them, induced so to do by their artful representations, to become victims to their injured
country; whereupon, such persons, to escape or avoid

the effects of its just resentment, followed and remain
with the British army, or lurk and conceal themselves
in secret places: and whereas the commandant of
Charlestown having sent beyond sea the wives and
families, which were in the said town, of all the
avowed friends of America; the several brigadiers
of militia were ordered, as a retaliation of such treatment, to send the wives and families, within their
respective districts, of all persons who had joined or
adhered to, and remained with the enemy, into their
lines: and whereas it is represented to me, in behalf
of the unhappy men who are with the British troops
or secreting themselves as aforesaid, that they are
now convinced, being reduced with their families to
great distress and poverty, that they relied on false
and specious engagements, and were flattered with
vain expectations and delusive hopes, and that they
are therefore anxious, if they may be admitted, to
return to their allegiance, and use their utmost exertions to support American independence. On
duly weighing and considering the premises, I have
thought fit, by and with the advice and consent of
the privy council, to issue this proclamation, offering, and I do hereby offer, to all persons who have
borne arms with the enemy, and who now adhere
to or are with them in this state, or are lurking or
concealing themselves in secret places in any part
of the state, a FULL and FREE PARDON and

OBLIVION, for such their offence of having borne arms with, or adhered to the enemy, upon the conditions following: that is to say, that such persons do, and shall, within thirty days after the date hereof, surrender themselves to a brigadier of the militia of this state, and engage to perform constant duty as privates, in the militia, for six months next ensuing the time of such surrender, and that they actually perform such duty. And I do further offer to the wives and children of such persons, upon their husbands or parents complying with the condition first abovementioned, license and permission to return to their habitations, and to hold and enjoy their property in this state without molestation or interruption. Provided always, that if such persons shall desert from the militia service within the time above limited, their families shall be immediately sent into the enemy's lines, and neither they or their husbands or parents, suffered to return to, or reside in this state. Nevertheless, I do except, from the pardon hereby offered, and from every benefit of this proclamation, all such persons, as having gone over to, or joined the enemy, were called upon by me in and by two several proclamations, to surrender themselves to a magistrate within forty days after the respective dates of those proclamations, in pursuance of an ordinance, entitled, ' An ordinance to prevent persons withdrawing from ' the defence of this state, to join the enemies there-

' of :' all such as were sent off or obliged to quit the state for refusing to take the oath required of them by law, who have returned to this country ; all those who subscribed a congratulatory address, bearing date on or about the fifth day of June, one thousand seven hundred and eighty, to General Sir Henry Clinton, and Vice-Admiral Arbuthnot, or another address, bearing date on or about the nineteenth day of September, one thousand seven hundred and eighty, to Lieutenant General Earl Cornwallis; all such as hold or have held any commission, civil or military, under the British government, and are now with the enemy; and all those whose conduct has been so infamous, as that they cannot, consistently with justice or policy, be admitted to partake of the privileges of Americans. Notwithstanding which last mentioned exception, such persons, if they should be deemed by me, or the governor and commander in chief for the time being, inadmissable to the rights and privileges of subjects, will not be detained as prisoners, but shall have full and free liberty, and a pass or permit to return. At a juncture, when the force of the enemy in this state, though lately considerable, is greatly reduced by the many defeats which they have suffered, and particularly in the late important action at Eutaw; when they are dispossessed of every post and garrison except Charlestown; when the formidable fleet of his most christian majesty, in Chesapeak-bay, and the combined armies of the king of France and of the United States, under the command of his Excellency General Washington, in Virginia, afford a well-grounded hope, that, by the joint efforts of their armies, this campaign will be happily terminated, and the British power in every part of the confederate states, soon totally annihilated; it is conceived, that the true and real motive of the offer hereby made, will be acknowledged. It must be allowed to proceed, not from timidity, to which the enemy affect to attribute every act of clemency and mercy on our part, but from a wish to impress, with a sense of their error, and to reclaim misguided subjects, and give them once more an opportunity of becoming valuable members of the community, instead of banishing them, or forever cutting them off from it; for even the most disaffected cannot suppose that the brave and determined freemen of this state have any dread of their arms.

WITH the persons to whom pardon is thus offered, the choice still remains, either to return to their allegiance, and, with their families, be restored to the favor of their country, and to their possessions, or to abandon their properties in this state forever, and go with their wives and children, whither, for what purpose, on whom to depend, or how to subsist, they know not...most probably to experience, in some strange and distant country, all the miseries and horrors of beggary, sickness and despair....This alternative is now, for the last time, submitted to their judgment...it will never be renewed.

GIVEN under my hand and the Great Seal, at the High Hills of Santee, this twenty-seventh day of September, in the year of our Lord, one thousand seven hundred and eighty-one, and in the sixth year of the independence of America.

J. RUTLEDGE.

By his Excellency's command,

JOHN SANDFORD DART, Sec'ry.

NOTE XXXII. PAGE 320.

CAMP, SOUTHERN ARMY, HIGH HILLS OF SANTEE,

August 20th, 1781.

THE subscribers commissioned officers serving in the southern army, beg leave to represent to the honorable Major General Greene, that they are informed, not only by current reports, but by official and acknowledged authority, that contrary to express stipulations in the capitulation of Charlestown, signed the twelfth day of May, 1780, a number of very respectable inhabitants of that town and others were confined on board prison-ships, and sent to St. Augustine, and other places distant from their homes, families and friends. That notwithstanding the general cartel settled for exchange of prisoners in the southern department, and agreed to the third of May last, several officers of militia and other gentlemen, subjects of the United States, have been, and still are detained in captivity ; that the commanding officer of the British troops in Charlestown, regardless of the principles, and even the express tenor of the said cartel, hath not only presumed to discriminate between the subjects of the United States prisoners of war, partially determining who were and who were not objects of exchange, but hath even dared to execute in the most ignominious manner, Colonel Hayne, of the militia of the state of South Carolina, a gentleman amiable in character, respectable in his connections, and of eminent abilities: and this violent act, as cruel as it was unnecessary and unjust, we are informed, is attempted to be justified by the imputed crime of treason, founded upon the unfortunate sufferer's having, in circumstances peculiarly distressing, accepted of what is called a protection from the British government.

If every inhabitant of this country, who, being bound by the tender ties of family-connections, and fettered by domestic embarrassments, is forced to submit to the misfortune of falling into the hands of the enemy, must therefore become a subject of such inhuman authority, and if such subjects are liable to be tried by martial law for offences against the said civil government of the British nation, their situation is truly deplorable ; but we conceive forms of protection which are granted one day, and retracted, violated, disclaimed or deserted the next, can enjoin no such condition or obligation upon persons who accept them. We consider the citizens of America as independent of the government of Great Britain as those of Great Britain are of the United States, or of any other sovereign power, and ,think it just the severities and indulgences to prisoners of war ought to be reciprocal. We, therefore, with submission, beg leave to recommend, that a strict inquiry be made into the several matters mentioned, and if ascertained, that you will be pleased to retaliate in the most effectual manner by a similar treatment of British subjects which are or may be in your power.

PERMIT us to add, that while we seriously lament the necessity of such a severe expedient, and commiserate the sufferings to which individuals will necessarily be exposed, we are not unmindful that such a measure may in its consequences, involve our own lives in additional dangers ; but we had rather forego temporary distinctions, and commit ourselves to the most desperate situations than prosecute this just and necessary war upon terms so unequal and so dishonorable.

We are, sir, with the greatest regard,
and most respectful sentiments of esteem,
your most obedient and most humble servants.
[Signed by all the officers of the army.]
The Honorable Major General GREENE.

NOTE XXXIII. PAGE 320.
PROCLAMATION.

By NATHANIEL GREENE, Esq. Major General, commanding the American Army in the Southern
Department.

WHEREAS Colonel Isaac Hayne, commanding a
regiment of militia in the service of the United States,
was taken prisoner by a party of British troops, and
after a rigorous detention in the Provost's prison at
Charlestown, was condemned and executed on the
fourth of this month, in the most cruel and unjustifiable manner, in open violation of the cartel agreed
upon between the two armies, for the release and
exchange of all prisoners of war; and it being no
less the duty than the inclination of the army to resent every violence offered to the good citizens of
America, to discountenance all those distinctions
which they have endeavored to establish, in making
a difference in various orders of men, found under
arms for the support of the independence of the
United States; and further considering that these violences are committed with a view of terrifying the
good people, and by that means preventing them
from acting in conformity with their political interests
and private inclinations; and that this method of trying
and punishing, in consequence of those distinctions, is
no less opposite to the spirit of the British, than it is
inclusive of an unwarrantable infringement of all the

laws of humanity, and the rights of the free citizens of the United States; from these considerations I have thought proper to issue the present proclamation, expressly to declare, ' that it is my intention ' to make reprisals for all such inhuman insults, as often as they shall take place.' And whereas the enemy seems willing to expose the small number of the deceived and seduced inhabitants, who are attached to their interests, if they can but find an opportunity of sacrificing the great number that have stood forth in defence of our cause; I farther declare, ' that ' it is my intention to take the officers of the regular ' forces, and not the seduced inhabitants who have ' joined their army, for the objects of my reprisals.'... But while I am determined to resent every insult that may be offered to the United States for having maintained our independence, I cannot but lament the necessity I am under of having recourse to measures so extremely wounding to the sentiments of humanity, and so contrary to the liberal principles upon which I wish to conduct the war.

GIVEN at the head-quarters at Camden, twenty-sixth of August, 1781, in the sixth year of American independence.

(Signed)   NATHANIEL GREENE.'

NOTE XXXIV. PAGE 341.

ARTICLES of TREATY between General MARION, in behalf of the State of South Carolina, and Major GANEY, and the inhabitants under his command, which were included in the Treaty made the seventeenth day of June, 1781.

ARTICLE I. Major Ganey and the men under his command to lay down their arms, as enemies to the state, and are not to resume them again until ordered to do so, in support of the interest of the United States, and of this state in particular.

II. WE will deliver up all negroes, horses, cattle, and other property that have been taken from this or any other state.

III. WE will demean ourselves as peaceable citizens of this state, and submit ourselves to be governed by its laws, in the same manner as the rest of the citizens thereof.

IV. WE do engage to apprehend and deliver up all persons within our district, who shall refuse to accede to these terms, and contumaciously persist in rebellion against this state.

V. WE will deliver up as soon as possible, every man who belongs to any regular line in the American service, and every inhabitant of North Carolina, of this, or any other state, who have joined us since the seventeenth of June, 1781, when the former treaty was made, or oblige them to go out of the district, and whenever they return, to take and deliver them into safe custody in any gaol within the state.

VI. Every man is to sign an instrument of writing professing his allegiance to the United States of America, and the state of South Carolina in particular ; and to abjure his Britannic majesty, his heirs, successors and adherents, and promise to oppose all the enemies of the United States, and the state of South Carolina in particular.

VII. All arms, ammunition, and other warlike stores, the property of the British, to be delivered up.

VIII. The above seven articles being agreed on, they shall have a full pardon for treasons committed by them against the state, and enjoy their property, and be protected by the laws thereof.

IX. Such men who do not choose to accede to these articles, shall have leave to go within the British lines, and to march by the twenty-fifth instant, and be safely conducted with such of their wives and children as may be able to travel, and carry or sell their property, except cattle, sheep and hogs, which they may dispose of, but not carry with them. Such women and children who cannot be removed, may remain until the first day of September next. The officers to keep their pistols and side-arms ; all other arms to be disposed of, and not carried with them. Each field-officer and captain to retain one horse, not exceeding twelve in the whole, and no other person to take with him any more horses that may be fit for dragoon service within the British lines.

WE have agreed to the before-mentioned nine articles, and have signed the same at Birch's-mill, on Peedee, this eighth day of June, 1782.

FRANCIS MARION,
Brigadier General,
State of South Carolina.

MICAJAH GANEY,
Major Loyalists, Peedee.

NOTE XXXV. PAGE 341.

HEAD-QUARTERS, August 13th.

SIR,

THE measure which I lately adopted, of sending a force to collect provisions on the Lower Santee, for the use of this garrison, was a necessary consequence of the conduct your party had thought proper to observe, in the prohibitions which prevented our receiving supplies of the kind from the country.

FROM the respect which I owe to the sentiments which appear to govern the present conduct of Great Britain towards America, I should have given a willing preference to any means less distressful to the country, by which this necessary purpose might have been obtained ; I am equally desirous to forbear the further prosecution of these measures ; and am ready to enter with you into any composition to that ef.

fect, which may, I think, be established on terms to the mutual advantage of both parties, affording to us a supply to our future necessities, and to you security from further depredation, and a voluntary compensation for what the force of arms has already given us in possession. The success which has attended this enterprize must convince you, that principles of benevolence and humanity are the true motives of a conduct, the moderation of which must appear striking to you.

I HOPE these considerations will induce you to accept a proposal so evidently advantageous to the interests of your own party ; and that you will in consequence order rice and other provisions to be sent into town, in quantities proportioned to our demand, which will be considerable, from the necessity of supplying the king's subjects who may think proper to remove from hence to the province of East-Florida.

IF, notwithstanding these offers, you think proper to adhere to your former line of conduct, the necessity which constrains will justify the measures which I shall be forced to take.

I have the honor to be, &c.

ALEX. LESLIE.

To Major General GREENE.

....

THE END.

....